VATICAN II
THE COMPLETE HISTORY

VATICAN II

THE COMPLETE HISTORY

Directed by Alberto Melloni

Edited by Federico Ruozzi and Enrico Galavotti
with contributions from Alberto Cadili, Davide Dainese, Maria Teresa Fattori,
Luca Ferracci, Patrizio Foresta, Saretta Marotta, Alberto Melloni,
Giuseppe Ruggieri, Riccardo Saccenti, Giovanni Turbanti

The John XXIII Foundation for Religious Studies, Bologna
www.fscire.it

Paulist Press
New York / Mahwah, NJ

Front jacket image by Trace Murphy
Jacket design by Lightly Salted Graphics

Copyright © 2015
Editoriale Jaca Book S.p.A., Milano
Fondazione per le scienze religiose, Bologna
All Rights Reserved
International Copyright handled by Editoriale Jaca Book S.p.A., Milano
First Italian Edition October 2015

Text Edited by Fscire/Jaca Book

Graphics by Jaca Book

Composition and Image Selection by The Good Company, Milano

Printing and Binding by Tecnostampa - Pigini Group Printing Division (Loreto - Trevi) Italy

Editoriale Jaca Book
Via Frua 11, 20146 Milano
tel. 02-48.56.15.20; fax 02-48.19.33.61
libreria@jacabook.it; www.jacabook.it

Translated into English for Paulist Press by Sean O'Neill and Bret Thoman

English translation copyright © 2015 by Paulist Press

Library of Congress Control Number: 2015941420

ISBN 978-0-8091-0624-0 (hardcover)

English-language Edition Published by Paulist Press
997 Macarthur Boulevard
Mahwah, New Jersey 07430
www.paulistpress.com

Contents

THE FORM OF VATICAN II
HISTORY, IMAGES, AND MAPS FROM THE TIME OF THE COUNCIL

Alberto Melloni

A Cloud of Questions

There are many questions regarding the Second Vatican Council: they are raised not just today or during the last pontificate, but from the very beginning—by the council's own admission. Why embark on a council when—as outlined by a popular encyclopedia of theology from the early years of the twentieth century— the pope, after Vatican I had defined papal primacy and infallibility, could have done anything he wanted, any way he wanted to?[1] It was legitimate to ask if an episcopate, which in January 1959—one hundred days after the end of the Pacelli pontificate—was still lethargic from the era of condemnations that had scourged Catholic theology with a doctrinal totalitarianism, subordinating the difficult search for truth to a police-like "regime," which an ecclesiology and history enthusiast like Father Congar bluntly called a "Gestapo."[2] Herein begin the new doubts. Why not a nice symposium at the "Cini Foundation," the future Paul VI reasoned, with the prudence that sometimes manifested itself as cleverness, when the revocation of his exile to Milan—and the papal tiara—were still far in his future?[3]

Nor would the questions lessen during the months of preparation. When the pope from Bergamo, "big old Angelo" as Pier Paolo Pasolini liked to call him,[4] spoke of "unity" and of "churches," not everyone believed that he knew the theological implications. Nor did they suspect that he was echoing some vague old paternalistic sentiment that the churches (especially Roman Catholic) often confused with the process of conversion from the worship of a divided self to the obedience to Christ's command to be one. Therefore, it became and remains legitimate to ask how a former nuncio like Roncalli could hand off the organization of "his" council to the heads of the dicasteries and the congregations of the Roman Curia. And why did he limit himself to flouting the lofty power of the Holy Office (presenting its list of *periti* rigorously selected from the divergent Roman schools that were in perpetual struggle among themselves, Ottaviani noted that "neither de Lubac or Congar" were on the list) only to require them to add precisely those two names…?[5] These issues became even more structural, because both those who lived through Vatican II and those who studied it asked if it made sense to create a "central" preparatory commission that did not coordinate a plan—a "project" [*progetto*] (in the language of the 1930s)[6]—but received stacks of paperwork from the other commissions that they rubber stamped. We know the crafty confidence of the pope who nominated a general secretary whom he thought would be replaced due to lack of tact and linguistic incompetence, as happened in Vatican I.[7] But would

such a replacement (which turned out not to be) be enough to transform a procedure designed for an assembly that would always give its approval into an instrument that would create a real encounter and confrontation, able to inspire and inflame an *aggiornamento*?

The flood of questions moved forward quickly even within the development of the council and of the relationship that the pope had to create with this body—distinct from his—and of which he was part. What did the immense gathering of fathers, the largest assembly of peers ever gathered on earth, understand about *Gaudet Mater Ecclesia*?[8] And what was the meaning of that short phrase—so "Roncallian"—pronounced on the eve of the opening of the council, among words about the moon and caressing one's children, in which he indirectly indicated that "it would not be over by Christmas" but would go on? What did he mean by saying they would meet "yet again" when this mortally ill Christian who touched the world so deeply knew he wouldn't be in the world much longer?[9] How should it proceed, after the pope decided to begin with the liturgy, when the famous "project" everyone was scrambling to create was lacking, perhaps for reasons more profound than those who missed it assumed?[10] What would happen when the council got hung up on the plural, *de fontibus*, over which there had been centuries of disputes, and the attempts to poison the wells of ecumenism?[11] Would the document on the Jews—which had been initially discarded (a case more unique than rare) by the Secretary of State during the preparatory phase and which reappeared on the agenda—be a strong point[12] or a snare for the Secretariat for Christian Unity, the only body ensuing from the invisible curial reforms implemented by John XXIII, which would have an enormous weight in redefining the ecumenical nature of Vatican II?[13]

In a council that witnessed the conclave—in which the council itself was on the agenda—that elected Pope Paul VI, questions no less relevant continued to echo.[14] A pope like Montini, with a tactical sense demonstrated on so many occasions, managed to set new procedures. But, having done so and having chosen the moderators, why did he become the protector of a minority—which included his most bitter enemies—and at the same time follow the "democratic" dream of a majority that tended towards unanimity instead of issuing a dispensation as his predecessor had in order to midwife that consensus which was the substance of conciliar decision-making?[15] When excitement over the quickening pace of reforms of the council was felt in the fall of 1963, when in just a few weeks liturgical reform, the principles of ecclesiology of communion, and the dismantling of an anti-ecumenical Mariology

1. *The Glorification of the Cross*, thirteenth-century fresco, David-Garedză Monastery Complex, Kakheti Province, Georgia (Archivio Jaca Book).

together.[19] But what outcome and what sense would it have made to search for the middle ground? The theology of divine revelation, the relationship with Israel, the irrevocable commitment to ecumenism by Rome, the mission of the church, and the freedom of the human conscience all marked unequivocal turning points on issues that the previous magisterium had dealt with—quite frankly—in a contrary manner: these themes injected, therefore, new energy of catholicity and theological awareness into the future of the church. Can the same be said of the documents that Döpfner sought to reduce to propositions?[20] And how should one judge *Gaudium et spes*, which split the majority of the council between those who saw it as the highpoint of a new outlook on the world and those who saw it as the refuse of potentially secularized optimism?[21]

Multiplying Questions upon Reception

The questions multiplied when the council began to be "received"; that is, the process by which decisions taken in all the great councils of history bring out historical and theological themes that did not always coincide with the priorities of the assembly.[22] The questions numbered in the thousands. They dealt with the responsibility of the bishops, who had lost that synergetic relationship with theologians that they will never get back, ever.[23] They affected lay men and women in their daily lives and in their enthusiasm for the Christian life regarding their "public presence." Was it the great victory of the modern age—or a moment of absolute cynicism and unshakable distrust, with no connection to the harshness (albeit sincere) that marked the popes named Pius?[24] They affected the religious communities within Catholicism: orders of ancient origin, monasteries born of thirst for God ever new, tattered parishes within Europe or elsewhere, young people with their priest, priest with young people, and so on.[25] Some were hoping the council would fulfill all their hopes and explain all their disappointments: both those with silly hopes of a Woodstock-like rebirth of the church, as well as those clinging to nostalgia and to Latin in the venerable name of tradition.[26] There were those disappointed by deeply theological issues, who feared the betrayal of the council and the return of Roman authoritarianism,[27] as well as those who saw in it rampant superficiality and the loss of the systematic theological references that had been their entire life.

The persistent questions pushed people on opposite sides of the pot where the church of the third millennium still cooks today: Ottaviani against Suenens on ecclesiological issues,

remarkably took place, did he go to Jerusalem for comfort and personal visibility or in order to add an ecumenical aspect to the agenda that was lacking?[16] As seen through the eyes of the minority, who in those early months of 1964 accused him of betraying the "small-minded" traditions of the previous two centuries in the name of the great ancient Tradition (was not this the point of the doctrinal totalitarianism of *Humani generis*?), did the pressure of those who chose to assault the conscience torment or irritate him?[17] All that the minority got was the inclusion of a handful of sentences in *Lumen Gentium*, but whether or not they were successful is a disputed question. Like the *Nota explicativa praevia* [explanatory note] that was read out loud to clarify the limiting interpretation regarding collegiality—which had no other authority than that of the commission that wrote it and which the Supreme Authority ordered merely to be "read"—was not a muzzle put on the council, had not a silly conservatism been fostered, had a violent compromise been proposed, intended only to produce doubts and trouble?[18]

More questions had arisen by the end of the council: was the "step"—as referred to by Congar—completed? Was the "leap forward" dreamed of by Pope John realized, begun, or did it move sideways? In the rush to finish the documents, it is clear that both developed and underdeveloped themes were mixed

2. Assisi, October 27, 1986. John Paul II together with representatives
of other faiths for the World Day of Prayer for Peace
(Archivio Jaca Book).

Paul VI against Lercaro on the council's reception within the dioceses, Lefebvre against Paul VI on liturgy, Küng against Ratzinger in theology, *Communio* against *Concilium* in dissemination. These were not issues of simple "disagreement" debated within fixed boundaries on an even playing field; instead, they shook the church violently to the ground. Incidents both relevant and petty were interrelated and indicative of the struggle for the watershed moment to silence discussion and end the story. Thus, the conclusion of the Sixties was marked by the end of a hypothesis by the reception of the council in the European churches,[28] the conference in Medellín, the "church of the Holy Spirit" knocking at the doors of the churches,[29] the withdrawal of the Tridentine missal in 1970—a sign of the Antichrist in the eyes of the traditionalists,[30] the non-canonization of John XXIII (or his subsequent canonization in 2013—the seal of its reception),[31] the Jubilee in 2000, the *mea culpa*, the elevation of the council which would lead the church of tomorrow,[32] and so on. It was against this background of discontent when in 2005 Benedict XVI rattled off a few sentences about hermeneutics (theological, of course) regarding Vatican II, some believed he had pulled the lever not against hermeneutics, but against the council itself. On that December at the beginning of his pontificate, Pope Benedict went back to a thesis he had penned in 1965 at the end of the council: he opposed a hermeneutic "of discontinuity and rupture," to one of "continuity and reform."[33] His statement was the consequence of his well-known theological position on the chronological and ontological preexistence of the universal church over the particular church.[34] Based on this assumption, on a "factual" level, the council may very well have overturned the claims of the papacies of previous centuries. Surely an academic like Ratzinger, aware of the boundaries of scientific disciplines, did not doubt that what happened historically must have been explained in the context of historical reconstruction. But the programmatically "ahistorical" nature of his position didn't take away the fact that on the "theological" level, the overturned magisterial statements, which although they had claimed for themselves an elevated doctrinal status, should not have affected and should not have touched the timeless essence of the church from which a reformable and immutable "continuity" in itself descended. This subtle Ratzingerian distinction—later popularized in a confrontation between continuity and discontinuity, with recourse to a simplistic understanding that certainly was not Benedict XVI's[35]—was not aimed at the historical level. It was

assumed that it dealt with ancillary—not theological—dimensions. The issue was if this ancillarity of history over theology should ever be discussed, because this is what affects the present and the future of Vatican II in the church.

The Council as an Event
Indeed, in 1988 the church historian, Giuseppe Alberigo, sought to evaluate Vatican II with the tools of history.[36] A student and friend of Hubert Jedin, the historian of the Council of Trent, Alberigo understood that historicity played a decisive role in every council. It was so for the pro- and anti-Photius councils which were understood differently after Francis Dvornik;[37] Chalcedon was reinterpreted in its time thanks to the studies of Aloys Grillmeier;[38] the Council of Constance benefited from the work of Brian Tierney and Alberigo himself;[39] after Joseph Gill, the Council of Florence was understood differently.[40] But it was especially so for Trent. The critical work of Hubert Jedin placed it within a context of real history and returned the long council to its historical place from the time of its anticipation (from the 1400s to 1545) to its realization (1545–1563).[41] The fundamental lesson of Jedin is that a council is never comprised of a sequence of small steps or chronologically aligned quotes of things that seem identical only to those who are ignorant of the contexts; rather, understanding the sources in accelerations and reductions qualify it and corroborate it (or contradict it) in what it can be in its iconic representation as bride of Christ.
Thus Alberigo launched and wrote and called others to write a history of Vatican II in five volumes (its size dictated the way those worked on and bound it) which sought to place the council within the context of history and historical issues. So it was not the reconstruction of the events that would generate facts and victories, because then it would become etiology and would only give cause to the winners—the point on which John O'Malley's subsequent history of the council rightly insisted on several occasions.[42] Nor was it simple narration—which also has an inestimable value, as readers of the articles of Fr. Giovanni Caprile in *La Civiltà Cattolica* directed by Tucci know[43]—because this would end up flattening time. But neither is it an exercise in hermeneutics: because this would suppose either the assumption of the *corpus* (even if such use has no less than mutilated the *corpus* of Vatican II from certain acts, such as the messages, which are usually excluded from the usual list of "sixteen" documents[44]) or the assumption of an interpretative paradigm that must be examined with the

2

tools proper to the theological, philosophical, or legal fields which one has chosen.[45]

All and only one history, then.[46] All and only history: freeing Vatican II from the conviction that it consisted only of the documents approved by it—of which there were not a few—but were a fruitful expression of a more complex generative dynamism, without which they were no longer "pure" or more "objective," but poorer and saying less. All and only history: understanding how time revealed how those who confused the multifaceted and colorful traditions of twenty centuries with the greyness of the nostalgia of an intransigent culture had become a minority. All and only history: overcoming the analysis of the trivial "political mechanics" of Vatican II[47] with the strength of the critical issues and of the historical question *par excellence*: understanding what happened and striving to understand why, allowing the study of the sources to imprint partial, fallible, incomplete, and doubtful judgments and truths in the scholar, while remaining continuously aware of what they allude to and from which they allow themselves to be questioned.[48]

Together with curious, malicious, theological, doctrinal, and political questions, the typical question on historical work has produced a history of Vatican II that was a watershed in the scholarly world and also in the way in which the church considered itself before the conciliar "visitation."[49] Fools are recognized by their reticence in citing those five volumes, which—while doing wrong to Otto Herman Pesch—can be done away with as an "initial" history of Vatican II,[50] but which are the only history that could have produced the development of critical and philological research unimaginable at fifty years from Trent or from Vatican II. True scholars of the history[51] of Vatican II know to place the council in the dimension of "event" which allows theologians—without reversed ancillarities, but in the distinction of scientific ends and not in their epistemological *quality*—to initiate a reflection on how the church has lived that season of evangelism.[52]

A Map

From that history, ways of studying the sources of the second half of the twentieth century have come out that are no less decisive than the research they prepared:[53] publications, historical studies, theological commentaries, archival research. And now this book. It seeks to accompany the reader through the stages of the council to discover, in its actual implementation, the journey of that event born from the primacy of John XXIII, which he announced on January 25, 1959, one hundred days after his election, and ended on December 8, 1965, on the 901st day of Paul VI's pontificate, after forty-five months of preparation that had come to naught, and thirty-eight months of celebration that saw sweeping changes and refutations in a relatively short time.

Through images of the council, this book seeks to add a visual dimension which is now an integral part of the historical disciplines and their specializations. Using the model of Jedin and his atlas of church history, it introduces in graphic format some procedures and dimensions of the conciliar itinerary from its preparation to its closing. It has recovered from photographic and cinematic archives the faces and stories of the major personages of Vatican II, and it exploits a body of collective historicizing with a few parallels in the historic-religious discipline and briefly in the historical one. It highlights aspects of the journey both local and global. This, too, uses an extensive reading of ecclesiastical, political, and conciliar geography as its point of reference. The Vatican II church is still European in its way of thinking, and the way it deals with its effective catholicity is not surpris-

3

ing—almost as if its future (symbolized by the election of the first non-European as bishop of Rome shifting its spiritual axis to the south and east in the second millennium) had come to announce its imminence.[54] Therefore, limiting the journey to the mention of bishops from outside Europe at Vatican II would be necessary, but insufficient.[55] In fact, there are other dimensions that influenced the council and its reception in parts of the vast world where Christianity was blossoming unnoticed by the core hierarchy and its edict. It is a model of intermediate collegiality which, after marking the character of the great church throughout the pentarchical ecclesiology of the fourth to sixth centuries and that of the *nationes* of the fifteenth century,[56] returns again to manifest itself in the working of the episcopal conferences. But they are not as they were in Italy or Spain in the 1950s (that is, spokespersons of the pope), nor as a buffer between Rome and the *intelligentsia* as in France, nor the large decision-making machines in Germany, nor as an expression of national identity as in Poland. The episcopal conferences were expressions of a form of church that sought not a shallow "democratization" of the model of ecclesiastical power, but a theological and canonical rethinking of the church within the churches in which and from which the universal church exists.[57] The strictly Dutch bishops in Indonesia—like the countless missionary bishops from the countries of old European Christianity—did not have the same level of education or theological culture as the bishops of the "third world" (as it is was called in the 1960s). Rather, the European missionary bishops were the voice of problems that were not "issues," much less to be managed paternalistically and authoritatively on a "case by case" basis by the congregations of the curia. Instead, they were "lights" of the gospel that illuminated the signs of the times with their being; they were glimmers of spiritual renewal that came from a time

that had been summarily condemned for nearly two centuries.[58]

Therefore, this history strives to provide confirmed and authoritative lists of participants at the council in different roles. It does not seek to give credit to the dull "official" lists that are full of additions, ideological exclusions, and errors that reveal the mindset of a centralism that does not correspond with the real catholicity of the churches in communion with Rome. The lists were quite difficult—and even risky—to compile because the sources that recorded them (in addition to an ideological mentality) had the added difficulty of adapting the old procedures to quickly changing ways of thinking. There was the ancient curial use, for example, of designating prelates with their Latin name, their diocese, and their order, or there was the Italianization of the actual names of the participants (a legacy of the fascist era).[59] Needless to say, this created a lot of confusion in the council, especially when dealing with names in which the first or the second word was the surname. The list of experts, hundreds of whom were named by their honorary titles, many in the last period of the council, was no less complex. In addition, among the observers and guests of the Secretariat for Christian Unity, some people are difficult to classify. For example, one was the interesting Romanian-Lebanese monk, André Scrima, who, as personal representative of the Patriarch Athenagoras, had a marginal status but a decisive role.[60]

But the bulk of the work offered here is that within the "time" of the council and the effort made to spread out the space—the most obvious dimension of a map of a journey—within time. It is within the time of the council in which those questions that I posed at the beginning were formed. The answers are given from time to time without having a picture of the future. In fact, when a participant arrived at the council on October 11, 1962, aware of the massive preparation and

3. St. Peter's Basilica, September 29, 1963, the opening of the second session of Vatican II. The council fathers take their seats as they await the entrance of Pope Paul VI, who decided the council would continue in spite of the death of John XXIII (photo: Pais/Archivio Rodrigo Pais–Ceub Università di Bologna).

faithful to the subordination of the bishops to curial rules, he must have thought it would be a very short council—perhaps a few weeks. He would have thought the council would have quickly approved the numerous documents—perhaps all seventy *schemata*. Though the *schemata* were overwhelmed by criticism in those summer weeks when they were read in preview, he would have thought they would go to a vote. Before these documents, Chenu and Congar inserted a short "message" full of openness and evangelical spirit, which in its beauty made clear the fear of being defeated in their hopes for a springtime of the Church.[61] When on November 21–22, the rejection of *De fontibus* suggested that the pope intended to protect the freedom of the majority in the council with the same calm decisiveness with which he allowed the curia to work on the preparation, the time horizon expanded.[62] The new preparations, which in January 1963 redefined the methods and "pastoral" aims of the council, also expanded the time of the council in which it was clear that Pope John would no longer be there. A further expansion of time came with the conclave, and then with the votes in October 1963. It gave a sense of the impressive ability of the council (not unlike that of the great ancient councils) to accelerate in doctrinal insight, with a thrust that created a lot of enthusiasm. In fact, in 1964 many thought they could bank on what they had obtained on the key theme of ecclesiology and thereby defeat the obstructionism of the minority who unexpectedly had the ear of Paul VI—not that this would be particularly significant for the pope and for his trusted theologian Fr. Carlo Colombo, but would serve that iconic unanimity which Montini believed politically essential in the post-council era.[63] And when *De Ecclesia* was approved, and it had to be decided what to do next in 1965, a few authoritative voices raised the possibility of prolonging the church in its conciliar state because it was not the duty of the isolated institution of the papacy to listen to and respond to the process of reception already begun before the end of the council with the first masses of reform; rather it was the duty of the communion of bishops.[64] When Vatican II closed on December 8, 1965, a history came to an end. In all, the open council had lasted 1,154 days following 1,354 days of preparation. Today, fifty years has not eroded the feeling that an extraordinary event took place in which everyone felt they were key players (ignoring those who felt that way) at which one looks with anger, affection, or attention.

Yet it was precisely the feeling of the "originality" of Vatican II that determined the position of authority of the assembly and of the papacy, the common sense of the theologians, and that of the common faithful, public opinion, and the international political opinion.[65]

The Multiple Idiosyncrasies of the Council

Like any council, the Second Vatican Council had its roots in a complex historical fabric that affected the unfolding of events and determined the way it was executed. No one came to the council of 1962–1965 with the same affirmation as was given to Cyril of Alexandria to safeguard the title *Theotokos*. But neither did Vatican II unfold without certain pressures and demands that have characterized all the great assemblies of Christianity; did not the threat of armed Muslims weigh on Constantinople in the 1430s?[66] Yet, this too, has to be evaluated based on the political and military issues in the context of geopolitical superpowers. Further, the impatience of the Germans that exploded in the general Fourth Lateran Council of 1215 did not represent the same form,[67] but issues of individual conscience and collective psychology did have a role in the ecumenical synod of the twentieth century. And if the sentiments of the old-Catholic minority that led to schism following Vatican I (very different from the schismatics opposed to Vatican II),[68] it is true that the split continues on in an historical scope in that line. And if the "invention" of the principle of collegiality aroused resistance and caution in Roncalli's and Montini's council, it was not unlike certain words, assumptions, and concepts foreign to the language of the New Testament from Chalcedon to Nicaea II.[69]

We could continue with endless analogies linking Vatican II to the multifaceted conciliar tradition of the East and West. We would do this not to establish arbitrary analogies, but to carry out the principal aim of history, which moves us in the opposite direction. It searches out miniscule distances with greater critical foresight and deeper recognition of the fact that when one moves the direction of the conciliar arc even a few degrees, the arrow of the decision shoots in directions different from what those who superficially cry "continuity" would have you believe.[70] One of the fruits of "historicizing" Vatican II (of which the "Bologna school," as its detractors sought to call it, was the main protagonist) was in fact that of bringing out features that were not belittled by institutional parallels connecting Vatican II to the synodal sequence of events of the Christian churches, but rather were more specifically highlighted in their scope, whether or not it was understood, and in their interrelation.[71]

In fact, if there have been fruits of the history of Vatican II, they have been that of stimulating both historical as well as theological research towards differential inquiry. Its effectiveness has been proven in many ways. For example, by now it has been accepted that the effect on the history of Vatican II of Roncalli's *intention* to convene a council without definitions and without condemnations has marked the assembly of the Church with the face of Christ and not with the face of heresy.[72] This intention opened the redefinition of the most difficult word of Vatican II—*pastoral*.[73] It exposed the trivial conceptions that would subordinate it to doctrine, as if precisely this semantic reshuffling (a scope no less than those regarding categories of person/substance or *auctoritas/potestas*) were not the key to understanding decisions of the council apparently based on other paradigms, such as the new attitude of the Magisterium towards Israel.

It is in defining these too often overlooked items in which the integral character of the council as an *event* emerges.[74] It was not the procedure that reached decisions; nor was it the wording of the decision itself that explained the weight of the issues glossed over by the assembly and the way in which it (through procedure and wording) effectively connected itself to the underlying intention, beyond the successful or failed efforts to articulate in a treaty-like structure *a posteriori* or in an *a priori* balance the parts, the themes, and choices.[75]

The overturning of the factual dimension of the decision-making process of Vatican II was in its language and in the way it expressed doctrinally significant and binding positions (the bishop as shaped by liturgy,[76] the symmetry between the intrinsic and asymmetric relationship with Israel and with other religions,[77] the hierarchy of truths,[78] Eucharistic ecclesiology,[79] the pneumatological dimension of baptism,[80] etc.).[81] It was parenthetical language, as Dossetti called it—or epideictic according to O'Malley. The register of Vatican II had a thickness derived from it being an effective expression of the conciliarity of the church.[82] So much so that when it is taken as mere stylistic words from the episcopal conferences' subsequent magisterial production or from papal oratory, it becomes sheer verbosity.[83]

The last of the specificities I would like to highlight is conciliar discourse as it pertained to the specific ecumenical nature of Vatican II.[84] It was certainly not an ecumenism designed concretely by the extension of imperial power, nor was it determined in the abstract from on high as according to the theory of Bellarmine.[85] Rather, it was a sought-after ecumeni-

cal attitude, marked by the presence of various denominations that confess the same Lord.[86] Yet, in a synodal friendship, the churches were not able to grasp its value, reducing that communion to multilateral negotiating tables, then to bilateral dialogues, and in the end to mere monologues conducted in the presence of one another.[87]

Self-understanding and Understanding

The tendency of the postconciliar magisterium to become consistently, not occasionally, *asynodal* (such is the problem of the churches) and the perennial humiliation of episcopal collegiality[88] (itself the result and cause of an excessively selective episcopacy according to the logic of self-interest), prompted high theology to isolate these idiosyncrasies of Vatican II, which instead can be kept together only on the historical level. This is the process that delineated the importance of the specificity of Vatican II and in the end contributed to the dispersal of its strength. In this process of the dehistoricization of Vatican II, no less important and serious in consequences as its historicization, some paradigms played such a large role as if they were autonomous.

The most significant was that of *reception*: from Congar to Beinert, interest in Vatican II's reception was certainly decisive, but it ended up nurturing a paradox. Given that its reception dealt with the responsibility of the local communities that selected what was important for their own vitality, the study of this phenomenon was wrongly directed towards the smallest level. Not the national church, but the local one; not the local church, but the specific community—this is where the historical work was talked about and sometimes practiced. As a result, there was the trivial endorsement of multiple items that became indescribable,[89] making it impossible to understand the reasons for the definitive or apparent loss and rejection of certain aspects of conciliar decisions and discourses (e.g. poverty).[90]

This tendency towards hyper-analysis leading *de facto* to aphasia is also joined by the assumption—equally uncritical—of the postulate that the ecclesiastical institution as such is the place to guard the connection between faith and dogma. For example, liturgical reform—attacked and defended on the trivial question as to the form of the missal[91]—had no purpose other than to offer a different way of closing the gap, which is to indicate the Eucharist as a place that molds duties and ministries, beginning from that of the bishop as guide of the community. Ecclesiology thus becomes engineering management and not a study of the conditions of Christian life, dredging

4. Pope John XXIII, photographed by Hank Walker, who was covering the council for *Life* magazine (photo: Hank Walker).

up the old conflicts between laxism and rigorism especially concerning the issue of access to the Eucharist as an exercise of the right of citizens of the Christian *politeia*.[92]

With respect to this process, the emphasis placed on rejecting the council (and on the reasons for the rejection) by that small-minded, spiritually autistic group had three devastating effects: keeping a large part of the troops of theologians idle before the walls of an empty sheepfold; encouraging non-conciliar conformism utilizing the tools of careerism; and, finally, pushing the papacy towards a form of nominalistic loyalty to the council which the artisans of the footnotes (adding references to the acts of the magisterium) created an art form that merits being studied as such.[93]

Shadows on the Threshold

This explains why discussion on the council in the decades since it took place have been primarily the reflections of the positions of the popes whose shadow is cast on each threshold, making its reading difficult. For example, in the 1985 extraordinary synod, Wojtyla refused Ratzinger's request of restoration and fine-tuned the episcopacies to the "great grace" thus providing a way of unity at little cost to Vatican II.[94] This constituted middle ground whose effects have been studied little. (Are the theses on the "definitive" magisterium the consequence? Or had the problem already been exhausted by the discussion of the *commissio parva* on the last re-reading before the promulgation of the new Code of Canon Law?)[95] Ten years after the preparation of *Ut unum sint*, a plan of discussion opened in which, excluding Archbishop Quinn's book which constituted one of the agendas of Francis' papacy,[96] progress was not made. Then in 2005, Ratzinger took the stage and gave a speech to the curia (sic!) in which the formula, continuity + reform vs. discontinuity + rupture opened the door to a series of squabbles of rare unproductiveness.[97] That is, until Francis's papacy—which began at the threshold of a half-century since the council. Bergoglio rarely references Vatican II, but he lives it in the name of an anti-nominalist reading of the council as a Latin American bishop and recovers some cornerstones such as the announcement of the Gospel and poverty.[98]

Give Back the Council

It is in this context that the question of the nature (?!) of doctrine[99] in the church fifty years after Vatican II is placed. Today, one out of three Christians has no denominational affiliation (or has more than one), and belonging to one or another established denomination is no longer discussed simply because the concepts are now void. The risk of a nostalgic vindication of the value of the council can be avoided, in fact, by fully accepting the responsibility that the council charged authority with, by meticulously censoring the recalcitrant resistance of the authorities themselves to those goads (the "*kentra*" in Acts 26:14) placed by real history on this era in which the pretexts of modernity focused on autonomy as a value, on the individual as a universal category, on rights as the common instance, no longer have any meaning.[100]

The schematic of an authority that strives to exert "control" over an unruly people who rise up to defend the autonomy of the individual as the engine of progressive history does not help in understanding why Vatican II remains distinctive after half a century. In an effort to reconcile a bourgeois culture bogged down by the weight of its own doubts (e.g. ecological capitalism, ethics based on individualism, etc.) the council met the twentieth century itself. This was the original feature that John XXIII, "with humble steadfastness of purpose," impressed on it in by prohibiting the use of the tools of definition as well as condemnation. Open to a new catholicity (also in the ecumenical sense) the council thereby became capable of speaking to the needs of a future time in which doctrines, styles, and tastes (the last of which is the only that has definitive weight today) could find a balance guaranteed by the responsibility of those invested in apostolic succession.[101]

CHRONOLOGY OF VATICAN II (1958–1965)

October 28: Cardinal Angelo Giuseppe Roncalli is elected pope, taking the name John XXIII.

May 17: The council's Antepreparatory Commission is appointed.

June 30: John XXIII receives the Antepreparatory Commission, chaired by Secretary of State Cardinal Domenico Tardini. Work begins.

October 30: Cardinal Tardini's first press conference on the council at Villa Nazareth (Rome).

March 28: The first native African bishop, Laurean Rugambwa of Tanzania, is elevated to the rank of cardinal at the consistory.

July 9: *Quaestionibus Commissionibus Praeparatoris Concilii Oecumenici Vaticani II positae* is drafted.

September 18: At New Delhi the Assembly of the World Council of Churches is opened. Five Catholic observers are sent.

December 25: Pope John XXIII issues the papal bull *Humanae Salutis*, announcing the council.

July 13: The pope authorizes the first set of *schemata* to be sent to the council fathers.

September 11: Radio message by John XXIII heightens anticipation of the council.

October 11: The formal opening of the Second Vatican Council in St. Peter's Basilica.

October 20: The council's message to the world is proposed and approved.

December 1–7: First examination of the *De Ecclesia* schema.

January 21: The Coordinating Commission meets to reorganize the agenda of the council.

May 10: John XXIII receives the Balzan Prize for Humanity, Peace and Fraternity among Peoples.

June 19: The cardinals meet in conclave to elect a successor to John XXIII.

58   59   60   61   62   63

October 9: Pius XII dies after a 19-year pontificate.

January 25: John XXIII announces the agenda for his pontificate: a synod for Rome, reform of the Code of Canon Law, the convocation of an Ecumenical Council.

June 18 : A letter goes out to the future council fathers asking for their views. Catholic universities and theology faculties worldwide are also consulted.

July 14: The pope decides to call the council "Vatican II."

February 20: Summaries of reports based on feedback from the bishops and other proposals are sent to the Roman congregations

June 5: Pope John issues the motu proprio *Superno dei nutu*, formally establishing the Preparatory Commission and the Central Preparatory Commission, to be chaired by the Secretary of State. The same day, the pope establishes the Secretariat for Christian Unity, headed by Cardinal Bea.

June 12: The beginning of the work of the Central Preparatory Commission, inaugurated by an address by John XXIII.

September 24: The Pan-Orthodox Congress of Rhodes opens.

February 2: John XXIII sets the beginning of the council for October 11, 1962.

August 6: The motu proprio, *Appropinquante Concilio*, establishes the regulations for the council.

October 4: John XXIII's pilgrimage to Loreto and Assisi.

October 13: The council's first General Congregation.

November 20: A majority rejects the draft of *De Fontibus Revelationis* prepared by the Theological Commission; the pope withdraws it and creates a joint committee with the Secretariat for Christian Unity.

December 8: The first session is adjourned.

January 6: John XXIII's letter *Mirabilis Ille* to the bishops on the new preparations.

April 11: The encyclical *Pacem in Terris* is published.

June 3: The death of John XXIII.

June 21: Cardinal Giovanni Battista Montini, Archbishop of Milan, is elected pope and takes the name Paul VI. He announces his intention to continue the council.

Summer: Discussion on the reform of the council regulations.

September 30: Resumption of the debate on *De Ecclesia*, guided by new moderators.

October 29: Vote on the inclusion of *De Beata Maria Virgini* in *De Ecclesia*.

November 30: The motu proprio *Pastorale Munus* on the powers and privileges granted to bishops is issued.

January 13: The council's constitution on the sacred liturgy is implemented.

April 2: The motu proprio *In Fructibus Multis* institutes the Pontifical Commission for Social Communications

September 23: Return of the head of St. Andrew, a relic that was stolen by Crusaders, to the Orthodox Church of Patras.

November 16: The text of the *Nota Explicativa Praevia* is read.

December 2: Paul VI goes to Bombay for the International Eucharistic Congress.

March 7: Promulgation of the decrees on concelebration and communion under both kinds.

October 4: Paul VI's speech to the United Nations in New York.

November 18: Approval and promulgation of the Dogmatic Constitution on Divine Revelation (*Dei Verbum*) and the Decree on the Apostolate of the Laity (*Apostolicam Actuositatem*). The canonization causes for Pius XII and John XXIII are opened.

December 7: Closing of the fourth session; approval and promulgation of the Constitution (*Gaudium et Spes*), the decrees on the missions (*Ad Gentes*) and the priesthood (*Presbyterorum Ordinis*) and the Declaration on Non-Christian Religions (*Nostra Aetate*). Joint Declaration of Paul VI and Athenagoras revoking the excommunications of 1054.

64

65

September 29: The opening of the second session.

October 8: Voting on *De Sacra Liturgia* begins.

October 30: Initial voting on *De Ecclesia.*

December 4: The closing of the second session; approval and promulgation of the Constitution on the Liturgy (*Sacrosanctum Concilium*) and the Decree on the Means of Social Communication (*Inter Mirifica*).

January 4–6: Paul VI's pilgrimage to the Holy Land. He meets with Ecumenical Patriarch Athenagoras.

January 15: The Coordinating Commission determines the number of schemas to be examined by the council.

September 14: Opening of the third session. Paul VI concelebrates Mass along with 24 council fathers.

November 14–21: Called "black week" because of the tensions over *De Ecclesia*, the decree on religious freedom, corrections to *De Oecumenismo*, and the definition of Mary as Mother of the Church.

November 21: The closing of the third session; the pope calls Mary "Mother of the Church"; the approval and promulgation of the Constitution on the Church *Lumen Gentium* and the decrees on ecumenism (*Unitatis Redintegratio*) and on the Eastern Churches (*Orientalium Ecclesiarum*).

February 1–6: The "Ariccia Schema," named after the neighborhood in Rome where the Joint Commission's subcommittees met to draft a new proposal for schema XIII.

September 14: Opening of the fourth period.

October 28: Approval and promulgation of the decrees on the Pastoral Office of Bishops (*Christus Dominus*), on religious life (*Perfectae Caritatis*), on priestly formation (*Optatam Totius*), and declarations on Christian education (*Gravissimum educationis*) and Religious Freedom (*Dignitatis Humanae*).

December 4: Ecumenical Liturgy of the Word at St. Paul Outside the Walls.

December 8: Final celebration; messages to humanity are read.

CHRONOLOGY OF 1959–1965. WORLD EVENTS

January 8: Charles de Gaulle becomes the president of the Fifth French Republic.

August 21: Hawaii becomes the fiftieth state of the United States of America

May 16: The physicist Theodore Maiman produces the first laser beam.

July 7: Italian Prime Minister Fernando Tambroni allows a pro-fascist group to hold its national congress in Genoa. Protesters are killed in clashes with police in Reggio Emilia.

October 10–14: OPEC is founded by Saudi Arabia, Iran, Iraq, Kuwait, and Venezuela.

December 14: The U.N. General Assembly approves resolution 1514, the Declaration on the Granting of Independence to Colonial Countries and Peoples.

March 13: The U.S. government launches Alliance through Progress, a vast program of economic assistance to Latin American states.

April 12: Soviet pilot Yuri Gagarin becomes the first human being to orbit the earth.

August 11–15: The government of the German Democratic Republic builds the Berlin Wall to prevent free passage between the East and West areas of the city.

December 26: The United Arab Republic dissolves after Syria secedes.

March 19: Bob Dylan's eponymous debut album is released.

July 12: The first Rolling Stones concert takes place at The Marquee Club in London.

October 1: James Meredith becomes the first African-American student to enroll at the University of Mississippi.

October 9: Uganda declares its independence.

October 15–28: The Cuban Missile Crisis.

June 11: The self-immolation in Saigon of Buddhist monk Thích Quảng Đức to protest the persecution of Buddhists by Vietnamese President Ngô Đình Diệm's government.

59

60

61

62

63

January 1–8: In Cuba, Fidel Castro and his followers overthrow Fulgencio Batista's regime.

March 17: Following the Chinese invasion of Tibet, the Dalai Lama abandons Lhasa and flees to India along with over 80,000 other refugees.

November 15: The German Social-Democratic Party meets in Bad Godesberg and formally renounces Marxism.

May 5: An American U2 reconnaissance plane is shot down on a mission over Soviet airspace and its pilot is arrested for spying.

June 15: Federico Fellini's *La Dolce Vita* is censored.

August 12: The launch of the Echo 1 satellite from Cape Canaveral begins the era of telecommunication.

November 8: Democratic Party candidate John Fitzgerald Kennedy is elected thirty-fifth president of the United States.

February 9: The Beatles debut at the Cavern Club, Liverpool.

April 11: The trial of Adolf Eichmann begins in Israel.

April 17–18: The Bay of Pigs Invasion.

September 17–18: U.N. Secretary General Dag Hammarskjöld dies in a plane crash in Rhodesia while on a mission to resolve the Congo Crisis.

March 18: The French Government and the Provisional Government of the Algerian Republic agree to the Évian Accords, ending the conflict that began in 1954.

April 16: The Chinese National Assembly adopts the 10-point austerity plan presented by Zhou Enlai.

August 5: Nelson Mandela is arrested and sentenced to five years in prison. He will not be released until 1990.

October 5: The first James Bond film, *Dr. No*, is released.

October 10–November 21: War between China and India.

May 25: Thirty-two African states found the Organization of African Unity to promote the development of their respective countries, defend their independence, and remove the remnants of colonialism.

June 16: Soviet cosmonaut Valentina Tereškova becomes the first woman in space.

August 28: The March on Washington for Jobs and Freedom. Martin Luther King delivers his "I Have a Dream" speech in front of the Lincoln Memorial.

November 22: U.S. President John F. Kennedy is assassinated in Dallas.

February 25: Cassius Clay (later Muhammed Ali) becomes boxing's world heavyweight champion for the first time.

April 10: Glenn Gould's last public concert in Los Angeles.

August 2–4: Following an alleged attack by North Vietnamese ships on the U.S military in the Gulf of Tonkin, the U.S. Congress approves a resolution authorizing President Johnson to use military force against North Vietnam.

September 4: Christian Democrat Eduardo Frei is elected president of Chile.

October 14: The Nobel Peace Prize is awarded to Martin Luther King.

October 16: China detonates its first nuclear device.

April: The European Communities, predecessor to the European Union, is formed by the merger of the EEC, ECSC, and EURATOM into one body, to take effect in 1967.

June 22: First U.S. air strike in North Vietnam.

July 16: The Mont Blanc Tunnel is opened by Presidents Giuseppe Saragat and Charles De Gaulle.

September 1: Pakistani troops penetrate India's territory.

October 3: Fidel Castro releases Ernesto "Che" Guevara's letter announcing his intention to leave Cuba to promote the revolutionary communist movement elsewhere.

November 21: The Berkeley Vietnam Day Committee stages a march of over 10,000 protesters.

64

65

October 9: In Italy, the landslide of Mount Toc into the reservoir created by the Vajont Dam produces a wave that overwhelms the town of Longarone, killing about 2,000 victims.

December 12: Kenya gains independence from the United Kingdom.

January 28: Andy Warhol opens his studio "The Factory" on East 47th Street in Midtown Manhattan.

April 1: The military junta in Brazil overthrows the democratically elected government of João Goulart beginning a period of government-sanctioned repression and torture of its opponents.

May 28–June 2: The Palestinian Liberation Organization (PLO) issues its Statement of Proclamation of the Organization in Jerusalem.

August 21: Palmiro Togliatti, the secretary of the Italian Communist Party, dies.

October 2: Pier Paolo Pasolini's film *The Gospel According to St. Matthew* is presented at the Venice Film Festival. A special screening is organized for the council fathers.

October 15: The Supreme Soviet removes Nikita Khrushchev from power; Leonid Brezhnev becomes secretary of the Central Committee of the Communist Party of the Soviet Union.

November 2: In Saudi Arabia, King Saud is dethroned and succeeded by his half-brother, Prince Faisal.

February 21: Malcolm X is assassinated in New York.

June 19: A coup in Algeria ousts President Ben Bella.

June: "Satisfaction" by the Rolling Stones is released in the United States.

September: President De Gaulle announces that France will leave NATO.

October: Jean Jacques Monod wins the Nobel Prize for medicine.

November: Mobutu Sese Seko seizes power in Congo.

December 30: Ferdinand Marcos is elected president of the Philippines.

1. The Ecumenical Councils of the First Millennium

1. Russian icon of Constantine with the bishops at the Council of Nicea, which was convened in the imperial palace in 325 (Archivio Jaca Book).

2. The condemnation of Arianism at the First Council of Nicea. Sixteenth-century icon, Monastery of St. Catherine of Sinai (Archivio Jaca Book).

The Greek noun *synodos* and the Latin *concilium* cover a wide range of meanings. In the Christian context, they were used originally to indicate meetings of believers and the buildings (churches) in which they were held and, subsequently, meetings of representatives of one or more communities presided over by a bishop. The origins of these assemblies are not clearly attested by sources and the history is spotty, but we can assume that it is just as ancient as that of Christian communities themselves. These kinds of assemblies probably originated as prayer meetings and became customary because of the need for such gatherings and the style of communion chosen, which consolidated the use of joint resolution of disciplinary or important doctrinal problems for the whole community. Galatians 2 is eloquent on this subject, as is Acts 14:27–28 and particularly Acts 15:1–35 in relation to the so-called Council of Jerusalem, gathering the different groups that based themselves on the teaching of Jesus and discussing issues related to the conversion of uncircumcised Gentiles to Christianity.

From the second and especially the third century, documentation on synods is more copious. With the Emperor Constantine and, more specifically, with the Council of Nicea in 325, a new era in the life of the so-called Great Church began, one marked by the ecumenical councils, occasions on which decisions were made organically and no longer by the authority of the emperor. The extreme complexity of the concept of "ecumenism" in the history of the first councils has led

LOCATIONS OF ECUMENICAL COUNCILS IN THE FIRST MILLENNIUM

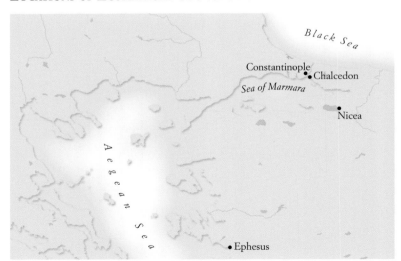

All eight councils were held in Constantinople or nearby cities, with the exception of Ephesus on the coast of Asia Minor.

3. The Basilica of Saint Irene in Constantinople, where the first Council of Constantinople was held (Archivio Jaca Book /Cigdem Kafescioglu).

4. Mosaic of the three visitors received by Abraham in Genesis 18 reflects a tradition of interpretation attested to by the first historian of the Council of Nicea, Eusebius of Caesarea, among others. In the *Demonstratio Evangelica* (V, 9), Eusebius says of the guests that one, "...is no angel...but one greater than an angel, the God and Lord who was seen...with two angels in human form." The representation of the three in this image is reminiscent of this exegesis (bamsphoto–Rodella).

3

to a distinction between the types of councils. Those summoned and/or chaired by the Roman or Byzantine emperor were ecumenical in that they were meetings of representatives of the churches from the whole Christian world, for example, Nicaea (325), Ephesus (431), and Chalcedon (451). Other councils were considered—not without controversy—to be ecumenical because of the topics discussed: Constantinople I (381), II (553), and III (6801), Trullo (691/2), Nicea II (787), Constantinople IV (both anti-Photian [869/70] and pro-Photian [879/80]).

Each of these assemblies had such distinct characteristics that sometimes it is difficult to make comparisons. Nevertheless, we can identify some common traits among the councils of the first millennium. First, reconstructed from the nature of the extant sources, initially expressed in epistles and anathemas and gradually collected in *corpora*, there is the approval of the definitions of faith (*horoi* or *termini*) and disciplinary canons with which the Church, once persecuted but now the dominant faith, adopts councils as the place where orthodoxy and orthopraxis are decided upon. This is the case with the councils between Nicea and Chalcedon, between Trullo and Nicaea II, and the two councils of Constantinople IV (869/870 and 879/880).

A second common feature consists of the participation in the councils of theologians and unbaptized laity, in addition to the bishops who were invited based on the organization of

4

> ▶ THE ECUMENICAL COUNCILS OF THE FIRST MILLENNIUM

325, Nicaea I—The creed, the condemnation of Arius, definition of the Son as consubstantial with the Father.

381, Constantinople I—The creed and doctrine on the Holy Spirit.

431, Ephesus—Definition of Mary as Mother of God against Nestorius.

451, Chalcedon—Only one Christ in two natures.

553, Constantinople II—Condemnation of Origenism.

680/1, Constantinople III—Doctrine of the two energies and wills of Christ.

691/2, Trullo—Canons on disciplinary matters such as the completion of decisions by the two previous councils.

787, Nicaea II—Defense of the veneration of holy icons.

5. Ruins of the Basilica of the Mother of God, where the Council of Ephesus was held.

6. One of the first icons of Mary as Mother of God, preserved in the monastery of St. Catherine of Sinai, VI–VII century. The Virgin and Child are enthroned between saints and angels, illustrating her glorification as Mother of God, defined by the Council of Ephesus (Archivio Jaca Book).

7. The Virgin nursing the Child, decorated prayer niche, from the monastery of St. Jeremiah, Saqqara, Egypt. Old Cairo Coptic Museum (Archivio Jaca Book).

the developing patristic church. At least some of the time, the Emperor Constantine (who had not yet been baptized) and his retinue of officials took part in the Council of Nicea in 325. Then consider Chalcedon, where the Emperor Marcian assigned the presidency of the council to nineteen of his commissioners. Even at Constantinople II (553)—the council that condemned the so-called Three Chapters, that is, the writings of Theodore of Mopsuestia, Theodoret of Cyrus, and Ibas, bishop of Edessa—officials selected by the Emperor Justinian preside. Consistent with this trend, Constantinople III (680/681)—the first council whose acts are formally signed by the emperor—basically meets to satisfy Emperor Constantine IV, who intended to gather some theologians together (as a result of the Lateran Council of 649) to discuss and resolve the issue of Monothelitism, a doctrine that asserts that Christ has two natures but only one will.

6

7

Two images demonstrate how iconographers highlighted differences that arose at the Council of Chalcedon. The icon of the monastery of Santa Catherine of Sinai in Palestine, depicts the suffering of Christ crucified. In the Armenian miniature, the triumph of the cross is emphasized.

8. *Crucifixion*, fragment of eighth-century icon, Monastery of St. Catherine in Sinai (Scala Archives/Deagostini Picture Library).

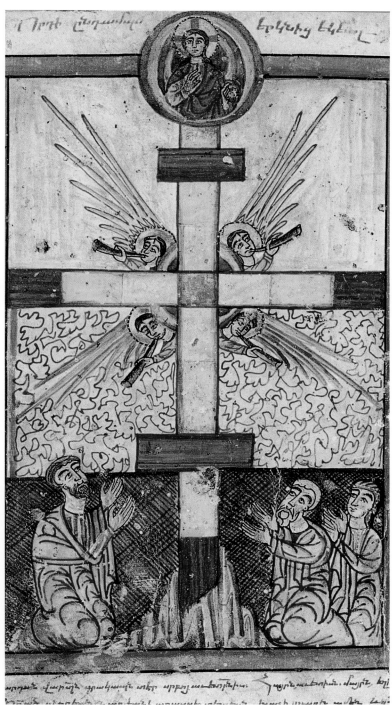

9. Exaltation of the Cross, Gospels of Vaspurakan, Sam Fogg Gallery, London (Archivio Jaca Book/ Isber Mehem).

21

11

The third common element in the councils of the first millennium may be the participation of representatives of monastic communities. This attests to the presence in the church, from the fourth century onwards, of a competitive charismatic component—that was an alternative to and often overlapped with the secular power of the bishops. Its weight affects conciliar history in various circumstances. The first time, significantly, it appears in the rejection expressed by many Eastern monks, of the definition of faith approved by Leo at the Council of Chalcedon. Then in the course of the councils of Constantinople II and III, during which there are tensions between the monastics, who were now ecclesiastically consolidated, and the bishops. These tensions on the conciliar level reach a peak after the iconoclasm controversy that upset the church in the East in the eighth and ninth centuries and formally ended only with the condemnation voted on in the council of Nicaea (787).

10. The imposing structure of Hagia Sophia in Istanbul. The Second Council of Constantinople met in one of its halls (Archivio Jaca Book / Cigdem Kafescioglu).

11. Late ninth-century miniature depicting the Emperor Justinian at the Second Council of Constantinople, which clarified Nicene teachings on the Holy Spirit (*Homilies*, Gregory Nazanzen, Paris Bibliothèque nationale de France) (Archivio Jaca Book).

12. *Justinian offers the Church of Hagia Sophia and Constantine offers the city to the Virgin Mary*. Mosaic above the southern gate of the narthex of Hagia Sophia, Istanbul. The emperors involved in both the First Council of Nicaea and Second Constantinople are depicted in this one image.

12

▶ REFERENCES TO THE FIRST ECUMENICAL COUNCILS IN VATICAN II DOCUMENTS

The constitutions of Vatican II that make the most reference to the councils of the first millennium are *Lumen Gentium* (LG) and *Orientalium Ecclesiarum* (OE). The first of these mentions the Nicene Creed (which is also quoted for its pneumatology in *Ad Gentes*, 4) and it is taken up again at the councils of Ephesus (431), Chalcedon (451), and Constantinople II (533) for its ecclesiology and Mariology (the latter doctrine is also employed at the end of Nicaea II [787], see LG 52, 57). There is also a reference to canon 4 of Nicaea (on the consecration of bishops) (325) over the status of bishops (LG 22) and, in this regard, LG 6–7 also mentions canons 6–7 of Nicaea (in relation to the bishops of Alexandria, Antioch, and Jerusalem, see LG 23).

Orientalium Ecclesiarum mentions the jurisdiction of the Eastern patriarchates decided on at Constantinople I (can. 2–3), Chalcedon (can. 9, 28), and Constantinople IV (869/70, can. 17, 21, see OE 7–13) and appeals to canon 18 of Nicaea (on deacons), to canon 6 of Chalcedon (concerning diaconal and priestly ordinations), and to canons 23 and 26 of Constantinople IV (869/70, the roles of bishops, priests, and deacons) in its deliberations on the sacraments (cf. OE 12–18).

It should also be noted that *Gaudium et Spes* invokes Chalcedon and the Councils of Constantinople II and III in the context of the interpretation of the Christology of Colossians 1:15 (the notion of Christ as the image of the invisible God, GS 22).

Finally, there is a reference to the end of Nicaea II and to can. 1 of Constantinople IV (869/70) in *Dei Verbum* (DV), about the concept of the apostolic tradition, regarding which the conciliar text refers to Judges 3 and II Thess 2:15 (DV 8).

13. Seventeenth-century icon of the Second Council of Nicaea, depicting the restoration of the use and veneration of holy images from the Novodevichy Convent in Moscow (Archivio Jaca Book).

14. Ruins of the church of Holy Wisdom in Nicaea, where the 787 council was held (Archivio Jaca Book/Cigdem Kafescioglu).

15–16. Monumental mosaic of the Deisis in the upper south gallery in Santa Sofia, Istanbul, dating from 1262. It is considered a masterpiece of Byzantine art, expressing the teachings of the Second Council of Nicaea on the Incarnation (Archivio Jaca Book Carlo Perogalli, Milan).

13

14

BIBLIOGRAPHY
G. D. Mansi, *Sacrorum Conciliorum Nova et Amplissima Collectio*, Florence-Venice 1759–1774; *Conciliorum Oecumenicorum Generaliumque Decreta, vol. I: The Oecumenical Councils. From Nicaea I to Nicaea II (325–787)*, Turnhout 2006; *Conciliorum Oecumenicorum Generaliumque Decreta, vol. II/1: The General Councils of Latin Christendom. From Constantinople IV to Pavia-Siena*, Bologna-Turnhout 2013, 1–71; *Concilium Universale Nicaenum Secundum. Concilii Actiones I–III, Herausgegeben von E. Lamberz*, Berlin-New York 2008; *Concilium Universale Nicaenum Secundum. Concilii Actiones IV–V*, Berlin 2012; *Concilium Constantinopolitanum A. 691/2 in Trullo Habitum (Concilium quinisextum), Herausgegeben* von H. Ohme, R. Flogaus, Ch.R. Kraus, Berlin 2013. For the basic secondary literature, see *Storia dei concili ecumenici*, edited by Giuseppe Alberigo, Brescia 1990, 5–178 and *The Oecumenical Councils*, op. cit. On "ecumenism," see also A. Melloni, "Concili, ecumenicità e storia," in *Cristianesimo nella storia*, 28 (2007), 509–542.

15

2. THE GENERAL COUNCILS OF LATIN CHRISTIANITY

The division between Latin and Eastern Christianity, sanctioned by the mutual excommunications between Rome and Constantinople in 1054, opened a long period during which the synodal institution acquired a major role in the development of the religious and political history of Latin Europe. The date of the break between the first and second stages coincided with the increasing pressure of the Gregorian Reform and the subsequent use of the synod as a regulatory instrument to develop and implement a thorough reform in the practice and in the structure of the life of the church. From this point until the Western schism and then up to the reforms of the sixteenth century, the synod and the council were a defining feature of life in Latin Christendom, in which rules and requirements were developed and adopted. The status of the many synods and councils that marked the life of Latin Christianity along this historical span is debated; in particular, any historical evaluation of the self-awareness that these assemblies of the Latin Church possessed is complex. Moreover, there are many opinions given by medieval authors, with different contexts and objectives, about the conciliar tradition of the Latin Church. For the canon lawyers of the twelfth century, the first four councils have a paradigmatic value: in the *Decretum*, Gratian, quoting Gregory the Great, put them in parallel with the four gospels (D. 15, c. 2). This medieval canonist, citing the

1. The enthronement of Photius, after his restoration by Constantinople IV (879–880). Twelfth-century miniature, National Library, Madrid (Archivio Jaca Book).

2. Lateran IV. From the *Chanson de la croisade des Albigeois* by William of Tudela and an anonymous collaborator. Bibliothèque nationale de France (Archivio Jaca Book).

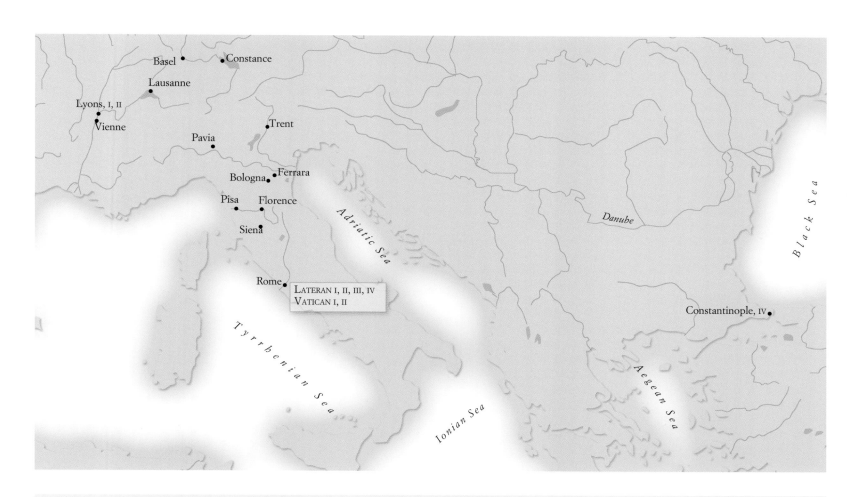

▶ THE GENERAL COUNCILS OF THE LATIN CHURCH

869/70, Constantinople IV—*Deposition of Photios.*

879/80, Constantinople IV—*Restoration of Photios.*

1040, Rome, *Measures against heresies.*

1050, Rome, *Rules against simony.*

1123, Lateran I—*Implementation of the Gregorian reform.*

1139, Lateran II—*Excommunication of Roger II of Sicily and condemnation of the Petrobrusians and the Henricians.*

1179, Lateran III—*End of the schism and implementation of the peace of Venice, condemnations of heresies.*

1215, Lateran IV—*Reform, discipline, and canonical structure of Christianity. Confession of faith against the Cathars; the doctrine of transubstantiation of the Eucharist; the rules regarding annual confession and communion.*

1245, Lyons I—*Deposition of Frederic II and call for the crusades.*

1274, Lyons II—*Decrees of Church reform.*

1311/2, Vienne—*Reform of the clergy, suppression of the Templars, the dispute over Franciscan poverty.*

1409, Pisa—*Election of Alexander V. Attempt to solve the Western Schism.*

1414/8, Constance—*End of the schism, condemnation of Jan Hus and John Wycliffe.*

1423, Pavia-Siena—*Implementation of the decisions of Constance.*

1431/49, Basel—*Decrees on reform and conciliarist theory.*

1437/49, Ferrara/Florence/Rome/Lausanne—*Attempt at union between the Latin and Orthodox churches.*

512/7, Lateran V—*Failed reform of the Church, the Curia, and cardinals.*

1545/63, Trent—*The reform of the Roman Catholic Church.*

1869/70, Vatican I—*Dogma of papal infallibility and the primacy of the Roman Pontiff.*

1962/5, Vatican II—*The renewal of the Roman Catholic Church.*

3. On Frederick II's orders, the Pisan fleet intercepts Genoese ships carrying prelates to Rome for the council called by Gregory IX. Fourteenth-century miniature from the *Cronica* of Giovanni Villani, from ms. Chigiano L.VIII.296, preserved at the Vatican Library.

3

Liber Diurnus, then qualified the first eight "holy" councils using the title *concilium universale* to emphasize their role in defining matters of faith (D. 16, c. 8). In contrast, at the Council of Constance in 1417, beside the first eight "universal councils," it also refers to the Fourth Lateran Council, the Council of Lyons, and the Council of Vienne as *concilium generale*. Fourteen years later in Basel, John of Segovia will add Lyons I, Pisa, and Siena to the list of general councils. In this context it should be noted that for Latin Christianity, councils considered major in terms of scope and importance are qualified as "universal" and "general," while the *ecumenical* (*oecumenicum*) remains the customary adjective for describing the councils chaired by the emperor or in which the East is represented, such as the Council of Ferrara-Florence whose agenda was reunion with the "Greeks."

Only in the sixteenth century, in order to strengthen the authority of Trent, did Robert Bellarmine, in *Controversia IV De Conciliis et Ecclesia Militante*, exclude the necessity of competition among the five patriarchates for the universality of the councils.

He will apply to councils the concept of being "ecumenical," which was first developed by the Jesuit Arnaldo Pontac, excluding from this the councils of the fifteenth century and promoting the three Lateran councils of the twelfth century that mark the end of the many crises between the papacy and the Empire.

The three Lateran councils of 1123, 1139, and 1179 had a different status than other important synods of the eleventh and twelfth centuries that were chaired by the popes, such as Reims (1049, 1119, and 1131), Clermont (1095 and 1130), Piacenza (1132), Pisa (1135), and Tours (1163). During the most intense period of the Gregorian reform, from the middle of the eleventh century to Lateran I, there were about seventy councils. They include those initiated by the pope's revitalization of the role of the Lenten synod, which did not always meet in Rome but took place in other areas of continental Europe because of the itinerancy of the Curia. Running alongside the growth of the role of the bishop of Rome, the synods convoked by the pope involved the whole of Latin Christendom and assume an ecclesiastical and

4, 5. Two images from the Chronicle of Giovanni Villani, preserved in the Vatican Library (Chigiano L.VIII.296). Fig. 4 illustrates the first Council of Lyons, during which Pope Innocent IV deposed the emperor Frederick II. Fig. 5 illustrates the Council of Vienne. In these images, the pope is in the center, a departure from the Byzantine tradition in which the emperor was depicted in the center.

4

5

6. Miniature depicting the first phase of the Council of Constance, during which John XXIII flees (bottom). Antonio Baldana, *De Magno Schismate*, c. 1420. Palatine Library, Parma (Archivio Jaca Book).

7. Election of Martin V in the final phase of the Council of Constance. Miniature from the book of Ulrich von Richental, *Das Concilium so zu Constanz gehalten ist worden des jars do man zalt von der geburdt unsers erlösers* M.CCCC.XIII. (Jar, Augsburg 1536).

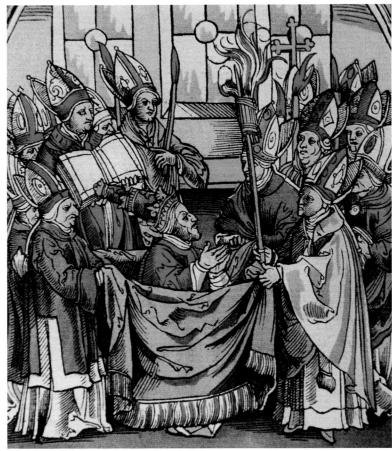

6

7

political importance of the highest order in terms of both the number and quality of the participants and because of the impact of the decisions taken therein. Because the papacy played a role in these reforms (synodal decisions have an impact on canonical jurisprudence) there is a certain "symbiosis of authority between the pope and the council." The synods formed the fulcrum of action by the Apostolic See in the reform of the Church, and in breaking free from imperial protection, throughout the so-called investiture controversy. These councils were not called, as in the first millennium, to address theological issues. Instead, they involve issues of discipline, imposing rules and prohibitions for simony, the sacraments, the life of the clergy, the crusades, usury, the church's sphere of action compared to that of the secular powers, and ended by imposing a hierocratic model on the Church. From the Fourth Lateran Council on (the most important of the Latin Middle Ages), it becomes easy to identify "major" synods, whose status of "general" (compared to ones from previous centuries) was recognized by their contempo-

raries: Lyons I and II, and Vienne, where in addition to bishops and abbots participants included representatives of chapters, mendicant orders, and universities. These were not meetings in which the discussion always bears the same weight: indeed the pope often convenes the council, leads it, formulates the canons, and promulgates them. Like papal decrees that become enshrined in canon law in a similar way to the implementation of teaching in the universities, the conciliar canons, which were promulgated publicly, were reviewed by the pope after the conclusion of the Assizes and subsequently sent to universities (Lyons I and II). The evolution of centralization of power in the papacy gradually changed the balance and the practices of the synod, which in the thirteenth century still was seen as an indispensable tool for affirming the will of the pope. Apart from dramatic moments, such as the resistance of the German bishops at Lateran IV or the harangues leading up to the deposition of the Emperor Frederick II at Lyons II, councils merely performed the function of ratification, so that after Vienne and the so-called

8. The burning of John Hus during the Council of Constance. Etching or woodcut.

9. Council of Basel. Image from J. Lenfant, *Histoire du concile de Constance*, Amsterdam, 1727.

10. Benozzo Gozzoli, fresco, Magi Chapel, Palazzo Medici Riccardi in Florence (1450). The Council of Florence was for the artists of the city a unique opportunity to get in touch with the costumes of the Byzantine court. The features of Benozzo's illustration of Melchior have traditionally been thought to depict Joseph, Patriarch of Constantinople, who died during the council. He is seen with part of his entourage in a Tuscan landscape (Archivio Jaca Book).

11. Lateran V. Image from *Concilium Lateranense V* MDXVII, ed. J. Mozzocchi, Rome, 1521.

12. Image probably of the thirteenth session of Council of Trent (July 15, 1563), San Vigilio Cathedral. Because of the summer heat, it was held in the nave, rather than a meeting hall. This is probably more accurate than most representations. 1563 canvas, probably from Venice; Musée du Louvre, Paris (Archivio Jaca Book).

12

"Babylonian captivity" of the popes at Avignon, they were no longer convened. The Western Schism caused an unexpected change: a council, thought to be a possible means of solution, was summoned after decades of failed attempts. The council of Pisa in 1409 was convened by the cardinals on both sides and elected a third pope; another council, convened in Constance from 1415 to 1417 with the support of Emperor Sigismund, affirmed the emperor's authority, deposed all three popes, and restored unity. Councils seemed able to resolve the problems of Christianity and the expectations of reform and unity within the church; from then on, they were held frequently. This impetus was lost in the councils in Pavia-Siena and Basel; the latter failed and was disavowed by the pope who transferred it to Ferrara and then to Florence. Eugene IV wished to celebrate the reunifi-

cation with the Eastern Church. However, this turned out to be short-lived and only brought about a rupture in the East, which was about to fall to the Ottoman Turks (1453). Distrust in the councils and conciliarist theories induced the pontiffs not to convene any synods until Lateran V (which scotched an attempt to hold a schismatic synod in Pisa-Milan, which France wanted for political reasons); this would contribute to a slowdown of preparations for the Council of Trent. It took thirty years after the start of the Lutheran crisis for the pope to convene a council. At Trent—which was held over eighteen years and included a number of restarts and changes of locale—in addition to defining the Catholic position on the doctrines disputed by the reformers, drew up a thorough disciplinary reform that held sway throughout the following three centuries. From the

13. The Council of Trent. Painting, Vatican Apostolic Palace (Biblioteca Apostolica Vaticana).

13

sixteenth to the eighteenth centuries, the Church was a model of organizational modernity and theological and missionary commitment. Thanks to exemplary figures such as Charles Borromeo, the Council of Trent fashioned a durable pastoral model. Only after the confrontation with the Enlightenment and with Josephism, after the upheaval of the French Revolution and the Napoleonic Wars, in the clash with modernity, would there be a council again, from 1869–70. At Vatican I, "errors" were condemned and a contemporary theological recasting of the figure of the pope was defined, with the approval of the teaching on infallibility and on the primacy of the Roman Pontiff over every Christian. Many Catholic theologians thought that, at least for their local churches, there should be no more councils. The suspension of the council for the Franco-Prussian war in the summer of 1870 and the fall of Rome to the forces for Italian reunification the following September 20, left the issue and the agenda open.

BIBLIOGRAPHY
The decrees of the Latin councils can be found in a critical edition in the *Corpus Christianorum: Conciliorum Oecumenicorum Generaliumque Decreta*, vol. II, 1–2, Turnhout, 2013; for an updated bibliography on the individual councils refer to their individual introductions. A bibliographic summary *Storia dei Concili Ecumenici*, edited by G. Alberigo, Brescia 1993. See also A. Melloni, "Concili, ecumenicità e storia" in *Cristianesimo nella storia*, 28 (2007), 509–542, J. Wohlmuth, *I Concili di Costanza (1414–1418) e Basilea (1431–1449)*, 219–281; A. Cadili, "Composizione, Ruoli e Formazione del Consenso nei Concili della Chiesa Latina Medievale (Secoli XI–XIII)," in *Cristianesimo nella storia*, 32 (2011), 963–1005.

3. The Synods of the Twentieth and Twenty-first Centuries

▶ **Some synods, councils, assemblies, and conferences of churches in the 20th and 21st century**

1905	London—*The Baptist World Congress*
1908	Lambeth Palace (London)—*Fifth Conference of the Anglican Communion*
1910	Edinburgh—*World Missionary Conference*
1917–1918	Moscow—*Great Council of Moscow and the Restoration of the Patriarchate*
1920	Lambeth Palace (London)—*Sixth Conference of the Anglican Communion*
1922	Berlin—*Synod of the Old-Prussian Union*
1924	Shanghai—*The Plenary Council of China (Roman Catholic)*
1925	Stockholm—*World Conference of the Movement for Practical Christianity*
1927	Lausanne—*World Conference on Faith and Order of the Church*
1930	Lambeth Palace (London)—*Seventh Conference of the Anglican Communion*
1933	Wittenberg—*The General Synod of the Evangelical Lutheran Church*
1934	Barmen—*The Synod of the Confessing Church*
1934	Dahlem—*Second Synod of the Confessing Church*
1935	Augsburg—*Third Synod of the Confessing Church*
1936	Bad Oeynhausen—*Fourth Synod of the Confessing Church*
1945	Treysa (Schwalmstadt) / Stuttgart—*Treysa Conference—Meeting of the Council of the German Evangelical Church (Lutheran, Reformed, and United Churches)*
1947	Lund—*Lutheran World Federation*
1948	Moscow—*Moscow Council in 1948 Chaired by Alessio*
1948	Amsterdam—*The General Assembly of the World Council of Churches*
1948	Lambeth Palace (London)—*Eighth Conference of the Anglican Communion*
1955	Evanston—*Second General Assembly of the World Council of Churches*
1955	Rio de Janeiro—*The General Conference of the Latin American Episcopal Council CELAM (Roman Catholic)*
1957	Bethlehem—*Unity Synod—Unitas Fratrum*
1958	Lambeth Palace (London)—*Ninth Conference of the Anglican Communion*
1961	New Delhi—*Third General Assembly of the World Council of Churches*
1961	Rhodes—*The Pan-Orthodox Conference*
1962–1965	Rome—*Vatican II*
1963	Rhodes—*Second Pan-Orthodox Conference*
1964	Rhodes—*Third Pan-Orthodox Conference*
1964–1969	Canterbury / York—*Synods of the Church of England*
1965	Addis Ababa—*General Council of the Churches of the Pre-Chalcedonian Orthodox Tradition*
1968	Uppsala—*Fourth General Assembly of the World Council of Churches*
1968	Medellín—*Second General Conference of the Latin American Episcopal Council CELAM (Roman Catholic)*
1968	Chambesy—*Fourth Pan-Orthodox Conference*
1968	Lambeth Palace (London)—*Tenth Conference of the Anglican Communion*
1971	Moscow—*Moscow Synod*
1973	Leuenberg—*Conference of the Lutheran, Reformed, and United Churches*
1975	Nairobi—*Fifth General Assembly of the World Council of Churches*
1978	Lambeth Palace (London)—*Eleventh Conference of the Anglican Communion*
1979	Puebla—*Third General Conference of the Latin American Episcopal Council CELAM (Roman Catholic)*
1983	Vancouver—*Sixth General Assembly of the World Council of Churches*
1986	Assisi—*Interreligious Assembly—World Day of Prayer for Peace*
1988	Lambeth Palace (London)—*Twelfth Conference of the Anglican Communion*
1988	Moscow—*Moscow Synod*
1991	Canberra—*Seventh General Assembly of the World Council of Churches*
1992	Santo Domingo—*Fourth General Conference of the Latin American Episcopal Council CELAM (Roman Catholic)*
1992	Porvoo—*European Conference of Twelve Lutheran Churches*
1998	Lambeth Palace (London)—*Thirteenth Conference of the Anglican Communion*
1998	Harare—*Eighth General Assembly of the World Council of Churches*
2000	Moscow—*Moscow Synod*
2006	Porto Alegre—*Ninth General Assembly of the World Council of Churches*
2007	Aparecida—*Fifth General Conference of the Latin American Episcopal Council CELAM (Roman Catholic)*
2008	Lambeth Palace (London)—*Fourteenth Conference of the Anglican Communion*
2009	Moscow—*Moscow Council*
2010	Grand Rapids—*The General Council of the World Communion of Reformed Churches*
2013	Busan—*Tenth General Assembly of the World Council of Churches*

1. Karl Barth's original manuscript of the Theological Declaration of Barmen, May 16, 1934. Written by Barth, who was Swiss Reformed, modified by Lutherans Hans Asmussen of Hamburg and Thomas Breit of Moncao. In the face of the Nazi regime and its attempt to control the churches in Germany, it stated that "Jesus Christ, according to the testimony of the Scriptures, is the only Word of God. We must listen to it alone." Its ecumenical intent can be seen by

the input from and adoption by different Protestant churches (Karl Barth-Archiv).

2. The All Russian Council, held by the Russian Orthodox Church in the Kremlin, 1917.

3. First Assembly of the World Council of Churches (WCC), Amsterdam, August 22 to September 4, 1948. Its theme was "Man's Disorder and God's

The twentieth and twenty-first centuries have been characterized, not only by large gatherings that are fundamental to the history of the Christian churches, but also by great aspirations, disappointments, and roadblocks on the ecumenical journey. This list—which is inevitably an overview—goes from the first Baptist World Congress in 1905, the first Protestant World Missionary Conference in Edinburgh in 1910, the Great Council of Moscow from 1917 to 1918, the Life and Work Congress in Stockholm in 1925, and the World Conference on Faith and Order in Lausanne in 1927, to the assemblies of the World Council of Churches, the Second Vatican Council of 1962–

1965, right up to the formation of the World Communion of Reformed Churches in 2010.

While differing from ecumenical councils mainly because of the nature of the non-binding decisions at their heart, the conferences arising from the ecumenical movement, particularly the assemblies of the World Council of Churches beginning with Amsterdam in 1948, mainly attempted to represent or make present the collegial element first of non-Catholic Christianity, and then of the whole of Christianity. However, if we look at the theological core of these assemblies—which did not become entangled with the legal and judicial aspects—they appear as

Design," and 147 churches from different denominations and countries were represented. At its most recent assembly held from October 30 to November 8, 2013, in Busan, South Korea, 345 members participated, discussing the theme "God of Life, Lead Us to Justice and Peace."

4. Opening ceremony of the Ninth Lambeth Conference of the Anglican Communion in London, held from July 23 to August 13, 1978. 450 bishops attended (Archivio Jaca Book/courtesy Lambeth Palace).

5. A group of bishops during the third general conference of the Latin American Episcopal Congress (CELAM), Puebla, Mexico, 1979. In his message to the conference, Pope John Paul II said, "It is a great consolation for the universal Father to note that you come together here not as a symposium of experts, not as a parliament of politicians, not as a congress of scientists or technologists, however important such assemblies may be, but as a fraternal encounter of Pastors of the Church" (Archivio Jaca Book /Giancarlo Giuliani).

4

5

of the 1930s (Barmen, Dahlem, Augusta, and Bad Oeynhausen), symbolically represented the churches' highest and densest opposition to totalitarianism and made possible the assembly of Treysa / Schwalmstadt, in 1945, which gave birth to the *Evangelische Kirche in Deutschland*. The first council of China in Shanghai and the assemblies of Medellín, Puebla, and Aparecida contributed to the awareness of the enlargement of Roman Catholic ecumenism in what were then considered Third-World countries. The conferences of the world federations of Protestants, such as the assembly of the Lutheran World Federation in 1947 and the general council in Grand Rapids, Michigan, which, in June 2010, created the World Communion of Reformed Churches, and the assemblies of Leuenberg and Porvoo tried, not without difficulty, to overcome the sectarian, national, and territorial divisions of the reform churches inherited from the fractures of the sixteenth century. The general council of the Eastern churches in Addis Ababa (1965), chaired by Emperor Haile Selassie, was the first-ever meeting of the pre-Chalcedonian churches (the Armenian, Syriac, Coptic, Ethiopian, and Malankara churches). Finally, the Pan-Orthodox conferences in Rhodes in 1961, 1963, and 1964 and in Chambesy in 1968, were preparatory meetings for the great Pan-Orthodox synod to be held in 2016, while the synods of Moscow concerned matters internal to the Russian church, with the important exception of the one in July 1948, which was convened at the height of the Stalinist regime to celebrate the 500th anniversary of the independence of the Russian Church, which ruled against participation in the meeting of the World Council of Churches.

stages in the journey towards unity of witness in the faith and in communal service. Among other things, consider the meeting in New Delhi in 1961, which was seen as an opportunity, together with the Second Vatican Council, to bear witness to the unity of Christians in the world and was the first assembly of the World Council of Churches to include the participation of Catholic observers. For its part, given the interest aroused beyond the boundaries of Roman Catholicism, Vatican II may well be called ecumenical in a fuller sense than Catholic theology has given to the term in the aftermath of the Council of Trent: in raising the problems of the Christian message and insisting on the issue of unity, it opened the debate on issues that transcend individual denominational traditions and affect all of contemporary Christianity. Because of the historical role played by Vatican II, in 1968 the World Council of Churches began to explore the theme of collegiality within the church and of the history of the councils. The wealth of historical forms into which the collegiality of Christian churches has been translated is expressed in the variety of synods of the twentieth and twenty-first centuries. Thus, some synods, such as those of the German Confessing Churches

6

8

9

6. World Day of Prayer for Peace in Assisi on October 27, 1986. Sixty-two religious leaders representing the major religions of the world gathered in Assisi to pray for peace, sharing in prayer and fasting. In his homily concluding the Week of Prayer for Christian Unity on January 25, 1986, Pope John Paul II had said, "On this solemn occasion I wish to announce that I'm about to initiate appropriate consultations with the heads, not only of different Christian churches and communions, but also of other world religions, in order to promote a special prayer meeting with them for peace in the city of Assisi, the place that the seraphic St. Francis transformed into a center of universal brotherhood (Archivio Fscire).

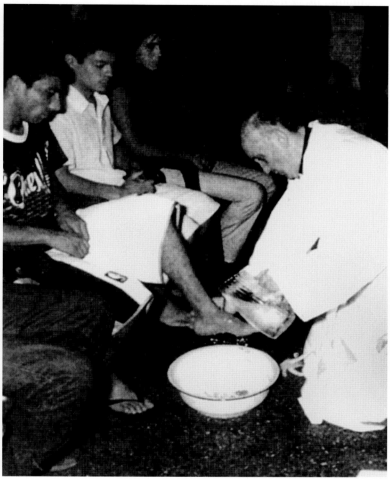

7

The centrality of the synodal and conciliar dimension responds, in a multifaceted, rich, and sometimes contradictory way, to the gospel and to the need for participation, co-responsibility and involvement in the life of the churches, emphasizing the fundamental equality of baptism with a new form of Christian presence in the post-ideological and secularized West and contributing significantly to the contemporary social and political awareness by gradually, even if not definitively, overcoming historical inequalities.

BIBLIOGRAPHY
Le Concile et les conciles. Contribution a l'histoire de la vie conciliaire de l'église, Chevetogne/Paris 1960; *Synod and Synodality. Theology, History, Canon Law and Ecumenism in New Contact*, edited by A. Melloni and S. Scatena, Münster 2005; G. Alberigo, *Transizione epocale. Studi sul Concilio Vaticano II*, Bologna 2009; "I sinodi: organi di governo e/o luogo di formazione del consenso nella Chiesa," edited by P. Hünermann and G. Ruggieri, in *Cristianesimo nella storia* 32 (2011).

7. Then-Archbishop of Buenos Aires, Jorge Mario Bergoglio, during the washing of the feet on Holy Thursday. He participated in The General Conference of Latin American Bishops' Council, held May 13–31, 2007 in Aparecida, Sao Paulo (Brazil). Bergoglio was appointed editor of the final text. At the time, he said, "The climate that led to the drafting of the document is an atmosphere of genuine and fraternal cooperation, mutual respect, that characterized the work, a work that has moved from the bottom up, not the opposite. To understand this we need to look at…three key points, the three 'pillars' of Aparecida. The first is: from the bottom to the top. This is possibly the first time a general conference of ours is not based on a prepackaged text but on an open discussion, which had begun before between CELAM and the Episcopal Conferences and continued" (photo Ansa).

8. The Fourteenth Lambeth Conference of the Anglican Communion, held at the University of Kent, Canterbury, July 2008. Rowan Williams, then the Archbishop of Canterbury, is seated at the center of the front table.

9. The Synod of Moscow, 2009, which elected Kirill I Patriarch of Moscow and all Rus'.

4. Conclude Vatican I or Call a New Council?

1. St. Peter's Basilica, 1870. The General Convocation of Vatican Council I, called by Pope Pius IX and interrupted by the outbreak of the Franco-Prussian War. This 1870 lithograph by Giacchino Altobelli shows the moment at which the dogmatic constitution was read by Bishop Antonio Valenziani of Fabriano. The document was discussed by the council from April 27 to May 8 (Museo Pio IX, Sinigallia).

2. Velletri Station. In March 1863, Pius IX traveled to Castel Gandolfo by train for the first time (photo Nazionale Ando Gilardi).

3. Rome, St. Peter's Square, July 1870. Pius IX promulgates the council's constitution on papal primacy and infallibility (photo Nazionale Ando Gilardi).

4. *Dictionnaire de Théologie Catholique* (Dictionary of Catholic Theology), 1908, where J. Forsen's entry for "Councils" claims that councils have been superseded by the dogma of papal infallibility ("are not necessary to the church") (Biblioteca G. Dossetti, Fscire).

5. Rome, February 11, 1933. Pius XI inaugurates Vatican Radio. On the far left is Guglielmo Marconi, the inventor credited with the invention of radio, who set up the station at the pope's request (*L'Osservatore Romano*).

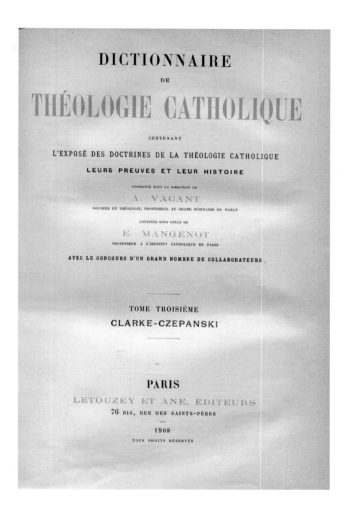

4

5

On October 20, 1870, after several weeks of uncertainty following the outbreak of the Franco-Prussian War, Pius IX suspended Vatican I *sine die* with the Apostolic Letter *Postquam Dei Munere*. It had only opened the previous year. The possibility of moving it, as was the Council of Trent, was not acceptable to the pope, who judged that the loss of his temporal power deprived him of the freedom essential to preside at a council. The suspension of Vatican I opened a whole range of issues, the complexity of which would be perceived fully only with the passage of time. For example, the fifty-one drafts left undiscussed, made it obvious that papal primacy and infallibility had not exhausted the council's agenda. In addition, its inability to continue the debate meant that its decisions concerning the papal office could not be fully digested and balanced with a discussion on the role of bishops in the church.

However, not all the preparatory material was lost. Some was merged into magisterial documents of Pope Leo XIII and some was taken up again during the development of the 1917 Code of Canon Law. But the declarations of the Second Vatican Council on primacy and infallibility had another unexpected effect: the emergence of the idea that papal primacy and infallibility made future councils useless. This did not escape the notice of Chancellor Bismarck, who in 1874 issued a circular noting the downgrading of bishops following Vatican I. Others noticed as well, such as the theologian Louis Billot, the lawyer Paul Hinschius, or the author of the entry under "Conciles" in the *Dictionnaire de Théologie Catholique* in 1908; they openly declared that the councils had been superseded now that the pope had ultimate power over all doctrinal or disciplinary matters. However, we should remember that, in spite of these developments, the manuals adopted in theological faculties and the 1917 Code of Canon Law, promulgated nearly half a century after Vatican I, confirmed the continued existence of councils as an institution.

Pius XI cleared up any doubt when he expressed his intention to resume and conclude Vatican I in the encyclical *Ubi Arcano* (1922). He followed this up in 1923 by a wide consultation of the Catholic episcopate on whether to resume the council, but he reserved to himself the setting of the agenda. However, despite encouraging signs, for reasons not completely understood, Pius XI suspended the project in May 1925.

The idea of convening a council took shape during the pontificate of Pius XII, who in March 1948, set up some preparatory commissions that began to lay out the preparatory drafts in absolute secrecy under the direction of the Holy Office. Pius XII intended more than a resumption and conclusion of Vatican I. Instead, he was thinking of a new council that would address a number of

6. July 19, 1943. Pius XII travelled to the damaged Basilica di San Lorenzo fuori le Mura and met with the people in the streets of Rome after the Allied bombings during the Second World War (Archivio Fscire).

6

urgent doctrinal and disciplinary issues. However, as the project progressed, important differences of opinion emerged regarding the kind of council to be held and whether it should be brief or open-ended. In addition, there was disagreement on which issues should be included in the agenda, such as the dogmatic definition of the assumption of Mary, a new condemnation of communism, or even the censure of some theological "deviations" that had been left out of other discussions. In January 1951, because of his advancing age as well as these uncertainties, Pius XII ordered that the project be set aside.

Of course the idea of a council, even after the indefinite suspension *sine die* of Vatican I in 1870, whether as a resumption or as a new council, was manifested even beyond the "official" attempts. For example, in 1910, Bishop Geremia Bonomelli, bishop of Cremona, said a new council was possible but "improbable," since the Holy See feared reprisals from bishops who might not want

to stay at the Vatican for an indeterminate period. But the need for a new council (as opposed to a resumption of Vatican I) was invoked in 1939 by Celso Costantini, Secretary of the Sacred Congregation for the Propagation of the Faith, who judged it essential, both to restore dignity to the bishops and as an opportunity to undertake a major restructuring of the Curia. In 1948, even Fr. Giovanni Calabria said he was convinced of the urgent need for a new council; Cardinal Schuster's dilatory response ("The idea of a council seems good. But it is a long and delicate undertaking, one that only Rome can implement...") did not keep him from reiterating that the bishops "could be gathered around the pope in some extraordinary assizes, as a council or nearly so, in order to bolster his cry for 'a war on war'." In the days following Pius XII's death, Fr. Zeno Saltini hoped that the new pope would "call a council in which all those who refuse to work and to act to remove all social injustice from the face of the earth are declared public sinners."

7. Don Zeno Saltini (1900–1981), founder of the Nomadelfia movement. In 1947, he settled his community in the former concentration camp at Fossoli (Modena). He later moved to Tuscany.

8. Dietrich Bonhoeffer (1906–1945), Lutheran pastor and member of the Confessing Church and director of the Finkenwalde Seminary. He fought against Nazi domination of the church, and for this he was imprisoned in 1943. He was executed by hanging on April 9, 1945 (Archivio Jaca Book).

9. Pope John XXIII's handwritten notes on an audience he had on November 2, 1958, with Cardinal Ruffini, archbishop of Palermo, during which he spoke of calling a council. Part of the note reads "Council. Preparation: Diocese of Rome" (Archivio Fscire).

In 1934, even Dietrich Bonhoeffer called for a council of all Christian churches, with the theme of peace as the agenda. Similarly, the Catholic theologian Max Josef Metzger wrote to Pius XII in 1939 a request to gather some authoritative representatives of various Christian denominations in Assisi to prepare for a council that would unite the church in order to finally make its commitment to peace credible.

A few days after his election, John XXIII stated his intention to organize a council. But with "humble resolve" he determined that the council called on January 25, 1959, would be a new one, thus concluding Pius IX's council, almost ninety years after its *sine die* suspension.

7

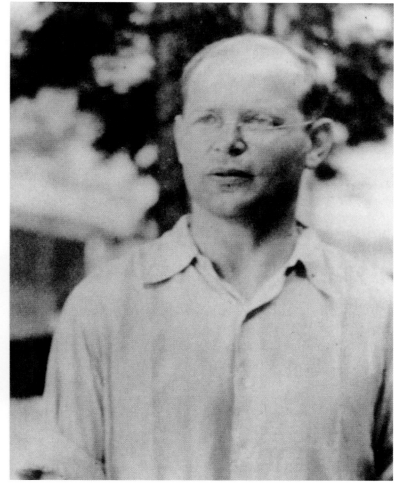

8

BIBLIOGRAPHY

Il Concilio Vaticano II. Cronache del Concilio Vaticano II edited by *La Civiltà Cattolica*, G. Caprile, vol. I/1, *L'annunzio e la preparazione, 1959–1962*, Rome 1966, 15–35; F.-C. Uginet, "Les projets de concile général sous Pie XI et Pie XII," in *Le deuxième concile du Vatican (1959–1965). Actes du colloque international de Rome (28–30 mai 1986)*, Rome 1989, 65–78; G. Butturini, *Alle origini del Concilio Vaticano secondo. Una proposta di Celso Costantini*, Pordenone 1988, 69–116; S. Casas, "Nouvelles données concernant la reprise de Vatican I sous Pie XI," in *Revue d'Histoire Ecclésiastique*, 104 (2009), 3–4, 828–855; A. von Teuffenbach, "Sulla via del Concilio Vaticano II: la preparazione sotto Pio XII," in *Pio XII e il Concilio*, Siena 2012, 75–180.

9

5. January 25, 1959: The Announcement

1

On January 25, 1959, in the sacristy of the Basilica of St. Paul Outside the Walls, after the closing celebration of the week of prayer for Christian unity, Pope John XXIII, who had been elected only three months before, met with the cardinals who were present at the ceremony. Cardinal Tardini later noted in his diary that it was "almost in the form of an ancient consistory." Pope John XXIII chose this opportunity to announce the plan for his pontificate: a synod for the Diocese of Rome (the first), a general council (according to the manuscript) for the universal Church, and a revision of the Code of Canon Law. The new pontiff, although elderly, resolutely chose to implement this decision that he had made virtually alone.

In the months before, several references made during discussions with various cardinals testify to how John XXIII had come to this decision, though subsequently he always described it as the illumination of the Holy Spirit. However, it was a decision made in solitude, communicated to the Sec-

retary of State, Cardinal Tardini, only when he was already convinced in his own heart: an act of papal discernment, made by one whose pontificate had been envisaged as merely transitional by the conclave.

Explaining his reasons to the cardinals on January 25, John XXIII in particular referred to his pastoral concerns, both as bishop of Rome and as pastor of the entire Church. On the one hand, he saw in modern times signs of positivity and hope, thanks to the progress made in many fields by humanity, but on the other hand, such progress seemed too often focused on material rather than spiritual things. Hence, the need to convene a general council to give the modern world the contribution of grace only the Church could offer: "Our Venerable Brethren and Beloved Sons! I announce before you, certainly trembling a little with emotion, but with humble resolve nonetheless, the name and the proposal of dual celebration: a Diocesan Synod for Rome, and an Ecumenical Council for the universal Church." It was the beginning of the

He devised three things: a Roman synod, an ecumenical council, and an update of the Code of Canon Law. He wants to announce these three points to the College of Cardinals after the ceremony at St. Paul's. I say to the Holy Father (who questioned me), 'I like new and beautiful things. Now these three points are beautiful, and the way of announcing them to the College of Cardinals is new (though linked to ancient papal traditions) and most opportune'" (Diary of Cardinal Domenico Tardini, January 20, 1959).

2. The text of Pope John's allocution, read to seventeen cardinals in the sacristy of St. Paul Outside the Walls. This image shows the first and last pages of the pope's handwritten manuscript (Archivio Fscire).

effort to update the life of the Church that had been expected by many people and in many places: "All came out well. I kept my continued communication with God in prayer," he noted in the pages of his diary at the end of that day.

Roncalli's idea of a council can be seen in the maturation of certain sensitivities and a feeling of urgency for the life of the Church in his personal biographical and spiritual path. Some direct references to the outlook in his speech on January 25 can be found, for example, in his radio message of Christmas 1958 (the image of the new Pentecost, the themes of unity and peace). Other "Roncallian fragments" emerge in those weeks in the course of speeches (at the Angelicum) or in private meetings with Cardinal Agagianian, with Fr. Giovanni Rossi, or with Secretary of State Tardini. During the audience with the latter, although Roncalli was said to be "very hesitant and uncertain," he was happily surprised by the response, "This surprise is more exciting than I could expect: 'Oh! But what an idea, a luminous and holy idea.'"

The reaction of the cardinals present in St. Paul's to the words of the pope was, as John XXIII was to relate with some irony, an "impressive, devout silence." Even in the months following, reactions came very slowly. For example, at the time the *Osservatore Romano* dedicated only a meager press release to the news. However, the media's response in the various countries and in religious magazines was livelier, as they began to dwell on what the convening of a council could mean. Many saw it as a hopeful sign for unity.

BIBLIOGRAPHY
Synopsis of the reporting on the speech in A. Melloni, Papa Giovanni. Un cristiano e il suo concilio, Turin 2009, 291–298; G. Alberigo, "L'annuncio del concilio. Dalle sicurezze dell'arroccamento al fascino della ricerca," in Storia del concilio Vaticano II, edited by G. Alberigo (Italian edition edited by A. Melloni), vol. I, Bologna 1995 (2012), 19–70; A. G. Roncalli—Giovanni XXIII, Pater Amabilis. Agende del pontefice 1958–1963, critical edition and annotation edited by M. Velati, Bologna 2007.

6. THE WORLD STAGE

1. On August 28, 1963, the Rev. Martin Luther King, Jr., at the civil rights March on Washington, where he delivers his famous speech, "I Have a Dream" (AFP/AFP/Getty Images).

2. Dallas, November 22, 1963. The presidential motorcade just before the assassination of John F. Kennedy, thirty-fifth president of the United States (© Corbis/Contasto).

3. A 1956 mural by the Mexican artist David Alfaro Siqueiros symbolized the violent dictatorships in Latin America (Archivio Jaca Book/© David Alfaro Siqueros, by SIAE 2015).

4. A demonstration in Havana after the resolution of the Cuban Missile Crisis in October 1962, which led to the embargo by the United States (Archivio Jaca Book/Gianni Costantino).

5. August 11–15, 1961. The German Democratic Republic (East Germany) erects the Berlin Wall (H. Cartier Bresson/Magnum/Contrasto).

6. March 1962. Joy in the streets of Algiers after the civil war gives Algeria its independence from France (Archivio Jaca Book).

7. Nikita Khrushchev and Leonid Brezhnev receive Fidel Castro in Moscow. The next year, on October 15, 1964, the Supreme Soviet dismisses Khrushchev and Leonid Brezhnev is elected secretary of the Communist Party of the Soviet Union (AP photo/Ansa).

8. The United States begins bombing Hanoi on June 22, 1965 (Foto Grazia Neri).

9. On November 11, 1965, Ian Smith founds the Republic of Rhodesia with the Unilateral Declaration of Independence and becomes Prime Minister. The ruling white minority dominates the country with an apartheid regime until the 1980s (John Downing/Express/Getty Images).

1

2

4

3

5

7

6

9

8

7. The Antepreparatory Commission and Proposals by the Bishops, Universities, and Roman Congregations

On May 17, 1959, members of an Antepreparatory Commission were appointed, to be presided over by Cardinal Domenico Tardini, Secretary of State and head of the Congregation for Extraordinary Ecclesiastical Affairs. All the secretaries of each congregation of the Roman Curia were members. Pericle Felici, an auditor of the Roman Rota, was appointed secretary. The decision to create such a commission, which was announced on the day of Pentecost, was a surprise and the novelty—the introduction of a preparatory stage prior to the preparation proper—can be seen in the word *antepreparatory*, a neologism created for the occasion, and in the choice of not leaving the management of this phase to the Holy Office (which was a real reform).

The commission's first meeting was on May 26, 1959. There were only five meetings: four in May and June of 1959, and one for a final assessment on April 8, 1960. However, the decisions made, which were probably the ones John XXIII wanted, were important and sufficient to start the preparation for the council—which proceeded at a suspiciously leisurely pace, given the age of the pope.

In addition to the general information on directions for the council (for example, choosing Latin as the language for the assembly, having a Catholic council rather than a unity council, and a council more pastoral than dogmatic), the main item on the agenda was how to organize the consultation of the bishops and of the Catholic universities. This time there would be a universal consultation, unlike what Pius IX had done previously for Vatican I and what Pope Pius XII planned to do for his council. In fact, this stage would be the first official act of preparation. On June 18, 1959, a letter went out to all the bishops of all the dioceses in the world asking the future council fathers for opinions, recommendations, and votes in "absolute freedom" in order to facilitate the preparation of the topics they would discuss. This was actually the result of some sleight of hand by the pontiff, who had extensively modified what the commission had decided. In fact, on May 26, Cardinal Tardini had outlined the way the procedures would work. It would be in the form of a questionnaire (the draft was entitled *Quaestiones Ponendae pro Futuro Concilio Ecumenico*), according to the tried and tested mindset of the Curia, which was more accustomed to being on the defensive. This was to determine which general, doctrinal, and moral errors the council could or should concentrate on. For example, one thing missing was the unfinished issue of ecclesiology from Vatican I, which had been omitted in order to discuss a draft

1. Opposite: Pope John XXIII (Archivio Fscire). On March 5, 1960, he noted in his diary, "The fact that it's 'cold and windy' has not prevented my reading interesting proposals for the ecumenical council from the bishops of the various rites of Greece and Asia Minor. Naturally, the variety of…attitudes is a reflection of the histories of the various countries and diverse races. The harmony is perfect, though…."

2. Rome, March 6, 1960. Pope John XXIII visits parishes in Roman neighborhoods. The faithful await his passing and feel particularly close to him (Fondazione Papa Giovanni XXIII, Bergamo). Roncalli will note in his diary, "Tonight a real triumph of popular piety and devotion to the pope. Perhaps never has there been such a respectful crowd. And children in the arms of their parents, and the enthusiastic crowd, men and women. I really had the impression that the Lenten liturgy and my simple words had touched everyone's heart, and that grace would operate in many innocent souls" (Diary of John XXIII, March 6, 1960).

3–4. Reproduction of the memo from the Secretary of State communicating John XXIII's wish that the commission not send a questionnaire to the council fathers, but conduct a "free" survey for the council agenda (Archivio Segreto Vaticano).

2

3

4

5. Rome, October 30, 1959. On the left, Cardinal Domenico Tardini, Secretary of State and President of the Antepreparatory Commission with Msgr. Pericle Felici (right), Secretary of the Commission, during the first press conference on the council, organized at Villa Nazareth. It is the first press conference in the history of the church. The journalists are informed on the state of preparations. In addition, this was the occasion of the announcement of the creation of a press office

to facilitate the relationship with the media and the dissemination of future news (©Archivio Storico Luce).

6. Rome, October 30, 1959. Journalists and religious attend the first press conference on the council. It is the first in the history of the Church (©Archivio Storico Luce).

5   6   7

by Fr. Kleutgen on bishops. However, Pope John, in contrast to his Secretary of State, personally dictated the line to follow, which was reflected in the text of the letter that was sent. In fact, his intention was to leave future council fathers freer to discuss the problems that they felt were urgent, without giving them a prepackaged list, and therefore without directing them in advance.

The *vota* requested of the bishops were not the only consultation. On May 29, the various departments of the Curia had started; all ten sent their *proposita et monita*. And on July 18, the Catholic universities were surveyed; 82.2 percent sent in their response of the *studia et vota*.

According to Canon 223 of the 1917 Code of Canon Law, which designated the legal members of future councils, more than 2,500 fathers were then consulted. The letters from both resident and titular bishops as well as from abbots began to arrive in the following months, but many of them came much later than the September 1 deadline. On March 21, 1960, the commission sent out another message in order to press those who had not responded. The month before, Tardini had written in a similar vein to the Roman congregations. Between July 1959 and the summer of 1960 about 77 percent responded.

The Secretariat then analyzed the letters and condensed the 9,438 proposals into a weighty *Analyticus Conspectus Consiliorum Votorum et Quae ab Episcopis Sunt et Data Prelates*. The suggested topics were painstakingly transcribed into two thick volumes, divided into eighteen sections, which reflected current thinking on the matter.

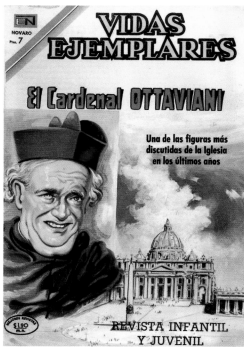

8

So when John XXIII appointed the commissions that were supposed to propose drafts for discussion by the council, this enormous amount of material was available to them. On February 11, 1960, the Secretariat of the Antepreparatory Commission drew up summary reports organized by geographic or linguistic areas. On March 12, this was followed by a much-slimmer, additional summary document, a final summary of the recommendations and suggestions of the bishops and

7. Alfredo Ottaviani (photo Pais/Archivio Rodrigo Pais–Ceub Università di Bologna). Pius XII made him cardinal in the consistory of 1953 and at the same time appointed him Pro-Secretary of the Holy Office. In November 1959, Ottaviani was appointed Secretary of the Holy Office.

8. A Spanish comic book about Cardinal Ottaviani (Archivio Fscire).

Stages of the Process and Preparatory Period before the Bishops' Vote

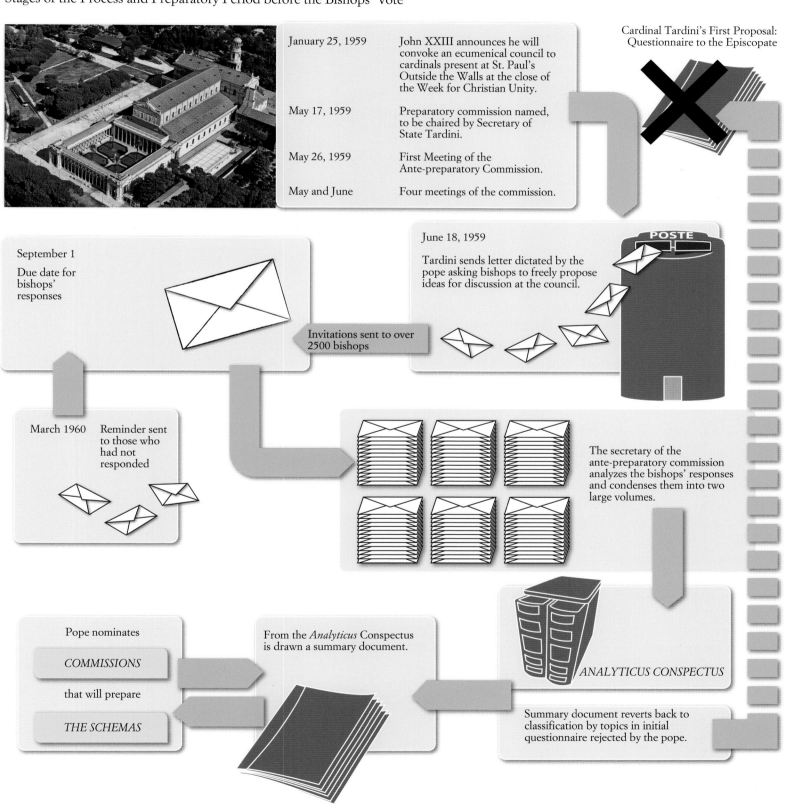

Cardinal Tardini's First Proposal: Questionnaire to the Episcopate

January 25, 1959	John XXIII announces he will convoke an ecumenical council to cardinals present at St. Paul's Outside the Walls at the close of the Week for Christian Unity.
May 17, 1959	Preparatory commission named, to be chaired by Secretary of State Tardini.
May 26, 1959	First Meeting of the Ante-preparatory Commission.
May and June	Four meetings of the commission.

June 18, 1959

Tardini sends letter dictated by the pope asking bishops to freely propose ideas for discussion at the council.

POSTE

September 1

Due date for bishops' responses

Invitations sent to over 2500 bishops

March 1960 — Reminder sent to those who had not responded

The secretary of the ante-preparatory commission analyzes the bishops' responses and condenses them into two large volumes.

ANALYTICUS CONSPECTUS

Pope nominates

COMMISSIONS

that will prepare

THE SCHEMAS

From the *Analyticus* Conspectus is drawn a summary document.

Summary document reverts back to classification by topics in initial questionnaire rejected by the pope.

prelates from around the world for the future council, consisting of eighteen folders organized by subject areas which later served to provide the discussion topics proposed to the various preparatory commissions, the so-called *Quaestiones Commissionibus Praeparatoriis Positae*. In the end, this document was used as the working basis for the preparatory commissions. Both of these summary documents were not included in the volumes of the *Acta et Documenta œcumenico Vaticano II apparando* in which the sources of this phase of Vatican II were published in 1960–1961.

This was a new way of consulting the future council fathers (the free universal consultation) that basically followed the old procedures: the responses were in fact organized along ideologically and historically well-defined criteria and these procedures resorted to the same approach as the theology manuals or the order of the Code of Canon Law. Beyond the purely quantitative data, which remains surprising, the input from the bishops represents a corpus that is quite heterogeneous and difficult to read. Some scholars believe that they were "prisoners of a preconciliar mentality," others are quick to see, "a self-portrait of the Catholic Church on the eve of the council": because in them one can find everything. For example, it is difficult to explain the reason why some responded late (Montini, the Cardinal of Milan, replied only on May 8, 1960) while the responses of the Latin American bishops do not in fact reflect the vivacity with which they later participated in the council sessions. Therefore, although the Roman administration of this endless material contributed at this stage to normalizing the proposals that had arrived (in this way, even the most innovative ideas lost the impetus that had driven them), retrospectively we can say that this consultation had the merit of starting a process of making the episcopate accountable, which had hitherto not been evident, and this would then leave things clear for the opening of the council.

BIBLIOGRAPHY

Acta et documenta Concilio Oecumenico Vaticano II apparando. Series I (Ante-praeparatoria), 4 vols., Vatican City 1960–1961; A. Melloni, "Per un approccio storico-critico ai consilia et vota della fase ante-preparatoria del Vaticano II," in *Rivista di Storia e Letteratura Religiosa*, 26 (1990), 556–576; (edited by) M. Lamberigts, Cl. Soetens, *À la Veille du Concile Vatican II. Vota et Réactions en Europe et dans le Catholicisme Oriental*, Leuven 1992; G. Alberigo, "Passaggi cruciali della fase ante preparatoria (1959–1960)," in *Verso il concilio Vaticano II (1960–1962)*, edited by G. Alberigo and A. Melloni, Genoa 1993, 15–42 (now also in G. Alberigo, *Transizione epocale. Studi sul Concilio Vaticano II*, Bologna 2009); É. Fouilloux, "La fase ante-preparatoria (1959–1960). Il lento avvio dell'uscita dall'inerzia," in *Storia del concilio Vaticano II*, edited by G. Alberigo (Italian edition edited by A. Melloni), vol. I., Bologna 1995 (2012), 71–176.

LEGEND

General statistical data
(b/a = c)
a = total contacted
b = total responses
c = percent responding

EUROPE

Country	a	b	c
Albania	3	0	0.0%
Austria	17	16	94.1%
Belgium	26	21	80.8%
Bulgaria	3	0	0.0%
Carpathia	0	0	0.0%
Czechoslovakia	19	0	0.0%
Denmark	1	1	100.0%
Estonia	0	0	0.0%
Finland	1	1	100.0%
France	130	110	84.6%
Gdansk	3	3	100.0%
Germany	54	41	75.9%
Gibraltar	1	1	100.0%
Great Britain	35	29	82.9%
Greece	5	5	100.0%
Holland	12	9	75.0%
Hungary	16	1	6.3%
Iceland	1	1	100.0%
Ireland	32	30	93.8%
Italy	367	316	86.1%
Latvia	4	2	50.0%
Lithuania	6	0	0.0%
Luxembourg	1	1	100.0%
Malta	3	3	100.0%
Monaco	1	1	100.0%
Norway	3	2	66.7%
Poland	51	42	82.4%
Portugal	28	23	82.1%
Romania	4	0	0.0%
Russia (Europe)	0	0	0.0%
Spain	89	83	93.3%
Sweden	2	1	50.0%
Switzerland	12	10	83.3%
Turkey (Europe)	3	3	100.0%
Yugoslavia	28	13	46.4%
Total Europe	961	769	79.9%

AFRICA

Country	a	b	c
Algeria	5	5	100%
Angola	5	5	100%
Cameroon	8	5	63%
Cape Verde Islands	1	1	100%
Congo	40	38	95%
Equatorial Africa	11	9	82%
Eritrea	3	2	67%
Ethiopia	4	3	75%
Gambia	1	1	100%
Ghana	7	5	71%
Guinea	3	3	100%
Kenya	9	8	89%
Liberia	2	1	50%
Libya	3	3	100%
Madagascar	13	13	100%
Mauritius	1	1	100%
Morocco	2	2	100%
Mozambique	6	6	100%
Nigeria	19	14	74%
Nyasaland	7	4	57%
Portuguese Guinea	1	0	0%
Reunion Island	1	1	100%
Rhodesia	14	10	71%
Ruanda-Urundi	7	6	86%
Seychelles	1	1	100%
Sierra Leone	2	2	100%
Somalia	2	2	100%
Southwest Africa	3	2	67%
Spanish Guinea	1	0	0%
Sudan	7	5	71%
Tanganyika	21	16	76%
Togo	2	1	50%
Tunisia	1	1	100%
Uganda	7	7	100%
Union of South Africa, Basutoland, Swaziland	28	25	89%
United Arab Republic (Egypt)	13	12	92%
West Africa	28	21	75%
Totals: Africa	289	241	83%

OCEANIA

Country	a	b	c
Australia	39	30	77%
Melanesia	4	1	25%
Micronesia	3	3	100%
Bismarck Archipelago	10	5	50%
New Zealand	5	3	60%
Polynesia	9	6	67%
Totals: Oceania	70	48	69%

GENERAL TOTALS

Catholic Hierarchy	1998/2593 (77%)	
Religious	101/156 (64.7%)	2099/2749 (76.3%)
Institutes of Higher Educ.	51/62 (82.2%)	
TOTAL	2150/2811 (76.4%)	

RESPONSES FROM INSTITUTES OF HIGHER EDUCATION

Roman Universities	14/14 (100%)
Catholic Universities outside Rome	24/32 (75%)
Faculties of Ecclesiastical Studies	8/11 (72.7%)
Faculties of Theological Studies in the U.S.	5/5 (100%)
TOTAL	51/62 (82.2%)

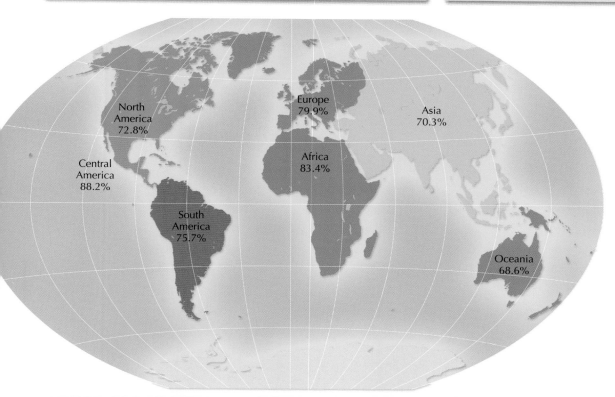

North America 72.8%
Central America 88.2%
South America 75.7%
Europe 79.9%
Africa 83.4%
Asia 70.3%
Oceania 68.6%

ASIA

Country	a	b	c
Arabia	2	2	100%
Burma	8	7	88%
Cambodia	1	1	100%
Ceylon	6	5	83%
China	116	56	48%
Cyprus	1	1	100%
Formosa	2	1	50%
India	80	63	79%
Indonesia	31	31	100%
Iran	4	4	100%
Iraq	12	11	92%
Japan	18	13	72%
Jordan	1	1	100%
Korea	10	5	50%
Laos	2	1	50%
Lebanon	26	22	85%
Malacca	3	3	100%
Pakistan	10	8	80%
Palestine	4	4	100%
Philippines	40	31	78%
Rhodes	1	1	100%
Siberia	0	0	0%
Syria	15	13	87%
Thailand	6	3	50%
Turkey (Asia)	1	1	100%
Vietnam	17	5	29%
Total Asia	417	293	70%

NORTH AMERICA

Country	a	b	c
Bermuda	1	0	0%
Canada	90	62	69%
Mexico	53	49	92%
United States	216	151	70%
Total North America	360	262	73%

CENTRAL AMERICA

Country	a	b	c
Bahama Islands British	1	1	100%
Honduras British	1	1	100%
West Indies	6	6	100%
Cuba	8	3	38%
Costa Rica	5	4	80%
Curaçao	1	1	100%
Dominican Republic	7	6	86%
El Salvador	6	6	100%
Guadeloupe	3	3	100%
Guatemala	12	12	100%
Haiti	8	7	88%
Honduras	6	5	83%
Nicaragua	6	6	100%
Panama	4	4	100%
Puerto Rico	2	2	100%
Total Central America	76	67	88%

SOUTH AMERICA

Country	a	b	c
Argentina	50	33	66%
Bolivia	21	15	71%
Brazil	167	132	79%
British Guyana	3	3	100%
Chile	25	20	80%
Colombia	54	38	70%
Ecuador	22	19	86%
Falkland Islands	1	0	0%
Paraguay	10	6	60%
Peru	36	29	81%
Uruguay	7	6	86%
Venezuela	24	17	71%
Total South America	420	318	76%

WORLD TOTALS

	a	b	c
EUROPE	961	769	79.9%
AFRICA	289	241	83%
ASIA	417	293	70%
NORTH AMERICA	360	262	73%
CENTRAL AMERICA	76	67	88%
SOUTH AMERICA	420	318	76%
OCEANIA	70	48	69%
Total	2593	1998	77%

Data source:
*Acta et Documenta
Concilio Oecumenico Vaticano II
Apparando*, Series I (*Antepraeparatoria*),
Indices, 206–433

8. MOVEMENTS, PERIODICALS, BOOKS

The announcement that a new council would be convened encouraged historians and theologians to reflect on issues that were supposed to go on the agenda. This phenomenon aroused the interest of many magazines and journals that had been working on these themes for decades and produced a rich harvest of studies and monographs by the most influential experts in the field.

1. *Irénikon* is published by the Benedictine monastery of Chevtogne and was founded in 1925 by Dom Lambert Beauduin.

2. *Istina* is the review of the Center for Ecumenical Studies founded in 1927 by the Dominicans to promote dialogue with Orthodox Christians.

3. *Nouvelle Revue Théologique* is a quarterly founded in 1865 by the Belgian priest Jean-Joseph Loiseaux.

4. *Theologische Quartalschrift*, founded in 1819 by German Catholic scholars, is the official journal of the theology faculty at the Catholic university of Tübingen and is the oldest German theology journal still in circulation.

5. *Theologische Zeitschrift* was founded by Karl Ludwig Schmidt in 1945 and is a quarterly published by the Faculty of Theology at the University of Basel.

6. *Theologie und Glaube*, founded in 1908 as the journal of the Theology Faculty at Paderborn and continues to be published under its auspices.

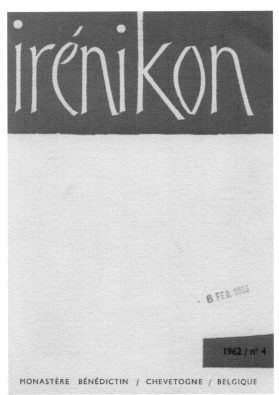

1

4

54

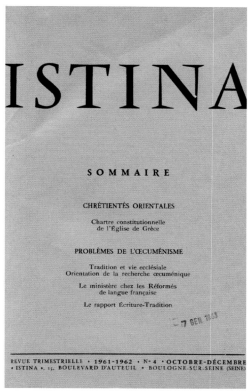

2

NOUVELLE REVUE THÉOLOGIQUE

MUSEUM LESSIANUM · SECTION THÉOLOGIQUE

94ᵉ ANNÉE   N° 7 JUILLET-AOUT 1962   TOME 84

SOMMAIRE

Les figures bibliques (suite). P. GRELOT	673
Mariage mixte et Concile. B. HÄRING, C.SS.R.	699
Un siècle d'Anthropologie préhistorique. Compatibilité ou incompatibilité scientifique du Monogénisme ? (suite). E. BONÉ, S.J.	709
« Mater et Magistra » : traductions et commentaires. C. MERTENS, S.J.	735

ACTES DU SAINT-SIÈGE :

Actes du Souverain Pontife :

Canonisation du Bhx Martin de Porrès, O.P. (Homélies du 6 mai 1962. Alloc. du 7 mai 1962) (E. B.)	738
Allocution du lundi 28 mai 1962 aux journalistes	739
Pour la paix en Algérie (Allocution du 3 juin 1962)	741
Bibliographie (voir en 2ᵉ et 3ᵉ pages la liste des ouvrages analysés)	743
Ouvrages envoyés à la rédaction	781

REVUE MENSUELLE PUBLIÉE SOUS LA DIRECTION DU
COLLÈGE PHILOSOPHIQUE ET THÉOLOGIQUE S.J. ST-ALBERT - LOUVAIN

ADMINISTRATION : CASTERMAN TOURNAI - PARIS

3

Theologische Zeitschrift

herausgegeben von der

Theologischen Fakultät der Universität Basel

Jahrgang 18   Heft 5   September–Oktober 1962

Inhalt:

Hebräische Erzählung und biblische Geschichtsschreibung. Von *Isac Leo Seeligmann*, Jerusalem	305
Pascals Denken zwischen Natur und Technik. Von *Walter Frei*, Basel . . .	326
Gnade und Natur. Der Einfluß der reformatorischen Theologie auf die Entwicklung der wissenschaftlichen Methode. Von *Thomas Torrance*, Edinburgh	341
Miszellen: Dieu fait sortir. Hiphil de *yāṣā*. Von *Paul Humbert*, Neuchâtel .	357
Rezensionen: J. Barr, Biblical Words for Time (*E. Eshing*); H. Graf Reventlow, Wächter über Israel (*O. Bächli*); R. de Vaux, L'archéologie et les manuscrits de la mer morte (*H.-J. Stoebe*); R. Schnackenburg, la théologie du Nouveau Testament (*Ch. Brütsch*); W. P. de Boer, The Imitation of Paul (*D. B. Pedersen*); J. N. Sevenster, Paul and Seneca (*E. Lohse*); Neotestamentica et Patristica. O. Cullmann zu seinem 60. Geburtstag (*J. J. Vincent*); W. M. Peitz & H. Foerster, Dionysius Exiguus-Studien (*L. Fischer*); J. B. Morrall, Gerson and the Great Schism (*M. A. Schmid*); H. Stroh, Luther jusqu'en 1520; R. Schwarz, Fides, Spes und Caritas beim jungen Luther (*H.-H. Schrey*); A. F. Modrevius, Opera omnia (*E.-W. Kohls*); L. Perriraz, Histoire de la théologie réformée française (*J. Roth*).	362
Notizen und Glossen. Zeitschriftenschau (Schweiz, Belgien, Deutschland, Frankreich, Großbritannien, Italien, Niederlande, USA). Personalnachrichten (Basel)	381

Verlag Friedrich Reinhardt AG., Basel

Einzelheft Fr. 5.—

5

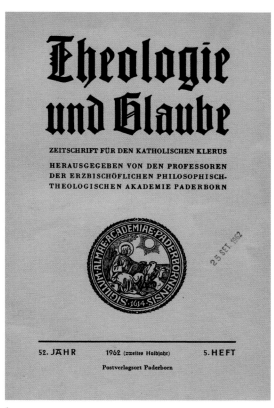

6

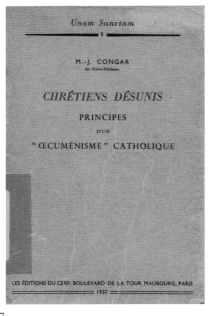

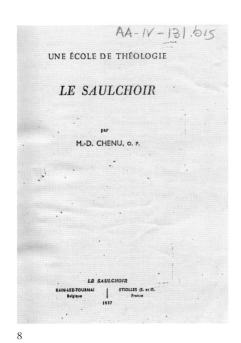

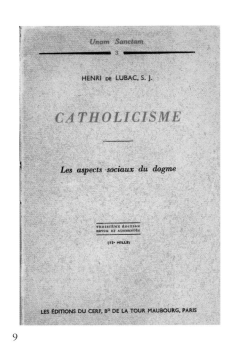

7

8

9

7. Y. M.-J. Congar, *Chrétiens désunis. Principes d'un "oecuménisme" catholique*, (*Unam Sanctam*, 1) Cerf, Paris 1937.
8. M.-D. Chenu, *Une école de théologie. Le Saulchoir*, Etiolles, Paris 1937.
9. H. de Lubac, *Catholicisme. Les aspects sociaux du dogme*, (*Unam Sanctam*, 3) Cerf, Paris 1938.
10. H. de Lubac, *Corpus Mysticum. L'Eucharistie et l'Église au Moyen Âge. Étude historique*, Aubier, Paris 1939.
11. H. Küng, *Konzil und Wiedervereinigung. Erneuerung als Ruf in die Einheit*, Herder, Wien-Freiburg-Basel 1960.
12. L. Jaeger, *Das ökumenische Konzil, die Kirche und die Christenheit. Erbe und Auftrag*, (*Konfessionskundliche Schriften des J.A.-Möhler-Instituts*, 4), Verlag Bonifacius, Paderborn 1960.
13. *Le Concile et les conciles. Contribution a l'histoire de la vie conciliaire de l'église*, Chevetogne-Cerf, Paris 1960.

10

11

12

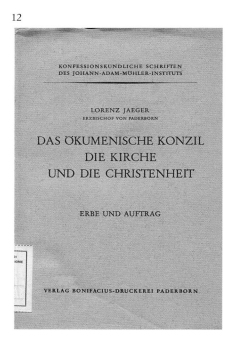

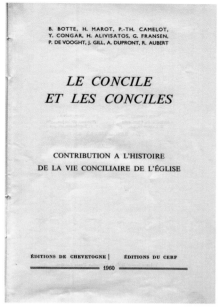

13

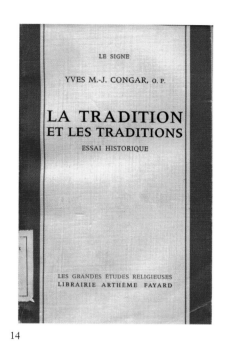

14

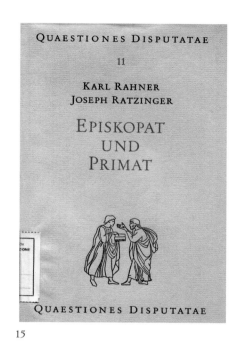

15

14. Y. M.-J. Congar, *La tradition et les traditions, vol: I. Essai historique; vol. II. Essai théologique, (Le Grandes Etudes Religieuses. Le Signe)*, Fayard, Paris 1960–1963.
15. K. Rahner, J. Ratzinger, *Episkopat und Primat, (Quaestiones disputatae, 11)*, Herder, Freiburg-Basel-Wien 1961.
16. *Conciliorum Oecomenicorum Decreta*, Centro di Documentazione, Istituto per le Scienze Religiose di Bologna, edited by J. Alberigo, P. P. Joannou, C. Leonardi, P. Prodi, Herder, Freiburg 1962.
17. Y. M.-J. Congar, *Aspects de l'oecuménisme*, (Études religieuses, n.756), La Pensée Catholique-Office Général du Livre, Bruxelles-Paris 1962.
18. Y. M.-J. Congar, *L'Épiscopat et l'Église universelle*, (*Unam Sanctam*, 39), Cerf, Paris 1962.

16

17

18

9. The Central Commission and the Preparatory Commissions

With the promulgation of the motu proprio *Superno Dei Nutu* on June 5, 1960, John XXIII instituted ten preparatory commissions that were to prepare drafts to be discussed in the council: 1) on theological issues; 2) on bishops and the government of dioceses; 3) on the governance of the clergy and the Christian people; 4) on religious; 5) on guidelines for the sacraments; 6) on the sacred liturgy; 7) on studies and seminaries; 8) on the Eastern Churches; 9) on the missions; and 10) on the apostolate of the laity. It also established three secretariats: one for relations with other churches and Christian communities, one for the media and the entertainment world, and one for economic and technical affairs. To coordinate the work, a Central Preparatory Commission was set up to consider the schemas produced. In general, the commissions referred back to the congregations of the Curia responsibility for their respective subjects, and on June 6, each was assigned the cardinal prefect of the appropriate congregation as presider. "The organization chart almost perfectly mirrored that of the Curia," which was seen as a victory, despite the fact that John XXIII had always publicly expressed his desire to avoid any confusion between the council and the Curia. Among the more notable exceptions were the commission for the apostolate of the laity, which did not have a corresponding department in the Curia, and the Secretariat for Christian Unity, an entirely new organization in terms of its origin, structure, and scope.

On July 9, 1960, the secretary of the Antepreparatory Commission gave the committee chairs the *Quaestiones Commissionibus Praeparatoris Positae*, with the assignment of topics to be addressed. Five key issues were assigned to the Theological Commission, which mirrored the congregation of the Holy Office and was chaired by its secretary, Cardinal Alfredo Ottaviani: the sources of revelation (a topic that included the question of the inspiration for biblical texts, the relationship between Scripture and Tradition, and historical-critical exegesis), the Church (the nature of the Church and the authority within it, the ecclesiology of bishops that had not been discussed at the First Vatican Council), supernatural principles in the moral sphere, marriage, and social doctrine. Because of its connection to the Holy Office, this commission claimed jurisdiction over any "doctrinal" matters, even those raised within other commissions, which in its opinion should deal with only the minor (or "pastoral" in a different sense from that of the pope) aspects of the topics assigned to them.

The commissions began working between the summer and

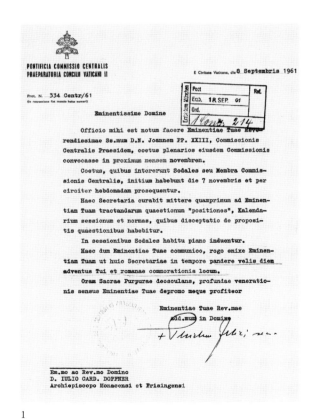

1. A letter from the secretary of the Preparatory Commission, Pericle Felici to Cardinal Julius Döpfner, archbishop of Munich and Freising, calling a work session of the central committee (Archivio Fscire).

2. A booklet with the list of members of the preparatory commissions, distributed by the Central Commission Secretariat (Archivio Fscire).

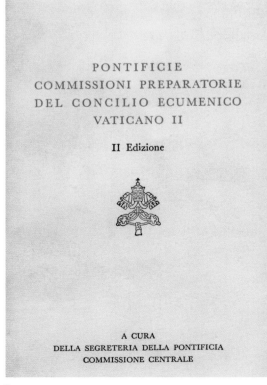

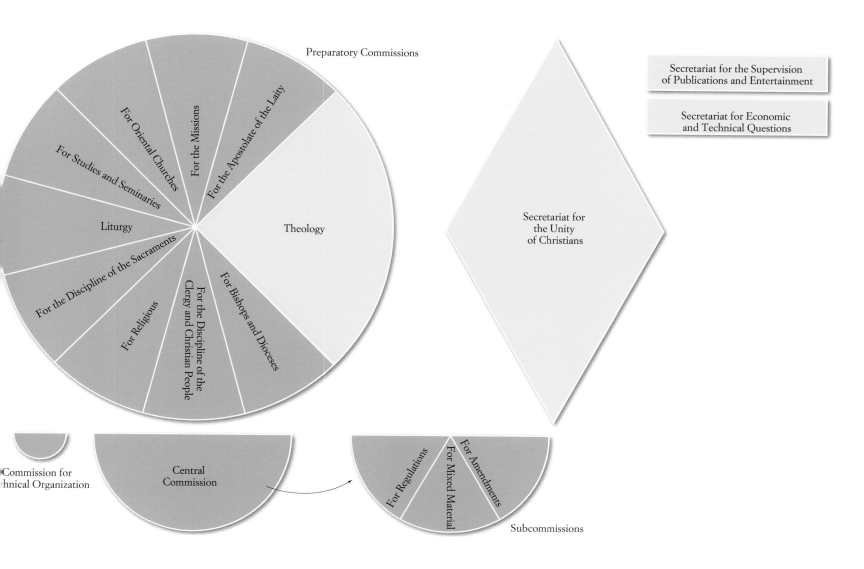

Preparatory Commissions

For the Apostolate of the Laity
For the Missions
For Oriental Churches
For Studies and Seminaries
Liturgy
For the Discipline of the Sacraments
For Religious
For the Discipline of the Clergy and Christian People
For Bishops and Dioceses
Theology

Secretariat for the Supervision of Publications and Entertainment

Secretariat for Economic and Technical Questions

Secretariat for the Unity of Christians

Commission for Technical Organization

Central Commission

For Regulations
For Mixed Material
For Amendments

Subcommissions

autumn of 1960—that is, before the formal inauguration of the preparatory period, in November 1960—internally organizing themselves into subcommittees corresponding to the different assigned topics. The result of the work of the subcommittees was evaluated in the plenary sessions, during which the texts to be sent to the Central Preparatory Commission were approved. This phase was to generate and set up a legacy of drafts and an idea of the council that would have a strong influence on the work of the council fathers.

The correspondence between preparatory commissions and Curial departments resulted in power plays. Each committee attempted to produce a draft for the most important issues dealt with by the relevant ministry, with the intention of obtaining from the council a solemn ratification of the definitions given to these issues in previous years, thus supporting the intransigent attitudes of the previous century. In this way, seventy drafts and documents were produced that claimed to standardize all the material with which the Roman Curia had been engaged over the years.

However, different ideas about the tasks that the council should have had also matured during preparation. The "new"

Secretariat for Christian Unity, presided over by Cardinal Augustin Bea, did not correspond to a department within the Curia, was not considered by the Antepreparatory Commission qualified to propose its own drafts to the council, and was not assigned any of the *Quaestiones* entrusted to other commissions. But far from being reduced to a body whose only task was "public relations" with other Christian denominations, the Secretariat did prepare drafts on crucial issues—which in some cases were the same as those being tackled by the Theological Commission—with the intention of dialogue with other Christian denominations and a renewal of the Church. In fact, in this way the Secretariat and the Theological Commission became the bearers of two council projects that were quite divergent: this opposition became apparent when the drafts were discussed in the Central Preparatory Commission.

The commission's first meeting took place in June 1961, but this was just an interim meeting. It was only at the meeting the following November that the Central Commission began to examine the first drafts submitted for its approval. The work then became progressively more intense and hectic, especially

3. Vatican City, January 23, 1962. Pope John XXIII, accompanied by Pericle Felice (left), secretary of the Central Commission, attended the proceedings of the Central Preparatory Commission (Archivio Fscire–Fondazione Papa Giovanni XXIII). The first plenary meeting was held on June 12, 1961, with the task of drafting the Regulations and examining the many topics. On the same day, the pope would note on his agenda, "First meeting of the Central Commission for the Council. I gave two speeches, one at the beginning and one at the end, and I greeted this happy beginning of the preparation for the Council. Followed the report of work already done by individual committees. They talked about the cardinal presidents of each. Overall satisfaction" (Diary of John XXIII, June 12, 1961).

when, on February 2, 1962, the pope decreed that the council would begin on October 11, 1962 when he issued the motu proprio *Consilium*.

The second plenary, first operational, session of the Committee, took place between November 7 and 12, 1961, and it decided to establish three subcommittees: one for the Regulations, to draft the council's procedural rules; the second "for mixed materials," with the task of coordinating the texts drawn up by the commissions in order to avoid repetition; and the third "for amendments" with the task of applying to the texts corrections proposed by the members of the central committee. The work of these last two subcommittees was the only filter between the preparation and the council. This filter, during the lively discussions on the schemas produced by the Theological Commission, would show that the passive unanimity expected by the congregations was not there.

Thus, there were 75 schemas (reduced to 60) developed by the commissions and submitted to the Central Commission. After examination by the Central Commission and the subcommittee, many were cancelled because they dealt with issues that they decided to reserve to the Holy See, with subjects that were better left to the Commission for the revision of the code of canon law (*Codex Iuris Canonici*), or because they were merged with each other. In the end, twenty-two preparatory schemas were actually approved by the council.

Right from the preparation stage, the commissions were the key body that was entrusted with the writing of documents to be discussed and approved. Their composition was therefore an important factor in the direction and outcome of the work of the council. The commissions were composed of members and advisers. The twelve commissions (including the Central Commission and the Ceremonial Commission) had 846 members in all (in fact only 842, since four overlapped in two of the commissions), of which 466 were members and 380 were advisers. At Vatican I there had been ninety-six advisers for five commissions. According to Felici's requirements, members would be the ones who had the right to vote and speak; the advisers had no vote and could intervene only if invited to do so. However, this distinction did not exist later in the daily work of the commissions.

Throughout the preparatory period the appointment of members and advisers was, in fact, controlled by the respective Curial congregations that they came from. With only one exception, no layman was appointed, not even in the commission appointed to discuss the apostolate of the laity. Not

3

▶ **The Central Commission Held a Total of Seven Sessions**

1) June 12–19, 1961: Discussion on the Regulations for the council, based on a questionnaire sent in advance to the members by the Secretary Archbishop Pericle Felici, who passed on to the council, to those who would be given the right to vote, what criteria should be followed when selecting experts, what rules to adopt when voting, which language to use, the possibility of making it easier for fathers to follow discussions in Latin, and which method to choose for recording the debates.

2) November 7–17, 1961: Discussion on the presence of non-Catholic observers from other Christian denominations and the beginning of the examination of the first documents submitted by the subcommittees. In particular, the following was discussed: the formula of the profession of faith prepared by the Theological Commission that the council fathers were to recite together at the beginning of the council; the draft on the "sources of Revelation"; some "pastoral" drafts, such as those on the clergy, on pastors, and on parishes.

3) January 15–23, 1962: Discussion of the drafts on moral order and on the deposit of the faith prepared by the Theological Commission; discussion of some drafts prepared by the Commission on the Sacraments (on the sacraments of Confirmation, Reconciliation, and Holy Orders) and the Commission for the Eastern Churches (on liturgical rites, on the Eastern patriarchs, on the use of local languages and on the sacraments).

4. Vatican City, January 23, 1962. The close of the third session of the Central Commission. In the photo, John XXIII delivers the keynote address: "Venerable Brethren and beloved sons, for the third time in the space of eight months you have come to Rome from all points of the earth to continue the work of preparation for the serious and challenging council. Before your eyes—but can we say?—In your hearts and minds is collected the magnificent contribution toward preparation offered by the entire episcopate of both East and West, from the Roman Curia, from the universities, and in agreement with excellent men of the clergy and laity of all backgrounds: all intended, with perfect pitch, to prepare the great event" (Archivio Fscire—Fondazione Papa Giovanni XXIII, Bergamo).

4

4) February 20–27, 1962: Discussion of the drafts developed by the Commission on Bishops (the division of dioceses, on Episcopal conferences, on the relationship between the bishops and congregations of the Roman Curia, on the relationships of bishops with parish priests), the Commission on the Clergy (on the care of souls, and on ecclesiastical precepts), the Commission for Eastern Churches (on ecclesiastical precepts, which would be postponed until the reform of the CJC), the Commission on Religious (on religious life, on religious congregations, on secular institutes), the Commission on Studies and Seminaries (drafts on vocations, on programs of study, and on ecclesiastical universities).

5) March 26–April 3, 1962: Discussion of the draft prepared by the Commission on the Liturgy, which addressed in different ways the general principles of liturgical renewal (the mystery of the Eucharist, the other sacraments and sacramentals, the reform of the Divine Office, the liturgical year, vestments, music, and sacred art). Each chapter was accompanied by some *Declarationes* that addressed and explained in more detail specific issues, whose relevance to the text of the council was discussed at length. Discussion on the drafts submitted by the Commission for the Missions (on the government of the missions, on missionary clergy, on religious, on the sacraments and liturgy in mission countries, on guidelines for the care of people, on studies in seminaries, on cooperation over the missions) and by the Secretariat for the Means of Social Communication.

6) May 3–12, 1962: Discussion of a draft prepared by the Commission on Bishops (on coadjutor bishops, on auxiliaries and the age limit for

the ministry, on the bishop's care for souls, on pastoral care in regions dominated by communism), of drafts from the Commission for the Clergy (on communism, on the catechism, on the censorship and approval of books, on judicial and punitive procedures), from the Theological Commission (a draft on marriage and matrimonial ethics and a draft on the Church), the Commission on Religious (on the renewal of religious life), drafts from the Commission on Sacraments (various texts on the legal aspects of marriage: impediments, consent, mixed marriages, the form of celebration, processes, and so on), the Commission for Eastern Churches (drafts on the faculties of bishops, on the catechism, on the calendar, and on the Divine Office).

7) June 12–20, 1962: Discussion of drafts prepared by the Commission on Studies and Seminaries (for example, on the formation of seminarians, on Catholic schools, on obedience to the teachings of the Church in religious studies); from the Theological Commission (various chapters of the draft on the Church, in particular on teaching and authority within the Church); various minor drafts on commissions, on bishops, on the clergy, on religious, on the sacraments, and on the Christian people. Discussion of the three drafts prepared on ecumenism by the Committee on the Eastern Churches, the Secretariat for Christian Unity, and the Theological Commission respectively (as the last chapter of the draft on the Church). Discussion of the draft on religious freedom prepared by the Secretariat for Christian Unity and the corresponding (but opposite) chapter on tolerance in the draft on the Church developed by the Theological Commission.

The following tables are collected from the preparatory commissions' data, as well as from lists published from time to time by the secretariat, with additions from other sources as needed. The president, secretary, and members of each committee are indicated. In addition to the members, consultors to the preparatory commissions were also reported. Members and consultors are listed in the order of the General Secretariat, which generally followed ecclesiastical rank. Each person's name is accompanied by his role in the episcopate or Curia, or other prominent post. Nationality is also indicated, generally referring to the main base of ministry or of nationality by birth. Each commission was assigned an agenda, assigned at the beginning of the work by the Secretariat in the preparatory document *Quaestiones commissionibus praeparatoriis Councils Oecumenicis Vatican II Positae*, as the detailed directions for each agenda. It also indicates the outlines actually prepared,

everything is clear regarding the criteria and methods used, but a broad look tells us how recognized experts were sought out, at least formally, covering the various subject areas that each commission would have to deal with, and with an explicitly international flavor. Some of them also took into account the need to represent different trends and opinions. However, we must consider that for many commissions, the actual work of writing the texts was conducted by a small number of collaborators belonging to the Roman universities and congregations of the Curia, while the other members and advisers were called together only to discuss and approve the work, so that Felici himself referred to them as honorary members. The commissions were heavily Eurocentric: about 80 percent of the members were European, the Italian contingent accounting for 25 percent, but the percentage rose to 37.71 percent taking into account those who were resident in Rome and in Vatican City (26.36 percent belonged to the Curia).

Another element that was interpreted by the commissions in a more or less rigid manner was the secrecy of the work that was imposed on those participating in the commissions. Congar lucidly captured the "political implications" of confidentiality in the pages of his diary: "The members of the commission who will work together in Rome, may, at the moment, at least, talk amongst themselves. So you can imagine a non-Roman world dispersed, fractured, subject to secrecy, and a Roman group, banding together and free to express themselves."

BIBLIOGRAPHY
V. Carbone, "Il Cardinale Domenico Tardini e la Preparazione del Concilio Vaticano II," in *Rivista di Storia della Chiesa in Italia*, 45 (1991), 42–88; A. Indelicato, "Formazione e Composizione delle Commissioni Preparatorie," in (edited by) G. Alberigo, A. Melloni, *Verso il Concilio (1960–1962). Passaggi e Problemi della Preparazione Conciliare*, Genoa 1993, 43–66; R. Burigana, M. Paiano, G. Turbanti, M. Velati, "La Messa a Punto dei Testi: Le Commissioni nella Fase Preparatoria del Vaticano II," in É. Fouilloux (edited by), *Vatican II Commence...Approches Francophones*, Leuven 1993, 28–53; J. K. Komonchak, "La Lotta per il Concilio Durante la Preparazione," in *Storia del concilio Vaticano II*, edited by G. Alberigo (Italian edition edited by A. Melloni), vol. I, Bologna 1995 (2012), 177–380.

CENTRAL PREPARATORY COMMISSION

PRESIDENT
John XXIII

SECRETARIES
General Secretary: Msgr. Pericle Felici
Adjunct Secretaries: Achille Lupi, Vincenzo Carbone, Fausto Vallainc, Nello Venturini, Emilio Governatori, Marcello Venturi, Nazareno Cinti, Antonio Pino.

MEMBERS

Card. Eugène Tisserant	Dean of the College of Cardinals; Prefect of the Congregation of Ceremonies; Pres. Pontifical Preparatory Commission on Ceremonies	FRA
Card. Clemente Micara	Vicar General, Diocese of Rome	ITA
Card. Giuseppe Pizzardo	Prefect of the Congregation of Seminaries and Universities; Pres. Preparatory Commission on Seminaries and Universities	ITA
Card. Benedetto Aloisi Masella	Prefect, Congregation of the Discipline of the Sacraments; Pres. of Preparatory Commission on the Sacraments	ITA
Card. Gaetano Cicognani	Prefect, Congregation of Rites; Pres. Prep. Commission on the Liturgy	ITA
Card. Giuseppe Ferretto	Sabina e Poggio Mirteto	ITA
Card. Manuel Gonçalves Cerejeira	Patriarch of Lisbon	PRT
Card. Achille Liénart	Lille	FRA
Card. Ignace Gabriel I Tappouni	Patriarch of Antioch in Syria	LEB
Card. Santiago Luis Copello	Chancellor of the Apostolic Chancery	ITA
Card. Grégoire-Pierre XV Agagianian	Patriarch of Cilicia (Armenian), Lebanon; Prefect, Congregation for the Propagation of the Faith	ITA
Card. James Charles McGuigan	Toronto	CAN
Card. Norman Thomas Gilroy	Sydney	AUS
Card. Francis Joseph Spellman	New York	USA
Card. Teodósio Clemente de Gouveia	Lourenço Marques	MOZ
Card. Jaime de Barros Câmara	São Paulo	BRZ
Card. Enrique Pla y Deniel	Toledo	ESP
Card. Manuel Arteaga y Betancourt	San Cristobal de la Habana	CUB
Card. Josef Frings	Cologne	GER
Card. Ernesto Ruffini	Palermo	ITA
Card. Antonio Caggiano	Buenos Aires	ARG
Card. Thomas Tien Ken-hsin	Peking (impeded); Apostolic Admin. of Taipei	TWN
Card. Valerio Valeri	Prefect, Congregation for Religious	ITA
Card. Pietro Ciriaci	Prefect, Congregation of the Council	ITA
Card. Carlos Maria de la Torre	Quito	ECU
Card. Giuseppe Siri	Genoa	ITA
Card. John Francis D'Alton	Armagh	IRL
Card. James Francis McIntyre	Los Angeles	USA
Card. Stefan Wyszyński	Gniezno and Warsaw	POL
Card. Fernando Quiroga y Palacios	Santiago de Compostela	ESP
Card. Paul-Èmile Léger	Montréal	CAN
Card. Valerian Gracias	Bombay	IND
Card. Giovanni Battista Montini	Milan	ITA
Card. Fernando Cento	Pres. Preparatory Commission on the Apostolate of the Laity	ITA
Card. Amleto Giovanni Cicognani	Secy. of State; Pres. Prep. Commission on Oriental Churches	ITA
Card. José Garibi y Rivera	Guadalajara	MEX
Card. Antonio Maria Barbieri	Montevideo	URY
Card. William Godfrey	Westminster	GBR
Card. Carlo Confalonieri	Secy. of the Sacred Consistorial Cong.	ITA
Card. Paul-Marie Richaud	Bordeaux	FRA
Card. Franz König	Vienna	AUT
Card. Julius Döpfner	Munich and Freising	GER
Card. Paolo Marella	Pres. of the Congregation of the Fabric of St. Peter; Pres. Prep. Commission on Bishops	ITA
Card. Gustavo Testa	Pro-pres. Commission for the Special Administration of the Holy See	ITA
Card. Aloisius Joseph Muench	Fargo	USA
Card. Albert Gregory Meyer	Chicago	USA

those presented to the central committee, and finally, schemas which, after the examination of the central committee and the internal reworking, were actually presented to the council in the appropriate volumes prepared by the secretariat.

In all tables, names are preceded by an honorific, which generally distinguishes the cardinals, bishops, religious, and lay people. In the case of multiple ministries or curial offices, that which is more relevant is indicated. Whenever possible, first names are included in the appropriate language—they are in Italian in the documents of the Secretariat. The same is done for the names of dioceses. When possible, the curial position or diocese in which a cleric was an auxiliary or apostolic delegate is indicated.

Card. Luigi Traglia	Vicar General, Diocese of Rome	ITA
Card. Peter Tatsuo Doi	Tokyo	JAP
Card. Bernard Jan Alfrink	Utrecht	NLD
Card. Rufino Jiao Santos	Manila	PHL
Card. Laurean Rugambwa	Bukoba	TZA
Card. José Humberto Quintero	Caracas	VEN
Card. Luis Concha Córdoba	Bogotà	COL
Card. Alfredo Ottaviani	Secy. Congregation of the Holy Office; Prep. Committee Theology	ITA
Card. Alberto Di Jorio	Pro-pres. Pontifical Comission for the Vatican City State; Pres. of Institute for Works of Religion; Pres. Administrative Secretariat for Preparation of the Council	ITA
Card. Francesco Roberti	Prefect of the Supreme Tribunal of the Apostolic Signature	ITA
Card. André-Damien-Ferdinand Jullien	Titular Archbishop of Corone	ITA
Card. Arcadio Larraona	Grand Penitentiary	ITA
Card. William Theodore Heard	Cardinal Deacon and Priest of San Teodoro	ITA
Card. Augustin Bea	Pres. Secretariat for Christian Unity	ITA
His Beatitude Stephanos I Sidarouss	Coptic Patriarch of Alexandria—Cairo	EGY
His Beatitude Maximos IV Saigh	Melkite Patriarch of Antioch—Damascus	SYR
His Beatitude Pierre-Paul Meouchi	Maronite Patriarch of Antioch	LBN
His Beatitude Alberto Gori	Latin Patriarch of Jerusalem	ISR
His Beatitude Paolo II Cheikho	Chaldean Patriarch of Babylonia	IRQ
Most Rev. Acacio Chacón Guerra	Mérida	VEN
Most Rev. Josip Antun Ujčić	Belgrade	YUG
Most Rev. Patrick Finbar Ryan	Port of Spain	TTO
Most Rev. Luis Chávez y González	San Salvador	SLV
Most Rev. Alfredo Silva Santiago	Concepción	CHL
Most Rev. Juan José Mena Porta	Asunción	PRY
Most Rev. Abel Isidoro Antezana y Rojas	La Paz	BOL
Most Rev. Donald Campbell	Glasgow	GBR
Most Rev. Octavio Antonio Beras	coad. Santo Domingo	DOM
Most Rev. Thomas Benjamin Cooray	Ceylon	IND
Most Rev. Peter McKeefry	Wellington	NZL
Most Rev. Marcel Lefebvre	Dakar	SEN
Most Rev. Karl Joseph Alter	Cincinnati	USA
Most Rev. Lawrence Leo Graner	Dacca	PAK
Most Rev. Daniel Eugene Hurley	Durban	ZAF
Most Rev. Juan Landázuri Ricketts	Lima	PER
Most Rev. Paul-Marie Maurice Perrin	Carthage	TUN
Most Rev. Franjo Šeper	Zagreb	YUG
Most Rev. Victor Bazin	Rangoon	MMR
Most Rev. François-Marie Poirier	Port-au-Prince	HTI
Most Rev. Michel-Jules Bernard	Brazzaville	COG
Most Rev. Paul Bernier	Gaspé	CAN
Most Rev. Martin John O'Connor	Pres. Pontifical Council for Social Communications; Pres. Prep. Secretariat for the Press	ITA
Most Rev. Bernard Yago	Abidjan	CIV
Most Rev. Jérôme Rakotomalala	Tananarive	MDG
Most Rev. Pierre Martin Ngô-dinh-Thúc	Hué	VNM
Most Rev. Albert Soegijapranata SJ	Semarang	IDN
Most Rev. Alphonse Verwimp	tit. of Gibba	ITA
Most Rev. Angelo Giuseppe Jelmini	Apostolic Admin. of Lugano	CHE
Most Rev. Johannes Theodor Suhr	Copenhagen	DNK
Most Rev. Leo Isidore Scharmach	Apostolic Vicar, Rabaul	PNG
Most Rev. Thomas Quinlan	Apostolic Vicar, Chunchon	KOR
Most Rev. Alfred Bengsch	Berlin	DEU
Fr. Benno Walter Gut	Abbot Primate, Benedictine Confederation	ITA
Fr. Michael Browne	Master General, Order of Preachers	ITA
Fr. Augustin Sépinski	Minister General, Friars Minor	ITA
Fr. Jean-Baptiste Janssens, SJ	Father General, Society of Jesus	ITA

CONSULTORS

Most Rev. José Da Costa Nuñes	Vice Chamberlain	ITA
Most Rev. Gabriel Acasius Coussa	Pro-Secretary of the Congregation for the Oriental Churches	ITA
Most Rev. Pietro Parente	Official of the Congregation of the Holy Office	ITA
Most Rev. Francesco Carpino	Official of the Sacred Consistorial Congregation	ITA
Most Rev. Pietro Sigismondi	Secy., the Congregation for Propagation of the Faith	ITA
Most Rev. Antonio Samorè	Secy., Congregation for Extraordinary Ecclesiastical Affairs	ITA
Most Rev. Dino Staffa	Secy., Congregation of Seminaries and Universities	ITA
Most Rev. Primo Principi	Secy., Congregation of the Fabric of St. Peter	ITA
Most Rev. Angelo Dell'Acqua	Deputy Secretary of State	ITA
Most Rev. Cesare Zerba	Secy., Congregation for the Sacraments	ITA
Most Rev. Pietro Palazzini	Secy., Congregation of the Council	ITA
Fr. Paul-Pierre Philippe, OP	Secy., Congregation for Religious	ITA
Most Rev. Enrico Dante	Secy., Congregation of Rites	ITA
Most Rev. Vittorio Bartoccetti	Secy., Supreme Tribunal of the Apostolic Signatura	ITA
Most Rev. Francis John Brennan	Dean, Roman Rota	ITA
Most Rev. Pietro Sfair	tit. of Nisibi	ITA
Msgr. Giuseppe Rossi	Regent, Apostolic Penitentiary	ITA
Msgr. Francesco Tinello	Regent, Apostolic Chancery	ITA
Most Rev. Silvio Romani	Sotto-Datario	ITA
Msgr. Ernesto Camagni	Chancellor of the Apostolic Brief	ITA
Most Rev. Pio Paschini	Honorary Rector, Lateran University	ITA
Msgr. Arthur Wynen	Judge Emeritus, Roman Rota	ITA
Msgr. Alberto Canestri	Judge Emeritus, Roman Rota	ITA
Msgr. Martino Giusti	Prefect, Vatican Secret Archives	ITA
Msgr. Alfredo Maria Cavagna	Confessor of John XXIII	ITA
Fr. Joaquin Anselmo Albareda, OSB	Prefect, Vatican Library	ITA
Fr. Pierre Salmon, OSB	Abbot, St. Jerome-in-the-City	ITA
Fr. Réginald Garrigou-Lagrange, OP	Professor of the Pontifical University of the Angelicum	FRA
Fr. Alberto Vaccari, SJ	Vice Rector, Pontifical Bibical Institute	ITA

SUBCOMMITTEES

SUBCOMMITTEE FOR REGULATIONS

President: Card. Francesco Roberti
Members: Cards. Jaime De Barros Câmara, André Jullien, Arcadio Larraona, William Theodore Heard
Secretary: Msgr. Vincenzo Carbone

SUBCOMMITTEE FOR MIXED MATERIAL

President: Card. Eugène Tisserant
Members: Cards. Giuseppe Ferretto, Achille Liénart, Ignace Gabriel I Tappouni, Aloisius Joseph Muench
Secretary: Msgr. Lauro Governatori

SUBCOMMITTEE FOR AMENDMENTS

President: Card. Carlo Confalonieri
Members: Cards. Clemente Micara, Santiago Louis Copello, Giuseppe Siri, Paul Émile Léger
Secretary: Msgr. Vincenzo Fagiolo

COMMISSION FOR TECHNICAL ORGANIZATION

President: Card. Gustavo Testa
Members: Cards. Francis Spellman, Fernando Quiroga y Palacios, Giovanni Battista Montini, Paul-Marie Richaud, Julius Döpfner, Paolo Marella, Luigi Traglia, Alberto De Jorio
Secretary: Most Rev. Pericle Felici
Subsecretaries: Msgrs. Sergio Guerri, Agostino Casaroli, Igino Cardinale

THEOLOGICAL COMMISSION
Headquarters: Palazzo Santa Marta

PRESIDENT
Card. Alfredo Ottaviani, Secretary of the Congregation of the Holy Office

SECRETARY
Fr. Sebastian Tromp, SJ, Prof., Pontifical Gregorian University

MEMBERS

Most Rev. Alfredo Vicente Scherer	Porto Alegre	BRA
Most Rev. Maurice Roy	Québec	CAN
Most Rev. Marcel-Marie Dubois	Besançon	FRA
Most Rev. Maxim Hermaniuk	Winnipeg (Ruthenian)	CAN
Most Rev. Giovanni Battista Peruzzo	Agrigento	ITA
Most Rev. John Joseph Wright	Pittsburgh	USA
Most Rev. Joseph Schröffer	Eichstätt	BRD
Most Rev. James Griffiths	Aux., New York	USA
Most Rev. Franjo Franić	Apostolic Admin. Split	YUG
Most Rev. Lionel Audet	Aux., Québec	CAN
Most Rev. Platon Kornyljak	Apos. Exarch of Germany for Ukrainian and Ruthenian Rite Catholics	BRD
Msgr. Antonio Piolanti	Rector, Pontifical Lateran University	ITA
Msgr. Pietro Pavan	Secy. of the Permanent Committee for the Social Weeks of the Italian Catholic; Prof. of Social Economics, Pontifical Lateran University	ITA
Msgr. Michael Schmaus	Pontifical Academy of Theology; Professor of Dogmatic Theology, University of Munich	BRD
Msgr. Lucien Cerfaux	Professor Emeritus of Sacred Scripture, Université Catholique de Louvain	BEL
Msgr. Joseph Fenton	Pontifical Roman Theological Academy; Catholic University of America	USA
Msgr. Gérard Philips	Professor, Université Catholique de Louvain	BEL
Msgr. Agostino Ferrari Toniolo	Prof., Labor Law, Pontifical Lateran University; Secy. of Permanent Committee on Catholic Social Weeks	ITA
Msgr. Salvatore Garofalo	Rector, Pontifical Urban University	ITA
Fr. Colombo Carlo	Prof., Major Seminary of Milan	ITA
Fr. Charles Journet	Prof. Major Seminary of Fribourg	CHE
Fr. Albert Michel	Editor, *Dictionnaire de theologie catholique* (DThC)	FRA
Fr. Luigi Ciappi, OP	Master of the Sacred Apostolic Palaces	ITA
Fr. Rosaire Gagnebet, OP	Prof., Pontifical University Angelicum	ITA
Fr. Louis-Bertrand Gillon, OP	Prof., Pontifical University Angelicum	ITA
Fr. Santiago Ramirez, OP	Prof., University of Salamanca	ESP
Fr. Karl Balić, OFM	Pontifical Roman College; Prof. of Maryology, Pontifical University Antonianum	ITA
Fr. Damian Van den Eynde, OFM	Rector, Pontifical University Antonianum	ITA
Fr. Agostino Trapé, OSA	Prof., College of St. Monica; Roman Curia	ITA
Fr. Edouard Dhanis, SJ	Prefect of Studies, Pontifical Gregorian University	ITA
Fr. Franz Hürth, SJ	Prof., Pontifical Gregorian University	ITA

CONSULTORS

Msgr. Johan Brinktrine	Theology Faculty, University of Paderborn	BRD
Msgr. George Joussard	Dean of Theology, Catholic University of Lyon	FRA
Msgr. Artur Janssen	Catholic University of Leuven	BEL
Msgr. Ugo Lattanzi	Pontifical Lateran University	ITA
Msgr. André Bride	Dean of Canon Law, Catholic University of Lyon	FRA
Msgr. Heribert Schauf	Prof. of Theology, German College	BRD
Fr. Ignaz Backes	Prof of Docmatic Theology, University of Trier	BRD
Fr. Philippe Delhaye	Prof, Catholic University of Lille	FRA
Fr. René Laurentin	Prof. of Theology, Catholic University of Angers	FRA
Fr. Leo Ambrose Ondrak, OSB	Abbot, St. Procopius Abbey	USA
Fr. Anastasio del S. Rosario OCD (Alberto Ballestrero)	Superior General, Discalced Carmelites	ITA
Fr. Yves Congar, OP	Università di Strasbourg	FRA
Fr. Michel Labourdette, OP	Dominican House of Studies	FRA
Fr. Raimond Sigmond, OP	rettore del pont. ateneo Angelicum ITA	
Fr. Umberto Betti, OFM	Pontifical University Antonianum	ITA
Fr. Alexander Kerrigan, OFM	Pontifical University Antonianum	ITA
Fr. Carlos José Boaventura Kloppenburg, OFM	Journal, *Brasileira*	BRA

Fr. Ermenegildo Lio, OFM	Pont. University Antonianum	ITA
Fr. Lorenzo Di Fonzo, OFM Conv	Pres., Pontifical Theology Faculty of St. Bonaventure	ITA
Fr. Dominic Unger, OFMCap	Capuchin College, Washington	USA
Fr. Bartolome Xiberta, OC	College of St. Albert	ITA
Fr. Filippo della SS. Trinita, OCD	Pres., Theological Faculty, Discalced Carmelites	ITA
Fr. Franz Dander, SJ	Theology Faculty, Innsbruck	AUT
Fr. Henri-Marie de Lubac, SJ	Prof., Fundamental Theology, Catholic University of Lyon	FRA
Fr. Gustav Gundlach, SJ	Pont. Gregorian University	ITA
Fr. Joaquin Salaverri, SJ	Pontifical University of Camillas	ESP
Fr. Ernst Vogt, SJ	Rector, Pontifical Biblical Institute	ITA
Fr. Jan Witte, SJ	Pontifical Gregorian University	ITA
Fr. Bernard Haring, CSsR	Prof, Moral Theology, Alphonsian Academy	ITA
Fr. Joseph Lècuyer, CSSp	Prof., French Seminary	ITA
Fr. Marcel Bélanger, OMI	Vice-rector, Catholic University of Ottawa	CAN
Fr. Emmanuel Doronzo, OMI	Prof., Dogmatic Theology, Catholic University of America	USA
Fr. Garces Narciso Garcia, CFM	Pres., Spanish Maryology Society	ESP
Fr. Domenico Bertetto, SDB	Pont. Theology Academy; Prof. of Dogmatic Theology, Pont. Salesian College	ITA
Fr. Giorgio Castellino, SDB	Prof. of Sacred Scripture, Pontifical Salesian College	ITA
Fr. Amedeo Rossi, CM	Spiritual Dir., Collegio Alberoni di Piacenza	ITA

Topics Assigned[1]
1. De fontibus revelationis[2]
2. De ecclesia catholica[3]
3. De ordine supernaturali praesertim in re morali[4]
4. De matrimonio[5]
5. De doctrina sociali[6]

Schemas Drafted[7]
1. Formula nova professionis fi dei
2. De fontibus revelationis
3. De ordine morali
4. De deposito fi dei pure custodiendo
5. De castitate, virginitate, matrimonio, familia
6. De ecclesia
7. De beata Maria virgine matre Dei et matre hominum

Appendix
1. De communitate gentium
2. De ordine sociali

Schemas Presented in the Council[8]
1. *Schema Constitutionis dogmaticae de fontibus Revelationis.*
2. *Schema Constitutionis dogmaticae de deposito Fidei pure custodiendo.*
3. *Schema Constitutionis dogmaticae de ordine morali cristiano.*
4. *Schema Constitutionis dogmaticae de castitate, matrimonio, familia, virginitate.*
5. *Schema Constitutionis dogmaticae de Ecclesia.*
6. *Schema Constitutionis dogmaticae de Maria Virgine, Matre Dei et matre hominum.*
7. *Schema Constitutionis doctrinalis de ordine sociali.*
8. *Schema Constitutionis doctrinalis de communitate gentium.*

1. *Quaestiones commissionibus praeparatoriis Concilii Oecumenicis Vaticani II positae*, in AD-P 2,1 408–409.
2. "Iuxta ea, quae a Summis Pontifi cibus recentius edita sunt, exponatur doctrina catholica de Sacra Scriptura (i.e. de sacrorum libr rum historicitate; de obsequio, quo Exegetae erga Traditionem sacram et Magisterium ecclesiasticum tenentur): novi de hac re errores damentur: simulque congruentes edantur normae, quibus Exegetae in Sacris Litteris iuxta sensum Ecclesiae intepretandi ducantur,"408.
3. "Constitutio de Ecclesia Catholica, a Concilio Vaticano I edita, compleatur et perfi ciatur, praesertim quoad: 1) Corpus Christus mysticum; 2) Episcopatum; 3) Laicatum," ibid.
4. "Doctrina catholica integre exponatur, praecipuis erroribus odierni reprobatis, nempe naturalismo, materialismo, communismo, laicismo," ibid.
5. "Novissimis Summorum Pontifi cum documentis attentis, doctrina catholica de matrimonio enucleetur atque pervagantes naturalismi errores reprobentur," ibid. 409.
6. "Doctrinae catholicae de re sociali concinna expositio edatur," ibid.
7. AD-P 3,1, 11–275.
8. The first four are in: *Schemata constitutionum et decretorum, de quibus disceptabitur in Concilii sessionibus*, Series 1, Vatican City: Typis polygl. Vaticanis, 1962, 7–154; the fifth and sixth: *Schemata constitutionum et decretorum…*, cit. Series 2, 7–122; the last two in: *Schemata constitutionum et decretorum, ex quibus argumenta in Concilio disceptanda seligentur*, Series 3, 1962, 5–66.

COMMISSION FOR BISHOPS AND THE GOVERNMENT OF DIOCESES

PRESIDENT
Cardinal Paolo Marella, prefect of the Congregation of the Fabric of St. Peter

SECRETARY
Most Rev. Giuseppe Gawlina, titular bishop of Madito

MEMBERS

Most Rev. Emile Maurice Guerry	Cambrai; Secy. of Assembly of Cardinals and Archbishops of France	FRA
Most Rev. Philippe Nabaa	Beirut and Jbeil (Melkite)	LBN
Most Rev. Ermenegildo Florit	coad. Florence	ITA
Most Rev. Casimiro Morcillo Gonzalez	Zaragoza	ESP
Most Rev. Jean-Marie Villot	coad. Lyon	FRA
Most Rev. John Joseph Krol	Philadelphia	USA
Most Rev. Alberto Castelli	Secy, Italian Bishops' Conference	ITA
Most Rev. Pierre Veuillot	coad. Paris	FRA
Most Rev. Michael John Browne	Galway and Kilmacduagh	IRL
Most Rev. Georges Léon Pelletier	Trois-Rivières	CAN
Most Rev. Leo Jozef Suenens	tit. Isinda	BEL
Most Rev. Vicente Enrique y Taracón	Solsona	ESP
Most Rev. Antoine Pierre Khoraiche	Saïda (Maronite)	LBN
Most Rev. Giuseppe Piazzi	Bergamo	ITA
Most Rev. Matthias Wehr	Trier	BRD
Most Rev. Joseph Gargitter	Brixen; Apostolic Admin., Trent	ITA
Most Rev. Jean-Édouard-Lucien	aux. Paris	FRA
Most Rev. Raul Primatesta	San Rafael	ARG
Most Rev. Luigi Maria Carli	Segni	ITA
Most Rev. George Patrick Dwyer	Leeds	GBR
Msgr. Giuseppe Pasquazi	Judge, Roman Rota; Consultor, Cong. of the Consistory	ITA
Fr. Fernand Boulard	Canon, Paris	FRA
Fr. Felice Cappello, SJ	Consultor, Cong. of the Consistory; Prof. of Canon Law, Gregorian University	ITA

CONSULTORS

Most Rev. Miguel Dario Miranda y Gomez	Mexico City	MEX
Most Rev. Demetrio Moscato	Salerno	ITA
Most Rev. Justin Daniel Simonds	coad. Melbourne	AUS
Most Rev. Leo Binz	Dubuque	USA
Most Rev. Marie-Joseph Lemieux	Ottawa	CAN
Most Rev. Helder Pessôa Câmara	aux. São Sebastião do Rio de Janeiro	BRA
Most Rev. Vincentas Brizgys	tit. Bosana	USA
Most Rev. Petar Čule	Mostar	YUG
Most Rev. Leo Richard Smith	aux. Buffalo	USA
Most Rev. Jerome Daniel Hannan	Scranton	USA
Most Rev. Narciso Arnau Jubany	aux. Barcellona	ESP
Most Rev. León Pablo Correa	Cúcuta	COL
Most Rev. Geraldo Fernandes Bijos	London	BRA
Most Rev. Thomas William Muldoon	aux. Sydney	AUS
Most Rev. Albino Mensa	Ivrea	ITA
Msgr. Julien Gouet	Secy., French Bishops	FRA
Msgr. Frans Lambrechts	Exec. Secy. Apostolate of the Sea	BEL
Fr. Emiliano Lucchesi	Abbot General, Vallombrosian Benedictines	ITA
Fr. Wilfrid Dufault	Superior General, Augustinian Assumptionists	ITA
Fr. Gaetano Stano	Procurator General, Conventual Franciscans	ITA
Fr. Jenaro Fernandez Echeverria	Procurator General, Augustinian Recollects	ITA
Fr. Giacomo Martegani	Italian Assistancy, Society of Jesus	ITA
Fr. Francesco Milini	Vicar General, Missionaries of St. Charles Borromeo	ITA
Fr. Karol Szrant	General Consultor, Redemptorists	ITA
Fr. Michiels Gommar, OFMCap	Prof., Lateran University	BEL
Fr. Tito di san Paolo della Croce	Passionist; Consultor of Congregation for the Consistory	ITA
Fr. Werenfried Van Straaten, OPraem	Abbot of Tongerlo (Antwerp)	BEL

Topics Assigned[1]
1. De dioceseon partitione[2]
2. De episcoporum potestate[3]
3. Praecipuae de animarum cura quaestiones[4]
4. De emigrantibus[5]

Schemas Drafted[6]
1. De dioeceseon partitione
2. De episcoporum coetu seu Conferentia
3. De rationibus inter episcopos et SS. Curiae Romanae Congregationes
4. De rationibus inter episcopos et parochos
5. De episcoporum coadiutoribus et auxiliaribus deque episcoporum cessation a munere pastorali
6. Praecipuae de animarum cura quaestiones
7. De rationibus inter episcopos et religiosos praesertim quoad apostolatus opera exercenda

Schemas Presented in Council[7]
– *Schema Decreti de episcopis ac de dioceseon regimine*
– *Schema Decreti de cura animarum*

---

1. *Quaestiones positae…*, cit. in: AD-P 2,1, 409.
2. "Ratio demerminetur qua dioceseon fi nes recognosci possint ita ut, Concilio espleto, earum partitio apte disponatur sub moderamine S. Congregationis Concistorialis vel alicuius Coetus a bea dependentis," ibid.
3. "Determinentur rationes: a) Episcopos inter et SS. Curiae Romanae Congregationes. Videatur quaenam facultates pro dioceseon regimine Episcopis stabiliter tribui possint; b) Episcopos inter et parochos. Institutum inamovibilitatis parochorum recognoscatur ita ut Episcopis, pro bono animarum, maior tribuatur agendi facultas; c) Episcopos inter et Religiosos. Exemptionis privilegio servato, curetur ut Religiosi magis, sub Episcoporum moderamine, in apostolatus opera incumbant et amplior cooperatio vigeat inter clerum dioecesanum et religiosos," ibid.
4. "Maxime odierni necessitatibus attendatur. Praeter ceteras, haec quoque perpendatur quaestio: de opportunitate instituendi in urbibus, frequentibus populo, paroecias personales quae dicuntur," ibid.
5. "Media apta expendatur, quae emigranti bus auxilium praestent ad fi dem moresque integre servandos," ibid.
6. AD-P 3,1.
7. *Schemata constitutionum et decretorum…*, cit. Series three, 67–180.

COMMISSION FOR THE DISCIPLINE OF THE CLERGY AND THE CHRISTIAN PEOPLE

President
Card. Pietro Ciriaci, Prefect of the Sacred Congregation for the Council

Secretary
Fr. Cristoforo Berutti, OP, consultor to the Sacred Cong. for the Council; professor of canon law, the Angelicum

Members

Most Rev. Charles de Provenchères	Aix	FRA
Most Rev. Roberto Ronca	tit. Lepanto	ITA
Most Rev. Enrico Nicodemo	Bari	ITA
Most Rev. Raffaele Baratta	Perugia	ITA
Most Rev. Alois Hudal	tit. Aela	ITA
Most Rev. Anton Vovk	Ljubljana	SVN
Most Rev. Laurent Koguian Sahag	aux. Beirut (Armenian)	LBN
Most Rev. William Philbin	Clonfert	IRL
Most Rev. Henri Mazerat	Fréjus–Toulon	FRA
Most Rev. Ernest John Primeau	Manchester	USA
Msgr. Pietro Mattioli	judge, Roman Rota	ITA
Msgr. Charles Lefebvre	judge, Roman Rota	ITA
Msgr. Jakob Weinbacher	Vicar General, Vienna	AUT
Msgr. Alessandro Gottardi	Pro-vicar General, Venice	ITA
Msgr. Simon Delacroix	Director General, Priests of the Sacred Heart	FRA
Msgr. Domenico Dottarelli	Parish of S. Eusebio–Roma	ITA
Msgr. Giuseppe D'Ercole	Prof., of the history of canon law, Lateran University	ITA
Msgr. Enrico Hoffmann	Member of Commission for the Supervision of the Tribunal for Marriage Process	ITA
Msgr. Luigi Piovesana	National Director, Apostolic Union of Clerics	ITA
Msgr. Walerian Meysztowicz	President, Polish Historical Institute	POL
Msgr. Peter Whitty	Pastor, Church of St. Dominic, Liverpool	GBR
Fr. Willy Onclin	Prof., Catholic University of Leuven	BEL
Fr. Herbert Linenberger	Director General, Missionaries of the Most Precious Blood	ITA
Fr. Wilhelm Möhler	Rector General, Pallotines	ITA
Fr. Mario Pinzuti, OSB	Olivetan Benedictines; Director of Institute for Scientific Book Restoration	ITA
Fr. Ludovico Bender, OP	Prof. of canon law, the Angelicum	ITA
Fr. Vittorio Costantini, OFMConv	Minister General, Conventual Franciscans	ITA
Fr. Agatangelo da Langasco, OFMCap	Capuchin; visitor appointed by the Holy See	ITA
Fr. Josef Grisar, SJ	Prof., Gregorian University	ITA
Fr. Eduardo Regatillo, SJ	Prof. of canon law, Catholic University of Comillas	ESP
Fr. Marcelino Cabreros de Anta, CMF	Prof. of canon law, Pontifical University of Salamanca	ESP
Fr. Klemens Tilmann, CO	Professor of religious education, University of Munich	BRD
Fr. Anselmo, FSC	Brothers of Christian Schools; Inspector of religious teaching in elementary and secondary schools in central Italy	ITA

Consultors

Most Rev. Eugeniusz Baziak	Archbishop of Lviv (Latin), apostolic admin. of Kraków	POL
Most Rev. Philip Francis Pocock	coad. Toronto	CAN
Most Rev. Luis del Rosario	Zamboanga	PHL
Most Rev. Santos Moro Briz	Avila	ESP
Most Rev. Arthur Douville	Saint-Hyacinte	CAN
Most Rev. Paul Taguchi Yoshigoro	Osaka	JAP
Most Rev. Charles Pasquale Greco	Alexandria	USA
Most Rev. Pio Alberto Fariña Fariña	Citarizo	CHL
Most Rev. Ernesto Corripio y Ahumada	Tampico	MEX
Most Rev. Luis Baccino	S. José de Mayo	URY
Most Rev. Miguel Raspanti	Morón	ARG
Most Rev. José Maximino Eusebio Dominguez y Rodriguez	aux. San Cristobal de la Habana	CUB
Msgr. Celestino Trezzini	Honorary prof., University of Friburg	CHE

Msgr. George Schlichte	Vice Chancellor, Archd. of Boston	USA
Msgr. Urban Krizomali	Abbot-Pastor of the collegiate church of Trogir Abbey	YUG
Msgr. Grazioso Ceriani	V.P., Pastoral Institute of the Lateran University	ITA
Msgr. Nicola Fusco	Pastor, Mount St. Peter's Church, New Kensington	USA
Msgr. Giovanni Catti	Director, Diocesan Catechetical Office of the Diocese of Bologna	ITA
Fr. Giovanni Battista Belloli	Diocesan Catechetical Office of the Diocese of Brescia	ITA
Fr. Lawrence McReavy	Prof. of Moral Theology and Canon Law, Ushaw College	GBR
Fr. André Brien	Dir., Higher Institute of Pastoral Catechetics of Paris	FRA
Fr. Jean Honoré	Dir., National Center for Religious Education, Paris	FRA
Fr. Hugo Aufderbeck	Priest of Diocese of Paderborn, member of Liturgical Xommission of the Bishops' Conference of Fulda, and of the Commission of Pastoral Theology for German-Speaking Countries	DDR
Fr. Lamberto De Echeverria	Prof. of Canon Law, Pontifical University of Salamanca	ESP
Fr. William M. Slattery, CM	Superior General, Congregation of the Mission	ITA
Fr. Jean-François Motte, OFM	Minister of the Friars Minor, French Province	FRA
Fr. Neil O'Connell, OFM	Prof. of Canon Law at the Pontifical University Antonianum	ITA
Fr. Giorgio Montico, OFMConv	Minister of the Conventual Franciscans, Italian Province	ITA
Fr. José Craveiro da Silva, SJ	Provincial and Visitor, Society of Jesus	BRA
Fr. Gottfried Heinzel, SJ	Prof., Moral Theology, University of Innsbruck	AUT
Fr. Henri Barrè, CSSp	Rector, Pontifical French Seminary	ITA
Fr. Milan Stanislav Ďurica, SDB	Prof., Salesian Theology Inst., Monteortone (Padua)	ITA
Fr. Giuseppe Muzio, SDB	Salesian, Director of the Salesian College of Villa Sora, Frascati	ITA
Fr. Carlo Tommaso Dragone, SSP	Superior, House of Writers, Albano Laziale	ITA

Topics Assigned[1]
1. De distributione cleri[2]
2. De inamovibilitate parochorum[3]
3. De habitu clericali[4]
4. De praeceptis ecclesiasticis[5]
5. De catechetica institutione[6]
6. De beneficiis ecclesiasticis[7]
7. De confraternitatibus[8]

Schemas Drafted[9]
1. De distributione cleri
2. De clericorum vitae sanctitate
3. De habitu et tonsura clericale
4. De paroeciarum provisione, unione, divisione
5. De obligationibus parochorum
6. De officiis et benefi ciis ecclesiasticis deque honorum ecclesiasticorum administratione
7. De patrimonio historico et artistico ecclesiastico
8. De parochorum obligationibus quoad curam animarum
9. De praeceptis ecclesiasticis
10. De catechetica populi christiani institutione
11. De cura animarum et communismo
12. De praevia librorum censura eorumque prohibitione
13. De censuris earumque reservatione
14. De modo procedendi in poenis in via administrativa infl igendis
15. De fi delium associationibus
16. De missarum stipendiis, de missarum onerum reductione, de piis ultimis voluntatibus
17. De promovendis ad ordines sacros iis qui fuerunt pastore seu ministri acatholici

Schemas Presented in Council[10]
–*Schema decreti de clericis*

---

1. *Quaestiones positae…*, cit., in: AD-P 2/1, 410.
2. "Rationes assignentur, quae clero aptius distribuendo faveant," ibid.
3. "Hoc institutum videatur cum Commissione de Episcopis ed de dioceseon regimine," ibid.
4. "An et quomodo, iuxta diversas regiones, sit immutandus," ibid.
5. "Examini subiciatur, ut nostris diebus magis aptetur, lex de die festivo, de ieiunio et abstinentia, de confessione et comunione paschali," ibid.
6. "a) Novus edatur catechismus, praecipua etiam continens elementa S. Liturgia, Historiae ecclesiasticae, necnon doctrina socialis; b) Catechesi pro adultis novum incrementum afferatur," ibid.
7. "An, quatenus et quibus criteriis institutum benefi ciale immutandum sit," ibid.
8. "Earum conformatio et statuta ita recognoscantur ut odierni necessitatibus effi cacius atque aptius respondeant," ibid.
9 AD-P, vol. 3,1.
10 *Schemata constitutionum et decretorum…*, cit. Series quarta, 27–42.

COMMISSION FOR RELIGIOUS

PRESIDENT
Card. Valerio Valeri, Prefect, Sacred Congregation for Religious

SECRETARY
Fr. Joseph Rousseau OMI, Consultor, Sacred Congregation for Religious and Seminaries

MEMBERS

Most Rev. Joseph-Martin Urtasun	Avignon	FRA
Most Rev. George Bernard Flahiff	Winnipeg	CAN
Most Rev. Girolamo Bartolomeo Bortignon	Padua	ITA
Most Rev. Arturo Tabera Araoz	Albacete	ESP
Most Rev. Joseph Mark McShea	Allentown	USA
Most Rev. Enrico Romolo Compagnone	Anagni	ITA
Fr. Jerome Gassner, OSB	Procurator General, Austrian Congregation (Benedictine)	ITA
Fr. Francesco Savarese, OM	Corrector General, Order of Minims	ITA
Fr. Joseph Mirande, SCI di Béth	Superior General, Society of Priests of the Sacred Heart of Bétharram	FRA
Fr. Gommaire van den Broeck, OPraem	Prior, Monastery of Saint-Bernard-de-Lacolle	CAN
Fr. Pietro Rutten, OSC	Procurator General, Canons Regular of the Holy Cross; commissioner, Sacred Congregation for Religious	ITA
Fr. Jules Fohl, OSB	Consultor, Sacred Congregation for Religious	ITA
Fr. Tomás Tascón, OP	Secretary General, Order of Preachers; Consultor, Sacred Congregation for Religious	ITA
Fr. Joaquin Sanchis, OFM	Definitor General for Spanish Language, Friars Minor	ITA
Fr. Pietro Tocanel, OFMConv	Prof. of canon law at the Pontifical Lateran University; Consultor, Sacred Congregation for Religious	ITA
Fr. Lazare D'Arbonne, OFMCap	Consultor, Sacred Congregation for Religious	ITA
Fr. Thomas Keulemans, OCarm	Secretary General VNPR Society	NLD
Fr. Pedro Abellan, SJ	Prof. of Moral Theology, Pontifical Gregorian University	ITA
Fr. Albert Van Biervliet, CSsR	Consultor, Sacred Congregation for Religious	ITA
Fr. Edward Louis Heston, OSC	Congregation of the Holy Cross, Procurator and General Postulator; Consultor, Sacred Congregation for Religious	ITA
Fr. Siervo Goyenece, CMF	Dean, Institute Utriusque Iuris, Pontifical Lateran University; Consultor, Sacred Congregation for Religious	ITA
Fr. Emilio Fogliasso, SDB	Professor, Pontifical Salesian College; Consultor, Sacred Congregation for Religious	ITA
Fr. Alvaro del Portillo	Secretary General, Opus Dei; Consultor, Sacred Congregation for Religious	ITA
Fr. Alessandro, FMS	Procurator and Postulator General, Marist Brothers	ITA

CONSULTORS

Most Rev. Louis-Severin Haller	Abbot Nullius of St. Maurice of Agaunum; Abbot Primate, Confederation of Canons Regular of St. Augustine	CHE
Most Rev. Bernardino Carlos Echeverria Ruiz	Ambato	ECU
Most Rev. Pacifico Maria Luigi Perantoni	Gerace	ITA
Msgr. André Baron	Rector, Convent of St. Louis of France; Vice President, Board of Governors, Congregation for the Propagation of the Faith	ITA
Fr. Patrick Francis Cremin	Prof., St. Patrick's College	IRL
Fr. Hubert Noots, OPraem	Abbot General, Premonstratensians	ITA
Fr. Sighard Kleiner, OCist	Abbot General, Cistercians	ITA
Fr. Gabriel Sortais, OCSO	Abbot General, Cistercians of the Strict Observance	ITA
Fr. Giuseppe Ricciotti, CRL	Consultor, Sacred Congregation for Religious	ITA
Fr. Armand François Le Bourgeois, CIM	Superior General, Eudists	FRA
Fr. Jean-François Barbier, OFM	Secretary General of dei CPR di Francia	FRA
Fr. Gérard Mulcahy, OFM	Rector, College of sant'Isidoro	ITA

Fr. Zaccaria da S. Mauro, OFMCap	Consultor, Sacred Congregation for Religious	ITA
Fr. Adolar Zumkeller, OESA	Prior, Hermits of St. Augustine, Munich	BRD
Fr. Beniamino della SS.ma Trinità, OCD	Definitor General, Discalced Carmelites; Commissioner, Sacred Congregation for Religious	ITA
Fr. Romaeus William O'Brien, OC	Prof. of Canon Law, Catholic University of America, Washington	USA
Fr. Vittore di Gesù e Maria, OCD	Definitor General, Discalced Carmelites; Consultor, Sacred Congregation for Religious	ITA
Fr. Robert Svoboda, MI	President of Caritas in Austria	BRD
Fr. Theodore Foley, CP	Consultor General, Passionists	ITA
Fr. André Guay, OMI	Procurator General, Missionaries of Mary Immaculate	ITA
Fr. Charles Corcoran, OSC	Prof. of Dogmatic Theology, Washington, DC	USA
Fr. John Mix, CR	Resurrectionists, St. Joseph's Church	USA
Fr. Candido Bajo, CMI	Assistant Director General, Claretians; Commissioner of the Sacred Congregation for Religious	ITA
Fr. Gerardo Escudero, CMI	Consultor, Sacred Congregation for Religious	ESP
Fr. Francesco Molinari, MS	Procurator General, Missionaries of Our Lady of La Salette; Commissioner, Sacred Congregation for Religious	ITA
Fr. Mario Piazzano, OSI	Procurator and Postulator General, Oblates of St. Joseph; Commissioner, Sacred Congregation for Religious	ITA
Fr. Gaston Courtois, FC	Procurator General, Brothers of Charity	ITA
Fr. Eugenio Fornasari, SSP	Society of St. Paul	ITA
Fr. Amadeo De Fuenmayor	Opus Dei; Prof of Civil Law, University of Madrid	ESP

Topics Assigned[1]
1. De vita religiosa renovanda[2]
2. De unione vel foederatione Institutoum religiosorum[3]
3. De privilegio exemptionis[4]
4. De habitu religioso[5]

Schemas Drafted[6]
1. De statibus perfectionis adquirendae
2. Pars prima: Doctrina de statibus perfections adquirendae
3. Pars secunda: Disciplina de renovatione vitae et operae in institutis status perfectionis adquirendae

Schema Presented in Council
– *Schema Constitutionis De statibus perfectionis adquirendae*[7]

---

1. *Quaestiones commissionibus…*, cit. AD-P 2,1 410–411.
2. "a) Constitutiones, 'Directoria,' 'Consuetudinaria' nostris temporibus melius aptentur; b) Media suggerantur ad incrementum institutionis religiosae Monalium et Sororum; c) Novitiorum institutio nostris temporibus aptetur novoque incremento augeatur; d) Spiritus religiosus fi rmetur atque disciplina praesertim in parvis communitatibus foveatur," ibid.
3. "a) Ad unitatem reducantur vel saltem in confoederationem copulentur familiae religiosae unius eiusdemque Instituti; b) In confoederationem uniantur Instituta Religiosa, quae fi nes eosdem vel similes persequuntur," ibid. 411.
4. "Normae determinentur, quae Religiosos magis immitti sinant in apostolatus opera, sub Episcoporum regimine. (Institutum exemptionis videatur una cum Commissione de Episcopis et doceseon regimine)," ibid.
5. "Habitus religiosus, sive virorum, sive mulierum, sit decens, simplex ac modestus, at temporum ac locorum aduncti necnon necessitatibus ministerii accomodatus," ibid.
6 AD-P 3,1, 431–495.
7 *Schemata constitutionum et decretorum…*, cit. Series Tertia, 181–281.

COMMISSION FOR THE DISCIPLINE OF THE SACRAMENTS

PRESIDENT
Card. Aloisi Masella, Prefect, Sacred Congregation for the Discipline of the Sacraments

SECRETARY
Fr. José Ramon Bidagor, SJ, Consultor, Sacred Congregation for the Discipline of the Sacraments; Prof., Pontifical Gregorian University

MEMBERS

Most Rev. José Garcia y Goldarez	Valladolid	ESP
Most Rev. Guido Luigi Bentivoglio	Catania	ITA
Most Rev. Antônio Maria Alves de Siqueira	coad. São Paulo	BRA
Most Rev. Armando Fares	Catanzaro e Squillace	ITA
Most Rev. Marcello Morgante	Piceno	ITA
Ascoli		
Most Rev. John George Chedid	Vicar for the Patriarch of Antioch (Maronite)	LBN
Most Rev. Lorenzo Miguelez	Dean Emeritus, Rota of the Apostolic Nunciature in Madrid	ESP
Msgr. Michele Toros	Apostolic Admin. "ad nutum sanctae sedis" of Gorizia	YUG
Msgr. Boleslaw Filipiak	Prelate Auditor of the Roman Rota	ITA
Msgr. William Doheney	Prelate Auditor of the Roman Rota	ITA
Msgr. Manuel Bonet y Muixi	Prelate Auditor of the Roman Rota	ITA
Msgr. Giovanni Pinna	Prelate Auditor of the Roman Rota	ITA
Msgr. José Miguel Pinto	Vicar General, Socorro y San Gil	COL
Msgr. Jacques Denis	Vicar General, Sens	FRA
Msgr. Clement Vincent Bastnagel	Prof., Catholic University of America, Washington	USA
Fr. Klaus Mörsdorf	Director, Canonical Institute of the University of Munich	BRD
Fr. Henri Wagnon	Prof., Catholic University of Leuven	BEL
Fr. Ulrico Beste, OSB	Prof., Pontifical College of S. Anselmo; Consultor, Congregation of the Holy Office	ITA
Fr. Pedro Lumbreras, OP	Prof., Pontifical College Angelicum; canon of the Apostolic Penitentiary	ITA
Fr. Vitomir Jelicić, OFM	Consultor, Sacred Congregation for the Sacraments	ITA
Fr. Adolf Pawel Ledwolorz, OFM	Definitor General, Friars Minor; Consultor, Pontifical Commission for the Authentic Interpretation of the Code of Canon Law	ITA
Fr. Antoine Delchard, SJ	Seminaries of the Mission of St. Martin d'Ablois	FRA
Fr. Jan Visser, CSsR	Prof., Pontifical College for the Propagagion of the Faith; Consultor, Sac. Cong. of the Holy Office	ITA
Fr. Henri Evers, SSS	Consultor, Sacred Congregation for the Sacraments	ITA
Fr. Antonio Peinador Navarro, CMF	Prof., Pontifical University of Salamanca	ESP

CONSULTORS

Most Rev. Danio Bolognini	Cremona	ITA
Most Rev. Alfonso Maria Ungarelli	tit. Azura; prel. nullius of Pinheiro	BRA
Most Rev. Enrique Rau	Mar del Plata	ARG
Most Rev. Valérian Bélanger	aux. Montréal	CAN
Most Rev. Juan Félix Pepén y Soliman	N.S. de la Altagracia en Higüey	DOM
Msgr. Luis Lituma	Canon, Cathedral of Lima	PER
Msgr. Jean Levillain	Curial Official of Paris	FRA
Fr. Gerhard Oesterle, OSB	Consultor, Sacred Congregation for the Sacraments	BRD
Fr. Stefano Gomez, OP	Consultor, Sacred Congregation for the Sacraments	ITA
Fr. Mark Said, OP	Prof., Pontifical University Angelicum	ITA
Fr. Guy Brisebois, OFM	Consultor, Sacred Congregation for the Sacraments; prof., Pontifical University Antonianum	ITA
Fr. Roberto Zavalloni, OFM	Prof., Pontifical Pastoral Institute, Lateran University	ITA
Fr. Miguel Fabregas, SJ	Consultor, Sacred Congregation for the Sacraments; prof. Pontifical Gregorian University	ITA
Fr. Karl Rahner, SJ	Prof., University of Innsbruck	AUT
Fr. Marcellino Zalba, SJ	Prof., Massimo Institute	ITA

Topics Assigned[1]
1. De confirmatione[2]
2. De poenitentia[3]
3. De ordine[4]
4. De matrimonio[5]
5. De sacerdoti bus qui defecerunt[6]

Schemas Drafted[7]
1. De sacramento confirmationis
2. De sacramento poenitentiae
3. De sacramento ordinis
4. De impedimentis ad matrimonium
5. De matrimoniis mixtis
6. De consensu matrimoniali
7. De forma celebrationis matrimonii
8. De processu matrimoniali
9. De praeparatione ad matrimonium
10. De sacerdotibus lapsis

Schemas Published[8]
– *Schema Decreti de matrimonii sacramento*

---

1 *Quaestiones commissionibus...*, cit. AD-P 2,1, 411–412.

2 "Casus determinentur, in quibus facultas administrandi hoc sacramentum concedatur sacerdotibus, qui sacro ministerio incumbant," ibid. 411.

3 "Casus determinentur, in quibus extendere expediat iurisdictionem ad confessiones sacramentales audiendas. De peccatis reservatis quaestio perpendatur," ibid.

4 "Disceptatur an et quomodo expediat veterem praxim instaurare quoad ordines minores et diconatum. De aetate, qua ordines maiores conferendi sint, et de interstitiis producendis," ibid.

5 "An et quomodo impedimentorum numerus minuendus sit et processus matrimonialis ad expeditiorem formam reducendus," ibid.

6 "Sacerdotum, qui defecerunt, infelix vita expendatur et, quod fi eri potest, aeternae ipsorum saluti consulatur," ibid. 412.

7 AD-P 3,1, 499–557.

8 *Schemata constitutionum et decretorum...*cit., Series quarta, Città del Vaticano, Typis polygl. Vaticanis, 1963, 175–207.

COMMISSION FOR THE SACRED LITURGY

PRESIDENT
Card. Amleto Giovanni Cicognani Prefect, Sacred Congregation for Rites

SECRETARY
Fr. Annibale Bugnini, CM, Prof. of Pastoral Liturgy at the Pastoral Institute, Pontifical Lateran University

MEMBERS

Most Rev. Joseph Goguè	Bassorah (Chaldean)	IRQ
Most Rev. Carlo Rossi	Biella	ITA
Most Rev. Juan Hervás y Benet	tit. Dora, prelate of Ciudad Real	ESP
Most Rev. Karel Justinus Calewaert	Gand	BEL
Most Rev. Franz Zauner	Linz	AUT
Most Rev. Henri Jenny	aux. Cambrai	FRA
Most Rev. Joseph Malula	aux. Léopoldville	COD
Msgr. Joaquim Nabuco	Consultor, Congregation for Rites	BRA
Msgr. Higini Anglès	Pres., Pontifical Institute of Sacred Music	ITA
Msgr. Joseph Maria Pascher	Prof. Emeritus, University of Munich	BRD
Msgr. Romano Guardini	Prof., Philosophy of Religion, University of Munich	BRD
Msgr. Giovanni Fallani	Pres., Pontifical Commission for Sacred Art	ITA
Msgr. Mario Righetti	Consultor, Congregation for Rites; Mitred Abbot, Nostra Signora del Rimedio	ITA
Msgr. Pietro Borella	Master of Ceremonies, Milan Cathedral	ITA
Msgr. Giovanni Schiavon	Master of Ceremonies, Basilica of San Marco, Venice	ITA
Fr. Enrico Cattaneo	Prof., history of liturgy, Univ. Cattolica del S. Cuore	ITA
Fr. Dragutin K. Kniewald	Prof. Emeritus of liturgy, University of Zagreb	YUG
Fr. John O'Connel	Liturgy editor, *The Clergy Review*	GBR
Fr. Johannes Quasten	Prof., Catholic University of America	USA
Fr. Josef Andreas Jungmann, SJ	Prof. Emeritus, University of Innsbruck	AUT
Fr. Gregorio Martinez de Antoñana, CMF	Vice Pres., "Junta Nacional de Apostolado Liturgico" of Spain	ESP
Fr. Giulio Bevilacqua, CO	Pastor	ITA
Fr. Giuseppe Pizzoni, CM	Dir., Pontificia Accademia Liturgica, Consultor, Congregation for Rites	ITA

CONSULTORS

Most Rev. Joseph Walsh	Tuam	IRL
Most Rev. Tadeusz Paweł Zakrzewski	Plock	POL
Most Rev. Kazimierz Jósef Kowalski	Chelmo	POL
Most Rev. Francis Xavier Muthappa	Coimbatore	IND
Most Rev. Otto Spülbeck	Meissen	DDR
Msgr. Salvatore Famoso	Chancellor, Archdiocese of Catania	ITA
Msgr. Michael Pfliegler	Prof., University of Vienna	AUT
Msgr. Johannes Wagner	Dir., Liturgical Institute of Trier	BRD
Fr. Antoine Chavasse	Prof., University of Strasbourg	FRA
Fr. Anton Hänggi	Prof., University of Fribourg	CHE
Fr. Percy Jones	Pres., Liturgy Commission, Archdiocese of Melbourne	AUS
Fr. Pierre Jounel	Prof., Liturgical Institute, Catholic University of Paris	FRA
Fr. Theodor Klauser	Prof., University of Bonn	BRD
Canon Aimé-Georges Martimort	Dir., Center for Pastoral Liturgy, France	FRA
Fr. Frederick McManus	Prof., Catholic University of America	USA
Fr. Jairo Mejia Gómez	Dir., Liturgical Apostolate of Colombia	COL
Fr. Ernesto Teodoro Moneta Caglio	Pres., Pontifical Ambrosian Institute of Sacred Music	ITA
Fr. Ignacio Oñativia	Prof. of Liturgy, Seminary of Vitoria	ESP
Fr. Theodor Schnitzler	Prof. of Liturgy, Seminary of Cologne	BRD
Fr. Valerio Vigorelli	Dir., School of Christian Art "Beato Angelico," Milano	ITA
Fr. Boniface Luykx, OPraem	Dir, Center for Pastoral Liturgy of Central Africa	COD
Fr. Bernard Botte, OSB	Dir. of Liturgy, Catholic Institute of Paris	BEL
Fr. Eugene Cardine, OSB	Prof. of musical paleography, Pontifical Institute of Sacred Music	ITA
Fr. Godfrey Diekmann, OSB	Editor, *Worship*	USA
Fr. Petrus Siffrin, OSB	Consultor, Congregation for Rites	BRD
Fr. Cipriano Vagaggini, OSB	Asst. Rector, Pontifical Atheneum of San'Anselmo	ITA
Fr. Ansgar Dirks, OP	Dir., Dominican Liturgical Institute	ITA
Fr. Pierre-Marie Gy, OP	Prof., Liturgical Institute, Catholic University of Paris	FRA
Fr. Lucas Brinkoff, OFM	Secy., Interdiocesan Liturgical Secretariat, Holland	NLD
Fr. Johannes Hofinger, SJ	Dir., East Asian Pastoral Institute	PHL
Fr. Herman Schmidt, SJ	Prof., Pontifical Gregorian University	ITA
Fr. Marcel Dubois, CSsR	Redemptorist	CAN
Fr. George de Lepeleere, SsCc	Prefect General of Studies, Congregation of the Sacred Hearts	ITA
Fr. Vincent Kennedy, CSB	Prof. of Sacred Liturgy, Medival Studies Institute of Toronto	CAN
Fr. Heinrich Kahlefeld, CO	Oratorian	BRD

Topics Assigned[1]
1. De calendario recognoscendo[2]
2. De Missa[3]
3. De Sacribus ritibus[4]
4. De Sacramentis[5]
5. De Breviario[6]
6. De lingua liturgica[7]
7. De vestibus liturgicis ad simpliciorem formam reducendis

Schemas Drafted
1. De sacra liturgia[8]

Schemas Presented in Council
– *Schema Constitutionis de sacra liturgia*[9]

---

1 *Quaestiones commissionibus…*, cit. in: AD-P 2,1 412.
2 "Apta criteria hac de re proponantur," ibid.
3 "Rationes edantru de textibus et rubricis recognoscendis," ibid.
4 "De reducendis ad sempliciorem formam Missa Pontifi cali, ecclesiae consecratione, campanarum bene-dictione etc," ibid.
5 "Baptismi, confi rmationis, extremae unctionis, matrimonii ritus ita recognoscantur, ut magis signifi cent ea quae effi ciutn," ibid.
6 "Aptetur Breviarium sacri ministerii necnon spiritualibus cleri necessitatibus," ibid.
7 "Diligenter perpendatur an expediat linguam vulgarem in quibusdam Missae et Sacramentorum adminis-trationis partibus permittere," ibid.
8 AD-P 3,2, 7–68.
9 *Schema constitutionum…*, cit. Series prima, 155–201.

COMMISSION FOR STUDIES AND SEMINARIES

PRESIDENT
Card. Giuseppe Pizzardo, Prefect, Cong. for Seminaries and Universities

SECRETARY
Fr. Paul Augustin Mayer, OSB, Rector, Pontifical Roman Athenaeum of Sant'Anselmo

MEMBERS

Most Rev. Marcelino Olaechea Loizaga	Valencia	ESP
Most Rev. Louis Marie de Bazelaire de Ruppierre	Chambéry	FRA
Most Rev. Paolo Botto	Cagliari	ITA
Most Rev. François Marty	Reims	FRA
Most Rev. Emile Arsène Blanchet	Rector, Istitut Catholique de Paris	FRA
Most Rev. Agostino Saba	Sassari	ITA
Most Rev. John Patrick Cody	coad. with succession, New Orleans	USA
Most Rev. António Ferreira Gomes	Porto	ESP
Most Rev. Sebastian Vayalil	Palai	IND
Most Rev. Thomas Lane Loras	Rockford	USA
Most Rev. François Nestor Adam	Sion	CHE
Most Rev. Giuseppe Carraro	Verona	ITA
Most Rev. Roger André Marcel Johan	Agen	FRA
Most Rev. Paolo Savino	aux. Naples	ITA
Most Rev. Giovanni Colombo	aux. Milan	ITA
Most Rev. Vincenzo M. Jacono	tit. Pataro	ITA
Most Rev. Francesco Bertoglio	tit. Paro	ITA
Msgr. Pier Carlo Landucci	Member, Pont. Academy of Theology	ITA
Msgr. Plinio Pascoli	Rector, Pont. Roman Seminary	ITA
Msgr. Carlo Figini	Pres., Pont. Theology Faculty of Milan	ITA
Msgr. Donal Herlihy	Rector, Pontifical Irish College	ITA
Msgr. Vincenzo Faraoni	Prof., Pont. Regional Seminary of Fano	ITA
Msgr. Rudolph G. Bandas	Consultor, Congregation for Seminaries and Universities	USA
Msgr. Roberto Masi	Prof. of Sacramental Theology, Pontifical Lateran University	ITA
Msgr. Antonio Angioni	Spiritual Director, Regional Seminary of Bologna	ITA
Msgr. André Combes	Prof., Pontifical Lateran University	ITA
Fr. Vicente Lores	Superior Gen., Diocesan Worker Priests, Madrid	ESP
Fr. Francesco Spadafora	Prof., Pontifical Lateran University	ITA
Fr. Hubert Jedin	Prof., University of Bonn	BRD
Fr. Pierre Girard	Superior General, Sulpicians	FRA
Fr. Benoît Lavaud, OP	Dominican House of Studies, Toulouse	FRA
Fr. Ilarino da Milano, OFMCap	Preacher to Papal Household	ITA
Fr. Gabriele M. Roschini, OSM	Pres. Theology Faculty, Pontifical Institute Marianum, Rome	ITA
Fr. Pablo Muñoz Vega, SJ	Rector, Pontifical Gregorian University	ITA
Fr. Paolo Dezza, SJ	Prof., Pontifical Gregorian University	ITA
Fr. Cornelio Fabro, CSS	Member, Pontifical Academy of Theology	ITA
Fr. Alfons Maria Stickler, ODB	Rector, Salesian Pontifical University	ITA

CONSULTORS

Most Rev. Alfredo Cifuentes Gomez	La Serena	CHL
Most Rev. Egidio Bignamini	Ancona	ITA
Most Rev. Norberto Perini	Fermo	ITA
Most Rev. Giuseppe D'Avack	Camerino	ITA
Most Rev. Patrick Aloysius O'Boyle	Washington	USA
Most Rev. Octaviano Márquez Tóriz	Angelopoli	MEX
Most Rev. Giuseppe Amici	Modena	ITA
Most Rev. Luis Manresa Formosa	Quezaltenango	GTM
Msgr. Francesco Olgiati	Prof., Catholic University of the Sacred Heart, Milan	ITA
Msgr. Bernhard Geyer	Albertus Magnus Institute, Bonn	BRD
Msgr. Giuseppe De Luca	Honorary Prelate	ITA

Msgr. Erich Kleineidam	Rector, Major Seminary of Erfurt	DDR
Msgr. William Joseph McDonald	Rector, Catholic University of America	USA
Msgr. Johann Gabriel	Consultor, Pontifical Commission for Biblical Studies	AUT
Msgr. Luigi Sonzogni	Rector, Bergamo Seminary	ITA
Msgr. John E. Steinmueller	Consultore, Pontifical Biblical Commission	USA
Msgr. Albert Lang	Prof., University of Bonn	BRD
Msgr. Arturo Duilio Pitton	Rector, Major Seminary, Padua	ITA
Msgr. Luigi Bettazzi	Prof., Regional Seminary of Bologne	ITA
Fr. Karl Adam	Prof. Emeritus, University of Tübingen	BRD
Fr. Andreas Bigelmair	Prof. Emeritus, University of Würzburg	BRD
Fr. Germano Martil	Rector, Pontifical Spanish College	ESP
Fr. Thomas Pierre Camelot, OP	Prof., Dominican House of Studies, Le Saulchoir	FRA
Fr. Vicente Beltrán de Heredia, OP	Prof. of Church History, Pontifical Univ. of Salamanca	ESP
Fr. Donato Baldi, OFM	Prof., Franciscan Biblical Institute in Jerusalem	ISR
Fr. Léopold Denis, SJ	Prof., Seminary of Mayidi	COD
Fr. Emile Jombart, SJ	Prof. of Canon Law	FRA
Fr. Stanislas de Lastapis, SJ	*Action populaire*	FRA
Fr. Laureano Suarez SchP.	Asst. General, Piarists	ITA
Fr. Louis Bouyer, CO	Prof., Catholic Institute of Paris	FRA
Fr. José Maria Albareda-Herrera	Rector, Catholic Univ. of Navarra	ESP
Prof. Francesco Vito	Rector, Catholic University of the Sacred Heart, Milan	ITA

Topics Assigned[1]
1. De vocationibus ecclesiasticis[2]
2. De studiis[3]
3. De disciplina[4]
4. Institutio spiritualis[5]
5. Institutio pastoralis[6]
6. De scholis catholicis[7]

Schemas Drafted[8]
1. De vocationibus ecclesiastici fovendis
2. De sacrorum alumnis formandis
3. De studiis academicis ab universitatibus tum catholicis tum ecclesiasticis provehendis
4. De scholis catholicis
5. De obsequio erga Ecclesiae magisterium in tradens discipinis sacris

Appendix
1. De lingua latina in studiis ecclesiasticis rite excolenda

Schemas Presented in Council
– *Schema constitutionis De sacrorum alumnis formandis*[9]
– *Schema constitutionis De scholis catholicis et de studiis academicis*[10]

---

1 Quaestiones commissionibus…, in: AD-P 2,1, 412–413.
2 "De vocationis ecclesiasticae natura. Rationes assignentur ad vocationes ecclesiasticas in pueris et adulescentibus fovendas," ibid. 412.
3 "Studiorum ratio seminariorum cuiusvis gradus et ordinis recognoscantur. Praesertim attendatur ad integritatem doctrinae tradendae pleno cum obsequio erga Ecclesiae Magisterium et ad rationem docendi s. Scripturam," ibid. 412–413.
4 "Praecipuis da hac re erroribus reiectis, qui speciosis nominibus et rationibus "autonomiam" quandam proclamant, aptiores ad clericos instituendos modi, iuxta Ecclesiae doctrinam, determinentur," ibid. 413.
5 "Spiritualis clericorum institutio iuxta temporum necessitates augeatur," ibid.
6 "Theologiae pastoralis studium foveatur una cum aptis et crebrioribus exercitationibus practicis," ibid.
7 "Huiusmodi argumentum ex integro pertractetur: a) de iure Ecclesiae scholas erigendi cuiusvis gradus et ordinis; b) de iure parentum eligendi scholas pro filiis; c) de officio Reipublicae sumptum ad rem necessarios suppeditandi. In huiusmodi scholis alimnorum institutio sive religiosa sive scientifica enixe curetur," ibid.
8 AD-P 3,2, 69–185.
9 Schemata constitutionum…, cit. Series Tertia, 209–275.
10 Ibid. 277–345.

COMMISSION FOR THE ORIENTAL CHURCHES

PRESIDENT

Card. Amleto Giovanni Cicognani, Secretary of State

SECRETARY

Fr. Athanasios G. Welykyi, OSBM, Pro-Rector, Ukrainian Pontifical College of St. Josaphat; Director, Analecta OSBM

MEMBERS

Most Rev. Ivan Bucko	Aposolic Visitor for Ukrainians of Byzantine Rite in Western Europe	ITA
Most Rev. Giacomo Testa	Pres., Pontifical Ecclesiastica Academy	ITA
Most Rev. Benedict Varghese Gregorios Thangalathil	Trivandrum (Syro-Malankarese) IND	
Most Rev. Joseph Parecattil	Ernakulam (Syro-Malankarese)	IND
Most Rev. Matthew Kavukattu	Changanacherry (Syro-Malankarese)	IND
Most Rev. Raphaël Rabban	Kerkuk (Chaldean)	IRQ
Most Rev. Ignace Antoine II Hayek	Aleppo (Syrian)	SYR
Most Rev. Ignace Ziadé	Beirut (Maronite)	LEB
Most Rev. Pierre Dib	Cairo (Maronite)	EGY
Most Rev. Alexandros Scandar	Assiut (Coptic Catholic)	EGY
Most Rev. Jesus Jacob Ghebre	Apostolic Exarch of Asmara; tit. Erythrum	ERI
Most Rev. Andrei Apollon Katkoff	tit. Nauplia; Byzantine Rite Ordinary in Rome	ITA
Most Rev. Ceslao Sipović, MIC	tit. Mariamme	GBR
Most Rev. Vasile Cristea	Pontifical Roman College	ITA
Most Rev. Garabed Amadouni	Apostolic Exarch of France (Armenian)	FRA
Fr. Teodoro Minisci, OSBI	Abbot of Grottaferrata	ITA
Msgr. Ovidio Bejan	Prelate Auditor, Roman Rota	ITA
Msgr. Clement Ignace Mansourati	Chorbishop, Procurator, Syrian Patriarchate	ITA
Msgr. Néophytos Edelby, BA	Secy. to Melkite Patriarch	SYR
Fr. Marko Japundži, OSF	Third Order of St. Francis	ITA
Fr. Anton Felix Gössmann, OSA	International College of St. Monica	ITA
Fr. Clemens Pujol, SJ	Prof., Pontifical Oriental Institute	ITA
Fr. Alphonse Raes, SJ	Pres., Pontifical Oriental Institute	ITA
Fr. Pelopida Étienne Stephanou, SJ	Prof., Pontifical Oriental Institute	ITA
Fr. Jerome Cornelis, AA	Editor of *Unitas*, Paris	FRA
Fr. Daniel Stiernon, AA	Prof. of Oriental Theology, Pontifical Lateran University	ITA

CONSULTORS

Most Rev. Michael Doumith	Sarba (Maronite)	LEB
Most Rev. Bojeslavs Sloskāns	Apostolic Admin., Minsk, Belarus	BEL
Msgr. Marian Strojny	Prelate Referendario of the Apostolic Signatura	ITA
Msgr. Sebastin Chereath	Dir., Holy Childhood Assoc.; Chancellor, Diocese of Trichur (Syro-Malabar)	IND
Msgr. Cesare Spallanzani	Archpriest, Vicar Forane of Bibbiano (Reggio Emilia)	ITA
Msgr. Stefano Bentia	Prof. of Canon Law	ITA
Msgr. Hanna Kaldany	Vicar Gen., Latin Patriarchate of Jerusalem; Pres. Latin Patriarch Tribunal	ISR
Fr. Francis Dvornik	Prof., Harvard University	USA
Fr. Pavlos Garò	Dir. of Catholic Press in Greece	GRE
Fr. Isaia Tumbas	Commissioner, Congregation for Oriental Rites; Rector, Church of Sant'Atanasio	ITA
Fr. Johannes Remmers	Pres., "Apostolate for Unification"	NLD
Fr. Arnold Van Lantschoot, OPraem	Vice-Prefect, Vatican Library	ITA
Fr. Livien Bauwens, OSB	Consultor, Subiaco Congregation	ITA
Fr. Thomas Becquet, OSB	Prior, Chevetogne	BEL
Fr. Germano Giovanelli, OSBI	Basilians of Grottaferrata	ITA
Fr. Meletius Wojnar, OSBM	Prof., Oriental Canon Law, Catholic University of America	USA
Fr. Athanase Hage, BC	Prof., Canon Law, Univ. of St. Joseph, Beirut	LEB
Fr. Pierre Benoit, OP	Prof. of Theology, Jerusalem	JOR
Fr. Feliks Bednarski, OP	Prof. Pontifical Angelicum Univ.	ITA
Fr. Angelico Lazzeri, OFM	Procurator General, Friars Minor	ITA
Fr. Basilio Talatinian, OFM	Prof. of Canon Law, Franciscan House of Studies, Jerusalem	JOR
Fr. Alfons Maria Mitnacht, OSA	Editor, *Der Christliche Osten*	BRD

Fr. Michal Lacko, SJ	Prof., Pontifical Oriental Institute	ITA
Fr. Giuseppe Valentini, SJ	Editor, *Letture*	ITA
Fr. Ivan Sofranov, CP	Writer	ITA
Fr. Elpide Stephanou, AA	Superior of Missions, Augustinian Assumptionists	GRE
Fr. Placido di s. Giuseppe, CMI	Consultor, Congregation for Oriental Churches	ITA
Fr. Dunstan Donovan, SA	Franciscan Friars of the Atonement	ITA
Fr. Maurice Blondeel, MAfr	Rector, Prof., of Theology, Seminary of St Anne, Jerusalem	JOR
Fr. Giovanni Malak, OP	S. Mark's, Cairo	EGY

Topics Assigned

"Commissio examini subiicere potest quaestiones:
a) de transitu ad alium ritum;
b) de communicatione in sacris cum christianis orientalibus non catholicis;
c) de modo reconciliandi orientales dissidentes;
d) Insuper praecipuas quaestiones disciplinares, quae pro ceteris Commissionibus indicatae sunt, relate tamen ad Ecclesias orientales"

Schemas Drafted[1]

1. De ritibus in Ecclesia
2. De patriarchis orientalibus
3. De communicatione in sacris cum christianis orientalibus non catholicis
4. De usu linguarum vernacularum in liturgiis
5. De Ecclesiae sacramentis
6. De Ecclesiae praeceptis
7. De facultatibus episcoporum
8. De catechismo et catechetica institutione
9. De Kalendario perpetuo et celebratione paschatis
10. De officio divino Ecclesiarum orientalium
11. De Ecclesiae unitate "ut omnes unum sint"

Schema Presented in Council

– *Schema decreti De Ecclesiis orientalibus*[2]

---

1 AD-P 3,2, 187–38.
2 Schemata constitutionum…, cit. Series quarta, 5–26.

COMMISSION FOR THE MISSIONS

PRESIDENT
Card. Grégoire-Pierre XV Agagianian, Patriarch of Cilicia (Armenian); Prefect, Congregation for the Propagation of the Faith

SECRETARY
Most Rev. David Mathew, tit. of Apamea in Bitinia

MEMBERS

Most Rev. Martin Lucas	tit. Aduli, Apostolic Delegate in Scandinavia	NLD
Most Rev. Victor Alphonse Sartre	Tananarive; tit. Beroë	MDG
Most Rev. Aurelio Signora	Prelate Nullius, Prelature of Pompei	ITA
Most Rev. John Kodwo Amissah	Cape Coast	GHA
Most Rev. Joachim Ammann	Abbot of Ndanda	TZA
Most Rev. Tarcisius Henricus van Valemberg	Apostolic Vicar, Pontianak, tit. Comba	IDN
Most Rev. José Lecuona Labandibar	tit. Vagada; Superior General, Spanish Institute of St. Francis Xavier for the Foreign Missions	ESP
Most Rev. Stanislaus Lokuang	Tainan	TWN
Fr. Heinrich Suso Brechter, OSB	Archabbot, Congregation of St. Ottilien for the Foreign Missions	BRD
Fr. Luciano Rubio, OESA	Prior General, Hermits of St. Augustine	ITA
Fr. Thomas Ohm, OSB	Congregation of St. Ottilien; Prof., Univ. of Münster	BRD
Fr. Rafael Moya, OP	Prof., Canon Law, Pontifical Univ. Angelicum	ITA
Fr. Alphonse Schnusenberg, OFM	Secy. General, Franciscan Missions	ITA
Fr. Pio Maria de Mondreganes, OFM	Consultor, Congregation for the Propagation of the Faith	ITA
Fr. Callisto Lopinot, OFMCap	Consultor, Congregation for the Propagation of the Faith	ITA
Fr. Pasquale D'Elia, SJ	Prof., Pontifical Gregorian University	ITA
Fr. Domenico Grasso, SJ	Prof. of Dogmatic Theology and Missionary Catechetics, Pontifical Gregorian Univ.	ITA
Fr. Jerome G. D'Souza, SJ	Assistant for India and East Asia, Jesuits	ITA
Fr. Johannes Rommerskirchen, OMI	Prof., Pont. Univ. Urbaniano	ITA
Fr. André Seumois, OMI	Prof. of Missiology, Pont. Univ. Urbaniano	ITA
Fr. Pierre Humbertclaude, SM	Procurator General, Marianists	ITA
Fr. Michael Schulien, SVD	Director, Lateran Museum	ITA

CONSULTORS

Most Rev. Celestine Joseph Damiano	Camden	USA
Most Rev. Joseph M. Antony Cordeiro	Karachi	PAK
Most Rev. Louis Joseph Cabana	tit. Cararallia	CAN
Most Rev. Juan C. Sison	Apostolic Admin., Neuva Segovia	PHL
Most Rev. Héctor Enrique Santos Hernández	Santa Rosa de Copán	HND
Most Rev. Ignacio Gregorio Larrañaga Lasa, OFMCap	Pingliang	ESP
Most Rev. Eberhard Hermann Spiess	tit. Cemeriniano; abbot nullius of Peramiho	TZA
Most Rev. Segundo García Fernández	Apostolic Vicar, Puerto Ayacucho	VEN
Msgr. James (Jim) Madden	Rector, St. Patrick's Seminary, Manly	AUS
Msgr. Klaus Mund	National Dir., Pont. Mission Society of Germania	BRD
Msgr. Alfons Johannes Maria Mulders	Dir., Nijmegen Institute for Mission Studies	NLD
Fr. Vincent Che-Chen-Tao	Prof., Canon Law, Pont. Univ. Urbaniano	ITA
Fr. Olaf Graf, OSB	Congregation of St. Ottielien	KOR
Fr. Antonino Abate, OP	Prof., Missiology Faculty, Pont. Univ. Urbaniano	ITA
Fr. Hermes Peeters, OFM	Definitor General, Franciscans	ITA
Fr. Giorgio Eldarov, OFM	Prof., Pont. Theology Faculty of St. Bonaventure	ITA
Fr. Timothy Lincoln Bouscaren, SJ	Consultor, Congregation for the Propagation of the Faith; Procurator General	ITA
Fr. Ludovico Bujis, SJ	Prof., Canon Law, Pontifical Gregorian University; Consultor, Cong. for the Propagation of the Faith	ITA
Fr. Luigi Civisca, SJ	Prof., Tokyo Seminary	JAP
Fr. Émile Gathier, SJ	Prof. of Religion Hindu Philosophy, Pont. Univ. Gregoriana	ITA

Fr. Hans Staffner, SJ	Rector, Seminary of Pune	IND
Fr. Caspar Caulfield, CP	Secy. for Missions, Passionists	ITA
Fr. Jean Soury-Lavergne, SM	Vicar Delegate and Superior, Seminary of S. Lèon, Païta	CHL
Fr. Bernard Fennelly, SSSp	Holy Ghost Missionary College, Kimmage-Dublin	IRL
Fr. Amand Reuter, OMI	Consultor, Congregation for the Propagation of the Faith; Director General of Studies, OMI	ITA
Fr. Georges Vromant, OMI	Prof., canon law and spiritual director, St. Charles Seminary	PHL
Fr. Giovanni Battista Tragella	Pont. Inst. of Sts. Peter and Paul and of Sts. Ambrose and Charles for the Foreign Missions; advisor, Pont. Missionary Union	ITA
Fr. Aelred Cauwe, MAfr	Asst. General, White Fathers	ITA
Fr. Johannes Beckmann, SMB	Prof. of Missiology, Univ. of Fribourg	CHE
Fr. François Legrand, CICM	Scheut Missionaries	ITA
Fr. Luigi Bisoglio, CM	Procurator General, Vincentians	ITA
Fr. Elias Dominguez Gomez, HMSS	Mercedarian	ESP

Topics Assigned[1]
1. De debito missionali[2]
2. De vocationibus missionariis[3]
3. De missionariis[4]
4. De clero indigena[5]
5. De rationibus inter dioceses et missiones

Schemas Drafted[6]
Proemium
1. De rigimine missionum
2. De disciplina cleri
3. De religiosis
4. De sacramentis ac de sacra liturgia
5. De disciplina populi christaini
6. De studiis clericorum
7. De cooperatione missionali

Schemas Presented in Council
– *Schema decreti De missionibus*[7]

---

1 Quaestiones commissionibus…, cit. in AD-P 2,1, 413–414.

2 "Determinentur et promoveantur illa opera, quibus catholici "debiti missionalis" pressius conscii evadant, illudque fidelius adimpleant," ibid. 413.

3 "Normae aptiores edantur ad promovendas fovendasque vocationes missionarias," ibid. 414.

4 "a) missionariurum institutio spiritualis et scientifica augeatur: atque "universalitatis spiritus" quam maxime foveatur; b) missionariorum, qui ad diversas familias pertinent, labores in ordinem, pro maiore animarum bono, disponantur," ibid.

5 "Quibus bonis rationibus clerus indigena augeri possit. Quorsum in rem catholicam inducantur ea quae ex civili singulorum populorum cultu bona acceptandaque videntur. Traditiones gentium, quae fidei moribusque catholicis non adversantur, quo obsequio excipienadae sint"

6 Ad-P 3,2 239–299.

7 Schemata constitutionum …, cit. Series Quarta, 347–369.

COMMISSION FOR THE LAY APOSTOLATE

PRESIDENT
Card. Fernando Cento

SECRETARY
Msgr. Achille Glorieux, Ecclesiastical Asst., Standing Committee, World Congress of the Lay Apostolate

MEMBERS

Most Rev. Evasio Colli	Parma	ITA
Most Rev. Ismaele Mario Castellano	Siena	ITA
Most Rev. Gabriel-Marie Garrone	Toulouse	FRA
Most Rev. Vincenzo Gilla Gremigni	Novara	ITA
Most Rev. Gabriel Bukatko	coad. Beograd; am. ap. Križevci	YUG
Most Rev. Manuel Larraín Errázuriz	Talca	CHL
Most Rev. Allen James Babcock	Grand Rapids	USA
Most Rev. Fulton J. Sheen	aux. New York; National Director, Society for the Propagation of the Faith	USA
Most Rev. Primo Gasbarri	aux. Velletri	ITA
Most Rev. Franz Hengsbach	Essen	BRD
Most Rev. Ferdinando Baldelli	Pres., Pontificia Opera Assistenza	ITA
Msgr. Aurelio Sabattani	Prelate Auditor, Roman Rota	ITA
Msgr. Ferdinando Prosperini	Eccles. Consultor, Secretariat for Morality	ITA
Msgr. Luigi Civardi	Canon, St. Peter's Basilica	ITA
Msgr. Emilio Guano	Eccles. Asst., Azione Cattolica	ITA
Msgr. Pietro Pavan	vice-pres. Standing Committee for Italian Catholic Social Weeks; Prof. of Social Economy, Pont. Lateran Univ.	ITA
Msgr. Agostino Ferrari Toniolo	Prof., Comparative Labor Law, Pont. Lateran Univ.; Secy., Permanent Committee for Italian Catholic Social Weeks	ITA
Msgr. Joseph Cardijn	Asst. General, Young Christian Workers	BEL
Msgr. Joseph Géraud	Procurator General, Sulpicians; Eccles. Asst. World Union of Catholic Men	ITA
Msgr. Jean Rodhain	Secy. General, "Secours Catholique"	FRA
Msgr. Santo Quadri	Asst. General, ACLI	ITA
Msgr. George G. Higgins	Dir., Dept. for Social Action, "Nationale Catholic Welfare Conference"	USA
Msgr. Jacques Bonnet	National Secy., Mission Ouvrière	FRA
Msgr. Antonius Cornelius Ramselaar	Rector, Archdiocesan Seminary of Apeldoorn	NLD
Msgr. Albert Stehlin	Pres., Deutschen Caritasverbands	BRD
Msgr. Gottfried Dossing	Dir., Bischöflichen Hilfswerk Misereor	BRD
Msgr. Ferdinand Klostermann	Pastoral Theology, Catholic Action Austria	AUT
Can. Albert Bonet y Marrugat	Secy. Gen., Catholic Action Spain	ESP
Fr. Anton Cortbawi	Pastor, Beirut	LEB
Fr. Henri Donze	Asst. Gen. Action Catholique	FRA
Fr. Wilhelm Bockler	Pastor, Düsseldorf	BRD
Fr. Albert Lanquetin	Asst., General, Rural Family Movement (MFR)	FRA
Fr. Cirillo Bernardo Papali, OCD	Prof., Pont. Univ. Urbaniano	ITA
Fr. Johannes Hirschmann, SJ	Prof. of Moral and Pastoral Theology, Theology Faculty, Frankfurt	BRD
Fr. Pablo Lopex de Lara, SJ	Instituto de literatura, S. José de Puente Grande	MEX
Fr. Roberto Tucci, SJ	Director, La Civiltà Cattolica	ITA
Fr. George Jarlot, SJ	Prof., Pont. Gregorian Univ.	ITA
Fr. Johannes Ponsioen, SCI	Institute of Social Studies, Den Haag	NLD
Fr. Giuseppe Menichelli, CM	Director, Roman Headquarters, Vincentians	ITA

CONSULTORS

Most Rev. Emanuele Trindade Salgueiro	Evora	PRT
Most Rev. Owen McCann	Cape Town	ZAF
Most Rev. Ambrose Rayappan	Pondicherry and Cuddalore	IND
Most Rev. Bernardin Gantin	Cotonou	BEN
Most Rev. Salvatore Russo	Acireale	ITA
Most Rev. Joseph Blomjous	Mwanza	TZA
Most Rev. Dragutin Nežič	Poreč i Pula	YUG

Most Rev. Bolesław Kominek	aux. Wrocław	POL
Most Rev. Bryan Gallagher	Port Pirie	AUS
Most Rev. Benedict Takahiko Tomizawa	Sapporo; Prefect of Karafuto	JAP
Most Rev. José Armando Gutiérrez Granier	aux. La Paz	BOL
Most Rev. Alfonso Toriz Cobián	Querétaro	MEX
Most Rev. Alexander Carter	Sault Sainte Marie	CAN
Most Rev. Reginald John Delargey	aux. Aukland	NZL
Most Rev. Manuel Fernández-Conde	Córdoba	ESP
Msgr. Charles-Édouard Bourgeois	General Director, Diocesan Center for Social Services, Trois-Rivières	CAN
Msgr. Luigi Ligutti	Observer from the Holy See to U.N. Food and Agriculture Org.	ITA
Msgr. William F. Kelly	Social Action Department, New York	USA
Msgr. Ferdinando Lambruschini	Prof. of Moral Theology, Pont. Lateran Univ.	ITA
Msgr. Luigi del Pietro	Secy., Azione Sociale Cristiana di Lugano	CHE
Fr. Henri Caffarel	Director, "Anneau d'or"	FRA
Fr. Victor Portier	Asst., Secrétariats Sociaux	FRA
Fr. Miguel Benzo	Asst. Catholic Action Spain	ESP
Fr. Raimondo Spiazzi, OP	Prof., Pont. Univ. Angelicum	ITA
Fr. Vincent-Alfons de Vogelaere, OP	Director, Sociale School Heverlee and Prof. at Hoger Instituut voor Verpleegkunde, Leuven	BEL
Fr. Salvatore Lener, SJ	Editor, La Civiltà Cattolica	ITA
Fr. Pedro Richards, CP	Asst. Secy., Movimiento Familiar Cristiano, Latin America	URY
Fr. Peter A. Pillai, OMI	Superior, Missionary Oblates of Mary Immaculate	LKA
Fr. William J. Ferree, SM	Second Assistant, Marianists	ITA

Topics Assigned[1]
1. De apostolatu laicorum[2]
2. De actione catholica[3]
3. De consociationibus[4]

Schemas Drafted
– De apostolatu laicorum[5]
1. Notiones generales
2. De apostolatu laicorum in actione ad regnum Christi directe provehendum
3. De apostolatu laicorum in actione caritativa
4. De apostolatu laicorum in actione sociali

Schema Presented in Council[6]
–*Schema constitutionis De apostolatu laicorum*

---

1 Quaestiones commissionibus…, cit. AD-P 2,1, 414.
2 "a) Ambitus et fines determinentur huius apostolatus: nec non erga Sacram Hierarchiam subiectio; b) Quibus aptioribus rationibus apostolatus laicorum hodiernis necessitatibus respondeat," ibid.
3 "1) Notio, ambitus et subiectio erga S. Hierarchiam pressius determinentur; 2) Eius constitutio ita recognoscatur ut nostris temporibus congruentius aptetur; 3) Determinentur rationes inter actionem catholicam et caeteras Consociationes (Congregationes Mariales, Pias Uniones, Uniones professionales, etc.)," ibid.
4 "Studeatur ut vigentium consociationum auctuositas, nostris hisce diebus, propositis finibus magis respondeat (Actio caritativa et socialis)," ibid.
5 AD-P 3,2, 301–429.
6 Schemata constitutionum…, cit. Series Quarta, 43–173.

SECRETARIAT FOR THE UNITY OF CHRISTIANS

PRESIDENT
Card. Augustin Bea

SECRETARY
Msgr. Johannes Willebrands, Founder, Secy., Catholic Conference on Ecumenical Questions

MEMBERS

Most Rev. Lorenz Jaeger	Paderborn	BRD/DDR
Most Rev. Joseph-Marie Martin	Rouen	FRA
Most Rev. John Carmel Heenan	Liverpool	GBR
Most Rev. François Charrière	Lausanne, Geneva and Fribourg	CHE
Most Rev. Emiel-Jozef De Smedt	Bruges	BEL
Most Rev. Gerard Marie van Velsen	Kroonstadt	ZAF
Most Rev. Pieter Antoon Nierman	Groningen	NLD
Most Rev. Thomas Holland	coad. Portsmouth	GBR
Msgr. Henri Ewers	Prelate Auditor, Roman Rota	ITA
Msgr. Joseph Höfer	Prof., Dogmatic History and Ecumenical Theology, Paderborn; German Embassy to the Holy See	ITA
Msgr. Michele Maccarrone	Prof., Church History, Pont. Lateran Univ.	ITA
Fr. Gustav Thils	Prof., Dogmatic Theology, Univ. of Leuven	BEL
Fr. Leo Rudloff, OSB	Abbot, Dormition Abbey, Jerusalem	ISR
Fr. Charles Boyer, SJ	Prof., Pontifical Gregorian University	ITA
Fr. Gerard M. Corr, OSM	London	GBR

CONSULTORS

Most Rev. William Andrew Hart	Dunkeld	GBR
Msgr. Hermann Volk	Prof., Dogmatic Theology, Univ. of Munster	BRD
Msgr. Eduard Stakemeier	Director, Johann Adam Möhler Institut, Paderborn	BRD
Msgr. Henri Francis Davis	St. Gregory, Bearwood	GBR
Msgr. John M. Oesterreicher	Director, Institute of Judaeo-Christian Studies	USA
Msgr. Janez Vodopivec	Prof., Pont. Univ. Urbaniano	ITA
Fr. Alberto Bellini	Prof., Diocesan Seminary of Bergamo	ITA
Fr. Johannes Feiner	Prof., Seminary of Coira	CHE
Fr. Franz Thijssen	Co-Founder, Catholic Conference on Ecumenical Questions	NLD
Fr. Pierre Dumont, OSB	Rector, Pontifical Greek College	ITA
Fr. Christophe Dumont, OP	Director, Istini Study Center	FRA
Fr. Jean Jérôme Hamer, OP	Rector, Dominican Faculty, Saulchoir	FRA
Fr. Gregory Baum, OSA	Seminary of Saint Basil, Toronto	CAN
Fr. Maurice Bévenot, SJ	Prof., Heythrop College	GBR
Fr. Gustave A. Weigel, SJ	Prof. of Fundamental Theology, Woodstock Theological Center	USA
Fr. George Tavard, AA	Mount Mercy College, Pittsburgh	USA
Fr. Edward Hanahoe, SA	Franciscan Friars of the Atonement	USA
Fr. Werner Becker	Oratorio of Leipzig	DDR
Fr. Stéphane Diebold, CM	Superior, Major Seminary, Montpellier	FRA
Fr. Pierre Michalon, PSS	Director, University Seminary, Lyon	FRA
Msgr. Jean-Francois Mathieu Arrighi	Clerk of the Secretariat	FRA
Fr. Thomas Stransky, CSP	Writer-Archivist of the Secretariat	USA

Topics Assigned
Le Quaestiones commissionibus praeparatoriis positae non prevedono temi specifici per questo segretariato[1]

Schemas Drafted[2]
1. De libertate religiosa
2. Necessitas orationis pro unitate christianorum maxime temporibus nostris
3. De oecumenismo catholico
4. De Verbo Dei

Appendix
De Judaeis

Schemas Presented in Council
– *Schema decreti de unione fovenda inter christianos*[3]

1 Quaestiones commissionibus …, cit., in AD-P 2,1, 408–415.
2 AD-P 3,2, 431–458.
3 Schemata constitutionum…, cit. Series Quarta, 371–391.

SECRETARIAT FOR PRESS AND MEDIA

PRESIDENT
Most Rev. Martin John O'Connor, Pres., Pontifical Commission for Motion Pictures, Radio, and Television

SECRETARY
Msgr. Andrzej Maria Deskur, Sub-Secretary, Pontifical Commission for Motion Pictures, Radio, and Television

MEMBERS

Most Rev. Ángel Herrera y Oria	Malaga	ESP
Most Rev. George Andrew Beck	Salford	GBR
Most Rev. Wilhelm Kempf	Limburg	BRD
Most Rev. Petrus Canisius van Lierde	Sacristan and Vicar General for His Holiness, Vatican City	BEL
Most Rev. René Louis Marie Stourm	Amiens	FRA
Most Rev. Abilio del Campo y de la Bárcena	Calahorra	ESP
Most Rev. Stefan László	Eisenstadt	AUT
Msgr. Salvador Canals	Consultor, Pontifical Commission for Motion Pictures, Radio, and Television	ITA
Msgr. Albino Galletto	Secretary, Pontifical Commission for Motion Pictures, Radio, and Television	ITA
Msgr. Mario Boehm	Consultant to *L'Osservatore Romano*	ITA
Msgr. Andrea Spada	Director, *Eco di Bergamo*	ITA
Msgr. Jean Bernard	Pres., Office Catholique International du Cinéma	FRA
Msgr. James Tucek	Director, Rome Press Office, National Catholic Welfare Conference	USA
Fr. Vicente Alberto Moreno Arango, SJ	Asst. Gen. for Latin America North	COL
Fr. Antonio Stefanizzi, SJ	Director, Vatican Radio	ITA
Fr. Emile Gabel, AA	Secy. General, International Catholic Union of the Press	FRA
Fr. Luigi Zanoni, SSP	Vicar and General Counsel, Society of St. Paul	ITA
Fr. George Frederick Heinzmann, MM	Director of Fides	USA

CONSULTORS

Most Rev. William Edward Cousins	Milwaukee	USA
Most Rev. Bernard James Sheil	aux. Chicago	USA
Most Rev. José Vincente Távora	Aracajù	BRA
Most Rev. Patrick Francis Lyons	Sale	AUS
Most Rev. James Aloysius McNulty	Paterson	USA
Most Rev. Albert Rudolph Zuroweste	Belleville	USA
Most Rev. Hebert Bednorz	coad. Katowice	POL
Most Rev. Èmilien Frenette	Saint-Jérôme	CAN
Most Rev. Alberto Devoto	Goya	ARG
Msgr. Zoltan Nyisztor	Priest; journalist	ITA
Msgr. Arthur Ryan	Pastor, St. Brigid's Church, Belfast	GBR
Msgr. Manuel Lopes de la Cruz	Journalist; Domestic Prelate to His Holiness	PRT
Msgr. José Jaquim Salcedo	Dir. General, Acción Cultural Popular Escuelas Radiofónicas	COL
Msgr. Justin Ortiz	Pres., Archbishop's Commission for Motion Pictures, Radio and Television	PHL
Msgr. Fausto Vallainc	Press Officer for the Central Preparatory Commission; Asst., National Association of Catholic Journalists	ITA
Msgr. Heric Klausener	Director, Information Office, Diocese of Berlin	DDR/BRD
Msgr. Karl Becker	Pres., Catholic Radio Office, Germany	BRD
Msgr. Timothy Flynn	Director, Information Office for Radio and Television, New York	USA
Fr. Jakob Haas	Catholic Asst., International Catholic Association for Radio and Television (Unda)	CHE
Fr. Karl August Siegel	Pres., Catholic Commission for Television, Germany	BRD
Fr. Raimon Pichard, OP	Catholic Asst., Radiodiffusion-Télévision Française	FRA
Fr. Frans Van Waesberge, OP	Provincial, Dominicans in the Netherlands	NLD
Fr. Agnellus Andrew, OFM	Catholic Asst. to State Radio and Television (BBC) of Great Britain	GBR

Fr. Mikhail-Petros Franzidis, OFM	Director, Centrale Catholique Egyptienne du Cinéma	EGY
Fr. Enrico Baragli, SJ	Staff, *La Civiltà Cattolica*	ITA
Fr. Jean Marie Poitevin, PME	Director, Secy. for Mission, International Catholic Office for Film; Director, Catholic Office for Film, Radio and Television of Canada	CAN

Topics Assigned[1]

1. Proponantur et illustrentur Ecclesiae doctrina de scriptis prelo edendis et de spectaculis moderandis
2. Illa incoepta et opera promoveantur quibus catholicorum conscientia ita effermetur, ut in huiusmodi institutionis mediis adhibendis, principia catholica ii perpetuo observent
3. Omnium catholicorum artificum ("specialisti, produttori, artisti, tecnici, gestori" etc.) recta conamina in ordinem ponantur, ut ea quae efficiuntur ed eduntur fidei moribusque congruent
4. Rationes declarentur, quibus media huiusmodi, apostolatus operibus apte serviant

Schemas Drafted

– De instrumentis diffusionis seu communicationis socialis[2]

Schema Presented in Council[3]

– *Schema constitutionis De instrumentis communicationis sociali*

COMMISSION FOR SACRED CEREMONIES

PRESIDENT
Card. Eugène Tisserant, Prefect, Congregation for Ceremonies
Most Rev. Beniamino Nardone, Secretary, Congregation for Ceremonies

MEMBERS

Most Rev. Federico Callori di Vignale	Chief Steward to His Holiness	ITA
Most Rev. Angelo Dell'Acqua	Substitute for the Secretary of State	ITA
Most Rev. Enrico Dante	Secretary of the Congregation for Rites	ITA
Most Rev. Mario Nasalli Rocca di Corneliano	Chief Chamberlain to His Holiness	ITA

CONSULTORS

Msgr. Giuseppe Calderari	Master of Pontifical Ceremonies	ITA
Msgr. Salvatore Capo	Master of Pontifical Ceremonies	ITA
Msgr. Adone Terzariol	Master of Pontifical Ceremonies	ITA
Msgr. Orazio Cocchetti	Master of Pontifical Ceremonies	ITA
Fr. Ildefonso Tassi, OSB	Prof. of Liturgy, Pont. Lateran Univ.	ITA
Fr. Roger Le Deault, CSSp	Prof. of Liturgy, Pontifical French Seminary	FRA

ADMINISTRATIVE SECRETARIAT

PRESIDENT
Card. Alberto Di Jorio, Pro-President, Commission of Cardinals for Vatican City State; President, Institute for the Works of Religion (IOR)

SECRETARY
Msgr. Sergio Guerri, Secy. Office for the Administration of the Goods of the Holy See; Special Administrative Delegate of the Holy See

MEMBERS

Msgr. Enrico Arato	Secy, Institute for the Works of Religion	ITA
Msgr. Ferrero Conti	Secretary for the Administration of the Assets of the Holy See	ITA
Msgr. Gaspare Cantagalli	Assigned to the Secretary of State	ITA
Count Enrico Pietro Galeazzi	Special Delegate for the Pontifical Commission for Vatican City State; General Director, Technical Services for Vatican City	ITA
Sig. Raffaele Quadrani	Secy. for Special Administration for the Holy See	ITA
Dr. Massimo Spada	Administrative Secretary, Institute for the Works of Religion	ITA
Dr. Luigi Mennini	Secy., Inspector, Institute for the Works of Religion	ITA
Dr. Fernando Musa	Chief Accountant, Vatican City State	ITA
Sig. Mario Seganti	Gardner, Apostolic Palaces	ITA
Sig. Francesco Vacchini	Engineer; General Manager, Technical Office of the Fabric of St. Peter	ITA

1 Quaestiones commissionibus …, cit., in AD-P 2,1, 415.
2 Ad-P 3,2, 389–429.
3 Schemata constitutionum…, cit. Series Prima, 203–248.

10. The Secretariat for Christian Unity

1. A press conference with Cardinal Bea, on the activities of the Secretariat for Christian Unity. International interest in the Secretariat was shown by the numerous requests for interviews and statements addressed to Bea. On the other hand, he realized the need for accurate information; in a letter to Pope John XXIII dated April 26, 1960, he supported the creation of a press office separate from *L'Osservatore Romano*, saying that an information office seemed

In his speech on January 25, 1959, John XXIII raised hopes with the announcement of the council and the references to unity with which it ended. The following year, the creation of the Secretariat for Christian Unity, together with the establishment of preparatory commissions, confirmed the importance that the dialogue with other churches had in Roncalli's vision of Vatican II. This was unprecedented in the organization of the Roman Curia and took place on the initiative of the rector of the Pontifical Biblical Institute, the German Jesuit Augustine Bea, who had been Pius XII's confessor. He became an advisor to the Holy Office a few months after Pope John, in his second consistory, created him cardinal. Bea, who had been following the ecumenical debate in Germany, had suggested to Lorenz Jaeger, the bishop of Paderborn and head of the German Bishops' Conference for "Una-Sancta-Arbeit," that they ask the pope to establish a Roman department dedicated to dialogue with the international ecumenical movement that would be the reference point for Catholic groups in the various countries on the topic of unity, and that he open the closed net of the magisterium that had condemned ecumenism as such and punished those theologians like Yves Congar who sought to establish the principles of Catholic ecumenism. Similarly, the Melkite Patriarch, Maximos IV, on May 23, 1959, during an audience with Pope John XXIII, made a proposal to the pope supporting the creation in Rome of "*une nouvelle congrégation ou une commission romaine spéciale* [a new congregation or special Roman commission]" responsible for "*tout ce qui touche à l'Oecuménisme* [everything related to ecumenism]," thus releasing it from the stranglehold of the Holy Office. In March and June 1959, the French Dominican Christophe Dumont had sent two notes to the Congregation for Oriental Churches that suggested the creation of such a congregation and creating two sections within Propaganda Fide, for relations with Orthodox and Protestants Christians respectively. These ideas may not have been implemented, but Jaeger's proposal was accepted three days later and Bea became president not of a congregation, but of a Secretariat with two sets of duties.

Johannes Willebrands of the Netherlands was appointed secretary. He had founded and led a Catholic Conference on ecumenical issues, which since 1952 had brought together theologians from different backgrounds (including very young scholars such as Joseph Ratzinger and Giuseppe Alberigo) who were sensitive to the expectations of Christian unity. Some of the Secretariat's members and advisers participated in the conference, such as Charles Boyer, Francis Davis, Christophe Dumont, Jerome Hamer, Joseph Höfer, and Franz Thijssen. Those who had had some contact with the conference, included Bishop Jaeger, Edward Stakemeier of Paderborn, Hermann Volk, François Charrière of Switzerland,

and other Swiss experts such as Johannes Feiner. In addition, there were Pierre Dumont and friends or monks of the ecumenical monastery of Chevetogne, and several North American theologians such as Gregory Baum, Thomas Stransky, Edward Francis Hanahoe, George H. Tavard, and Gustave Weigel.

The mission of the Secretariat during the preparatory phase was threefold: to work on their drafts, to open a dialogue with other churches, and to invite their observers to the council. A critical point on this agenda concerned the Orthodox churches; this was part of the job of the Congregation for the Eastern Church but for the purpose of proselytizing. On the eve of the first session this became a responsibility of the Secretariat.

Confidence in Bea convinced John XXIII, after an interview with Jules Isaac, to entrust to the Secretariat the task of preparing a draft on the Jews that would abolish the catechesis of contempt. However, the Central Preparatory Commission shelved the draft in June 1962, pending a political decision by the Secretary of State. It was then put back on the agenda of Vatican II between the end of the first period and the first session, following the pope's intervention, as requested by Bea.

Where other preparatory commissions for the council, according to the motu proprio *Superno Dei Nutu* of June 5, 1960, were assigned specific *quaestiones* to develop, the Secretariat for Christian Unity was not. The theological commission presided over by Cardinal Alfredo Ottaviani, Prefect of the Holy Office, interpreted this as confirmation of the subordinate role of Bea's department and its inability to present drafts independently for discussion in council. In short, he considered it a mere "information office." However, the pope's intent and what happened in practice was the allowance of greater room for maneuver and discussion. This was confirmed by the fact that they had sent in their own drafts and had then been transformed into a segment of the council without voting rights in the sessions. During the first session of the council, the passage of the revised draft on Divine Revelation to a joint committee composed of members of the Theological Com-

necessary "because of the vast echo that steps related to unity arouse, and the possibility of misunderstandings and falsehoods that would be particularly harmful to the movement for unity" (Bernhard Moosbrugger, Zürich in *Erneuerung in Christus. Das Zweite Vatikanische Konzil (1962–1965) im Spiegel Münchener Kirchenarchive*, Hrsg. A. R. Batloog, C. Brodkorb, P. Pfister, Verlag Schnell und Steiner, Regensburg 2012).

mission and the Secretariat showed how the ecumenical theme and its management by the Secretariat were ancillary but fundamental in the design of conciliar renewal.

The creation of the Secretariat shows that Pope John saw the necessity of an agile, distinct, and independent instrument of the Curia to whom he had entrusted the rest of the preparation. This was foreign to the idea of a council that, over the course of a few weeks, would approve drafts and condemnations prepared by the Roman congregations and their theological schools.

In fact, the preparatory phase of the council was characterized by a permanent tension between Bea's Secretariat and Ottaviani's Theological Commission. In the first two months of 1961, the Theological Commission rejected proposals to establish joint committees. Not only did it believe that it had an exclusive say in matters of doctrine, but it also expected that other commissions would refrain from commenting on them. The members of the Secretariat for Christian Unity instead had adopted as their method the development of proposals, which were first sent to various committees, then developed as drafts, thus challenging the hegemony of the Holy Office of which the Theological Commission was the representative prior to the council.

In fact, within the Secretariat there were fifteen subcommittees at work, composed of four or five members and chaired by a bishop as monitor. In each subcommittee a text was prepared by a bishop or a theologian and subsequently communicated, almost always by letter to the other members for comments, which were used for a *relectio* of a document submitted to the plenary session. The committees studied: 1) the issue of membership of the Church and the state of baptized non-Catholics; 2) the nature of the Church (God's people) and its hierarchical structure (the role of the bishops in the universal Church and episcopacy as a sacrament); 3) individual and community conversions; the restoration of the lay diaconate; 4) the universal priesthood of the faithful and the role of the laity in the Church; 5) Church-State relations and Christian tolerance (religious freedom); 6) the Word of God; 7) the relationship between Scripture and Tradition in the Church;

2. A meeting of the Secretariat for Christian Unity presided over by Cardinal Bea (da M. von Galli, B. Moosbrugger, *Das Konzil und seine Folgen*, Verlag C.J. Bucher AG, Luzern und Frankfurt/M 1966).

8) liturgical questions: the abandonment of Latin and the centrality of the Eucharist, communion under both kinds, concelebration, and *communicatio in sacris*; 9) mixed marriages; 10) a new formula for the Octave of Prayer for Christian Unity in January; 11) the ecumenical problem according to the viewpoint of the World Council of Churches; 12) the relationship with Judaism; 13) the Secretariat as a permanent body after the council; 14) the preparation of an ecumenical directory (list of practical guidelines); 15) the invitation of non-Catholics to the council.

In addition to the issues that were more clearly linked to the Secretariat's agenda there were: *De Ecumenismo Catholico*, written in competition with the chapter on the return to unity in the Theological Commission's *De Ecclesia* and the Commission for Oriental Churches' text *De Unitate Ecclesiae*, which was replaced during the debate, so that they became the council decree *Unitatis Redintegratio*; the issue of religious freedom that should have been dealt with by a Joint Committee that was boycotted by Ottaviani and Tromp, but then merged into *Dignitatis Humanae*; *De Judaeis* which was shelved in the preparatory phase and then formed the general chapter of *Nostra Aetate*. There was powerful tension with the group chaired by Bea over the problem of the relationship between Scripture and Tradition: for example, on November 22, 1962, when the draft of *De Fontibus Revelationis* was shelved by a papal exemption to the Regulations and a new *De Revelatione* was entrusted to the joint committee, it was understood that what appeared to be only an "address in the city of Rome" for the ecumenists had been a decisive factor in the reforming flavor of the council.

BIBLIOGRAPHY
J. Komonchak, "La lotta per il concilio durante la preparazione," in *Storia del concilio Vaticano II* edited by G. Alberigo (Italian edition edited by A. Melloni), vol I, Bologna 1995 (2012),177–380; *Verso il Concilio Vaticano II (1960–1962). Passaggi e problemi della preparazione conciliare*, edited by G. Alberigo, A. Melloni, Genova 1993; M. Velati, "Un indirizzo a Roma." La nascita del Segretariato per l'unità dei cristiani (1959–1960)," in *Il Vaticano II fra attese e celebrazione*, edited by G. Alberigo, Bologna 1995, 75–118; *Dialogo e rinnovamento. Verbali e testi del Segretariato per l'unità dei cristiani nella preparazione del concilio Vaticano II (1960–1962)*, edited by M. Velati, Bologna 2011.

11. SETTING UP THE COUNCIL: ST. PETER'S BASILICA TRANSFORMS INTO A COUNCIL HALL

On November 7, 1961, when Pope John XXIII announced the creation of new organizations, he included the formation of a Technical and Organizational Commission on the list as a subset of the more general Central Commission. It was presided over by Cardinal Gustavo Testa and Archbishop Pericle Felici, who was appointed its secretary, and assisted by three other secretaries, Sergio Guerri, Agostino Casaroli, and Igino Cardinale. The tasks of the commission included the preparation and layout of the Council Hall. This meant organizing St. Peter's Basilica, bearing in mind some basic needs: over 2,000 seats for the council fathers; provisions for celebrating the solemn ceremonies; space for the observers; and reconfiguring St. Peter's so that it could still be used in a limited way both for regular liturgical activities and for visits by the faithful.

Vatican I, which had already used St. Peter's as its Council Hall, had had sizable logistical problems. The layout of the hall in the right-hand aisle of the transept, which had been built about a century before by architect Count Virginio Vespignani—traces of which can be found in the space around the great temporary hall for the Vatican Ecumenical Council (1874)—was a disaster in terms of its acoustics. The organization of councils had always been complex.

In the first months of 1962, work started on the restoration and set up with the cleaning of the great fifteenth-century central bronze door, the stucco on the vault, and a updating of the lighting and flooring. But transforming the basilica into the Council Hall posed too many problems for the technical team from the congregation for the maintenance of St. Peter's, led by engineer Francesco Vacchini.

In the Council Hall, six different systems were installed: lighting, television, telephone, copiers, sound, and finally one for registration, with everything installed and lined with sound-absorbent materials from the company Sadi of Verona, in order to avoid acoustical problems that could interfere with the work of the hall. The fundamental issue of recording data (for example, from the fathers' personal details to the general register of participants, from accounting for those present in the hall to the counting of the votes) was brilliantly solved thanks to punch-card technology made available by Olivetti-Bull, which offered the useful and unprecedented ability to perform calculations and make comparisons between different periods. Recording and amplification were entrusted to Philips, the Dutch company that had been a leader in the field since 1891, under the watchful eye of the staff of Vatican Radio, who were responsible for all audio issues for the dura-

tion of the council and had thirty years' experience in radio. Therefore, in addition to thousands of meters of damask and velvet, hundreds of feet of gold fringes and various other fabrics, structures and metal scaffolding from the Dalmine Innocenti company, rubber sheeting for the seats in the tiers provided by the firm Joco of Glasgow, and 150 cubic meters of spruce, it was necessary to manage the 65,000 meters of telephone lines used in Vatican City, along with the thousands of feet of coaxial cable for video, radio, and television, and individual items of equipment: for example the recording equipment with its booths, the four large recorders, the telephone system and switchboard, the thirty speakers, the forty microphones and the control rooms, not to mention the independent lighting of the basilica provided by forty 2,000-watt lights; from the cameras placed on the cornices of the hall, to eighty-six other lamps that provided proper lighting for color filming and television coverage, using power upwards of two thousand kilowatts distributed among 10,000-watt spotlights—the amount of power that was usually required to illuminate the whole of Vatican City. Thus, the resulting

1

1. St. Peter's Basilica. Preparation of the hall (from *Aula Sancta Concilii*, edited by the Segreteria Generale del Concilio Ecumenico Vaticano II, Roma 1967).

2. Sketch of the high-backed seats with desks (from *Aula Santa Concilii*).

3. St. Peter's Basilica, October 8, 1962. Arrangements for the council are in evidence as Archbishop Felici and the engineer and project supervisor Vacchini of the technical office of the Congregation for the Fabric of St. Peter give journalists a guided tour of the basilica to update them on the adaptation of the basilica (© Archivio Storico Luce).

4. The council fathers seated on the benches during the opening ceremony for the second session (photo: Pais/Archivio Rodrigo Pais–Ceub Università di Bologna).

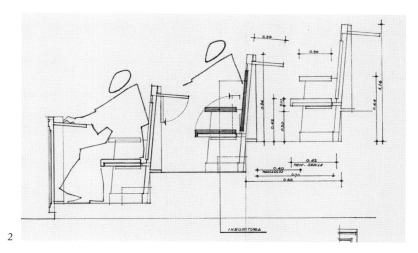

2

3

▶ THE POPE'S CLOSED-CIRCUIT TELEVISION

Inside the basilica, in addition to the operator stations and RAI (Radiotelevisione Italiana) cameras, the installation of an additional television system that was of "far more modest proportions" went ahead: there were two Philips transistor cameras, positioned high up in the tiers on which the fathers of the council sat. This in turn was connected to an amplification system and synchronized in the Ottoboni repository, a space isolated from the basilica; this constituted the closed-circuit television system for the pontiff. Coaxial cables, in fact, linked the footage from the hall with a TV in Pope John XXIII's study. The system gave the pope the opportunity to directly follow the unfolding of the work of the council whenever he wanted, without presiding personally over the congregations. From his studio—as Roncalli himself related during several audiences in which he explained to those present the service offered by his "private television"—he could be simultaneously the director of his own private film and the program's only viewer: through a series of commands he could in fact directly adjust not only the point of view from which to follow the discussion, by selecting the first or second camera, but also control their horizontal and vertical movements, and the adjustment of the lens and focus, so as to have total control over the viewing experience.

The pope alluded to his private "viewing" in several audiences: for example, those on November 7 and November 14, 1962 (as reported in *L'Osservatore Romano* on November 7 and 17, 1962).

Even Cardinal Tisserant mentioned the closed-circuit system in his welcome speech on behalf of the cardinals, on December 23, 1962, in the Clementine Hall, "Your Holiness has followed our general congregations, thanks to modern technology, and has been able to intervene with his decisions, when the interpretation of the Regulations or the very aims of the council required the kind and guiding word from the revered head of the Church."

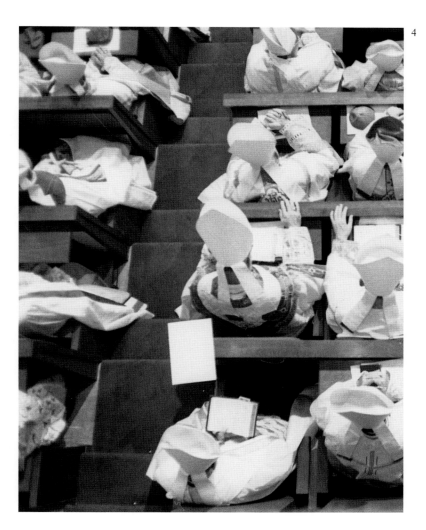

4

▶ **LAYOUT OF MEETING SPACE**

1. Altar
2. Papal Throne
3. Presidential Council's Table
4. Cardinals Moderators' Table
5. Secretary General and Secretaries' Table
6. Tables for Workers at the General Secretariat and Printing Office
7. Pulpit for general communications and announcements
8. Seats for the Cardinals
9. Seats for the Patriarchs
10. Seats for the council fathers
11. Raised tribune in the side arches
12. Tribune of St. Andrew for auditors

13. Tribune of St. Longinus for observers
14. Tribune of St. Helena
15. Tribune of St. Veronica

A. Passages giving direct access from the center aisle to the seats
B. Stairs giving access to the passage behind the upper back seats of the council fathers and the tiers
C. Data processing
D. Sound and recording booth
E. Snack bars and rest rooms
F. First aid station

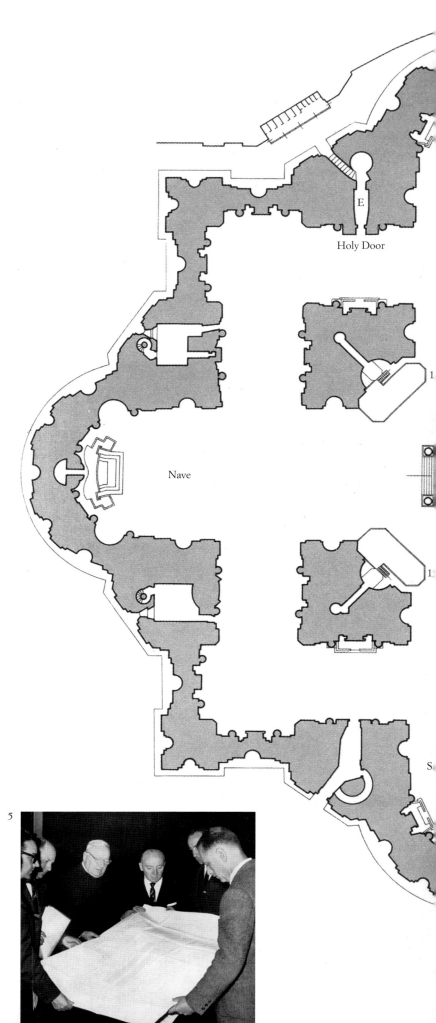

5. St. Peter's Basilica. Card. Gustavo Testa examines the technical layout in the hall (from *Aula Sancta Concilii*).

electrical system and lighting were useful for filming and sufficient to ensure that everyone on the benches could read the documents, but they were also designed to conform to the aesthetic of the basilica. The structures were not in fact supposed to look like extraneous add-ons to the basilica, so that the participants might forget the place where the whole of Catholicism came to meet but, rather, to ensure that the architecture of the basilica continued to dominate.

The changes that the basilica had to undergo during those months—it was closed to the public from September 27 until October 11 to allow the completion of the final set-up work—were such that the day after the opening, when three hundred journalists who had been accredited by the council's press office visited the Council Hall, almost all the world's media reported on it enthusiastically with photos, news, and impressive technical data. With the help of the chief language groups of the press office, journalists could see for themselves the efforts that were being made to adapt St. Peter's to the needs of both council fathers (comfortable seats, good visibility, health services, sanitation, and refreshment) and the members of the media who would be present in the hall. The arrangements provided the means to film the event from forty-one different television stations positioned along the entire perimeter of the basilica and the surrounding areas, forty-one different points of view from which viewers worldwide could follow the public sessions from a privileged position and for the first time receive images within a council.

BIBLIOGRAPHY

Aula Sancta Concilii, edited by the General Secretary of the Vatican II Ecumenical Council, Rome 1967; K. Wittstadt, *Alla vigilia del concilio, in Storia del concilio Vaticano II*, edited by G. Alberigo (Italian edition edited by A. Melloni), vol. I, il Mulino, Bologna 1995 (2012), 429–518; F. Ruozzi, *Il concilio in diretta. Il Vaticano II tra informazione e partecipazione*, il Mulino, Bologna 2012.

6. The council snack bar (Archivio Fscire). Cardinal Suenens recalled, "The council consisted of a long series of speeches in Latin with interventions concentrated down to eight minutes, but there was also the opportunity for informal exchanges among bishops, *periti*, and observers. In the free time between sessions, they could be found in the snack bars, precious places to refresh thoughts and continue discussions over a cup of coffee. I made a rule for myself to go there for a few minutes every day to breathe in the atmosphere" (L.-J. Suenens, 1993). Originally, there were two such snack bars. The council fathers humorously dubbed one "Bar Jonas" (pictured) and the other "Bar Abbas." A third snack bar for women, "Bar Nun," added for the second session, was mostly unused (photos of Bishop Hermann Volk / Dom- und Diözesanarchiv Mainz Bestand: 4 5.4).

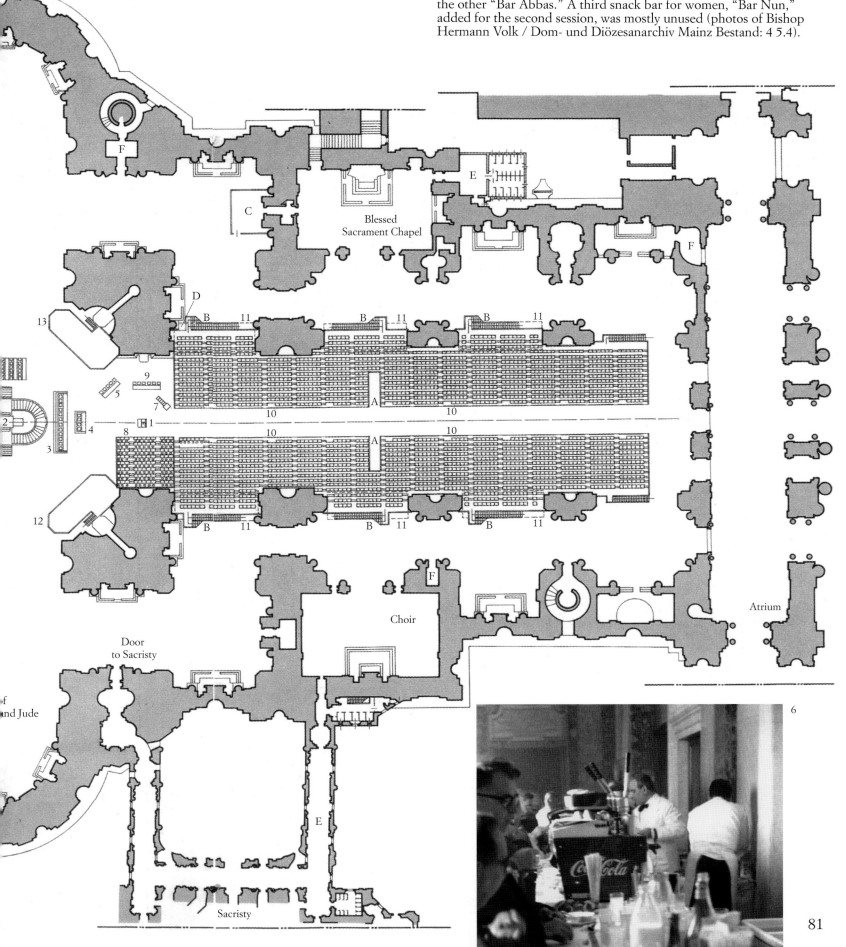

81

12. The Composition of the Assembly

Among Vatican II's many firsts compared to previous councils was the number of its participants. In fact, never before had there been a council that gathered together such a number of council fathers, especially since they represented almost all the nations of the world a mere seventeen years after the end of World War II. To be fully aware of the importance of this, we must compare it with the Council of Trent, where the number of participants from one period to the next only amounted to a few dozen, mostly Spanish and Italian bishops. At Vatican I there were about seven hundred participants.

Canon 223 of the 1917 Code of Canon Law had formalized who was entitled to participate in councils: cardinals, even those without episcopal status, patriarchs, residential and titular bishops, abbots, and superiors of religious orders. At the time of Vatican II's opening, there were about 2,800 individuals who could have taken part in the council; by the end of the council, because of new appointments, this figure came close to more than three thousand. In fact, the actual number of participants in Vatican II varied between 2,400 and 2,600 fathers (representing over 80 percent of the total). For the first time in history, most of them arrived by plane. There were absences: some bishops could not reach Rome because of their age. Other factors prevented some bishops—mostly auxiliaries—from leaving their sees. The number of bishops from communist countries who were either prevented from attending or imprisoned amounted to a small percentage, but it was significant. Just before the opening of the council, John XXIII initiated some patient diplomatic outreach so that even bishops from behind the Iron Curtain could come to Rome; he received a partial but positive response. Even in spite of these absences, the gathering of fathers at Vatican II was by far the most diverse ever achieved by a council, mostly because of the number of nations represented. Europeans were no longer the major component, although they still represented a third of the council fathers present, a number that is larger if we count bishops from mission areas. Several European countries (France, Germany, Italy, Spain) were overrepresented compared to some countries in the Americas where some bishops governed dioceses as large as some Italian regions, or other non-European states like the Philippines with a high density of Catholics. Conversely, Africa's number of participating bishops was high in proportion to its number of baptized Catholics. However, participation by national episcopates, without discounting individual contributions, cannot be reduced to

---

▶ Participants in General and Ecumenical Councils

(Source: N. Venturini, *I convocati al concilio ecumenico Vaticano II—dati statistici* in ASV, Carte Bea, b. 18)

Lateran IV (1215) = 404 + 800 abbots
Vatican I (1869–70) = 764
Chalcedon (451) = 600
Lateran II (1139) = 500
Basel-Ferrara-Florence (1431–45) = 354
Nicaea II (787) = 300
Lateran I (1123) = 300
Lateran III (1179) = 300
Constance (1414–18) = 300
Trent (1545–63) = 255
Nicaea I (325) = 250
Lyons II (1274) = 200
Ephesus (431) = 198
Constantinople III (680–81) = 174
Vienne (1311–12) = 170
Constantinople II (553) = 164
Constantinople I (381) = 150
Lyons I (1245) = 150
Constantinople IV (869–70) = 102
Lateran V (1512–17) = 94

▶ Length of Ecumenical and General Councils

(Source: N. Venturini, *I convocati al concilio ecumenico Vaticano II—dati statistici* in ASV, Carte Bea, b. 18)

Trent: 17 years, 11 months, 21 days
Basel-Ferrara-Florence: 14 years, 7 days
Lateran V: 4 years, 10 months, 6 days
Constance: 3 years, 6 months, 17 days
Constantinople II: 10 months, 9 days
Vatican I: 7 months, 10 days
Vienne: 6 months, 20 days
Constantinople IV: 4 months, 23 days
Constantinople I: 3 months
Lyons II: 2 months, 10 days
Nicaea I: 2 months, 5 days
Lateran II: 1 month
Nicaea II: 29 days
Constantinople II: 28 days
Ephesus: 25 days
Chalcedon: 24 days
Lateran I: 19 days
Lateran IV: 19 days
Lyons I: 19 days
Lateran III: 14 or 17 days

1. Rome Station, October 7, 1962. Cardinal Stefan Wyszyński, primate of Poland, arrives in Rome for the opening of the council, accompanied by fourteen Polish bishops, including a young Karol Wojtyla. Meeting them are Cardinal Raúl Silva Henríquez (Santiago, Chile), assistant secretary of state, Archbishop Angelo Dell'Acqua, members of the laity, and many journalists covering the arrival of the bishops from behind the Iron Curtain (photo Pais/Archive Rodrigo Pais–Ceub University Bologna). "Our presence at the council is required for the whole Church, and at the same time, our presence—that of the Polish bishops—is necessary for the Catholic Church in Poland. Participation in the council is something new in the consciousness of the whole Church, especially for bishops [who are there]. We are convinced that we must create together a new face for the Church, a face for which humanity yearns so earnestly" (Karol Wojtyla, speech of October 5, 1962).

2. The council fathers meet in St. Peter's (Archivio Fscire).

3. Two bishops, one from Tanzania and the other from the United States, talk before entering the Council Hall (Archivio Fscire).

4. The apostolic constitution calling the Second Vatican Council, *Humanae Salutis* (Biblioteca G. Dossetti, Fscire). "To a world which is lost, confused, and anxious because of the constant threat of new frightful conflicts, the forthcoming council is called to offer a possibility for all men of good will to turn their thoughts and proposals toward peace…" (John XXIII, *Humanae Salutis,* 9).

mere quantitative factors. For example, in spite of the fact that they made up the highest number of participants, the Italian bishops did not make much of a mark in council debates. The same can be said of the Spanish bishops, who were particularly reluctant to accommodate supporters of renewal in the council. Even the U.S. episcopate did not register much, outside of the debate on religious freedom. Conversely, small nations such as Belgium and the Netherlands, which did not have a large episcopal presence, gave valuable input on many aspects of the council discussions. As for the bishops from Eastern Europe, Vatican II undeniably gave them a podium where they could break free from the image of the "Church of silence." For fathers from Africa or Latin America—that is, from countries that had been colonized by European powers—participation in Vatican II was a factor in the growing self-awareness of their own relevance and equal dignity within

1

2

3

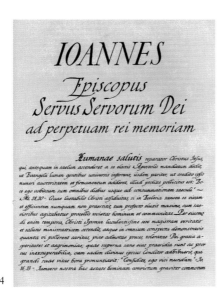

4

the Church. The first cardinal of color had been created only in 1960, and for some non-Europeans the council was the harbinger of their subsequent inclusion in the ranks of the Roman Curia.

Such a vast assembly also required new procedures, since only a small number of council fathers were involved in committee work. Instead of dividing themselves into commissions, the assembly elected commission members, thus excluding most of the bishops from the afternoon work. For the majority of fathers, the only commitment remaining was that of participating in the general congregations in St. Peter's. Besides the council itself, another—and just as important—opportunity

for discussion and debate developed within the colleges or the Roman residences, where meetings or conferences were held on the topics on the agenda. This other "council" produced a fundamental reshuffling of the bishops from all continents, either according to language or common feelings regarding the guidelines that had developed in the Council Hall. In this context, what surfaced was clearly the importance of the role of the *periti*, that is, the theologians and counselors who participated in every aspect of the council, albeit in an advisory capacity and without voting rights, either in the hall or in the meetings of the commissions. These were largely—but not exclusively—European scholars who taught in prestigious

COUNCIL FATHERS OF VATICAN II

	Present	Absent	Dioceses Vacant	Total Dioceses	Cardinals Present	Cardinals Absent
Europe (including Russia, the Balkans, and the East)	479	88	116	683	21	2
North America	66	16	2	84	0	0
Latin America	51	32	12	95	0	0
Africa (not including Algeria and Egypt)	9	4	2	15	0	0
Asia	39	19	6	64	0	0
Australia and the Pacific	14	5	1	20	0	0
TOTAL	658	164	139	961	21	2

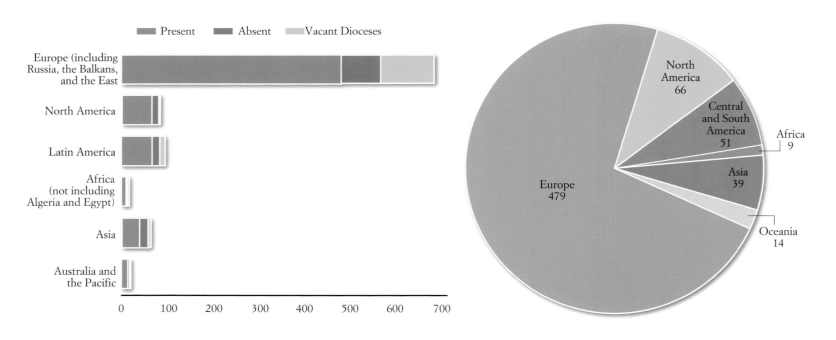

FATHERS PRESENT AT VATICAN COUNCIL II*

Continent	Session I (October - December 1962)			Session II (September - December 1963)			Session III (September - November 1964)			Session IV (September - December 1965)			Totals
	Eligible	Participants	%	Eligible	Participants	%	Eligible	Participants	%	Eligible	Participants	%	Total Council Fathers
Europe	1087	917	84.36	1057	916	86.66	1053	921	87.46	1064	949	89.19	1060
Asia	374	298	79.68	437	302	69.10	449	297	66.14	448	311	69.41	408
Africa	295	265	89.83	335	303	90.44	336	284	84.52	332	311	93.67	351
North America	403	346	85.86	409	332	81.17	422	334	79.14	426	362	84.97	416
Central and South America	573	470	82.02	606	485	80.03	633	475	75.03	644	529	82.14	620
Oceania	75	63	84.00	78	59	75.64	78	59	75.64	76	64	84.21	74
Tot.	2807	2359	84.30	2922	2397	82.03	2971	2370	79.77	2990	2526	84.48	2929
Superior Generals	97	90	92.79	100	91	91.00	103	96	93.20	103	99	96.11	129
TOT.	2904	2449	84.33	3022	2488	82.32	3074	2466	80.22	3093	2625	84.86	3058

Data from the General Secretariat of the Council, (ASV)

COUNCIL FATHERS BY CONTINENT OF ORIGIN

Continent	Total Council Fathers	Population	Catholics	% of Catholics in Total Population	No. of Faithful per Council Father
Europe	1060	560.000.000	232.000.000	41.5	218.868
Asia	408	1.543.000.000	32.000.000	2.7	78.431
Africa	351	224.000.000	21.000.000	9.4	59.829
North America	416	227.600.000	73.300.000	32.2	176.202
Central and South America	620	161.400.000	137000000	84.8	220.968
Oceania	74	15.000.000	3.000.000	20.3	40.541
Tot.	2929	2.731.000.000	498.300.000		170.126

EUROPEAN PARTICIPATION AT VATICAN II

Country	Total Council Fathers	Country	Total Council Fathers	Country	Total Council Fathers
Austria	16	Greece	6	Monaco (Principality)	1
Belgium	27	Ireland	31	Norway	3
Bulgaria	2	Iceland	1	Holland	15
Czechoslovakia	5	(In Italian totals, 28 curial cardinals are included)	451	Poland	59
Denmark	3			Portugal	29
Danzig	3			Spain	87
Finland	2			Sweden	1
France	144	Yugoslavia	28	Switzerland	11
Germany (E. and W.)	61	Latvia	3	Turkey	3
		Lithuania	1	Hungary	12
Gibraltar	1	Luxembourg	2	USSR (Ukraine)	1
Great Britain	48	Malta	3		

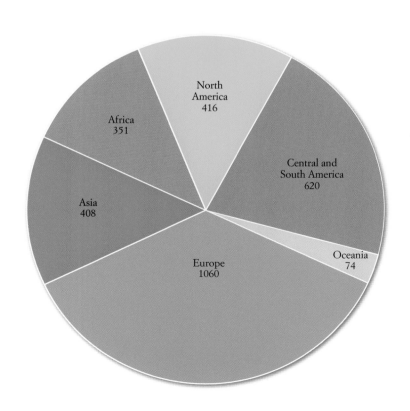

North America 416

Africa 351

Asia 408

Europe 1060

Oceania 74

Central and South America 620

faculties throughout the world or who had faced in previous decades mistrust and hostility because of their commitment to theological renewal that took into account the fundamental developments taking place in society.

The novelty of the presence of observers from other Christian Churches was huge: these were delegates and guests from non-Catholic denominations who had been invited by the Secretariat for Christian Unity to attend the proceedings of the assembly of bishops. Their involvement was the result of strenuous efforts at mediation by the Secretariat, especially toward the Orthodox churches, which raised the ecumenical credibility of the Roman Catholic Church to an unparalleled level, overcoming the resistance of the Holy Office and other departments of the Curia. On a regulatory level, observers were not intended to play an active role in the council, but their presence undoubtedly constituted an important ecclesiological and theological factor, indirectly contributing to the development of the schemas, whose preparatory texts were delivered to them as discussion evolved within the council.

From the second session onwards, even some lay auditors took part in Vatican II (by the end there were about fifty) and were invited to attend the council sessions. However, their overall contribution was far more marginal than that of the observers. They were certainly inspired by the desire to give feedback on the evolution of the role of the laity in the Church. At the same time they were disempowered from the outset by both the choice of who should be involved (mostly leaders of the most important Catholic organizations), and by the excess of formalities and controls through which they had to wade in order to intervene.

What was missing, compared to the councils of the past, were Catholic monarchs and representatives of civil powers, but these followed the council and intervened through informal channels and through the relationships between the bishops and their embassies.

NORTH
AMERICA

416 Council Fathers

CENTRAL
AND SOUTH
AMERICA

620 Council Fathers

Bibliography
Cl. Prudhomme, "Les évêques d'Afrique noire anciennement française et le Concile," in É. Fouilloux (edited by), *Vatican II commence…Approches Francophones*, Leuven 1993, pp. 163–188; Cl. Soetens, *L'apport du Congo-Léopoldville (Zaïre), du Rwanda et du Burundi au concile Vatican II*, 189–208; R. Aubert, "Organizzazione e funzionamento dell'assemblea," in *Storia della Chiesa*, XXV/1, *La Chiesa del Vaticano II (1958–1978)*, edited by M. Guasco, E. Guerriero, F. Traniello, Cinisello Balsamo 1994, 159–187; G. Alberigo, *Transizione epocale. Studi sul Concilio Vaticano II*, il Mulino, Bologna 2009, 325–350; H. Raguer, "Fisionomia iniziale dell'assemblea," in *Storia del concilio Vaticano II*, edited by G. Alberigo (Italian edition edited by A. Melloni), vol. 2, Bologna 1996, 193–258.

Iceland
1

Norway
3

Finland
2

Great Britain
48

Sweden
1

Ireland
31

Danzig
2

Latvia
3

Lithuania
1

Holland
15

EUROPE

1060 Council Fathers

Belgium
27

Poland
59

Ukraine
1

Luxembourg
2

Germany
61

Czechoslovakia
5

Switzerland
11

Austria
16

Hungary
12

Portugal
29

Yugoslavia
28

Spain
87

Bulgaria
2

Princ. Monaco
1

Italy
451

Gibraltar
1

Turkey
3

Greece
6

Malta
3

ASIA

408 Council Fathers

AFRICA

351 Council Fathers

OCEANIA

74 Council Fathers

13. The Council Hall and the Placement of the Participants

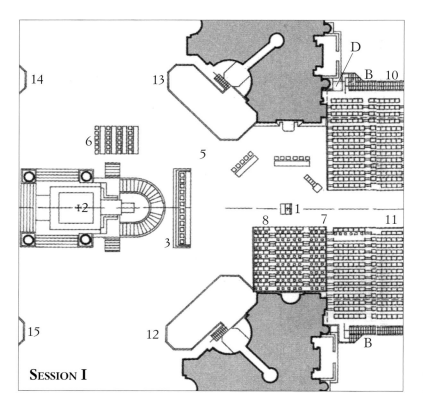

Session I

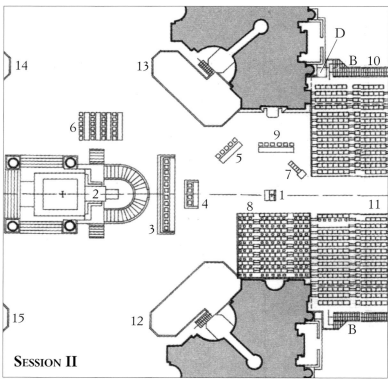

Session II

On May 15, 1962, after a long period of planning, the work of changing the central nave of the Vatican basilica into the Council Hall began. The original construction project underwent many significant changes, but always according to the wishes of the Holy Father, who was aware of the symbolic significance of certain technical choices. For example, at first the papal throne was placed in front of the Bernini baldacchino, covering the staircase leading to the crypt with the tomb of Peter. Pope John immediately ordered that the throne be moved back, in order to maintain free access to the tomb, which thus became an integral part of the Council Hall. In its new position under the baldacchino, the papal throne was a simple red and gold armchair taken from the Hall of Blessings, without its own canopy, placed at a height of one meter and seventy centimeters from the floor of the basilica.

For the celebration of Masses and the daily enthronement of the Gospel—on the same small gold throne used at Vatican I—it was originally planned that a portable altar, a legacy of Cardinal Rampolla, would be used, placed in a central position for the liturgy and then moved to the side during the general congregations. However, John XXIII firmly forbade this solution, which made the daily liturgy appear like a "paren-

▶ **Layout of Council Hall**

1. Altar
2. Papal throne
3. Table for the Presidential Council (10–12 members)
4. Table for the Cardinals Moderators
5. Table for the Secretary General and Secretaries
6. Tables for General Secretariat and from second session on, the Press Office workers
7. Pulpit for general communications and ads
8. Seats for the Cardinals
9. Seats for the Patriarchs
10. Seats for the Council Fathers
11. Raised tribune in side arches
12. Tribune of St. Andrew for Auditors (from the second session on)

13. Tribune of St. Longinus for Observers
14. Tribune of St. Helena
15. Tribune of St. Veronica

A. Passages allowing direct access from the center channel to the aisles
B. Stairs giving access to the passage in the upper back seats of the council fathers and the raised stands
C. Information processing center
D. Sound and central recording booth
E. Snack bars and restrooms
F. First aid station

1. Opening ceremony of the council. In this photo we can see the papal throne placed under the baldacchino, allowing free access to the tomb of St. Peter (photo Pais/Archivio Rodrigo Pais–Ceub Università di Bologna).

2. Cardinal Julius Döpfner talks with Cardinal Giuseppe Pizzardo (© Archivio Storico Luce).

3. The altar at the front of the nave. Each morning the Gospel was enthroned on this altar (Archivio Fscire).

4. Every section had an *assignator locorum*. "The *assignator locorum* has a very specific role, starting at the entrance to the basilica. Each bishop is assigned to a hierarchically ordered place, according to precise criteria regarding the importance of the office he occupies.... The basilica is large, and the seats of the fathers are divided into numbered sections. Even the seats are numbered, left and right....But there are many places and sectors. The fathers forget, and early on, no one knew where to go. So the *assignator locorum* guides them. Each sector has an *assignator* who is in charge of about seventy or eighty bishops. However, his task does not end when all are seated. He has other jobs: he will distribute and then collect and deliver cards to the processing center, he will distribute and collect ballots, and remain vigilant when the fathers vote" (Maurilio Guasco, *Una giornata di Vaticano II*).

4

5

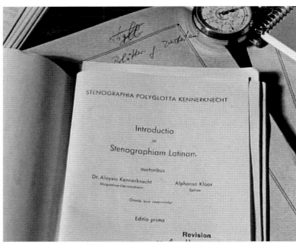

5. *Left:* Young seminarians and priests in a Latin shorthand class taught by the German professor Aloys Kennerknecht.
Right: Their textbook. "Ironically, the conservatism of the Vatican in which they lived required that some students of Roman colleges act as Latin stenographers for the council and fix the speeches of the bishops at a time when there were working tape recorders. But we were told that it had been so at Vatican I, and so it had to be at Vatican II" (Giuseppe Ruggieri, *Ritrovare il concilio*).

thesis" to the beginning of each day of the council. Instead, he demanded a fixed altar, smaller but placed in the middle of the nave where the stalls began, that is, almost in the midst of the council fathers. Every morning the book of the Gospels (a precious illuminated manuscript from the Vatican Library dated 1472) would be solemnly brought out and remain during the course of the general congregations.

In front of the papal chair was placed the bench for the ten cardinals who, under Article 4, paragraph 1 of the *Ordo Concilii* of the first period, constituted the presider's council. They had the task of ensuring compliance with the regulations, to resolve any doubts and procedural difficulties, and to moderate the general congregations in turn, according to seniority, giving the floor to the various speakers, holding votes and giving direction to the council mostly through the general secretary, Pericle Felici. It was composed of cardinals: Bernard Jan Alfrink, Achille Liénart, Antonio Caggiano, Josef Frings, Norman Thomas Gilroy, Ignace Gabriel I Tappouni, Francis Joseph Spellman, Enrique Pla y Deniel, Ernesto Ruffini, and Eugéne Tisserant. From the second session on, this group was not dissolved, but rather, in compliance with Paul VI's new regulations, was augmented. This was the result of a proposal that various experts, including Giuseppe Dossetti, had worked on. From the second period a panel of four moderators was introduced (Cardinals Grégoire-Pierre Agagianian, Julius Döpfner, Giacomo Lercaro, and Leon-Joseph Suenens), which had a similar function to the papal legates at the Council of Trent and could determine the order and duration of the debates. The presider's council, which Pope Paul set up simultaneously, had ten to twelve members, adding Albert Gregory Meyer, Giuseppe Siri, and Stefan Wyszyński. Pla y Deniel had resigned, and in the fourth session, Lawrence Shehan would replace Meyer, who had died. Though it no longer had responsibility for moderating the sessions, it would continue to monitor compliance with the regulations, resolving difficulties and doubts that would arise from time to time. Together with the General Secretariat, it would decide on crucial points, such as how the votes were to be cast in October 1963. At other times an overlap of responsibilities emerged, such as at the end of the third session, on November 19, 1964, when voting on the draft on religious freedom was postponed until the next session.

From the second session on, a new table for the moderators was prepared in the hall in front of the main table, which was in the meantime expanded to accommodate the new members and raised up on a three-step platform so that it would remain visible behind the moderators. At the beginning of the fourth session, an additional place was added to the presider's table for the pope, slightly elevated above the others. Visually, therefore, he became the real chairman of the council assembly during the public sessions. It was from here that Paul VI addressed the fathers on October 5, 1965, about his visit to the United Nations in New York, and where he presided over the general congregations of November 10 and December 4, 1965. Consequently, during this last period of the council, the papal throne was removed, along with its drapery and tapestry (measuring 3.60 x 4.7 yards). From the second session on, Paul VI had wanted this behind his throne, hanging from the top of Bernini's baldacchino, so that an image of the Madonna could be placed in the Council Hall.

To the left of the presider's and the moderators' tables, the general secretary and his five undersecretaries had their desk, which was oblique to the hall and behind which, lined up next to the confessionals, were placed four tables to accommodate officials of the General Secretariat, members of the council's press office, and the stenographers. Of these last, half were clerics (twenty out of a total of forty-one, which rose to forty-four in the fourth session—however during the first period only fifteen were employed). Half were young students from colleges and seminaries in Rome, selected by their respective deans from among the best students representing every nationality, in order that the Latin words—mangled by the pronunciation of the different speakers—could be understood. They spent the months leading up to the council learning to transcribe the Latin words according to stenographic specifications, alternating three shifts per day during the congregations. The courses were organized by Aloys Kennerknecht, professor at the Mainz University, who created a system to adapt the standards of German stenography to the language of Cicero. A comparison of the recordings, however, shows that stenography (which was also used at Vatican I) was soon superseded. Eventually the stenographers mainly worked on transcribing recordings, which were on double reels to avoid missing anything when tapes were changed.

Assignatores locorum also came from the Roman seminaries, who, since the opening ceremony on October 11, had had the task of accompanying the fathers to their places, assigned according to careful criteria that placed the bishops who were more senior in years since consecration and the importance of the see they governed, nearer the front. As Maurilio Guasco,

6. A technician in the control room monitors the acoustics in the basilica, which had caused many problems during Vatican I (*Aula Sancta Concilii*).

7. A view of the council hall during the second period (photo Pais/Archivio Rodrigo Pais–Ceub Università di Bologna). In a circular letter to his community, Hélder Câmara writes, "In St. Peter's Basilica there are large tiers, as you have seen in the photos. Each of them seats about a hundred bishops. I'm in the second tier, behind the

cardinals, to the left of the altar. My number is 128 (which means that in all the world, only 127 archbishops were appointed before I was)" (Hélder Câmara, *Le notti di un profeta*).

8. Seats for the observers, and behind, the diplomatic corps, during the opening ceremony of the first period. During general congregations, observers were seated in the tribune of St. Longinus (from *Concilium Oecumenicum Vaticanum II*, edizione Istituto Luce–edizione Ancora, Roma-Milano, ed. by S. Garofalo, 1963).

a young *assignator*, writes, it was not uncommon to hear "protests from those who seemed to have been downgraded relative to their merits, preferring to seek justice immediately, without waiting for paradise, where all hierarchies will be overturned and the last shall be the first!" The seats reserved for the bishops were arranged symmetrically on either side of the aisle with an overall length of ninety meters, on stands of ten or more levels, which banked up thirty centimeters progressively to ensure that all the fathers could see. The tiers were divided into sectors (which were numbered equally). Each *assignator* was assigned the care of about seventy to eighty bishops, and dealt with, among other things, collecting the texts of the presentations, checking the list of those present and who could vote, verifying that the cards were compiled accurately, and correcting possible errors. The processing system could only read marks made with a special black graphite pencil that each father had at his place. It would have nullified the card if the vote had been marked with a normal pen.

Each sector was also equipped with a microphone for speeches, located at the first place in the bottom row, where the *assignator* usually sat; often the *assignator* became responsible for passing notes or documents between the fathers in order to set up meetings or make agreements.

The central corridor of the hall was about 5.60 meters wide, but two passageways, about halfway down the stairs, allowed one to cross the room quickly without having to go the whole length of the aisle. In this way, the *assignatores* with ballot papers could quickly reach the processing center next to the chapel of the Blessed Sacrament, so that they could quickly pass the results of the ballots to the presider's table. During the most hectic stages of the council, particularly in the fourth session, there could be more than ten votes in a morning.

The cardinals' places—seats with attached kneelers and wooden writing desks with red cushions, to distinguish them from the green reserved for bishops—were placed in a stairway at the front of the stands, opposite the statue of St. Peter and to the right of the papal throne. During the first session, the Eastern patriarchs sat on green seats in the first sector, behind the benches of the cardinals. This aroused fierce protests by patriarchs of the Eastern Rite Churches who stood upon their dignity, saying that they were superior to the cardinals of the Roman Church. The problem was solved from the second session onwards by creating for them a special seven-seat grandstand in front of the Cardinals, with the same color drapery.

The experts attending the council were placed at the back of the hall, in the last two of the six stands, which were elevated by building high walls around the arches that faced the central nave from the side aisles of the basilica. The non-Catholic observers were accommodated in a position of privilege, and were placed, much to their surprise, on the grandstand of St. Longinus, to the left of the papal throne, from where they were able to follow the work of the council even better than some of the bishops. Similarly, from the second session on, the auditors who were invited as representatives of the lay faithful were placed opposite, in the grandstand of St. Andrew, next to the cardinals' seats. In the second session, the auditors were all male, but from the third session on, both lay and religious women were added, and a comfortable spot was set aside for them in the so-called Rezzonico monument area.

BIBLIOGRAPHY
Aula Sancta Concilii, edited by the General Secretariat of the Second Vatican Ecumenical Council, Vatican City 1967; K. Wittstadt, *Alla vigilia del concilio, in Storia del concilio vaticano II*, edited by G. Alberigo (Italian edition edited by A. Melloni), vol. I, Bologna 1995 (2012), 498–517; M. Guasco, *Una giornata di Vaticano II, in Le deuxième Concile du Vatican (1959–1965). Actes du colloque organisé par l'École française de Rome en collaboration avec l'Université de Lille III, l'Istituto per le scienze religiose de Bologne et le Dipartimento di studi storici del Medioevo e dell'età contemporanea de l'Università di Roma-La Sapienza (Rome, 28–30 Mai 1986)*, Rome 1989, 443–462.

6

7

8

14. The Eve of the Council

The drafts developed by the Preparatory Commissions, discussed by the Central Commission and modified by the Subcommittee for Amendments, would have been sent to the council fathers between July and November 1962. In fact, the subcommittee continued to work on the preparatory drafts even after the council had begun.

The first folder that the fathers received in the mail, just a few weeks before leaving for Rome and after explicit requests from John XXIII, contained only seven of the drafts. Until then, most of the bishops (about 97 percent) had been unaware of the preparations. The choice and order of the drafts was determined by the review by the Subcommittee for Amendments (without returning them to the Central Committee), and it was assumed that they were ready for speedy adoption in a short council—the pope was old and therefore it was thought that the assembly would last for only one session and soon close. The documents forwarded in this first consignment were: 1) the draft of the dogmatic constitution on the sources of revelation, *De Fontibus Revelationis*; 2) the draft of the dogmatic constitution on the preservation of the purity of the deposit of faith, *De Deposit Fidei*; 3) the draft of the dogmatic constitution on Christian moral order, *De Ordine Morali Christiano*; 4) the draft of the dogmatic constitution on chastity, marriage, family, and virginity, *De Castitate, Matrimonio, Familia et Verginitate*; 5) the draft of the constitution on the sacred liturgy, *De Sacra Liturgia*; 6) the draft of the constitution on the means of social communication, *De Instrumentis Communicationis Socialis*; 7) the draft decree on the unity of the Church prepared by the Committee on the Eastern Churches, *De Ecclesiae Unitate*.

For the council fathers leaving for Rome, this dossier constituted the first real working papers they had to deal with. The fathers had been told that they could send comments by September 15, with the idea that the documents would be ready for approval a month later. Few did, and in general, the reception of this first series of drafts (of which as many as four—the dogmatic constitutions—came from the Theological Commission) was not homogeneous. Alongside the few positive responses, there were uncertain reactions and very critical positions taken.

Some theologians who were to have a central role in the editing of the various documents of the council (Yves Congar, Karl Rahner, Joseph Ratzinger, Edward Schillebeeckx, Henri de Lubac, Marie-Dominique Chenu, Hans Küng) were able to communicate comments to their own bishops.

Even some of the bishops were dissatisfied with the outcome of the preparatory work. This was dealt with by actions of members of the Preparatory Commission, who had anticipated how things would fall. This malaise had already found voice in the Lenten letter written by the young Belgian Cardinal, Leon-Joseph Suenens, whom John XXIII valued and had received in audience. The pope had asked him for a memorandum on the work of a council that was intended to be more pastoral and missionary than one consistent with the commissions' plans. Suenens's draft identified two areas that in his opinion would have to be the subject of conciliar debates: the first concerned the Church *ad intra* and covered various issues of internal reform; the second was to encompass the relations of the Church *ad extra* and therefore with society and with other Christian denominations. Therefore, the council must offer an opportunity to develop a new missionary impulse in the Church and to renew the apostolate deeply. After Suenens gave the Pope his views, John XXIII wanted a group of cardinals to discuss them. A meeting was arranged with Julius Döpfner, Achille Liénart, Giovanni Battista Montini, Giuseppe Siri, and Suenens; they met at the beginning of July at the Belgian College. The result was the preparation of a new draft. The group then met several more times before the council, when the drafts distributed showed everyone how urgent it was that preparations be restarted.

Suenens was not the only one among the cardinals of the central committee to be worried. On April 18, Archbishop Denis Eugene Hurley, Bishop of Durban in South Africa and hero of resistance to apartheid, had sent Suenens a note containing his criticisms of the preparations, asking the cardinal to intercede with the pope or members of the Central Preparatory Committee to reduce the topics the council would cover to the most relevant issues. Cardinal Josef Frings of Cologne also voiced his views in the May session of the Central Committee, asking that a special subcommittee be set up to reorganize and simplify all the preparatory drafts.

At the end of August, the bishop of Montreal, Cardinal Paul-Émile Léger, sent Döpfner the text of a petition to be sent to John XXIII asking him to intervene in order to give the council a different perspective from the one that had emerged from the preparatory drafts. Léger asked the bishop of Monaco and other European cardinals to sign his text, in particular Alfrink from Utrecht, König from Vienna, Montini from Milan, Liénart from Lille, and Suenens from Mechelen-Brussels.

Beyond these contacts and exchanges, once they had received

1

the first conciliar drafts, many bishops in individual countries began to question their content. In some cases, meetings were organized to discuss the issue, so that they would not arrive at the council unprepared. In Germany, the new bishop of Mainz, Hermann Volk, gathered a small group of theologians including Rahner, Ratzinger, and Otto Semmelroth to examine them analytically.

In the Netherlands, Archbishop Wilhelmus Bekkers of 's-Hertogenbosch took the initiative of consulting some theologians beforehand so that they could formulate a common judgment on the drafts. He then assembled the Dutch bishops, including missionaries who had returned to attend the council, to discuss them together and undertake joint initiatives. Schillebeeckx was asked to write observations on the drafts in

2–3. October 4, 1962. The faithful await Pope John XXIII, on the occasion of his double pilgrimage to the shrines of Loreto and Assisi for the imminent opening of the council (photo Pais/Archivio Rodrigo Pais–Ceub Università di Bologna). That evening, the pope wrote, "In my life, this date is to be written in gold. It is the pilgrimage that I wanted to make—and a few days were enough to conceive it, do it, and succeed, with the help of the Lord—as well as the Madonna of Loreto and St. Francis of Assisi—as a plea for extraordinary grace for the Second Vatican Council….I write that this day, in fact, will remain one of the most holy and happy in my humble pontificate" (John XXIII, October 4, 1962).

4. Pope John XXIII on the train to Loreto and Assisi, with the president of the Consiglio Amintore Fanfani (photo Pais/Archivio Rodrigo Pais–Ceub Università di Bologna). This would be the first time since the 1870 annexation of Rome by the Italian state that a pope would leave the local area. Radio and television had live coverage of the entire pilgrimage, showing the enthusiasm of the faithful. John XXIII would write in his diary on October 6, "Communication by the press from all over the world increases dramatically the reasons for my complacency before the Lord for the success of spiritual teaching of the day—the pope's pilgrimage to Loreto and Assisi" (John XXIII, October 6, 1962).

▶ JOHN XXIII'S PREPARATIONS

From June to October, after the monopoly of the preparatory bodies gave the council a very specific shape, the pontiff returned as a player on the scene, with several private and public actions that demonstrated his diplomatic skills. He listened to the fears of some bishops and replied in his own way: the radio message of September 11 was part of his plan that would culminate with the opening speech on October 11. The preparation of *Gaudet Mater Ecclesia*, because of the importance that Pope John placed on it, eclipsed other issues (such as the *ordo concilii*, which was very close to the spirit of Vatican I, and which the pope promulgated without, in fact, reading it).

Another undisputed protagonist in this phase was the media, which, as October 11 drew near, began to devote more time and space to the event. The press, the radio, but in particular Italian television, which with Eurovision and its nearly six million active subscribers, was able to reach sectors of public opinion that had hardly been tapped by journalism and provide TV stations around the world with first-hand material.

Unlike other television stations in the world, RAI took viewers by the hand and, through a series of historical insights aired during prime time on Church history and the history of the councils, led them to a better understanding of Vatican II, thus contributing to an increased sense of expectation among the public. On Sunday, September 30, RAI, in agreement with the Catholic film and television centers, aired a live interview with Felici, which allowed him to explain the final preparations and the work done so far by the commissions. The interview, "Vigilia di Concilio" (The Eve of the Council), was aired on the National Program at 11:40, just after the usual broadcast of the Mass.

Even the dual pilgrimage of atonement to Loreto and Assisi that Pope John XXIII decided to undertake on October 4— despite his final illness having been diagnosed—fell within the "spiritual preparation" for the imminent opening of the council. Once again, television helped to turn it into a real media event: it was the first time since 1870 that a pope had traveled from Rome across the former Papal States that now were part of Italy. The welcome that Pope John XXIII received on this trip from civil authorities represented symbolically and visually the end of Vatican isolation, as the television journalists did not fail to point out. RAI followed the path of the Pontifical entourage closely, and then-Prime Minister Amintore Fanfani also joined the procession. The cameras positioned along the way documented the crowds waiting impatiently for the train to pass as it made its way through many small towns, each of which was eager for the pope to stop. As can be seen in the series of black and white photos, the inhabitants turned out in numbers, either along the platforms or on the roofs of the stations, when the pope passed, and expressed all their devotion, their support, and their feeling of closeness.

2

7

5–6. Moments during the pilgrimage (photo Pais/Archivio Rodrigo Pais–Ceub Università di Bologna).

7. RAI, in connection with Eurovision, aired a live broadcast of Pope John XXIII's message to the faithful of the world, a month before the council. "In the course of three years of preparation, an array of chosen minds assembled from all parts of the world and of every tongue, united in sentiments and in purpose, has gathered together so abundant a wealth of doctrinal and pastoral material as to provide the episcopate of the entire world, when they meet beneath the vaults of the Vatican basilica, themes for a most wise application of the Gospel, teaching of Christ which for twenty centuries has been the light of humanity redeemed by His blood" (Message of John XXIII, September 11, 1962).

3

5

4

6

more detail, observations (*Animadversiones*) that were copied and distributed to all the bishops of the council, once they had arrived in Rome. Schillebeecks's *Animadversiones* for the Dutch episcopate resulted in the scrapping of the preparatory drafts that showed the irrelevance and lack of awareness embedded in the scope of discussions left over from the last century, and convinced many bishops of the impossibility of working with the Preparatory Commissions' drafts.

Similar initiatives took place in other countries. During these weeks, in various environments and contexts, the idea was conceived for the council to send an initial message to the world, which would be approved by the council fathers in the fourth general congregation on October 20.

Suenens's text, with the *ad intra* and *ad extra* distinction, was certainly used by John XXIII to draft his radio message to the faithful throughout the world, delivered on September 11, 1962, a month before the opening of Vatican II. The message was broadcast on Eurovision, and it echoed strongly among both future council fathers and public opinion. Opening with an observation regarding the "great anticipation of the ecumenical council," the pope recognized that "The ecumenical council is about to assemble, seventeen years after the end of World War II. For the first time in the history, the council fathers will belong, in reality, to all peoples and nations. Each will bring his own contribution of intelligence and experience, to cure and to heal the wounds of the two conflicts that have profoundly changed the face of all countries." He noted that "Where the underdeveloped countries are concerned, the Church presents herself as she is. She wishes to be the Church of all, and especially the Church of the poor."

BIBLIOGRAPHY
A. Riccardi, "La tumultuosa apertura dei lavori," in *Storia del concilio Vaticano II*, edited by G. Alberigo (Italian edition edited by A. Melloni), vol. 2, Bologna 1996 (2012), 21–86; L.-J. Suenens, "Aux origines du Concile Vatican II," in *Nouvelle Revue Théologique*, 107 (1985), 3–21; G. Routhier, "Les réactions du cardinal Léger à la préparation de Vatican II," in *Revue d'histoire de l'Église de France*, 80 (1994), 281–301.

15. ORDO CONCILII: THE TWO REGULATIONS

The convocation of a new council in 1959 raised the question of how an assembly of nearly three thousand members would work. Clearly, when the pope decided that the council would not re-open Vatican I, which was interrupted in 1870, but instead would be celebrated as Vatican "II," it should have its own "Ordo."

"The Regulations" were developed by a specific sub-committee of the Central Preparatory Commission, based on the mistaken assumption that the council would be of short duration and would be composed of many fathers who were willing to vote on anything submitted to them with papal approval. The head of the sub-committee was Cardinal Francesco Roberti, a canon lawyer, who developed the standards of conduct for the sessions by reworking those used in Vatican I. At the end of the preparation phase, John XXIII then promulgated the motu proprio *Appropinquante Concilio* (August 6, 1962), establishing the *Ordo Concilii Oecumenici Vatican II Celebrandi*. It was published only a month later and the council fathers received a copy the very day the council opened. The first part of the Regulations outlined the rules regarding the council fathers, the experts, and the observers from other Christian churches. The second part related to the procedures of the council, the need for confidentiality, the language to be used at the council, discussions in the Council Hall, the examination of drafts, and the possibility of introducing new topics. The third part contained rules regarding the conduct of solemn sessions, general congregations, and commissions.

The headquarters of the council was to be in the nave of the basilica of St. Peter. Following the Nicene tradition, the book of the Gospels would be enthroned at the center of the hall. Each session of the council would open with the celebration of Mass and the prayer of the Fourth Council of Toledo, known by its opening word, "*Adsumus.*" Latin was the only language allowed in the debates in the General Congregation and for keeping records of the proceedings. It defined those who were entitled to participate (resident and titular bishops and other clergy members listed in Article 223 §1 of the 1917 Code of Canon Law), and all those who were present at the sessions

1. The Council President's table, and in the foreground, the moderators' table (from *Das Konzil und seine Folgen*).

2. Pericle Felici, secretary of the council (from *Das Konzil und seine Folgen*).

3. The council fathers during the second period of Vatican II (photo Pais/Archivio Rodrigo Pais–Ceub Università di Bologna).

3

from an organizational point of view. The Ordo expected that the council would be headed by a presiding council composed of ten cardinals (which increased to twelve in 1963). Those who took part were Dean Eugène Tisserant, Achille Liénart (Lille), Ignace Gabriel I Tappouni (Patriarch of Antioch of the Syriac Catholic Church), Norman Thomas Gilroy (Sydney), Francis Spellman (New York), Enrique Pla y Deniel (Toledo), Josef Frings (Cologne), Ernesto Ruffini (Palermo), Antonio Caggiano (Buenos Aires), and Bernard Jan Alfrink (Utrecht).

The Regulations also set up a general secretary, Archbishop Pericle Felici, who was in charge, just as in the preparatory phase. At the beginning of the council, John XXIII was joined by five undersecretaries from different countries: Philippe Nabaa (Beirut and Jbeil for the Melkites), Casimiro Morcillo Gonzalez (Zaragoza), Jean-Marie Villot (Archbishop of Lyon), John Krol (Philadelphia), Wilhelm Kempf (Limburg). At the council, they were responsible especially for the task of giv-

ing the floor to members who wished to speak and for holding votes, but they did not have powers to interrupt the debates, provided they were short and did not go into much detail.

At the beginning of the second working period, Pope Paul VI (who as a council father had had firsthand knowledge of the "the regulatory inconsistencies" of the first period) ordered the enactment of new Regulations that redefined the powers of the executive committee, which had proved unsuitable for the management of such a complex assembly. The committee was then exclusively assigned the task of verifying compliance with council Regulations and resolving any disputes. The running of the council was entrusted to a new college of four moderators with the powers of papal legates: Paul VI chose Cardinals Grégoire-Pierre XV Agagianian who was Armenian by birth and was a member of the Curia, Julius Döpfner, Archbishop of Munich and Freising, Giacomo Lercaro, Archbishop of Bologna, and Leon-Joseph Suenens, Archbishop of Mechelen-Brussels. It

The process for Council documents: from preparation to promulgation.

1962
John XXIII

1963–65
Paul VI

Presidential
council
10 members
2 in the second
period)

+

direction
4 moderators

COORDINATING COMMITTEE (FROM 1963)
11 CONCILIAR COMMISSIONS

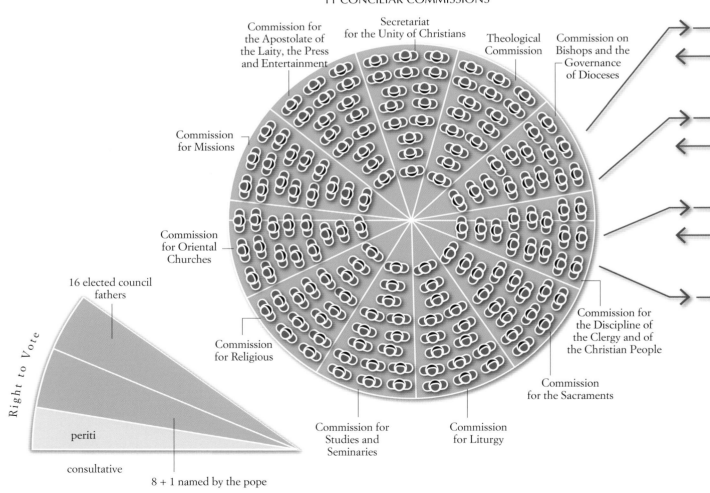

Commission for
the Apostolate of
the Laity, the Press
and Entertainment

Secretariat
for the Unity of Christians

Theological
Commission

Commission on
Bishops and the
Governance
of Dioceses

Commission
for Missions

Commission
for Oriental
Churches

16 elected council
fathers

Right to Vote

periti

consultative

8 + 1 named by the pope

Commission
for Religious

Commission for
Studies and
Seminaries

Commission
for Liturgy

Commission for
the Sacraments

Commission for
the Discipline of
the Clergy and of
the Christian People

COMPOSITION OF A COMMISSION

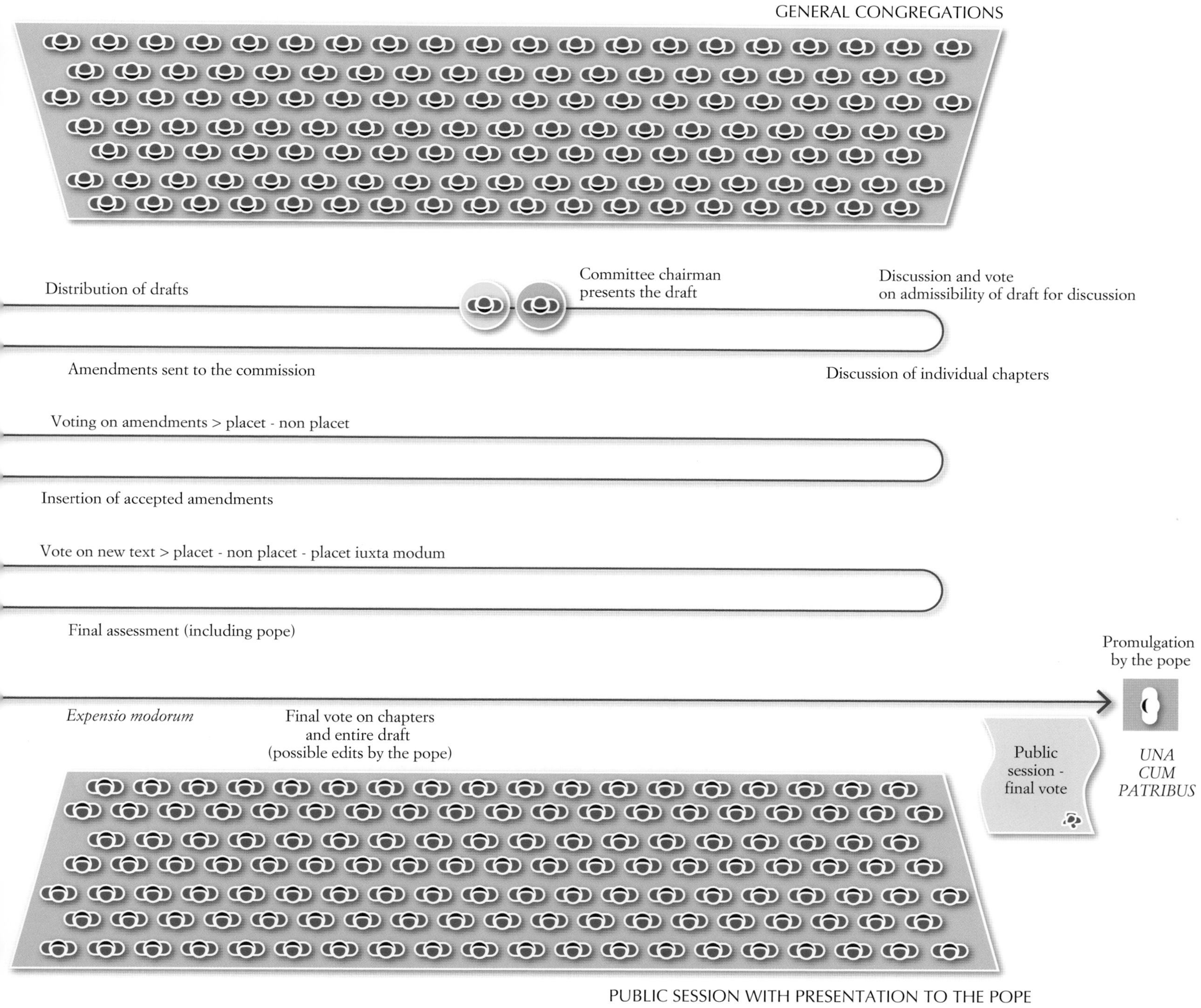

GENERAL CONGREGATIONS

Distribution of drafts

Committee chairman
presents the draft

Discussion and vote
on admissibility of draft for discussion

Amendments sent to the commission

Discussion of individual chapters

Voting on amendments > placet - non placet

Insertion of accepted amendments

Vote on new text > placet - non placet - placet iuxta modum

Final assessment (including pope)

Promulgation
by the pope

Expensio modorum

Final vote on chapters
and entire draft
(possible edits by the pope)

Public
session -
final vote

*UNA
CUM
PATRIBUS*

PUBLIC SESSION WITH PRESENTATION TO THE POPE

▸ The Television as a Player in the Events of the Council

Television did not just play an informative role, but entered directly into the council, influencing and affecting an assembly that proved agreeable to debate outside the Council Hall. One example is the interview with the constitutionalist Costantino Mortati, whose opinion, at the urging of Alberigo, helped to break the deadlock that came about due to the vagueness of the Regulations in the first session. In the first episode, which aired one month from the opening of the council, on November 10, 1962, Alberigo interviewed Costantino Mortati and questioned him on some issues related to the *Ordo Concilii*. In the interview, Mortati, a professor of constitutional law, explained some cases on which the council Regulations remained rather vague. In particular, he focused on the lack of a rule that would allow a vote on the principles that inspired the draft after it had been debated in the general congregations, thus separating it out from other assemblies "in which the Regulations expressly provided for a vote at the conclusion of the general introductory discussion before the examination of the individual provisions." His opinion, which was broadcast on television, as Alberigo remembered a few years later, proved useful in providing technical elements to get around that lacuna and it encouraged the presider of the council to order an indicative vote on the draft of *De Liturgia*, four days after the transmission of the episode, on November 14. The "silence of the Regulations" in the case of a negative indicative vote, for Mortati, would make "the interpreter's task very difficult," but not impossible given the assembly's degree of autonomy. The interview was also reflected in the choice on November 19 and it provided a way out of the impasse caused by not reaching the quorum of two-thirds in the vote on *De Fontibus*.

Bibliography
F. Ruozzi, *Il concilio in diretta. Il Vaticano II tra informazione e partecipazione*, Bologna 2012; D. Viganò, *Il Vaticano II e la comunicazione*, Rome 2013; F. Ruozzi, "La chiesa a concilio. Uomini e problemi. L'officina bolognese e la RAI-TV" (November—December 1962), in *Cristianesimo nella storia*, 34 (2013), 611–670.

▸ "So How Does the Council Work?" Alberigo Explains on Television

The group of scholars at the Documentation Center at Bologna, led by Giuseppe Dossetti, worked hard during the years of the council, preparing materials, memos, and notes, and making changes to documents, from proposals by Cardinal Lercaro and other fathers. But even before that, between the months of September and December 1962, Giuseppe Alberigo, Paolo Prodi, and Boris Ulianich broadcast two television series for RAI (*1962 Year of the Council* and *The Church in Council. The Men and the Problems*), with the idea that it was necessary to provide the public with some more general background first and then give a breakdown of the progress of the first session, in order to make the discussions more comprehensible, since they were often complicated by technical and specialized language. In fact, the overall success of the council also generated an understanding in public opinion throughout the world of what was happening inside the Council Hall at St. Peter's.

On November 10, on Channel 2, at 10:20 p.m., the first episode of the series *The Church in Council* aired. In it, scholars from Bologna analyzed the opening day of October 11 and those first weeks, and did not shy away from explaining the Vatican II Regulations, remembering that it was first of all a tool and "how each tool can be changed, as had already happened at Vatican I, and that there may also be exceptions to the rule." At the beginning of the broadcast, Alberigo, who was sitting behind a desk, tried to explain how the council operated: "During the preparatory work, among the other commission, there was also a small but important group that was in charge of preparing the Regulations for the council. The results of this commission, which was composed of a small number of influential cardinals of the Roman Curia, were not sent to the council for discussion, but instead were submitted to the pope for approval, and he in fact issued a motu proprio on August 6 last year agreeing the rules for the celebration of the council. In other words, he issued the Regulations. It is therefore a papal act that the council fathers are required to observe, but over which they have no control. This system was already in place at the First Vatican Council, whereas all previous councils had never had any real Regulations. In Christian antiquity, the first councils were governed primarily by the procedures of the Byzantine court. In the Late Middle Ages, the councils had found a way of establishing a set of internal rules that were sufficiently autonomous, which also allowed them to nominate their officials, that is, those who held special functions within the council. Naturally, the bishop of Rome always exerted his prerogatives, by convening, transferring, dissolving the council and promulgating the decisions that had been taken by the majority of fathers."

4. Title of television broadcast *1962 anno del concilio* (1962, Year of the Council), edited by Giuseppe Alberigo, with Pierre Riches and designed to give insight into the history of the council (Tech RAI).

5. The Swiss theologian Hans Küng (1928–) in an interview on the work of the council (Teche RAI).

6. The German historian Hubert Jedin (1900–1980), interviewed on the history of the Council of Trent (Teche RAI).

7. The French Dominican theologian Yves Congar (1904–1995), interviewed on the first four ecumenical councils (Teche RAI).

was a pared-down group with powers to guide the assembly and indirectly act as a bridge between the Council Hall and the commissions. The choice of these moderators answered the need to find a balance between the representative of the Roman Curia and the bishops who had emerged as real leaders of the majority of the assembly in the first period.

After the new preparation for the council took place during the break between sessions, the Second Vatican Council restarted in September 1963, chaired by Paul VI. It took advantage, therefore, of the new Regulations, which had been influenced by the suggestions from the Franco-German group and by proposals put forward by Giuseppe Dossetti (who, as vice-secretary of the Christian Democrats, between 1945 and 1951, had had frequent contact with the then-replacement Secretary of State, Montini).

Since its first version, the Ordo had governed the presence of observers sent by the Christian Churches separated from the Catholic Church: they could attend the general congregations and the public sessions but could not intervene in the debate or vote, even if they were bishops. The observers were also bound to the rule of confidentiality imposed on the work, which would only be partly mitigated after 1963; it was subsequently superseded.

The council worked collaboratively. At a less visible level, there was the work of the ten conciliar commissions and the Secretariat, each consisting of twenty-four members (sixteen elected council fathers plus eight appointed by the pope, which then became nine as decided by John XXIII, thus bringing membership to twenty-five) and experts chosen by the commissions.

The members had the right to speak and vote, while the experts had, pursuant to the Regulations, an advisory function. In reality, many of these would eventually play a key role in drafting the final documents. The commissions had the task of reworking the "schemata" (the term used to distinguish conciliar draft texts throughout their editorial process) and if necessary revising the structure in the light of the debate in the hall. Discussions within the General Congregation took place at another level and were conducted in the presence of all the council fathers; these were open to all. A speaker appointed by the respective commissions introduced the discussion on the topic on the agenda, initiating the debate; the timing of the speeches had to be strictly adhered to and the precedence of the speakers respected their ecclesiastical dignity (cardinals went before archbishops, archbishops before bishops, and so on).

The fathers had to register well in advance for the discussion and could speak provided they could gather a significant proportion of supporters—which varied in the course of the work—for their proposed comments. The drafts were then analyzed and discussed chapter by chapter and fathers could vote in three possible ways: *placet, non placet,* or *placet juxta modum* (a conditional consent to the introduction of certain changes, which were to be specified in writing). The speaker was expected to respond to the presentations and to the amendments presented in the hall: if the assembly agreed with the proposals that emerged during the debate, they had to be sent back to the relevant commission to be integrated into the draft. The acceptance or rejection of a draft or parts of it required a majority of

7

two thirds of the fathers, and the voting took place through a new processing system using punch cards. Minutes were drawn up of all the meetings and there was—unprecedented in the history of the councils—a full audio recording.

After the general congregations, the last operating level was represented by the "public sessions," that is, the general congregations that took place in the presence of the pope and of the people, in the course of which a solemn and definitive vote was held on the conciliar documents. In *sessio publica*, the fathers listened to the reading of the document that had already been approved in the hall and, after the reading, which was performed by the Secretary General, the congregation was asked to express a *placet* or *non placet*. After that, the pope promulgated the document.

The formula of enactment was originally supposed to follow that of Vatican I but was modified in 1963 and 1964 to give the sense of communion between the successor of Peter and the successors of the apostles, so that the pope signed the various documents "*una cum patribus.*"

The documents were distinguished from one another according to kind, without changing their theological qualification: at Vatican II four constitutions on the most fundamental issues were in fact approved; twelve decrees and declarations, in which the principles of renewal were articulated; and two messages, one voted on in the hall at the beginning of the council and the other, which had no papal promulgation, was read in St. Peter's Square at the end of Vatican II and approved by acclamation.

Constitutions, decrees, and declarations thus arose from a process that was traditional and parliamentary in nature: each draft was entrusted to the commission responsible for the subject for initial analysis, which concluded with the majority of the commission expressing a joint opinion and referred to the general congregation by an appointed speaker. In the general congregation, the bishops discussed and proposed changes, orally or in writing. These were collected and sent to the commission, examined, grouped together, and then accepted or rejected.

At this point the draft, along with the proposed amendments, was sent back to the general congregation, which reexamined the changes. Those that were accepted came back for the last time to the commission, which formalized the text and sent the draft back to the general congregation for a positive or negative vote on each chapter and on the draft as a whole. From this moment, the draft was ready for the solemn session in which it was again voted on, approved, and promulgated.

BIBLIOGRAPHY
Ordo Concilii Œcumenici Vaticani II celebrandi, Vatican City, 1962; *Ordo Concilii Œcumenici Vaticani II celebrandi. Editio altera recognita*, Vatican City, 1963; *Acta et Documenta Concilio Oecumenico Vaticano II apparando*, IV/1, Vatican City, 1988, 11–284; P. Levillain, *Le mécanique politique de Vatican II. La majorité et l'unanimité dans le Concile*, Paris 1975; G. Alberigo, "Dinamiche e procedure nel Vaticano II. Verso la revisione del Regolamento del Concilio, 1962–1963," in *Cristianesimo nella storia*, (1992), 115–164 (then in *Transizione epocale*, op. cit., 183–228); G. Alberigo, "La preparazione del Regolamento del Concilio Vaticano II," in *Vatican II commence…Approches francophones*, edited by É. Fouilloux, Leuven 1993, 75–104 (then in *Transizione epocale*, op. cit., 161–182).

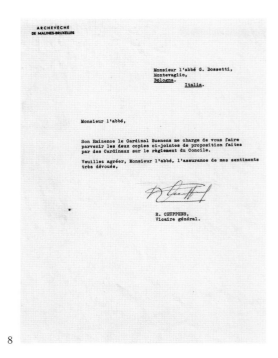

8

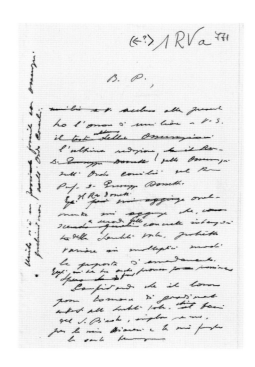

9

8. Cardinal Léon-Joseph Suenens' proposals sent to Giuseppe Dossetti, Cardinal Giacomo Lercaro's theologian (Archivio Fscire).

9. Giuseppe Dossetti's manuscript with the proposed revision of the Regulations (Archivio Fscire).

10. The council fathers vote (Archivio Fscire).

11–12. Samples of ballots used by the council fathers (Archivio Fscire).

13. Joseph Bonacini, bishop of Bertinoro, watching the processing of data in the office (from *Il Concilio Vaticano II*, 3 vol., Fratelli Fabbri Editori, Milan 1966).

14. The data processing center (from *The Pope and the Council*).

10

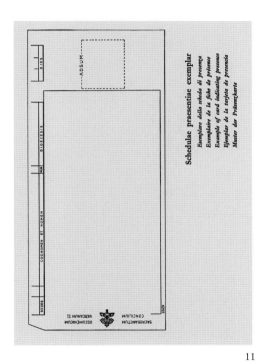

11

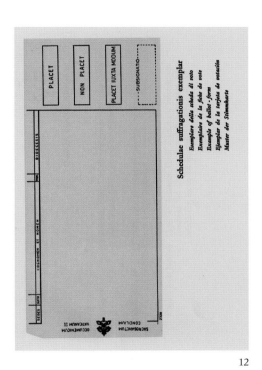

12

13

14

16. October 11: Gaudet Mater Ecclesia

2

The solemn opening of the council occurred on October 11, 1962. The council fathers vested in the "sala delle lapidi" near St. Peter's Basilica. There were some last-minute problems as it became apparent that there were no chairs for the cardinals. At 8:30 a.m., the long procession toward the basilica began and cameras rolled to transmit the events as they unfolded, first via Eurovision, then as a worldwide broadcast. The fathers proceeded in sixes, with an order of precedence that had the abbots general enter first, followed by the prelates nullius, bishops, archbishops, primates, patriarchs, and cardinals. The procession of the long line was slow and lasted nearly an hour. Last came the pope, wearing precious vestments and carried in the *sedia gestatoria*, and as the *Veni Creator* was sung the liturgy commenced, led by the polyphony of the Sistine choir. Then the pope addressed the congregation of bishops—though it

had been many hours since their arrival at the Vatican.

The opening speech of the council delivered by John XXIII—referred to by its opening words, *Gaudet Mater Ecclesia*—constitutes one of the acts of major importance not only of the pontificate of John XXIII, but also of papal teaching in the twentieth century. With this address, Roncalli marked a watershed in the way the Catholic Church had defined its understanding of the gospel and its own position in the world. The main preparation for this speech, which the pope wrote in the summer of 1962, is connected to John XXIII's plan for the council. From its announcement in January 1959 to its actual opening in 1962, this gradually came into focus through a series of speeches in which the pope suggested that the new council was not to be seen as a "project," but should open a season of *aggiornamento* whose essential elements it was the bishops' duty to define. The pope

1. The procession of council fathers went from the halls of the Vatican Palace, through the Scala Regia, across St. Peter's Square, and into the basilica (*Concilium Oecumenicum Vaticanum*).

2. October 11, 1962. The procession of bishops at the opening of the first session of the council (Archivio Fscire).

3. Pope John XXIII descends the Scala Regia at the conclusion of the procession of council fathers (*Concilium Oecumenicum Vaticanum*).

4. Pope John XXIII in prayer (*Concilium Oecumenicum Vaticanum*).

5. Pope John XXIII wrote his much-anticipated opening speech, *Gaudet Mater Ecclesia*, in his own hand in Latin. The Italian television network translated it into Italian for its viewers. It is a "theological pearl," that would mark a change in the atmosphere that had prevailed during the preparatory work (Pais/Archivio Pais–Ceub Università di Bologna).

referred several times to the image of a new Pentecost, signifying both the weight of expectations inherent in the future council, and the need to allow for open discussion among the bishops and not prepackaging the final decrees of Vatican II. The pope's attitude aroused alarm in some sectors of Catholicism. The freedom of movement granted by the pope had actually been employed by the preparatory bodies mainly to process a number of drafts that were aimed at summarizing the convictions expressed by the magisterium in previous decades, not at incorporating the renewal produced by and expressed in the contexts of biblical exegesis, the liturgical movement, the ecumenical movement, the return to the study of the fathers of the Church, or the experiences of the lay apostolate.

However, John XXIII did not give up his firm determination to give the council and the fathers the same freedom exercised by the Curia in preparation for the council—an idea that he wanted to reiterate in his speech, which he had written with his own hand, without external editors, to celebrate his responsibility as head of the Church.

The pope began by placing Vatican II within the great tradition of the councils, which had been called to reflect the historic dynamism of which that tradition, in turn, was part. In that sense, John XXIII manifested the belief that he was bringing about a historical

6. Pope John XXIII gives the "Sermon of the Moon" (Fondazione Papa Giovanni XXIII, Bergamo). "This evening's spectacle will always remain in my memory as it will in yours. Let us honor the images of this evening, that we might always feel the way we do now, as we expressed them before Heaven and earth: faith, hope, charity, love of God, love of our brothers. Together they help in the peace of the Lord in performing good works. When you go home, you'll find your children there. Give them a hug and say, 'This is from the Pope.' You will find tears that need to be dried; do something, say a kind word. The Pope is with us, especially in times of sadness and bitterness" (John XXIII, Sermon of the Moon, October 11, 1962).

Following page:
7. St. Peter's Square, October 11, 1962. Catholic Action organized a candlelight vigil to mark the opening of Vatican II, as the Christians in Ephesus had done fifteen centuries earlier. The crowd came together in the square and they appeared as a large cross made up of torches (Archivio Fscire).

5

6

moment to which no one could respond by hiding or reiterating dated attitudes. Thus, he distanced himself from those he called "prophets of doom" who could only see harmful things resulting. By not providing the agenda for Vatican II, the pope was stating that the new council—as many bishops had requested—would not have to busy itself with defining new dogmas or ratifying the condemnations recently expressed by the magisterium, but instead by making "a leap forward" towards a "deeper penetration" of the Gospel, according to teaching that was, and wanted to be, "primarily pastoral." In that adjective—*pastoral*—could be found the new profile of the council that John XXIII was pointing to: not to be thought of as inferior to the dogmatic, but a way of stating the consistent Christian truth through its existence that could only be completely understood through the mystery of Christ. Finally, he introduced a distinction, which had been essential to his language since 1902, between substance and accidents, between the "substance" of doctrine and its "appearance." By this, he indicated what the council should concern itself with, because if they were simply going to repeat things that had already been said, then "there was no need for a council."

And so, in the face of errors, he counseled that the Church should resort to the "medicine of mercy" rather than the "weap-

ons of severity." In the face of the divisions among Christians he pointed to a threefold unity—of Catholics, of Christians, and of the human family—that did not distinguish, in the evangelistic sense, between those levels. This was an idea that, on the evening of October 11th, in his famous "Sermon of the Moon," he referred to as "the search for what unites us," and placed the papacy at the service of all ("My person counts for nothing; I am a brother who became a father [...] but everything, fatherhood and brotherhood is a gift of God, everything, everything").

The speech, which was of the utmost importance for the council and for the history of the Church, was not fully understood at the time, but over the course of the weeks, when the council fathers delved into theological issues of a larger scale, they grasped the strength of those conditions with which Roncalli "opened" Vatican II, in all senses.

BIBLIOGRAPHY
John XXIII, *Il concilio della speranza*, Introduction and notes by A. and G. Alberigo, Padua 2000[2]; G. Alberigo, *Dalla Laguna al Tevere. Angelo Giuseppe Roncalli da San Marco a San Pietro*, Bologna 2000, 157–190; A. Melloni, *Papa Giovanni. Un cristiano e il suo concilio*, Turin 2009, 299–335; A. G. Roncalli-John XXIII/G. B. Montini-Paul VI, *Lettere di fede e amicizia. Corrispondenza inedita (1925–1963)*, edited by L. F. Capovilla and M. Roncalli, Rome-Brescia, 2013; G. Sale, *Giovanni XXIII e la preparazione del Concilio Vaticano II nei diari inediti del direttore della "Civiltà Cattolica" padre Roberto Tucci*, Milan-Rome 2012.

▶ THE SERMON OF THE MOON

The opening ceremony was broadcast in its entirety by RAI on the National Program and linked to Eurovision's network (and for a short period in the afternoon was also broadcast worldwide) and commented on by a single voice, that of Luca Di Schiena, who beat every European record for the longest live broadcast by a single reporter. "For hours on end," Schiena would remember a few years later, "I practiced in order to get straight in my mind the faces, the dress, and the resumes of all the most prominent characters to be able to distinguish patriarchs from archbishops, bishops from superiors general of religious orders; to recognize miters, crowns, dalmatics, copes, chasubles, and all the complex variety of sacred vestments of the Eastern Rite. It was constant and methodical training, using photos of the cardinals and bishops in the foreground. By covering the captions, I forced myself, by staring at the face of each, to remember the name and the biography. Five hours is a length that would scare even the most practiced orator."

None of the media missed coverage of such a global event, but it was the images transmitted by the television that were to have the greatest impact on public opinion. Through those same images, viewers were able to observe the real universality of the Catholic Church, but they also lifted the veil on the catholicity of the Catholic Church. For the first time, people could see the faces and hear the words of the African, Chinese, Latin American, Northern European, and Asian bishops with their different vestments and liturgies, behind which were different sensitivities and priorities.

The television would play a leading role in the reception of the council and was particularly close to events on the evening of October 11. That evening, Catholic Action from Roman parishes organized a procession: members, the faithful, and clergy gathered to celebrate the opening of Vatican II in the same way the Christians in Ephesus had celebrated the third ecumenical council fifteen centuries before. There were three simultaneous marches to the basilica, which formed a striking large cross made up of torches in the center of St. Peter's Square, around the obelisk erected during Pope Sixtus V's pontificate. RAI-TV followed this event with a special broadcast, "The Council: Zero Hour," which was to begin with a live candlelight vigil for a few minutes, and transmitted those images from Rome to the whole country transforming them into a common visual heritage. The pope was not expected to make a speech, but his secretary, Archbishop Loris Francesco Capovilla, invited the pope to peek through the window at the crowd and persuaded the pope to give them his blessing.

According to the agreed-upon schedule, the pope would come out to bless those present, but he had forgotten that he wouldn't be adding anything to his comments made at the morning ceremony. Instead, John XXIII unexpectedly improvised a speech that encompassed all the points that he had made that morning in the keynote address, *Gaudet Mater Ecclesia*. In fact, it so happened that the coverage from St. Peter's had ended just moments before the pope decided to look out of his window. The live feed from the square was already over, but RAI's technicians and Luca Di Schiena, the anchor for the transmission, understood what was happening and restored the connection with the Vatican that had just been closed. Just when they were tuning in to the National Program, RAI sent viewers the image and voice of Pope John XXIII, whose words then passed into history as the "Sermon of the Moon." He spoke of unity and brotherhood, he invited the crowd to "hug their children," and he alluded to the fact that the duration of the council would be much longer that anyone thought at the time. The perceptiveness of the RAI journalists enabled them to preserve what in a few minutes would leave an indelible mark on that day and on John XXIII's whole pontificate.

7

17. The Liturgy and Ceremonies of October 11

The liturgy has always been an integral part of every council. In a sense, a council is itself a liturgical act and many of its historical functions—the inclusion of the creed, the trial of writings against Church teaching, the attempts to reform the Church—have liturgical characteristics. In the conciliar tradition of the Roman Catholic Church in particular (as well as for the Byzantine, Slavic, and Russian synods), the ceremonies of the council have the function of communicating ideas through discussion and allowing them to change as the sessions proceed.

This was true at Vatican II. Overall, it was a short council, but during it liturgical reform came into force. It was a council that the faithful were able to observe through television, which ultimately transmitted the liturgy of the council itself, presenting a particular point of view along with an explana-

tion, which conditioned the perceptions of eyewitnesses and contributed to establishing a faithful picture of events for those who were not present.

The ceremony was designed exactly according to the Regulations, in the mistaken conviction that the council would yield lightning approvals. Therefore, it was modeled on ceremonies based on the *Ordo in Concilio Plenario Servandus*, which came from that of the papal chapels and, in some respects, from the tradition of the ceremonies of the papal court. This structure was overlaid with some personal choices by the council popes: Pope John XXIII in the first period and Paul VI in the other three.

The opening ceremony on October 11, 1962, began with a long procession beginning outside the basilica and drawing

1. October 11. The council fathers process across St. Peter's Square (Pais/Archivio Rodrigo Pais–Ceub Università di Bologna).

2. Pope John XXIII in the *sedia gestatoria* entering the basilica at the end of the procession (Pais/Archivio Rodrigo Pais–Ceub Università di Bologna).

2

in hundreds of council fathers and assistants (the bishops had vested inside the palace, which was used as a kind of mega-sacristy) to the bronze door. From there they crossed the fan-shaped stairway and entered St. Peter's through the main door. The pope brought up the rear of the procession, in rich pontifical vestments, carried in the *sedia gestatoria*. The liturgy began with the *Veni Creator* and was dominated by polyphony.

The ritual of "obedience" to the pope was a typical act from the medieval court and from the conclave, and was consistent with post-Tridentine ecclesiology. After the profession of faith, made by John XXIII and by Pericle Felici on behalf of the fathers, one by one the cardinals and Eastern patriarchs, two archbishops, two bishops, and two superiors general repre-

senting their confreres, knelt before the throne and kissed the pope: the cardinals and patriarchs kissed his hand, the bishops and archbishops his right knee, and the superiors general his foot. The ornaments in the hall drew from the decorative tradition of the Baroque, while the benches were quite simple. The bishops wore the *cappa magna* and the miter. These were symbols of a priesthood that remained, however, silent. As the theologian Yves Congar wrote in his diary, "The liturgical movement has not arrived in the Roman Curia. This huge assembly does not say anything, does not sing anything. It is said that the Jews are the people of the ear, and the Greeks of the eye. But here there is only the musical eye and ear: there is no liturgy of the Word. Not one spiritual word. I know that now a Bible will be enthroned, to preside over the council.

3–4. Inside the council hall. The faithful, political authorities, and members of the diplomatic corps following the opening ceremony of Vatican II (Pais/Archivio Rodrigo Pais–Ceub Università di Bologna).

5. Cardinal Eugène Tisserant, Dean of the College of Cardinals, celebrated the Mass of the Holy Spirit followed by the ritual enthronement of the gospel book and the ritual obedience offered by the council fathers to the pope. Many would be impressed by the spectacle of the ceremony, but disappointed in its

3

4

5

liturgical aspects. Among these, Yves Congar, who barely found a place from which to follow the ceremony would write, "It is said that the Jews are the people of the ear, and the Greeks of the eye. But here there is only the musical eye and ear: there is no liturgy of the Word. Not one spiritual word. I know that now a Bible will be enthroned, to preside over the council. BUT WILL IT SPEAK?" (Yves Congar, October 11, 1962).

6–7. The council fathers take their places on the benches (Pais/Archivio Rodrigo Pais–Ceub Università di Bologna).

6

7

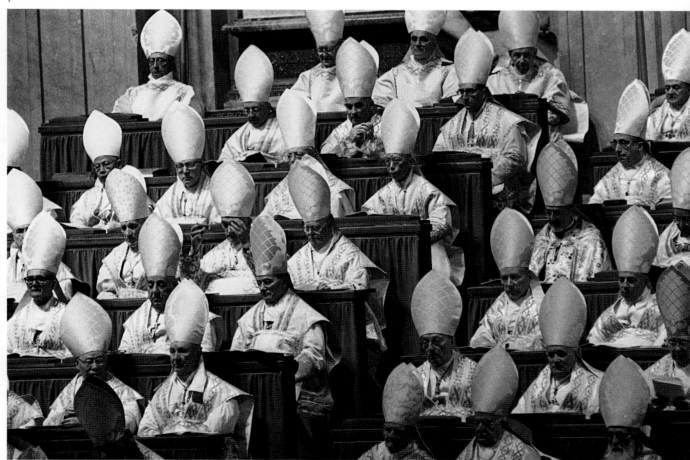

8–9 Moments from the opening liturgy and ceremonies (Pais/Archivio Rodrigo Pais–Ceub Università di Bologna). After descending from the *sedia gestatoria*, Pope John XXIII kneels at the altar, prior to intoning the *Veni Creator*. On his right, Cardinal Alfredo Ottaviani (photo 9). At the end of the day, the pope would note in his diary, "This day

8

BUT WILL IT SPEAK? Will it be heard? Will there be any time given to the Word of God?" The French theologian felt so oppressed by the ritual, which he found "feudal and as if from the Renaissance," that he left his seat immediately after the epistle, and then, before the pope delivered his speech, said, "I'm sorry…we seem to have wanted a style of celebration that is alien to the truth of things. What would it have been like if these 2,500 voices had been able to sing the Creed together, or even better the entire Mass, instead of the elegant warbling of those salaried professionals?" Although the opening ceremony with about three thousand people was inevitably a solemn occasion that would elicit a certain "observance of etiquette" and a "certain pomp," it also made it clear to many observers that "the time when the Church had close ties with feudalism"—as Congar noted somewhat angrily in the

pages of his diary—"when it held temporal power, and popes and bishops were lords who held court, protected artists, and aspired to a splendor similar to that of the Caesars: all this the Church, in Rome, has never repudiated. Disentangling itself from the era of Constantine had never been part of the program….Pius IX still reigns. Even Boniface VIII still reigns, and has taken a place superior to that of Simon Peter, the humble fisher of men."

The meeting between fathers from different local churches sparked comparisons. Neophytos Edelby, a young Melkite bishop born in Aleppo, was surprised to note that almost every council father came accompanied by a *socius* or associate to help carry his things, and he wrote in the pages of his private diary that "we too could certainly have worn great pontifical robes. But we decided to put on only the *epitrachílion* and

marks the solemn opening of the ecumenical council. The news is all over the papers and is in the hearts of all of Rome. I thank the Lord that I was not unworthy of the honor of opening [the council]" (Diary of John XXIII, October 11, 1962).

9

omophorion. We don't regret it." At the end of the ceremony, although his dress made him stand out from the crowd, on a pragmatic level, his choice made it "easier to bear a ceremony of more than five hours in a reduced set of vestments." But this did not stop him from criticizing the seating arrangements: "Despite all our efforts, it was not possible to get Rome to grant to the patriarchs the rank that was accorded to them by the early ecumenical councils. But we do not despair that one day it can be obtained. The absence of our patriarch was noted. Those in the know quickly guessed that health was not the only reason."

As of October 13, 1962, by the will of John XXIII, every general congregation was introduced by the celebration of weekday Mass and the rite of enthronement of the Gospel. During the general congregations, the fathers who were bishops wore the purple *mantelletta*, bishops of the Eastern rite wore their own appropriate robes, while religious wore the habit of their order. Despite their short duration, Masses were perceived as a delay: some fathers, who had already said Mass early in the morning, skipped it in order to meet with each other in the side aisles. Pope John wanted Mass to be celebrated, not only following the Roman rite, but periodically, also according to the Eastern Catholic rites. The choice of celebrants followed consistent geographical-continental criteria. For many fathers it was the first time they saw non-white bishops celebrate the Roman rite, and the Eastern liturgy contained rituals, prayers, vestments, and languages that were strange to many prelates. The Masses that were celebrated, sometimes following the Eastern-rite liturgical calendar, the Melkite and Maronite, the Armenian, Malabar, Coptic, or Syro-Antiochene rites, also had

10–14. The faithful, journalists, cameramen, photographers, and curious onlookers in St. Peter's Square and the via della Conciliazione follow the opening ceremonies (Pais/Archivio Pais–Ceub Università di Bologna).

10

11

12

an educational benefit that was enhanced by the TV coverage. It showed that the use of living languages did not diminish the sense of the sacred and did not debase dogmas. The Melkites in particular offered written explanations and commentaries in Latin, and during the Mass and the Assembly, some Latin prayers were introduced (the Gloria, the Creed, the Our Father, and so on).

BIBLIOGRAPHY

N. Edelby, *Il Vaticano II nel diario di un vescovo arabo*, edited by R. Cannelli, Cinisello Balsamo–Milan 1996; A. Riccardi, "La tumultuosa apertura dei lavori," in *Storia del concilio Vaticano II*, edited by G. Alberigo (Italian edition edited by A. Melloni), vol. 2, Bologna 1996 (2012), 21–86; Y. Congar, *Mon Journal du Concile*, presented and annotated by E. Mahieu, t. I: 1960–1963, t. II: 1964–1966, Paris 2002 (Italian translation: Cinisello Balsamo–Milan 2005).

13

14

18. First Steps

1. Cardinal Achille Liénart, bishop of Lille, took the floor from the Executive Committee and asked for a postponement of the council vote for members of conciliar commissions. "On the agenda is the election of committee members. Cardinal Liénart asks that the election be postponed. This intervention was unexpected…; he is

When the council opened, few really paid attention to the deep meaning of the words spoken by John XXIII in the speech that he had prepared long before and written in his own hand during the previous months. It was only in the course of the council discussions that gradually his words began to be cited and fully understood.

Other events showed that the bishops would not be content merely to approve the drafts provided by the Preparatory Commissions. At the end of the opening session, a booklet was distributed to the assembly that would be used at the next congregation, on Saturday, October 13, for the election of the commissions. In anticipation of the session, many bishops themselves prepared lists of candidates for each commission. This had not been anticipated: the fathers had been given a list of the members of the council and another with members of the Preparatory Commissions so that they could get down to work. In fact, time was short. On Saturday morning when Felici, the secretary of the council, announced from the pulpit that voting would begin, the fathers would have had to start filling the sixteen boxes with sixteen names for each of the ten committees. In fact, the bishops were being asked to copy the names of those chosen during council preparations.

While many were about to write something else on their papers, Cardinals Achille Liénart of Lille followed by Josef Frings of Cologne, both members of the council presidency, took the floor, abruptly changing the agenda: they asked for a reasonable postponement of the voting to give the council fathers and national conferences time to prepare lists of suitable candidates from which the council fathers could choose with greater awareness. The applause with which this proposal was received demonstrated the general attitude of the assembly who wished "to talk and discuss." The applause was rightly regarded as a vote by acclamation for the point of order the two cardinals had raised. Thus, in the following hours, various bishops' conferences agreed to come up with stronger sets of candidates. The smaller conferences proposed only a few names and not for all commissions. The Congregation of the Holy Office also circulated the names of trusted men to be proposed as candidates. Different views surfaced, among which, on the one hand was the list prepared by the bishops' conferences from central and northern Europe, and on the other the lists from the Italians and Spaniards which had some curious reversals (Lercaro, a leading liturgist, was voted onto the "transalpine" list). In the elections, many candidates on the list from northern Europe prevailed.

According to the Regulations of the council, each of the ten committees should be composed of twenty-four members, of which sixteen were elected and eight appointed by the pope. John XXIII added another member, thus bringing the committees' membership to twenty-five.

Among the first acts the council presidency submitted to the council fathers was a proposal for a message to the world, *nuntius ad omnes homines et nationes*, at the opening of the meeting. The idea of an initial message by the council to the world had emerged in the previous weeks for fear that the council would simply follow what the Preparatory Commissions had already prepared. In particular, the French Dominican Marie-Dominique Chenu had spoken to Yves Congar and Karl Rahner and had developed a draft that was circulated among the council fathers in the days immediately preceding the opening of the council. The council's message was revised by Archbishop Emile Maurice Guerry along with three other French bishops (Cardinal Achille Liénart, Archbishop Alfred Ancel, and Archbishop Gabriel-Marie Garrone). In the end, it was actually presented to the council fathers, and was discussed and promulgated at the very beginning of the council, on October 20, as the first public act by the council assembly. The message had some impact on public opinion and had an impact, even if not immediately, on how the work went ahead. Eventually it would be left out in many editions of the documents of Vatican II. As then-Archbishop of Cotonou in Benin, Bernardin Gantin noted: "The eyes of the world were on the council. We were no longer closed in, in our little rooms."

Since their first days in Rome, the council fathers and theologians were engaged in various meetings outside the hall: meetings of episcopal conferences, transnational groups that met to organize their participation in the council with information services, informal groups to maintain the discussion on forgotten issues such as poverty. Some meetings of bishops and *periti* also had higher ambitions; for example, several German and French bishops gathered with their *periti* to discuss doctrinal drafts that were upcoming in the Council Hall and took into consideration a proposal for an alternative draft on revelation drawn up by two theologians, Karl Rahner and Joseph Ratzinger. Commissioned by the same group, Congar prepared a "preface" to this new draft. Even Jean Daniélou prepared some material for this purpose and Cardinal Suenens asked Archbishop Gerard Philips, professor of ecclesiology, to prepare an alternative draft on the Church, even though this issue was not yet on the agenda and the preparatory schedule had not yet been distributed.

While these council fathers from northern Europe met, Cardinal Siri of Genoa also attempted to organize parallel meetings between the Italians and Spaniards, including the U.S. bishops. They had opposing objectives and were suspicious of these young applauded by those who understand the meaning and importance.... Speaking with some council fathers, it was found that the decision is considered normal and a good sign of the courage of the assembly, and of laziness and lack of preparation on the part of the Secretariat" (Diary of Carlo Ferrari, October 13, 1961).

theologians, including Ratzinger, who was mocked because of his appearance and his speaking voice.

The African bishops, along with those from South and Central America, and from the so-called Third World, engaged themselves more slowly in the dynamics of the council. Fr. Gauthier, who was supported by Bishops George Hakim and Charles-Marie Himmer as well as Cardinal Pierre-Marie Gerlier, took the initiative of arranging a series of meetings between the bishops of the poorest countries so that the council could also hear their voice. The group was inspired by a part of John XXIII's radio message on September 11, and called themselves the "Church of the Poor." Their objective was to raise awareness among the council fathers of the issues of poverty and underdevelopment, issues that they regarded as the most urgent and the most able to engender reform in the Church. Even bishops who did not have time to attend were represented: Cardinal Lercaro, for example, brought Fr. Giuseppe Dossetti to Rome to keep abreast of those discussions.

BIBLIOGRAPHY

A. Duval, *Le message au monde, in Vatican II commence...Approche franco-phones*, Leuven 1993, 105–118; M.-D. Chenu, *Notes quotidiennes au Concile*, édition critique and introduction by A. Melloni, Paris 1995; A. Melloni, "Ecclesiologie al Vaticano II (autunno 1962–estate 1963)," in *Les commissions concili-ares à Vatican II. Colloque de Leuven et Louvain-la-Neuve*, edited by J. Famerée, J. Grootaers, M. Lamberigts, Cl. Soetens, Leuven 1996, 91–179; A. Riccardi, "La tumultuosa apertura dei lavori," in *Storia del concilio Vaticano II*, edited by G. Alberigo (Italian edition edited by A. Melloni), vol. 2, Bologna 1996 (2012), 21–86; G. Alberigo, "Un concile à la dimension du monde: Marie-Dominique Chenu à Vatican II d'apres son journal," in *Marie-Dominique Chenu. Moyen-Âge et modernité*, Paris 1997, 155–172.

1

2. The Jesuit, Karl Rahner (1904–1984), *peritus* at the council (Archivio Fscire).

3. Marie-Dominique Chenu (1895–1990) (Archivio Fscire) first thought of a message of the council fathers to the world. "I thought that there should be an initial declaration of the council, a 'message' to all people, Christians or not, setting out the purpose and dimensions of the current world situation....This would be in the style and consistent with the frequent speeches of John XXIII, in particular his message of September 11" (Diary of Marie-Dominique Chenu, September 10–25, 1962).

4. Joseph Ratzinger, *peritus* for the Archbishop of Cologne, Cardinal Josef Frings, at the time of the council (Archivio Fscire).

2

3

4

19. QUONIAM MULTI: THE COMMISSIONS

According to the Regulations, the council would have had to appoint commissions to examine the corrections to the texts proposed by the council fathers. Before the work of the council began, the entire Curia, the secretary general, and even many experts thought that the conciliar commissions ought to match substantially the groups that had already worked on the texts. Thus, Vatican II could be completed in a few weeks.

But the two presiding cardinals, Achilles Liénart and Josef Frings, taking the pope's speech into account, gave a presentation in which they asked for more time for other nominations in the episcopacy and to foster a climate of "mutual trust" among bishops. The response was surprising: it was greeted by unexpected and thunderous applause. The two speeches—of the pope and the two cardinals—changed the course of the council. The episcopal conferences presented thirty-four lists, thus allowing entry into the commissions of people, some of whom were new and more representative of the theology of the episcopate rather than of Rome. Forty-three percent of those elected had not participated in the preparatory phase.

For each of the ten commissions, the council fathers elected sixteen members, to which were added nine appointed by the pope, bringing the total number to twenty-five members for each commission. Nearly a third of those elected were European: twenty-two Italians, sixteen Frenchmen, eleven Germans, and ten Spaniards. The Latin American episcopate had only twenty-seven elected members (including seven Brazilians), North America twenty-six, Asia sixteen (six Indian), and Africa seven.

Of the ninety fathers chosen by John XXIII, twenty-seven were Italian: to these were added members of the bishops' conferences from Poland, Switzerland, Portugal, and Africa. As a result of these appointments, Italian, Spanish, and U.S. bishops were present in all the commissions. The chairmen, appointed by the pope, were confirmed as those of the preparatory period. There was also a general list of *periti*, which was updated during the council as new experts were nominated, who, for their expertise or good will, were gradually added to the list.

During the first period, on October 22, John XXIII also decided to assimilate into the conciliar commissions the Secretariat for Christian Unity, which the first council Regulations included under "technical administration." However, it maintained its original composition—including those who were not bishops, and therefore were not council fathers like their counterparts—and retained their advisers—some of whom were, in fact, council fathers. Through the Secretariat, the opinions on the drafts of observers from other churches could be heard in the general congregation.

In response to many requests, at the end of the second period, Paul VI decided to expand the number of members on each committee to thirty, adding five to each, four to be elected and one to be nominated by the pope. An exception was the commission for Eastern Churches, which already had twenty-seven; because of previous changes, it was therefore increased by only three. Another exception was the Secretariat for the Unity of Christians. It had had only eighteen members and was increased by another twelve. New members were not integrated into the Committee on the Liturgy, because with the approval of the Constitution on the Sacred Liturgy in 1963, its activities had effectively ceased.

1. A meeting of the theological commission, chaired by Cardinal Ottaviani (photo by Bishop Hermann Volk, Mainz / Archiv der Deutschen der Provinz Jesuiten adpsj). The Belgian Dominican Edward Schillebeeckx described the first meeting in his diary: "First meeting of the new theological commission, chaired by Ottaviani. Ottaviani, Tromp, Parente, Peruzzo appear worried. Ottaviani announces that Cicognani has received 160 letters (in late September) and one hundred are against the theological schema! He says it was the product of hard work, that it's a good schema. Tromp talks about a smear campaign started by Rahner and Schillebeeckx (our text is on the table, mine in English). Parente then asks the committee to launch a counteroffensive!! A sad silence. Then Peruzzo (eighty-four years old) intervenes and says 'I saw the beginning of Modernism. Now we see a new Modernism in action, and we must push it back firmly.' Cardinal Léger (Canada) can't help himself and explodes in anger: 'I can't work under these pressures and insinuations. I resign'" (Diary of Edward Schillebeeckx, November 13, 1962).

2. A meeting of the joint committee (photo by Bishop Hermann Volk, Mainz / Archiv der Deutschen Provinz der Jesuiten adpsj).

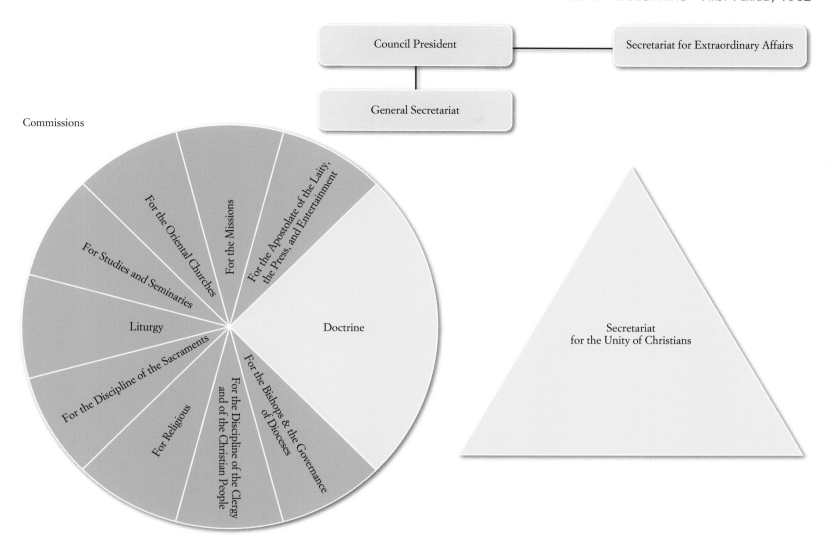

Commissions

The conciliar commissions, through their functions and through the development of the work of Vatican II, were thus bodies that were particularly sensitive to the breadth of the assembly. It was there that the most heated discussions took place on what changes to make, or not make, to the drafts to be discussed in the Council Hall. Those commissions, especially those discussing doctrine, played an important part: such as in the declarations on the theological qualification of documents and the "*nota explicativa praevia*" on the constitution *De Ecclesia*, which was read in the Council Hall at the request of the pope, and which the minority always tried to have regarded as a "document" or even as part of *Lumen Gentium*.

20. The Secretariat for Extraordinary Affairs

Since the first congregations of the council, the General Secretariat had organized the procedural aspects of the sessions: John XXIII's prediction that the Secretary General, Archbishop Pericle Felici, would soon be replaced because of his limited knowledge of languages as had his predecessor at Vatican I, did not come true. He instead immediately showed that he had no power over the debate unless it was on his own initiative—as happened on the first day when Cardinals Achille Liénart and Josef Frings asked that the election of commissions be stopped. Indeed, although the executive council met three days after the council had started, it then met only rarely in the weeks that followed.

To many commentators, the weakness of the executive council and John XXIII's decision not to participate in the meetings, spoke of a council that had no guide, no time for discussion, and no agenda. The failure of commissions to meet—which, according to the Regulations should have occurred only after the debates had finished—gave a sense during the first few weeks that the council was going around in circles.

Some of these fears were well founded. John XXIII had to intervene directly on several occasions, with powers of exemption or by decisions, to resolve procedural impasses, including the issue of voting against the discussion of the Ottaviani commission's draft on the "sources of revelation," which did not reach the two-thirds majority required by the Regulations. This would have forced the council to discuss a text that would never have been approved.

However, an inconspicuous guiding hand did intervene at times: throughout the first period, the so-called Secretariat for Extraordinary Affairs was in play. It was a limited consultation body that gathered a few cardinals from whom John XXIII—who had included it in the Regulations during the summer as the only variation from the structure inherited from Vatican I—asked for various decisions.

The Secretariat for Extraordinary Affairs was chaired by Secretary of State Cardinal Amleto Cicognani, and its members were Cardinal Giuseppe Siri (Genoa), Stefan Wyszyński (Gniezno-Warsaw), Giovanni Battista Montini (Milan), Julius Döpfner (Munich and Freising), Albert Gregory Meyer (Chicago), Léon-Joseph Suenens (Malines-Brussels), and Carlo Confalonieri, a member of the Curia and former secretary of Pius XI. It was an authoritative and representative assembly which convened in audience with Pope John XXIII on October 16, 1962, and received directly from the pope a mandate substantially broader than what was allowed in the Regula-

1

tions. The pope asked them to identify in the works of the sessions major points of importance to develop, to review any additional themes and how acceptable they were compared to those included in the preparatory drafts, and to make suggestions about issues or drafts that were difficult to resolve. On that occasion, John XXIII also entrusted them with reviewing a reminder by Cardinal Bea, President of the Secretariat for Christian Unity, which called for a broader reorganization of the work and the agenda of the council in order to reorient it towards the "eminently pastoral nature" of the teaching defined in the keynote address of October 11. Two days later, Cardinal Montini gave the Secretary of State a long document in which he outlined his proposals for restructuring the council's agenda. Moreover, many of the cardinals from the Secretariat were aware of the "project" prepared by Cardinal Suenens and presented in its turn to John XXIII on how to divide the documents the council would have to approve into two subject areas—the Church *ad intra*, and the Church *ad extra*. In the meeting devoted to considering Bea's document, the Secretariat for Extraordinary Affairs came up with three

1. Cardinal Giuseppe Siri, archbishop of Genoa (Archivio Fscire). On November 5, 1962, Pope John XXIII wrote in his diary: "Individual council fathers are making long comments without having even seen the detailed work, which must be done by the committees that will prepare the final texts of proposals to be submitted to a vote! Ultimately, it makes one uncertain and perplexed about the speed with which the work might be done. At this rate, the whole of 1963 will take care of everything the world desires. The temptation of impatience spreads! Therefore, we must see our way clear to change the system in order to facilitate good work and the preparation of resolutions" (*Diary of John XXIII,* November 5, 1962).

In an interview with Robert Trisco of the Catholic University of America that aired late in the evening of November 10, 1962 as the first episode of the television series *The Church in Council,* the historian of the Council of Trent, Paolo Prodi, tried to give historical context to the role of commissions, highlighting any innovations:

Paolo Prodi: "Had the commissions' working methods already been adopted in previous councils?"

Robert Trisco: "In the first Vatican Council, for the first time in the history of these ecumenical assemblies, there were fixed standing commissions. Four were first established by Pope Pius IX, but their members were all elected at the general assembly by the council fathers. In fact, this procedure was not genuinely representative, as might be expected, because although members of different nationalities had been elected in the commissions, those fathers who were opposed to the declaration—opposed to the definition of papal infallibility—were completely excluded from the composition of the most important one, namely the commission on faith. This maneuver has been criticized by historians as the most serious problem in the First Vatican Council."

Paolo Prodi: "Then, professor, what is the main difference between the current council and Vatican I, with regard to the commissions?"

Robert Trisco: "The most striking difference between the First and the Second Vatican Councils, in terms of the commissions, is the elections system. This time, according to the instructions provided in advance by the Holy Father, the members of the council assembly elected only sixteen members for each committee. And then the pope appointed nine others, not including the chairman. This change may be motivated by a desire to avoid further manifestations of intolerance, such as those that arose in 1869. The appointment by the pope of one-third plus one acquires a special significance, because a two-thirds majority is required to ratify the actions of the commission. In the First Vatican Council a majority of half plus one was considered sufficient."

Paolo Prodi: "The commissions should therefore reflect the general assembly in its vastness and complexity. In this context, what are the functions and the importance of the chairmen of the individual commissions?"

Robert Trisco: "The chairmen of these commissions are the same cardinals who chaired the preparatory commissions that drew up the drafts later approved by the Central Preparatory Commission, and which are now being discussed in the council. In this way, as well as through the appointment and election to the commissions of some of the former members of the advisers to the preparatory commissions, some continuity has been ensured between the preparation and implementation stages of the council. On the other hand, more than one observer has emphasized that these chairmen were chosen in the first place because they were and still are the leaders of the Sacred Congregations of the Roman Curia. Now it is likely that the prelates at the center of the Church see problems differently than bishops around the world. These chairmen certainly enjoy great privileges through the wide-ranging powers conferred on them by the pope in the Regulations. Each commission chairman may appoint a vice chairman to help him or take his place in his absence. He may appoint the commission's secretary from among the experts of the council, he can establish the discussion and voting methods to follow at the commission meetings, and he can choose which fathers or external experts to consult. He also decides what modern languages can be used. The chairman may appoint a speaker who is responsible for presenting and explaining the original draft and subsequent amendments to the general congregations. Finally, he can prepare the draft revision by incorporating the amendments that have been accepted by the general congregations. But we must remember that the influence of the chairman is limited by the rule that requires a two-thirds majority for all decisions made by the commission."

tasks: to discuss the theme of the "Church as mystery"; to guide the decisions of the council in a "pastoral" sense; and to redefine the powers of the executive council. This would give Vatican II a different complexion. There were still other recommendations aimed at drastically reducing the drafts being discussed by the commissions that were not accepted but gave a sense that there could be a different kind of conciliar consensus than what had been imagined by those who had laid the groundwork for the council.

Nevertheless, although the Secretariat for Extraordinary Affairs did not deal with the crisis on the sources of revelation, it decided that all drafts should be submitted first to a general vote before moving on to the discussion of chapters and articles. Even more important was that, in the crucial session on November 30, a list of twenty drafts was approved on which all the future work of the council was to be focused. It was presented to the council fathers on December 5, three days before the close of the session, and it was the first order of business for the future of the council, an order of business that few would have imagined in October.

BIBLIOGRAPHY
G. Alberigo, "Concilio acefalo? L'evoluzione degli organi direttivi del Vaticano II," in *Il Vaticano II. Fra attese e celebrazione,* edited by G. Alberigo, Bologna 1995, 193–240.

21. Governing Bodies and Commissions of the Council

COUNCIL OF PRESIDENTS

Card. Eugène Tisserant	Dean of the College of Cardinals	
Card. Achille Liénart	Lille	FRA
Card. Ignace Gabriel i Tappouni	Patriarch of Antioch in Syria	
Card. Norman Thomas Gilroy	Sidney	AUS
Card. Francis Joseph Spellman	New York	USA
Card. Enrique Pla y Deniel[1]	Toledo	ESP
Card. Josef Frings	Cologne	DEU
Card. Ernesto Ruffini	Palermo	ITA
Card. Antonio Caggiano	Buenos Aires	ARG
Card. Bernard Jan Alfrink	Utrecht	NLD

ADDED IN SECOND PERIOD

Card. Giuseppe Siri	Genoa	ITA
Card. Stephan Wyszyński	Gniezno-Warsaw	POL
Card. Albert Gregory Meyer[2]	Chicago	USA

ADDED IN FOURTH PERIOD

Card. Lawrence Joseph Shehan	Baltimore	USA

1. Participated only in the first period of the council.
2. Participated only in the second and third periods of the council.

GENERAL SECRETARIAT[1]

GENERAL SECRETARY

Most Rev. Pericle Felici	tit. Samosata	ITA

UNDERSECRETARIES

Most Rev. Philippe Nabaa	Beirut and Jbeil (Melkites)	LEB
Most Rev. Casimiro Morcillo González	Zaragoza	ESP
Most Rev. Jean-Marie Villot	coad. Lyon	FRA
Most Rev. John Joseph Krol	Philadelphia	USA
Most Rev. Wilhelm Kempf	Limburg	DEU

1. Lists edited by the Secretariat of the Council report from the second period only.

The following tables contain data collected on the conciliar commissions, as well as from the lists published from time to time by the organs of the Secretariat, with additions from other sources when necessary.

For each committee, the president, secretary, and members are indicated. The names of the members are sorted based on the votes received in the election, integrating them with the members appointed by the pope.

For the elected members the votes received are indicated. Also included are nationalities (generally following the locations of their ministries or sees) and the council sessions in which they participated in their commission.

The number of committee members was established by a special provision of the Regulations, which John XXIII and Paul VI reviewed on several occasions. However, we must consider that these were dynamic organizations, and reality does not always correspond to what was preserved on paper; side by side with the most active members can be found the names of those whose participation was nominal. The schemas that each commission was responsible for are listed: those included in the list of December 1962, those provided after the reorganization of the work of the council by the Coordination Committee in January 1963, and those actually brought to the council hall for discussion and approved.

In all tables, names are preceded by the honorific that generally distinguishes the cardinals, bishops, religious, and lay people. The offices and statuses listed are as they were during the period to which the table refers. If one held several curial offices or ministries, the most significant are shown.

Whenever possible, first names have been rendered in the appropriate modern language. The same is done for names of dioceses. In the case of bishops, where possible, their office in the curia or diocese where they were auxiliaries or apostolic delegates is indicated.

OFFICES OF THE GENERAL SECRETARIAT

OFFICE I: DE SACRIS RITIBUS

Most Rev. Enrico Dante, Prefect of Pontifical Ceremonies, Secretary of the Congregation for Rites

OFFICE II: DE NEGOTIIS PERAGENDIS

NOTARIES

Most Rev. Giuseppe Rossi, tit. Palmira[1]
Most Rev. Annibale Ferretti
Most Rev. Cesare Federici
Most Rev. Raffael Boyer
Most Rev. Alfredo Parisella
Most Rev. Luigi Piovesana

PROMOTORS

Most Rev. Salvatore Natucci
Most Rev. Giuseppe D'Ercole
Most Rev. Giovanni Carrara[2]

SCRUTATORS

Most Rev. Arturo De Jorio
Most Rev. Gerard Rogers
Most Rev. Giuseppe Casoria
Most Rev. Ernesto Civardi
Most Rev. Giovanni Sessolo

1. Third period.
2. Second and third periods only.

OFFICE III: DE ACTIS SCRIBENDIS AC SERVANDIS

Section A	Most Rev. Vincenzo Carbone
	d. Nello Venturini
Section B	Most Rev. Achille Lupi
	Most Rev. Mariano De Nicolò
Section C	Most Rev. Vincenzo Fagiolo
	Most Rev. Marcello Venturi
	D. Giannino Zuliani[3]
Section D	Most Rev. Emilio Governatori
	Most Rev. Nazareno Cinti
	D. Luciano Tosti
	Gianni Malpassi[4]
	Gino Falconetti[5]

Interpreters

Most Rev. A. Lupi, Most Rev. E. Ulinski, Most Rev. E. Francesco Davis, d. A. Koulik, d. J. Feiner, d. F. Thijssen, d. G. Corbon, Fr. E. Lanne OSB, Fr. Anian OSB Cam, Fr. A. da Hebo OFM, Fr.. G. Corr OSB, Fr.. G. Weigel SJ, Fr. M. Bévenot SJ, Fr. D. O'Hanlon SJ, Fr. G. Novack AA, Fr. P. Michalon PSS[6]

Latinists

Most Rev. A. Tondini; Most Rev. G. Del Ton, Most Rev. G. Zannoni, Fr. C. Egger CRL, Most Rev. I. Parisella, Most Rev. R. Gallicani, Most Rev. G. Coppa

OFFICE IV: DE REBUS TECHNICIS

Fr. Antonio Stefanizzi, SJ
Francesco Vacchini
Mauro Ercole

3. Second and third periods only.
4. Part of third period.
5. Part of third period.
6. The last three only in the third period. In the fourth, official interpreters were reduced to two: Most Rev. Achille Lupi e Most Rev. Edmondo Ulinski.

SECRETARIAT FOR EXTRAORDINARY AFFAIRS[1]

PRESIDENT

Card. Amleto Giovanni Cicognani, Secretary of State

MEMBERS

Card. Giuseppe Siri	Genoa	ITA
Card. Stephan Wysziński	Gniezno-Warsaw	POL
Card. G. Battista Montini	Milan	ITA
Card. Carlo Confalonieri, Consistory	Secretary of the Congregation for the	
Card. Julius Döpfner	Munich	DEU
Card. Albert Gregory Meyer	Chicago	USA
Card. Léon-Joseph Suenens	Malines-Brussels	BEL

SECRETARY

Most Rev. Pericle Felici, Secretary-General for the Council

1. Established by the council Rules of 1962.

COMMISSIONE DI COORDINAMENTO[1]

PRESIDENT

Card. Amleto Giovanni Cicognani Secretary of State

MEMBERS

Card. Achille Liénart	Lille	FRA
Card. Grégoire Pierre xv Agagianian	Prefect, Congregation for the Propagation of the Faith	
Card. Francis Spellman	New York	USA
Card. Giacomo Lercaro	Bologna	ITA
Card. Giovanni Urbani	Venice	ITA
Card. Carlo Confalonieri	Secretary for the Congregation for the Consistory	
Card. Julius Döpfner	Munich	DEU
Card. Léon-Joseph Suenens	Malines-Brussels	BEL
Card. Francesco Roberti	Prefect of the Apostolic Signatura	

1. Established by John XXIII after the first period, it began work in January 1963. Meetings were attended by Secretary-General Pericle Felici, the secretaries of the council, with the assistance of Most. Rev. V. Fagiolo.

DELEGATES (OR MODERATORS)[1]

Card. Grégoire Pierre XV Agagianian	Prefect, Congregation for the Propagation of the Faith	
Card. Giacomo Lercaro	Bologna	ITA
Card. Julius Döpfner	Munich	DEU
Card. Léon-Joseph Suenens	Malines-Brussels	BEL

1. Established by Paul VI in his reform of the Rules in 1963.

DOCTRINAL COMMISSION

PRESIDENT
Card. Alfredo Ottaviani, Secretary of the Congregation of the Holy Office

VICE-PRESIDENTS
Card. Michael Browne
Most Rev. André Charue[1]

SECRETARY
Fr. Sebastian Tromp SJ, Professor, Pontifical Gregorian University

MEMBERS

Elected October 1962[2]

Most Rev. Joseph Schröffer	Eichstatt	BRD	1761	****
Most Rev. Gabriel-Marie Garrone	Toulouse	FRA	1738	****
Card. Franz König	Vienna	AUT	1670	****
Most Rev. Jan van Dodewaard	Haarlem	NLD	1537	****
Most Rev. Alfredo Vicente Scherer	Porto Alegre	BRA	1465	****
Card. Paul-Émile Léger	Montréal	CAN	1258	****
Most Rev. Ermenegildo Florit	Florence	ITA	1244	****
Most Rev. John Francis Dearden	Detroit	USA	1189	****
Most Rev. André Charue	Namur	BEL	1138	****
Most Rev. John Joseph Wright	Pittsburgh	USA	1138	****
Most Rev. Marcos Gregorio McGrath	Panamá	PAN	1116	****
Most Rev. James Griffiths	aux. New York	USA	1077	**__
Most Rev. Maurice Roy	Québec	CAN	994	****
Card. Rufino Jiao Santos	Manila	PHL	813	****
Most Rev. Franjo Šeper	Zagreb	YUG	788	****
Most Rev. Giovanni Battista Peruzzo*	Agrigento	ITA	741	*___
Most Rev. Hermann Volk	Mainz	BRD		_***

* Only for the first period, then replaced by Most Rev. H. Volk.

Papal Appointment October 29, 1962[3]

Card. Michael Browne				****
Most Rev. Pietro Parente	Congregation of the Holy Office	ITA		****
Most Rev. Francisco Barbado y Viejo	Salamanca	ESP		**__
Most Rev. Georges Léon Pelletier	Trois Rivières	CAN		****
Most Rev. Franjo Franić	Split-Makarska	YUG		****
Most Rev. Michael Doumith	Sarba (Maronites)	LBN		****
Most Rev. Francesco Spanedda	Bosa	ITA		****
Fr. Benno Gut OSB	Abbot Primate, Benedictine Confederation			****
Fr. Anicetus Fernandez OP	Master General, Dominicans			****

Elected November 28, 1963[4]

Most Rev. Alfred Ancel	Lyon	FRA	1491	__**
Fr. Christopher Butler, OSB	Abbot President, English Benedictine Congregation	GBR	1448	__**
Most Rev. Jozef-Maria Heuschen	aux. Liège	BEL	1160	__**
Most Rev. Luis Enríquez Jiménez	aux. Caracas	VEN	831	__**

Papal Appointment January 8, 1964

Most Rev. Antonio Poma	Mantova	ITA	_	__**

Other Additions[5]

Most Rev. Hermann Volk	Mainz	BRD		_***
Most Rev. Anastasio García Granados	aux. Toledo	ESP		__**
Fr. Anastasio del Santo Rosario OCD (Antonio Ballestrero)	Prior General, Discalced Carmelites	ITA		__**

Preparatory Drafts Proposed by the Council Secretariat (December 5, 1962)[6]

1. De divina revelatione
2. De ecclesia
3. De B. Maria Virgine matre Dei et hominum
4. De deposito fidei pure custodiendo
5. De ordine morali
6. De castitate, virginitate, matrimonio, familia
7. De ordine sociali et de communitate gentium

1. From the third period.
2. AS 1, 1 225–226.
3. AS 1, 1 559.
4. AS 2, 6 306.
5. Bishop Hermann Volk was appointed to the commission to replace Bishop G. B. Peruzzo, who died on July 20, 1963. Bishop Grenados and Fr. Anastasio del Santo Rosario replace Bishop J. Griffiths, who died on February 24, 1964, and Bishop Francisco Barbado y Viejo, who died on April 29, 1964.
6. Schemata constitutionum et decretorum ex quibus argumenta in concilio disceptanda seligentur, in AS 1,1 90–95.

Drafts Assigned by the Coordinating Commission (January 1, 1963)[7]

1. De divina revelatione
2. De ecclesia
3. De B. Maria Virgine, matre ecclesiae
4. De ecclesiae principiis et actione ad bonum societatis promovendum[8]

Documents Produced

Dogmatic Constitution on the Church *Lumen gentium* (Nov. 21, 1964)
Dogmatic Constitution on Divine Revelation *Dei verbum* (Nov. 18, 1965)
Pastoral Constitution on the Church in the Modern World *Gaudium et spes* (Dec. 7, 1965)

7. Elenchus schematum constitutionum et decretorum de quibus disceptabitur in concilii sessionibus, in AS 5,1 201.
8. Together with the Committee for the Lay Apostolate.

COMMISSION FOR BISHOPS AND THE GOVERNANCE OF DIOCESES

PRESIDENT
Card. Paolo Marella, Prefect, Congregation for the Fabric of St. Peter's

VICE PRESIDENTS
Card. James McIntyre
Card. José María Bueno y Monreal

SECRETARY
Most Rev. Lauro Governatori

MEMBERS

Elected Session One[1]

Most Rev. Emile Maurice Guerry	Cambrai	FRA	1807	***
Most Rev. Hermann Josef Schäufele	Freiburg im Breisgau	BRD	1658	****
Most Rev. Michael Browne, OP	Galway and Kilmacduagh	IRL	1634	****
Most Rev. Pierre Marie Veuillot	coad. Paris	FRA	1592	****
Most Rev. George Patrick Dwyer	Leeds	GBR	1582	****
Card. James Francis McIntyre	Los Angeles	USA	1384	****
Most Rev. Miguel Miranda y Gomez	México	MEX	1303	****
Most Rev. Karl Joseph Alter	Cincinnati	USA	1287	****
Most Rev. Marie-Joseph Lemieux	Ottawa	CAN	1285	****
Most Rev. Alberto Castelli	Secy, Italian Bishops' Conference	ITA	1237	****
Most Rev. Giuseppe Piazzi	Bergamo	ITA	1054	*___
Most Rev. Raul Francisco Primatesta	San Rafael	ARG	1035	****
Most Rev. Joseph Gargitter	Bressanone	ITA	999	****
Most Rev. Pablo Correa León	Cucuta COL	918	****	****
Most Rev. Louis Mathias	Madras e Mylapore	IND	745	***_
Card. José María Bueno y Monreal	Seville	ESP	722	****

Papal Appointment October 29, 1962[2]

Most Rev. Peter Tatsuo Doi	Tokyo	JPN		****
Most Rev. Leo Binz	Saint Paul	USA		****
Most Rev. Francesco Carpino	congreg. concistoriale	ITA		****
Most Rev. Victor Bazin	Yangon	MMR		*___
Most Rev. Ignace Antoine II Hayek	Aleppo in Syria	SYR		****
Most Rev. Angelo Fernandes	coad. Dehli	IND		****
Most Rev. Jérôme Louis Rakotomalala	Tananarive	MDG		****
Most Rev. Narciso Jubany Arnau	aux. Barcelona	ESP		****
Most Rev. Luigi Carli	Segni	ITA		****

Elected November 28, 1963[3]

Most Rev. James Patrick Carroll	aux. Sydney	AUS	1738	__**
Most Rev. Eduard Schick	aux. Fulda	BRD	1475	__**
Most Rev. Alfredo Viola	Salto	URY	1173	__**
Most Rev. Owen McCann	Cape Town	ZAF	960	__**

Papal Appointment January 8, 1964

Most Rev. Venedictos Printesis	Athens	GRC	__**

Other Additions[4]

Most Rev. Józef Gawlina	Bishop Emeritus, Polish Military	POL	_*__
Most Rev. Luis Del Rosario	Zamboanga	PHL	_***
Most Rev. Petar Čule	Mostar	YUG	__**
Most Rev. Charles-Marie Himmer	Tournai	BEL	___*

1. AS 1,1 225–226
2. AS 1,1 559.
3. AS 2,6 306–307.
4. In the second period, Bishop Gawlina and Bishop Del Rosario replaced Bishop Piazzi, who died on August 8, 1963, and Bishop Bazil. In the third period, Bishop Cule replaced Bishop Mathias, who died on August 3, 1965.

Preparatory Drafts Proposed by the Council Secretariat (December 5, 1962)[5]

1. De episcopis et dioceseon regimine
2. De cura animarum

Drafts Assigned by the Coordinating Commission (January 30, 1963)[6]

1. De episcopis et dioceseon regimine
2. De cura animarum

Documents Produced

Decree on the Pastoral Office of Bishops *Christus dominus* (October 28, 1965)

5. Schema constitutionum . . . , cit. AS 1,1 92.
6. Elenchus schematum constitutionum…, cit. AS 5,1 201.

COMMISSION ON ORIENTAL CHURCHES[1]

PRESIDENT
Card. Amleto Giovanni Cicognani, Secretary of State

VICE PRESIDENTS
Card. Fernando Quiroga y Palacios
Most Rev. Gabriel Bukatko

SECRETARY
Fr. Atanasij Hryhor OSBM, Superior General, Basilian Order of St. Josaphat

MEMBERS

Elected Session One[2]

Most Rev. Ambrozij Andrew Senyshyn	Philadelphia (Ukrainians)	USA	1432	***
Most Rev. Giuseppe Perniciaro	aux., Eparchy of Piana degli Albanesi (Italo-Albanese)	ITA	1264	***
Fr. Joannes Hoeck OSB	Abbot President, Bavarian Congregation (Benedictine)	BRD	1167	***
Most Rev. Antoni Baraniak	Poznaň	POL	1116	***
Most Rev. Maximos IV Saïgh	Antioch (Melkites)	SYR	1112	***
Most Rev. Gabriel Bukatko	coad. Beograd	YUG	1101	***
Most Rev. Joseph Parecattil	Ernakulam (Syro-Malabarese)	IND	1096	***
Most Rev. Néophytos Edelby	aux. Antioch (Melkites)	SYR	1036	***
Most Rev. Matthew Kavukattu*	Changana-Cherry (Syro-Malabarese)	ITA	724	***
Most Rev. Manuel da Silveira d'Elboux	Curitiba	BRA	1009	***
Most Rev. Ivan Bučko	ap. visitor to Ukrainians in Western Europe		896	***
Most Rev. Andrés Sapelak	ap. visitor, Ukrainians in Argentina		837	***
Card. Fernando Quiroga y Palacios	Santiago di Compostela	ESP	818	***
Most Rev. Benedict Varghese Gregorios Thangalathil	Trivandrum (Syro-Malankarese)	IND	810	***
Most Rev. Bryan Jospeh McEntegart	Brooklyn	USA	754	***
Most Rev. Martien Jansen	Rotterdam	NLD	753	***

* Replaced Most Rev. Theodorus Minisci, Abbot of Santa Maria di Grottaferrata.

Papal Appointment October 10, 1962[3]

Most Rev. Stephanos I Sidarouss	Alexandria (Coptic)	EGY		***
Most Rev. Piérre Paul Meouchi	Antioch (Maronite)	LBN		***
Most Rev. Alberto Gori	Jerusalem (Latin)	PSE		***
Most Rev. Paul II Cheikho	Babylon (Chaldean)	IRQ		***
Most Rev. Ignace Pierre XVI Batanian	Cilicia (Armenian)	LBN		***
Most Rev. Joseph Rabbani	ap. admin. Homs (Syrian)	SYR		***
Most Rev. Asrate Mariam Yemmeru	Addis Abeba (Ethiopian)	ETH		***
Most Rev. Giovanni Battista Scapinelli de Leguigno	tit. Laodicea ad Libanum	ITA		***
Most Rev. Hyakinthos Gad	ap. exarch of Greece	GRC		***

Elected November 28, 1963[4]

Most Rev. Maurice Baudoux	Saint Boniface	CAN	1684	—*
Most Rev. Ignace Ziadé	Beirut (Maronite)	LBN	1677	—*
Most Rev. Charlese-Marie De Provenchères	Aix	FRA	1323	—*

1. Active only during the first three months of the council until the final approval of the decree *Orientalium ecclesiarum* in the public session on November 21, 1964.
2. AS 1,1225–226.
3. AS 1,1 559.
4. AS 2,6 306–307; the committee already had twenty-seven members so only three additional were needed to reach thirty. There was no additional papal appointment.

Other Additions[5]

Card. Gustavo Testa	Secretary of the Congregation for Oriental Churches	ITA	—**
Most Rev. Josyf Slipyj	Lviv (Ukrainian)	UKR	—**

Preparatory Drafts Proposed by the Council Secretariat (December 5, 1962)[6]

1. De ecclesiis orientalibus

Drafts Assigned by the Coordinating Commission (January 30, 1963)[7]

1. De ecclesiis orientalibus

Document Produced

Decree on the Catholic Churches of the Eastern Rite *Orientalium ecclesiarum* (November 21, 1964)

5. Prior to the second period, Cardinal Testa was named Secretary of the Congregation for Oriental Rites.
6. Schemata constitutionum …, cit. in AS 1,1 92.
7. Elenchus schematum …, cit. in AS 5,1 201.

COMMISSION FOR THE DISCIPLINE OF THE SACRAMENTS

PRESIDENT
Card. Benedetto Aloisi Masella, Prefect, Congregation for the Discipline of the Sacraments

VICE PRESIDENTS
Most Rev. Armando Fares
Most Rev. José García y Goldarez

SECRETARY
Fr. Raimondo Bidagor SJ

MEMBERS

Elected Session One[1]

Most Rev. José García Goldaraz	Valladolid	ESP	1737	***_
Most Rev. Josef Schneider	Bamberg	BRD	1673	***_
Most Rev. Joseph McGucken	San Francisco	USA	1602	***_
Most Rev. Franz von Streng	Basel and Lugano	CHE	1407	***_
Most Rev. Armando Fares	Catanzaro	ITA	1400	***_
Most Rev. Valérien Bélanger	aux. Montréal	CAN	1345	***_
Most Rev. Antônio Maria Alves de Siqueira	aux. São Paulo	BRA	1210	***_
Most Rev. Críspulo Benítez Fontúrvel	Barquisimeto	VEN	1030	***_
Most Rev. Jan van Cauwelaert	Inongo	COD	973	***_
Most Rev. Alexandre Renard	Versailles	FRA	963	***_
Most Rev. Aníbal Maricevich Fleitas	aux. Asunción	PRY	946	***_
Most Rev. Pierre-Marie Puech	Caracassonne	FRA	931	***_
Most Rev. Francis Reh	Charleston	USA	890	***_
Most Rev. Lucas Katsu Saburo Arai	Yokohama	JPN	854	***_
Most Rev. Thomas William Muldoon	aux. Sydney	AUS	846	***_
Most Rev. Marc-Armand Lallier	Marseille	FRA	788	***_

Papal Appointment October 29, 1962[2]

Most Rev. Guido Luigi Bentivoglio	Catania	ITA	***_
Most Rev. Angelo Dell'Acqua	Deputy Secretary of State		***_
Most Rev. Caesare Zerba*	Secretary of the Congregation for the Discipline of the Sacraments	ITA	***_
Most Rev. Paul Yoshigoro Taguchi	Osaka	JPN	***_
Most Rev. Danio Bolognini	Cremona	ITA	***_
Most Rev. João Chedid	Patriarcal Vicar of Maronites in Brazil	BRA	***_
Most Rev. Marcello Morgante Ascoli	Piceno	ITA	***_
Most Rev. Michael Kien	Samophithak	THA	***_
Most Rev. Juan Félix Pepén y Soliman	N.S. de la Altagracia en Higüey	DOM	***_

* Created cardinal Feb. 22, 1965.

Elected November 28, 1963[3]

Most Rev. Juan Hervás y Benet	Ciudad Real	ESP	1470	—*_
Most Rev. John Edward Taylor	Stockholm	SWE	1463	—*_
Most Rev. Pieter Moors	Roermond	NLD	1257	—*_
Most Rev. Joannes de Reeper	pref. Ngong	KEN	1178	—*_

Papal Appointment January 8, 1964

Most Rev. Afonso Espino y Silva	Monterrey	MEX	—*_

Due to the decision to defer the issue of the sacrament of marriage to the revision of the Code of Canon Law, the commission ceased activity during the third period

1. AS 1,1 260.
2. AS 1,1 559.
3. AS 2,6 306–307.

Preparatory Drafts Proposed by the Council Secretariat (December 5, 1962)[4]
1. De matrimonii sacramento

Drafts Assigned by the Coordinating Commission (January 30, 1963)[5]
1. De matrimonii sacramento

Documents Produced
(none)

---

4. Schemata constitutionum et decretorum ex quibus argumenta in concilio disceptanda seligentur, in AS 1,1 90–95.
5. Elenchus schematum constitutionum et derectorumde quibus disceptabitur in concilii sessionibus, in AS 5,1 201.

COMMISSION FOR THE DISCIPLINE OF THE CLERGY AND THE CHRISTIAN PEOPLE

President
Card. Pietro Ciriaci, Prefect of the Congregation for the Council

Vice Presidents
Card. Alfonso Castaldo
Card. Joseph Elmer Ritter

Secretary
Fr. Alvaro del Portillo, Secretary General of Opus Dei

Members

Elected Session One[1]

Most Rev. Henri-Marie Mazerat	Angers	FRA	1493	****
Most Rev. Alfred Bengsch	Berlin	DEU	1368	****
Most Rev. Henric Maria Janssen	Hildesheim	BRD	1315	****
Most Rev. Miguel Raspanti	Morón	ARG	1240	****
Most Rev. León Lommel	Luxembourg	LUX	1174	****
Card. Joseph Elmer Ritter	Saint Louis	USA	1165	****
Most Rev. Philip Francis Pocock	coad. Toronto	CAN	1160	****
Most Rev. Lawrence Joseph Shehan*	Baltimore	USA	1135	**___
Most Rev. Luis Baccino	San José de Mayo	URY	1129	****
Most Rev. Guillaume Marie van Zuylen	Liège	BEL	1107	****
Most Rev. Norberto Perini	Fermo	ITA	1076	****
Most Rev. Enrico Nicodemo	Bari	ITA	1066	****
Most Rev. Agnelo Rossi**	Ribeirão Preto	BRA	1045	****
Most Rev. Vicente Enrique y Tarancón***	Solsona	ESP	929	****
Most Rev. François Marty	Reims	FRA	869	****
Most Rev. Emanuele Trindade Salgueiro	Èvora	PRT	851	****

* Created cardinal February 22, 1965.
** Made archbishop of São Paulo on January 11, 1964, created cardinal on February 22, 1965.
*** Became bishop of Oviedo April 12, 1964.

Papal Appointment October 29, 1962[2]

Card. Alfonso Castaldo	Naples	ITA		****
Most Rev. Thomas Benjamin Cooray*	Colombo	LKA		****
Most Rev. Paul Nguyên-van-Binh	Saigon	VNM		****
Most Rev. Pietro Palazzini	Secretary of the Congregation for the Council	ITA		****
Most Rev. Charles Pasquale Greco	Alexandria	USA		****
Most Rev. Pio Alberto Fariña Fariña	aux. Santiago del Chile	CHL		****
Most Rev. Ángel Temiño Saiz	Orense	ESP		****
Most Rev. Ernesto Corripio Ahumada	Ciudad Victoria–Tamaulipas	MEX		****
Most Rev. José Maximio Eusebio Domínguez y Rodríguez	Matanzas	CUB		****

* Created cardinal February 25, 1965.

Elected November 28, 1963[3]

Most Rev. Bernardin Gantin	Cotonou	BEN	1587	—**
Most Rev. Paul Rusch	ap. admin. Innsbruck	AUT	1510	—**
Most Rev. Julio Rosales	Cebu	PHL	1426	—**
Most Rev. William John Conway*	Armagh	GBR	1371	—**

* Created cardinal February 25, 1965.

Papal Appointment January 8, 1964

Most Rev. Antoine Pierre Khoraiche	Sidone (Maronites)	LBN		—**

Other Additions[4]

Laurentius Satoshi Nagae	Urawa	JPN		—**

1. AS 1,1 225–226.
2. AS 1,2 559.
3. AS 2,6 306–307.
4. In the third period, Bishop Satoshi Nagae replaced the Bishop Joseph Shehan, who moved to the Secretariat for the Unity of Christians.

Preparatory Drafts Proposed by the Council Secretariat (December 5, 1962)[5]
1. De clericis

Drafts Assigned by the Coordinating Committee (January 30, 1963)[6]
1. De clericis

Documents Produced
Decree on the Ministry and Life of Priests *Presbyterorum ordinis* (December 7, 1965).

---

5. Schemata constitutionum et decretorum ex quibus argumenta in concilio disceptanda seligentur, in AS 1,1 92.
6. Elenchus schematum constitutionum et derectorum de quibus disceptabitur in concilii sessionibus, in AS 5,1 201.

COMMISSION FOR RELIGIOUS

President
Card. Valerio Valeri, Prefect of the Congregation for Religious

Vice Presidents
Card. Juan Landázuri Ricketts
Most Rev. Karl Leiprecht

Secretary
Fr. Joseph Rousseau OMI

Members

Elected Session One[1]

Most Rev. Gérard Huyghe	Arras	FRA	1804	****
Most Rev. Karl Leiprecht	Rottenburg	BRD	1736	****
Most Rev. Arturo Tabera Araoz	Albacete	ESP	1587	****
Most Rev. Girolamo Bortignon	Padova	ITA	1321	****
Card. Juan Landázuri Ricketts	Lima	PER	1145	****
Most Rev. George Beck	Salford	GBR	1099	****
Fr. Benedikt Reetz, OSB	Abbot President, Beuronese Congregation (Benedictine)	BRD	1089	***_
Most Rev. Bernardino Echeverría Ruiz	Ambato	ECU	1053	****
Most Rev. George Bernard Flahiff	Winnipeg	CAN	1045	****
Most Rev. Edward Daly	Des Moines	USA	1040	***_
Most Rev. Benedict Takahiko Tomizawa	Sapporo	JPN	1019	****
Most Rev. Joseph-Martin Urtasun	Avignon	FRA	1000	****
Fr. Augustin Sépinski, OFM	Minister General, Franciscans	FRA	934	****
Most Rev. Thomas Cahill	Cairns	AUS	919	****
Most Rev. Joseph Mark McShea	Allentown	USA	907	****
Most Rev. Paolo Botto	Cagliari	ITA	884	****

Papal Appointment October 29, 1962[2]

Most Rev. Lorenz Jäger*	Paderborn	BRD		——
Most Rev. Paul Pierre Philippe	Secretary, Congregation for Religious	FRA		****
Most Rev. Louis Séverin Haller, CRA	Abbot of Saint-Maurice	CHE		****
Most Rev. Enrico Compagnone	Anagni	ITA		****
Most Rev. Dominic Vendargon	Kuala Lumpur	MYS		****
Most Rev. Ceslao Sipović, MIC**	tit. Mariamme	POL		****
Fr. Sighard Kleiner OCist	Abbot General, Cistercians	AUS		****
Fr. Jean-Baptiste Janssens, SJ	Superior General, Jesuits	BEL		***_
Fr. Renato Ziggiotti SDB	Rector Major, Salesians	ITA		***_

* Since Bishop Jäger was already part of the Secretariat for the Unity of Christians, he was replaced early on by Bernard Mels, Archbishop of Luluabourg.
** Superior General of Marian Fathers of the Immaculate Conception as of July 2, 1963.

Elected November 28, 1963[3]

Most Rev. Gerald McDevitt	aux. Philadelphia	USA	1543	—**
Most Rev. Bernhard Stein	aux. Trier	BRD	1454	—**
Most Rev. Luigi Borromeo	Pesaro	ITA	1240	—**
Most Rev. Joseph Marie Cordeiro	Karachi	PAK	1222	—**

Papal Appointment January 8, 1964

Most Rev. Pacifico Perantoni, OFM	Lanciano e Ortona	ITA		—**

Other Additions[4]

Most Rev. Bernard Mels	Luluabourg	Congo		****
Most Rev. Cornelius Lucey	Cork and Ross	IRL		——*
Fr. Pedro Arrupe, SJ	Superior General, Jesuits	ESP		——*
Fr. Luigi Riccieri	Rector Major, Salesians	ITA		——*

---

1. AS 1,1 260.
2. AS 1,1 559.
3. AS 2,6 307.
4. After the first period, Bishop Mels replaced Bishop Jäger. Later, Bishops Salinas Fuenzalida and Lucey replaced Bishop Daly, who died on November 23, 1964, and Abbot Reetz, who died on December 28, 1964. Fr. Arrupe succeeded Fr. Janssens, who died on October 5, 1964, and Fr. Riccieri succeeded Fr. Ziggiotti, whose term as general of the Salesians ended In April 1965.

Preparatory Drafts Proposed by the Council Secretariat (May 5, 1962)[5]

1. De statibus perfectioni adquirendae (seu De Religiosis)

Drafts assigned by the Coordinating Commission (January 30, 1963)[6]

1. De religiosis

Documents Produced

Decree on the Renewal of Religious Life *Perfectae caritatis* (October 28, 1965)

---

5. Schemata constitutionum et decretorum ex quibus argumenta in concilio disceptanda seligentur, in AS 1,1 93.

6. Elenchus schematum constitutionum et derectorum de quibus disceptabitur in concilii sessionibus, in AS 5,1 201.

COMMISSION FOR MISSIONS

PRESIDENT

Card. Grégoire-Pierre XV Agagianian, Patriarch of Cilicia (Armenians); Prefect, Congregation for the Propagation of the Faith.

VICE PRESIDENTS

Most Rev. Vittore Sartre
Most Rev. José Lecuona Labandibar

SECRETARY

Most Rev. Saverio Paventi

MEMBERS

Elected Session One[1]

Most Rev. Jean Zoa	Yaoundé	CMR	1403	****
Card. Laurean Rugambwa	Bukoba	TZA	1347	****
Most Rev. Guy Riobé	coad. Orléans	FRA	1229	****
Most Rev. Fulton Sheen	aux. New York	USA	1216	****
Most Rev. Aurelio Signora	Prelate Nullius of Pompei	ITA	1110	****
Most Rev. Alfonso Manuel Escalante y Escalante	ap. vicar Pando	BOL	1062	****
Card. Thomas Tien Ken-Sin	Beijing; ap. admin. Taipei	CHN	1042	****
Most Rev. Maurice Perrin	Carthage	TUN	954	****
Most Rev. Alfonso Maria Ungarelli	prelate nullius Pinheiro	BRA	930	****
Most Rev. Gaetano Pollio	Otranto	ITA	871	****
Most Rev. Mariano Rossel y Arellano	Guatemala	GTM	860	***_
Most Rev. Juan Sison	coad. Nueva Segovia	PHL	801	****
Most Rev. Pius Kerketta	Ranchi	IND	801	****
Most Rev. José Lecuona Labandibar	Superior General, St. Francis Xavier Spanish Institute for Foreign Missions	ESP	766	****
Most Rev. Luciano Pérez Platero	Burgos	ESP	744	*___
Most Rev. Oscar Sevrin	emeritus Raigarh-Ambikapur	IND	706	****

Papal Appointment October 29, 1962[2]

Card. Manuel Gonçalves Cerejeira	Patriarch of Lisbon	PRT		****
Most Rev. Lawrence Leo Graner	Dacca	BGD		****
Most Rev. Pietro Sigismondi	Secretary of the Congreagtion for the Propagation of the Faith			****
Most Rev. Victor Alphonse Sartre	Emeritus, Tananarive	MDG		****
Most Rev. Bernard Yago	Abidjan	CIV		****
Most Rev. Pierre-Martin Ngô-dinh-Thûc	Huê	VNM		****
Most Rev. Albert Soegijapranata	Semerang	IDN		*___
Most Rev. Stanislaus Lokuang	Tainan	TWN		****
Fr. Léo Deschâtelets OMI	Superior General, Oblates of Mary Immaculate	CAN		****

Elected November 28, 1963[3]

Fr. Johannes Schütte SVD	Superior General, Divine Word Missionaries	BRD	1645	—**
Most Rev. Eugene Louis D'Souza	Bhopal	IND	1417	—**
Most Rev. John William Comber MM	Superior General, Foreign Mission Society of America (Maryknoll),	USA	1063	—**
Most Rev. Ignatius John Doggett	vic ap. Aitape	PNG	833	—**

Papal Appointment January 8, 1964

Most Rev. Charles Cavallera	Nyeri	KEN		—**

---

1. AS 1,1 225–226.
2. AS 1,1 559.
3. AS 2,6 306–307.

Other Additions[4]

Most Rev. Adolf Bolte	Fulda	BRD	_***	_***
Most Rev. Emanuel Mabathoama	Maseru	LSO	—**	—**
Fr. Gerald Mahon	Superior General, St. Joseph's Missionary Society of Mill Hill	GBR	—*	—*

Preparatory Drafts Proposed by the Council Secretariat (December 12, 1962)[5]

1. De missionibus

Drafts Assigned by Coordinating Commission (January 30, 1963)[6]

1. De missionibus

Documents Produced

Decree on the Missionary Activity of the Church *Ad gentes* (December 7, 1965)

---

4. Bishop Bolte and Fr. Schütte (the latter only for the third period) replaced Bishop Pérez Platero, who died on June 14, 1963, and Bishop Soegijapranata, who died on July 22, 1963. In the final period, Fr. Mahon replaced Bishop Rossell y Arellano, who died on December 10, 1964.

5. Schemata constitutionum et decretorum ex quibus argumenta in concilio disceptanda seligentur, in AS 1,1 95.

6. Elenchus schematum constitutionum et derectorum de quibus disceptabitur in concilii sessionibus, in AS 5,1 201.

LITURGICAL COMMISSION

PRESIDENT

Card. Arcadio Larraona Saralegui, Major Penitentiary

VICE PRESIDENTS

Card. Paolo Giobbe
Card. André-Damien Jullien

SECRETARY

Fr. Ferdinando Antonelli OFM

MEMBERS

Elected Session One

Most Rev. Franz Zauner	Linz	AUT	2231	**—
Most Rev. Carlo Rossi	Biella	ITA	1954	**—
Most Rev. Karel Justinus Calewaert	Ghent	BEL	1919	**—
Most Rev. Henri Jenny	aux. Cambrai	FRA	1792	**—
Most Rev. Otto Spülbeck	Meissen	GER	1553	**—
Most Rev. Francis Grimshaw	Birmingham	GBR	1515	**—
Most Rev. Paul Hallinan	Atlanta	USA	1347	**—
Most Rev. Wilhelm van Bekkum	Ruteng	IDN	1338	**—
Most Rev. Joseph Albert Malula	aux. Léopoldville*	COD	1083	**—
Card. Giacomo Lercaro	Bologna	ITA	1082	**—
Most Rev. Alfred Pichler	Banjaluka	YUG	1023	**—
Most Rev. Enrique Rau	Mar del Plata	ARG	1018	**—
Most Rev. Franciszek Jop	aux. Sandomierz	POL	872	**—
Most Rev. Jesús Enciso Viana	Majorca	ESP	835	**—
Most Rev. Joseph Albertus Martin	Nicolet	CAN	804	**—
Most Rev. Cesario D'Amato OSB	Abbot, St. Paul Outside the Walls	ITA	795	**—

* As of July 7, 1964.

Papal Appointment

Card. Paolo Giobbe	Apostolic Datary	ITA		**—
Card. André Damien Jullien	Dean, Roman Rota	FRA		**—
Card. Joaquín Anselmo Albareda y Ramoneda	Prefect, Vatican Library	ESP		**—
Most Rev. Enrico Dante	Secretary, Congregation for Rites	ITA		**—
Most Rev. Bernardo Fey Schneider	coad. Potosi	BOL		**—
Most Rev. Ramón Masnou Boixeda	Vic	ESP		**—
Most Rev. Willem Bekkers	's-Hertogenbosch	NLD		**—
Fr. Jean Prou OSB	Abbot President, Solesmes Congregation (Benedictine)	FRA		**—
Fr. Peter Schweiger SMF	Superior General, Claretians			**—

Its work completed in the second period, new members were not elected on November 11, 1963.

Preparatory Drafts Proposed by the Council Secretariat (December 5, 1962)[1]

1. De sacra liturgia

Drafts Assigned by the Coordinating Commission (January 30, 1963)[2]

1. De sacra liturgia

Documents Produced

Constitution on the Sacred Liturgy *Sacrosanctum concilium* (December 4, 1963)

---

1. Schemata constitutionum et decretorum ex quibus argumenta in concilio disceptanda seligentur, in AS 1,1 90–95.

2. Elenchus schematum constitutionum et derectorum de quibus disceptabitur in concilii sessionibus, in AS 5,1 201.

COMMISSION FOR SEMINARIES, STUDIES, AND CATHOLIC SCHOOLS

PRESIDENT
Card. Giuseppe Pizzardo, Prefect, Congregation for Seminaries and Universities; Secretary of the Congregation of the Holy Office

VICE PRESIDENTS
Card. Jaime De Barros Câmara
Most Rev. Dino Staffa

SECRETARY
Fr. Augustin Mayer OSB

MEMBERS

Elected Session One[1]

Most Rev. Patrick Aloysius O'Boyle	Washington	USA	2059	****
Most Rev. Alfredo Silva Santiago	Concepción	CHL	1750	****
Most Rev. Marcelino Olaechea	Valencia	ESP	1495	****
Most Rev. Joseph Höffner	Münster	BRD	1462	****
Most Rev. Jules Daem	Antwerp	BEL	1177	****
Most Rev. Michal Klepacz	Łódź	POL	1152	****
Most Rev. John Patrick Cody*	aux. New Orleans	USA	1123	****
Most Rev. Giovanni Colombo**	aux. Milan	ITA	1090	****
Most Rev. Argaña Ramón Bogarín	San Juan Bautista de las Misiones	PRY	947	****
Most Rev. Denis Eugene Hurley	Durban	ZAF	930	****
Most Rev. Antoine-Marie Cazaux	Luçon	FRA	927	****
Most Rev. Emile-Arsène Blanchet	Saint-Dié	FRA	914	****
Most Rev. Octaviano Márquez y Tóriz	Puebla de los Ángeles	MEX	899	****
Most Rev. Vicente Marchetti Zioni***	aux. São Paulo	BRA	804	****
Most Rev. Arrigo Pintonello	Military Ordinariate, Italy	ITA	802	****
Most Rev. Marius Paré	Chicoutimi	CAN	781	****

* Bishop of Chicago as of June 14, 1965.
** Ordinary as of August 10, 1963; created cardinal February 22, 1965.
*** Bishop of Bauru as of March 25, 1964.

Papal Appointment October 29, 1962[2]

Card. Jaime de Barros Câmara	São Sebastião do Rio de Janeiro	BRA	****
Most Rev. Ernesto Sena de Oliveira	Coimbra	PRT	****
Most Rev. Gregorio Modrego y Casáus	Barcelona	ESP	****
Most Rev. Justin Daniel Simonds	coad. Melbourne	AUS	****
Most Rev. John Christopher Cody	London	CAN	****
Most Rev. Tulio Botero Salazar	Medellín	COL	****
Most Rev. Dino Staffa	Secretary, Congregation for Seminaries and Universities	ITA	****
Most Rev. Giuseppe Carraro	Verona	ITA	****
Most Rev. Paolo Savino	aux. Naples	ITA	****

Elected November 28, 1963[3]

Most Rev. Franz Jáchym	coad. Vienna	AUT	1674	—**
Most Rev. Loras Thomas Lane	Rockford	USA	1581	—**
Most Rev. Bernard Patrick Wall	Brentwood	GBR	1150	—**
Most Rev. José Maurer	Sucre	BOL	1050	—**

Papal Appointment January 8, 1964

Fr. Paul Joseph Hoffer	Superior General, Marianists	FRA	—**

Other Additions[4]

Most Rev. François-Nestor Adam	Sion	CHE	—**
Most Rev. František Tomášek	ap. admin. Prague	CZE	—*

Preparatory Drafts Proposed by the Council Secretariat (December 5, 1962)[5]
1. De sacrorum alumnis formandis
2. De studiis academicis et de scholis catholicis

Drafts Assigned by Coordinating Commmission (January 30, 1963)[6]
1. De sacrorum alumnis formandis
2. De scholis catholicis

Documents Produced
1. Decree on Priestly Training *Optatam totius* (October 28, 1965)
2. Declaration on Christian Education *Gravissimum educationis* (October 28, 1965)

1. AS 1,1 260–261.
2. AS 1,1 559.
3. AS 2,6 306–307.
4. In the third period, Bishop Adam replaced Bishop John Christopher Cosy, who died on December 12,1963. In the last period of the council, Bishop Tomášek of Prague would be added, bringing the number of commission members to thirty-one.
5. Schemata constitutionum et decretorum ex quibus argumenta in concilio disceptanda seligentur, in AS 1,1 90–95.
6. Elenchus schematum constitutionum et derectorum de quibus disceptabitur in concilii sessionibus, in AS 5,1 201.

COMMISSION FOR THE APOSTOLATE OF THE LAITY, FOR THE PRESS AND ENTERTAINMENT

PRESIDENT
Card. Fernando Cento Major Penitentiary

VICE PRESIDENTS
Card. Raul Silva Henriquez
Most Rev. Martin John O'Connor

SECRETARY
Most Rev. Achille Marie Glorieux

MEMBERS

Elected Session One[1]

Most Rev. Franz Hengsbach	Essen	BRD	1849	****
Most Rev. Jacques Ménager	Meaux	FRA	1530	****
Most Rev. José Armando Gutierrez Granier*	aux. La Paz	BOL	1509	****
Card. Stefan Wyszyński**	Gniezno–Warsaw	POL	1455	——
Most Rev. Ángel Herrera y Oria***	Malaga	ESP	1362	****
Most Rev. Stefan László	Eisenstadt	AUT	1246	****
Most Rev. Evasio Colli	Parma	ITA	1223	****
Most Rev. William Edward Cousins	Milwaukee	USA	1169	****
Most Rev. John Edward Petit	Menevia	GBR	956	****
Most Rev. Martin John O'Connor	Rector, Pontifical North American College	USA	890	****
Most Rev. Manuel Larraín Errázuriz	Talca	CHL	871	****
Most Rev. Gerardus Henricus De Vet	Breda	NLD	866	****
Most Rev. Eugênio De Araújo Sales	ap. admin. Natal****	BRA	832	****
Most Rev. Joseph Blomjous	Mwanza	TZA	810	****
Most Rev. Paul Yü Pin	Nanking	CHN	783	****
Card. Raúl Silva Henriquez	Santiago del Chile	CHL	780	****

* Named bishop of Cochabamba August 19, 1965.
** Replaced by Thomas Morris, who had 672 votes.
*** Created cardinal, February 22, 1965.
**** As of July 9, 1964, ap. admin. of São Salvador da Bahia.

Papal Appointment October 29, 1962

Most Rev. Antonio Samorè	Secretary of the Congregation for Extraordinary Ecclesiastical Affairs	ITA	****
Most Rev. Ismaele Mario Castellano	Siena	ITA	****
Most Rev. Eduard Nécsey	ap. admin. Nitra	SVK	****
Most Rev. Herbert Bednorz	coadj. Katowice	POL	****
Most Rev. René-Louis-Marie Stourm	Sens	FRA	****
Most Rev. Bolesław Kominek	aux. Breslavia	POL	****
Most Rev. Sebastian Vallopilly	Tellicherry	IND	****
Most Rev. Emilio Guano	Livorno	ITA	****
Most Rev. Luigi Civardi	tit. Tespia	ITA	****

Elected November 28, 1963[2]

Most Rev. José Pedro da Silva	aux. Lisbona; coadj. Goa and Damão (India)*	PRT	1632	—**
Most Rev. Manuel Fernández-Conde	Cordoba	ESP	1491	—**
Most Rev. Allen James Babcock	Grand Rapids	USA	1387	—**
Most Rev. Hélder Pessôa Camara**	aux. Rio de Janeiro	BRA	1100	—**

* Bishop of Viseu as of February 13, 1965.
** Bishop of Olinda e Recife as of March 12, 1964.

Papal Appointment January 8, 1964

Fr. Wilhelm Möhler, SAC	Rector General, Pallotines	DEU	—**

Other Additions[3]

Most Rev. Thomas Morris	Cashel and Emly	IRL	672	****

Preparatory Drafts Proposed by the Council Secretariat (December 5, 1962)[4]
1. De laicis
2. De instrumentis communicationis socialis

Drafts Assigned by Coordinating Commission (January 30, 1963)[5]
1. De apostolatu laicorum
2. De instrumentis communicationis socialis
3. De ecclesiae principiis et actione ad bonum societatis promovendum (with the Doctrinal Commission)

Documents Produced
1. Decree on the Instruments of Social Communication *Inter mirifica* (December 4, 1963)
2. Decree on the Apostolate of the Laity *Apostolicam actuositatem* (November 18, 1965)
3. Pastoral Constitution on the Church in the Modern World *Gaudium et spes* (December 7, 1965)

1. AS 1,1 225–226.
2. AS 2,6 306–307.
3. Bishop Thomas Morris replaced Cardinal Wyszyńki, who had resigned.
4. Schemata constitutionum et decretorum ex quibus argumenta in concilio disceptanda seligentur, in AS 1,1 93, 95.
5. Elenchus schematum constitutionum et derectorum de quibus disceptabitur in concilii sessionibus, in AS 5,1 201.

SECRETARIAT FOR THE UNITY OF CHRISTIANS

PRESIDENT
Card. Augustin Bea

VICE PRESIDENTS
Most Rev. John Carmel Heenan
Most Rev. Emiel-Jozef De Smedt

SECRETARY
Most Rev. Johannes Willebrands tit. Mauriana

At the beginning of the Council, the Secretariat for Christian Unity was added to the other conciliar commissions by an act of John XXIII. Members were elected as for other commissions, and it retained the same composition as it had in the preparatory period, with the addition of four new members. Not all members were necessarily bishops or council fathers; in the second period they were included in a separate list. Here we also consider them separately.

MEMBERS

Most Rev. Lorenz Jäger	Paderborn	BRD	****
Most Rev. Joseph-Marie Martin	Rouen	FRA	****
Most Rev. John Carmel Heenan	Liverpool	GBR	****
Most Rev. François Charrière	Lausanne, Geneva and Fribourg	CHE	****
Most Rev. Emiel-Jozef De Smedt	Bruges	BEL	****
Most Rev. Gerard van Velsen	Kroonstad	ZAF	****
Most Rev. Pieter Antoon Nierman	Groningen	NLD	****
Most Rev. Thomas Holland	coad. Portsmouth	GBR	****

Members Added During the First Period[1]

Most Rev. Angelo Prinetto	ap. admin. of Loreto	ITA	****
Most Rev. Andrei Apollon Katkoff	tit. Nauplia	USSR	****
Most Rev. Clément Ignace Mansourati*	aux. Antioch (Syrians)	LBN	
Fr. Teodoro Minisci	Abbot of Santa Maria di Grottaferrata	ITA	****

* Named bishop July 6, 1963.

Additions During First Intersessional Period[2]

Most Rev. Angelo Rotta	tit. Thebes (Greek)	ITA	_**_
Most Rev. Lawrence Joseph Shehan	Baltimore	USA	_***

Elected November 28, 1963[3]

Most Rev. Maxim Hermaniuk	Winnipeg (Ukrainians)	CAN	1641	—**
Most Rev. Charles Herman Helmsing	Kansas City	USA	1406	—**
Most Rev. John Willem Gran	coad. Oslo	NOR	1351	—**
Most Rev. Pedro Catero Cuadrado*	Huelva	ESP	1148	—**
Most Rev. Ernest John Primeau	Manchester	USA	1127	—**
Most Rev. Leo Arlindo Lorscheider	Santo Angelo	BRA	952	—**
Most Rev. Gilbert Ramanantoanina	Fianarantsoa	MDG	947	—**
Most Rev. Donal Raymond Lamont	Umtali	RSR	911	—**

* Bishop of Saragoza as of May 20, 1964.

Papal Appointment January and February 1964[4]

Most Rev. Raphaël Rabban	Kerkük (Chaldeans)	IRQ	—**
Most Rev. William Andrew Hart	Dunkeld	GBR	—**
Fr. Basil Herman Heiser OFM	Superior General, Conventual Franciscans	USA	—**
Fr. Omer Degrijse CICM	Superior General, Congregation of the Immaculate Heart of Mary	BEL	—**
Card. José Humberto Quintero	Caracas	VEN	—**
Most Rev. Gabriel Wilhelmus Manek	Endeh	IDN	—**
Most Rev. Leonard Joseph Raymond	Nagpur	IND	—**
Most Rev. Josef Stangl	Würzburg	BRD	—**

Other Additions[5]

Most Rev. Luigi Centoz	Vice Chamberlain of the Apostolic Chamber	ITA	—*

---

1. Conciliar commissions by the Secretariat, 1962. The last three members chosen by the pope were from among the members of the Prepartory Commission for the Oriental Churches (cf. Caprile 2, 2, 68).
2. During the second period, members of the Secretariat included Cardinals Marella, Head, and Antoniutti, but as of the third period, they were designated "honorary members" and did not affect the total members of the Secretariat. Dearden (Detroit–USA) was also named, but he was already part of the Doctrinal Commission and did not participate in the work of the Secretariat.
3. AS 2,6 307.
4. Cfr. Caprile 3, 281, 319.
5. Bishop Centoz replaced Bishop Rotta, who died on February 1, 1965.

SECRETARIAT MEMBERS WHO WERE NOT COUNCIL FATHERS

OCTOBER 1962

Most Rev. Henri Ewers,	auditor, Roman Rota
Most Rev. Joseph Hoefer.	Prof. of Dogmatic History and Ecumenical Theology, University of Paderborn, Germany
Most Rev. Michele Maccarrone,	Prof. of Church history at the Pontifical Lateran University
Fr. Gustave Thils,	Prof. of Dogmatic Theology, University of Louvain, Belgium
Fr. Leo Rudloff OSB,	Abbot of Dormition Abbey, Palestine
Fr. Charles Boyer SJ,	Prof. at the Pontifical Gregorian University
Fr. Gerard M. Corr OSM,	Great Britain

Added after the First Period

Fr. Édouard Beauduin,	Director, Oeuvre d'Orient, Belgium
Fr. Hans Gerard Remmers,	Founder Catholic Union and Prof. of Ecumenism, University of Munster, Germany
Fr. Emmanuel Lanne,	Monastery of Chevetogne, Belgium
Fr. George C. Anawati OP,	Islamic studies
Fr. Joseph Gill SJ,	Great Britain
Fr. Alfonso Raes SJ,	Rector, Pontifical Oriental College

Additional Listing

Most Rev. William Andrew Hart	Dunkeld, Scotlanda
Most Rev. Hermann Volk	Mainz, Germany
Most Rev. Eduard Stakemeier	Director, Johann Adam Möhler Institut of Paderborn, Germany
Most Rev. Henry Francis Davis	Great Britain
Most Rev. John M. Oesterreicher	Director, Institute of Judaeo-Christian Studies, USA
Most Rev. Janez Vodopivec	Prof. Pontifical University Urbaniano
Fr.. Alberto Bellini	Prof. of Episcopal Seminary of Bergamo, Italy
Fr. Johannes Feiner	Prof., Seminary of Coira, Switzerland
Fr. Franz Thijssen	Holland
Fr. Pierre Dumont OSB	Rector, Pontifical Greek College
Fr. Christophe Dumont OP	Director, Istina Center for Studies, France
Fr. Jean Jérôme Hamer OP	Rector, Dominican Faculty at Saulchoir, France
Fr. Gregory Baum OSA	Saint Basil Seminary, Toronto (Canada)
Fr. Maurice Bévenot SJ	Prof., Heythrop College, England
Fr. Gustave A. Weigel SJ	Prof. of Fundamental Theology, Woodstock College, USA
Fr. George H. Tavard AA	Mount Mercy College, Pittsburgh, USA
Fr. Edward F. Hanahoe SA	USA
Fr. Werner Becker	Oratory of Leipzig, Germany
Fr. Stéphane Diebold CM	Superior, Major Seminary of Montpellier, France
Fr. Pierre Michalon PSS	Director of University Seminary of Lyon, France
Msgr. Jean-Francois Mathieu Arrighi	Clerk of the Secretariat, France
Fr. Thomas Stransky, CSP	Writer-Archivist of the Secretariat, USA

Preparatory Drafts Proposed by the Council Secretariat (December 5, 1962)[6]
1. De unione fovenda inter christianos

Drafts Assigned by Coordinating Commission (January 30, 1963)[7]
1. De oecumenismo

Documents Produced
1. Decree on Ecumenism *Unitatis redintegratio* (November 21, 1964)
2. Declaration on the Relation of the Church to Non-Christian Religions *Nostra aetate* (October 28, 1965)
3. Declaration on Religious Liberty *Dignitatis humanae* (December 7, 1965)

PLENARY SESSIONS OF THE SECRETARIAT FOR CHRISTIAN UNITY
(Source: *L'Osservatore della domenica*, 1966)

PREPARATORY PHASE
1960
November 14–15: Rome, Biblical Commission
1961
February 6–9: Ariccia (Rome), Casa Gesù Divin Maestro
April 16–21: Ariccia (Rome), Casa Gesù Divin Maestro
August 26–31: Bühl-Baden (Germany), Sisters of the Most Holy Savior
November 27–December 2: Ariccia (Rome), Casa Gesù Divin Maestro
1962
March 6–7: Rome, palazzo della Cancelleria

COUNCIL SESSIONS
1962—Session One
Weekly meetings, Grand Magisterium of the Equestrian Order of the Holy Sepulchre of Jerusalem
1963—Session Two
Weekly meetings, Grand Magisterium of the Equestrian Order of the Holy Sepulchre of Jerusalem and at the English College
1964—Session Three
Several times a week in the boardroom of the Palazzo di San Luigi dei Francesi
1965—Session Four
Bi-weekly meetings at the offices in the via dell'Erba, 1

INTERSESSIONAL MEETINGS
1963
May 12–19: Rome, Grand Magisterium of the Equestrian Order of the Holy Sepulchre of Jerusalem
1964
February 24–March 7: Ariccia (Rome), Casa Gesù Divin Maestro
1965
February 28–March 6: Ariccia (Rome), Casa Gesù Divin Maestro
May 10–15: Rome, Secretariat for the Unity of Christians (via dell'Erba, 1)

---

6. Schemata constitutionum et decretorum ex quibus argumenta in concilio disceptanda seligentur, in AS 1,1 95.
7. Elenchus schematum constitutionum et directorum de quibus disceptabitur in concilii sessionibus, in AS 5,1 201.

22. The Discussion on the Liturgy

In the summer of 1962, when the future council fathers received the first seven drafts from the Secretary of the Preparatory Commission, they found among them the *schema* (the Latin name for these drafts) of the constitution *De Sacra Liturgia*. This draft was in fifth place, which meant that those who had prepared the council intended that it deal with other dogmatic issues first, and then get around to this document. Instead, John XXIII wanted the council to start with this draft, the only one out of all the preparations to be discussed and approved without any radical changes. *De Sacra Liturgia* did not come about because of the mentality of the Roman schools but sprang from the "liturgical movement." This movement advocated for freeing the liturgy from Baroque practices by restoring the purity of the traditional liturgy in order to bring it back to its ancient spiritual value,

thus overcoming the ritualism that had grown in recent years, and thus making it as a place for "active participation" (Pius X had already pointed to this, without developing the ecclesiological implications). Unlike other movements—such as the biblical movement, the ecumenical movement, and the patristic studies movement—which had also aroused suspicions, the liturgical movement had been encouraged by Rome. Pius XII, in the encyclical *Mediator Dei* (1947), had already legitimized the liturgical movement by launching a series of reforms, including that of the Triduum, especially the Easter Vigil. On the eve of the council, however, many still believed that only the Eastern Churches united to Rome could use living languages (Greek, Arabic, Slavic languages) and that the Catholic Church should instead preserve the ancient Latin language, even though it was dead.

1. (Opposite) The Chapel for the Dominican Sisters of Vence, near Nice, designed by Henry Matisse at the end of the 1940s and dedicated June 25, 1951, anticipated the work of the council. Influenced by the journal *L'Art Sacré*, which was edited by the Dominicans in Paris, the sisters agreed with Matisse in every detail. From the image, we can see that the altar is placed to be visible to both the nuns' choir and the visitors' section in the chapel (BAMSphoto–Rodella/© Succession Matisse, by SIAE 2015).

2. Le Corbusier, the Modernist architect, accepted the proposal of the Commission of Sacred Art of Besançon to rebuild the shrine of Notre Dame du Haut near the border between France and Germany, which had been destroyed by the war. Although an agnostic, Le Corbusier committed himself to follow the symbolic and liturgical dictates of his clients, and created a building that is a masterpiece of the Modernist school. Here we see how the convex interior apse forms a concave wall outside, to accommodate an external altar in order to accommodate the large numbers of pilgrims who would visit the shrine (BAMSphoto–Rodella/© FLC e AONDH, by SIAE 2015).

3. The 37th Eucharist Congress held in Munich, 1960. The Congress gave visibility to the liturgical movement, thanks to the work of liturgist Joseph Andreas Jungmann that Cardinal Wendel incorporated into his pastoral letter. The images broadcast on television showed the mass as a concrete symbol of unity. Jungmann raised the veil on the true universality of the Church and on the achievements of the liturgical movement before the world.

2

3

When, in obedience to the will of the pope, the draft of *De Sacra Liturgia* opened the conciliar debates on October 22, 1962, the assembly deemed it a topic whose time had come. The draft, in which the Amendments Subcommittee of the Central Preparatory Commission had heavily intervened, had been weakened compared to the work done by the Preparatory Commission. Fr. Annibale Bugnini, secretary of that commission and one of the most qualified Italian liturgists who had worked on the background *declarationes utili* so that the historical and theological foundation of the proposed reforms could be understood, had been ousted from the council's Liturgical Commission. In his place, Fr. Antonelli, who was close to the theological culture of Cardinal Alfredo Ottaviani, was appointed. Within the commission, the northern European bishops chose Giacomo Lercaro, a prominent figure in the liturgical movement, whom the Italians had not wanted to nominate. The Apostolic Constitution, *Veterum Sapientia*, signed by John XXIII in February 1962, introduced distinctions between the language of prayer, the language of the theological schools, and the language of the Roman magis-

4. Results of vote on *De sacra liturgia,* November 14, 1962.

5. Priestly vestments from the liturgical art studio of Yaounde, Cameroon. The Church in Africa has sought to encourage liturgical renewal that would integrate the symbols and forms of African

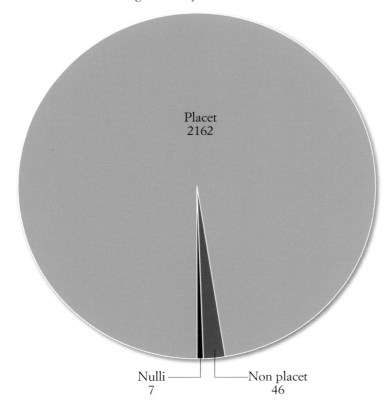

Placet
2162

Nulli
7

Non placet
46

4

terium. This intimidated some fathers who were struggling with a text that should clearly have gone beyond the monopoly of Latin, which was decidedly not a common shared language. Anyone who had heard the unintelligible Latin spoken in the national accents of the bishops in the hall was aware of this.

The discussion, which was made somewhat clumsy by the first set of council Regulations, took place slowly and with difficulty for many weeks, while the commission went ahead collecting the proposed amendments and correcting the text. This went on during the first session until November 14, 1962, and took up fifteen general congregations, in which 328 fathers commented. Another 253 did so in writing.

There was a sizable but not exclusive contribution from the bishops of countries where the liturgical movement was thriving. In the debate, the problem of the use of modern languages was touched upon as well as the principles for how to adapt the liturgy—concelebration, communion under both species—but especially the role of the bishop as primary liturgist. This would result in the rise of what, after the ecclesiological reform, would be called the local church. Other subjects discussed included reforming the liturgical books (the missal, the breviary, and the ritual). In this first crucial step in the discussion, resistance emerged from some members of the Council Commission, from the Sacred Congregation of Rites, and from the Holy Office, but these were in the minority. The majority who were for reform were thus able to win the day. Although there were some internal

tradition. Here we have three basic shades in a color scheme that is an African symbol of the human conditions. Geometric shapes and figurative art trace continuity between Christianity and African cosmology: a man and "cosmic circles," the oval and shells, symbols of fertility and life, which are joined to the cross, the symbol of our salvation (E. Mveng, *Art négre ou art chrétien?* Rome 1967).

variations, it was a measure of how far the reform had extended when, on November 14, 2,162 voted *placet,* and forty-six *non placet*, with seven invalid votes, thus approving the guiding criteria of *De Sacra Liturgia*, "which, with due prudence and knowledge, would tend to make the various parts of the liturgy more vital and formative for the faithful, in accordance with the pastoral needs of our time." On December 7, at the end of the first period of work, the pope ensured that this draft would be treated as the most important among all the deliberations of the council and the prospects of renewal that it had been developing: "It was no accident that the council began with the draft of *De Sacra Liturgia*: the relationship between man and God. That is, the highest order of relations that should be established on the solid foundation of revelation and of the apostolic teaching."

BIBLIOGRAPHY
A. Bugnini, "De sacra liturgia in prima periodo Concilii Oecumenici Vaticani II," in *Ephemerides Liturgicae*, 77 (1963), 3–18; "'Traditio et progressio.' Nel ricordo di mons. Annibale Bugnini," *Rivista Liturgica*, 6 (2012); M. Lamberigts, "Il dibattito sulla liturgia," in *Storia del concilio Vaticano II*, edited by G. Alberigo (Italian edition edited by A. Melloni), vol. 2: *La formazione della coscienza conciliare. Il primo periodo e la prima intersessione, ottobre 1962–settembre 1963*, Bologna 1996 (2012), 130–198; M. Paiano, "Il rinnovamento della liturgia: dai movimenti alla chiesa universale," in *Verso il Concilio Vaticano II (1960–1962). Passaggi e problemi della preparazione conciliare*, edited by G. Alberigo and A. Melloni, Bologna 1993, 67–140; A. G. Martimort, *Les débats liturgiques lors de la première période du concile Vatican II, in Vatican II commence….Approches Francophones*, edited by É. Fouilloux, Leuven 1993, 291–314.

▸ **THE VOICE OF THE AFRICAN BISHOPS**

In the second episode of *The Church in Council. The Men and the Problems* aired by RAI on November 24, Alberigo tried to provide a key to understanding the debate that occurred on the liturgical draft, using the voices of various council fathers, including that of African, Archbishop Joseph Malula, auxiliary bishop of Léopoldville (Congo), in order to try to understand the relationship between liturgy and the local churches in Africa.

Giuseppe Alberigo: "The council has dedicated its first weeks of work to discussing one of the leading drafts coming out of the preparatory work, namely the draft on the sacred liturgy. In recent weeks, voting on the amendments has been going on, that is, on the changes to this draft, and it is legitimate to expect that the same draft could be voted on in the final session on December 8. Clearly, this was not a random choice, but rather a choice rich in significance, because of the proper pastoral approach that has been given to the council right from the start. […] Can we ask what problems the council has before it regarding the liturgy? It is widely believed that one problem dominates all the others, and is a fundamental condition for the development of Christianity in our times. What place does the liturgy have in the relationship between Christianity and people of color, people who are from a

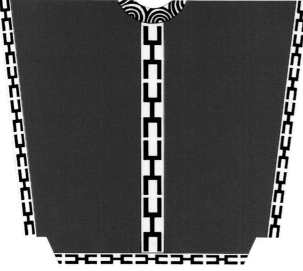

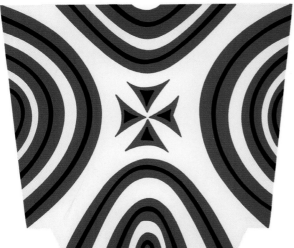

5

different civilization? We put this question to Archbishop Malula, auxiliary of the Congolese diocese of Leopoldville and a respected member of the council's Liturgical Commission."

Archbishop Joseph Malula: "At its base is the fundamental problem of the incarnation, the mystery of Christ in the soul of non-Western peoples. The Church by her nature is not linked to any culture. As the guardian of truth, she meets all the positive values of all cultures. Not only does she respect them, but increasingly the Church wants to make these values its own, wants to elevate and integrate them into the Christian dynamism for which Christ praises the Father. For the peoples of Africa in particular, evangelization must be undertaken with sensitivity, with the religious aspirations that exist in the soul of the African peoples. These aspirations existed before evangelization and constituted, as it were, a preparation, almost an expectation of Christ's message. Liturgical renewal can certainly bring us much help in bringing about this incarnation. Until now, evangelization took place for us through Western liturgy, but we believe that through the council's conclusions, we will be able to appeal to our own religious sensibilities, our traditional values, to integrate them into the liturgy and so enable us to bring about evangelization, by means of our traditions and our own sensibility. For example, we have already tried once to offer an experience of paraliturgy. I know very well that this is not really liturgy as it is normally understood, but it is an experience of paraliturgy. On Good Friday we tried to mourn our Lord in the way our people mourn their dead. So the cross was placed on a large table and I called the faithful who had come to kneel around this table. With their songs and their purely indigenous musical instruments, these faithful really achieved something that touched the heart of all of us, through the lively spontaneity and passion with which they expressed their religious sentiments. And all this took place in my Church, with great success. Certainly, it is only paraliturgy. We know perfectly well that it is the Mass, the Holy Mass that is the center of liturgical life, and so we strive to explain the mystical body to our people. It is quite easy because we rely mainly on the idea that our people have of family. This concept has its foundations in the clan, and so we explain that the mystical body is the great family of the children of God, so that all we do is elevate the concept that they have of the family and enlarge it in Christ. And so we help the people to attend Mass really as a community, as God's clan, a family that comes together to praise the Lord with their big brother, Christ, with their songs and accompanied by their traditional instruments. So we work to incorporate liturgical renewal into Christ's message because this is where its foundation lies in the concepts and in the traditions of our own people."

23. November 21: The Rejection of the Draft on the Sources of Revelation

On November 14, the same day that discussion on the draft on the liturgy ended and the document was returned to the commission for amendment, the debate on the second draft of the document concerning the sources of revelation began. It occupied the council until November 21. *De Fontibus*—as it came to be called—was a turning point in the maturation of the council's consciousness of itself. In fact, Vatican II would take possession of itself, of its natural purpose, conforming to the intentions of John XXIII that had not been incorporated into the work of the preparatory committees, with the exception of the Liturgical Commission and the Secretariat for Christian Unity.

The draft on the sources of revelation, prepared by the Theological Commission, was meant to ratify the condemnations regarding exegesis that had been issued over the previous six decades, and to make permanent the repression of movements that were condemned at the beginning of the twentieth century, such as "modernism." By indicating the "sources of revelation" as either Scripture or tradition, this draft went beyond the scope of Trent. It not only deepened the gulf with the Reformation churches, but it condemned the theology that, through historical-critical exegesis and spiritual reading of the Bible, proposed a deeper understanding of the text and of its value in the life of the Church.

Ever since the previous summer when it went out to the council fathers, *De Fontibus* had raised fierce criticism because of its one-sidedness and theological shortcomings, such as the famous "*animadversiones*" that Edward Schillebeeckx compiled for the Dutch bishops. The perceptions of its shortcomings were such that, in the early days of the council, the German and French bishops who believed that the draft was beyond repair had asked some theologians, particularly Karl Rahner and Joseph Ratzinger, to prepare a new draft of the dogmatic constitution that would address these issues in a completely different way.

When, on November 14, Cardinal Alfredo Ottaviani introduced the presentation of the draft on the sources of revelation prepared by his commission (represented by Archbishop Salvatore Garofalo), he already knew of the existence of alternative drafts and tried to warn the council fathers. Both he and Garofalo did not limit themselves to introducing the draft, but mounted a stout defense, which opened the door to more open and severe criticism, supporting the need to quash the draft and start from scratch. Eight cardinals agreed: Bernard Alfrink, Augustin Bea, Joseph Frings, Franz König, Achille Liénart, Paul-Émile Léger, Léon Joseph Suenens, and Joseph Ritter. John XXIII noted in his diary that day, "We expect a quarrel to start up. On the one hand, the document (the preparatory draft) does not take into account the precise intentions of the pope in his speeches on the council and to the council. On the other, eight cardinals together discredit the main point of the proposal. May the Lord help us and unite us." After several days of discussions, by which time the different positions were clarified, the presider decided to take a vote on whether the will of the council was to drop the draft (with a two-thirds majority voting *placet*) or not (by voting *non placet*). It was a solemn decision because discarding one of the preparatory drafts meant questioning all the preparations that had been made by the Roman congregations. For some, such as Cardinal Giuseppe Siri, it was a real drama: "It will be a serious matter," he noted in his diary on the eve of the vote, "if tomorrow the draft falls! Lord, help us! Holy Virgin, St. Joseph, pray for us! You can get *cunctas haereses sola interemisti in universo mundo*."

The majority of the fathers voted for the interruption of the debate and therefore for the rejection of the draft—as could have been predicted from the prevalence of presentations against it—1,368 out of 2,209 fathers voting for the rejection of the prepared document, and 822 for its continuation. But 105 votes were still needed for a quorum. And so, by default, according to the Regulations—which had not even imagined such an eventuality—the council would have had to discuss a document that the vast majority did not agreed with.

In the following hours and during the night of November 21, John XXIII, urged by some cardinals including the Canadian Léger, departed from the Regulations and ordered that the new text be drafted by a joint commission composed of members of the Doctrinal Committee along with some from the Secretariat for Christian Unity. The Holy Office, "supreme" by definition, had lost its monopoly on doctrine in the Church, and the pope had used the power of primacy that "exalted not only the capacity for initiative but gave even greater value to that of listening. In even more relevant terms it can be said that the synodal nature of Petrine primacy found concrete expression." John XXIII's decision did not pose a risk, therefore, to the freedom of the bishops, but rather returned freedom to the council, which had had it taken away in that particular case, by predefined Regulations that had not been open for discussion: "Without even putting it in writing, the council had made perhaps one of the most important changes in the

1

1. Part of the introduction to the Bible printed by Gutenberg, the first book printed on a press, sec. XV. Stampato Barberini AAA. VI. 16–17 f. lr. (Biblioteca Apostolica Vaticana).

2. Manuscript pages from Pope John's diary for November 14, 1962: "Interesting discussions about the sources of revelation. We expect a quarrel to start up. On the one hand, the document (the preparatory draft) does not take into account the precise intentions of the pope in his speeches on the council and to the council. On the other, eight cardinals together discredit the main point of the proposal. May the Lord help us and unite us." (Diary of John XXIII, November 14, 1962). On the 19th he would instead note: "Interesting listening today to all the voices of the council. They are largely critical of the proposed schemes (of Card. Ottaviani) that together reveal the arrogant tone and the persistence of a mentality that cannot free itself from a pedantic tone. Semi-blindness in one eye shadows the vision of the whole. Of course, the reaction is strong, sometimes too strong. But I think a good understanding will ultimately prevail" (Diary of John XXIII, November 19, 1962).

evolution of doctrine in the Catholic Church: the option for more 'pastorally relevant' doctrine": the "modernist crisis" came to an end that night.

Bibliography
J. R. Geiselmann, *Die Heilige Schrift und die Tradition*, Freiburg 1962; H. Sauer, *Erfahrung und Glaube. Die Begründung des pastoralen Prinzips durch die Offenbarungskonstitution des II. Vatikanischen Konzils*, Frankfurt a.M. 1993; G. Ruggieri, "Il primo conflitto dottrinale," in *Storia del concilio Vaticano II*, edited by G. Alberigo (Italian edition edited by A. Melloni), vol. 2, Bologna 1996–2012, 259–294; R. Burigana, *La Bibbia nel concilio. La redazione della costituzione* Dei verbum, Bologna 1998; E. Fouilloux, *Une Eglise en quête de liberté. La pensée catholique française entre modernisme et Vatican II (1914–1962)*, Paris 1998; C. Theobald, "Le développement de la notion des 'vérités historiquement et logiquement connexes avec la Révélation' de Vatican I à Vatican II," in *Cristianesimo nella storia*, 21 (2000), 37–70; C. Theobald, *La Réception du Concile Vatican II: I. Accéder à la source*, Paris 2009.

24. The "Decembrists" and De Ecclesia. The End of the First Session

During the last weeks of the first period, the council was engaged in examining three drafts. The first was an objectively insignificant one, regarding modern means of mass communication. This draft was prepared by the Secretariat for the Press and the Entertainment, which followed the usual outline indicating the apostolic opportunities and moral dangers of the media. The second draft, which had been kept back because of its design and style, had been prepared by the Committee on Eastern Churches and covered the Churches of Eastern rites and the issue of Uniatism, a concept that proposed that Churches that had detached themselves from the Orthodox communion "return" to communion with Rome. The third draft was "what, in the opinion of almost all the bishops, was the *raison d'être* of the council" (G. Ruggieri): *De ecclesia*. This had been prepared by the Theological Commission of the Holy Office, and was eleven chapters and eighty-two pages long. It was destined to arouse the same reservations that had caused the draft on sources of revelation to founder: it ignored the work of exegetical and patristic study, lacked a comprehensive understanding of the relationship between Christ and the Church, gave no room to the college of bishops, which even the Code of Canon Law pointed to as the repository of full and supreme power in the Church. During the XXXI General Congregation on December 1, while introducing the draft in the Council Hall and before presentation by Bishop Frane Frani of Split, Alfredo Ottaviani recited the criticisms he expected, to the amusement of the assembly: "Those who had prepared the schema took care to make it most pastoral, biblical, and understandable to many. But you can expect to hear the usual litany from the council fathers: it is not ecumenical but scholastic, it is not pastoral but negative, and so on, and so on" (see AS, I/IV, 121–122). The great theologians of the council—Jorge Medina, Yves Congar, Edward Schillebeeckx, Karl Rahner, Joseph Ratzinger, and others—had already highlighted the weaknesses of the proposal, and the Belgian theologian Archbishop Gerard Philips, in what would be published in January as an article in the *Nouvelle Revue Théologique* spoke of "two ecclesiologies," one concerned legalism and the other with communion, which confronted each other in the draft ("Deux tendances dans la théologie contemporaine").

But the debate on *De Ecclesia*, held from December 1 to 7, with seventy-seven presentations, was also an opportunity to express the vision of the council and of the Church, right before a conclave that everyone assumed would be sooner rather than later. Modifying the language of the October Revolution, some newspapers spoke of the "Decembrists" of that session: Augustin Bea, Giovanni Battista Montini, Léon-Joseph Suenens, Giacomo Lercaro, Franz König, Jan Bernard Alfrink, Julius Döpfner, Maximos IV, Michael Doumith, Alfred Ancel, Emiel-Jozef De Smedt. The Latin Americans expressed their thoughts on the matter, behind which was the work of theologians such as Carlo Colombo, Giuseppe Dossetti, Joseph Lécuyer, and Otto Semmelroth, plus Congar, Philips, Ratzinger, Schillebeeckx, and Rahner.

Philips, in consultation with Montini, had been commissioned by Cardinal Suenens to draw up the framework for an ad hoc project, aimed at improving *De Ecclesia*; this project was more a work in progress to be easily "digested" even by the minority and by the theological commission, but the *animadversiones* of Schillebeeckx and Rahner had a much clearer goal: "the elimination of the preparatory draft and the spirit that had dominated it," because "the concept of theology that was reduced almost exclusively to apologetics and biblical exegesis not employed in order to lay out the mystery in all its fullness, but to confirm the teaching of the Magisterium, finds its most significant application in *De ecclesia*," as Dossetti wrote in his memoir on the ecclesiological project that developed in those weeks.

Through Cardinal Fring, Ratzinger, one of his young theologians, had criticized the lack of "catholicity" in the draft, which depended on recent papal teaching and ignored both the Greek and the ancient Latin tradition. It fell instead to Cardinal Suenens, on December 4, to put forward his suggestive proposal that not only the draft, but the whole of the council, should hinge on two axes: the vitality of the Church *ad intra* and relations of the Church *ad extra*, thus addressing the issue of the Church in dialogue with the world. This proposal had the backing of Cardinal Montini, so that—among the possible contenders—he implicitly set out the conditions of his pontifical plan regarding the council, thus breaking with the theology that prevailed within the Curia. On December 6, Cardinal Lercaro made "the last great keynote speech," which was prepared by Dossetti, and instead stated that the "poverty of Christ," and the "poverty of the Church," held the new key for proposing "an essentially biblical vision of the Church." The archbishop of Bologna asked that they concentrate on the poor as privileged recipients of the Gospel and thus on poverty as the fundamental mystery of the Church: "If the theme of this council is the Church, we can and we must ensure that we have wording that most conforms to the eternal truth of the Gospel and is most appropriate to the historical situation of our time: the theme of the council is the Church, particularly as the Church of the poor, of all the millions and millions of individual poor people, and collectively of the poor peoples of the whole earth."

1. Cardinal Giacomo Lercaro, archbishop of Bologna (1891–1976) (Archivio Fscire).

2. Cardinal Bea in conversation with the German Lutheran theologian Oscar Cullmann (from *Das Konzil und seine Folgen*).

3. Cardinal Léon-Joseph Suenens with Dom Hélder Câmara (from L. J. Suenens, *Souvenirs et espérances*, Fayard, Paris 1991).

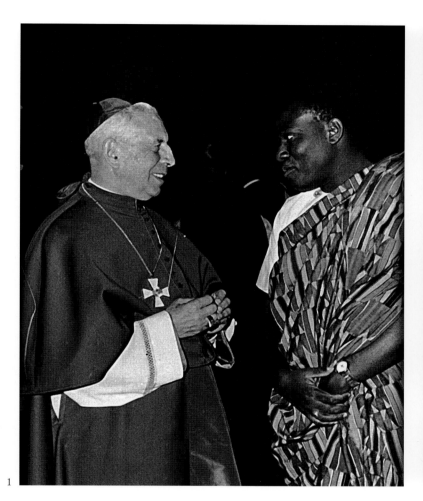

BIBLIOGRAPHY
J. A. Brouwers, *Vatican II. Derniers préparatifs et première session. Activités conciliaires en coulisses, in Vatican II commence…Approches francophones*, edited by É. Fouilloux, Leuven 1993, 353–368; M. Lamberigts, "Una pausa: i mezzi di comunicazione sociale," in *Storia del concilio Vaticano II*, edited by G. Alberigo (Italian edition edited by A. Melloni), vol. 2, Bologna, 1996 (2012), 295–308; G. Ruggieri, "Il difficile abbandono dell'ecclesiologia controvertista," in *Storia del concilio Vaticano II*, edited by G. Alberigo (Italian edition edited by A. Melloni), vol. 2, Bologna, 1996 (2012), 309–384; A. Melloni, "Ecclesiologie al Vaticano II (Autumn 1962–Summer 1963)," in *Les commissions conciliaires à Vatican II*, edited by M. Lamberigts, Cl. Soetens, J. Grootares, Leuven 1996, 91–179; G. Alberigo, "Giuseppe Dossetti al Concilio Vaticano II," ora in *Transizione epocale*, Bologna 2009, 393–502.

25. Mirabilis Ille and New Preparation

1

1. John XXIII, Christmas Day, 1962, celebrating Mass in his private chapel in the Vatican (Fondazione Papa Giovanni XXIII, Bergamo). "I think back to my letter to all the council bishops in the world that cost me much. I wanted it to be personal, all thought and heart, from the Pope's pen. And I thank the Lord that I succeeded" (Diary of John XXIII, January 8, 1963).

On December 5, while discussions were taking place on *De Ecclesia*, the council fathers finally received the list of the twenty drafts that the council would have to discuss in future sessions. It was the result of a painstaking pruning and selection of the seventy preparatory texts that had still been on the program as late as October 11, 1962. The document was called *Schemata constitutionum et decretorum ex quibus argumenta in concilio disceptanda seligentur*: an eleven-page document compiled by the General Secretariat of the council, which was trying to preserve the "Roman" flavor of the preparations.

On December 6, the Secretary of State, Cardinal Amleto Cicognani, distributed the rules that had been approved by the pope for the work that was to take place between the sessions. This document established a "Coordinating Commission" composed of leading cardinals of the Curia and resident cardinals, which would have to divide the list of twenty drafts among the individual commissions. Cicognani's plan laid out that each commission would take charge of the drafts that fell within its competence; these had already been prepared by the Preparatory Commissions and the commissions would rework them making them shorter or combining them as they saw fit. The resumption of the council was scheduled for May 1963, although no exact date had been set. This gave the go-ahead to what was considered a proper "fresh preparation for the council," with the institution of a group that would ensure the continuation rather than the deconstruction of the debate between sessions when the bishops returned to their dioceses. Meanwhile, on December 8, the first session ended with Pope John XXIII's speech, "a resigned farewell to his council, that he would never see gathered again" (G. Ruggieri). He asked that "each bishop, although he would be taken up with pastoral care, should continue to study and develop the drafts available to him, along with the other material that would be sent in due time." It was Roncalli's way of saying that not everything should be left in the hands of the Curia department heads.

Many had faced the problem of how to make good use of those months of downtime; however, the scope of this new phase was laid out in the letter *Mirabilis Ille*, which was sent by the pope to each individual bishop. He had begun working on it immediately after Christmas (it was anticipated in his speech to the Sacred College on December 23, in which he once again reminded them of "the dynamic perspective" with which to view the work of Vatican II). It was dated on the Epiphany, and John XXIII had devoted himself personally and with great care to its preparation, in order to encourage the council fathers to stay "in tune" with the spiritual climate of the council, even during the intersessional period, and he reaffirmed the initial inspiration outlined in the opening speech on October 11.

As in his letter of April 15, 1962 to all bishops, *Omnes Sane*, where he called the episcopate to personal sanctification as a form of preparation for the opening of Vatican II, the pontiff in *Mirabilis Ille* asked them "to keep the zeal for the council alive during the long months between sessions, during which the bishops would be distant from Rome, and above all, far from each other, in the wake of the "positive impact" of the inaugural address. The Coordinating Commission, which was mentioned in the letter, met for the first time between January 21 and 27, 1963. The members had been given the task of reporting on the drafts, following this allocation:

Cardinal Amleto Cicognani: Eastern Churches, ecumenism, missions (later assigned to Cardinal Confalonieri);

Cardinal Achille Liénart: sources of revelation, the deposit of faith;

Cardinal Francis Joseph Spellman: liturgy, marriage, and chastity;

Cardinal Giovanni Urbani: clergy, lay apostolate, modern media, the sacrament of marriage;

Cardinal Carlo Confalonieri: seminaries, Catholic schools;

Cardinal Julius Döpfner: bishops, pastoral care, religious;

Cardinal Léon-Joseph Suenens: the Church, the Virgin Mary, moral order, social order.

While the Secretary of State, Cardinal Cicognani, pushed for the reinstatement, at least in their essential content, of the preparatory drafts; other cardinals, such as Suenens, Döpfner, and Liénart demanded complete reworking of all the drafts, especially the highly important doctrinal drafts. Some amalgamation brought the new list to sixteen drafts, plus one on the Church and the modern world, and the preparatory draft on morality was discarded. The new program for the council, therefore, provided a structure divided as follows:

1. Divine revelation
2. The Church
3. The Blessed Virgin Mary, Mother of the Church
4. The bishops and the government of dioceses
5. Ecumenism
6. The clergy
7. Religious

8. The apostolate of the laity
9. The Eastern churches
10. The sacred liturgy
11. The care of souls
12. The sacrament of marriage
13. The formation of the clergy
14. Catholic schools
15. The missions
16. The means of social communication
17. The principles and the action of the Church to promote the good of society

The individual commissions then began to work as directed by the Coordinating Commission. Some commissions that were working on doctrinal issues, such as the Commission for the Apostolate of the Laity, and the Secretariat for Christian Unity (which had been definitively recognized, by Pope John XXIII, as a true and proper conciliar commission with the power to present its drafts) worked assiduously in the following months, meeting several times in plenary session. Other commissions, such as those for bishops, clergy, seminaries, and religious, opted for the revision work to be performed in Rome by some of their members and some trustworthy theologians appointed by the presider, thus marginalizing the other members of the commission who lived far from the Eternal City.

Between March 25 and 29, the Coordinating Commission reconvened to review how the reworking of the drafts was progressing, which were still underway, or which had just been set on a new footing. The convening of the second period, given the worsening of the pope's health, was then moved to September. The texts revised by the individual commissions and examined the Coordinating Commission, once the pope had given them the green light, had to be sent to the council fathers before the summer. In this context, given the time pressure, the Coordinating Commission would have had to meet for another session in early June. However, on June 3, 1963, after a long illness, John XXIII died. Work then stopped, and was suspended pending the election of a successor, who under the law would have to decide whether to reconvene the council.

BIBLIOGRAPHY

G. Ruggieri, "Il difficile abbandono dell'ecclesiologia controvertista," in *Storia del concilio Vaticano II*, edited by G. Alberigo (Italian edition edited by A. Melloni), vol. 2, Bologna, 1996 (2012), 309–384; J. Grootaers, "Il concilio si gioca nell'intervallo. La 'seconda preparazione' e i suoi avversari," in *Storia del concilio Vaticano II*, edited by G. Alberigo (Italian edition edited by A. Melloni), vol. 2, Bologna 1996 (2012), 385–558; E. Galavotti, "Il concilio continua. Giovanni XXIII e la lettera 'Mirabilis Ille'," in *Tutto è grazia*, edited by A. Melloni, 115–169 (with a synopsis of the editing process).

1. Divine Revelation.

1. La Maiestas Domini *nell'abside centrale di San Clemente a Tahull, Museo di Catalogna, Barcellona.*

2. Saint Francis and the poor man, *miniature in the manuscript of the* Legenda Major, *Istituto Storico dei Cappuccini, Roma. 3. Fra Angelico,* The Coronation of Mary, *The Louvre, Paris, detail. 4. Simone Martini,* The Dream of St. Ambrose (*also known as St. Martin in Meditation*), *San Martino Chapel, Lower Basilica of St. Francis in Assisi, detail. 5. Eero Saarinen, apse of MIT Chapel, Cambridge, Massachusetts, 1950–1955. 6. A catechism lesson in Peruvian village. 7. Missionaries of Charity attending the Eucharistic Congress held in Charlotte, North Carolina. 8. Maestro dei Mesi, September, Museo del Duomo, Ferrara. 9. Kiev (Ukraine), St. Sophia Cathedral, Christ distributes communion to the apostles under both species. 10. Le Corbusier, exterior south wall of the chapel of Notre-Dame du Haut, Ronchamp (France). 11. Wiligelmo, detail of doorway, Modena Cathedral. 12. Raphael,* The Marriage of the Virgin, *1504, Pinacoteca di Brera, Milano. 13. Robert Bresson (1907–1999), who did a film adaptation of George Bernanos' novel,* The Diary of a Country Priest. *14. Christ teaching the apostles, Chapel of St. Aquilino in the basilica of San Lorenzo Maggiore, Milano. 15. Detail from the illustrated frontispiece of an edition of the* Brevísima relación de la destrucción de las Indias *by Bartolomé de Las Casas, Seville, 1552. 16. Labyrinth embedded in the right side of the portico of St. Martin's Cathedral, Lucca. 17. Filippo Brunelleschi, detail of the façade of the Ospedale degli Innocenti, Florence. (All images Archivio Jaca Book/© FLC e AONDH, by SIAE 2015 per foto n.10)*

THE 17 DRAFTS

2. The Church

3. The Blessed Virgin, Mother of the Church

4. The bishops in their dioceses

5. Ecumenism

6. Clergy

7. Religious

8. The Apostolate of the Laity

9. The Eastern Church

10. The sacred liturgy

11. Care of souls

12. The sacrament of matrimony

13. The formation of the clergy

14. Catholic schools

15. The missions

16. The Means of Social Communication

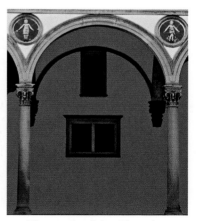

17. The work of the Church to promote the good of society

26. The Bishops' Residences

During the antepreparatory stage, the asset managers of the Holy See had made provision for the arrangement of the offices of the General Secretariat at no. 10 Via Serristori and supplied them with the minimum equipment necessary. In the early 1960s, this would have been typewriters with keyboards for different languages, photocopiers, typesetting machines, and a multigraph printing machine. At the same time, they made provision for staffing and the payment of out-of-pocket expenses.

In the preparatory phase, a special administrative secretariat headed by Cardinal Alberto di Jorio went into operation. Archbishop Sergio Guerri was appointed as secretary with some lay people as members, the first to be part of a preparatory body. The secretariat's aim was to resolve all problems relating to the administration of the council. In fact, even before it was set up, the Secretariat had to pay the expenses of the antepreparatory period, including those for the functioning of the various commissions and for the equipment and services required: mail, stationery, office furniture, and the reimbursement of travel expenses. In the beginning it ran the small offices of the preconciliar commissions, organized the hall for the congregations and other meeting rooms for the various committees, and sometimes took charge of organizing travel arrangements for the members of the preparatory commissions. Afterwards it took charge of implementing the projects approved by the technical and organizational commission, such as the preparation of the hall in the basilica. Engineer Francesco Vacchini, manager of the technical office of the Fabric of St. Peter (which at the time had the status of a congregation) was asked to sift through contracts and arrange for payments for supplies.

The Secretariat organized a complete data archive of the council fathers, bound in folders, divided by country and continent, which included a résumé, data on each father, and photographs. From this register stemmed the list of the fathers, which in its different editions was modeled on the *Annuario pontificio* that contained the names of the Curia, their various locations, and the Latin spellings of their names; this caused endless problems and misunderstandings. The register was necessary for the administrative checking of the assembly, an issue that had always been of the utmost importance and that was being faced for the first time by the financial authorities of a state that was barely thirty years old. With the data on episcopal ordinations, it was also possible to assign seating and arrange for members' transportation to and from Rome, which in many cases was organized directly by the fathers or

in some cases by their governments (Sometimes these were affected by political issues, which, for example, were faced by the Brazilian bishops after the 1964 coup).

The problem of housing about eight thousand people participating in various capacities at the council was particularly

1. Aerial view of the via della Conciliazione going into St. Peter's (BAMSphoto –Rodella).

2. The Domus Mariae, headquarters of the women's Catholic Action. During the council, Brazilian, Hungarian, and African bishops, among many others, were housed here. It became, in the words of Dom Hélder Câmara, "A place of evangelical conspiracy and nonviolent revolution." He writes, "I have integrated myself into a group of African bishops staying at the Domus. It was not easy. Yesterday one of them told me, responding to the use of the words paganism and pagan when referring to indigenous Africans, 'We are not pagans. Paganism is the absence of God. Our people, even though superstitious, are full of God'" (Hélder Câmara, *Le notti di un profeta*).

▶ THE FATHERS' LEISURE TIME

In addition to the transportation service within the city of Rome, the administrative secretariat also organized health and emergency services, phone services, postal services, and catering. In the Council Hall, two snack bars were set up, one on the left side of the hall, in the space that housed the sacristy of the Chapel of the Blessed Sacrament, and the other on the right, in the passage between the choir chapel and the sacristy of the basilica. Subsequently, a third snack bar specifically for the auditors was installed during the third session, in the space below the monument to Clement XIII. In fact, the Council Hall's snack bars (which had biblical names: Bar-Abbas and Bar-Jonah) formed, like many other places in Rome during the council, important meeting areas. However, they also became one of the most dangerous sources of distraction: the opening initially scheduled for 10:30 was later postponed by half an hour just to delay, as much as possible, the mass exodus that was inevitably created as soon as they opened. Every morning during the council, on average 2,200 hot drinks were consumed (coffee, lattes, or tea, consuming a total of 120 liters of milk daily), 1,400 cold drinks (including cola, orange, bitter orange, lemonade, mineral water, iced tea, and iced coffee) and 6,000 pastries (croissants, biscuits, slices of cake, pastries). These were served by a snack bar staff consisting of thirteen waiters and three managers. During the four sessions, the telephone switchboard operators worked a total of 3,115 hours; the four messengers worked 5,588 hours.

2

complex. Many fathers settled in the colleges where they had studied. Other groups stayed in about forty institutions and national ecclesiastical colleges in Rome: east of the Via dell'Aurelia at the Latin American College or the Domus Mariae, the American College near the Trevi Fountain, the French seminary behind Largo Argentina, the Belgian College near the Quirinal, the English College in Via Giulia, and so on. The large motherhouses and headquarters of various orders and ancient monasteries hosted council fathers or groups of fathers. In many places, since this was prior to the change in the rules on concelebration, it was necessary to use small portable altars so that each bishop could celebrate his Mass at dawn, before breakfast in order to observe the Eucharistic fast. Often a bishop who had just finished his Mass (in about fifteen minutes) then acted as altar server to others until breakfast time.

Many fathers were able to cover the costs of travel and accommodation themselves, including about 140 bishops and their assistants from the United States—in all about four hundred people—who rented three hotels for themselves, including the Grand Hotel, which became Cardinal Francis Spellman's headquarters. However, at least 1,342 fathers, almost half of the 2,860 participants, sought and obtained from the Vatican reimbursement for room and board for themselves and their staffs. There were the Latin American bishops (414 out of a total of 520 during the first period), Africans (239 out of 331), Asians (238 out of 345), but also Europeans (Poles and Yugoslavs). In addition, 201 out of 546 bishops residing in Italy asked to have their accommodation paid for. About a third of the council fathers (937) requested a contribution toward all or part of their travel expenses to the Holy See, which also chartered transportation, such as the sleeper car reserved for the Polish bishops.

The economic effort was not inconsiderable: from the preparation stage to the fourth session more than four and a half billion lire (over 2.5 million U.S. dollars) was spent. This

HOSPITIA ET INSTITUTA
CONCILIARIBUS PATRIBUS EXCIPIENDIS

1 HOTEL LE ANFORE - Viale Tito Livio, 7 - Tel. 348.333
2 HOTEL AMERICANA DI ROMA
Via Aurelia, Km. 16,900 - Tel. 620.680 - 622.1000
3 HOTEL CAESAR AUGUSTUS
Corso Francia, 200 - Tel. 320.254
4 HOTEL DERBY - Largo delle Sette Chiese - Tel. 515.567
5 HOTEL NORDLAND - Via A. Alciato - Tel. 626.457
6 HOTEL BOTTICELLI - Via Clemente III - Tel. 6274.279
7 HOTEL CASTEL SANT'ANGELO
Piazza Adriana, 12 - Tel. 651.237
8 HOTEL MEDICI - Via Flavia, 96 - Tel. 471.319
9 HOTEL NOVA DOMUS - Via G. Savonarola, 38 - Tel. 318.141
10 DOMUS MARIAE - Via Aurelia, 481 - Tel. 620.061
11 ISTITUTO MARIA RIMOLDI
Via Teulada, 36 - Tel. 355.700
12 FIGLIE DELLA PRESENTAZIONE
Via Gregorio VII, 166 B - Tel. 632.943
13 SUORE DEL PREZIOSISSIMO SANGUE
Via S. Maria Mediatrice, 8 - Tel. 631.759
14 RESIDENZA ADELE DI TRENQUELLEON
Via Biagio Pallai, 4 - Tel. 533.179
15 VILLA LITUANIA - Piazza Asti, 25 - Tel. 780.014
16 ISTITUTO S. TOMMASO DI VILLANOVA
Viale Romania, 7 - Tel. 870.274
17 CASA MATER IMMACULATA
Via Monte del Gallo, 36 - Tel. 630.863
18 OSPIZIO S. MARTA - Città del Vaticano - Tel. 698
19 COLLEGIO PORTOGHESE
Via Banco di S. Spirito, 12 - Tel. 652.013
20 COLLEGIO CAPRANICA - P.za Capranica, 98 - Tel. 674.435
21 PENSIONATO ROMANO
Via della Traspontina, 18 - Tel. 561.286
22 CASA MADONNA DI FATIMA
Via G. Cerbara, 40 - Tel. 510.996
23 SUORE FRANCESCANE DI CRISTO RE
Via Torre Rossa, 80 - Tel. 6223.239
24 HOTEL PENSIONE ARISTEIA
Piazza Adriana, 12 - Tel. 659.202
25 SEMINARIO FRANCESE - Via S. Chiara, 42 - Tel. 651.526
26 PROCURA S. SULPIZIO
Via Quattro Fontane, 113 - Tel. 470.820
27 S. LUIGI DEI FRANCESI
Via S. Giovanna d'Arco, 5 - Tel. 653.629
28 COLLEGIO IRLANDESE - Via SS. Quattro, 7 - Tel. 735.690
29 COLLEGIO S. ALFONSO - Via Merulana, 31 - Tel. 733.720
30 COLLEGIO S. COLOMBANO - Corso Trieste, 57 - Tel. 846.603
31 OBLATI DELLA B. VERGINE IMMACOLATA
Via Aurelia, 290 - Tel. 6370.251
32 CHIERICI DI S. VIATORE
Via Sierra Nevada, 60 - Tel. 996.284
33 PP. MARISTI - Via A. Poerio, 63 - Tel. 580.613
34 CURIA GENERALIZIA O.F.M.
Via S. Maria Mediatrice, 5 - Tel. 632.241
35 COLLEGIO S. ANTONIO
Via Merulana, 124 - Tel. 770.551
36 DELEGAZIONE DI TERRA SANTA
Via M. Boiardo, 16 - Tel. 776.308
37 CONVENTO DEI SS. QUARANTA
Via S. Francesco a Ripa, 20 - Tel. 583.321
38 CONVENTO S. FRANCESCO A RIPA
Piazza S. Francesco d'Assisi, 8 - Tel. 5819.020
39 SUORE DI NOSTRA SIGNORA
Via della Camilluccia, 687 - Tel. 324.260
40 STIMMATINE FRANCESCANE
Viale Marconi, 446 - Tel. 5571.265
41 MISSIONARI DELLA CONSOLATA
Via Mura Aurelie, 11 - Tel. 632.616
42 COLLEGIO LEGIONARI DI CRISTO
Via Aurelia, 677 - Tel. 620.672
43 COLLEGIO PIO LATINO AMERICANO
Via Aurelia, 511 - Tel. 6224.641
44 COLLEGIO PIO BRASILIANO
Via Aurelia, 527 - Tel. 620.172
45 COLLEGIO FILIPPINO - Via Aurelia, 490 - Tel. 6220.873

95

46 COLLEGIO S. GIOSAFAT
Passeggiata Gianicolo, 7 - Tel. 636.369
47 SALVATOR MUNDI
Via Mura Gianicolensi, 67 - Tel. 582.860
48 MISSIONI ESTERE DI PARIGI
Piazza G. Fabrizio, 1 - Tel. 846.551
49 IST. MARCHESA GERINI
Va Tiburtina, Km. 10 - Tel. 419.141
50 CASA PALLOTTI - Via Pettinari, 64 - Tel. 6568.843
51 IST. MISSIONI ESTERE - Corso d'Italia, 36 - Tel. 848.044
52 PONTIFICIO COLLEGIO SPAGNOLO
Via Torrerossa, 2 - Tel. 6220.990
53 COLLEGIO GERMANICO UNGARICO
Via S. Nicola da Tolentino, 13 - Tel. 479.333
54 IST. MADRI PIE - Via Alcide de Gasperi, 4 - Tel. 631.967
55 HOTEL RITZ - Piazza Euclide - Tel. 805.751
56 COLLEGIO S. GIROLAMO - Via Tomacelli, 132 - Tel. 671.050
57 COLLEGIO OLANDESE
Via Ercole Rosa, 1 - Tel. 573.923
58 HOTEL DE LA VILLE
Via Sistina, 69 - Tel. 688.941
59 HOTEL COLUMBUS
Via della Conciliazione, 33 - Tel. 565.435
60 FRATERNITA' SACERDOTALE
Via della Camilluccia, 24 - Tel. 340.043
61 MISSIONARI DELLO SPIRITO SANTO
Piazza S. Salvatore in Campo, 57 - Tel. 652.041
62 HOTEL FLORA - Via Veneto - Tel. 462.151
63 GRAND HOTEL - Via V. E. Orlando - Tel. 489.011
64 RESIDENCE PALACE - Via Archimede, 69 - Tel. 878.341
65 HOTEL AMBASCIATORI - Via Veneto - Tel. 480.451
66 COLLEGIO INGLESE - Via Monserrato, 45 - Tel. 651.829
67 COLLEGIO ASS. A.C.I. - Via N. Piccolomini, 32 - Tel. 634.641
68 PADRI BIANCHI - Via Aurelia, 269 - Tel. 632.314
69 COLLEGIO MARYKNOLL - Via Sardegna, 83 - Tel. 465.700
70 COLLEGIO S. ANSELMO
Via Porta Lavernale - Tel. 573.569
71 HOTEL EXCELSIOR - Via Veneto, 12 - Tel. 489.031
72 COLLEGIO BEDA - Viale S. Paolo, 18 - Tel. 551.758
73 PONT. COLLEGIO CANADESE
Via IV Fontane, 117 - Tel. 480.754
74 MISSIONARI SS. CUORE
Va S. Cuore di Maria, 5 - Tel. 878.189
75 HOTEL MICHELANGELO
Via Stazione di S. Pietro, 14 - Tel. 631.251
76 FIGLI DI MARIA IMMACOLATA
Via del Mascherone, 5 - Tel. 653.857
77 PADRI PASSIONISTI
Piazza SS. Giovanni e Paolo, 13 - Tel. 736.841
78 COLLEGIO DEL VERBO DIVINO
Via dei Verbiti, 1 - Tel. 570.059
79 COLLEGIO INT. DEI SS. CUORI
Via S. Erasmo, 2 - Tel. 754.071
80 RETRAITE DU SACRE COEUR
Via Ulisse Seni, 2 - Tel. 580.446
81 FRANCESCANE MISSIONARIE DI MARIA
Via Giusti, 12 - Tel. 733.898
82 FRANCESCANE DELLA PENITENZA
Via Cassia, 645 - Tel. 3070.657
83 SAC. DEL S. CUORE DI GESU'
Via Casale S. Pio V, 20 - Tel. 620.864
84 COLLEGIO POLACCO - Piazza Remuria, 2 - Tel. 573.936
85 PADRI ROSMINIANI - Via Porta Latina, 17 - Tel. 750.377
86 MISSIONARI DEL S. CUORE
Via Aventina, 3 - Tel. 573.949
87 MISSIONARI DEL S. CUORE
Via Asmara, 11 - Tel. 813.741
88 COLLEGIO S. PATRIZIO - Via Piemonte, 60 - Tel. 465.716
89 COLLEGIO PP. MARIANISTI - Via Corsica, 1 - Tel. 864.358
90 COLLEGIO LEONIANO
Via Pompeo Magno, 21 - Tel. 359.946

IL SERVIZIO GENERALE DI AUTOPULLMAN PER IL TRASPORTO DEGLI ECC.MI PADRI CONCILIARI E' AFFIDATO ALLE DITTE:
SIRET - Piazzale Clodio, 45 - Telefono: 383.064 - 389.498
LUSTRISSIMI - Viale Pinturicchio, 94 - Telefono: 305.208 - 398.180

96

3. Map of Rome, showing the distribution of the council fathers' residences (Archivio Segreto Vaticano).

4. A busload of council fathers arrives for a general congregation (from *Das Konzil und seine Folgen*). The bishop of Pesaro complained about the lack of a service car to transfer the fathers at St. Peter's: "They said that the Holy See had arranged for a service car for all the council fathers, but the latest is that each has to find their way to the Vatican on their own. Big problem! Will it be a problem every day?" (Diary of Luigi Carlo Borromeo, October 11, 1962).

4

▶ Council Expenses (in Lire)

Costs incurred during the antepreparatory period:	9,776,683
Costs incurred during the preparatory period:	349,974,323
Costs incurred during the first session period:	618,266,695
Costs incurred during the second session period:	899,182,375
Costs incurred during the third session period:	1,129,069,007
Costs incurred during the fourth session period:	1,138,221,605
Costs incurred for the Council Hall and equipment:	417,517,045
Total	**4,562,007,733**

288,439,490:	total printing costs for the four sessions and the preparatory period
1,281,259,308:	travel expenses
1,497,220,619:	living expenses
1,067,794,588:	general expenses for the operation of the secretaries and commissions

(Source: *Attività del segretariato amministrativo 1959–1965*, rel. mons. Luigi Esposito, 10 giugno 1967—ASV, Conc. Vat. ii, b.368, f.1)

included general operating expenses, travel reimbursements, and equipment. The Holy See received offers from the faithful and the wealthier bishops' conferences such as the Americans and the Germans, who contributed a million Deutschmarks to council expenses.

Since there was not enough space in the religious institutions to accommodate all of the participants, it was necessary to draw up agreements with hotels. A total of 139 places were involved. These were selected by the heads of the Secretariat and those in charge of pilgrimages, the *Peregrinatio Romana ad Petri Sedem*, the office that had managed the Holy Year in 1950 and the hospitality for the preparatory phase, and which kept a file with the addresses in Rome of all the council fathers that was updated annually.

The financial management of the assembly, which had been particularly significant at the Council of Trent, did not impact Vatican II greatly. The organization was limited to extrinsic matters, such as meals and laundry arrangements. In addition, the clothing of some council fathers was replaced or repaired by nuns, items that had arrived in Rome in a "truly miserable" state, as the Secretariat's technical report stated at the end of the council's fourth session.

The cardinals and the Eastern patriarchs used their own cars or ones provided by the Vatican fleet. Some bishops had their own cars, and observers were assisted by the Secretariat for Christian Unity. However, most of the assembly travelled by means of the transportation service contracted out to two companies (SIRET and Lustrissimi), who made available about sixty small- and medium-sized buses and a few cars. Each vehicle had a number, a permit, and a prearranged itinerary to take the council fathers from their accommodations between eight and nine in the morning to St. Peter's Square, parking in Bernini's colonnade. Then in late morning, they took them back to their residences where the bishops ate their meals in common before devoting the afternoon to lectures and meetings. From the second period on, Paul VI subscribed to *Avvenire d'Italia*, edited by Raniero Valle. This became—for many who knew Italian thanks to their theological studies in Rome or had been coming for visits since the 1930s—the essential tool for understanding what had been said in Latin (incomprehensible because of national accents) in the Council Hall. In many houses in the evening, the TV provided the opportunity to see the daily recap of the council broadcast by RAI and presented by Luca Di Schiena, which provided a key to the discussions in St. Peter's to nearly four million subscribers in 1962. This number would grow to more than six million by 1965.

5. Cardinal Lercaro's pass, giving him free access to the Vatican for the council (Archivio Fschire).

6. The area around the Piazza Navona in Rome. The church is Sant'Agnese in Agone (BAMSphoto—Rodella).

5

6

▶ THE CARDINALS

The cardinals, especially the Italians, had residences in Rome which they normally used during their stays and which they also retained during the council. Some stayed in the Vatican itself, but others chose accommodations that were more discreet and that were free, as normally happens during conclaves. During the first period, Cardinal Giovanni Battista Montini stayed at the Lombardy Seminary; Cardinal Giacomo Lercaro stayed with the Benedictine nuns of St. Priscilla on Via Salaria; Cardinal Franz König at the Salvator Mundi nursing home belonging to the Sisters of the Divine Savior in Via delle Mura Gianicolensi, where some subcommittees met. After his appointment as cardinal, Charles Journet stayed at the Swiss Guards' accommodations.

Colleges and national seminaries were the places where the meetings of the various episcopal conferences were mostly held. Many bishops conferences met at Domus Mariae on the Via Aurelia: most of the Brazilian bishops and many Italians stayed here (the Italian bishops' conference, which had never been convened until the council, had its headquarters in the Via della Conciliazione).

At Domus Mariae also the important group of secretaries and the representatives of the episcopal conferences of the world met: it was an informal group, founded and coordinated by Archbishop Roger Etchegaray, secretary general of the French Episcopal Conference, which gradually became a very important reference point for the development of the debates.

At the Pontifical Teutonic College of Santa Maria dell'Anima, on the street of the same name near Piazza Navona, not only the German bishops and experts, but any German-speaking fathers and advisers gathered. No. 30, Via Santa Maria dell'Anima, behind Piazza Navona, was host instead to the headquarters of IDOC, the documentation center run by the Dutchman, Alting von Gesau, where, in 1968, the "Pro Union" Center would be set up, which was where the Dutch theologian Edward Schillebeeckx often lectured.

For the duration of the council, the Belgian College was a meeting place of a different caliber. Here Fr. Gauthier's group of the Church of the poor gathered, from the first period on, and it was here that meetings were held around the moderators, Archbishop Gerard Philips, assistant secretary of the Doctrinal Commission of the council, and Cardinal Leon-Joseph Suenens.

In the council's press room, information was sorted and categorized among the news agencies. This material was often useful for guiding the bishops and theologians who wrote columns for the periodicals (such as Yves Congar, Joseph Ratzinger, and Giovanni Caprile). Here they met the representatives from the international press, who, in some cases, wrote under pseudonyms, such as Fr. Francis X. Murphy, aka Xavier Rynne, whose books became best sellers.

BIBLIOGRAPHY
Aula Sancta Concilii, edited by the general secretariat of the Second Vatican Ecumenical Council, Rome 1967; Concilio Ecumenico Vaticano II, "Attività del Segretariato Amministrativo 1959–1965, relatore: mons. Luigi Sposito, Vaticano, June 10, 1967," in ASV, Concilio Vaticano II, binder 368, file. 1; G. Caprile, *Il concilio Vaticano II. Cronache del Concilio Vaticano II edite da "La Civiltà Cattolica." Il primo periodo (1962–1963)*, Rome 1968, 287–288; O. J. Beozzo, "Il clima esterno," in *Storia del concilio Vaticano II*, edited by G. Alberigo (Italian edition edited by A. Melloni), vol. 1, Bologna 1995 (2012), 381–428.

27. Host Sites for Commissions, Episcopal Conferences, Groups, and Others

Although the general congregations were held in St. Peter's Basilica, which was suitably equipped with grandstands and platforms, a large number of council sites scattered around Rome and its surroundings were no less influential than the Council Hall itself as work progressed. At the Council of Trent it was customary for the bishops to discuss among themselves in the mornings and listen to theologians in the afternoons, all in the Council Hall. However, at Vatican II, this custom was abandoned. Dialogue with and listening to the experts occurred in other places and times—sometimes even taking place far from Rome in a kind of centripetal motion, which intensified in the course of the work. For example, the Antepreparatory Commission met at the Apostolic Palace in the apartments of the secretary of state, and when the pope wished to intervene they met in the pontiff's private library (where Paul VI had had *The Resurrection* by Perugino hung). The Central Commission had its headquarters at no. 10 via Serristori, near the Via della Conciliazione. Significantly, the other commissions instead were based at the headquarters of the Curia at no. 12 Piazza Pio, just where the Via della Conciliazione began. The Commissions for the Discipline of the Clergy, for Religious, and for Studies and Seminaries met at no. 3. The Commissions for Liturgy, for Sacraments, and for Bishops met at no. 10. The Theological Commission was located at the Holy Office at Piazza Cavalleggeri. Similarly, the Commission on the Eastern Churches was also located at the Congregation for Oriental Churches on Via dei Corridori, with the Commission for the Missions at no. 48 Piazza di Spagna, center for the Propaganda Fide congregation. The Commission on the Lay Apostolate was located in the palace of the Chancery of Apostolic Briefs, in the square of the same

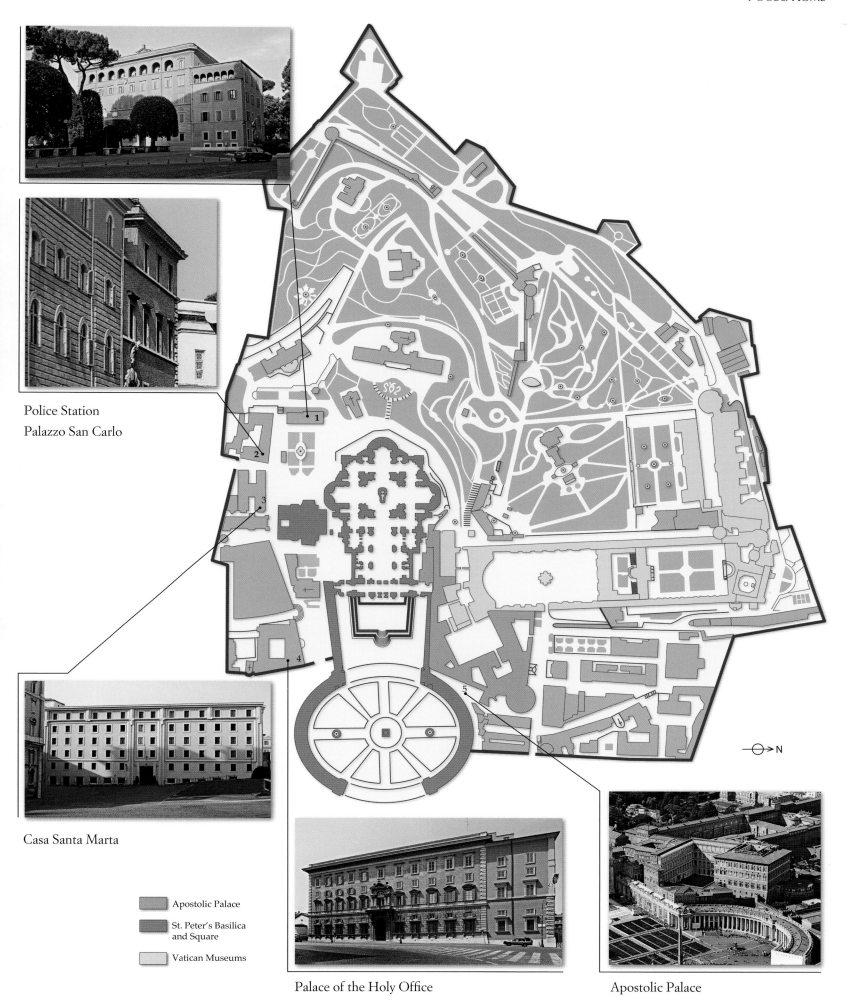

Police Station

Palazzo San Carlo

Casa Santa Marta

Apostolic Palace

St. Peter's Basilica
and Square

Vatican Museums

Palace of the Holy Office

Apostolic Palace

153

1–3. St. Peter's Square and the Piazza of Pius XII, at the beginning of the Via della Conciliazione (BAMSphoto—Rodella).

name, where Cardinal Cento lived and ran the Center, and at Trastevere, in the Palace of the Congregations of Piazza St. Callixtus, the headquarters of COPECIAL, the Standing Committee for International Congresses for the Lay Apostolate. The Secretariat for Christian Unity was housed in the building on Via dei Corridori, but with its own entrance. The Secretariat for the Press and the World of Entertainment was located instead in the San Carlo building, within the Vatican walls, while the Commission for Ceremony was in Via della Rotonda.

The preparatory committee meetings were held in different places—often in the old building of Santa Marta in the Vatican, which, even before the later restructuring that John Paul II had wanted for the conclave, could accommodate several dozen people. Subcommittees had some, but not total, freedom of location, but not all—Fr. Sebastian Tromp, secretary of the Theological Commission, recalls in his diary misunderstandings and discussions that came about because of a meeting of the subcommittee that was convened at the Gregorian, instead of at the Holy Office. The Secretariat for Christian Unity also showed its logistical asymmetry: the first informal meeting took place between members and consultants for example in September 1960 in Gazzada (Varese), at the annual Catholic Conference on Ecumenical Issues.

During the council, the governing bodies and the conciliar commissions were almost all set up in the Santa Marta building in the Vatican. The only exceptions were the Commission on Religious and the Secretariat for Christian Unity, which retained their headquarters in Via dei Corridori.

The Press Office, the first in the history of the Church and of the council, was placed at no. 12 Via Serristori.

The locations of the work of the council subcommittees and informal working groups were even more varied and included the houses where the bishops and experts were staying.

Fr. Congar's diary testifies to the many places throughout Rome where sessions, meetings, and gatherings were held: the Belgian Pontifical College (35 Via G. Pagano), the Brazilian Pontifical

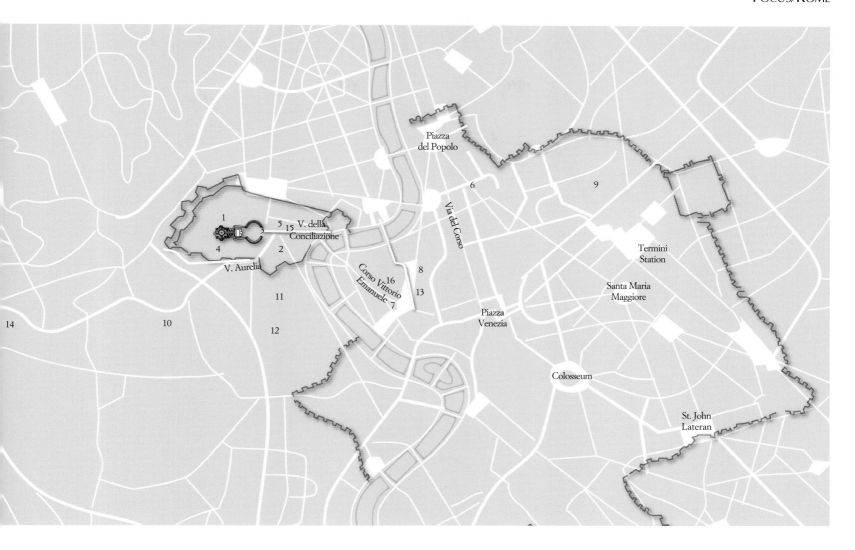

College (527 Via Aurelia), the Pontifical North American College (in the grounds of Villa Gabrielli al Giancolo), the Villa Mater Dei belonging to the German dioceses (at 10 Via delle Mura Aureliane), the Polish Pontifical College (2 Piazza Remuria), and the Pontifical French Seminary (42 Via di Santa Chiara). Even the mother houses of some religious orders were able to offer hospitality to the work of a subcommittee or working group.

From the preparation stage on, there were sessions on most days that became necessary and that took place outside Rome: the preparatory Theological Commission had already organized a special session of the subcommittee on *De Ecclesia*, in July 1961, at the Pauline Fathers' House in Ariccia in the Alban Hills, which then became the headquarters for several crucial meetings for editing *Gaudium et Spes* and other documents.

In the week between February 3 and 9, 1964, a group of experts from the Secretariat for Christian Unity gathered at the motherhouse of the Sisters of Bethany of the Holy Spirit in Rome, in the Monte Mario neighborhood, where Archbishop Willebrands lived, to work on *De Libertate Religiosa*. In January and February of 1964 in Zurich, Switzerland, at the Jesuit community that published the magazine *Orientierung*, the first meeting took place of the joint subcommittee (the Doctrinal Commission and the Commission for the Apostolate of the Laity) to discuss the chapter on the laity in the draft of *De Ecclesia*. This was followed, at the same location, by a meeting of the drafting committee of the Joint Commission to discuss the draft on the Church in the modern world. In February 1965, the latter committee organized a two-week working session, again in Ariccia, to which all the members of the two constituent commissions, the Doctrinal Commission and the Commission for the Lay Apostolate, were invited, plus a large number of experts involved in drafting the document, a total of more than a hundred people. In the week between January 11 and 16, 1965, experts from the Commission on the Missions gathered for a residential working session in the house of the Fathers of the Divine Word at Lake Nemi, south of Rome. The commission met here in plenary session between March 19 and April 3. These examples show how council locations were divided up.

BIBLIOGRAPHY
Y. M. J. Congar, *Le Concile au jour le jour*, Paris 1963–1966, 4 vols.; X. Rynne, *Letters from Vatican City. Vatican Council II. Background and Debates*, London 1963; X. Rynne, *The Debates and Decrees of Vatican Council II*, London 1964–1966, 3 vols.; G. Caprile, *Il concilio Vaticano II. Cronache del Concilio Vaticano II edite da "La Civiltà Cattolica,"* Rome 1966–1969, 5 vols.; *Storia del concilio Vaticano II*, edited by G. Alberigo (Italian edition edited by A. Melloni), Bologna 1995–2001, 5 vols.

28. The Conclave

As had happened before, the duration of the Second Vatican Council extended beyond one pontificate (in this case, to two) and involved both its convener John XXIII, and his successor Paul VI. Obviously—wrote Hubert Jedin, historian of the Council of Trent—"the differences in formation, personality, and experience between John XXIII and Paul VI," would mean that the council would be oriented differently: on the one hand, Pope John, who had guaranteed the total freedom of the Curia during the council preparations, would have granted the same freedom to the assembly and have been swayed by the majority. But, Paul VI, whom the Curia opposed before the conclave, was not going to exacerbate this situation. Instead, he would want unanimous council decisions that would silence any recriminations. In the midst of the council, John XXIII fell ill and died. The 1963 conclave marked the transition between the stages.

The first period between sessions was marked by the death of Pope John XXIII on June 3, closing what most of the cardinals who had elected him in 1958 thought of as a "transitional" pontificate. His illness had not prevented him publishing an encyclical just fifty-three days before his death, *Pacem in Terris*, in which, speaking for the first time to all men of good will (not just to the members of the Church), "he overcame the secular theology of war, and denied that there could ever be a 'just' war in the atomic age" (a condemnation of war the council never managed to agree on); he received the Balzan Prize, for "humanity, peace, and brotherhood among peoples," the pillars of Roncalli's message to the embassies of the United States and the Soviet Union in Rome, averting the impasse of the Cuban missile crisis and the outbreak of nuclear war.

The suffering and the death of Pope John was lamented by all, including Chief Rabbi Elio Toaff in St. Peter's Square, and was followed by television stations worldwide, resulting in a consensus about the impact he had made. The Archbishop of Canterbury, speaking to RAI, said, "We, and indeed all of our churches, have the impression we too have lost our pope."

It was clear from the start how "council and conclave" were "inextricably linked," and that the Council Hall—as Cardinal Eugène Tisserant explained to the French ambassador—played a role in the selection of the candidates (including the Italians, Giovanni Battista Montini and Giacomo Lercaro) and leaders (such as Augustin Bea, Josef Frings, Achille Liénart, and Léon-Joseph Suenens).

Montini's candidacy was feared by the Spanish dictator Francisco Franco (who prayed against his election), by the German Chancellor Konrad Adenauer, and on the Italian right by the President of the Republic Antonio Segni, and Luigi Gedda. He had crossed swords with the leaders of the Roman Curia who nine years earlier had moved him out of the secretariat of state by promoting him to archbishop of Milan; they were willing to vote for Lercaro rather than have him as pope. Instead Montini entered the conclave on June 19 as the favorite and on the 21st was made pope, taking the name Paul VI, thanks to a compromise with Lercaro. As a Belgian diplomat wrote, "the council has made the conclave."

The death of John XXIII on June 3, 1963, had meant that, according to the canonical prescriptions, Vatican II had to be suspended, but Pope Paul VI announced on June 27 not only that Vatican II should continue, but that it would resume work the following September 29: "It is the first thought of my apostolic ministry," to honor the "guarantees" that had previously been given and, in the climate of consensus, he would not fail to grow the seed that the council and Pope John had sown.

As Archbishop Montini—no one knows how involved he had been in Pius XII's council plans—he was among those who had expressed concern about the absence of a precise plan of work for the Second Vatican Council and had kept a low profile. As pope, however, he immediately intervened in the conciliar process by changing the Regulations and favoring a judicious pruning of the drafts that were to be discussed.

Above all, he established a new relationship between the pope and the council, acting directly both from a procedural standpoint, and on the merits of the drafts in question. Montini conceived his role as essentially that of a guarantor of harmony within the council, which from the second period of work on, was seriously threatened by the resistance of a minority of tenacious council fathers who were resistant to renewal.

Paul VI intervened several times in order to give guarantees to the minority, even at the cost of compromising the relationship with "his" majority. Five times he withdrew topics from the council agenda if he considered it prudent to decide himself—for example, the reform of the Curia, artificial contraception, nuclear deterrence, clerical celibacy, the functioning of the synod—which would have otherwise remained in limbo.

How he dealt with a proposal that the council canonize John XXIII was emblematic of his attitude as presider of Vatican II. He deferred it in favor of the regular canonization process, along with a regular process for Pius XII. In 2014, Pope Francis fulfilled the desire of the council by canonizing John XXIII—and beatifying Paul VI.

2. Giovanni Battista Montini, archbishop of Milan, was one of the major players during the first period of the council. Elected pope on June 21, 1963, he chooses the name Paul VI. Two days prior to the coronation, *L'Osservatore Romano* made public his decision to continue Vatican II, establishing Sunday, September 29, as the date for the resumption of the Council (photo Pais/Archivio Pais–Ceub Università di Bologna).

BIBLIOGRAPHY

Paolo VI e i problemi ecclesiologici al Concilio, International Colloquium of Study (Brescia, September 19–21, 1986), Brescia-Rome 1989; G. Alberigo, "Imparare da sé.' L'esperienza conciliare," in *Storia del concilio Vaticano II*, edited by G. Alberigo (Italian editing edited by A. Melloni), vol. 2, Bologna 1996 (2012), 613–634; A. Melloni, *Il conclave. Storia dell'elezione del Papa*, Bologna 2001 (2005, 2013); E. Galavotti, *Processo a Papa Giovanni. La causa di canonizzazione di A.G.* *Roncalli (1965–2000)*, Bologna 2005; A. G. Roncalli-Giovanni XXIII, *Pater amabilis. Agende del pontefice, 1958–1963*, critical edition and annotation by M. Velati, Bologna 2007; G. Alberigo, *Transizione epocale. Studi sul Concilio Vaticano II*, Bologna 2009, pp. 95–134; A. Melloni, *Pacem in terris. Storia dell'ultima enciclica di Papa Giovanni*, Rome-Bari 2010; J.-D. Durand, "La storiografia conciliare su Paolo VI," in *Giovanni XXIII e Paolo VI. I due papi del Concilio*, edited by Ph. Chenaux, Vatican City, 2013, 129–152.

29. THE MODERATORS

The eight weeks of work during the first period had been an effective test of the council Regulations. Right from the first sessions, the development of a council that was effectively open and not merely a rubber stamp approving the preparatory drafts brought out the limits of the ordo, primarily those sections that defined the powers of the council's governing bodies. It can truly be said that the problems began with the first session. The ten-cardinal presidential council of Vatican II, who had taken as their model the council that had taken place ninety years earlier, had no say over the voting of the conciliar commissions, but was the source from which the request to defer them was voiced. A few weeks later the pope directly addressed the solution to the impasse that had been created by the vote on the draft *De Fontibus*, which had been rejected by the Assembly by an insufficient—according to the letter of the Regulations—majority of votes, but at the same time was unequivocal in expressing the deep feelings of most of the Council fathers.

In addition to the presidential council and the more active Secretariat for Extraordinary Affairs, which was composed of seven members and chaired by the Secretary of State, John XXIII created a third structure that would guide the period between the sessions: the Coordinating Commission. This group was to reorganize the council agenda, especially in light of the guidelines that emerged during the debates. They apparently took over from the Central Preparatory Commission, which had become obsolete when the council began its work: instead of working downstream from the preparatory commissions and merely dealing with slight changes and objections, it was upstream of the council commissions, structuring their work.

As a member of the Central commission and of the Secretariat for Extraordinary Affairs, as well as an expert in ecclesiastical government, Cardinal Montini understood very well that the risk of ending in an impasse had been averted by this step. So at the time of his election to the papacy in June 1963, while he gave important assurances to the Curia regarding the reform process, Paul VI also decided to tackle the problem of how to run Vatican II and its "many-headed authority structure." The pope decided on a revision of the Regulations, which he completed in only two months.

At first the new pope had seemed inclined to rely on a single cardinal in the person of Cardinal Leon-Joseph Suenens, archbishop of Malines-Brussels. Then he was convinced that it was appropriate to appoint more than one, and added Car-

dinals Grégoire-Pierre XV Agagianian, prefect of the Congregation De Propaganda Fide, and Julius Döpfner, archbishop of Munich and Freising. To these he added Cardinal Giacomo Lercaro, archbishop of Bologna. He announced these appointments on September 12, 1963, by the letter *Quod Apostolici* addressed to Cardinal Eugène Tisserant. At the same time Paul VI announced the dissolution of the Secretariat for Extraordinary Affairs, the elevation of twelve members to the presidential council, and the setting up of a Group of Four "delegates" or "moderators" of the council, to whom, as the pope wrote, "we will give the responsibility of directing the work of the council: they will take turns in leading the discussions of the general congregations, while always maintaining and ensuring the freedom of the council fathers, indeed, ensuring the order and clarity of what is said in the council either individually or severally."

The pope did not want to abolish the presidential council, thus angering its members (some had been his opponents in the conclave, such as Cardinal Giuseppe Siri, while others had voted for him, such as Cardinal Tisserant), but did not want to choose from among them the legates that the Council Hall needed. On the other hand, he wanted to be faithful to what emerged as a majority from the council.

Alongside Agagianian, who was a respected figure in the Curia but not too invested in the preparatory drafts, he appointed Suenens, Döpfner, and Lercaro, who, because of the harmony of their views, would be jokingly called "the Synoptics." During the summer, all three had provided the pope with ideas and notes on the work in general (Suenens) and on the Regulations (Döpfner and Lercaro). The experts they consulted—from Gerard Philips and Yves Congar, to Karl Rahner, Otto Semmelroth, or Giuseppe Dossetti (who, for a short period, was secretary of the moderators)—guaranteed that the work had a solid theological basis. By nominating Agagianian and Lercaro to the Coordinating Commission, Paul VI designed a structure for the work that would allow the council to make decisions and be truly representative.

BIBLIOGRAPHY
L.-J. Suenens, *Ricordi e speranze*, Cinisello Balsamo 1993, 134–137; R. Aubert, "Organizzazione e funzionamento dell'assemblea," in *Storia della Chiesa*, XXV/1, *La Chiesa del Vaticano II (1958–1978)*, edited by M. Guasco, E. Guerriero, F. Traniello, Cinisello Balsamo 1994, 187–213; J. Grootaers, "Il concilio si gioca nell'intervallo. La 'seconda preparazione' e i suoi avversari," in *Storia del concilio Vaticano II*, edited by G. Alberigo (Italian edition edited by A. Melloni), vol. 2, Bologna 1996 (2012), 385–558; G. Alberigo, *Transizione epocale. Studi sul Concilio Vaticano II*, Bologna 2009, 183–228.

1. The four moderators of the council. From left, Cardinals Grégoire-Pierre XV Agagianian, Giacomo Lercarco, Julius Döpfner, and Léon-Joseph Suenens.

2. Cardinal Lercaro with Suenans on the left (Archivio Fscire).

3. At the presidents' table, Cardinal Eugène Tisserant confers with Cardinal Agagianian (© Archivio Storico Luce).

4. The moderators' table in front of the council presidents' table. In the foreground, Cardinal Agagianian talks with Cardinal Ottaviani, at the left end of the table, Cardinal Tisserant with Cardinal Lercaro (© Archivio Storico Luce).

30. The Council Reopens. Votes on Issues of Collegiality

1. St. Peter's Basilica, September 29, 1963. Paul VI enters the Council Hall. Instead of being carried in the *sedia gestatoria*, he makes his way down the aisle on foot, the council fathers applauding as he passes (photo Pais/Archivio Rodrigo Pais–Ceub Università di Bologna).

On September 29, 1963, the second period opened. During this session, the press would play a role as disseminator of information and views and would have significant influence over the progress and implementation of the council itself outside the Council Hall in St. Peter's.

The ceremony was less triumphalist than the year before: the fathers could arrive at the basilica singly or enter in procession. Paul VI made his entrance on foot and not in the *sedia gestatoria*. But not everyone appreciated these attempts at simplification. For example, Yves Congar observed a Church still unwilling to give up the pomp of the past: "The pope is about to make his entrance. Before

he arrives his court enters: the Swiss guard carrying halberds, cardinals with priestly (or diaconal) adornments, done up in very tall miters, prelates in purple and red, servers dressed as though from the sixteenth century, the insignia-holders (carrying the papal tiara and the miter), finally the pope, attended by a deacon and subdeacon, with canopy-bearers. The pope wears the precious miter: he enters on foot. Gradually, as he advances down the nave, those in the rows of benches he passes begin to applaud, which shocked me very much."

In his opening address, the pope drew attention mainly to the draft on the Church, which would be discussed at

2. St. Peter's Basilica, September 29, 1963. The ceremony opening the second session is broadcast by Eurovision. Compared to the opening of the first session, the second seems more subdued. The bishops had the choice of entering the basilica individually and sitting without regard for seniority or of processing in before the pope (photo Pais/Archivio Rodrigo Pais–Ceub Università di Bologna).

3. St. Peter's, September 29, 1963. Cardinal Tisserant presides at the opening ceremony. After the profession of faith and ritual promise of obedience, the pope will read his speech: "You, venerable brothers…are like the apostles themselves, drawing your origin from the apostolic college. In this you are their true heirs." (photo Pais/Archivio Rodrigo Pais–Ceub Università di Bologna).

3

the beginning of the second session and was one of the fundamental steps of the whole council. In addition, he introduced the theme of "dialogue." There was already a draft on this, which would become the encyclical *Ecclesiam Suam*. The Church would have to establish a new relationship with the other Christian churches and with the modern world. Archbishop Enrico Bartoletti called the speech "important and crucial for the work of the council. He has clarified the issue, shown us the attitude to have, and given us a clear roadmap without the possibility of further misunderstandings," without, however, "having the immediacy of Pope John."

On September 30, Cardinals Alfredo Ottaviani and Michael Browne, chairman and vice chairman of the Doctrinal Commission respectively, presented the new draft in a changed atmosphere, in which the bishops had learned "to say 'no' calmly, and without fear." *De Ecclesia* had been completely rewritten by the Doctrinal Commission during the intersessional period, based on the draft prepared by Gerard Philips, a Belgian theologian trusted by Cardinal Suenens. Although the text retained passages from the preparatory draft that were deemed "harmless," it presented an entirely new perspective: it did not keep the legal structure of the Church in the foreground, it did not merely

4–5. The opening ceremony of the second session of the council (photo Pais/Archivio Rodrigo Pais–Ceub Università di Bologna).

6–7. Moments from the ceremony (photo Pais/Archivio Rodrigo Pais–Ceub Università di Bologna).

4

5

6

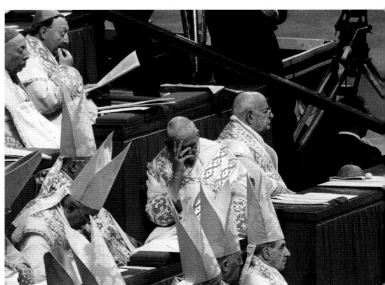

7

8. Five questions (Archive Fscire) "This occurred to me tonight… Dr. Tonino Rubbi… dined with us. On the bus in Bologna, he overheard two women talking, first making a comment on 'Ruby, who killed Oswald.' Then, commenting on the council she said 'I can't understand why the bishops still continue to talk!'" (Giacomo Lercaro, Letter, November 29, 1963).

9. Letter of the Secretary Pericle Felici to the council fathers on the program of work to prepare for the second session (Archive Fscire).

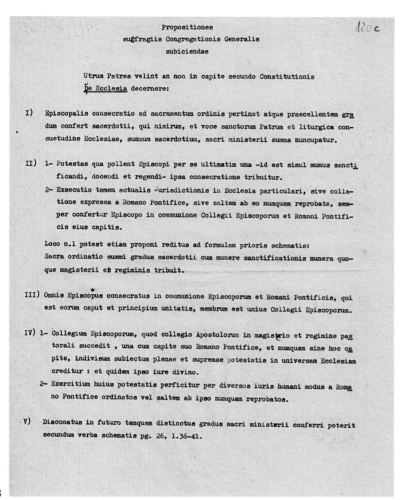

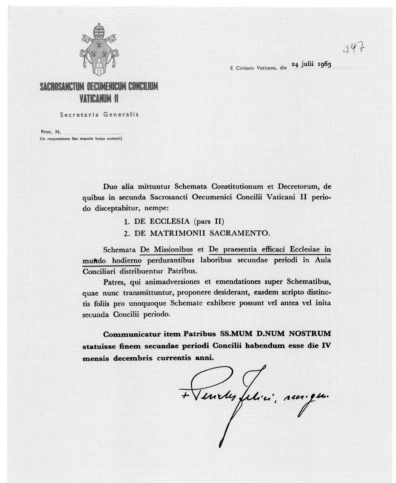

8

9

state the principle of authority, and it did not restrict the principle of salvation to the Catholic Church. In the new draft, the Church's nature was described as that of a mystery, with a Trinitarian perspective: the concept of the "mystical body" remained, but with a liturgical dimension. Moreover, the draft opened relations with other Christian Churches, thanks to the definition of baptism. The paragraphs devoted to the episcopate were developed further, stressing the ancient formula of the Church founded on the faith of Peter and the apostles, who together formed an apostolic "college." Thus, the foundations of affirmation of the principle of collegiality were laid along with an ecclesiology of communion.

However, the council discussion was long and bitter. It introduced the theme of the biblical models of the Church, including that of the "people of God." The episcopate was thought of as a sacrament in which jurisdiction over the universal Church is attributed to the bishops precisely because they are bishops of local churches; there was broad consensus on this, but several cardinals and bishops intervened to defend the meaning of the pontifical mandate in the definition of the bishop. It was difficult to understand the will of the council. "The council is like a stutterer," commented Giuseppe Dossetti, "who cannot formulate coherent words and phrases: the danger is that the Curia will take advantage of this with the excuse that because they have to somehow finish up the discussion, they will vote on anything."

The fact that the *placet juxta modum* could only be used for a whole chapter of a draft and not for individual amend-

10

ments, and also that the changes required could be interpreted further complicated the overall direction of the general debate and the orientation of the assembly. It was Dossetti, de facto secretary of the moderators, thanks to his previous experience as a member of the assembly, who thought about the possibility of submitting a series of guiding principles to the fathers: not rules, but guidelines on which the commission could base a rewrite of the text. The proposal was opposed by the minority, which countered by appealing directly to the pope. The questions, developed earlier by Dossetti and by Carlo Colombo—Paul VI's trusted theologian—and then revised in its second formulation by Gerard Philips, Charles Moeller, and Albert Prignon, asked if the fathers had agreed to the proposals that the council had defined 1) that the episcopal consecration constituted the maximum degree of the sacrament of Orders; 2) that every bishop who was consecrated and in communion with the pope was part of the "body of bishops"; 3) that the college of bishops is successor to the apos-

tolic college and as such, together with the pope, had the supreme authority in the universal Church; 4) that the fullness of power was of divine right. To these—in the fifteen days that passed between the announcement of the vote and the actual casting—was also added a question asking for 5) the restoration of the permanent diaconate as a distinct degree of the sacrament of holy orders open to those who were married.

Once the debate on the second chapter had ended, the announcement of the vote on October 15 raised alarm bells for the Secretary General, Archbishop Felice. He turned to the Secretary of State, Amleto Cicognani, and they went to Paul VI, who blocked the vote and had the printed ballot cards burned. Paul VI ordered a meeting of all the leaders of the council, moderators, presiders, Coordinating Commission, and secretary. On October 23, thanks to Cardinal Eugène Tisserant, dean of the College of Cardinals, this super-commission approved the questions, which Cardinal Ottaviani had sought to return to the Doctrinal Commis-

10. A rare representation of "The People of God" found in Marc Chagall, *The Exodus from Egypt* 1931. Ink drawing on paper, Musée national Chagall, Nizza (© Chagall®, by SIAE 2015).

11. The Church represented by the apostles gathered around Christ in a mosaic in the apse of S. Pudenziana (403–417), completed during the pontificate of Innocent I. Christ sits on a throne surmounted by a glorious cross studded with precious stones, recalling Rev 21:18–21, with the symbols of the evangelists, surrounded by the apostles and two maidens holding the victorious crown of martyrdom. (Archivio Jaca Book).

11

sion responsible for the draft in order to have it prepare a new version. On October 29—after a new meeting of the super-commission and an article in the newspaper *Il Quotidiano* on Ottaviani, who was against collegiality—with the consent of the pope it was decided to put it to a vote, which occurred on October 30: on all five there was a very large majority (1,717 for and 408 against, which became 525 over married diaconate). Taking note of the outcome of the vote, the Doctrinal Commission was able to revise the text of the draft that would become the Dogmatic Constitution *Lumen Gentium*.

BIBLIOGRAPHY
V. Carbone, "L'azione direttiva di Paolo VI nei periodi II e III del Concilio Ecumenico Vaticano II," in *Paolo VI e i problemi ecclesiologici al Concilio*, Brescia 1989, 80–82; A. Melloni, "L'inizio del secondo periodo e il grande dibattito ecclesiologico," in *Storia del concilio Vaticano II*, edited by G. Alberigo (Italian edition edited by A. Melloni), vol. 3, Bologna 1996 (2012), 19–132; A. Melloni, "Procedure e coscienza conciliare al Vaticano II. I voti del 30 ottobre 1963," in *Cristianesimo nella storia. Saggi in onore di G. Alberigo*, edited by A. Melloni, D. Menozzi, G. Ruggieri, M. Toschi, Bologna 1996, 313–396; G. Alberigo, "Giuseppe Dossetti al Concilio Vaticano II," in *Transizione epocale*, Bologna 2009, 393–502.

31. THE LITURGICAL REFORM

In his opening address to the second session, Paul VI followed John XXIII in giving a special emphasis to liturgical reform. Among the themes of the council, said the pope, "the sacred liturgy holds a meaning that is undoubtedly prominent and overflowing with charity. Since it has been discussed at length and extensively during the first session, we hope that now it will be brought to a very happy conclusion." And that is what happened. At the end of the second period, on December 4, 1963, during the public session, the council approved the first constitution and the first decree of Vatican II since the message to the world of the previous year, along with the Decree on the Media of Social Communication (*Inter Mirifica*, approved with 1,960 votes in favor and 164 *non placet*). This brought to fruition the reform initiated by the liturgical movement beginning in the late nineteenth century, which had already seen some results during Pacelli's pontificate: for example, the founding of the *Centre de Pastorale Liturgique* in 1943, the encyclical *Mediator Dei* of 1947, the Center of Italian Liturgical Action, and the *Institut Liturgisches Trier* in Germany). At the Congress of Mechelen, in 1909, the Benedictine Lambert Beauduin, who later founded the ecumenical experience at Chevetogne, and Professor Gottfried Kurth had spoken of "liturgical ignorance," of the importance of the missal as a prayer book, and of the experiments in Italy by Abbot Caronti to provide the faithful with access to their liturgical heritage. In 1957, Cipriano Vagaggini, liturgist and consultant to the council for the Liturgical Commission, explained that liturgical reform was imposed because it was "simply a consequence of the nature of the Church, which was at the same time human and divine, unchangeable and changeable. Its human aspect is subject to changes, to deficiencies, to phase shifts, with lapses that are more or less obvious, and therefore it is also subject to subsequent adjustments, improvements and reforms that are more or less significant. [...] The liturgy is no exception to this general law of the Church's life. Within it there is a core that is divine and immutable: the sacraments and the Eucharistic sacrifice in their substance. Everything else, strictly speaking, could change." As if to confirm Vagaggini's intuition, the vote of the bishops during the preparatory phase of Vatican II came in: one quarter were related to the liturgy and encouraged a process of reform that the Preparatory Commission would put in place, that the Central Preparatory Commission would substantially accept, and that the council fathers would reinforce in the discussion that marked the first period of the council in 1962.

The revised text was discussed by the relevant commission and voted on, together with the examination of *De Ecclesia*: it was voted on chapter by chapter and approved as a whole (even by Marcel Lefebvre who later became an opponent). On December 4, the 400th anniversary of the end of the Council of Trent, the constitution *Sacrosanctum Concilium* was voted on in the public session, and was promulgated by Paul VI with the new formula of approval.

Because it was not related to the controversy over strictly ecclesiological issues, the constitution introduced important principles: it highlighted the function of the bishop as icon of Christ the first liturgist; it established the "Eucharistic" principle of the Church and therefore the completeness of the local church; the Eucharist celebrated in the Church was recognized as a "sacrament of unity," that is "the holy people united and ordered under their bishops" (no. 26); although the production of general rules on the liturgy remained the prerogative of Rome, local episcopal conferences also had a role; and the introduction of the languages spoken in some parts of the ritual had the function of initiating a process that would be even more rapid and mature than what was expected. It was enough to "read the document carefully to see that it opened, and not closed doors."

The reform was enacted the following autumn and touched the experience of the whole people of God: the council and the reform, as even the Lefebvrian minority in a polemical sense would have guessed, would become one. In a few short months, the level of participation and the position of the celebrant became a lived experience. Even concelebration was accepted without difficulty.

In order to implement the reform, the pope made a historic decision: he entrusted the pace of the reform not to a congregation but to a *Consilium ad Exsequendam Constitutionem de Sacra Liturgia*. Between 1964 and 1975, it was responsible for editing the books that were the basis for translations into national languages and minority languages backed by legislation by the episcopal conferences.

BIBLIOGRAPHY
Giuseppe Alberigo, "'*Una cum patribus.*' La formula conclusiva delle decisioni del Vaticano II," in *Ecclesia a Spiritu Sanctu edocta. Mélanges théologiques. Hommage à Mgr Gérard Philips*, Gembloux 1970, 291–319; A. Bugnini, *La riforma liturgica 1948–1975*, Rome 1983; R. Kaczynski, "Verso la riforma liturgica," in *Storia del concilio Vaticano II*, edited by G. Alberigo (Italian edition edited by A. Melloni), vol. 3, Bologna 1998 (2013), 209–276; M. Paiano, "Il rinnovamento della liturgia: dai movimenti alla chiesa universale," in *Verso il concilio Vaticano II (1960–1962). Passaggi e problemi della preparazione conciliare*, edited by G. Alberigo and A. Melloni, Genoa 1993, 67–140; E. Galavotti, "Verso una nuova era liturgica. Appunti sul contributo di Cipriano Vagaggini al concilio Vaticano II," in *Teologia in un regime di simboli. Scritti in onore di Cipriano Vagaggini (1909–1999)*, edited by M. Ferrari and G. Remondi, Camaldoli 2011, 56–93.

1. The Second Vatican Council's Constitution on the Sacred Liturgy, published by Typis Polyglottis Vaticanis (Archivio Fscire).

2. The liturgical reform in action: Cardinal Julius Döpfner celebrates the liturgy according to the new rite (photo Gustl Tögel, Munich; da *Erneuerung in Christus*)

SACROSANCTUM OECUMENICUM CONCILIUM
VATICANUM SECUNDUM

CONSTITUTIO
DE SACRA LITURGIA

TYPIS POLYGLOTTIS VATICANIS
MCMLXIII

1

2

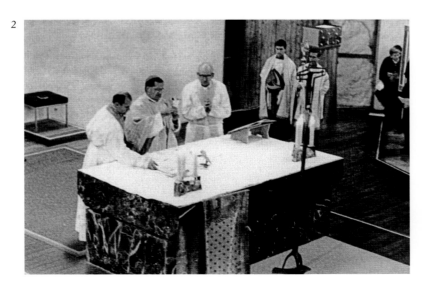

▶ *"UNA CUM PATRIBUS."* THE FORMULA FOR CONFIRMATION OF THE DECISIONS OF VATICAN II

The Regulations of Vatican II, published on August 6, 1962 with John XXIII's motu proprio *Appropinquante Concilio*, stipulated that, when he had decided to confirm the decisions of the council, the pope would pronounce the following formula: *"Decreta et canones modo lecta placuerunt Patribus, nemine dissentiente (vel si quis forte dissenserit, tot numero exceptis) Nosque, sacro approbante Concilio, illa ita decernimus, statuimus atque sancimus, ut lecta sunt"*. This formula remained unchanged even in the *editio altera recognita* of the Ordo, a second version of the Regulations approved by Pope Paul VI in September 1963, which included a number of amendments based on the difficulties encountered during the first session. It was not until the second session that the pope resorted to reading the formula, since none of the documents had been finalized previously. The formula literally repeated that described in paragraph VIII of the Regulations for the First Vatican Council, published on November 27, 1869.

However, it highlighted a distance between the bishop of Rome and the bishops of the council, which made them seem as if they were two bodies and not one unit. Paul VI entrusted a small group of theologians, historians, and canonists (including Carlo Colombo, Hubert Jedin, Giuseppe Dossetti, Klaus Mörsdorf, and Karl Rahner) with the task of coming up with a formula that was theologically more appropriate. Paul VI used it on December 4, 1963 and continued to use it until the fourth session (despite the fact that section fifty of the Regulations of Vatican II had never been formally amended), with an emphasis on mutual acceptance between the authority of the pope and the decisions of the synod, a step that was derived from the ancient council tradition: *"In nomine et sanctissimae individuae Trinitatis Patris et Filii et Spiritus Sancti. Decreta, quae in hac sacri sancta et uniersali synodo Vaticana secunda legitime congregata modo lecta sunt placuerunt Patribus. Et Nos, apostolica a Christo Nobis tradita potestate, illa, una cum venerabilibus Patribus, in Spiritu Sancto approbamus, decernimus et statuimus, et quae ita synodaliter statuta sunt ad Dei gloriam promulgari iubemus."*

3

5

3. An Eastern Rite celebration in the council (photo: Giordani / in *Il concilio Vaticano II*).

4. A liturgy in the Coptic Alexandrian Rite.

5. The rite of enthroning the Gospel book, presided over by Paul Nousseir, Coptic Bishop of Minya. On the ceremony closing the second session, Hélder Câmara commented, "The solemn closing of the session was anticipated by a long Vigil Mass....When we arrived in St. Peter's, we were at exactly the same height as the colossal equestrian statue of Constantine. Whoever said that the age of Constantine was over? Throughout the ceremony—it seemed like a nightmare—I could almost see and feel the stone horse galloping to the Basilica, carrying the emperor who has become the sorry symbol of what we want to overcome, but which is still very much alive" (Hélder Câmara, 59° Circolare, Rome, December 4/5, 1963).

6. St. Peter's Basilica, February 25, 1965. Paul VI concelebrates the Eucharist with the twenty-six new cardinals created in the consistory of February 22 (Archive Fscire). The option for concelebration was one of the liturgical reforms approved in the second session. In fact, the opening ceremony for session three was presided over by Paul VI along with twenty-four concelebrants from nineteen different countries, to symbolize that, as the pope himself wrote, "The council was a representation of the universal church gathered in unity of mind and will." Bishop Luigi Carlo Borromeo of Pesaro, during the discussion on concelebration, wrote this critical comment on his agenda, "We lack priests, and on holy days of obligation some have to run here and there all morning, celebrating two or three times in order for the faithful to hear Mass—and we're talking about concelebration at a time like this?" (Diary of Luigi Carlo Borromeo, November 5, 1962).

4

6

32. Jerusalem and Ecumenism

1. Paul VI leaves for the Holy Land, flying on the Italian airline, Alitalia. It would be the first trip outside of the borders of Italy taken by a pope in years, ushering in an era of papal trips (photo Pais/ Archivio Rodrigo Pais—Ceub Università di Bologna).

1

On December 4, 1963, during a speech in Latin that concluded the second session, Paul VI announced that between January 4 and 6, 1964, he would go on a pilgrimage to the Holy Land. The main purpose of this trip—the first of his pontificate—was mostly religious "to honor Jesus Christ in the land that his coming to the world made holy," as the pope wrote in a note on September 21, 1963. To this objective lesser aims were added: to give attention to places considered holy throughout the long history of the Catholic Church; to pray for peace "in that blessed and troubled land"; to move toward an ecumenical meeting with the representatives of other Christian denominations; and to bring hope of a rapprochement with the great monotheistic religions of Judaism and Islam.

It was a project whose success was not facilitated by either the ecclesiastical or the political context. First, when the second session of the council completed the final text of the Decree on Ecumenism, it was still unsatisfactory. The parts dedicated to the relationship between the Church and Judaism and to religious freedom had not even been discussed. Most of all, the postponement of the initial vote and its success had created anxiety in both the majority and in Paul VI.

On the political side, the pope's visit meant he would cross the two states, Israel and Jordan, which had fought during the war of 1948–1949. The Holy See had diplomatic relations with neither of them and did not wish the pope's visit to look like the prologue of recognition. Paul VI was well aware of this, and did not concede anything either to King Hussein of Jordan nor to the Israeli authorities—he never uttered the word *Israel* throughout the entire trip. To President Zalman Shazar he defended the actions of Pius XII during World War II, which had come under fire from Rolf Hochhuth's play, *The Deputy*. He had already done so in writing to the *Tablet* on the opening day of the conclave of 1963.

Thus understood, the pope's pilgrimage played out "in the most important places sanctified by the evangelical mysteries of our Lord," from Jordan (Jordan, Bethany, the Holy Sepulchre, Gethsemane) to Israel (Nazareth, the Sea of Galilee, the Upper Room) and from Israel to Jordan (Bethlehem). The most significant events were: the crowd that broke the Jordanian police's security cordons and pressed against the pope during the Way of the Cross to the Holy Sepulchre; the holy hour in Gethsemane; the

2. January 4, 1964. Paul VI in the streets of Jerusalem. At the close of the second session of the council, Paul VI had announced to the fathers his intention to make a pilgrimage to the Holy Land, a decision he had arrived at much earlier, soon after his election (Archivio Fscire).

3. Jerusalem, January 5, 1964. Paul VI and the Ecumenical Patriarch of Constantinople, Athenagoras. Although for the pope, the purpose of his pilgrimage to the Holy Land was strictly spiritual, symbolic gestures and the ensuing media attention gave the trip an ecumenical dimension that would affect the council. During the third period of the council, the patriarchate of Constantinople would send observers for the first time (Archivio Fscire).

homily at Nazareth, which touched upon the theme of work and the Beatitudes; and the homily at Bethlehem with a declaration of "immense sympathy" for the world and an invocation to Christ for the unity of the Church.

However, the theme of ecumenism became the heart of the journey, as the Ecumenical Patriarch Athenagoras wanted. He went to Jerusalem to welcome the pope with the Metropolitan Bishop Benedictos. This act, which could have amounted to a reinforcement of the status quo, overturned the difficulties that had prevented the patriarchy from appointing observers and had prevented the Catholic Church from engaging in the ecumenical movement. It had been organized by a White Father from the Secretariat, Pierre Duprey, and the meeting was a success. After their embrace, which was destined to become an icon of the ecumenical journey of the twentieth century, they prayed the Our Father together in Latin and Greek. The next day they read together chapter 17 of the Gospel of John, the priestly prayer of Jesus "that they may be one," and each expressed the hope that they could restore full communion and be able to take communion together in the near future at the same Eucharistic table.

Undoubtedly the meeting in Jerusalem—the "offspring and fruit" of the council—accelerated the ecumenical commitment of the Church of Rome, which in later years brought about—on the Catholic side—a new relationship with the Anglicans, the start of the collaboration with the ecumenical council of Churches (which Paul VI visited in Geneva in 1969), and the lifting of the excommunications between Rome and Constantinople on December 7, 1965. Another result of the papal visit of 1964 was the founding of the Ecumenical Institute of Tantur, built between Bethlehem and Jerusalem and opened in 1971.

Bibliography
Il pellegrinaggio di Paolo VI in Terra Santa 4–6 gennaio 1964, Vatican City 1964; *Tomos Agapis. Vatican-Phanar 1958–1970*, Rome-Istanbul 1971; V. Martano, *Athenagoras, il patriarca (1886–1972). Un cristiano fra crisi della coabitazione e utopia ecumenica*, Bologna 1996; C. Soetens, "Entre Concile et initiative pontificale. Paul VI en Terre sainte," in *Cristianesimo nella storia*, 19 (1998), 333–365; G. Alberigo, "Conclusione. La nuova fisionomia del concilio," in *Storia del concilio Vaticano II*, edited by G. Alberigo (and A. Melloni), vol. 3, Bologna 1998 (2013), 513–535; U. Ulrike, "Paolo VI in Terra santa," in *Il Regno—Documenti* 15 (2000), 64–72; V. Martano, *L'abbraccio di Gerusalemme. Cinquant'anni fa lo storico incontro tra Paolo VI e Athenagoras*, Milan 2014.

33. THE DÖPFNER PLAN

The second period of the council had been characterized by challenging discussion of the draft of *De Ecclesia*, which lasted throughout the month of October 1963, the discussion of the draft of *De Episcopis*, between November 5 and 15, and the draft of *De Ecumenismo*, from November 18 to the end of the period. Meanwhile, there had also been the voting and final approval of liturgical reform in the Constitution on the Liturgy and the Decree on the Means of Social Communication. Regarding the seventeen drafts that were established in the program at the beginning of 1963, there was still much to do. The commissions had started working on revising the texts with guidance from the Coordinating Commission, but their drafts were yet to be discussed.

There was widespread fear that such a vast program could constitute a risk to the council itself, as many issues had not been aired properly. In addition, because many bishops did not want to be away from their dioceses for too long, Paul VI hoped that the whole council could conclude with the third session.

There were various proposals to make this happen. In particular, since the end of the first period, Cardinal Julius Döpfner, with the help of Hubert Jedin and Giuseppe Dossetti, had been putting forward various ideas for shortening the work program, which were linked to the reform of the Regulations. On June 30, 1963, the day of his pontifical coronation, Paul VI received him in audience and urged him to prepare a more comprehensive plan. After the second period, this was again a hot topic. It was discussed during the meeting of the Coordinating Commission on November 20, 1963, and Döpfner was commissioned to revise his plan and present it at the next meeting on December 29.

In order to conclude the council in 1964, Döpfner asked that only six major drafts be moved forward: the drafts on the Church, on bishops, on revelation, on the lay apostolate, on ecumenism, and on the Church in the modern world. As for the other drafts, deemed less urgent, the commissions would be asked to reduce them to "propositions" which would then be passed, with a conciliar mandate, to special committees after the council for final processing and application, following the parliamentary principles of "delegated legislation."

At its meeting on January 15, 1964, the Coordinating Commission established more specifically the procedure for each draft. Those on revelation, on the Church and on ecumenism, which had already been discussed in the Council Hall, had to be revised in accordance with what had been decided and

voted on. Regarding the draft on Ecumenism, the Secretariat for Christian Unity would have to decide whether the last two chapters dealing respectively with the Jews and religious freedom were to be kept in the draft, or pulled out into independent texts. Similarly, for the draft on the Church in the modern world, a more definitive text was expected from the relevant commission.

The other drafts, those on the Eastern Churches, on the missions, on clergy, religious, and on the lay apostolate and seminaries would be reduced to the fundamental principles or canons; those on Catholic schools and on the sacrament of marriage would be reduced to simple "votes" to be presented to the relevant postconciliar bodies. Most of these drafts, which had been reduced to brief propositions, would not even be discussed in the hall, but sent to the bishops for their observations and then, once they had been reworked based on that feedback, put to a vote.

The commissions were disappointed in these directives. Their draft texts, once they had been approved by the Coordinating Commission, were sent to the council fathers during the summer of 1964, with the idea that they would be voted on. Because of the short deadline, only the Commission for the Apostolate of the Laity had produced a text of propositions that was sufficiently articulate, and the Coordinating Commission agreed to submit it to a brief discussion by the fathers.

Even more changes were made to the Regulations to try to reduce the number of presentations on each topic. In order to speak, one had to sign up least five days before the debate. Presentations that repeated similar arguments could be canceled by the moderators. Authorization to make presentations could also be requested at the time of the discussion, once those planned had concluded, but these requests had to be signed by at least seventy fathers. Moreover, the number of commission members was also increased, partly by new elections, partly by pontifical appointment.

Based on these directives and the work done on individual drafts, at its meeting on April 17, 1964, the Coordinating Committee established in general terms the program for the next period of the council. But by the next meeting of the commission, it was already becoming obvious that the issues on the agenda could not be voted on without a free and open debate in the Council Hall.

On June 26, Döpfner put forward the proposal for a "brief discussion" of the minor drafts. This was then taken up again, with the support of Cardinal Léon-Joseph Suenens, in Sep-

1. The moderators: Cardinals Giacomo Lercaro, Julius Döpfner, and Léon-Joseph Suenans, jokingly referred to as "The Synoptics" (photo *Jesus*).

2. The historian of the Council of Trent and *peritus* of Vatican II, Hubert Jedin (Archivio Fscire).

On the Church

On Bishops

On Revelation

On the Apostolate of the Laity

On Ecumenism

On the Church in the Modern World

Other Drafts

Referred to Post-conciliar Committees

So it was that, in response to pressure from many bishops and episcopal conferences, moderators agreed to a day of discussion for the "minor" drafts.

But this was not enough for the bishops.

In a joint meeting of the council's governing bodies on October 7, 1964, the possibility of concluding the council within the year was discussed at length. When the "short" discussion that had been planned began on one of the smaller drafts, on the clergy, it was subjected to so much criticism that it was clear that a comprehensive review was needed. Similar reactions were foreseen for the other drafts. In addition, there was the problem of the extensive draft on the Church in the modern world, which would have required a long discussion and careful review. In a new meeting of the governing bodies on October 15, Lercaro brought to light strong pressure from the assembly for freer discussion. In the end, an inevitable fourth session was accepted and the "Döpfner plan" was effectively abandoned.

Bibliography
J. Grootaers, "Le rôle de Mgr. G. Philips à Vatican II," in *Ecclesia a Spiritu Sancto edocta. Mélanges théologiques en hommage à Mgr Gérard Philips*, Gembloux 1972, 343–380; G. Alberigo, "Concilio acefalo? L'evoluzione degli organi direttivi del Vaticano II," in *Il Vaticano II tra attese e celebrazione*, edited by G. Alberigo, Bologna 1995, 193–238; Kl. Wittstadt, "Vorschläge von Julius Kardinal Döpfner an Papst Paul VI. zur Fortührung der Konzilsarbeiten (July 1963)," in *Fe I teologia en la història. Estudis en honor d'E. Vilanova*, Montserrat 1997, 565–584; E. Vilanova, "L'intersessione (1963–1964)," in *Storia del concilio Vaticano II*, edited by G. Alberigo (Italian edition edited by A. Melloni), vol. 3, Bologna 1998 (2013), 367–512.

tember, when work was about to begin again. It was hoped that the new rules for discussions that had been introduced would make things leaner and more effective, and would therefore allow for a brief debate on the drafts.

34. The Bishops

Paragraph 1 of section 2 of the Regulations made clear who should participate in the council. In fact, it quoted from the Code of Canon Law (canon 223, §1) and from the Eastern Rite code (canon 168, §1); indeed, it introduced nothing new since Vatican I. Instead, it solidified a tradition and a discussion that took place in 1869 about those who should be summoned. So the code repeated the following: "*Vocantur ad Concilium in eoque ius habent suffragii deliberativi: 1) S. R. E. Cardinales, etsi non Episcopi; 2) Patriarchae, Primates, Archiepiscopi, Episcopi residentiales, etiam non dum consecrati; 3) Abbates vel Praelati nullius; 4) Abbas Primas, Abbates Superiores Congregationum monasticarum, ac supremi Moderatores religionum clericalium exemptarum, non autem aliarum religionum, nisi aliud convocationis decretum ferat. §2. Etiam Episcopi titulares, vocati ad Concilium, suffragium obtinent deliberativum, nisi aliud in convocatione expresse caveatur.*" In the motu proprio *Cum Gravissima* of April 15, 1962, Pope John conferred episcopal dignity on all the cardinals, ordaining as bishops all those who were not yet ordained, and in May 1963 he also added the apostolic prefects to those called to the council, even if they were not bishops. According to the code, the titular bishops (those bishops who, unlike resident bishops, retain the title over a diocese but not jurisdiction over it), were invited to attend with the right to vote, adding, "unless stated otherwise." At Vatican I, Pius IX had in fact been in doubt as to whether they should be called, and then decided in the affirmative. It was the same for Vatican II.

In 1962, there were 1,619 resident archbishops and bishops and 975 titular bishops (for the most part apostolic vicars, nuncios, and auxiliary bishops). Together with eighty-seven cardinals and patriarchs and ninety-seven superiors general of religious orders and congregations who were called to take part in the council, there was a total of 2,900 participants. Of these, between 2,400 and 2,450 attended the first session. Most of the nuncios and apostolic delegates remained at home, as did some auxiliary bishops. Here it is worth remembering that among the resident Italian bishops, 42 percent were absent; over 11 percent were absent of those from the United States and Brazil. There were nearly three hundred bishops who ultimately failed to participate in even one session of Vatican II. Ill health and the infirmities of age were among the reasons given. In addition, some were prevented from attending by the political regimes of their countries. To overcome this, thanks to a suggestion from Giorgio La Pira, the Holy See tried to begin a dialogue with the Chinese government through its embassy in Cairo.

One of the first fathers to arrive was the bishop Antonie Barbieri, Archbishop of Montevideo, who arrived in Rome toward the end of September. Some bishops never arrived in Rome, as in the case of John Hogan Forest of Bellary in India who died after reaching Naples. Others were only able to participate in part of the council, such as the Jesuit Aston Chichester, archbishop emeritus of Salisbury, Rhodesia, who died in the atrium of the basilica on October 24, 1962, just one hour before the beginning of the sixth general congregation. In one of the first entries of the *Diario del concilio* [Diary of the Council]—the weekly series on the National Program presented by journalist Luca Di Schiena which followed the work of the council from 1962 to 1965—RAI aired a news report on the youngest and oldest bishops at Vatican II, thirty-four-year-old Alcides Mendoza Castro, bishop of Abancay in Peru, and Alfonso Carinci, secretary emeritus of the Congregation of Rites. Carinci had been born in 1862, had served as an altar boy at Vatican I, and died aged 101 years at the end of the second session, on December 5, 1963.

The program, in addition to passing on trivia, unwittingly touched on an issue that was not to be underestimated, in terms of the debate and the voting, or the generational exchanges that were witnessed in the various sessions: 296 new bishops were appointed during the years of the council (one hundred seven Europeans, but also thirty-eight Asians, forty-four Africans, forty-three North Americans, sixty Central and South Americans, and four from Oceania). In fact, there was a significant turnover among the bishops who attended, with deaths and new appointments. Over 250 council fathers died between 1962 and 1965. By the end of the first session, five cardinals had already died (that is, since December 25, 1961), twelve archbishops, forty-eight bishops, and one superior general. Seven of these had died at the start of the council (including three in Rome). This figure rose to 142 by the end of the third session, to which we must add eighty-two in 1965 (including five cardinals: Giulio Bevilacqua, Maurilio Fossati, Pierre-Marie Gerlier Paul, Albert Gregory Meyer, and Clemente Micara). The appointments were always higher by comparison, so that the number of members came to exceed 3,000. At the third session, for example, 150 bishops participated in Vatican II for the first time. Despite this, it was the period in which regions with the lowest numbers of participants were proportionally most affected, due to the decline of the fathers from Africa, Asia, and Latin America.

Again it was RAI TV, that realized how the figure of the bishop—the "specialist among them all" according to the famous definition by Jean Guitton—was the real protagonist of the event,

COUNCIL FATHERS APPOINTED DURING THE COUNCIL

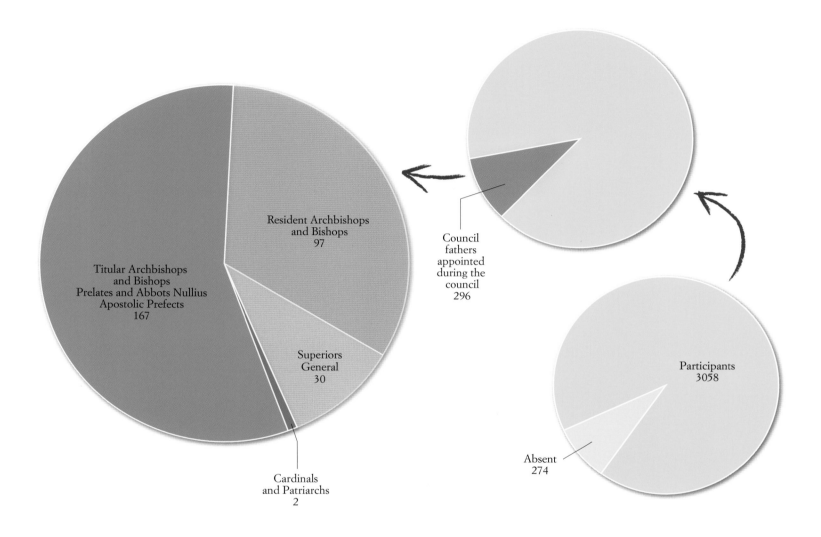

▶ **DISTRIBUTION OF PARTICIPATING FATHERS BY DATE OF BIRTH**

(Source: J. L. Martín Descalzo, *Un periodista en el Concilio. Primera etapa*, Madrid 1963)

Fathers born before 1871	9
Between 1871 and 1880	124
Between 1881 and 1890	418
Between 1891 and 1900	521
Between 1901 and 1910	981
Between 1910 and 1920	604
After 1920	24

COUNCIL FATHERS NOMINATED DURING THE COUNCIL

Countries and Continents	Cardinals	Residential Archbishops	Titular Archbishops	Residential Bishops	Titular Bishops	Prelates and Abbots Nullius	Apostolic Prefects	Superiors General	Totals
Belgium	-	-	-	1	-	-	-	-	1
England	-	-	1	2	3	-	-	-	6
Finland	-	-	-	-	1	-	-	-	1
France	-	-	-	4	5	-	-	-	9
Holland	-	-	-	-	1	-	-	-	1
Hungary	-	-	-	-	3	-	-	-	3
Ireland	-	-	-	2	-	-	-	-	2
Italy	1	2	1	7	17	2	-	30	60
Latvia	-	-	-	-	1	-	-	-	1
Lithuania	-	-	-	-	1	-	-	-	1
Poland	-	-	-	1	8	-	-	-	9
Portugal	-	-	-	1	2	-	-	-	3
Romania	-	-	-	-	1	-	-	-	1
Spain	-	-	-	2	2	-	-	-	4
Switzerland	1	-	-	-	-	-	-	-	1
Yugoslavia	-	-	-	-	3	-	-	-	4
Europe	**2**	**3**	**2**	**20**	**48**	**2**	**-**	**30**	**107**
Burma	-	1	1	-	-	-	-	-	2
Cambodia	-	-	-	-	1	-	-	-	1
Ceylon	-	-	-	1	1	-	-	-	2
Formosa	-	-	-	-	-	-	1	-	1
India	-	-	-	4	5	-	1	-	10
Indonesia	-	1	-	1	-	-	-	-	2
Iraq	-	-	-	-	1	-	-	-	1
Japan	-	-	-	-	1	-	-	-	1
Jordan	-	-	1	-	2	-	-	-	3
Korea	-	-	-	3	-	-	-	-	3
Lebanon	-	-	1	-	-	-	-	-	1
Pakistan	-	-	-	-	1	-	-	-	1
Palestine	-	-	-	-	1	-	-	-	1
Philippines	-	-	-	3	1	-	-	-	4
Thailand	-	-	1	-	2	-	1	-	4
Vietnam	-	-	1	-	-	-	-	-	1
Asia	**-**	**2**	**5**	**13**	**15**	**-**	**3**	**-**	**38**
Angola	-	-	-	1	-	-	-	-	1
Burundi	-	-	-	-	1	-	-	-	1
Cameroon	-	-	1	2	-	-	1	-	4
Central Afr. Rep.	-	-	-	2	-	-	1	-	3
Chad	-	-	-	1	-	-	1	-	3
Congo (Belg.)	-	1	-	2	-	-	-	-	3
Congo (French)	-	-	-	-	1	-	-	-	1
Dahomey	-	-	-	1	-	-	1	-	2
Ivory Coast	-	-	-	1	-	-	-	-	1
Kenya	-	-	-	1	-	-	-	-	1
Libya	-	-	-	-	1	-	-	-	1
Madagascar	-	-	-	1	1	-	-	-	2
Malawi	-	-	-	1	1	-	-	-	2
Mali	-	-	-	2	-	-	-	-	2
Mozambique	-	-	-	-	1	-	-	-	1
Nigeria	-	-	1	1	1	-	1	-	4
South Rhodesia	-	-	-	1	-	-	-	1	2
Spanish Guinea	-	-	-	-	1	-	-	-	1
Tanzania	-	-	-	2	-	-	1	-	3
Togo	-	-	-	2	-	-	-	-	2
Uganda	-	-	-	1	1	-	-	-	2
Upper Volta	-	-	-	1	-	-	1	-	2
Zambia	-	-	1	1	-	-	-	-	2
Africa	**-**	**1**	**3**	**25**	**8**	**-**	**7**	**-**	**44**

Countries and Continents	Cardinals	Residential Archbishops	Titular Archbishops	Residential Bishops	Titular Bishops	Prelates and Abbots Nullius	Apostolic Prefects	Superiors General	Totals
Canada	-	-	-	-	8	-	-	-	8
Mexico	-	-	-	5	1	-	-	-	6
United States	-	-	-	4	25	-	-	-	29
North America	**-**	**-**	**-**	**9**	**34**	**-**	**-**	**-**	**43**
Costa Rica	-	-	1	-	-	-	-	-	1
Cuba	-	-	-	1	2	-	-	-	3
El Salvador	-	-	1	-	-	-	-	-	1
Honduras	-	-	-	-	2	-	-	-	2
Panama	-	-	-	2	-	-	-	-	2
Puerto Rico	-	-	-	1	-	-	-	-	1
Central America	**-**	**-**	**2**	**4**	**2**	**2**	**-**	**-**	**10**
Argentina	-	-	-	6	2	-	-	-	8
Brazil	-	-	-	8	10	5	-	-	23
Chile	-	-	-	-	3	1	-	-	4
Colombia	-	-	-	2	2	-	-	-	4
Equador	-	-	-	1	3	-	-	-	4
Peru	-	-	-	1	1	-	-	-	2
Uruguay	-	-	-	1	-	-	-	-	1
Venezuela	-	-	-	2	2	-	-	-	4
South America	**-**	**-**	**-**	**19**	**24**	**7**	**-**	**-**	**50**
Australia	-	-	-	1	1	-	-	-	2
New Guinea	-	-	-	-	-	-	1	-	1
Polynesia	-	-	-	1	-	-	-	-	1
Oceania	**-**	**-**	**-**	**1**	**2**	**-**	**1**	**-**	**4**
Totals	**2**	**6**	**12**	**91**	**133**	**11**	**11**	**30**	**296**

FATHERS UNABLE TO PARTICIPATE IN THE COUNCIL

Countries and Continents	Cardinals	Residential Archbishops	Titular Archbishops	Residential Bishops	Titular Bishops	Prelates and Abbots Nullius	Apostolic Prefects	Totals
Albania	-	-	-	-	3	-	-	3
Belgium	-	-	-	-	3	-	-	3
Bulgaria	-	-	-	1	1	-	-	2
Czechoslovakia	-	-	-	3	5	-	-	8
Denmark	-	-	-	1	-	-	-	1
England	-	-	-	1	4	-	-	5
France	-	1	3	3	17	-	-	24
Germany	-	-	1	-	2	-	-	3
Holland	-	-	1	-	2	1	-	4
Hungary	1	-	-	2	4	-	-	7
Ireland	-	-	-	3	4	-	-	7
Italy	-	1	3	1	6	-	2	13
Latvia	-	-	-	-	1	-	-	1
Lithuania	-	-	-	1	2	-	-	3
Poland	-	-	-	3	7	-	-	10
Portugal	-	-	-	1	1	-	-	2
Romania	-	-	-	2	-	-	-	2
Spain	-	-	-	4	3	1	-	8
Switzerland	-	-	-	-	1	-	-	1
Yugoslavia	-	1	-	1	1	-	-	3
Europe	**1**	**3**	**8**	**27**	**67**	**2**	**2**	**110**
Burma	-	-	1	-	-	-	-	1
Ceylon	-	-	-	-	1	-	-	1
China	-	3	-	15	3	3	-	24

Countries and Continents	Cardinals	Residential Archbishops	Titular Archbishops	Residential Bishops	Titular Bishops	Prelates and Abbots Nullius	Apostolic Prefects	Totals
Korea	-	-	-	1	-	-	-	1
Hong Kong	-	-	-	1	-	-	-	1
India	-	-	2	-	2	-	-	4
Indonesia	-	-	-	-	1	-	-	1
Iraq	-	1	1	-	-	-	-	2
Japan	-	-	-	-	1	-	-	1
Lebanon	-	1	1	-	4	-	-	6
Pakistan	-	-	-	1	-	-	-	1
Palestine	-	-	1	-	1	-	-	2
Philippines	-	2	-	1	3	-	-	6
Syria	-	1	1	-	-	-	-	2
Vietnam	-	1	1	12	3	-	-	17
Asia	**-**	**9**	**8**	**31**	**19**	**3**	**-**	**70**
Congo (Belgian)	-	-	-	-	1	-	-	1
Tanzania	-	-	-	-	3	-	-	3
Union of South Africa	-	-	-	-	1	-	-	1
Africa	**-**	**-**	**-**	**-**	**5**	**-**	**-**	**5**
Canada	-	-	2	3	9	-	-	14
Mexico	-	-	1	3	5	-	-	9
United States	-	2	-	3	14	-	-	19
North America	**-**	**2**	**3**	**9**	**28**	**-**	**-**	**42**
Costa Rica	-	-	-	1	-	-	-	1
Cuba	-	1	-	1	-	-	-	2
Dominican Republic	-	-	-	2	-	-	-	2
El Salvador	-	-	-	-	1	-	-	1
Haiti	-	-	-	-	1	-	-	1
Honduras	-	-	1	-	-	-	-	1
Panama	-	-	-	-	1	-	-	1
Puerto Rico	-	-	-	1	1	-	-	2
Central America	**-**	**1**	**1**	**5**	**4**	**-**	**-**	**11**
Argentina	-	-	-	-	3	-	-	3
Brazil	-	2	1	5	7	-	-	15
Chile	-	-	-	-	2	-	-	2
Colombia	-	1	2	-	2	2	-	7
Equador	-	-	-	1	1	2	-	4
Peru	-	-	1	-	2	-	-	3
South America	**-**	**3**	**4**	**6**	**17**	**4**	**-**	**34**
Australia	-	-	-	-	1	-	-	1
Melanesia	-	-	-	-	1	-	-	1
Oceania	**-**	**-**	**-**	**-**	**2**	**-**	**-**	**2**
Totals	**1**	**18**	**24**	**78**	**142**	**9**	**2**	**274**

COUNCIL FATHERS DECEASED DURING COUNCIL

Countries and Continents	Cardinals	Residential Archbishops	Titular Archbishops	Residential Bishops	Titular Bishops	Prelates and Abbots Nullius	Apostolic Prefects	Totals
Belgium	-	-	-	1	5	-	-	6
Czechoslovakia	-	-	-	1	-	-	-	1
England	-	3	1	1	1	-	-	6
France	2	2	-	6	9	-	-	19
Germany	-	-	1	2	5	-	-	8
Holland	-	-	2	-	1	-	-	3
Hungary	-	-	-	1	1	1	-	3
Ireland	1	-	-	3	1	-	-	5
Italy	6	5	10	25	12	1	4	63
Lithuania	-	-	-	1	-	-	-	1
Poland	-	-	1	4	5	-	-	10
Portugal	-	2	-	2	-	-	-	4
Romania	-	-	-	1	-	-	-	1
Spain	-	3	-	8	2	1	-	14
Switzerland	-	-	-	1	-	-	-	1
Turkey	-	1	-	-	-	-	-	1
Yugoslavia	-	1	-	1	-	-	-	2
Europe	**9**	**17**	**15**	**57**	**43**	**3**	**4**	**148**
Burma	-	1	-	-	-	-	-	1
Formosa	-	-	-	1	-	-	-	1
India	-	1	-	2	1	-	-	4
Indonesia	-	1	1	-	-	-	-	2
Iraq	-	-	-	-	1	-	-	1
Japan	-	-	-	-	1	-	-	1
Lebanon	-	-	-	1	3	-	-	4
Palestine	-	-	1	-	-	-	-	1
Philippines	-	1	1	1	-	-	-	3
Syria	-	-	1	-	-	-	-	1
Thailand	-	-	-	-	1	-	-	1
Asia	**-**	**4**	**4**	**5**	**7**	**-**	**-**	**20**
Burundi	-	-	-	-	1	-	-	1
Congo (Belgian)	-	-	-	4	1	-	-	5
Egypt	-	-	1	2	-	-	-	3
Libya	-	-	-	-	1	-	-	1
Madagascar	-	-	-	1	1	-	-	2
Malawi	-	-	-	-	1	-	-	1
Nigeria	-	1	-	-	-	-	-	1
Rwanda	-	-	-	1	-	-	-	1
Senegal	-	-	-	-	-	1	-	1
Southwest Africa	-	-	1	-	-	-	-	1
Tanzania	-	-	2	-	-	-	-	2
Union of South Africa	-	-	1	1	1	-	-	3
Upper Volta	-	-	-	1	-	-	-	1
Africa	**-**	**1**	**3**	**11**	**7**	**1**	**-**	**23**
Canada	-	3	-	1	2	-	-	6
Mexico	-	-	-	1	-	-	-	1
United States	1	2	1	5	11	-	-	20
North America	**1**	**5**	**1**	**7**	**13**	**-**	**-**	**27**
Cuba	1	-	-	-	-	-	-	1
Guatemala	-	1	-	-	-	-	-	1
Haiti	-	-	1	-	-	-	-	1
Honduras	-	-	-	1	1	-	-	2
Panama	-	1	-	-	-	-	-	1
Puerto Rico	-	-	-	1	-	-	-	1
Central America	**1**	**2**	**1**	**2**	**1**	**-**	**-**	**7**
Argentina	-	2	-	2	-	-	-	4
Bolivia	-	-	-	-	1	-	-	1
Brazil	-	1	1	3	1	-	-	6
Chile	-	-	-	2	1	-	-	3
Colombia	-	-	-	1	1	-	-	2
Ecuador	-	-	-	1	1	-	-	2
Peru	-	1	1	-	-	-	-	2
Uruguay	-	-	-	1	-	-	-	1
South America	**-**	**4**	**2**	**10**	**5**	**-**	**-**	**21**
Australia	-	2	1	1	1	-	-	5
New Guinea	-	-	-	-	1	-	-	1
New Zealand	-	-	-	1	-	-	-	1
Oceania	**-**	**2**	**1**	**2**	**2**	**-**	**-**	**7**
Totals	**11**	**35**	**27**	**94**	**78**	**4**	**4**	**253**

COUNCIL FATHERS BY AGE (AS OF 1965)

Country & Continent	Total Cardinali	Average Age
Austria	1	60
Belgium	2	72
England	6	75
France	3	68
Germany	1	60
Holland	1	52
Ireland	40	76
Italy	1	60
Poland	1	65
Portugal	1	64
Spain	1	77
Switzerland	5	75
Yugoslavia	1	65
Total—Europe	**64**	**74**
Ceylon	1	64
Formosa	1	73
India	1	65
Japan	1	57
Lebanon	2	79
Philippines	1	87
Syria	1	75
Total—Asia	**8**	**72**
Algeria	1	62
Egypt	1	48
Tanzania	1	61
Union of S. Africa	1	58
Upper Volta	1	53
Total—Africa	**5**	**56**
Canada	3	64
Mexico	1	76
United States	5	73
Total—North America	**9**	**70**
Argentina	1	76
Brazil	4	72
Chile	1	58
Colombia	1	74
Equador	1	92
Peru	1	52
Uruguay	1	73
Venezuela	1	63
Total South America	**11**	**70**
Australia	1	69
Total Oceania	**1**	**69**
Total	**98**	**72**

Country & Continent	Total Residential Archbishops	Average Age
Austria	1	73
England	6	60
France	16	65
Germany	3	54
Greece	3	46
Hungary	1	75
Ireland	3	66
Italy	59	67
Malta	1	80
Poland	2	53
Portugal	3	61
Spain	11	69
Turkey	1	81
Yugoslavia	5	66
Total Europe	**115**	**66**
Burma	2	63
Formosa	2	64
India	16	62
Indonesia	6	53
Iran	2	62
Iraq	6	59
Japan	1	71
Jordan	1	68
Korea	3	58
Lebanon	6	59
Pakistan	3	56
Palestine	2	67
Philippines	5	67
Singapore	1	64
Syria	7	60
Vietnam	1	55
Total Asia	**64**	**61**
Angola	1	82
Basutoland	1	61
Burundi	1	66
Cameroon	1	41
Central African Rep.	1	58
Chad	1	48
Congo (Belgian)	5	54
Congo (French)	1	48
Dahomey	1	43
Egypt	2	63
Ethiopia	1	61
Ghana	1	61
Ivory Coast	1	49
Madagascar	3	53
Malawi	1	60
Mali	2	50
Morocco	2	72

Country & Continent	Total Residential Archbishops	Average Age
Mozambique	1	50
Nigeria	3	65
Rwanda	1	51
Senegal	1	44
South Rhodesia	1	60
Tanzania	2	63
Togo	1	40
Uganda	1	66
Union of South Africa	3	55
Zambia	1	54
Total Africa	**44**	**57**
Canada	13	64
Mexico	10	70
United States	26	68
Total North America	**49**	**67**
Costa Rica	1	55
Cuba	1	63
Dominican Rep.	1	59
El Salvador	1	64
Guatemala	1	56
Honduras	1	48
Nicaragua	1	81
Panama	1	44
Puerto Rico	1	43
Trinidad and Tobago	1	84
Total Central America	**10**	**60**
Argentina	10	61
Bolivia	2	72
Brazil	25	59
Chile	4	62
Colombia	6	64
Ecuador	2	69
Paraguay	1	76
Peru	2	59
Venezuela	2	70
Total South America	**54**	**62**
Australia	6	66
New Zealand	2	75
Total Oceania	**8**	**68**
Total	**344**	**63**

Country & Continent	Total Titular Archbishops	Average Age
Austria	3	63
Belgium	4	67

Denmark	1	54
England	4	66
France	12	66
Germany	1	62
Holland	2	74
Ireland	2	59
Italy	45	64
Poland	1	62
Portugal	3	66
Spain	2	73
Switzerland	1	77
Turkey	1	78
Total Europe	**82**	**65**

Burma	1	41
Formosa	2	55
India	4	59
Iran	1	50
Japan	1	54
Jordan	1	43
Korea	1	52
Lebanon	3	68
Pakistan	2	48
Philippines	3	52
Syria	4	58
Thailand	1	51
Vietnam	3	53
Total Asia	**27**	**55**

Algeria	1	53
Angola	1	53
Cameroon	2	57
Congo (Belgian)	1	58
Egypt	2	55
Kenya	1	54
Liberia	1	53
Madagascar	2	69
Nigeria	1	51
Tanzania	1	60
Tunisia	1	47
Union of S. Africa	1	62
Zambia	1	55
Total Africa	**16**	**57**

Canada	4	60
Mexico	3	53
United States	3	66
Total North America	**10**	**60**

Costa Rica	1	51
Dominican Rep.	1	54
El Salvador	1	50
Honduras	1	56
Panama	1	53
Total Central America	**5**	**53**

Argentina	2	62
Bolivia	1	53
Brazil	8	59
Chile	3	64
Colombia	4	71
Equador	1	53
Paraguay	1	55
Peru	1	54
Uruguay	2	65
Venezuela	2	55
Total South America	**25**	**61**

Australia	3	53
Total Oceania	**3**	**53**

Total	**168**	**61**

Country & Continent	Total Residential Bishops	Average Age
Austria	6	58
Belgium	6	59
England	19	62
Finland	1	68
France	66	61
Germany	20	63
Gibraltar	1	65
Greece	1	67
Holland	7	57
Hungary	3	71
Ireland	20	67
Italy	183	64
Luxemburg	1	72
Malta	1	75
Monaco	1	60
Norway	1	45
Poland	9	62
Portugal	10	57
Spain	48	64
Sweden	1	51
Switzerland	5	68
Yugoslavia	10	61
Total Europe	**420**	**63**

Burma	6	55
Ceylon	5	58
Formosa	9	61
Hong Kong	2	69
India	56	60

Indonesia	20	55
Iran	1	81
Iraq	4	56
Japan	13	61
Jordan	1	68
Korea	8	55
Lebanon	9	64
Malaysia	3	58
Pakistan	6	66
Philippines	18	53
Syria	3	59
Thailand	1	60
Vietnam	8	59
Total Asia	**173**	**59**

Algeria	3	66
Angola	5	55
Basutoland	2	49
Burundi	3	50
Cameroon	7	47
Cape Verde Island	1	55
Central African Rep.	3	53
Chad	3	48
Congo (Belgian)	33	56
Congo (French)	2	63
Dahomey	4	51
Egypt	2	51
Ethiopia	2	59
Gabon	1	54
Gambia	1	53
Ghana	6	54
Guinea	1	46
Ivory Coast	5	53
Kenya	8	54
Madagascar	12	58
Malawi	5	55
Mali	4	56
Mauritius	1	65
Mozambique	7	54
Niger	1	46
Nigeria	17	58
Reunion Island	1	50
Rwanda	3	52
Senegal	2	50
Seychelles	1	66
Sierra Leone	2	59
Somalia	1	56
South Rhodesia	4	53
Tanzania	14	22
Togo	3	47
Uganda	7	56
Union of S. Africa	15	60

Country		
Upper Volta	5	59
Zambia	7	58
Total Africa	**204**	**55**
Canada	40	59
Mexico	42	54
United States	111	63
Total North America	**193**	**60**
Bahamas	1	56
British Honduras	1	55
Costa Rica	2	49
Cuba	3	48
Curaçao	1	59
Dominican Rep.	1	47
El Salvador	4	63
Guadalupe Island	2	65
Guatemala	6	61
Haiti	3	67
Honduras	2	53
Jamaica	1	70
Nicaragua	4	62
Panama	3	42
Puerto Rico	2	49
Trinidad and Tobago	3	55
Total Central America	**39**	**57**
Argentina	38	53
Bolivia	5	61
Brazil	105	53
Chile	13	56
Colombia	26	55
Ecuador	8	62
Guiana	4	63
Paraguay	2	60
Peru	15	54
Uruguay	8	57
Venezuela	13	53
Total South America	**237**	**54**
Australia	18	62
Micronesia	1	66
New Zealand	2	47
Total Oceania	**21**	**61**
Total	**1287**	**59**

Country & Continent	Total Titular Bishops	Average Age
Austria	4	60
Belgium	13	64
Bulgaria	2	71
Czechoslovakia	4	71
Denmark	1	69
England	9	57
Finland	1	40
France	37	64
Germany	33	61
Greece	2	63
Holland	5	60
Hungary	7	61
Iceland	1	68
Ireland	1	74
Italy	85	62
Latvia	1	70
Lithuania	1	71
Luxemburg	1	76
Malta	1	74
Norway	2	66
Poland	44	57
Portugal	8	55
Romania	1	60
Spain	17	61
Switzerland	3	74
Yugoslavia	10	53
Total Europe	**294**	**61**
Arabia	2	64
Borneo	3	57
Cambodia	2	51
Ceylon	2	54
Formosa	1	50
Hong Kong	1	65
India	10	55
Indonesia	3	63
Iraq	1	38
Jordan	2	61
Laos	3	53
Lebanon	3	53
Pakistan	1	50
Palestine	1	47
Philippines	16	55
Thailand	6	53
Vietnam	3	60
Total Asia	**60**	**55**
Algeria	1	61
Burundi	1	60
Congo (Belgian)	3	52
Congo (French)	1	56
Egypt	4	61
Ethiopia	4	56
Gabon	1	59
Liberia	1	48
Libya	2	61
Madagascar	1	38
Malawi	1	50
Mali	1	80
Nigeria	1	33
Reunion Island	1	69
Somalia	1	75
Southwest Africa	2	53
Spanish Guinea	2	50
Sudan	2	56
Tanzania	4	53
Uganda	3	57
Union of S. Africa	1	62
Zambia	1	54
Total Africa	**39**	**56**
Bermuda	1	76
Canada	29	57
Mexico	8	61
United States	90	58
Total North America	**128**	**58**
Costa Rica	2	56
Cuba	4	58
Dominican Rep.	1	57
El Salvador	3	48
Guatemala	3	52
Haiti	1	45
Honduras	1	55
Nicaragua	3	64
Panama	2	59
Puerto Rico	2	61
Trinidad and Tobago	2	60
Total Central America	**24**	**56**
Argentina	14	52
Bolivia	14	58
Brazil	66	56
Chile	10	57
Colombia	11	50
Ecuador	10	54
Paraguay	9	56
Peru	20	56
Uruguay	3	53
Venezuela	11	61
Total South America	**168**	**56**
Australia	8	52
Melanesia	6	58
Micronesia	2	60
New Guinea	11	56
New Zealand	2	50
Polynesia	8	59
Total Oceania	**37**	**56**
Total	**740**	**58**

Country & Continent	Total Prelates and Abbots Nullius	Average Age
Austria	1	70
Hungary	1	59
Italy	6	68
Switzerland	1	51
Total Europe	**9**	**65**
Canada	1	50
United States	1	49
Total North America	**2**	**50**
Honduras	2	56
Total Central America	**2**	**56**
Brazil	7	48
Chile	1	48
Colombia	1	70
Peru	5	52
Total South America	**14**	**51**
Australia	1	61
Total Oceania	**1**	**61**
Total	**28**	**56**

Country & Continent	Total Apostolic Prefects	Average Age
Austria	1	65
Holland	2	63
Italy	3	65
Switzerland	1	65
Total Europe	**7**	**64**
India	5	60
Indonesia	2	60
Malaysia	1	65
Thailand	1	65
Hong Kong	1	65
Formosa	3	65
Total Asia	**13**	**62**
Algeria	1	65
Bechuanaland	1	46
Cameroon	1	55
Central African Rep.	1	65
Chad	1	49
Congo (Belgian)	2	60
Dahomey	1	65
Guinea	1	50

Country & Continent		Average Age
Kenya	1	50
Libya	1	65
Mali	1	50
Nigeria	3	62
Portuguese Guinea	1	50
Tanzania	1	50
Union of S. Africa	4	51
Upper Volta	1	65
Zambia	1	50
Total Africa	**23**	**56**
Canada	1	59
Mexico	1	65
United States	2	64
Total North America	**4**	**63**
Colombia	7	59
Ecuador	2	65
Falkland Islands	1	75
Peru	1	60
Total South America	**11**	**62**
New Guinea	2	59
Total Oceania	2	59
Total	**60**	**60**

Country & Continent	Total Superiors General	Average Age
Total	**125**	**59**

(Sources: *Osservatore della domenica*, 1966; secretary of Vatican II and *Il Concilio Vaticano II. Cronache del Concilio Vaticano II* edited by *La Civiltà Cattolica*, by Giovanni Caprile 1965–69).

1. Some of the faithful wait for the fathers to leave the Council Hall (Archivio Fscire).

1

and planned a series of discussions to be broadcast in the summer of 1962, in particular by dedicating one series to *Who is the bishop?* It was a series of episodes aimed at illustrating for the general public the figure of the bishop in all its pastoral, social, and historical aspects—and it delved into the issue in some depth. The transmission tried to fill the knowledge gap that was evident, at least among Italians, from the investigation carried by the program among the faithful themselves, in which they were asked to describe, on camera, the role of their pastors. A certain fragility was present (the lack of any "episcopal movement," as has been pointed out) that would be partly reflected even in the document that Vatican II dedicated precisely to the episcopal ministry, the Decree *Christus Dominus*. This was despite the introduction of major innovations that "supported" a typically twentieth-century level of theological maturation that also appears in the constitution *Lumen Gentium*, to which the decree is closely linked in relationship of dependency.

BIBLIOGRAPHY
J. Hamer, "Notes sur la collégialité épiscopale," in *Revue de sciences philosophiques et théologiques*, 44 (1960), 40–50; I Padri presenti al Concilio Ecumenico Vaticano II, edited by the Secretary General of the Council, Vatican City 1966; R. Aubert, "Organizzazione e funzionamento dell'assemblea," in *Storia della Chiesa: La Chiesa del Vaticano II (1958–1978)*, vol. XXV/1, edited by M. Guasco, E. Guerriero, F. Traniello, Cinisello Balsamo 1994, pp. 159–226; G. H. Raguer, "Fisionomia iniziale dell'assemblea," in *Storia del concilio Vaticano II*, vol. 2, Bologna 1996 (2012), 193–258; M. Faggioli, *Il vescovo e il concilio. Modello episcopale e aggiornamento al Vaticano II*, Bologna 2005.

35. RELIGIOUS ORDERS

The canon law in force at the time, in accordance with the tradition of the Latin Church, allowed for certain others to be present at the council: abbots and prelates nullius, abbot primates, abbots who were superiors of monastic congregations, but also of the superiors of "exempt" orders (that is, those under papal rather than episcopal jurisdiction). But religious congregations that were not composed of clerics and those who came under diocesan law had to receive an invitation. This had already happened at Vatican I, when Pius IX called to the council superiors of major religious orders, like the Benedictine liturgist and ultramontanist Prosper Guéranger, abbot of Solesmes. At the beginning of October 1962 Pope John XXIII also invited (in technical terms, extended a "concession" to participate) the superiors of some non-exempt religious families, who had more than one thousand professed members, to which he added four missionary congregations. And so those who were seated in the Council Hall of Vatican II included the superiors of the Congregation of the Sacred Hearts, the Marist Fathers, the Monfort fathers, the Oblates of Mary Immaculate, the clerics of Saint Viator, the Marianists, the Congregation of Holy Cross, the Assumptionists, the Priests of the Most Holy Sacrament, the Claretian Missionaries of the Sacred Heart of Jesus, the Oblates of St. Francis de Sales, the Missionaries of Our Lady of La Salette, the Priests of the Sacred Heart of Jesus, the Sons of the Sacred Heart of Jesus (from the African Missions of Verona), the Congregation of the Immaculate Heart of Mary (Scheut Missionaries), Salvatorians, the Consolata Mission Institute of Turin, the Missionaries of the Holy Family, the Society of St. Paul, and the Little Work of Divine Providence. To these, then, were added the Missionaries of Africa (White Fathers), the Society of African Missions, the Society of St. Joseph of Mill Hill for the foreign missions and the Society of St. Columban for Chinese missions. Religious communities were thus a substantial presence. Apart from religious (about 500) who were bishops and the superior general of the Congregation of the Holy Spirit who was at Vatican II as a diocesan bishop, in St. Peter's there were 940 religious present, that is, about 38 percent of the assembly: ninety-seven were the superiors general of religious orders and congregations who were called for the first session. The largest groups were the Friars Minor (ninety), the Capuchins (fifty-five), the Jesuits (fifty-one), the Salesians (fifty-one), the White Fathers (forty-four), the Congregation of the Holy Spirit (forty-one), the Benedictines (thirty-seven), the Dominicans (thirty-six), and the Oblates of Mary Immaculate (thirty-four). In addition to these, there were the *periti* or experts, including some of the great theologians of the council.

The religious from exempt orders who were present at the council belonged to six different groups: canons regular (for example, the Congregation of the Most Holy Savior, Premonstratensians, Crosiers), monks (the Benedictine confederation, the Cistercians, the Trappists, the Carthusians, the Basilians, and so on), mendicants (Dominicans, the Friars Minor, the Conventual Franciscans, the Capuchins, the Discalced Carmelites, the Third Order of St. Francis, and so on), regular clergy (Theatines, the Barnabites, Jesuits, Somaschi fathers, the Ministers of the Sick, the Clerics Regular Minor of St. Francis Caracciolo, clerics of the Mother of God, and the Piarists), the clerical religious congregations (the Congregation of Christian Doctrine, the Marianists, the Passionists, Redemptorists, the Rosminians, the Salesians, the Divine Word Missionaries, and so on) and societies following common life without vows (the Vincentians and Pallotines).

Despite this great presence, the decree on religious life, *Perfectae Caritatis* was not one of the great documents of the council. The proposal to reduce it to a series of "proposals," which was put forward in the Coordinating Commission in January 1963, was not adopted: one decree (which was approved in last session with 2,325 votes in favor, and four against, in its fifth draft) which was one of the few contributions that was theologically qualified was that of the Canadian ecumenist Jean-Marie Roger Tillard on poverty. Other issues—the priestly ordination of teaching brothers such as the Marist brothers—were inserted into the document at the last minute without theological foundation.

1. St. Anthony the Abbot, paint on wood, 18th Century, Coptic Museum, Cairo (Archivio Jaca Book).

2. Saint Benedict, assisted by an angel, gives his Rule to Abbot John I (914–934). Rule of St. Benedict and other texts (914–934), Montecassino Abbey Archive. Cod. Casin. 175, 2 (Archivio Jaca Book).

3. Saint Francis, fresco by the Master of Cimabue, Basilica of Saint Francis of Assisi, Lower Church (Archivio Jaca Book).

4. Pope Paul III approving the Constitutions of the Society of Jesus, handed to him by St. Ignatius. Painting in the sacristy of the Gesú in Rome by an anonymous artist (Archivio Jaca Book).

1

2

3

4

Ordini religiosi	Cardinali, patriarchi, arcivescovi e vescovi residenziali e titolari	Prelati non vescovi	Totale generale		Ordini religiosi	Cardinali, patriarchi, arcivescovi e vescovi residenziali e titolari	Prelati non vescovi	Totale generale
Friars Minor*	89	1	90		Hermits of St. Augustine*	4	1	5
Capuchins*	54	1	55		Eudists	5	-	5
Jesuits*	50	1	51		Pallottines	5	-	5
Salesians*	49	2	51		Servites *	4	1	5
White Fathers	44	-	44		Basilian Alepians*	3	1	4
Congregation of the Holy Spirit	41	-	41		Basilian Salvatorians*	3	1	4
Benedictine Confederation*	14	23	37		Basilian Chouerites	3	1	4
Dominicans*	34	2	36		Order of the Holy Cross*	3	1	4
Oblates of Mary Immaculate	34	-	34		Marian Hill Missionaries	4	-	4
Vincentians	29	-	29		Missionaries of the Holy Family	4	-	4
Society of the Divine Word*	24	2	26		Xaverians	2	2	4
Redemptorists*	24	1	25		Third Order Regular of St. Francis*	2	2	4
Society of Foreign Missions of Paris	24	-	24		Barnabites*	2	1	3
Society of African Missions	21	-	21		Sylvestrines *	2	1	3
Missionaries of the Sacred Heart	17	1	18		Conventual Franciscans*	2	1	3
Marists	14	-	14		Marianists*	2	1	3
Passionists*	13	1	14		Mercedarians*	2	1	3
Pime Fathers	14	-	14		Missionaries of Our Lady of La Salette	3	-	3
Maryknoll	11	2	13		Missionaries of St. Francis de Sales	3	-	3
Cistercians*	2	10	12		Oblates of St. Francis de Sales	3	-	3
Scheut Missionaries	12	-	12		Order of the Most Holy Trinity*	2	1	3
Priests of the Sacred Heart	11	-	11		Premonstratensians*	2	1	3
Mill Hill Fathers	11	-	11		Society of St. Patrick	3	-	3
Picpus Fathers	9	1	10		Somaschi Fathers*	2	1	3
Montfort Fathers	10	-	10		Sulpicians	3	-	3
Discalced Carmelites*	8	1	9		Antonians of Aleppo*	1	1	2
Claretians	9	-	9		Clerks Regular of the Mother of God*	1	1	2
Congregation of the Holy Cross	8	-	8		Josephites of Asti	1	1	2
Comboni Missionaries	8	-	8		Spanish Institute of St. Francis Xavier	2	-	2
Carmelites of the Ancient Observance*	5	2	7		Mechitharists of Venice *	2	-	2
Recollects	6	1	7		Mechitharists of Vienna	2	-	2
Colomban Fathers	7	-	7		Missionaries of the Precious Blood	2	-	2
Assumptionists	6	-	6		Missionaries of the Sons of the Sacred Heart	1	1	2
Basilians of St. Josaphat*	5	1	6		Foreign Mission Society of Quebec	2	-	2
Consolata Missionaries	6	-	6		Yarumal Society for the Foreign Missions	2	-	2
Missionaries of St. Paul (Melkite)	6	-	6		Antonians of St. Ormizda of Chaldeans*	1	1	2
Augustinian Canons*	2	3	5		Resurrectionists	2	-	2

Antonians of St. Isaiah (Maronite)*	-	1	1
Lebanese Antonians (Maronite)*	-	1	1
Olivetans*	-	1	1
Vallombrosans*	-	1	1
Camillians*	-	1	1
Adorno Fathers*	-	1	1
Carthusians*	-	1	1
Italian Congregation of Basilian Monks*	-	1	1
Missionaries of the Sacred Hearts	-	1	1
Congregation of Camaldolese Hermits*	-	1	1
Camaldolese Hermits of Mt. Corona*	-	1	1
Disciples of the Lord	1	-	1
Christian Doctrine Fathers*	-	1	1
Sons of the Immaculate Conception, Luçon	1	-	1
Franciscan Family of St. Joseph	1	-	1
Josephites of Murialdo	1	-	1
Order of Imitation of Christ	1	-	1
Cavanis Fathers	1	-	1
Institute of Our Lady of Guadalupe	1	-	1
Minims*	-	1	1
Missionaries of the Holy Spirit	1	-	1
Missionaries of St. Joseph of Mexico	1	-	1
Bethlehem Fathers	1	-	1
Scarboro Foreign Mission Society	1	-	1
Monks of St. Paul the Hermit*	-	1	1
Opus Dei	-	1	1
Teutonic Order*	-	1	1
Little Brothers of the Poor	1	-	1
Priests of the Sacred Heart of Betharram	1	-	1
Priests of St. Basil	1	-	1
Discalced Augustinians*	-	1	1
Rosminians	1	-	1
Piarists*	-	1	1
Portuguese Overseas Mission Society	1	-	1
Stigmatines	1	-	1
Theatines*	-	1	1
Trappists*	-	1	1

* Exempt orders
Source: *I convocati al Concilio Ecumenico Vaticano ii*, edited by N. Venturini; ASV, Carte Bea, b. 18.

BIBLIOGRAPHY

Il Concilio Vaticano II. Cronache del Concilio Vaticano II edite da "La Civiltà Cattolica"—Quarto periodo 1965, edited by G. Caprile, vol. V, Rome 1969; R. Aubert, "Organizzazione e funzionamento dell'assemblea," in *Storia della Chiesa: La Chiesa del Vaticano II (1958–1978)*, vol. XXV/1, edited by M. Guasco, E. Guerriero, F. Traniello, Cinisello Balsamo 1994, 159–226; H. Raguer, "Fisionomia iniziale dell'assemblea," in *Storia del concilio Vaticano II* edited by G. Alberigo (Italian edition edited by A. Melloni), vol. 2, Bologna 1996 (2012), 193–258; *Les Religieux et le Concile Vatican II. Colloque International, Rome, November 12–14, 2014* (forthcoming).

36. Eastern Rite Catholics

The impressive procession of bishops that marked the opening of the Second Vatican Council on October 11, 1962, made visible the variety of ritual traditions historically encompassed within the Catholic Church. Alongside the bishops from American, African, Asian, and European countries who entered St. Peter's, there were also those wearing different vestments, showing that they belonged to Churches whose tradition was not Latin. All these bishops came under the general description of "Oriental." The Orthodox churches that had entered into communion with Rome at various times and ways were distinguished by the designation "Uniate." These definitions, however, had accumulated a host of expressions that were really very different.

John XXIII was particularly aware of this. In 1925, he had been sent to Bulgaria to attempt a union, which failed; he knew from the history of ancient Constantinople how complex many of the Eastern Churches were. "The East does not exist except in the generalizing classifications of Westerners," Roncalli had said as Patriarch of Venice. The group of "Eastern" Catholics at the council was actually very heterogeneous. There were about sixty fathers from the Middle East, representing six Catholic patriarchates (Armenian, Chaldean, Maronite, Melkite, Syrian, and Coptic); there were about fifteen Ukrainian bishops of the Greek-Catholic rite representing two million, both in Europe and in the Americas. Since the *vota*, the latter had as a priority the issue of condemning communism and felt that they could play a decisive role in relations with Orthodox churches. Other groups were convinced of this too: the Maronites, Armenians, Syrians, and especially the Melkites, who wanted to mark "the place of those who were absent," that is, the Orthodox church of Constantinople, which from the third period on was represented only by a personal delegate from the Patriarch Athenagoras. These were churches that had resisted "Romanization" and were in tune with John XXIII in maintaining that it was dangerous to think of new dogmas that would increase the gap with the Orthodox Churches.

However, in order to guarantee the presence of observers (other than bishops) from the areas under Soviet influence, the Secretariat for Unity and the nuncio in Ankara initiated contact with the Soviet Union that led to some resistance from the Ukrainians, who adhered—as indeed a large part of the Hungarian and Polish Catholics did—to a vision of extreme resistance against communist regimes. John XXIII had initiated confidential negotiations to encourage the participation in the council of all those bishops who were imprisoned behind the Iron Curtain: not even the release of Archbishop Josyp Slipyj of Lviv in the Ukraine, which was the first important result of these negotiations, could change the mind of those who believed that the Church should not engage in dialogue with the Kremlin for any reason.

Other "Easterners," such as the Maronites, contributed to the discussion on the unity of the Church, while the Melkites, particularly through the Patriarch Maximos IV, showed how different they were by demanding that a seat be reserved for them in the Council Hall which would place them ahead of the cardinals, and also by refusing to speak in Latin. The liturgical heritage and discipline of these Churches (the use of living languages, concelebration, communion under both kinds, married clergy) played a role in opening the eyes of many bishops who had considered the East remote; and it allowed them to have an experience of collegiality, which was part of their tradition, but which revealed a way of exercising *comunio ecclesiarum* that had been forgotten in the Latin Church.

1. Eastern rite bishops enter the council on opening day, October 11 (photo Pais/Archivio Rodrigo Pais–Ceub Università di Bologna).

2. A group of Eastern council fathers at the council. From left to right, Romanian, Ukrainian, Italian-Albanian, and Russian (from *Il Concilio Vaticano II*).

3, 4. Eastern rite bishops await the start of the opening ceremony for the second session of the Council (photo Pais/Archivio Rodrigo Pais–Ceub Università di Bologna).

3

4

BIBLIOGRAPHY

Discorsi di Massimo IV al Concilio, Bologna 1968; I. Dick, "Vatican II et les Églises orientales catholiques," in *Le deuxième concile du Vatican (1959–1965)*, Rome 1989, 615–625; R. Morozzo della Rocca, "I 'voti' degli orientali nella preparazione del Vaticano II," in *À la veille du Concile Vatican II. Vota et réactions en Europe et dans le catholicisme oriental*, edited by M. Lamberigts and Cl. Soetens, Bibliotheek van de Faculteit der Godgeleerdheid, Leuven 1992, 119–145; R. Aubert, "Organizzazione e funzionamento dell'assemblea," in *Storia della Chiesa*, XXV/1, *La Chiesa del Vaticano II (1958–1978)*, edited by M. Guasco, E. Guerriero, F. Traniello, and Cinisello Balsamo 1994, 173–174; N. Edelby, *Il Vaticano II nel diario di un vescovo arabo*, edited by R. Cannelli, and Cinisello Balsamo 1996; H. Raguer Riccardi, "Fisionomia iniziale dell'assemblea," in *Storia del concilio Vaticano II*, edited by G. Alberigo (Italian edition edited by A. Melloni), vol. 2, Bologna 1996 (2012), 193–258.

	Residential cardinals, patriarchs, archbishops, bishops	Titular archbishops and bishops	Subtotal	Prelates (not bishops)	Total	Faithful	Proportion of council fathers to faithful
Melchites	13	9	22	3	25	397,600	15,500
Ukrainians	8	10	18	1	19	5,374,000	282,800
Maronites	10	3	13	3	16	870,000	54,300
Chaldeans	12	1	13	1	14	190,000	13,500
Armenians	7	7	14	–	14	97,100	6,900
Syrians	6	4	10		10	80,000	8,000
Malabars	7	–	7	–	7	1,349,000	192,700
Copts	4	2	6	–	6	82,800	13,600
Etiopians	3	1	4	–	4	59,200	14,800
Romanians	2	1	3		3	1,572,000	524,000
Italo-Albanians	1	1	2	1	3	70,400	23,400
Syro-Malankars	2	–	2	–	2	118,000	59,000
Russians	–	2	2	–	2	3,000 (outside Russia)	1,500 (outside Russia)
Hungarians	1	–	1	–	1	215,000	215,000
Yugoslavians	–	1	1	–	1	56,300	56,300
Ruthenians	–	1	1	–	1	35,000	35,000
Bulgarians	–	1	1	–	1	9,400	9,400
Greeks	–	1	1	–	1	2,800	2,800
TOTALS	76	45	121	9	130 (4.6% of council fathers)	10,582,500	

37. THE PERITI

Section 9 of the fifth chapter of the motu proprio *Appropinquante Concilio*, published on August 6, 1962, on the Regulations of the Synod Assembly, outlines the authority of the pope to appoint theologians, canon lawyers, and other specialists as consultants or *periti* to the council. In section 10 it is clear that these *periti* could participate in the general congregations but could speak only if asked. In fact, although at the Council of Trent and previous councils, the theologians had had occasion to speak in front of the council fathers gathered in the general congregations, at Vatican II this never happened in the Council Hall. Despite this, the *periti* made crucial contributions at the council, not only in the preparation of documents in conciliar commissions, but also in shaping and guiding the opinions of the fathers through events that unfolded outside of St. Peter's, such as the study meetings held by episcopal conferences or groups, or interviews given to journalists. In this regard, on September 15, 1964, in the middle of the discussion on the controversial chapter 3 of *De Ecclesia*, Paul VI updated the standards to which the *periti* should adhere. According to some council fathers, the *periti* were too busy holding "conferences that facilitated and disclosed certain tendencies." Among the numerous prohibitions contained in these standards was one related to giving interviews, and the consequent risk of losing one's position as *peritus* to the council (AS, vol. III, t. 1, 24, 157).

Section 11 of the Regulations also allowed individual council fathers to make use of personal *periti*, who would follow them to Rome without the right to participate in the general congregations and meetings of the commissions while being equally bound to secrecy about the debates and the internal council discussions to which their bishops allowed them access. These private *periti* did not always have a peripheral role: Giuseppe Dossetti, for example, who at the beginning of the second session took his place as secretary of the board of moderators during a brief but crucial phase, only received papal approval of his appointment from the third session on.

The first list of *periti*, published on September 28, 1962, contained 224 names. The number increased during the council sessions, between groups and individual nominations that were announced from time to time in the interim, eventually reaching a total of 480. From the start, the nominees, despite the fact that they came from more than thirty different countries, belonged to the Curia and were members and consultants from the various preparatory commissions as well as professors from universities in Rome, thus revealing a council controlled by Roman factions fighting among each other. Eighty-five were Italians (including forty-four from the Curia), with a hundred other Europeans coming mainly from France, Spain, and Germany, while there was only one from Africa

(Egypt) and seven from Asia (two from Lebanon, one from Jordan, one from Syria, one from Turkey, one from China, and one from India). There were sixteen Americans, three Canadians, two Brazilians and one Argentinian, with eighty-four professors from universities, colleges, institutes, and Roman houses of religious orders, and fifty-three, mostly canon lawyers, who were already consultants or members of the Roman Congregations. National and cultural representation was never a goal. There were not many missionary theologians, no pastors and as a whole, most of the appointments were Europeans. The almost complete absence of theologians and canon lawyers from mission areas was also linked to finances; it was cheaper and easier to appoint specialists who already lived in Rome. In fact, of the 224 initially appointed, more than half came right from the heart of Catholicism in Rome.

Yet it was precisely these *periti* who brought to the conciliar documents the influence of the biblical, liturgical, and patristic movements that had emerged and were being established from the beginning of the nineteenth century and had become a key factor in the almost silent renewal of the three decades prior to council. The influence of Central European and French theological schools was particularly strong, like those of Louvain, Innsbruck, Tübingen, Lyon, and the Dominicans from the Saulchoir. Among the theologians of the "German school" (although Franz Hürth and Heribert Schauf, representatives of the rigid Roman scholastic approach, were also Germans) were Joseph Jungmann, and Johannes Wagner, of the liturgical movement, and Eduard Stakemeier, from the Ecumenical Institute at Paderborn, as well as Bernhard Häring, forerunner of the renewal of moral theology. The German contingent also had the church historian Hubert Jedin, a scholar of the Council of Trent, Joseph Ratzinger, who had accompanied Cardinal Frings in the first session as a private *peritus* then received a papal appointment as an expert from the second period onwards, and especially Karl Rahner, one of the most crucial theological influences on Vatican II, who, because of his authority, caused the downfall of several draft documents, and presented alternative projects in collaboration with other *periti*, that were theologically more open. Among these were various French theologians who had a strong influence on the work of the council, such as Yves Congar, Jean Daniélou, and Henri de Lubac, who were all part of the *nouvelle théologie* movement that had been suppressed during Pius XII's pontificate.

John XXIII personally insisted that they be summoned to the council as *periti*, especially Congar and de Lubac, so that the council could also dialogue with different positions and theological concepts. Other theologians played a role without finding the

Top row, left to right, the *periti* Carlo Balič (1899–1977), Edward
Schillebeeckx (1914–2009), Henri de Lubac (1896–1991); bottom
row, left to right, Gregory Baum (1923–), Yves Congar (1904–1995),
Jean Daniélou (1905–1974) (from *Das Konzil und seine Folgen*).

acceptance that in several cases (Daniélou, Ratzinger, Congar, de Lubac, Grillmeier) was confirmed by their creation as cardinals in later pontificates: for example, the Dominican Marie-Dominique Chenu was never appointed *peritus* and was closely scrutinized by the Holy Office. Nevertheless, he still contributed enormously to the council, making himself available to several French bishops and bishops' conferences (For example the first draft of the Message to the World was his idea and was approved by the fathers a few days after the opening of the council on October 20, 1962). At the end of the fourth session, Paul VI (who during that session particularly took advantage of the work of his personal advisor Carlo Colombo, and ran almost everything past him at the end of the council during the review of the council's most controversial drafts) wanted to make a public tribute to the hidden services rendered by the experts at the council by inviting some to participate at the concelebration of a Mass on November 18, 1965.

BIBLIOGRAPHY

M.-D. Chenu, *Notes quotidiennes au Concile*, edited by A. Melloni, Paris 1995; Y. Congar, *Mon Journal du Concile*, 2 vols., Paris 2002; H. de Lubac, *Carnets du Concile*, t. 1 and 2, introduction and notes by L. Figoureux, Paris 2007; G. Alberigo, "Giuseppe Dossetti al concilio Vaticano II," in *Transizione epocale*, Bologna 2009, 393–502; *The council notes of Edward Schillebeeckx 1962–1963*, edited by K. Schelkens, Leuven 2011; G. Valente, *Ratzinger al Vaticano II*, Cinisello Balsamo 2013.

A

Name	I	II	III	IV
Abate A., OP	I	II	III	IV
Abellán P., SJ	I	II	III	IV
Ahern B., CP	I	II	III	IV
Albareda G. M.	I	II	III	IV
Alting von G. L.				IV
Anglés P. I.	I	II	III	IV
Antonelli F., OFM	I	II	III	IV
Arrighi G., OP		II	III	IV
Augustin F.		II	III	IV

B

Name	I	II	III	IV
Baker J.	I	II	III	IV
Balic C., OFM	I	II	III	IV
Bandas R.	I	II	III	IV
Baragli E., SJ	I	II	III	IV
Barahana G., SJ		II	III	IV
Baraúna G., OFM			III	IV
Barbosa R. Z.			III	IV
Barry G., OMI	I	II	III	IV
Barry M.	I	II	III	IV
Bartoccetti V.	I	II	III	IV
Baum G., OESA	I	II	III	IV
Baum W.	I	II	III	IV
Bednarski F., OP		II	III	IV
Behrendt A.			III	IV
Bejan O.	I	II	III	IV
Bélanger M., OMI	I	II	III	IV
Belloli G. B.	I	II	III	IV
Beniamino della SS. Trinità, OCD	I	II	III	IV
Benoit P., OP		II	III	IV
Bergin C. E.		II	III	IV
Bernard J.	I	II	III	IV
Bertrams W., SJ			III	IV
Berutti C., OP	I	II	III	IV
Beste U., OSB	I	II	III	IV
Betti U., OFM			III	IV
Bevilacqua G., OSFN	I	II	III	IV
Bidagor R., SJ	I	II	III	IV
Bogliolo L., ODB		II	III	IV
Boillat F.	I	II	III	IV
Bonet y Muixi E.	I	II	III	IV
Bonet Marrugat A.	I	II	III	IV
Borella P.			III	IV
Bosler R.	I	II	III	IV
Boulard F.	I	II	III	IV
Boyer C., SJ	I	II	III	IV
Brennan F.	I	II	III	IV
Breysse M., SS	I	II	III	IV
Brezanoczy P.	I	II	III	
Bugnini A., CM	I	II	III	IV
Buijs L., SJ	I	II	III	IV
Burke A.	I	II	III	IV

C

Name	I	II	III	IV
Caloyeras D., OP	I	II	III	IV
Camagni E.	I	II	III	IV
Camelot T., OP	I	II	III	IV
Canals S.	I	II	III	IV
Cancouet M.		II	III	IV
Capovilla L.			III	IV
Carbone V.	I	II	III	IV
Cardijn J.		II	III	
Carley J.		II	III	IV
Cardinale I.	I			
Carpenter H.			III	IV
Casaroli A.	I	II	III	IV
Casoria G.	I	II	III	IV
Castellino G., SDB	I	II	III	IV
Cecchetti I.	I	II	III	
Cerfaux L.	I	II	III	IV
Ceriani G.	I	II	III	IV
Chavasse A.	I	II	III	IV
Che-Chen-Tao V.	I	II	III	IV
Chereath S.	I	II	III	IV
Ciappi L., OP	I	II	III	IV
Cik S.			III	IV
Civardi E.	I	II	III	IV
Clark A.	I	II	III	IV
Clark R. A.	I	II	III	IV
Coffey J.	I	II	III	IV
Colombo C.	I	II		
Combes A.	I	II	III	IV
Congar Yves, OP	I	II	III	IV
Connell F. J., CSsR	I	II	III	IV
Connolly J.	I	II	III	IV
Connolly N. P.		II	III	IV
Conway D.			III	IV
Cottier M. M., OP				IV
Courtney Murray J., SJ		II	III	IV
Cremin P.	I	II	III	IV
Crepeault P.-E.	I	II	III	IV
Crovella E.	I	II	III	IV
Crump F., OMI			III	IV
Cummins J.		II	III	IV
Curran C. A.			III	IV

D

Name	I	II	III	IV
Dale R., OP			III	IV
Daly C.			III	IV
Daly J., CSSp			III	IV
Daniélou J., SJ	I	II	III	IV
D'Ascenzi G.				IV
Davis C.			III	IV
Davis H.-F.	I	II	III	IV
de Clercq C.	I	II	III	IV
Defresne M.		II	III	IV
Delacroix S.		II	III	IV
Delhaye P.		II	III	IV
Delly E.			III	IV
del Portillo A., Opus Dei	I	II	III	IV
Del Ton G.		II	III	IV
de Lubac H., SJ	I	II	III	IV
Denis H.		II	III	IV
Denis J.	I	II	III	IV
D'Ercole G.	I	II	III	IV
De Riedmatten H., OP		II	III	IV
Deskur A.	I	II	III	IV
Devine T. F.	I	II	III	IV
Dezza P., SJ	I	II	III	IV
Dhanis E., SJ	I	II	III	IV
Di Biagio A.	I	II	III	IV
Diekmann G., OSB		II	III	IV
Dietz D., OMI				IV
Di Fonzo L., OFM	I	II	III	IV
Dirks A., OP	I	II	III	IV
Dockx I., OP		II	III	IV
Doheny W.	I	II	III	IV

Name	I	II	III	IV
Dossetti G.			III	IV
Drew B.		II	III	IV
Driscoll A., OP		II	III	IV
Dubarle D., OP				IV
Dumont C., OP	I	II	III	IV
Duroux B., OP			III	IV

E

Name	I	II	III	IV
Ebben B., OP				IV
Egger C., CRL	I	II	III	IV
Eid E.	I	II	III	IV
Eldarov G., OFM	I	II	III	IV
Etchegaray R.			III	IV
Evers E., SSS	I	II	III	IV
Ewers H.	I	II	III	IV
Extross J.	I	II	III	IV

F

Name	I	II	III	IV
Fabro C., CPS	I	II	III	IV
Fagiolo V.	I	II	III	IV
Faltin D., OFM	I	II	III	IV
Fazzalaro F.	I	II	III	IV
Felici A.	I	II	III	IV
Fenton J.	I	II	III	IV
Fernandez Gennaro del S. Cuore, ORSA	I	II	III	IV
Ferrari Toniolo A.	I	II	III	IV
Ferraro N.	I	II	III	IV
Fiedler E.	I	II	III	IV
Filipiak B.	I	II	III	IV
Finucan J.	I	II	III	IV
Flynn F., CP			III	IV
Flynn K., OFM				IV
Flynn M. F.	I	II	III	IV
Flynn M. J.		II	III	IV
Fohl J., OSB	I	II	III	IV
Foucreault L.			III	IV
Freschi A.				IV
Frison B., CMF		II	III	IV
Frutaz A. P.	I	II	III	IV

G

Name	I	II	III	IV
Gagnebet M.-R., OP	I	II	III	IV
Gagnon E., PSS			III	IV
Gallagher T., OP				IV
Galletto A.	I	II	III	IV
Gambari E., SMM	I	II	III	IV
Garcia M.		II	III	IV
Garofalo S.	I	II	III	IV
Gavazzi E., OSB	I	II		
Geraud J., SS	I	II	III	IV
Gervais J., OMI			III	IV
Gheddo P., PIME			III	IV
Gibson A.				IV
Gibson L.	I	II	III	IV
Gillespie P.	I	II	III	IV
Gillon L., OP	I	II	III	IV
Giovannelli A.	I	II	III	IV
Giovanetti A.	I	II	III	IV
Girard P., PSS			III	IV
Giusti M. A.	I	II	III	IV
Glazik J., MSC			III	IV
Glorieux A.	I	II	III	IV
Goossens P.		II	III	IV
Gössman F., OESA	I	II	III	IV
Gottardi A.	I			
Gouet J.		II	III	IV

Name	I	II	III	IV
Governatori L.	I	II	III	IV
Goyeneche S., CMF	I	II		
Graneris G.	I	II	III	IV
Grasso D., SJ	I	II	III	IV
Graves L.			III	IV
Greco G., SJ			III	IV
Grillmeier L., SJ		II	III	IV
Groot J.			III	IV
Guardini R.		II	III	IV
Guay A., OMI		II	III	IV
Guerri S.	I	II	III	IV
Guglielmi A.				IV
Gutierrez A., CMF	I	II	III	IV

H

Name	I	II	III	IV
Haas J.	I	II	III	IV
Hacault A.	I	II		
Hafouri G.		II	III	IV
Hamer J. J., OP	I	II	III	IV
Hammel P.		II	III	IV
Häring B., CSsR	I	II	III	IV
Haubtmann P.		II	III	IV
Herlihy D.	I	II		
Heston E., CSC	I	II	III	IV
Hickey J.	I	II	III	IV
Higgins G.	I	II	III	IV
Hiret M.				IV
Hirschmann J., SJ	I	II	III	IV
Hnlica P., SJ	I	II		
Hoffmann H.	I	II	III	IV
Hoppe P.		II	III	IV
Howard J. J.	I	II	III	IV
Hrynchyshyn M., CSsR			III	IV
Hunt W.		II	III	IV
Hurley M.	I	II	III	IV
Hürth F., SJ	I			

I

Name	I	II	III	IV
Iglesias D.	I	II	III	IV
Ilarino da Milano, OFM	I	II	III	IV
Iparraguirre I., SJ	I	II	III	IV

J

Name	I	II	III	IV
Jedin H.	I	II	III	IV
Jelici V., OFM	I	II	III	IV
Johnson J.	I	II	III	IV
Jordan P., OSB			III	IV
Jungmann J., SJ	I	II	III	IV

K

Name	I	II	III	IV
Keeler W. K.	I	II	III	IV
Kelley J.		II	III	IV
Kelly J. P., CSSp		II	III	IV
Kenneth P.				IV
Kernweiss K.			III	IV
Kerrigan A., OFM	I	II	III	IV
Khalife I., SJ	I	II	III	IV
King J., OMI		II	III	IV
Klempa S., OPraem	I	II	III	IV
Kloppemburg B., OFM	I	II	III	IV
Klosterann F.	I	II	III	IV
Köster W., SJ			III	IV
Kowalsky N., OMI			III	IV
Küng H.	I	II	III	IV

L

Name	I	II	III	IV
Labourdette M., OP	I	II	III	IV
Lafortune P.	I	II	III	IV

Name	I	II	III	IV
Lambert B., OP			III	IV
Lambruschini F.	I	II	III	IV
Landi A.	I	II	III	IV
Landucci P. C.		II	III	IV
Lattanzi U.	I	II	III	IV
Laubacher J., SS		II	III	IV
Laurentin R.	I	II	III	IV
Le Bourgeois A., CJM		II	III	IV
Lebret J., OP			III	IV
Lecuyer J., CSSp	I	II	III	IV
Ledwolorz A., OFM	I	II	III	IV
Leetham C.		II	III	IV
Lefebvre C.	I	II	III	IV
Leinfelder P.	I	II	III	IV
Lentini S.	I	II	III	IV
Lessard R.	I	II	III	IV
Levesque C. H.	I	II	III	IV
Ligutti L.	I	II	III	IV
Limoges R.		II	III	IV
Lio E., OFM	I	II	III	IV
Loizeau E.	I	II	III	IV
Lonergan B., SJ			III	IV
Lopes Da Cruz E.	I	II	III	IV
Lores V.,	I	II	III	IV
Lumbreras P., OP	I	II	III	IV
M				
Maccarrone M.	I	II	III	IV
MacKenzie R., SJ			III	IV
Madden J.			III	IV
Malak J.	I	II	III	IV
Maly E.	I	II	III	IV
Manteau-Bonamy H.				IV
Mansourati I.	I			
Mariani B., OFM			III	IV
Mariani G.	I	II	III	IV
Martegani G., SJ				IV
Martil G.,	I	II	III	IV
Martimort G.	I	II	III	IV
Martinez de Antoñana G., CFM	I	II	III	IV
Mascarenhas Roxo R.			III	IV
Masi R.	I	II	III	IV
Massimi G.				IV
Mathieu C.			III	IV
Mattioli P.	I	II	III	IV
Mauro A.	I	II	III	IV
Mayer A., OSB	I	II	III	IV
McCormick J.	I	II	III	IV
McDevitt A.		II	III	IV
McDonald W.	I	II	III	IV
McGraw J.	I	II	III	IV
McManus F.	I	II	III	IV
McReavy L.	I	II	III	IV
Medeiros S. H.	I	II	III	IV
Medina Estevez G.	I	II	III	IV
Mejia G.		II	III	IV
Mestre G.		II	III	IV
Miano V., SDB				IV
Michiels G., OFM	I	II	III	
Mitchel G.		II	III	IV
Mitnacht A., OESA		II	III	IV
Mizzi E., OCD	I	II	III	IV
Moëller C.		II	III	IV
Molinari P., SJ		II	III	IV

Name	I	II	III	IV
Morisset B.			III	IV
Morlion F., OP			III	IV
Mörsdorf N.		II	III	IV
Moss Tapajoz I.			III	IV
Mouroux J.				IV
Moya R., OP	I	II	III	IV
Müehlen H.				IV
Mulders A.	I	II	III	IV
Muñoz Vega P., SJ	I	II		
Mura E., RSV		II	III	IV
Murphy F.X., CSsR		II	III	IV
Murray E.			III	IV
N				
Nabuco J.	I	II	III	IV
Naud A.		II	III	IV
Neuner J., SJ		II	III	IV
Nicet J., FSC		II	III	IV
Nicolau M., SJ				IV
Novarese L.				IV
O				
O'Connel J.	I	II	III	IV
O'Connell M.				IV
O'Connor D., MSsST	I	II	III	IV
O'Keefe D.		II	III	IV
Olivier B., OP		II	III	IV
Olmedo D., SJ		II	III	IV
O'Mara J.	I	II	III	IV
Onclin W.	I	II	III	IV
Overath J.	I	II	III	IV
P				
Pagani C.				IV
Paik D.		II	III	IV
Papali C., OCD	I	II	III	IV
Paradis W. H.	I	II	III	IV
Pascoli P.	I	II	III	IV
Pasquazi G.	I	II	III	IV
Pavan P.	I	II	III	IV
Paventi S.	I	II	III	IV
Pecoraio E.	I	II	III	IV
Peeters H., OFM	I	II	III	IV
Peinador A., CFM	I	II	III	IV
Permentier W.		II	III	IV
Perrault A.-M., OP	I	II	III	IV
Persich N.	I	II	III	IV
Pfister P., SJ		II	III	IV
Philipon M., OP		II	III	IV
Philips G.	I	II	III	IV
Pietrobelli A.	I	II	III	IV
Pinna G.	I	II	III	IV
Piolanti A.	I	II	III	IV
Piovesana L.		II	III	IV
Pironio E.			III	IV
Placido di S. Giuseppe, OCarm	I	II	III	IV
Polzin L.		II		
Pozzi R.	I	II	III	IV
Prignon A.		II	III	IV
Pujol C., SJ	I	II	III	IV
Putz J., SJ		II	III	IV
Q				
Quadri S.	I	II		
Quinn J. S.	I	II	III	IV
R				
Radenac H.	I	II	III	IV

Name	I	II	III	IV
Raes A., SJ	I	II	III	IV
Rahner K., SJ	I	II	III	IV
Ramirez G., OP	I	II	III	IV
Ramselaar A.	I	II	III	IV
Ratzinger J.		II	III	IV
Rawden J.	I	II	III	IV
Regatillo E., SJ	I	II	III	IV
Reuter A., OMI	I	II	III	IV
Rigaux B., OFM		II	III	IV
Righetti M.	I	II	III	IV
Robitaille D.	I	II	III	IV
Rodhain J.	I	II	III	IV
Rodriguez M. J.	I	II	III	IV
Romani S.	I	II	III	IV
Romita F.	I	II	III	IV
Roschini G., OSM		II	III	IV
Rosemeyer R.		II	III	IV
Rossi G.	I	II	III	IV
Rousseau J., OMI	I	II	III	IV
Ryan A.				IV
S				
Sabattani A.	I	II	III	
Sala L.,	I	II	III	
Salaverri G., SJ	I	II	III	IV
Salmon P., OSB	I	II		
Sanchis J., OFM	I	II	III	IV
Sauras E., OP	I	II	III	IV
Schauf E.	I	II	III	IV
Schierano M.				IV
Schmaus M.	I	II	III	IV
Schürmann H.				IV
Schwarcz-Eggenhofer A.	I	II	III	IV
Semmelroth O., SJ			III	IV
Sennot R.	I	II	III	IV
Sessolo G.				IV
Seumois A., OMI	I	II	III	IV
Seumois X., PA		II	III	IV
Shea G. W.	I	II	III	IV
Shea J. T.				IV
Shook L. K., CSB				IV
Siegel C. A.		II	III	IV
Sigmond R., OP	I	II	III	IV
Sikora L.	I	II	III	IV
Smulders P., SJ		II	III	IV
Spada A.	I	II	III	IV
Spallanzani C.				IV
Spence F. G	I	II	III	IV
Spiazzi R., OP			III	IV
Springhetti E., SJ	I	II	III	IV
Stack J. J.	I	II	III	IV
Stakemeier E.	I	II	III	IV
Stankevicius J.			III	IV
Stano G., OFM	I	II	III	IV
Stefanizzi A., SJ	I	II	III	IV
Steinmueller J.	I	II	III	IV
Stephanou P., SJ	I	II	III	IV
Stickler A., SDB	I	II	III	IV
Streiff J.			III	IV
Suarez L., SP	I	II	III	IV
Suen Jing-Chyan F.		II	III	IV
Sullivan J.	I	II	III	IV
Surlis P.				IV
Swain J., SJ				IV

Name	I	II	III	IV
T				
Talatinian B., OFM	I	II	III	IV
Tascon T., OP	I	II	III	IV
Tavard G., AA	I	II	III	IV
Tchao Yun-Koen P.		II	III	IV
Teusch J.			III	IV
Thils G.	I	II	III	IV
Tillard J.-M., OP			III	IV
Tilmann C., CO	I	II	III	IV
Tinello F.	I	II	III	IV
Tobin T.	I	II	III	IV
Tocanel P., OFM	I	II	III	IV
Tondini A.	I	II	III	IV
Toomey J.	I	II	III	IV
Trapé A., OESA	I	II	III	
Trezzini C.	I	II	III	IV
Trisco R.	I	II	III	IV
Tromp S., SJ	I	II	III	IV
Tshibangu T.		II	III	IV
Tucci R., SJ	I	II	III	IV
Turrado L.		II	III	IV
V				
Vaccari A., SJ	I	II	III	IV
Vagaggini C., OSB	I	II	III	IV
Valentini L.	I	II		
Vaivods J.			III	IV
Van den Broeck G., OPraem	I	II	III	IV
van den Eynde D., OFM	I	II	III	IV
van Leewen B., OFM		II	III	IV
van Rijen L., MSC			III	IV
van Roessel F., CICM		II	III	IV
van Straelen H., SVD				IV
Verardo R., OP	I	II	III	IV
Vermeersch L., PA	I	II	III	IV
Viganò Cattaneo E., SDB	I	II	III	IV
Violardo G.	I	II	III	IV
Visser J., CSsR	I	II	III	IV
Vogt V., OMI		II	III	IV
Volkmann W.				IV
Von Euw C.	I	II	III	IV
Von Phul Mouton R.	I	II	III	IV
W				
Wagner J.	I	II	III	IV
Wagnon E.	I	II	III	IV
Welykyj A., OSBM	I			
White P.	I	II	III	IV
Whitty P.	I	II	III	IV
Willebrands J.	I	II		
Wirz G.	I	II	III	IV
Witte J., SJ	I	II	III	IV
Wojnar M., OSBM	I	II	III	IV
Worlock T.			III	IV
Wuenschel E., CSsR		II	III	IV
Wulf F., SJ			III	IV
X				
Xiberta B., OC	I	II	III	IV
Y				
Yzermans V. A.		II	III	IV
Z				
Zaccaria di San Mauro, OFM	I	II	III	IV
Zalba M., SJ				IV
Zannoni G.	I	II	III	IV
Zcrypszak O.			III	IV

38. OBSERVERS AND GUESTS

1. Cardinal Augustin Bea (1881–1968) (Archivio Fscire).

2. Lutheran theologian Oscar Cullman (1902–1999). During an interview with RAI at the conclusion of the council, he said, "This council has been distinguished not only by the documents adopted, but also by the spirit that animated it from start to finish. This is why I consider it to have been a special privilege to be able to live as a guest and Protestant observer to the council, in close daily contact with the council fathers" (Archivio Fscire).

3. The prior and subprior of the ecumenical community of Taizé, Roger Schutz and Max Thurian, were observers at the council, with Cardinal Bea and Pope John XXIII. The council gave many Italian bishops the opportunity to expand their contacts and knowledge (Archive Fscire).

In addition to preparing the drafts for the synod discussions, among the responsibilities of the Secretariat for Christian Unity, which had been newly created by John XXIII in March 1960 and was included among the preparatory commissions of the council, was also the task of contacting other Christian denominations and inviting them to send their own representatives to the council. This invitation had many precedents in the history of the councils, the most recent of which was at Vatican I. Pope Pius IX had written with this purpose to the other Christian Churches (it was more a request to "return" than a simple invitation), but received a flat refusal. Thanks to the efforts of the Secretariat, led by Augustin Bea, this time the invitation found wide and growing acceptance. In fact, the number of observers to Vatican II grew with each successive period, with fifty-four delegates (including eight guests) at the first session, sixty-eight (nine guests) at the second, eighty-two (thirteen guests) at the third and one hundred six (sixteen guests) at the fourth. The observer delegates were chosen to emphasize that these guests were representatives of

their Churches, distinguishing them from guests of the Secretariat who represented only themselves (among the latter, for example, were Roger Schutz and Max Thurian from the ecumenical monastic community of Taizé, and Oscar Cullmann). The coverage of the group compared to the totality of the Christian churches, both geographically and confessional, was not exhaustive. The negative response to the invitation from Constantinople and other Orthodox Churches meant that Protestants were better represented. Only the Baptists were absent; the Baptist World Alliance was the only one of the Protestant Churches to decline the invitation to send a delegate, but its president, Joseph H. Jackson, participated as a guest. Moreover, observers came predominantly from the continents of the northern hemisphere, with obvious repercussions on the spectrum of issues that were close to their hearts.

The first session was attended by fourteen representatives of the Orthodox and Eastern Churches compared to forty delegates from the ecclesial communities founded during the

4. Andrei Scrima, personal observer for the Ecumenical Patriarch Athenagoras.

5. Seating for the observers and guests in the council (photo: Bernhard Moosbrugger, Zürich; from *Erneuerung in Christus*).

5

Reformation. Six delegates came from the non-Chalcedonian Churches, while there was no representative from the Orthodox Churches who were in communion with the Ecumenical Patriarchate of Constantinople, which had not yet prepared itself for a common response to the invitation. There were eight Russian delegates of three different jurisdictions, each antagonistic toward the others, including the Russian Episcopal Synod Abroad, which separated after 1917 from the patriarchate of Moscow because of its monarchical legitimism. The presence of delegates from Moscow, thanks to the political will of the Kremlin, co-opted the Holy Synod of Constantinople because of its initial hesitation and caused difficulties for the patriarch, while simultaneously provoking the hostility of the eastern delegates who had come together in Rome and who saw in it Soviet propaganda and a lack of respect by the Holy See toward the so-called "Church of silence."

Although at the time of the council all the Orthodox Churches had entered the World Council of Churches, at the Second Vatican Council (including the fourth period) the number of their observers remained limited. During the second period, only the Church of Georgia, represented by the delegates from Moscow, was added; in the third period, the Ecumenical Patriarchate of Constantinople and Alexandria finally sent their delegates (including the personal representative of the Patriarch Athenagoras, Archimandrite André Scrima); during the fourth period the observers of Serbia and Bulgaria arrived. The patriarchates of Antioch and Jerusalem, and the Churches of Romania, Cyprus, Greece, Poland, and Czechoslovakia did not attend the council.

Initially, the observers were only to serve as conduits of information to their Churches, but soon their presence and contributions proved vital for the development of the council. Increasingly they began to take part in the council sessions, and were sought out by the media for interviews and comments. RAI-TV made known to Italian society (and its bishops) the voices and faces of these protagonists who were often ignored, and they appeared on television screens in prime time. At the reception hosted in their honor by the Secretariat for the opening of the first session, the Lutheran Edmund Schlink, responding on behalf of everyone to Cardinal Bea's welcome speech, acknowledged that, "we realize that what has been sent to us are the same draft documents that the council fathers received, and that Your Eminence is giving us the opportunity to express our opinion on them. We know that we owe this opportunity personally to His Holiness who, following the dictates of his own heart, has created a new atmosphere of openness and serenity toward the non-Roman Churches." In fact, the observers did have the same documents as the council fathers, without exception, and they also attended all the general congregations, but not the meetings of the commissions, to which not even the vast majority of bishops had access. They were able to follow completely the course of the work just like the other members of the council, and perhaps even more since the Secretariat had made Latin translators available to them, both for documents and for the presentations in the Council Hall. Every Tuesday afternoon, the Secretariat organized a special meeting of the observer delegates and guests, during which a theologian or bishop with particular expertise explained the meaning and the editorial history of the drafts that were currently being debated by the council. These meetings gave observers the opportunity to advance proposals and observations on the texts under discussion, which often were welcomed by members of the Secretariat and conveyed to the Council Hall through the intervention of a council father who acted as spokesman for them.

Although joint action and collective proposals were excluded on principle—since the observers were independent representatives of their own Churches—they began meeting regularly and separately, every Monday morning in the Methodist Church on the Tiber for common prayer and to come to an agreement—with some effort—on whose turn it was to speak on behalf of the groups at the receptions and hearings. They also met in smaller groups to exchange information and discuss how to proceed. Increasingly, on specific issues, they formed convergences that went beyond their denominational boundaries: an example of such collaboration is the petition filed on October 1, 1965, on mixed marriages. In this sense, the observers who had taken part continuously in more conciliar periods, and therefore were more used to the mechanisms of the council, played an important role. Among them also some theologians of great importance stood out, like Kristen Skydsgaard and Oscar Cullmann. The attention of observers focused primarily on documents that addressed the theological issues that had characterized the sectarian disputes in past centuries, such as *De Revelatione*, *De Ecclesia*, and *De Ecumenismo*. These documents provoked a lively discussion among them on draft XIII on the dialogue between the Church and the modern world, which only the Ecumenical Council of Churches considered a key document.

The invitation of observer delegates and their presence at the council had important repercussions on a purely existential

Churches, alliances, communion, conventions, federations, councils, and institutions represented*	Observers, delegates, or guests of the Secretariat with country of origin	Sessions attended**
World Alliance of Churches (Reformed and Presbyterian)	Robert McAFEE BROWN (USA)	II
	Allan McARTHUR (United Kingdom)	III
	Richard H. N. DAVIDSON (Canada)	IV
	Angus W. MORRISON (United Kingdom)	II
	James NICHOLS (USA)	I
	John K. S. REID (United Kingdom)	IV
	Hébert ROUX (France)	I, II, III, IV (representing the Protestant Federation of France)
	Douglas W. D. SHAW (United Kingdom)	I
	Vittorio SUBILIA (Italy)	I (a), II (a), III, IV
	John Newton THOMAS (USA)	III
International Association for Liberal Christianity and Religious Freedom	James Luther ADAMS (USA)	I (a)
	Albert W. CRAMER (The Netherlands)	IV
	Heije FABER (The Netherlands)	IV (a)
	Dana McLEAN GREELEY (USA)	I, II
	L. J. VAN HOLK (The Netherlands)	I, II, III, IV
	George Huntston WILLIAMS (USA)	II (a), III (a), IV (a)
Armenian Apostolic Church (Holy See of Cilicia)	Vardapet KAREKIN SARKISSIAN (Lebanon)	I, III, IV
	Ardavazt TERTERIAN (France)	II, III, IV
Armenian Apostolic Church (Mother See of Holy Etchmiadzin)	Grigor BEKMEZYAN (USSR)	II, III, IV
	Zgon V. DER HAGOPIAN (Italy)	IV
	Parkev KERVOKIAN (USSR)	II, III, IV
Holy Apostolic Assyrian Church of the East	George W. LAMSA (USA)	III
	Quashisha Isaac REHANA (USA)	III
Coptic Orthodox Church of Egypt	ANTONIOS (Egypt)	IV
	Pakhoum A. EL-MOHARAKY (Egypt)	II
	Farid EL-PHARAONY (Egypt)	II, IV
	Youhanna GUIRGUIS (Egypt)	I, IV
	Marcos Elias ABDEL-MESSIH (Canada)	III
	SAMUIL (Egypt)	III
	Mikhail TADROS (Egypt)	I

Church of South India	Arnold Henry LEGG (India)	II, III
	Pereji SOLOMON (India)	IV
Evangelical Church in Germany	Wolfgang DIETZFELBINGER (West Germany)	III (a), IV (a)
	Edmund SCHLINK (West Germany)	I, II, III, IV
Lutheran Church, Missouri Synod	Oswald C. J. HOFFMANN (USA)	III (g), IV (g)
	Carl S. MEYER (USA)	IV (g)
	Walter F. WOLBRECHT (USA)	IV (g)
	Stanley I. STUBER (USA)	I (g), II (g)
Bulgarian Orthodox Church	JOAN (Petrov Nikolov) (Bulgaria)	IV
Russian Orthodox Church (Moscow Patriarchate)	Nikolaj AFINOGENOV (USSR)	I (a), II (a), IV
	Vitalij BOROVOIJ (USSR)	I, II, III, IV
	Jakov ILIČ (USSR)	II
	JUVENALIJ (Vladimir Poiarkov) (USSR)	IV
	Boris NELUBIN (Sweden)	III, IV (a)
	VLADIMIR (Vladimir Kotliarov) (USSR)	I
	Liverij VORONOV (USSR)	III, IV
Russian Orthodox Church (Synod of Karlovitz)	AMVROSIJ (Amvrosij Pogodin) (Italy)	III, IV
	ANTONIJ (Bartoševič) (Sweden)	I, II
	Sergej GROTOFF (Italy)	I (a), II (a), III (a), IV (a)
	Igor TROYANOFF (Sweden)	I, II, III, IV
Ethiopian Orthodox Church	Haile Gabriel DAGNE (Ethiopia)	II
	DIMETROS (Melake Selam Dimetros Gebremariam) (Ethiopia)	II
	Petros Gabre SELASSIE (Israel)	I, IV
	Sergew Hable SELASSIE (Ethiopia)	IV
	Haile Mariam TESHOME (Ethiopia)	I
Georgian Orthodox Church	Vitalij BOROVOIJ (USSR)	II, III, IV
Serbian Orthodox Church	Dušan KASIČ (Yugoslavia)	IV
	Lazar MILIN (Yugoslavia)	IV
Mar Thoma Syrian Church of Malabar	ATHANASIUS (Thomas) (India)	IV
	CHRYSOSTOM (Philipose Oommen) (India)	III
	C. P. MATHEW (India)	II
Syrian Orthodox Church of India	T. S. ABRAHAM (India)	III

Syrian Orthodox Church of India	C. T. EAPEN (India)	IV
	Korah PHILIPOS (India)	II
United Church of Christ in Japan	Tetsutaro ARIGA (Japan)	IV
	Masatoshi DOI (Japan)	II (representing the CEC), III (g)
Old-Catholic Church (Utrecht Union)	Herwig ALDENHOVEN (Sweden)	III (a)
	Werner KÜPPERS (West Germany)	II (a), IV (a)
	Peter J. MAAN (The Netherlands)	I, II, III, IV
Religious Society of Friends	A. BURNS CHALMERS (USA)	III
	William HUBBEN (USA)	I (a)
	Douglas V. STEERE (USA)	II, III, IV
	Richard ULLMANN (United Kingdom)	I
Anglican Communion	Najib Atallah CUBA'IN (Israel)	IV
	Peter DAY (USA)	IV (a)
	Harold DE SOYSA (Ceylon)	I, II
	Stanley ELEY (United Kingdom)	II (a)
	Eugène R. FAIRWEATHER (Canada)	III, IV
	John FINDLOW (Greece)	III, IV
	Frederick C. GRANT (USA)	I
	Ernst JOHN (India)	III
	John W. LAWRENCE (United Kingdom)	IV (a)
	John R. H. MOORMAN (United Kingdom)	I, II, III, IV
	Bernard PAWLEY (United Kingdom)	I, II, III, IV (a)
	Howard E. ROOT (United Kingdom)	II (a), III (a), IV (a)
	John R. SATTERTHWAITE (United Kingdom)	IV
	Massey H. SHEPHERD (USA)	III (s)
	Clement W. WELSH (USA)	IV
	William J. WOLF (USA)	I (a), II
	Alphaeus ZULU (Sudafrica)	II (a)
Community of Taizé	Roger SCHUTZ (France)	I (g), II (g), III (g), IV (g)
	Max THURIAN (France)	I (g), II (g), III (g), IV (g)
World Pentecostal Conference	David DU PLESSIS (USA)	III (g)

Australian Council of Churches	Frank Leslie CUTTRISS (Australia)	IV
Ecumenical Council of Churches	Paul A. ABRECHT (Sweden)	IV (a)
	Jerald C. BRAUER (USA)	III, IV (representing the World Lutheran Federation)
	Masatoshi DOI (Japan)	II, III (g)
	Victor E. W. HAYWARD (Sweden)	IV (a)
	Zachariah Keodirelang MATTHEWS (Sweden)	III
	Nikos A. NISSIOTIS (Sweden)	II, III, IV
	Patrick RODGER (Sweden)	IV (a)
	John SADIQ (India)	II
	Paul VERGHESE (Sweden)	IV (a)
	Lukas VISCHER (Sweden)	I, II, III, IV
International Council of Congregationalists	Elmer J. F. ARNDT (USA)	II (a)
	George B. CAIRD (United Kingdom)	I, II, III, IV
	Edgar H. S. CHANDLER (USA)	IV (a)
	Douglas HORTON (USA)	I, II, III, IV
	Ruben H. HUENEMANN (USA)	IV (a)
	Ralph D. HYSLOP (USA)	IV (a)
	Stuart LE ROY ANDERSON (USA)	IV (a)
	Robert V. MOSS (USA)	I (a)
	Heiko A. OBERMAN (USA)	I (a), II (a), III (a), IV (a)
	Howard SCHOMER (USA)	II (a)
	Bard THOMPSON (USA)	III (a)
	John R. VON ROHR (USA)	III (a)
	George Huntston WILLIAMS (USA)	I (a), II, III, IV substitute delegate for the IARF

World Council of Methodists	William R. CANNON (USA)	III (a), IV (a)
	Fred Pierce CORSON (USA)	I, II, III (a), IV
	Robert E. CUSHMAN (USA)	I (a), II (a), III (a), IV (a)
	Franz HILDEBRANDT (USA)	I (a)
	David Alan KEIGHLEY (Italy)	II (a), III (a), IV (a)
	Reginald KISSACK (United Kingdom)	I (a)
	Franklin H. LITTELL (USA)	III (a)
	José MIGUEZ-BONINO (Argentina)	I (a), II (a), IV (a)
	Walter G. MUELDER (USA)	III
	Emer P. NACPIL (Philippines)	IV (a)
	Albert C. OUTLER (USA)	I, II, III, IV
	Philip POTTER (United Kingdom)	III (s)
	Harold ROBERTS (United Kingdom)	I, II, III, IV
	Ernest Gordon RUPP (United Kingdom)	IV (a)
	Lee F. TUTTLE (USA)	II (a)
	Max W. WOODWARD (United Kingdom)	II (a), III (a), IV (a)
National Council of the Churches of Christ in the United States	Robert C. DODDS (USA)	IV (g)
	William A. NORGREN (USA)	II (g), III (g), IV (g)
World Convention of the Churches of Christ	Jesse M. BADER (USA)	I
	William G. BAKER (United Kingdom)	II, III
	William Barnett BLAKEMORE (USA)	III, IV
	Basil HOLT (South Africa)	IV
	Howard E. SHORT (USA)	III (a)
National Baptist Convention	Joseph M. JACKSON (USA)	I (participated in first session only)
Evangelische Michaelsbruderschaft	Wilhelm SCHMIDT (West Germany)	III (g), IV (g)
World Federation of Lutherans	Jerald C. BRAUER (USA)	III (representing the CEC), IV (a)
	Oscar CULLMANN Università La Sorbona / Università di Basilea (West Germany)	I (g), II (g), III (g), IV (g)

World Federation of Lutherans	Friedrich W. KANTZENBACH (West Germany)	IV (a)
	Walter LEIBRECHT (USA)	I (a)
	George A. LINDBECK (USA)	I, II, III (a)
	Warren A. QUANBECK (USA)	II (a), III, IV
	Sven SILÉN (Sweden)	II (a), III, IV
	Kristen Ejner SKYDSGAARD (Denmark)	I, II, III, IV
	Hagen A. K. STAACK (USA)	IV (a)
	Seppo Antero TEINONEN (Finland)	IV (a)
	Vilmos VAJTA (France)	I (a), II, III (a), IV
Protestant Federation of France	Hébert ROUX (France)	I e II (representing the World Alliance of Reformed Churches), III, IV
	Marc BOEGNER (France)	III (g), IV (g)
Reformed Churches in the Netherlands	Gerrit Cornelis BERKOUWER (The Netherlands)	I (g), II (g), III (g), IV (g)
Orthodox Theological Institute of St. Sergius (Paris)	CASSIEN (Sergej Sergeevič Bezobrazov) (France)	I (g), II (g), III (g)
	Alexis KNIAZEFF (France)	IV (g)
	Nicolas AFANASSIEFF (France)	IV (g)
	Pavel EVDOKIMOV (France)	IV (g)
Ecumenical Patriarchate of Constantinople	Maximos AGHIORGOUSIS (Italy)	III, IV
	EMILIANOS (Tiamidis) (Sweden)	IV
	Panteleimon RODOPOULOS (USA)	III
	John ROMANIDES (USA)	III
	André SCRIMA (France, personal representative to Patriarch Athénagoras)	III, IV
Greek-Orthodox Patriarchate of Alexandria	Vasso CANAVATIS (Egypt)	IV
	Nicodimos GALIATSATOS (Egypt)	IV
	Cyrillos KOUKOULATIS (Greece)	III
	Theodoros MOSCONAS (Egypt)	II (g), III (g), IV
Syrian-Orthodox Patriarchate of Antioch	Ramban Zakka B. IWAS (Syria)	I, II
	Saliba SHAMOON (Syria)	III, IV
St. Vladimir's Orthodox Theological Seminary (New York)	Nicholas ARSENIEV (USA)	IV (g)
	Alexander SCHMEMANN (USA)	I (g), II (g), III (g), IV (g)

level. Through them, many council fathers for the first time found themselves talking about theological issues in the presence of other denominations. In the Council Hall the sight of observers, who occupied a central place at the table of the council presider, had to bring into question the motives for the separation of millions of Christians from the Catholic Church and its consequences for the overall state of Christianity and the world. "I had tears in my eyes when I met the observers for the first time here," wrote an emotional Congar in November 1962, when, during the first audience with the observers on October 13, 1962, John XXIII had confessed that "at that providential and historic moment" on the day of the inaugural session of the council, "on seeing your group, and each of you individually, I got comfort from your presence. Let us not go too far. Let us be content for now to note the fact. And if you wish to read what is in my heart, maybe you will find there much more than words can say."

Through the efforts of the Secretariat for Christian Unity, Vatican II gave credibility to the Catholic Church (which since the 1920s onwards had disowned and often punished every form of "Catholic ecumenism"). In addition to the ecumenical openness of the council documents, taking this line also opened the door to a series of symbolic acts of great significance, such as the meeting between Paul VI and Athenagoras in January 1964 in Jerusalem, or the return to Patras in September 1964 of the relic of St. Andrew which had been stolen by the crusaders, right up to the final documents of the council, or the ecumenical prayer celebrated by Paul VI together with observers on December 4, 1965, and the historic lifting, on December 7, 1965, of the mutual excommunications between Rome and Constantinople from 1054.

BIBLIOGRAPHY

M. Velati, *Una difficile transizione. Il cattolicesimo tra unionismo ed ecumenismo*, Bologna 1996; L. Vischer, "Il concilio come evento del movimento ecumenico," in *Storia del concilio Vaticano II*, edited by G. Alberigo (Italian edition edited by A. Melloni), vol. 5, Bologna 2001 (2015), 493–546; M. Velati, *Separati ma fratelli. Gli osservatori non cattolici al Vaticano II (1962–1965)*, Bologna 2014.

This map represents the principal churches and other Christian confessions invited to send representatives to the council as observers.

11 Geneva

12 Canterbury

14 Houston

1. The Emperor Justinian offering the Church of Hagia Sophia and the city of Constantinople to the Virgin Mary. Mosaic in lunette above the southern gate of the narthex of Hagia Sophia.
2. The Red Monastery, built in the fourth century and named for the Egyptian Saint Pishay. Its name comes from the color of the outside walls built of red brick.
3. Detail of the fresco in the apse of the the Monastery of Mar Musa, Damascus.
4. Micheta-Samtavro, Kartli, Georgia. Chapel dating back to the fourth century.
5. Church of Saint Hripsimé, seventh century, Vagharspat, Armenia.
6. Rila Monastery, view of courtyard with portico and part of the church. It burned down in 1833, but was rebuilt beginning in 1834. It houses the icon of St. Ivan of Rila.
7. The cruciform church of St. George (Bete Giyorgis), which was carved from limestone in Lalibela, Ethiopia.
8. Monastery of the Patriarchate of Peč, near Kosovo, center of Servian spirituality. The church is dedicated to St. Demetrius.
9. Trinity Cathedral, built over the tomb of St. Sergius at Sergiev Posad, about 70 kilometers from Moscow, a spiritual center of the Russian Orthodox Church.
10. Door of All Saints' Church, or the "Castle Church" at Wittenberg. The painting above the door dates to 1858 and depicts Martin Luther on the left with a German bible, Philipp Melanchthon on the right holding the Augsburg Confession.
11. Geneva, monument to the Reformation.
12. Interior of Christ Church in Canterbury.
13. Evangelical Church of Germany.
14. *Jesus Saves* is the title of a photograph by Wim Wenders taken in Houston. The Protestant place of worship emphasizes the saving action of Jesus.

(All images, Archivio Jaca Book)

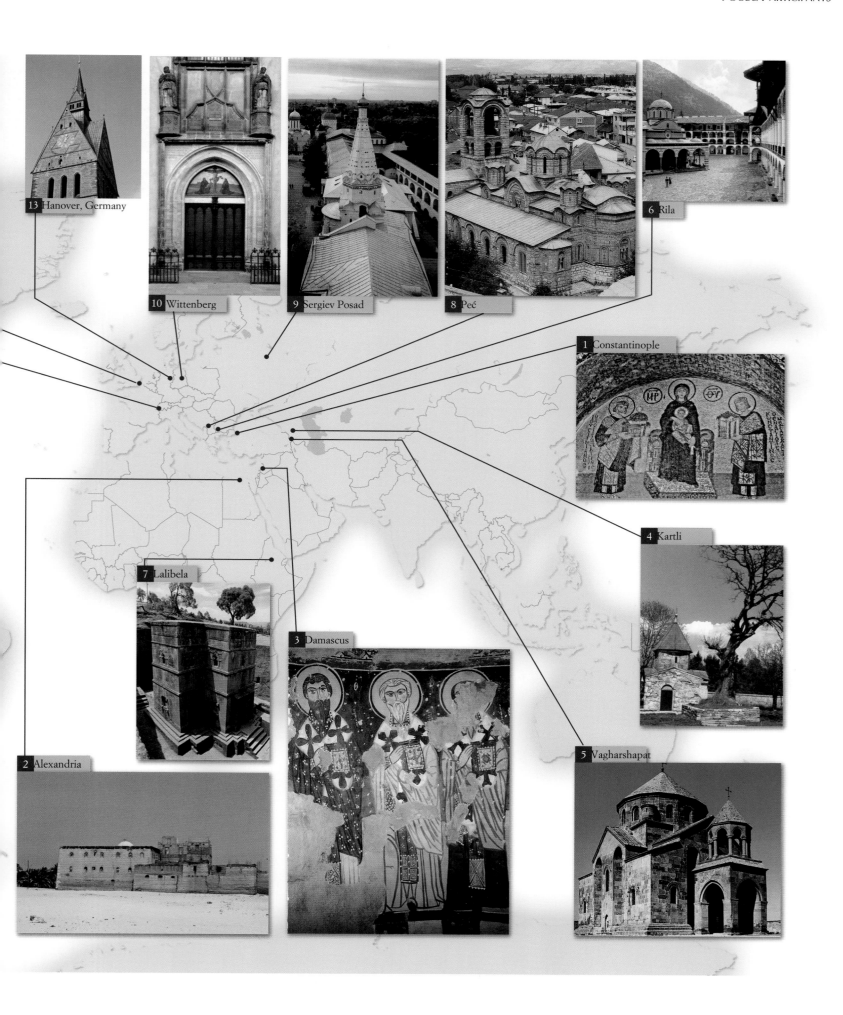

13 Hanover, Germany

10 Wittenberg

9 Sergiev Posad

8 Peć

6 Rila

1 Constantinople

4 Kartli

7 Lalibela

3 Damascus

5 Vagharshapat

2 Alexandria

39. INFORMAL GROUPS

1. An informal meeting during the council (from *Das Konzil und seine Folgen*).

2. Cardinal Lercaro, archbishop of Bologna, at a papal audience with Pope John XXIII, along with the *peritus* Giuseppe Dossetti, October 1, 1962. Dossetti had come to Rome during the first session to attend meetings of the group, the "Church of the Poor," for his bishop. The

Vatican I had been heavily influenced by informal pressure groups. Regarding the council and its agenda, the theme of infallibility had been invoked by magazines and newspapers. Even the maximalist interpretation of that papal infallibility and primacy, as well as the schism of the Old Catholic Church, had been affected by groups and environments that were able to represent themselves in the public arena of the council.

Instead, at Vatican II, an eloquent effect of the freedom that John XXIII had intended to ensure throughout the duration of the council was represented by the influence of the informal groups that formed, including bishops, theologians, lay people, and representatives of movements.

In a council of *aggiornamento* with "pastoral" goals, communication was not limited to the Council Hall. In the history of Vatican II, we see how important the various groups of fathers became. These had either been predefined or were named according to the jargon in use at the time: "the Central European Bloc," "the Conference of Delegates," "the Group of Religious Superiors," "the Group of Religious Bishops," or "the Group of Missionary Bishops." Some of these groups even had "headquarters" where they could be seen at different times of the afternoon or evening or on the weekends, during times when the council was adjourned. In retrospect, one of the most famous informal groups of Vatican II began to gather at the Belgian College in Rome: the group that came together as the Church of the Poor, taking as their inspiration a phrase in John XXIII's radio message of September 11, 1962, when he said that the Church undertook to be especially "of the poor." It was further inspired by the work of Fr. Paul Gauthier, the rector of the seminary in Dijon, who in

1954 had moved to Nazareth after the Suez War and founded the Fraternity of the Companions of Jesus the Carpenter. The participants were bishops, theologians, and lay people who sympathized with the experience of the worker-priests or who rejected the definition of a Church aligned with the capitalist social order. The Church of the Poor group developed various proposals. However, despite the encouragement given directly by Paul VI to Cardinal Lercaro in the fall of 1963, this group was unable to either succeed in establishing a Secretariat, or change the direction of the council documents, with the sole exception of *Lumen Gentium* 8.3. At the end of the council they established the "Pact of the Catacombs," named for the Catacombs of Domitilla, where it was signed on November 16, 1965 by forty bishops who renounced titles, insignias, palaces, ornamentation, and other symbols of opulence.

Another very significant group was "Coetus Internationalis Patrum" which assembled many traditionalist bishops (the Spanish contingent being the most notable) along with all the ultraconservatives, who organized some of the most significant obstructionist moves in the Council Hall. It was founded and animated primarily by Geraldo de Proença Sigaud, Archbishop of Diamantina (Brazil); he had two important collaborators in the Frenchman, Marcel Lefebvre, and the Italian, Luigi Maria Carli. Coetus Internationalis Patrum did not want to influence the drafting of a single document or develop any single issue, but held the conservative line. They methodically fought against the premise of renewal and rejected all requests for reform, warning against what they called the spirit of Neo-Modernism (which would later be used by the Lefebvrian schismatics). They were group met at the Belgian College and was chaired by Cardinal Paul Pierre-Marie Gerlier (Archivo Fscire). Yves Congar also participated in their meeting on November 30, 1962, and commented, "Meeting at the Belgian College with bishops of the group discussing the topic of the Church of the poor….This is truly beautiful: some of these people show the true image of freedom. These men work for a holy cause, perhaps the most important. It is almost beyond belief that the

council quibbles, while men expect something from this assembly on peace, world hunger, the dignity of the world. Msgr. Mercier tells me, however, that even this group wanted to remove strong, concrete references from the letter he wrote to the pope, for example, "I have neither gold nor silver…," and proposals to have pectoral crosses and rings of non-precious metal, or to refrain from using luxury cars" (Diary of Yves Congar, November 30, 1962).

3

4

5

6

politically tied to the right and fought unsuccessfully for a denunciation of communism (which was opposed by many Eastern bishops who supported the anthropological inconsistency of the Marxist-Leninist ideology) and submitted a counterproposal of their own against the draft on religious freedom.

3. Some images of some who became famous after the council for their attention to contemporary concerns and dedication to a life of poverty: Dorothy Day with her staff preparing an edition of the *Catholic Worker*. In 1933, she founded the Catholic Worker movement in the United States to aid the poor. Her cause for beatification was recently opened (Archivio Jaca Book/photo courtesy Henry Beck).

4. The Abbé Pierre founded the Emmaus movement in the 1950s for the homeless. Here he is pictured with one of their vans (Archivio Jaca Book).

BIBLIOGRAPHY
H. Raguer, "Fisionomia iniziale dell'assemblea," in *Storia del concilio Vaticano II*, edited by G. Alberigo (Italian edition edited by A. Melloni), vol. 2, Bologna 1996 (2012), 220–247; C. Lorefice, *Dossetti e Lercaro. La Chiesa povera e dei poveri nella prospettiva del Concilio Vaticano II*, Cinisello Balsamo 2011; M. Lamberigts-L. Declerck, "La contribution de la 'squadra belga' au Concile Vatican II," in *Anuario de Historia de la Iglesia*, 21 (2012), 157–183; M. Mennini, "Paul Gauthier e la povertà della chiesa durante il Vaticano II. La faticosa ricerca di un consenso," in *Cristianesimo nella storia*, 34 (2013), 1, 391–422; Ph. Roy-Lysencourt, "Histoire du *Coetus Internationalis Patrum* au concile Vatican II," in *Laval théologique et philosophique*, 69 (2013), 2, 261–279.

5. Sister Magdeleine of Jesus, drawn to the spirituality of Charles de Foucauld, founded the Little Sisters of Jesus, who share the lives of the poor and foster friendship among people of different religions. Here she is in the Algerian desert. In 1964, during the council, her congregation was recognized formally by the Church (Archivio Jaca Book/Archives nationales du monde du travail – Emmaus International).

6. Joseph Wresinski, founder, International Movement ATD Fourth World, dedicated to the fight against poverty (Archivio Jaca Book/ photo: L. Prat).

40. The Bishops' Conferences

Many national or transnational bishops found in the council an opportunity for constant activity and some, like the Italian bishops, a reason to organize a bishops' conference that they had never had before.

Particularly at the beginning of the council, the contacts that most of the bishops had were restricted to small groups: their confreres from their own country or ministry of origin, individuals from their own order, or who spoke the same language (for example, the bishop of Brixen participated in the meetings of the German-speaking group).

The bishops' conferences that had been around for the longest time were responsible for organizing debates on the issues under discussion, often with the *periti* most directly involved in the drafting of the documents. The secretaries of various bishops' conferences took care of special bulletins containing the documents, the assessments, expert opinions, and discussions in committee, so as to facilitate the formation of opinions that would then come out in the Council Hall.

The national episcopacies and conferences were not normally coherent groups, and within them could be found very different positions. During the council, although their role strengthened, relations among bishops of different countries and combinations also began to intensify according to the sensibilities of each, and mixed groups arose that were more or less influential in organizing the consensus of the council fathers on specific topics.

The Regulations did not define any function for the episcopal conferences yet they played an important role in determining the character of the council (the commissions voted on lists that originated from within them) and the gathering of opinions. From the second period on, Archbishop Roger Etchegarray, secretary general of the French Episcopal Conference, promoted and led coordination between the general secretaries of the various episcopal conferences, which met periodically at the Domus Mariae in the afternoons when there were no council meetings. This also allowed messages to circulate in the hall.

Many of the presentations by the council fathers were prepared within groups of bishops who arranged them in such a way as to give more strength to their positions: the Regulations, which allowed cardinals to speak first (then the archbishops, then bishops, and so on) in fact allowed only limited planning of the debate. In this way, some episcopacies, although not numerous, were able to exert considerable influence. For example, this was the case with the few bishops from Belgium whose primate Léon-Joseph Suenens was also among the moderators. Because

1

of this their residence, the Belgian College near the Quirinal, soon became a reference point for all those council fathers and *periti* who wanted fresh information on the progress of the drafting of the different documents on which the Belgian *periti*, who were present in every commission thanks to the prestige of the professors from Louvain such as Archbishop Gerard Philips, assistant secretary of the theological commission, together provided information.

A similar point can be made about the Dutch episcopate, led by Cardinal Bernard Jan Alfrink, who was distinguished from the beginning by the positions he took regarding the preparatory drafts. The international bulletin of documentation produced by the Dutch pressroom throughout the council, and then in subsequent years, was an essential reference point for information.

Among the European episcopates that had significant weight, not least because of their large numbers, were the French and German episcopates on the one hand, and the Italian and Spanish on the other. From the beginning, the first two found forms of collaboration that went against the mentality behind the preparatory drafts but were in favor of a complete update. Among the French bishops, it is worth remembering the importance of Cardinal Achille Liénart, Cardinal Paul Richaud, bishops Jacques-Eugène Ménager, Jacques Martin, Alfred Ancel, and Gabriel Garrone. They had great theologians available, like Yves Congar, Marie-Dominique Chenu (who was appointed as expert by a former student of his from Madagascar), Michel Labourdette, Jean Daniélou, and Henri de Lubac. Among the Germans, those who had a particularly important role included

1. The Polish bishops. At center, the Primate of Poland, Cardinal Stefan Wyszyński. In the second row, to the left, the young Bishop Karol Wojtyla (photo *Jesus*).

2. Rome, Fiumicino Airport, December 1962. The U.S. bishops board a Pan Am plane for their return home (© Archivio Storico Luce).

2

Cardinals Julius Döpfner, who was appointed a moderator in 1963, Josef Frings, Franz Hengsbach, the Austrian Franz König, who could avail themselves not only of the collaboration of the Jesuit theologians Karl Rahner, Alois Grillmeier, Otto Semmelroth, and Johann Hirschmann, but also of secular priests such as Joseph Ratzinger, Heribert Schauf, or the Redemptorist Bernhard Häring. The German-language bishops also held frequent meetings during intersessional periods and acted in agreement both in the debates in the hall and in the work of the commissions. Their contribution to the council was crucial, especially in the drafts that were more theological in nature, such as the ones on revelation, on the Church, and on ecumenism. On the draft on the Church in the modern world, they maintained a position that was more critical to the end, despite support from the Bishop of Essen, Archbishop Hengsbach, for the work that the commission had done. At the beginning of the last period of the council, Rahner had some very harsh criticisms of the draft that were generally shared by the German bishops. Only a thorough revision of the text convinced them to approve it.

The Spanish and Italian episcopates were two huge groups with leading figures from the council minority and conservative personalities like Cardinal Ernesto Ruffini of Palermo, Giuseppe Siri of Genoa, or the Bishop of Segni, Archbishop Luigi Maria Carli (who was one of the most active members of *Coetus Internationalis Patrum*, the most organized group among the minority); they would have nothing to do with liturgists like Cardinal Giacomo Lercaro of Bologna who was also a moderator. Other bishops such as Archbishop Luigi Bettazzi Ivrea who asked for the canonization of Pope John in the hall, or Joseph Gargitter who proposed that the opening chapter of *Lumen Gentium* should be on the people of God, belonged to a band of silent episcopates that changed their position in the council meetings. In this regard, the support of important Italian prelates such as Archbishop Pietro Parente on the issue of collegiality or of Archbishop Ermenegildo Florit, bishop of Florence, on biblical issues, appeared to all, including Paul VI, as an important indicator of the fate of the council.

The Spanish bishops, led by the influential Cardinal of Madrid, Morcillo Gonzalez, presented themselves to the council as a homogeneous group with conservative tendencies. One of their objectives was to curb the draft on religious freedom which was incompatible with the national-Catholic regime of Francisco Franco. However, there were also Spanish bishops who were in solidarity with the majority, such as Archbishop Gonzalez Moralejo, who was most open to con-

ciliar renewal and who played a major role in the drafting of *Gaudium et Spes*.

Of the bishops' conferences of Eastern Europe—those behind the "Iron Curtain"—various bishops were prevented by their governments from participating in the council. The primate of Hungary had taken refuge in the U.S. Embassy in Budapest, others were in prison. The senior Archbishop of Lv'ov, Josyp Slipyj, the last bishop of that region, had been freed because Khruschev relaxed some restrictions. But the Polish delegation, with the primate Cardinal Stefan Wyszynski, who had been a member of the Executive Committee in 1963 and later also of the Secretariat for Extraordinary Affairs, did participate and had bishops on many commissions, but not on the Doctrinal Commission. Some of those who were most active were Michal Klepacz, Herbert Bednorz, Boles aw Kominek, Józef Gawlina, and from the third period on, the Bishop of Krakow, Karol Wojtyla, who, according to Congar who discussed draft XIII with him, emanated a "radiant fluency."

Unlike the Spanish and European conservatives, the Poles demanded a full affirmation of religious freedom to assert against the claims of an oppressive state which in the East amounted to communist ideology.

In the Americas, the U.S. bishops, which constituted the largest national group after the Italians, had a bishops' conference that was well organized and efficient, led by Cardinal Francis Spellman of New York, who was often sensitive to the voice of the minority. Cardinal Spellman, Cardinal Albert Gregory Meyer of Chicago, and Cardinal Lawrence Shehan of Baltimore played an important role in the governing bodies of the council. Many other U.S. bishops were appointed to the conciliar commissions and some had an important role in them (John Francis Dearden, John Joseph Wright, and Henry James Griffiths in Doctrinal Commission; James Francis McIntyre in the one on bishops; Ernest John Primeau and Shehan in the Secretariat; Joseph Elmer Ritter in the one on clergy). Although there were different positions held on many theological issues, on religious freedom, the U.S. bishops argued with conviction the thesis of the Jesuit John Courtney Murray, who having been condemned in the 1950s, was at Vatican II the inspiration behind the episcopate that sought legitimacy in a pluralist society. Many bishops and particularly Spellman, who was the Apostolic Vicar for the U.S. Armed Forces, spoke against the condemnation of atomic deterrence.

The Canadian bishops were almost all part of the majority. One who played a decisive role in some of the key moments of the council was Cardinal Paul Émile Léger, bishop of Montreal who, although he had not been included in the governing bodies of the council, was particularly authoritative. The Canadian bishops were not present in all the commissions, but they had strong representation in the Doctrinal Commission with Archbishop Maurice Roy and Archbishop Georges Pelletier, in addition to Léger. Also important was the role played by Archbishop Maxim Hermaniuk within the Secretariat and that of Archbishop Albertus Joseph Martin in the Commission on the Liturgy.

The actions of the Central American episcopate, which had members in only a few of the commissions, were marked by strong personalities like that of Bishop Sergio Mendez Arceo of Cuernavaca, who, in the Council Hall, was the protagonist of some particularly strong presentations, on religious freedom, on the Church, on clerical celibacy, and on psychoanalysis; the Bishop of Panama, Archbishop Marcos Gregorio McGrath, who was very active in the Doctrinal Commission, and the two Ecuadorean bishops Archbishop Leonidas Eduardo Proaño Villalba, Bishop of Riobamba, and Archbishop Pablo Muñoz Vega, SJ, auxiliary bishop of Quito. They were active, along with all the bishops of Latin America, in the Latin American Episcopal Conference or CELAM. Other episcopates, from Brazil, Chile, or Argentina, were numerically very substantial and therefore carried great weight. In particular, the Brazilian bishops, who were staying mostly at the "Domus Mariae," soon became the main leaders of the group of representatives from the episcopal conferences that were also staying there. They were present in all the commissions, and thus when they got together they could get an idea of the complex progress of the work: Cardinal Antonio Caggiano, bishop of Buenos Aires, was a member of the Executive Committee; the Brazilian Archbishop Alfredo Scherer had been elected to the Doctrinal Commission which then added the Venezuelan Archbishop Luis Eduardo Enríquez Jiménez; the Commission on Bishops had the Argentinian Archbishop Raúl Francisco Primatesta and Colombian Pablo Correa León; those in the Commission for the Apostolate of the Laity were Bolivian Archbishop José Armando Gutierrez Granier, Chileans Manuel Larrain Errazuriz, and Raul Silva Henriquez and Brazilian Archbishop Eugênio de Araújo Sales; the members of the Secretariat included Brazilian Archbishop Aloisio Lorscheider Leo and Venezuelan José Quintero Parra. If we consider the votes that were sent in prior to the council, the majority of these bishops seemed disinclined to support the renewal proposed by Roncalli (and therefore it is not surprising that de Proenca Sigaud, bishop of Diamantina, was

one of the cofounders of *Coetus Internationalis Patrum*). However, the experience of the council was for many one of radical conversion, illuminated by figures such as Dom Hélder Pessôa Câmara.

In the African episcopate, the majority of bishops were missionaries and they therefore were more representative of their culture of origin or religious order; they found at Vatican II a precious opportunity to be aware of their identity and their role in the continent. Despite the fact that there were some larger groups (such as the Congolese episcopate, as well as those from South Africa, Tanzania, Nigeria, Madagascar, and Egypt), neither the French-speaking African delegates nor those who spoke English had a role in the governing bodies of the council or on the Doctrinal Commission. In the Commission on the Missions there were five African bishops, including some strong personalities, such as the bishop of Durban, Daniel Eugene Hurley, the bishop of Kroonstadt in South Africa, Gerard Marie van Velsen, the delegate from Cotonou, Bernardin Gantin, Cardinal Lauren Rugambwa from Bukoba (Tanzania), Joseph Blomjous from Mwanza (Tanzania), and the Congolese Joseph Malula, auxiliary of Leopoldville. But it was, the Bishop of Dakar, Mgr. Marcel Lefebvre, who emerged as one of the most influential leaders of *Coetus Internationalis Patrum* and of the small minority who continued to vote against some drafts (not the liturgical reform, which Lefebvre passed, but the documents on religious freedom, ecumenism, and religions).

The bishops from Asia belonged to different worlds. In the countries of the Middle East, there were Christian Churches of very ancient lineage, linked to Rome but with their own rites and canonical traditions. While these bishops asked the council for more explicit recognition of the dignity of their traditions, they brought to the other fathers an experience of ecumenical dialogue and compared themselves with the Orthodox Christian Churches with whom they shared the minority status within Islamic countries. Also the Arab populations to which their communities belonged were subject to the deep tensions caused by the birth of the state of Israel, which made them hostile to a document on Judaism that did not have, as *Nostra Aetate* would have later, chapters on Islam and the great religions. The difference in ritual separated these bishops into groups, which were sometimes able to organize themselves: the largest groups were those of the Melkite and Maronite bishops of Syria and Lebanon. Among the Melkites, the personality of the Patriarch of Antioch Maximos IV Sayegh stood out and he played a leading role in various discussions in the Council

3. A group of African bishops (photo: Riccardi/from *Il Concilio Vaticano II*).

4. The bishops from India (from *Il Concilio Vaticano II*).

5. Dom Hélder Câmara, vice president of the Latin American Episcopal Council (CELAM) and archbishop of Recife since 1964 (Archivio Fscire). "There are with us in the Domus Mariae, an archbishop, a bishop, and two lay people that the communist government [of Hungary] allowed to come to the council. The archbishop is an old man, marked by suffering, impressive for virtue and holiness. A few days ago, in the hallway, he wanted to kiss my hands. I rejected him kindly. I said in Latin: 'Archbishop, I am your brother.' Then followed the amusing comment of which I was reminded today: 'But it was revealed to me that one day you will be a cardinal.' Almost jokingly, I asked him: 'Was the revelation of God or of men?'" (Hélder Câmara, *Le notti di un profeta*).

6. The afternoon conferences were a time for the bishops to have important meetings to compare and discuss ideas brought up in the General Congregation (Archivio Fscire).

Hall. But just as important was the work of bishops Nephytos Edelby, Denys Hayek, and Antonio Philippe Nabaa, who was appointed one of the secretaries of the council. Among the Maronites, in addition to the Patriarch of Antioch, Paul Peter Meouchi, there were also important bishops such as Michael Doumith, Ignace Ziade, and Abdallah Nujaim. Their activity concentrated on the Commission for the Eastern Churches, but there were Middle Eastern bishops in the commissions, such as the Doctrinal Commission and the Secretariat.

The bishops of Central Asia, the Far East, and Oceania, who were often numerically small and unconnected to each other, as such did not have a particularly important role in the work of the council. The Indian episcopate was particularly large and was composed mainly of missionary bishops. Some of them played an important part, especially in the Commission on the Missions, but their presence, although not widespread, was also significant in other commissions, like the one on the laity, the one on bishops, and the Secretariat for Christian Unity. There were also very many Chinese bishops (who were united in a group called *Coetus Episcoporum Sinensium*), but they lived mostly in exile after the establishment of the four autonomous regions in the People's Republic and the repression of anti-communist preaching. Archbishop Paul Yü Pin, bishop of Nanking, played an important role in the Commission for the Apostolate of the Laity, while the bishop of Taiwan, Archbishop Stanislaus Lokuang, was a member of the Commission for the Missions and was an active representative of the conciliar minority.

The Philippine episcopate was also rather large and was led by the authoritative figure of Cardinal Rufino Santos, who was bishop of Manila and a member of the Doctrinal Commission. It was also represented in the Commissions for the Missions and the Commissions on Clergy and on Bishops. As for the Australian bishops, Cardinal Norman Thomas Gilroy, Archbishop of Sydney, was a member of the presiding body of the council. Australian bishops were also present in various commissions, particularly those on seminaries, on the sacraments, on religious, and on bishops. For linguistic and cultural reasons, they were more linked with the U.S. bishops, and often followed their position on issues. Among them there were important personalities, like the conservative Bishop of Fesseë, Thomas William Muldoon, who often found himself isolated from the rest of the Australian episcopate since he was largely open to conciliar renewal.

BIBLIOGRAPHY
V. A. Yzermans, *American Participation in the Second Vatican Council*, New York 1967; W. Dushnyck, *The Ukranian-Rite Catholic Church at the Ecumenical Council, 1962–1965*, New York 1967; Ph. Levillain, "Les épiscopats de l'Europe de l'Est à Vatican II," in *Documentation sur l'Europe centrale*, 11 (1973), 81–98; G. Battelli, "Alcune considerazioni introduttive per uno studio sui vescovi italiani al Concilio Vaticano II," in *Le deuxième concile du Vatican (1959–1965)*, Rome 1989, 267–279; J. Jacobs, *Les Pays-Bas et le Concile Vatican II, in Sources locales de Vatican II*, edited by J. Grootaers and Cl. Soetens, Louvain 1990, 47–58; A. Stacpoole, "Sources for recording British participation in the Second Vatican Council," in *Sources locales de Vatican II*, cit., 67–80; A. Michel, "L'épiscopat français au deuxième concile du Vatican," in *Le deuxième concile du Vatican (1959–1965)*, cit., 281–296; Cl. Soetens," La 'Squadra Belga' au concile Vatican II," in *Foi, gestes et institutions religieuses au XIXe et XXe siècles*, Louvain-la Neuve 1991, 159–169; *À la veille du Vatican II. Vota et réactions en Europe et dans le catholicisme oriental*, edited by M. Lamberigts and Cl. Soetens, Louvain 1992; Cl. Prudhomme, *Les éveques d'Afrique noire anciennement française et le Concile, in Vatican II commence...*, edited by E. Fouilloux, Louvain 1993, 163–188; Cl. Soetens, *L'apport du Zaire, du Rwanda et du Burundi au Concile Vatican II*, cit., 189–210; R. Aubert, "Organizzazione e funzionamento dell'assemblea," in *Storia della Chiesa: La Chiesa del Vaticano II (1958–1978)*, vol. XXV/1, edited by M. Guasco, E. Guerriero, F. Traniello, and Cinisello Balsamo 1994, 159–226; A. Lazzarotto, "I vescovi cinesi al concilio," in *Experience, Organisation and Bodies at Vatican II*, edited by M. T. Fattori, and A. Melloni, Leuven 1999, 67–86; P. Paulikkan, "Asian Contribution to the Second Vatican Council: The Story from the Subcontinent and the Oriental Churches in the Middle East," in *Revisiting Vatican II. 50 years of Renewal*, edited by S.G. Kochuthara, vol. I, Bangalore 2014, 132–146.

3

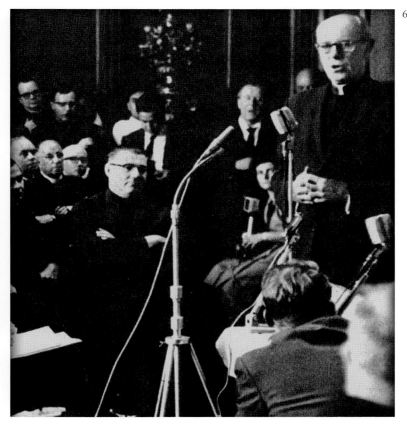

41. Journalists, Television, and the Media. The Council outside the Hall

1

Vatican II was the first council in the history of the church that took place under the eyes of TV and movie cameras and received radio coverage, in a century that has been defined as "Media-eval." For the first time, the whole world was able to watch live coverage of the council sessions and be informed at the same instant in which the event was taking place. World public opinion developed an awareness of the council to a degree and level that would have been unthinkable, for example, at Vatican I, which took place only a century before. Regarding the role played by magazines, newspapers, and audiovisual media, it is no coincidence then that people were talking about it in terms of having an "influential audience."

At noon on October 5, 1962, when the new headquarters of the council press office were opened in Via Serristori, it was obvious to everyone that the Holy See understood that it was no longer viable in the society of the 1960s to handle infor-

mation using the established methods of the past. In fact, in the century of the media, it was impossible to think of spoon-feeding council news or limiting distribution exclusively to what *L'Osservatore Romano* published or what Radio Vatican broadcast, as if the secular press did not exist.

The last council had actually contributed to the reach and limits of censorship and ecclesiastical secrecy with unexpected results. Despite the fact that the press had spread internationally, the lack of a central management and dissemination of information on the part of the Holy See had the effect that journalists interested in the council went looking for news "too often by consulting sources that were poisoned by partisan passions." The controversies or scoops disseminated in their articles could not be stopped even by attempts such as that of Father D'Alzon, the founder of the Augustinian Assumptionists, who sent 400 letters to various countries as bulletins

1. RAI's cameras broadcast the opening ceremony of Vatican II live. Many of the *periti* or council fathers resorted to television to follow the ceremonies (Photo: Pais/Archivio Rodrigo Pais–Ceub Università di Bologna). On October 11, 1962, Neophytos Edelby, adviser and secretary of Patriarch Maximos IV Saigh, noted, "At 7:30 we were gathered in the Great Hall of the memorials in the Vatican to participate in the procession. The patriarch did not participate in this solemn session. He could see it on television. There were more than

2,500 bishops and superiors general" (Diary of Neophytos Edelby, October 11, 1962).

2. Reading a press release on the work of the general congregation to reporters (Archivio Fscire).

3. Cameras focused on the council (Bernhard Moosbrugger, Zurich; from *Erneuerung in Christus*).

or newsletters on the council; it only highlighted the limited scope of this strategy. Even the *Rivista del cinematografo*, in presenting the coverage that broadcast media were offering of Vatican II, opened an article on the subject by quoting the words of Luis Veuillot who, in his diary of Vatican I, commented rather harshly about "those strangers who are here simply to stare," concluding succinctly, "I am talking about all these people who know nothing or talk nonsense."

Politicization of the news or the search for sensationalism had not been absent from Vatican I. However, in order to avoid leaving the news of the council in the hands of the media, and given the special relationship that was established between Pope John XXIII and journalists from the earliest days of his pontificate, the issue was how to enable and facilitate the press so it could follow the preparation stages first and then the council event itself. The solution was to set up a press

office so that the Vatican could handle and "control" the news flow and the relationship with the media. It was the Secretary of State, Domenico Tardini, who announced it during what is remembered as the Holy See's first press conference in history, on October 30, 1959. After some public announcements, it began operating on April 18, 1961, as the press office of the Central Preparatory Commission. Archbishop Pericle Felici announced to journalists the opening of the location at 12 Via Serristori, which, in October 1962, became the council press office. Once Vatican II had finished, it became the site of the current Vatican press office.

The opening of Vatican II—a huge event—was witnessed by more than 1,200 journalists who were accredited by the Holy See and had come from all five continents. The services of RAI television were used and disseminated by another sixty-six different international organizations. The flow of news and coverage of the event that the public expected was therefore considerable. Dutch Catholic Radio, KRO—Katholieke Radio Omroepverenéging—showed up at the council with an impressive setup, which was coordinated by the Rome correspondent Jan Dykgraaf who, thanks to the work of numerous technicians, a radio transmitter, and an antenna, managed to broadcast constant audio and video updates on the events. Radio and television stations then collaborated directly and frequently with the Council Documentation Centre in Rome (IDoc).

The summaries that were disseminated in the beginning were rather sketchy. There were few understandable news items that enabled journalists to inform their audiences of what was happening. Although the attitude of secrecy and the dominance the Holy Office had had only a few years before was finally broken, the complaints of journalists about the lack of information on what was happening at the council were, with different shades and gradations, widespread among all the media. In the aftermath of the council, the keyword on information, "despite the press office that had just opened, was still 'confidential'." This impenetrable secrecy was so strong as to induce Raniero La Valle, the young director of *The Future of Italy*, to become the spearhead of an initiative in 1963 to request more information. At the same time many other similar external initiatives were materializing.

During the years of preparation and the first session, the public's interest was such that the various international networks, although they were devoid of first-hand information, still managed to find more or less informal channels of information. For the first time, news agencies began to specialize, and through them were broadcast the first press conferences with the cardinals or bishops involved in the preparation who were not averse to being interviewed and televised through multiple television networks. This created the effect of free circulation of information: the newspapers were watching what the magazines were reporting, which in turn reported on the debates that sprang up spontaneously, which were heavily influenced by the press conferences of some prelates who had attended or whose audio recording or video footage could be accessed. The conferences and interviews with the fathers engaged in the council thus became an important tool for journalists, especially radio and television journalists, because they offered a direct source that all the media could draw on liberally. Many of these were not only recorded in audio and video, but also included in the documents of the

council. As the *Future of Italy* program noted during the first session, "one of the characteristics of the first period of the work of the council, even though they occurred outside of the council itself, was the press conferences." Although the presentations of the fathers during the general congregations were confidential and the press releases very "parsimonious" on the real opinions expressed, "there was always someone who gave out more than a glimmer about the actual substance of the 'things the Council was dealing with'; so there were some, in fact many, council fathers who were willing to talk" and "the means they used were the press conferences." The news agencies organized themselves to facilitate the collection and dissemination of information: for example, 30 Via Silvieri was the home of RICI, the Romanae Informationes Catholicae Internationalis, formed by Kathpress (Austria), KNA (Germany), and KIPA (Switzerland). KNP (Netherlands) and CIP (Belgium) also joined them. The documentation and information centers for the bishops conferences or for religious congregations were set up to follow the proceedings, such as the documentation center of the Catholic Church of the Netherlands or CCC, the information center of the Canadian episcopate; there were also Brazilian, Spanish, French, American, German, Italian, and Pan-African Centers as well as the information centers for the Oblates of Mary Immaculate, the White Fathers, or the Society of Divine Word.

In the afternoons this kind of activity by the speakers at the council, and especially by the theologians, was so intense that on September 15, 1964, a list was distributed among the council fathers with rules to be followed by the *periti*, which Paul VI had already sent to the Coordinating Commission at the end of December 1963. It recommended '"objectivity" and especially "prudence" in speaking of the council, as well as refraining from criticism in the debate, and also prohibited the formation of currents of opinion, the public defense of their own ideas, and giving interviews. It sounded like a formal warning regarding the intense *extra aulam* activity on the part of the *periti*, and even a threat that, if the rules were not respected, they would lose their position. Evidently the directive was intended to establish good practice that would be strictly adhered to during those years, but it was annoying nonetheless.

Through the interviews, those who were in the vanguard of theological, biblical, liturgical, and ecumenical thought, the representatives of the bishops conferences and the voices of the observers, were finding new opportunities to make themselves heard. There are hints of this in the private diaries of the fathers and the *periti* who tracked the numerous weekly appointments with the radio, newspapers, and international television. The television gave faces to the names, so that as the weeks went by they became increasingly recognizable to the somewhat lethargic Italian Catholic populace who were used to identifying the Church with the image of the pope. Transalpine theologians who had been condemned a few years earlier, under Pacelli's pontificate, bishops of the local churches (from Africa to Asia), non-Catholic observers, and representatives of other denominations, each took their turn appearing onscreen. Some became real media leaders: in the preparatory phase, Cardinal Augustin Bea was sought out by radio and television from the international networks for news on his Secretariat. So were Léon-Joseph Suenens, Julius Döpfner, theologians like Yves Congar and Hans Küng, and observers and guests such as Oscar Cullmann and Roger Schutz. RAI-TV became a real instrument of the conciliar majority and, despite initial reluctance, some members of the minority had to adapt to using it too. In addition, the weekly television reports and analyses reported by the daily newspapers helped some fathers to take the temperature of the discussions of the council, which were not always understood in Latin and which was spoken with many different accents and inflections.

If the information conveyed by the small screen exerted some influence within the council, this was even more true outside of it. We can understand how the information media (television, radio, and print) affected the council debate and the perception of this on the part of public opinion through the debate that the group *De Religionibus Non Christianis* was having in February 1965. Congar noted in his diary that "the Arabs of the Middle East (we've got their vivid reactions to hand) have been championed by propaganda in Arabic made by Israeli radio: many people are listening to what they are saying. And the radio repeats the refrain: the council has recognized the innocence of the Jews." The usefulness of proper dissemination of news by the media can be perceived, in fact, in precisely those moments or events that touched sensitive issues in the balance of relationships with others. So on September 15, Congar could finally note, "The pope also wanted the Muslim world to be better informed not only on this issue but generally on the work of the council. What we are trying to do is give good information and to explain things on the radio, to gather some people who are competent and influential to affect public opinion in a positive way."

If the general media were able to engage public opinion, orientating it to the formation of hopes and expectations, and the magazines and specialized periodicals were able to make a contribution to the bishops, thus affecting the same debates, through the thoughts expressed in their pages, this confirms that they all seemed to have acted in unison and made their presence felt, at different levels, both inside and outside of the Council Hall in St. Peter's, thus giving a new dimension to the sessions in terms of information and participation.

BIBLIOGRAPHY

L. Veuillot, *Rome pendant le concile*, 2 vols., Paris 1872; E. L. Heston, *The Press and Vatican II*, Notre Dame–London 1967; C. Ceccuti, *Il concilio Vaticano I nella stampa italiana (1869–1870)*, Rome 1970; *Paolo VI e i problemi ecclesiologici al concilio*, Brescia 1989; R. Laurentin, *L'information au Concile, in Le deuxième concile du Vatican (1959–1965)*, Rome 1989, 359–378; M. Marazziti, *I papi di carta. Nascita e svolta dell'informazione religiosa da Pio XII a Giovanni XXIII*, Genoa 1990; J. Grootaers, "L'information religieuse au début du Concile," in Fouilloux (editor), *Vatican II commence…Approches Francophones*, Leuven 1993, 211–234; A. Melloni, "Lo spettatore influente. Riviste e informazione religiosa nella preparazione del Vaticano II (1959–1962)," in *Il Vaticano II fra attese e celebrazione*, edited by G. Alberigo, Bologna 1995, 119–192; J. O. Beozzo, "Il clima esterno," in *Storia del concilio Vaticano II*, edited by G. Alberigo (ed. A. Melloni), Bologna 1995, 381–428; A. Melloni, *L'altra Roma. Politica e S. Sede durante il concilio Vaticano II (1959–1965)*, Bologna 2000; F. Ruozzi, *Il concilio in diretta. Il Vaticano II e la televisione tra informazione e partecipazione*, Bologna 2012.

42. The Auditors and Pastors

During the preparatory phase of the council, the laity were not called on to collaborate directly in the work of the commissions, with the exception of Professor Francesco Vito, who was included in the Commission for Studies and Seminaries.

A general "theology of the laity" was articulated through the international organizations of the lay apostolate and various other initiatives, in particular a series of reports sent to the preparatory bodies (the meeting in Freiburg of Pax Romana on July 17, 1960; the establishment of a "special group" within the conference of International Catholic Organizations). The Commission on the Apostolate of the Laity—the only one without a congregation behind it, because it was thought that a congregation of the laity could be founded after the council—included lay members only after the close of the first session of the council. A delegation of lay people identified as such attended the opening ceremony on October 11, 1962, along with diplomats and journalists, but they did not participate in the discussions, with the exception of those who were part of the non-Catholic observers' group.

It was Paul VI, former ecclesiastical assistant to the Italian Catholic University Federation, who wanted the presence of a group of auditors representing the Catholic laity for the second council period. In mid-September 1963, Archbishop Casimiro Morcillo González, archbishop of Zaragoza and undersecretary of the council, gave an interview to Radio Popular in which he anticipated what the pontifical position would be: "It is almost certain that a number of lay auditors—and this is a good word for them, auditors, not observers, will be invited to the council. A small number, of course. How many? It would be premature to say. A limited number, and probably chosen from among those who preside over International Catholic organizations…."

At first, there were thirteen auditors, all of whom were male. The place reserved for them in the hall was on the rostrum in front of the column of St. Andrew. Most of them came from apostolate organizations working internationally or from the governing bodies of the Standing Committee of the International Congresses for the Lay Apostolate (The COPECIAL, of which Vittorino Veronese was president) and from the Conference of International Catholic Organizations (OIC), but they had been appointed by the pope as individuals. The number of auditors in subsequent sessions increased progressively through new appointments and, for a limited number of general congregations, other lay people were added, with the title of "invitees" until they totaled forty-three men and women, as well as ten religious auditors, who followed the work of the council from the

same rostrum as the laity. Fifty priests were also admitted to the Council Hall in 1964. Together with the observers they had the function of widening the debate to all those areas, which were outside the hall, but not irrelevant. In opening the third period of the council, Paul VI commented on the enlargement of the group of auditors, saying that he wanted it this way, not only to show "fatherly feelings towards all categories of the People of God," but also "to ensure that within the Christian community there would be greater harmony, collaboration, and charity."

The idea of adding some women auditors, so that "irreplaceable female cooperation" would be present—no women had been members of the preparatory bodies or of the commissions of the council—had been put forward during the second period of the council by Cardinal Léon-Joseph Suenens, who had reminded the assembly that "women, if I'm not mistaken,

1. Dialogue between a council father and some auditors during a break in the council (from *Die Tür ist geöffnet, Das Zweite Vatikanische Konzil—Leseanleitungen aus Frauenperspektive*, Hg. Theologische Kommission des Katholischen Deutschen Frauenbundes e.V., Aschendorff Verlag, Munster 2012).

2. A group of lay auditors (from *Das Konzil und seine Folgen*).

2

constitute half of humanity." Others, like Metropolitan Bishop Josyf Slipyj, found this step incomprehensible to the Eastern tradition; still other bishops supported the motion, and some had asked that female auditors be sent from countries whose bishops were prevented from attending. During the second intersessional period, Vittorino Veronese had requested an increase in the number of auditors to give them more representation, a presence that the large international committees were accustomed to, and which, from his experience at UNESCO, also had a political value.

It was only on September 8, 1964, less than a week before the resumption of work, that Paul VI (who had forgotten that a woman, Empress Irene, had convoked Nicaea II), made the decision and had communicated to a group of religious from the diocese of Albano, "We have given orders that some qualified and devoted women also assist, as auditors, at several of the solemn rites and several of the general congregations of the upcoming third session of the Second Vatican Ecumenical Council. At those congregations, issues may be raised in discussion that particularly affect the life of women. In this way we will have present for the first time, perhaps, in an ecumenical council some women, a small number of women—obviously—but significant as symbolic female representatives." The list of the names of the new lay auditors, and of the lay and religious women, that the pope had appointed was forwarded by Secretary of State Amleto Cicognani to Archbishop Pericle Felici on September 12, but the invitations were not sent out until September 21. On September 14, when, in his opening speech for the session Paul VI addressed a greeting to the auditors, he was unaware of their absence.

The first woman auditor was Marie Louise Monnet, who was appointed on September 20; three days later, the names of all the other eight religious and seven lay people (a number that increased in the fourth session) were made public; again, the international confederations, the associations, and some religious women from the various continents were represented. Apart from two war widows appointed because they were witnesses of the horrors of armed conflicts and of aspirations for peace, none of them had ever been married. There was a request in October 1964 by some lay Americans that Barbara Ward, the English Baroness known as Lady Jackson, be asked to speak to the council on the issue of international aid, but the request was denied by the secretariat of the council. Only in the fourth period were José and Luz-Marie Álvarez-Icaza Manero, a Mexican married couple, invited to attend the council congregations.

The liturgical presence of the auditors was passive, like that of most of the bishops, and only after the approval of the liturgical reform, on September 16, 1964, did the four auditors receive communion during the council Mass.

Although the pope's words had suggested a limited presence by the female auditors, they followed all the work together with the male auditors. They met regularly to study the issues debated in council, and were associated with some of the commissions, although it was in the commission for the lay apostolate and then the commission for developing draft XIII that they played a role. However, the religious women, who in addition to the weekly meetings of the entire group met separately, were never allowed to take part in the meetings of the Commission on Religious.

The wish expressed by some fathers to be able to listen to lay people express themselves in the council, was granted only on December 3, 1963, not in a discussion, but in the session to commemorate the fourth centenary of the closing of the Council of Trent. On this occasion, Jean Guitton and Vittorino Veronese spoke. The first layperson to speak on a subject on the council's agenda was Patrick Keegan, president of the World Movement of Christian Workers. On October 13, 1964, he spoke in English on the draft on the lay apostolate, although only at the end of the discussion. Although Keegan's speech constituted a useful precedent, the auditors continued to ask for non-symbolic recognition, particularly in the debate on draft XIII, whose subject was the role of the Church in the modern world. On October 26, the lay auditors wrote a letter to moderators in which they asked that one of their representatives be allowed to speak on draft XIII, proposing, based on their unanimous choice, Maria Pilar Bellosillo, president of the World Union of Catholic Women's Organizations, stressing that the speech of a woman who presided over an organization of more than thirty million members worldwide demonstrated well the increased role of women in the Catholic laity. The speech was accepted, but the presence of a woman at the ambo was not, so on November 10, 1964, the Argentinian, Juan Vazquez, President of the International Federation of Catholic Youth Organizations, spoke in Spanish on the mission of the laity in the modern world.

On November 5, James Norris, president of the International Catholic Commission on Migration, delivered a speech to the Council Hall on the problem of poverty in the world, not as a representative of the auditors, but at the request of the delegates of the Episcopal Conferences who had written to Paul VI on October 16. The laity took the floor before the council assembly a total of six times. The last speech by a lay auditor was on October 13, 1965, by the Togolese auditor, Eusèbe Adjakpley, in addition to the final vote of thanks to the pope and to the council fathers which was given by Veronese who acted as spokesman.

On November 17, 1964, a pastor from Madrid, Marcos Louis, spoke to the council as a representative of the pastors who were auditors at the council. On September 19, Cardinal Amleto Cicognani had informed Felici of the pope's desire that some representatives of the secular clergy take part in the general congregations when the issue on the agenda was priestly life. In the end, about fifty priests were appointed, some of whom were present for the first time on October 13, although their presence was little more than a formality.

During the solemn session on November 18, 1965, Paul VI gave a copy of *Apostolicam Actuositatem*, the decree on the lay apostolate, to three male auditors and three female auditors, symbolizing the mandate for its implementation.

BIBLIOGRAPHY
R. Goldie, "La partecipazione dei laici ai lavori del Vaticano II," in *Presenza Pastorale*, 55 (1985, 4, 128–147; G. Caprile, *Il concilio Vaticano II. Cronache del Concilio Vaticano II edite da "la Civiltà Cattolica" a cura di Giovanni Caprile*, vol. III–IV, Rome 1968; G. Turbanti, *La presenza e il contributo dei laici al Concilio Vaticano II, in Vittorino Veronese dal dopoguerra al Concilio: un laico nella chiesa e nel mondo*, Rome 1994, 179–196; *Storia del concilio Vaticano II*, edited by G. Alberigo (Italian edition edited by A. Melloni), vol. 3, Bologna-Leuven 1998 (2013) and vol. 4, Bologna 1999 (2013); G. Turbanti, *Un concilio per il mondo moderno. La redazione della costituzione pastorale "Gaudium et spes" del Vaticano II*, Bologna 2000; *"Tantum aurora est." Donne e Concilio Vaticano II*, edited by M. Perroni, A. Melloni, S. Noceti, Berlin 2012.

Male Auditors	Sessions		
Eusèbe Adjakpley (Togo) *Regional Secretary for Africa from the International Federation of Catholic Youth*		III	IV
Jose Alvarez Icaza Manero (Mexico) *President, with his wife, of the Latin American Secretariat of Movimiento* *Familiar Cristiano*			IV
Chacko Kadankavil Chacko (India) *Director of the Governing Institute of Engineering from Trivandrum, Kerala*			IV
John Chen (Hong Kong) *Chairman of the Diocesan Council for the Apostolate of the Laity in Hong Kong*		III	IV
Mieczyslaw De Habicht (Poland / Switzerland) *Permanent Secretary of the Conference of International Catholic Organizations*	II	III	IV
Raoul Delgrange (Belgium) *President of the International Catholic Child Welfare Bureau*			IV
Leon R. De Rosen (France)		III	IV
Frank Duff (Ireland) *Founder and President of the Legion of Mary*			IV
Paul Fleig (Germany) *President of the World Union Catholic teachers*		III	IV
Luigi Gedda (Italy) *President of the International Federation of Catholic Doctors*		III	IV
Silvio Golzio (Italy) *President of the Governing Council of the Standing Committee of the International Congress for* *the Apostolate of the Laity*	II	III	IV
Jean Guitton (France) *Member of the Académie Française*	II	III	IV
José Maria Hernandez (Philippines) *National President of Catholic Action*		III	IV
Emilio Inglessis (Greece) *Executive Director of the International Federation of Catholic Men*	II	III	IV
Patrick Keegan (UK) *President of the World Movement of Christian Workers*		III	IV
Jean Larnaud (France) *Secretary of the International Catholic Coordinating Centre for UNESCO*	II	III	IV
Raimondo Manzini (Italy) *Director of L'Osservatore Romano and President of the International Union* *of Catholic Press*	II	III	IV
James Norris (USA) *President of the International Catholic Migration Commission*	II	III	IV
Bartolo Perez (Brazil) *President of Jeunesse Ouvriere Catholique International*		III	IV
Henri Rollet (France) *President of the International Federation of Catholic Men and the* *Social Commission of the Conference of International* *Catholic Organizations*	II	III	IV
Stephen Boleslav Roman (Czechoslovakia / Canada) *Entrepreneur*		III	IV
Stefan Swiezawski (Poland) *Professor of Philosophy at the Catholic University of Lublin*		III	IV
Ramon Sugranyes de Franch (Spain) *President of Pax Romana and the Conference of International Catholic Organizations*	II	III	IV
Auguste Vanistendael (Belgium) *General Secretary of the International Confederation of Christian Trade Unions*	II	III	IV
Juan Vazquez (Argentina) *President of the International Federation of Catholic Youth*	II	III	IV
Vittorino Veronese (Italy) *Former Director of UNESCO and former President of the First and Second World Congress for the* *Apostolate of the Laity*	II	III	IV
Francesco Vito (Italy) *Rector of the Catholic University of Milan and Vice President of the International Federation of* *Catholic Universities*	II	III	IV
Walter von Löe (Germany) *President of the Fédération Internationale des Mouvements d'Adultes Ruraux Catholiques*			IV

* Joseph M. Fitzgerald (USA), International President of the Serra Club, attended the council as a permanent invitee, but not as an auditor.

Martin H. Work (USA) *Executive Director of the National Council of Catholic Men*			IV
Female Auditors			
Constantina (Laura) Baldinucci, SCCG (Italy) *Superior General of the Institute of Maria Santissima Bambina and President of the Italian* *Federation of Hospital Sisters*		III	IV
Maria Pilar Bellosillo (Spain) *President of the World Union of Catholic Women's Organizations*		III	IV
Jerome Marie Chimy, SSMI (Canada)			IV
Amalia Dematteis, widow of Cordero Lanza di Montezemolo (Italy) *National President of the Foundation of Spiritual Assistance to the Armed Forces*		III	IV
Marie Sabine de Valon, RSCJ (France) *Superior General of the Dames du Sacre Coeur and President of the International Union of* *Superiors General*		III	IV
Gertrud Ehrle (Germany) *President of Katholischen Deutschen Frauenbund and committee member of the World Union of* *Catholic Women's Organizations*			IV
Cristina Estrada Carrera-Pesas, ACI (Spain) *Superior General of the Handmaids of the Sacred Heart and the first President of the Union of* *Major Superiors of Italy*		III	IV
Claudia (Anna) Feddish, OSBM (USA) *Superior General of the Sisters of the Byzantine Order of St. Basil the Great*		III	IV
Marie Henriette Ghanem, SSCC (Lebanon) *Superior General of the Sisters of the Sacred Hearts of Jesus and Mary and the President of the* *Assembly of major superiors of Lebanon*		III	IV
Rosemary Goldie (Australia) *Executive Secretary of the Permanent Committee of International Congresses for the Apostolate of* *the Laity*		III	IV
Suzanne Guillemin, DC (France) *Superior General of the Daughters of Charity of St. Vincent de Paul*		III	IV
Marie de la Croix Khouzam, RESC (Egypt) *Superior General of the Sisters of the Sacred Heart and President of the Union of the Teaching* *Religious of Egypt*		III	IV
Luz Maria Longoria Gama, wife of Alvarez-Icaza (Mexico) *President, with her husband, of the Secretariat of the Latin American Movimiento* *Familiar Cristiano*			IV
Ida Marenghi-Marenco, widow Grillo (Italy) *President of the Union of Women from the Italian branch of Catholic Action*		III	IV
Catherine McCarthy (USA) *President of the National Council of Catholic Women*		III	IV
Alda Miceli (Italy) *President of the Italian Women's Centre and Central President of the Secular Institute of the* *Missionaries of the Kingship of Christ*		III	IV
Marie-Luise Monnet (France) *President of the Mouvement International d'Apostolat des Milieux Sociaux Indépendants*		III	IV
Margarita Moyano Llerena (Argentina) *President of the World Federation of Catholic Young Women*			IV
Gladys Parentelli (Uruguay) *President of the women's branch of the Movimiento Internacional de la Juventud Agrícola y Rural* *Católica*			IV
Anne-Marie Roeloffzen (Netherlands) *Secretary of the World Federation of Catholic Young Women*		III	IV
Karolina Hedwig von Skoda (Czechoslovakia / Switzerland) *Founder and President of Equipes Internationales de Renaissance Chrétienne*			IV
Juliana Thomas, ADJ (Germany) *General Secretary of the Union of Superiors General of Germany*		III	IV
Mary Luke Tobin, SL (USA) *Superior General of the Sisters of Loretto and President of the Conference of Major Religious* *Superiors of Women of the United States*		III	IV
*Maria H.C. Vendrick (Netherlands)		III	IV

* Participated as an auditor at the council from the third session and was one of the most active delegates, despite the fact that she is not included in the list published in the *Acta*, which is incomplete, or in the more detailed Chronicles of Caprile, which counts twenty-nine male auditors and twenty-three women. She was deleted from the official photos because she refused to wear a veil and was wearing short sleeves.

43. The Discussion on De Ecclesia: Between the Intersessional and the Third Period

On September 14, 1964, the third period opened. For a time, it was thought by many—including the pope—to be the last. Images of the ceremony broadcast by RAI on Eurovision showed one of the first results of the liturgical reform, a concelebrated Mass, a custom that had remained in the Byzantine Churches but had not been widespread in the West for six centuries. Paul VI concelebrated along with twenty-four council fathers from nineteen countries. The area around the Altar of Confession in St. Peter's Basilica was enlarged for the occasion and the role of the choir of the Sistine Chapel was reduced, thus allowing the opportunity for the assembly to participate in the liturgy. The difference from the previous two solemn opening ceremonies, in 1962 and 1963, was evident. Thanks to the continuous relations between Rome and Constantinople that had been fostered by the Secretariat for Christian Unity, particularly by Fr. Pierre Duprey, Patriarch Athenagoras decided to send his own delegates along with those of other Orthodox and Nestorian churches as observers, so that their numbers rose from sixty-eight in the second period to eighty-three in the third (including guests and alternates). The lay people admitted to the council as auditors also increased in number (twenty-one), in addition to the auditors from the international lay organizations. What dominated the discussion in the third period was *De Ecclesia*, which would be overwhelmingly approved in a few weeks and become the Dogmatic Constitution on the Church, *Lumen Gentium*.

The draft had caused a stir since the announcement of the council. It had moved from the first to the second session and as the votes came in on October 30, 1963, a strong drive towards an ecclesiology of communion was revealed. The intersessional period was spent trying to establish an agenda for the vote on the text, especially the third chapter on episcopal collegiality, which troubled the minority, since, as they stated to the pope, it implied a reduction in the authority of the bishop of Rome. In May 1964, Paul VI himself sent thirteen proposals to the Doctrinal Commission and appointed a special committee to revise the chapter, in reaction to the pressure that a small group continued to exert against the intentions that had inspired the constitution. Archbishop Pericle Felici's opinion was that because of the gravity of the matter and the resulting discussions, "thirty-nine votes should be used for examining the crucial chapter, paragraph by paragraph, while twenty-three votes could be used for everything else in the document: the Church as mystery, God's people, the laity, the universal call to holiness, the Blessed Virgin Mary." The attempt to alarm the council was also fueled by the press; even *L'Osservatore Romano* published an article on June 7 that contributed to heightening the tensions and fears of the pontiff. Even the Italian episcopate listened to the objections raised by the *Coetus Internationalis Patrum*, raising the suspicion that the council was being limited to Vatican I's decisions on papal primacy.

On September 13, the day before the third session's opening ceremony, a note that was personally addressed to the Holy Father was delivered to Paul VI on the draft of the constitution *De Ecclesia*, in which a group of fathers warned the pope about the dangers of the text and the need to postpone the most controversial points to a later date. It became evident that the campaign against the third chapter was coming to a head, intensifying Paul VI's fears so that he launched another round of consultation.

Voting on the chapter began one week after the start of the session, on September 21, after four presentations to the hall by Franić, König, Parente, and Henríquez. This made the foundation of the opposition public, and when the vote on the most controversial parts of the chapter was held on September 22, support for the opposition did not even reach 15 percent of the council fathers' votes. Despite this outcome, opponents

▶ **Synopsis historica constitutionis dogmaticae Lumen Gentium, edited by G. Alberigo and F. Magistretti, Bologna 1975**

In December 1964, Giuseppe Dossetti and the Bologna group of the "Centro di Documentazione" decided to write the *Synopsis historica constitutionis dogmaticae Lumen Gentium*, a study edition of the constitution *De Ecclesia*, designed as a working tool and aimed at providing guidance for the implementation of Vatican II.

The project, which Paul VI approved of, came out of a recognition of the importance of the process that led to the approval of the document (giving synopses of the different versions), and the need to relate it not only to the other approved documents, but also to the conciliar and papal teaching of the past (the Vatican-I constitution *Pastor Aeternus* and Pius XII's encyclical *Mystici Corporis*), in order to show the continuity with and in particular the differences from the previous ecclesiology.

2. Chapter 1, paragraph 8 of *De Ecclesia*. In the amended text a significant change was introduced. In the previous version, it stated that the church of Christ "is" (*est*) the Catholic Church, in the revised text it says that it "subsists in" (*subsistit in*) the Catholic Church.

1. Patras, Greece, September 26, 1964. The relics of St. Andrew, stolen in 1462 by Crusaders, are returned to Greece by a delegation from Rome led by Cardinal Bea. In this photo, the delegation of the Orthodox Metropolitan of Patras leads a procession through the streets after the ceremony. On September 23, the 86th General Congregation opened with a ceremony in honor of the apostle Andrew. The ecumenical significance of this event had been anticipated by Paul VI on June 23, when he promised to send a special delegation to Patras bearing the sacred relic (from Augustin Kardinal Bea, *Wegbereiter der Einheit. Gestalt, Weg und Wirken in Wort, Bild und Dokument aus Zeugnissen von Mitarbeitern und Weggenossen. Veröffentlicht unter dem Protektorat von Lorenz Kardinal Jaeger*, Verlag Winfried-Werk, Augsburg 1972).

of collegiality did not cease their criticism but resorted to a "war of votes" in the final vote on the whole chapter, that is, they launched a campaign in favor of a *placet juxta modum* vote, so that the draft would not receive a two-thirds majority in favor and would call into question the whole chapter. But even this tactic did not produce the desired results. The tensions that these clashes within the council had produced, however, did have an important aftermath: acceptance of some other requests from this minority would not in fact come from the council, but from the pope himself, who wanted almost unanimous approval, a wish he had often expressed.

BIBLIOGRAPHY

J. Grootaers, "La collégialité vu au jour le jour en la IIIème session conciliaire," in *Irenikon*, 138 (1965), 2, 183–194; *Paolo VI e i problemi ecclesiologici al Concilio*, Brescia 1989; J. A. Komonchack, "L'ecclesiologia di comunione," in *Storia del concilio Vaticano II*, edited by G. Alberigo (Italian edition edited by A. Melloni), vol. 4, Bologna-Leuven 1999 (2013), 19–118.

44. The "Black Week"

The end of the third period of the council was marked by a dramatic moment of tension at Vatican II. Borrowing a phrase from the newspapers, people were referring to it as the "black week." The expression came from the Dutch bishop of 's-Hertogenbosch, Wilhelmus Marinus Bekkers, who spoke of it as "sombre semaine." It was repeated by the Italian periodical *La Civiltà Cattolica*, while Xavier Rynne confined himself to calling it "Black Thursday," in language reminiscent of the stock market crash of 1929. It indicated the incidents, misunderstandings, and the impasse of that particular period in 1964, which was an "event within the event" (Luis Antonio G. Tagle).

In the previous weeks, the "Döpfner plan" had largely failed because the council fathers wanted to examine all the arguments carefully. Approval of *De Ecclesia* could and, according to many fathers, should resolve other decisions (such as would otherwise be left to synods of bishops, for example). And the minority—who were against chapter 3 of *Lumen Gentium* and had resorted to obstructionist tactics bordering on parliamentary filibustering—believed that it was even more necessary to curb the spirit of renewal that had overcome the crucial theological obstacle of collegiality. They would continue to exert pressure on the pope, airing their grievances, and availing themselves of the support of the Secretary General, Archbishop Pericle Felici. In the last days of the third session, the council still had to discuss and vote on drafts covering religious life, priestly formation, Christian education, and the sacrament of marriage. There would also be preliminary voting on the drafts on religious freedom and on relations with non-Christian religions, and a decisive vote on the Church, Ecumenism, and Eastern Churches. Saturday, November 21 was the last scheduled public session of the period; the previous week all discussions and voting had to be concluded and the drafts ready to be promulgated.

In this turbulent atmosphere, on the last week of work, "one had the impression," as Giuseppe Alberigo wrote, "of an attempt to slow down the renewal which the council had pursued from the start and limit the capacity for initiative that the assembly had painstakingly built in the first two years of its existence."

First on the agenda was the Constitution on the Church, which had now been approved. On the morning of Monday, November 16 (three days before Paul VI donated his tiara to raise funds for the poor), the eve of the final vote on the hierarchical structure in the third chapter of *De Ecclesia*, Archbishop Pericle Felici warned that "by mandate of higher authority," that is, the pope, a *Nota Explicativa Praevia* would be read out in the hall. Technically it was an explanation of the criteria to use when voting, but it was announced as if it were an introductory and restrictive interpretation of the text on collegiality. It is even reported as such in some accounts of Vatican II.

Carlo Colombo, Paul VI's theologian, proposed this *Nota* (which was prepared in secret by the Theological Commission in meetings that had excluded theologians), and it was intended to reassure the minority of the good intentions of the text. In fact, in the weeks before, the pope had been subjected to intense pressure to prevent the chapter being approved. Paul VI did not yield, but he tried to find a way to garner the widest possible consensus on the text. The contents of the *Nota*, and the authoritative way in which it was presented, actually managed to satisfy many of the fathers who were in the minority and irritate some fathers and theologians of the majority beyond measure. Joseph Ratzinger, who was Cardinal Josef Frings's expert, worked to examine the possibility of an intervention in the hall by the archbishop of Cologne against the *Nota* threatening to vote against the Constitution on the Church by way of protest, but this idea was withdrawn. In the end, the outcome of the vote was in fact largely favorable (2,099 votes in favor, 46 against, 1 null), despite the ambiguity of the issue involved. That remained even on Thursday when there was the final vote on the entire document and Archbishop Felici pointed out that the text would be "understood" according to what had been delineated in the *Nota Praevia*, which would then be inserted in the documents of the council, making it a council document. On November 21, the Dogmatic Constitution on the Church, *Lumen Gentium*, was approved with 2,151 votes in favor and 5 against.

The other incident involved religious freedom. On Thursday November 19 (Rynne's "Black Thursday"), voting on the draft on religious freedom was canceled at the last minute. The draft had already been distributed the previous Tuesday and, after a long process of reworking, was ready for a vote, but some fathers in the minority group (in particular the Spanish group, who were against the declaration) had asked, through a formal administrative appeal, that the vote be postponed. And so, within the limits of available time, the vote was postponed until the next session. Since the board had already finished the new wording on October 24, this was a "political" postponement. The proposal of the executive council and the moderators, who wanted to consult the assembly, was contested, and so Cardinal Eugène Tisserant, after consulting only the cardinals on the executive board who were present in the hall and without asking the moderators, announced that the vote would undoubt-

1. Paul VI in conversation at the presidents' table with Cardinal Eugène Tisserant (photo: Giordani).

2. The *periti* Joseph Ratzinger and Yves Congar (photo: Hermann Volk, Mainz/Archiv der Deutschen Provinz der Jesuiten ADPSJ).

edly be delayed. So when the speaker, the Belgian Archbishop Emiel-Jozef De Smedt, presented the draft to the Council Hall, a draft they would not be voting on, there was copious thunderous applause that sounded like a protest for a postponement that would not endanger the text, as the majority feared, but would improve it.

There was a confirmation of these fears concerning the fate of the Decree on Ecumenism, which had been voted on chapter by chapter and only needed an overall vote. On the same day, Thursday, November 19, Felici announced the vote for the next day; but warned that the text had been further modified with last-minute corrections, clearly made by or on behalf of the pope, without discussion. It was then realized that the corrections introduced were not substantial. After considering the possibility of postponing approval of the decree, Paul VI had in fact received and downplayed the reservations of some fathers of the minority group who had approached him or his closest advisers. These had been passed to the Secretariat (in a hectic round of consultations and compromises between Willebrands, Thils, Lanne, Duprey, Bea, Felici, and Dell'Acqua), which had received nineteen of them, and had the difficult task of explaining to the observers who saw in them an arbitrary use of the primacy. In fact, the pope's actions showed that he had given into pressure from the minority, but that did not stop

the council. The Decree on Ecumenism, *Unitatis Redintegratio*, was formally approved in the fifth session on November 21 (2,137 votes in favor and 39 against), together with *Lumen Gentium* and the decree on the Eastern Churches, *Orientalium Ecclesiarum* (2,110 votes in favor and 39 against).

The last case concerned Mariology. The council, being faithful to its mandate, had not wanted to publish proclamations of dogmas or Marian titles, not even the title "Mater Ecclesiae," which in itself did not pose any problems but would open a discussion on the universal mediation of grace which had already been a source of division in the 1950s. In his closing speech for that period, Paul VI used the title "Mother of the Church" for the Virgin Mary, a gesture that seemed harmless to some, authoritarian to others.

BIBLIOGRAPHY
J. Feiner, "The nineteen changes inserted to the text of the Decree on Ecumenism at the request of Pope Paul VI on November 19, 1964," in *Commentary on the Documents of Vatican II*, edited by H. Vorgrimler, Freiburg a.M. 1969, 159–164; J. Grootaers, "Le crayon rouge de Paul VI," in *Les Commissions Conciliaires à Vatican II*, edited by M. Lamberigts, Cl. Soetens, J. Grootaers, Leuven 1996, 316–352; P. Duprey, "Paul VI et le décret sur l'oecumenisme," in *Paolo VI e i problemi ecclesiologici al concilio*, Brescia 1998; L. A. G. Tagle, "La tempesta di novembre: la 'settimana nera'," in *Storia del concilio Vaticano II*, diretta da G. Alberigo (Italian edition edited by A. Melloni), Bologna 1999 (2013), 417–482.

45. THE LAST INTERSESSIONAL PERIOD AND THE STUMBLING BLOCK OF REVELATION

On November 21, 1964, during the solemn session that closed the third period, the Constitution on the Church (*Lumen Gentium*), and the decrees on ecumenism (*Unitatis Redintegratio*) and Eastern Churches (*Orientalium Ecclesiarum*) were approved. This is how the last intersessional period opened. Paul VI had in fact agreed to hold a fourth and final period of council work. On January 4, 1965, the reopening of the session was set for September 14; the months from December 1964 to January 1965, and the following September were crucial. Despite the tensions of the third period, especially the new openly confrontational relationship that had arisen between the majority and the minority, and although the link had weakened between the pope and the majority, which a year earlier had elected Montini pope and continued to carry out further work on the council, the third session had shown that a profound renewal of Catholic ecclesiology was possible, without losing the essential heritage of doctrine. But much work was still to be done: not only was there a long agenda of issues to be considered (during the previous three sessions only five documents, plus the message to the world, had been approved; in the fourth, eleven drafts would be discussed and approved, plus the final messages), but many of the issues on the table still had open questions. The work of the commissions in the last intersessional period was thus critical to preparing the ground for the conclusion of the council: "The brisk, if not hectic, pace of the fall of 1965 would have been determined, in fact, by the plethora of texts that had been developed in the intersessional period," Alberigo writes, and, as in the last period of the

Council of Trent, it gave the assembly "an impression […] of 'yes-men,' who seemed to emerge in various contexts in Rome in the aftermath of the announcement on January 25, 1959."

The magazines and newspapers continued to analyze the events of the previous few months, the results achieved, the clashes between the various groups, the pope's actions, and the attempt to control the council (see, for example, the strong criticisms expressed within the Dutch bishops' conference) but attention—thanks to a print campaign specially designed by *L'Osservatore Romano*—moved mainly from the council to the pope. What also contributed to this was Pope Paul VI's pilgrimage to India, and Bombay, in early December (2–5), 1964, on the occasion of the 38th International Eucharistic Congress.

Again, some members of the minority tried to induce Paul VI to impose changes that the commissions did not want. And Paul VI showed his dissatisfaction with the progress and the drafting of some documents, especially Draft XIII, to such an extent as to involve—as we learn from the private journals of various stakeholders—external individuals in order to gain votes (for example, he asked Maritain for observations on religious freedom) or by indirectly suggesting actions. In 1965, Paul VI started work on a *Lex Ecclesiae Fundamentalis*, which—in spite of the ecclesiology of *Lumen Gentium*—should have and could have provided a new basis for a higher-level canon law at the council rather than being subordinate to it, as John Paul II did when he promulgated the new *Codex Iuris Canonici*.

On the other hand, an authoritative voice from the majority introduced an issue that contrasted the council, "according to John" and the council "according to Paul." On February 23, 1965 (the day after the consistory in which Paul VI created twenty-seven cardinals), Giacomo Lercaro held a conference in Rome on the subject *Guidelines for Research on John XXIII*. It was drafted entirely by Giuseppe Dossetti who was his personal *peritus* and was for a short time secretary of the moderators in the council, and touched a raw nerve regarding the relationship between the pope and council: "I would not be so sure that everything that Pope John actually expected from the council and generally advocated as the historical and religious task of our generation has already been achieved or is about to be realized or is at least now heading towards progressive deployment, without the possibility of reversions, interruptions, and partial contradictions." Despite the fact that the Bolognese Cardinal had not read the conclusions of his speech, in which he proposed that the council canonize John XXIII, according to an ancient practice (which had already been suggested by the Pole, Bejze, and the Italian, Bettazzi), his

1. Paul VI promulgates the Constitution on the Church, *Lumen Gentium*, during a solemn session of the council on November 21, 1964 (Archivio Fscire).

2. Cardinals Albert Meyer and Ernesto Ruffini, influential members of *Coetus internationalis partum* (from *Il Concilio Vaticano II*).

2

words had an impact. In the meantime, on March 7 the work of the council became public and one of the first reforms was demonstrated quite visibly: on that Sunday that the celebration of the Mass according to the renewed rite began and Paul VI himself celebrated in Italian, in a Roman parish, with the altar facing the faithful. On April 9, the creation of the papal Secretariat for Non-Believers was announced, a choice that became part of the climate of reconciliation and dialogue with non-believers, in opposition to a certain party that was still hoping that the council would condemn communism. As the presider, Cardinal König had said, "we are not trying to pick a fight with atheism, not even militant atheism, but […] to establish contact in order to engage in a dialogue on the intellectual level, to make a concerted effort in favor of peace."

The work of the intersessional period was dogged by the deadlines imposed by the secretary general and by the *Promemoria* drafted by Felici for the pontiff, in which the drafts were set out based on their various stages of discussion and voting that they had reached; this factor actually influenced the progress of the work. In general, after the collection and classification of the observations and the votes and after examination by the experts, the work passed to subcommittees and finally to discussion in the plenary commission. The new drafts instead had to be examined by both the Coordinating Commission, and the pope, before they were sent to the fathers.

This was one of the times when the young Karol Wojtyla became known and there was more work for a theologian like Congar,

who gave a crucial contribution to the preparation of various documents: he participated in the draft on the Church in the modern world, and the ones on religious freedom, non-Christian religions, the clergy and the missions.

However, it was in this climate, characterized by the minority exerting pressure on the pope and by the position the Secretary General Felici took at the expense of the Coordinating Commission, that corrections to the draft on revelation were discussed. In the third period, it was not ready in time for a vote on the new wording, which was delivered to the fathers on November 20, 1964, so it was postponed until the fourth period. January 31, 1965, was set as the deadline for sending in new votes. In the subcommittee, the prevailing idea was to maintain the balance of the positions that had already been reached, but in the early months of 1965, two powerful opposing forces emerged. On the one side, the *Coetus Internationalis Patrum* went on the attack asking—through Cardinal Siri—that tradition and the Magisterium of the Church should be stated to be "primary and above all other means of interpretation." On the opposite side, however, were some professors from the Biblical Institute who asked that the "meaning of tradition" be defined, and by distinguishing the literary genres in the interpretation of biblical texts, "the different value of truth contained in scripture" also be defined. Paul VI seemed able to defend himself from the demands of *Coetus*, which raised the question of unanimity, but as Willebrands mentioned to Congar, who then noted it in his diary, "a council has the tools to win against the opposition and overcome the objections of the minority. The pope doesn't" (August 25–27, 1965).

On September 14, the fathers returned to Rome for the fourth time. The pontiff had decided this would be the last period. However, given the enormous work that awaited the fathers, and the complete and comprehensive discussion of all the drafts that still remained open, this was not so obvious, and there were many who were in favor of putting off some issues or setting aside the most difficult topics.

BIBLIOGRAPHY
H. Sauer, *Erfahrung und Glaube. Die Begründung des pastoralen Prinzips durch die Offenbarungskonstitution des II. Vatikanischen Konzils*, Würzburg 1993; R. Burigana, *La Bibbia nel concilio. La redazione della costituzione "Dei Verbum" del Vaticano II*, Bologna 1998; G. Alberigo, "Grandi risultati—ombre di incertezza," in *Storia del concilio Vaticano II*, edited by G. Alberigo (Italian edition edited by A. Melloni), vol. 4, Bologna 1999 (2013), 649–671; G. Turbanti, "Verso il quarto period," in *Storia del concilio Vaticano II*, edited by G. Alberigo (Italian edition edited by A. Melloni), vol. 5, Bologna 2011 (2015), 23–72.

46. "MINOR" DRAFTS

1. "Minor" documents approved by the council were used to contextualize fundamental issues such as the relationship of the church to the world. In the image, a symbol of the globalization of finance (Archivio Jaca Book/Giorgio Bacchin, designer).

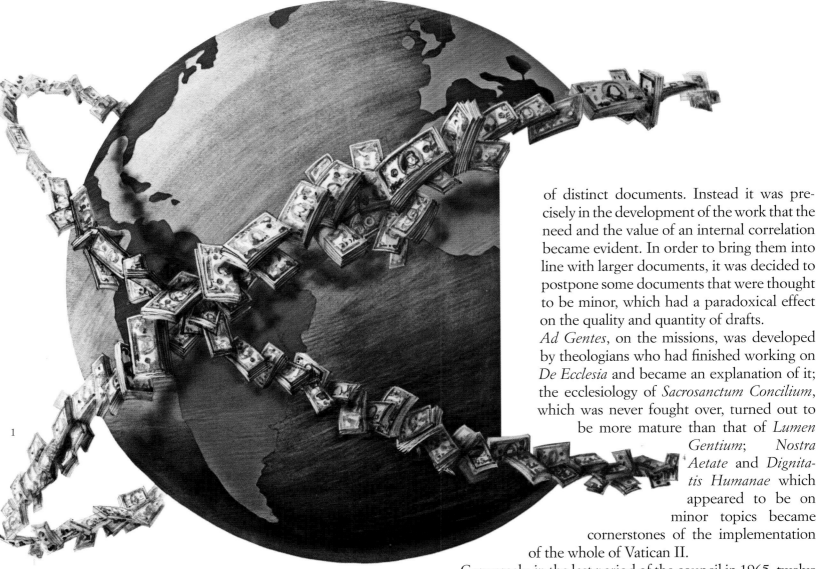

1

of distinct documents. Instead it was precisely in the development of the work that the need and the value of an internal correlation became evident. In order to bring them into line with larger documents, it was decided to postpone some documents that were thought to be minor, which had a paradoxical effect on the quality and quantity of drafts.

Ad Gentes, on the missions, was developed by theologians who had finished working on *De Ecclesia* and became an explanation of it; the ecclesiology of *Sacrosanctum Concilium*, which was never fought over, turned out to be more mature than that of *Lumen Gentium*; *Nostra Aetate* and *Dignitatis Humanae* which appeared to be on minor topics became cornerstones of the implementation of the whole of Vatican II.

Conversely, in the last period of the council in 1965, twelve of the eighteen texts of the conciliar corpus were approved. So, inevitably, the last three months of the council took on the characteristics of a headlong rush to vote on and promulgate the last drafts.

At the opening of Vatican II, the question soon arose about the kind of documents that the council would approve and, consequently, their different theological qualification. From previous conciliar history, Vatican II borrowed the kinds of constitutions that would be used for the basic topics (revelation, the Church, liturgy, and the relationship with the world), and the kinds of decrees that would be dedicated to issues on which the council was to provide the doctrinal framework and guide subsequent reforms. Instead, what was introduced were the kinds of declarations, which, at least in intention, were to be limited to shorter statements. For years, the messages used at the opening and closing of the council, were not considered to be council documents. The design of how the documents were organized was theoretical and still suffering from a concept of the council as a library

Two of these were very large—the Dogmatic Constitution *Dei Verbum*, which arose from a discussion that had gone on since 1962, and the Pastoral Constitution *Gaudium et Spes*, which had been rewritten many times over before coming to a vote—and a sequence of very short and reworked documents. In fact, the Decree on the Pastoral Office of Bishops *Christus Dominus* was promulgated, but had had to wait for the approval of *Lumen Gentium* for orientation. Decrees on the renewal of religious life *Perfectae Caritatis*, on priestly formation *Optatam Totius* and on the ministry and life of priests *Presbyterorum Ordinis*,

2. An oil pipeline crosses a shantytown on the outskirts of a Third World city. Recent history has underscored the growing inequality between rich and poor in the availability of resources (Archivio Jaca Book).

2

postulated a renewal of the process of formation for clerics and religious, but with aims and means that would prove inadequate to the face of the crisis of the clergy and religious that would suddenly emerge shortly thereafter. The Decree on the Apostolate of the Laity *Apostolicam Actuositatem*, provided the orientation for the movement for the apostolate of the laity, but still did not appropriate the doctrine on the common priesthood of the baptized. The Decree on Missionary Activity of the Church *Ad Gentes*, had abandoned the Third-World (and somewhat triumphalist) approach that had marked its introduction to the council, in order to discover the character and mission of the whole Church.

So two statements by the council were approved in addition to *Gravissimum Educationis* (which was an amalgamation of the classic discourse on Catholic schools with the principles of Christian education): they had in common the fact that they were the product of separating out parts of the draft on ecumenism that were found to be sensitive. Both deeply renewed the attitude of the Church on these issues, to the point that they did not quote many recent Church documents as the others had

done in abundance. The declaration *Nostra Aetate* was drawn up in order to change the relationship with Judaism, and to it had been added chapters on the great non-Christian religions, so as to make the relationship between Judaism and the Church like a sacrament compared to the others.

The declaration *Dignitatis Humanae* upheld the principle of religious freedom and the immunity of personal conscience as indispensable elements in the affirmation of human dignity. Precisely because of the asymmetry of these principles with respect to the ideology of Christianity and nostalgia for that regime, they were particularly opposed by the minority among the council and then by the openly or secretly hostile environment at Vatican II.

BIBLIOGRAPHY
R. Aubert, *Lo svolgimento del Concilio,* in *Storia della Chiesa,* XXV/1, *La Chiesa del Vaticano II (1958–1978),* edited by M. Guasco, E. Guerriero, F. Traniello, San Paolo, Cinisello Balsamo 1994, 326–335; P. Hünermann, "Le ultime settimane del concilio," in *Storia del concilio Vaticano II,* edited by G. Alberigo (Italian edition edited by A. Melloni), vol. 5, Bologna 2001 (2015), 371–491; G. Alberigo, *Breve storia del concilio Vaticano II (1959-1965),* Bologna 2005 (2012²), 128–158; J. W. O'Malley, *What Happened at Vatican II?* Cambridge, MA 2008, 45–54.

47. The Documents of the Secretariat for Christian Unity: From Ecumenism to Religious Freedom and Non-Christian Religions

The draft on ecumenism prepared by the Secretariat for Christian Unity was approved during the third session, using the text that had been amended with last-minute revisions by the pope. Although this had caused tensions within the council among the same observers who had contributed to the drafting, the most significant ecumenical theologian, Yves Congar, admitted that the document had lost "its virginity or a certain purity," and showed its intrinsic theological irrelevance: "the good words that we multiply are not enough to eliminate the unpleasant impression many have of it. So I carefully reread these three chapters of *De Ecumenismo*. Their substance, their own content is unchanged. If we read them for the first time, ignoring the episode of which we speak, we do not see in this strong and frank statement by the unanimous Catholic Church, the thoughts of the Holy Father, or his intentions for ecumenism. No! The text is not depleted." The decree laid the foundations of the commitment of the Catholic Church on its ecumenical journey, connecting "Christian unity above all with the renewal of the Church" and raising the question of doctrinal and theological differences and the disciplines of Christian history. The acceptance of the variety of charisms, the hierarchy of truth, the "complementarity of traditions" and the abandonment of hostilities and proselytism, the divestiture of the terminology of division and the adoption of fraternity came about "by invoking the ancient basic truth of Christianity on the sacrament of baptism" (Bea) and "accepting that the ways and the methods of articulating the faith can be different but complementary and that the truth of Christian doctrine can have different degrees of proximity to the core of revelation." (Alberigo).

The draft that had been discussed in the second period of the council was accompanied by two other chapters that were no longer part of the decree on ecumenism: the chapter on the relationship with the people of Israel and the one on religious freedom would, in fact, have had a place of their own in the council process.

John XXIII, in response to the solicitation of Jules Isaac, and thanks to his experience as a Vatican diplomat during the Holocaust, asked the Secretariat to prepare an outline on the Jews. The Preparatory Commission had excluded it from the council's agenda, for political reasons that arose from fears, both of Arab churches and fundamentalist anti-Semitism. At the request of the pope, the Secretariat had nevertheless reintroduced it, as a chapter in the draft on ecumenism and wanted to abandon the catechesis of contempt, and free the issue from preaching about "deicide."

Another subject that emerged, equally complex and full of implications, was the issue of religious freedom that was in fact "up to the fourth period […] fiercely debated and […] then accepted with an overwhelming majority." This chapter was also debated vigorously in the Central Preparatory Commission. Unlike the thoughts expressed in the drafts of the Preparatory Theology Commission, the Secretariat's draft argued that fully accepting religious freedom was a necessary condition for ecumenical dialogue, while the commission took to itself what Cardinal Alfredo Ottaviani's maintained, that even though one might not call "error," that which could at best be "tolerated," one should also not give it the same weight of "truth." The issue should have been discussed at the preparatory stage but no commission had yet been set up; the Secretariat inserted its proposals into a chapter of *De Ecumenismo*.

This draft was discussed in the Council Hall in November 1963, but due to lack of time, the last two chapters, those concerning religious freedom and relations with Judaism, were postponed. Only the proposals made in writing were used for a first revision; the Coordinating Commission decided, during the intersessional period, to separate out those chapters and make the two "declarations" autonomous, destined to be approved in the following period as though they were secondary issues. Several times the secretary general, Archbishop Pericle Felici, the secretary of state, Cardinal Amleto Cicognani, and even Paul VI asked for concessions aimed at appeasing the minority who would never accept the way in which the council had short-circuited anti-Semitic attitudes, the theology of religions, and the immunity of the conscience. Several fathers raised objections. Representatives of Middle Eastern churches fought against what would become *Nostra Aetate*, which was consistent with the position of their governments, and against the declaration on religions that had had several chapters added on the major religions, which they said could facilitate the recognition of the state of Israel. The minority fought instead against a repudiation of anti-Semitic, anti-Jewish, or substitutionist preaching that was implied by the declaration. The American episcopate and the Polish bishops wholeheartedly supported the statement on religious freedom, while some Italian bishops and many Spaniards believed that one must concede the possibility of confessional states existing. The Joint Committee's revision—which was the method used in the first period to allow bishops in commissions, where Holy Office's ideas were strongest, to be heard—was reversed

1. In 1956, Pius XII approved publication of a new *Ordo Hebdomadae Sanctae* or order of worship for the liturgies of Holy Week. While the new *Ordo* had important changes, the Good Friday prayer for the "perfidious," or faithless, Jews remained. The faithful were instructed to kneel as they did for the other petitions; formerly they remained standing for this petition alone. In 1959, John XXIII interrupted the Good Friday liturgy and asked that the prayer be repeated without

the word *perfidis*. Priests updated their copies of the liturgical books with a stroke of the pen (Archivio Fscire).

2. Proposed amendments to the Declaration on Religious Freedom (Archivio Fscire).

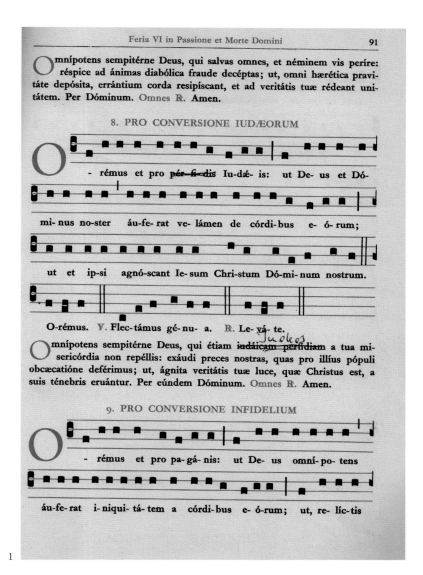

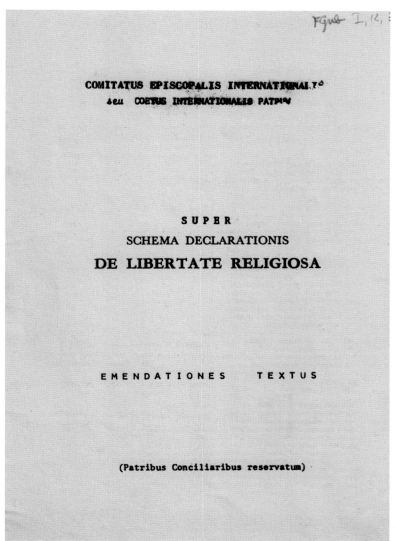

for these two drafts: Archbishop Felici asked Cardinal Augustin Bea that the revision of the two drafts be entrusted to two joint committees, made up of Secretariat and Doctrinal Commission members. But Paul VI, on Bea's insistence, prevented the removal of the two issues from the Secretariat's agenda. In the fall of 1964 the draft of *Dignitatis Humanae* had been largely reworked under the guidance of the American Jesuit Fr. John Courtney Murray, according to which the problem of religious freedom was to be placed not so much in terms of rights to be granted to the Catholic faith, but in terms of individual rights of freedom, which had to be respected by the political authority without considering the merits of the religious choices made by each person. These rights included

"no coercion" and "no duress" to a person's religious profession, the only exceptions being issues of public order and the common good. The assembly made its voice heard in favor of the positions on religious freedom as indivisible good during "Black Week," pending a postponement so that the text could be improved. With regard to Murray's position, the French theologians, particularly Congar, asked that the issue of human freedom be placed in the context of salvation history. Paul VI asked that the civil aspect of religious freedom, which was a fundamental right of the person, be distinguished from the moral aspect that for the individual believer provided a limit to one's conscience. It was not possible to think that the right to freedom had the same value within the Church as it had for

3–5. Pamphlets against the declaration *Nostra Aetate* were distributed in the council (Archivio Fscire).

6. A memo from Pericles Felici reminding the council participants about the policy regarding distribution of publications, brochures, and circulars among the council fathers (Archivio Fscire).

7. On the right, John Courtney Murray, SJ (1904–1967), with Gustave Weigel, SJ (1906–1964) at Woodstock College in Maryland.

8. A council father reads the report of the discussion on *Nostrae Aetate* in *L'Avvenire d'Italia* (Archivio Fscire). The editor of the paper, Raniero La Valle, recalled, "I went down to Rome at the beginning

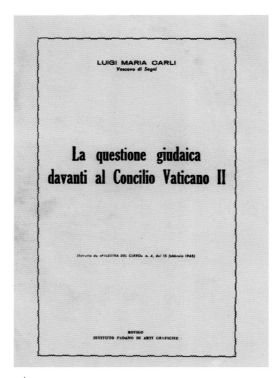

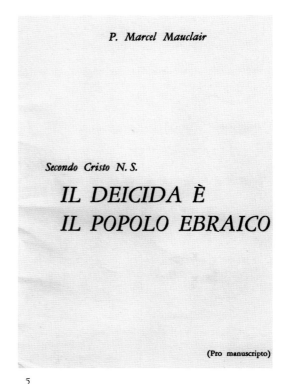

3

4

5

the state. The new draft, which was revised as recommended, was finally sent to the fathers. There was an opportunity for further discussion in the hall and then further critical comments. In fact, the minority opposed to the draft did not give up and, right up to the end, made requests to Paul VI for drastic changes or to quash the text. So there was further reworking of the text, which was then approved and promulgated in December 1965. Even the draft on Judaism was extensively revised after discussion in the hall during the third period. In order to acknowledge the concerns and threats of political retaliation, the declaration was included in the broader context of the relations of the Church with non-Christian religions, therefore including a chapter on Islam and one on Eastern religions, without realizing that the intrinsic asymmetrical bond between Judaism and the Church had become a reality. The condemnation (*damnat*) of anti-Semitism was contested by the fathers from the minority: on October 11, 1965, a few days before the final vote, *Coetus Internationalis Patrum* distributed a pamphlet in the hall ("Suggestiones circa suffragationes mox faccenda de Schemate: 'De Ecclesiae abitudine ad religiones non christianas'") which called upon fathers to vote *non placet*. Faced with this radical opposition the Secretariat, at the request of Paul VI, proposed that the

Circa poi le distribuzioni private, che i Padri e i Periti intendono effettuare a domicilio, sarebbe conveniente, per il principio asserito all'inizio di questo pro-memoria, che se ne informasse per tempo la Presidenza del Concilio, tramite la Segreteria Generale, rimettendo in pari tempo copia di quanto si intende distribuire.

24 giugno 1964

6

condemnation (*deplorat*) be minimized, and this gained some consensus among the small fringes of the minority who continued to apply pressure on the pope against *Nostra Aetate*. Even the principle of interreligious dialogue was challenged, of the second session and began reporting the daily news of the council. We participated, if possible, in all the meetings and press conferences, and we had contact with numerous council fathers, some of whom passionately followed the discussions: Suenans, Dosetti, Don Clemente Riva. Father Benedict Calati, prior of the Camaldolese welcomed us to his monastery on Celio hill in Rome, where he would meet with many bishops and cardinals. So we could see the documents and interventions in order to understand what was really happening….*L'Avvenire d'Italia* was distributed to 2,500 of the council fathers, so that by reading our newspaper, they could have a comprehensive idea of what was happening" (Raniero La Valle, editor, *L'Avvenire d'Italia*).

7

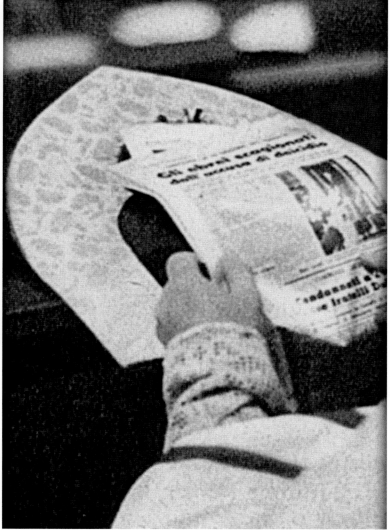

8

while the assembly in those weeks was filled with anti-Semitic pamphlets. On October 15, it came to the final vote on the declaration on relations with non-Christian religions, first on individual chapters and then on the whole document, which garnered only 243 *non placet* votes.

The declaration *Nostra Aetate* was then promulgated during the seventh public session on October 28, 1965, on the initiative of the Secretariat itself, which feared potential uneasiness among the assembly.

Despite the fact that these two texts are described only as "declarations," they represent two of the most important documents of the council, in that they define, in principle, a profound renewal of the church's position on two highly relevant issues.

BIBLIOGRAPHY

P. Ladrière, *Le décret du concile Vatican II sur l'oecuménisme, ouverture et blocage. Vers de nouveaux oecuménismes*, edited by J.-P. Williame, Paris 1989; G. Alberigo, "Grandi risultati. Ombre di incertezza," in *Storia del concilio Vaticano II*, edited by G. Alberigo (Italian edition edited by A. Melloni), vol. 4, Bologna 1999 (2013), 649–674; P. Hünermann, "Le ultime settimane del concilio," in *Storia del concilio Vaticano II*, edited by G. Alberigo (Italian edi-tion edited by A. Melloni), vol. 5, Bologna 2001 (2015), 371–492; S. Scatena, *La fatica della libertà. L'elaborazione della dichiarazione "Dignitatis humanae" sulla libertà religiosa del Vaticano II*, Bologna 2004; N. Lamdan, A. Melloni (eds.), *Nostra Aetate: Origins, Promulgation, Impact on Jewish-Catholic Relations*, Berlin 2007.

48. COMPLETING GAUDIUM ET SPES

In the eyes of many of the participants, the pastoral constitution *Gaudium et Spes* was one of the most anticipated documents of Vatican II. It marked the laying to rest of the Church's complete antagonism towards modernity and the transition to a church that was capable of listening to and respecting the history of the men and women for whom modernity was simply the times in which they found themselves. The drafting of the document was particularly tortuous. Unlike the other documents, it had not been incubated during the preparatory period. In that phase, the drafts on social and individual moral order did not form a basis for the work even in a polemical sense.

John XXIII had repeatedly expressed the idea that the council should also attend to the problems of contemporary society. Cardinal Léon-Joseph Suenens had already thought, prior to the council, that this could be achieved by dividing the topics of the council between those that were focused on the *ad intra* and *ad extra* activity of the church. This concept had an important influence in the planning of the draft, which was decided by the Coordinating Commission after the first period, the seventeenth on their list. In fact, the commission recognized the thematic overlap between some drafts developed by the Doctrinal Commission and the document drawn up by the Commission for the Apostolate of the Laity, in view of the "social doctrine": marriage, state laws, the economy, and peace. Thus, what was outlined was a proposal for a unitary document that included these core subjects, which was to be entrusted to both of the commissions. This new draft was then added to the list of documents on the new council agenda with the title *De Ecclesiae et Principiis Actione ad Bonum Societatis Promovendum*. Based on the position it occupied it began to be commonly referred to as "schema XVII."

Some members of the two committees were designated to work on this new schema and in the first months of 1963 the document, which included a doctrinal chapter on mankind and its supernatural vocation, also had five chapters devoted to a particular range of issues: society, the family, politics, economics, peace, and war. The result was a simple summation of the social doctrine taught in previous decades by the ecclesiastical magisterium.

This abstract and doctrinal formulation was soon abandoned: two documents already covered the same ground. There was the principle of the "signs of the times" in *Pacem in Terris*, which was issued by Pope John XXIII in April, 1963, and the principle of "dialogue," as set out by Pope Paul VI at the start of the second period and then developed the following year in the encyclical *Ecclesiam Suam*.

During the summer of 1963, a group of theologians who had been called together by Cardinal Suenens had been assigned the task of reviewing the theological basis of schema XVII and proposed a new text that focused on the idea of the "mission" of the church in the world. In November 1963, the job of reworking the document started all over again: the working group was expanded and became an autonomous organization. The Chairman of the Central Subcommittee was the young bishop of Livorno, Archbishop Emiliano Guano; at the helm of the editorial committee was the Redemptorist Fr. Bernard Häring, a theologian who was very unpopular with the Holy Office. In a restricted meeting that took place in Zurich in February 1964, a new draft was prepared, centered on the unity of mankind's vocation, the dynamism of the redemption wrought by Christ in humanity, and the "signs of the times" as signs of salvation present in history. It was a draft that was richer and better thought out theologically, and it moved much of the previous material into appendices, the so-called "*Adnexa*" which now covered the family, culture, politics, economics, war, and peace.

In the third period of the council, the schema (which in the renumbering of the projects became Schema XIII) was discussed for the first time in the Council Hall. Many appreciated its openness, its breadth, and the way it spoke to a modernity, which until then had remained alien and the object of condemnation. Others criticized the draft for being too positive toward the modern world, and its lack of emphasis on the contradiction that the Christian message represented. The openness to "dialogue," was criticized by the minority, in particular relating to the family and to the problem of birth control, to economic life, and to the use of modern weapons. Fr. Häring, who had already been criticized by the Doctrinal Commission, was harshly attacked by some fathers during the discussion and was removed from office and replaced by the French Archbishop Pierre Haubtmann.

Haubtmann, once again, began from scratch. He prepared a text that had a more Christological basis, concentrating on the one hand on the theology of earthly realities, and on the other the actions of Christians in society. This text was discussed in an extended session of the Joint Committee held at Ariccia in early February 1965. One individual who had a particularly important role on this occasion was the Archbishop Karol Wojtyla of Krakow who had begun to actively cooperate with praises of Archbishop Wojtyla to Guano, but he seemed not to have understood and did not respond. I repeated it to our secretary who commented that Wojtyla would soon become a cardinal (Diary of Henri de Lubac, April 5, 1965).

4. New York, October 4, 1965. Paul VI speaks before the General Assembly of the United Nations as an "expert in humanity." He extends his personal greetings as well as those of the council. It is on this occasion that he declares "No more war, war never again. It is peace, peace which must guide the destinies of peoples and of all mankind." Back in Rome, the council fathers follow the visit enthusiastically. "We see on television the pope's arrival in New York, live. At the very moment of the event, we are witnesses. Fantastic!" (Diary of Yves Congar, October 4, 1965).

1

2

3

the commission. He presented an alternative text, which had been drafted in the previous months in Poland. It proved to be very important in reorienting Haubtmann's draft to be more ecclesiological and to give a more realistic account of the evil in the world; in particular, Archbishop Wojtyla's text stressed the evil of modern atheism and its aggressive attack on the faith. The Belgian Archbishop Philips had a fundamental role at this point in the editing of this draft, as he had had for the document on the church, but because of ill health, undoubtedly due to the excessive work of those months, he did not manage to follow the document through to the end of the drafting process and was forced to relinquish his role as editor.

A long introduction was also added to the draft outlining the condition of modern mankind and the most urgent problems facing it. This was intended as a sign of the pastoral perspective of the document and expressed the will of the commission not to begin from abstract doctrinal principles, but from the concrete human condition, in the belief that the mystery of the incarnation of Christ was in some way present in it. The "*Adnexa*" were also integrated into the draft, which until then had had a more ambiguous position. In this way, it took on decidedly larger dimensions.

The schema was discussed again among the fathers at the beginning of the last period of the council, and it gained many supporters, but still there were many critics. Many fathers noticed

4

5. A group of bishops, mostly from the United States, voted *non placet* on chapter 5, the second part of Schema XIII (Archivio Fscire).

6. The assembly line in an automobile factory. The unskilled work, the monotony, the repetitiveness of which the assembly line was emblematic, led workers in some areas to engage in violent protests at the end of the 1960s (Archivio Jaca Book; Giorgio Bacchin, designer).

a certain vagueness and theological superficiality overall. Others felt there was excessive optimism toward earthly realities, which neglected the negative aspects and the dramatic dimension of evil. Many pointed to the lack of biblical study of the issues addressed, and the sociological and almost journalistic style that was used when talking about certain things, which was hardly suitable for a council document. The Germans had expressed strong reservations about the economic and social issues covered by the draft, which was particularly driven by the judgment of Karl Rahner and by an article by Joseph Ratzinger, but Archbishop Léon-Arthur Elchinger wrote to Yves Congar that "the Germans will no doubt be less critical than they were in danger of being. [...] They recognize that the text is imperfect, but it is the beginning of a dialogue with the world and not an absolute, conclusive doctrine." Archbishop Gabriel-Marie Garrone, who became chairman of the Central Subcommittee after Archbishop Guano but was forced to step down for health reasons, emphasized several times that many of these defects were in fact due to the pastoral nature that the commission had wanted to give to the draft and the fact that the document aimed at starting an effective dialogue with modern mankind. Moreover, he warned, the document's pastoral nature did not relegate it to a secondary field of action by the Church, but rather gave it a profound and intrinsic theological purpose, for which the mystery of redemption is anchored in the incarnation of salvation within humanity's history.

However, the most radical criticisms had to do with the final chapters on the most urgent problems of the modern world, and in particular those relating to marriage, birth control, peace, and war. The new draft was criticized for the prudential and possibilist positions it had taken up regarding the defensive use of modern weapons, nuclear deterrence, and the arms race, but many other bishops, in particular those from the United States, forcefully requested that it refrain from any condemnation of modern weapons so as not to embarrass the governments of countries that were on the front lines deterring threats from communist countries. Another section that came under insistent criticism was the statement in the draft in favor of conscientious objection to military service and the praise of nonviolence. During the weeks when the council discussed the topic of war, Paul VI made his trip to New York, where on October 4 he delivered his speech at the United Nations as "an expert in humanity." This was a real council event: not only did the fathers follow the pope's address live, but they decided to include the text in the documents of Vatican II, which certainly affected the debate in the Council Hall, giving it new direction

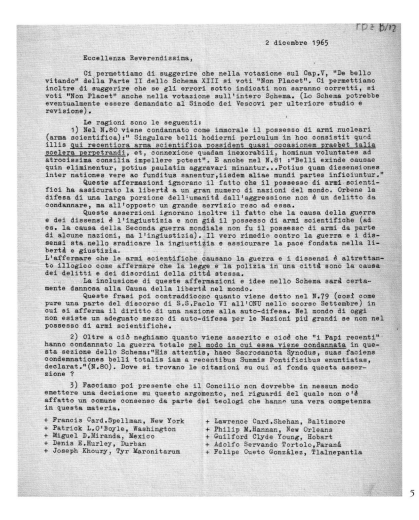

that appeared less radical than those that had been formulated in *Pacem in Terris*, two years before.

Regarding marriage, it was feared that, insisting on conjugal love as a fundamental principle, the text would open the way to a relativization of the traditional doctrine of indissolubility and also by neglecting to strongly reiterate the primary goal of procreation would lend itself to lax interpretations about the use of nonnatural means of birth control. These subjects were particularly sensitive to the public because at that time the contraceptive pill was entering the market in many countries, and there were open, lively debates even among Catholic moralists. Up to the last day before the final vote (which occurred on December 6 in the 168th and final working session) the opposition repeatedly sought to prevent approval for a document they thought contrary to traditional teaching and harmful for the Church and for the Christian faith. However, the document corresponded to a specific intention that many of the council fathers had expressed during the council: to open dia-

6

logue with the world again and learn to view the history of mankind with a more positive and involved attitude, taking into account its joys and hopes, its suffering and anxieties, according to the original intentions of the pastoral constitution. The final form of the draft was voted on in the last few days before the close of the council, and despite the strong opposition of some sections of the conciliar minority, the Pastoral Constitution on the Church in the Modern World *Gaudium et Spes* gained approval with a large majority of votes and was promulgated, together with the declaration *Dignitatis Humanae*, and the decrees *Ad Gentes* and *Presbyterorum Ordinis*, on December 7, in the ninth and last formal session. After its publication, many theologians pointed out the many theological limitations in the pastoral constitution. However it is undoubtedly a key document in the teaching of the council, as an expression of openness to the world and to history that the council fathers considered from the outset to be a fundamental component of their work.

BIBLIOGRAPHY
P. Hünermann, "Die Frage nach Gott und der Gerechtigkeit. Eine kritische dogmatische Reflexion auf die Pastoralkonstitution," in *Visionen des Konzils. 30 Jahre Pastoralkonstitution "Die Kirche in der Welt von heute,"* hrsg. Von G. Fuchs, A. Lienkamp, Münster 1997, 123–144; G. Turbanti, *Un concilio per il mondo moderno. La redazione della costituzione pastorale "Gaudium et spes" del Vaticano II*, Bologna 2000; P. Hünermann, "Le ultime settimane del concilio," in *Storia del concilio Vaticano II*, diretta da G. Alberigo (Italian edition edited by A. Melloni), vol. 5, Bologna 2001 (2015), 371–492.

49. Controversies: Subjects Taken on by the Pope

1. The half-empty assembly room at the end of a General Congregation (Archivio Fscire). "There were many surprises in the pope's speech. After praising the Roman Curia, he announced that there would be imminent reform, starting with the Holy Office, that the causes for the beatification of Pius XII and John XXIII would be introduced…and he announced a Jubilee Year to be observed

1

During the council, the complex redefinition of the agenda was made first by the Secretariat for Extraordinary Affairs and then by the Coordinating Commission. The latter evaluated the individual drafts before submitting them for discussion in the Council Hall. In general, there were never any difficulties regarding the specific topics that had been developed by commissions, which enjoyed a degree of autonomy in setting out the documents entrusted to them and in defining the topics for discussion. If anything, what was discussed was which draft seemed the most appropriate for a given topic, and the intention, which was more or less openly declared, was to attribute it to one or other of the commissions depending on the guidelines that had been set for them. For example, for a long time it was uncertain whether the issue of religious freedom would be included in the draft on the Church in the modern world and entrusted it to the competent joint committee made up of members of the Doctrinal Commission and the Commission for the Apostolate of the Laity, or if it would instead be added to the draft on ecumenism, which would come under the Secretariat for Christian Unity.

However, there were some cases in which the pope intervened directly with his authority, requesting that the council refrain from addressing certain issues that were more delicate or complex, on

which he intended to express himself directly or because—as in the case of the condemnation of communism—he believed them to be unrelated to the pastoral nature of Vatican II.

His interventions were expressed, from time to time, in different ways and had different outcomes, including on the corrections requested or imposed on texts.

The reform of the Curia. The council dealt with the relationship between the Petrine ministry and the authority of the college of bishops. This could have involved a thorough reform of the Curia's operations. Instead, the Roman Curia, which as a whole had opposed the election of Paul VI, in fact was saved by the pope himself from being reformed by the council. On September 21, 1963, just weeks after his elevation to the papacy, Pope Paul assured the Curia that he would work with them on reform. Despite momentous episodes, such as the *J'Accuse* of Cardinal Josef Frings against the Holy Office and the passionate defense by Cardinal Alfredo Ottaviani, the decree on the bishops and the relevant commission provided only some general indications. Therefore, Paul VI proceeded with the initial reform of the Congregation of the Holy Office (transformed into the Congregation for the Doctrine of the after the council. You can see from this the pope's strategy, making concessions to the right and to the left, he wants to preserve the unanimity of the episcopate in love" (Diary of Neophytos Edelby, November 18, 1965).

2. Boris Kustodiev (1878–1927), *The Bolshevik*, 1920 (Moscow, Tretyakov Gallery). Symbolic representation of Bolshevism as a giant towering over everything, from the center of political power to the church. The giant resembles Lenin (1970–1924) and demonstrates an indomitable determination (Archivio Jaca Book).

Faith by the December 7, 1965 motu proprio *Integrae Servandae*, which also did away with the index of prohibited books) and with the reform set out in the Apostolic Constitution *Regimini Ecclesiae Universae*, issued on August 15, 1967. The Curia was reformed again by John Paul II, in part by the new Code of Canon Law, and then again in the reorganization of 1988. In 2013, during the conclave that elected Pope Francis, the issue was again considered central.

The Synod of Bishops. The draft on the bishops prepared by the special commission beginning with the initial version of 1964, made provision for the setting up of the Episcopal Synod (*Synodus Episcoporum*), as a representative body of the college of bishops that would help the pope in governing the universal church. In order to calm the debate between the majority and the minority, Paul VI instituted the Synod, without involving the conciliar commission or the council, following a suggestion by the presider of the council, Cardinal Paolo Marella. Archbishop Antonio Samore from the Extraordinary Affairs section of the secretary of state prepared the motu proprio *Apostolica Sollicitudo*, which was issued on September 15, 1965, right at the beginning of the last period of the council, when the draft on the ministry of bishops had yet to be voted on. It was an individual action, which some saw as a way to meet the expectations of the council, but which established a synod without any power over its agenda or its decisions.

Clerical celibacy. The celibacy of candidates for the priesthood in the Latin Church (Eastern Rite Catholic churches had always had a married priesthood) was the subject of discussion when *Lumen Gentium*, which restored the married diaconate, showed that even the church of Rome considered a return to the ancient practice. In fact, the needs of many regions of the world posed the problem of how to provide a sufficient number of priests to preserve the pastoral care of the territory. The text of the draft on the priesthood presented to the fathers in November 1964 merely recommended celibacy, but for some fathers this was ambiguous and inadequate. In October 1965, when the text was again questioned, Paul VI, through Cardinal Eugène Tisserant, sent a letter to the office of the presider in which he explicitly asked the council fathers to avoid any discussion on the subject and to entrust it to the presider so that it would be subject to pontifical prudence in the future. Subsequently, Paul VI issued the encyclical *Sacerdotalis Coelibatus* (June 24, 1967), in which the custom of the Roman

church of choosing its clerics from among celibates was reaffirmed. However, exceptions have been made in individual cases for former non-Catholic clergymen to be ordained to the Catholic priesthood, even if their spouses were still alive.

The Bomb. In time of nuclear deterrence, one subject that the council had to face was that of peace, not only in the sense indicated by the ancient doctrine of ecclesiastical public law which condemned war and saw in it the penalty of modern apostasy, but especially in the sense of Pope John's *Pacem in Terris*, which denied that in the "atomic age," war could be an instrument of justice. The attempt by various fathers to arrive at a total condemnation of war and nuclear deterrence was only partially successful. *Gaudium et Spes*, in fact, explicitly condemned all-out war, but on the issue of deterrence, which the American bishops considered essential regarding the threat of the USSR, there was no ruling by the council. The pope's presentation to the United Nations, in fact, may have been a cry for "No more war," but he presented it as a fruit of sin that was impossible to eliminate from human history.

Birth control. The production of the first hormonal contraceptive—a progesterone pill that interfered with female fertility—had raised questions about the completely negative position taken by Pius XI on its use. In the spring of 1963, John XXIII set up a commission to study the matter, and the topic was touched upon in the draft on the Church in the Modern World, in the chapter on married life. Paul VI feared that a brutal

3. Invitation to October 27, 1964 conference in the Borgo Santo Spirito organized by Father Ermenegildo Lio on "De pillulis sic dictis anti-baby"—the birth control pill (Archivio Fscire).

discussion would open up and so he reactivated the commission established by Pope John XXIII, increasing the number of its members and consultants and asked them to formulate a reasoned opinion for him. At the same time, he informed the conciliar commission that he would deal with this issue personally—numerous interventions of the conciliar commission showed that a majority was in favor of cautiously opening up the issue. During the drafting of *Gaudium et Spes*, the pope intervened directly with the commission to avoid a text that could be interpreted as some kind of openness to the use of contraceptives by Catholics, and the council suspended its judgment. In July 1968, against the advice of the majority of the commission, Paul VI issued the encyclical *Humanae Vitae*, which condemned birth control by nonnatural methods. The encyclical was greeted with bitter controversy and was not accepted, even by those who thought its standards had become irrelevant.

Condemnation of communism. The request for a new condemnation of communism was widely supported in the voting of the bishops in the antepreparatory phase. This accorded with a subject that was felt at the ideological level and over which there was no fear of stepping on anyone's toes. However, John XXIII had excluded doctrinal condemnations; the presence of observers from the church of Moscow and especially the bishops from socialist-governed countries discouraged any explicit mention of a condemnation that was already present and had been observed for decades. It was only in the draft on the Church in the modern world, thanks to the contribution of Archbishop Karol Wojtyla, that the topic was linked with the problem of atheism and spoken about with disapproval. Paul VI himself, even in the face of repeated requests from the bishops of *Coetus Internationalis Patrum* and a petition from about a quarter of the fathers, was still opposed to an explicit doctrinal condemnation of communism.

The relationship between Judaism and the Church. The theme of the relationship with Judaism could have been dropped from the council agenda. During the preparatory period, the short text *De Judaeis*, which was drawn up by the Secretariat for Christian Unity, was rejected and Cardinal Amleto Cicognani made a statement ridiculing it saying that if they were to take that approach then they would end up with a document on Islam too. At the request of Cardinal Augustin Bea, John XXIII reintroduced the subject, which then appeared in section 4 of the declaration *Nostra Aetate*.

```
SEGRETARIATO               Romae, die 21 Octobris 1964.
Piazza di Sant'Uffizio 6
Tel. 561.232
Roma

Excellentissime ac Reverendissime Domine,
     Nomine plurium Patrum Conciliarium variarum nationum te,
magna cum reverentia, invito ad CONFERENTIAM quam habebit
     REV.MUS D. PATER ERMENEGILDO LIO, O.F. MIN.
Professor Universitatis Antonianae in Urbe et Peritus Concilii
     de themate magni momenti:
     CIRCA SCHEMA DE MATRIMONII SACRAMENTO: QUAESTIONES  ·
     MATRIMONIALES MORALES PRAESENTIS MOMENTI
     (De pillulis sic dictis "anti-baby")
     Conferentia haec erit Feria 3ª, 27 Octobris, hora 17.00 in
aula cuius ingressus est Via della Conciliazione 33, vel Borgo
Santo Spirito 75.  Lingua erit latina.
     Condiciones acusticae aulae optimae sunt.
               Religiose te, Ex.me ac Rev.me Domine saluto.
                    Add.mus in Domino.
               +Gerardus de Proença Sigaud,Arch.pus Adamantinus
                    Secretarius

Nota.  Usque ad finem huius Sessionis Conciliaris habebitur
eodem loco et hora eadem, singulis Feriis tertiis, conferentia
secundum mentem traditionalem Theologiae.
     Haberi possunt "modi" et alia scripta eiusdem mentis, in
"Segretariato" ut supra omnibus diebus feriis, hora 17 ad 18,30.
```

3

Bibliography
B. Häring, K. Rahner, *Riflessioni sull'enciclica "Humanae vitae"*, Rome 1968; J. Grootaers, "*Humanae Vitae* et la réactions dans les pays du Tiers monde," in *Pour relire "Humanae Vitae." Déclarations èpiscopales du monde entier. Commentaires théologiques*, Gembloux 1970, 51–66; G. Turbanti, "Il problema del comunismo al Concilio Vaticano II," in *Vatican II in Moscow (1959–1965)*, edited by A. Melloni, Leuven 1997, 147–187; M. Franzinelli, R. Bottoni, *Chiesa e guerra. Dalla "benedizione delle armi" alla "Pacem in terris"*, Bologna, 2005; J. Madiran, *"L'accordo di Metz." Tra Cremlino e Vaticano*, Roma 2011; J. O. Beozzo, "Intervenções episcopais desaparesidas dos Acta Synodalia do Vaticano II: a ordenação presbiteral de homens casados e o celibato eclesiástico," in *Cristianesimo nella storia*, 34 (2013), 41–56; E. Galavotti, "Sulle riforme della Curia romana nel Novecento," in *Cristianesimo nella storia*, 35 (2014), 849–890.

4. Udine, 1949. Notice of excommunication for those who support the Communist Party, following the decree from the Holy Office (Archivio Fscire).

5. A symbolic image: an atomic bomb explosion in a beaker (© Yves Forestier/Sygma/Corbis/Contrasto).

AVVISO SACRO

CURIA ARCIVESCOVILE DI UDINE

DOPO IL DECRETO DEL SANTO UFFIZIO CONTRO IL COMUNISMO ATEO.

E' peccato grave:

1° Iscriversi al Partito Comunista.
2° Favorirlo in qualsiasi modo, specialmente col voto.
3° Leggere la stampa comunista.
4° Propagare la stampa comunista.

Quindi non si può ricevere l'assoluzione da questo peccato se non si è pentiti e fermamente disposti a non commetterlo più.

Chi tacesse in Confessione questo peccato, commetterebbe un sacrilegio.

Quanto si è detto per il Partito Comunista vale anche per gli altri Partiti che fanno causa comune con esso, e per tutte quelle Associazioni che da esso dipendono: Camera del Lavoro - Fronte della Gioventù Comunista Italiana - U. D. I. (Unione Donne Italiane) - Federterra - A. P. I. (Associazione Pionieri Italiani).

E' scomunicato:

Chi, - iscritto o no al Partito Comunista, - ammette la dottrina marxista, atea ed anticristiana e ne fa propaganda, perchè **Apòstata dalla Fede** e **non** può essere **assolto** che dalla Santa Sede.

Il Signore illumini e conceda ai colpevoli in materia tanto grave, il pieno ravvedimento, poichè è in pericolo la stessa salvezza nell'eternità.

4

5

On December 6, the fathers of the council gathered in St. Peter's for the final general congregation, to rate the individual chapters of the constitution *Gaudium et Spes* which followed the final vote on the entire text, which was formally approved in a public session a day later on December 7, together with the decrees on the missions *Ad Gentes*, on the priesthood *Presbyterorum Ordinis* (PO), and the Declaration on Religious Freedom *Dignitatis humanae*, the vote (the last, number 544) was accompanied by the singing of the choir of the Sistine Chapel. In November, Paul VI decided that the council would end on December 8, the feast of the Immaculate Conception and the anniversary of the opening of Vatican Council I (December 8, 1869). A series of gestures enriched those last days of the council, in addition to the ceremonies of those days.

On December 4, in the presence of observers from other churches, Pope Paul presided at an interfaith Liturgy of the Word at St. Paul Outside the Walls. During the council, the observers had attended the Masses and prayers, which was previously not allowed. But on this occasion they played an active part and their faith was publicly recognized. The readings (Psalm 27, Romans 29:10–18 and 15:1–6) were read by a French Catholic, an American Methodist, and a Greek Orthodox. In his homily, the pope did not comment on the chosen texts from the Old and New Testaments, but he instead spoke of the closeness that had been established between the fathers and observers, thanks to the daily meetings and personal interactions during the years of the council: "Gentlemen, dear observers, allow me to call you by the name that has taken four years of an ecumenical council to come to: brothers, brothers and friends in Christ!"

December 7 witnessed not only the last public session, at which the last documents were promulgated, but another event that would mark the history of relations between East and West. After the last vote, in the presence of Metropolitan Meliton of Heliopolis, Johannes Willebrands, head of the Secretariat for Christian Unity, read from the ambo the Joint Declaration of Paul VI and Athenagoras lifting the anathemas dating back to the eleventh century. The pope and the patriarch, on an equal footing, solemnly declared that they deplore the mutual excommunication of 1054 and "regret the offensive words, the reproaches without foundation, and the reprehensible gestures" which had led to the rupture of ecclesial communion. Once again the work of the Secretariat and in particular Fr. Pierre Duprey had brought about this stunning result, achieved in a few weeks, although it remained uncertain until just a few days prior. At the same time, in the patriarchal basilica in Istanbul, in the presence of the patriarch and papal delegates led by Cardinal Lawrence Shehan of Baltimore, they proclaimed a joint statement by the mouth of the Secretary of the Holy Synod. After the reading of *Dell'Ambulate*

1. St. Peter's Basilica, December 7, 1965. Johannes Willebrands, head of the Secretariat for Christian Unity, reads the Joint Declaration of Paul VI and Athenagoras that lifted the anathemas of 1054 (*L'Attività della Santa Sede nel 1965*, Tipografia Poliglotta Vaticana, Città del Vaticano 1965).

2. St. Peter's Basilica, December 7, 1965. Paul VI and Orthodox Metropolitan Heliton of Heliopolis embrace after the lifting of the mutual excommunications (*L'Attività della Santa Sede nel 1965*).

3. St. Peter's Square, December 8, 1965. The closing ceremony of Vatican II (*L'Attività della Santa Sede nel 1965*).

▶ CÂMARA'S DREAM

"Then I told him [Montini] about the other dream: the word *council* should be understood by the people as a 'union of the Churches.' We cannot allow the council to end without unequivocally demonstrating our decision to open the doors and our hearts to our separated brothers and to all humanity. And I presented him with an entirely new version of the prayer for unity. I removed everything spectacular. I told Montini:

'Eminence, imagine St. Peter's Square overflowing with people. Suddenly, after the bells of the Basilica ring, a speaker (briefly, skillfully, and expressively) invites all those present—indeed the entire world—to accompany the prayer for unity which the pope will say together with the leaders of all the great Christian families.

'And there will be music, but only music. Yet it will be chosen in such a way that is pleasing and suitable in order to create the best framework for what is about to be experienced. Obviously, it will be exciting and suspenseful. And we will see and hear the pope pray—together with great (non-Catholic) Christian leaders—an evangelical prayer of power and great beauty.

'Then, another speaker (someone clear-headed, appropriate, and adequate) will announce something even more powerful: an encounter of the Christian families with Israel, a biblical prayer for spiritual unity and peace in the world. It will be made more suspenseful by utilizing a brief period of waiting with music of a different type and style.

'At first the pope will speak alone. He will ask the Jews for forgiveness for the centuries of persecution committed against them by Christians....Then he will embrace the Chief Rabbi with the embrace of peace. And together—with the Christian leaders and the Chief Rabbi—they will recite a prayer of Solomon.

'Then there will be the third break of the speaker—always in the right measure. He will announce a prayer for spiritual unity and peace in the world in union with the great non-Christian religions.

'Music will continue to play a key role. It will not become tedious because it will not be repetitive; each time the music will be in a different style. And there will be prayer in union with all the greats [whom] I believe will accept the pope's invitation....

'Finally, in conclusion, the speaker will announce that the pope will offer a gesture toward men of no faith—those without God. Due to the impossibility of their being present to pray together, the Vicar of Christ will speak on their behalf. The music will be completely different.

'And the pope's prayer should express absolute respect toward nonbelievers and a heartfelt invocation that those present seek to do good and reach the truth in light....' Montini believes the realization of this dream to be perfectly possible and plausible."

(Dom Hélder Câmara, 20th Circular Letter, Rome, November 2, 1962)

3

in dilectione by Cardinal Augustin Bea, cancelling the mutual excommunications, there was an exchange of peace and a symbolic embrace between Paul VI and Melito, which was greeted by a long applause of the assembly and preserved in the audio recording: the council solemnized that decision. The moment thus became one of the most intense of Vatican II on a symbolic level. This renewal of the Roman Catholic Church's ecumenical commitment was not only a spiritual gesture—the relics of St. Andrew, which had been taken by Crusaders in 1462, were returned to the Orthodox Church of Patras.

The final session of the Second Vatican Council was held in St. Peter's Square on the morning of December 8, with a solemn papal Mass, without concelebrants, as might have been expected: Pope Paul VI was assisted by the Papal Almoner and the Sacristy Prefect just as he would have been in the papal chapel, and two clerics of the papal court chanted the readings and the Gospel.

237

4. The French philosopher Jacques Maritain receives Paul VI's "Message to Men of Thought and Science" at the conclusion of Vatican II (*L'Attività della Santa Sede nel 1965*).

5–6. Messages are delivered to representatives of the groups addressed: Women, workers, and the poor (*L'Attività della Santa Sede nel 1965*).

4

5

The fourth and final period of the council closed with an event of great visual impact, characterized by sometimes-hectic activity. For the last time, the commissions had worked to make the final amendments to the texts, and the assembly was gathered together again to vote. The moments of great discussions and the epic battles seemed to give way to fatigue. Many of the texts that had been approved had indisputable innovative power, but there was fear that the impetus of this initiative had weakened. Decisions made by the pope alone—the statutes of the synod of bishops, hormonal contraception, clerical celibacy—were issues that seemed closed. The pope's presentation to the United Nations that had blocked the path to a condemnation of nuclear deterrence, the refusal to canonize John XXIII and leave his cause, along with Pius XII's, to the regular process, had disappointed some of the majority. But even the minority complained about the failure to condemn communism. Even the blessing of the foundation stone of a church dedicated to "Mary Mother of the Church"—the formula that the council had not wanted to use in order to avoid new Marian titles—was not a concession that carried much weight for the minority who had to endure the discussion of *Nostra Aetate* and *Dignitatis Humanae* during the last period of the council.

Even the proclamation of the seven messages on behalf of the council would be the subject of discussion. The messages were not directed to humanity as such, as was the message to the world

of October 20, 1962, but to seven specific categories of people, defined using divisions that came in part from the social doctrine that was already in place: rulers, scientists, artists, women, workers, the poor, the sick and the suffering, and the young. They were addressed on behalf of the council ("We, the fathers of the twenty-first ecumenical council of the Catholic Church, address ourselves in this solemn moment"), but the council had no hand in writing these messages and they were approved by acclamation without discussion. The cardinals who should have read them received the text, which was prepared by the pope himself with some collaborators (including Jacques Maritain), only the day before.

However, they appeared to be a great innovation and exhibited openness to the public, even if they were a step backwards compared to the renewal ushered in by *Gaudium et Spes* on the theme of dialogue with contemporary mankind.

Câmara had envisioned a grand ceremony of *mea culpas*: the pope would come out from St. Peter's on his own and ask forgiveness for papal authoritarianism towards the bishops, who would forgive him and then join him. Together they would ask forgiveness from the laity; then all together would ask forgiveness from other Christians, and these together from the Jews and then from believers of other religions; and then all together from women. The final liturgy of the council was not like that. For example, Fr. Otto Semmelroth wrote in his diary that it was "very long and not

7. Paul VI celebrates the closing of the council with the council fathers and *periti* (photo Giodani). The pope is holding the *ferula* commissioned for the closing of the council by the Neapolitan artist, Lello Scorzelli. Pope Paul's successors, John Paul I and John Paul II, continued to use it, but Benedict XVI used one previously used by Pius IX. Pope Francis has resumed use of the Scorzelli *ferula*.

8. All the council fathers were given a commemorative gold ring (Archivio Fscire). "It was announced that the Holy Father would offer a 'gold ring' to each council father....Imagine a gold-plated man's ring (of iron or bronze), without a gemstone, shaped like a miter with an image of Christ and Saints Peter and Paul at either side....I have no delusions; it is heavy. The majority will continue to use [rings with] precious stones. But the Pope continues to teach....For me, the new ring...even has a fun side. The child in me likes to use it because it is a curiosity! Not taking anything away from its tastefulness and finesse, it's reminiscent of the rings from cigars that children put on their fingers, or the ring that you put around a carrier pigeon's leg (Hélder Câmara, 88th Circular Letter, Rome, December 6/7, 1965).

as rich as I would have liked." For others the avenue that fascism had built, destroying a neighborhood of Rome in order to create a triumphalist prospect of St. Peter's, gave the opposite feeling. The bishops were open to returning to their dioceses to begin the post-conciliar work. For Paul VI, thus ended the opening years of a very demanding pontificate. Two types of transition characterized his approach: acceleration and braking. Among those who left the council were Albino Luciani, who would succeed Paul VI, and Karol Wojtyla, who would ascend to the papacy in 1978. Among the theologians returning home was Joseph Ratzinger, who would be elected pope in 2005. Vatican II, "the greatest grace of the twentieth century," as John Paul II called it, ceased to be only an event and became one with its implementation which would, in fact, take some time to become embedded.

BIBLIOGRAPHY
P. Kizeridis, *Il dialogo tra le Chiese ortodossa e cattolica dal 1920 fino all'abolizione delle reciproche scomuniche (7 dicembre 1965)*, Rome 1966; *L'evento e le decisioni. Studi sulle dinamiche del Concilio Vaticano II*, edited by M. T. Fattori and A. Melloni, Bologna 1997; *Volti di fine concilio. Studi di storia e teologia sulla conclusione del Vaticano II*, edited by J. Doré, A. Melloni, Bologna 2000 (in particular Cl. Soetens, "Les messages finaux du Concile," 99–114); P. Hünermann, "Le ultime settimane del concilio," in *Storia del concilio Vaticano II*, edited by G. Alberigo (Italian edition edited by A. Melloni), vol. 5, Bologna 2001 (2015), 371–492; G. Alberigo, "Conclusione e prime esperienze di ricezione," in *Storia del concilio Vaticano II*, op cit., 547–576; G. Alberigo, *Transizione epocale. Studi sul Concilio Vaticano II*, Bologna 2009.

51. CALENDAR OF THE CONGREGATIONS

Legend
PS = Public Session
GC = General Congregation

FIRST SESSION (October 11–December 8, 1962)

No.	Date	Liturgical Rite	Gospel Enthroned by	Celebrant (nationality)	President/Moderator	Fathers Present	Oral Interventions	No. of Votes	
-----	------	-----------------	---------------------	-------------------------	---------------------	-----------------	--------------------	--------------	
PS	10/11/1962	Roman;	P. Felici (Italy)	E. Tisserant (Italy)	John XXIII	Seats had not yet been assigned, attendance not taken	–	–	
GC 1	10/13/1962	Roman	P Felici (Italy)	E. Florit (Italy)	E. Tisserant	Due to brevity of GC, no attendance taken	2	–	
GC 2	10/16/1962	Roman	P. Felici (Italy)	C. Morcillo Gonzales (Spain)	E. Tisserant	2381	4	1	
GC 3	10/20/1962	Roman	P. Nabaa (Lebanon)	M. Jansen (Holland)	A. Liénart	2344	38	1	
GC 4	10/22/1962	Roman	C. Morcillo Gonzales (Spain)	L. Jaeger (Germany)	N. Gilroy	2356	21	–	
GC 5	10/23/1962	Roman	J. Villot (France)	J. Krol (USA)	F. Spellman	2363	18	–	
GC 6	10/24/1962	Byzantine Melkite	J. Krol (USA)	P. Nabaa (Lebanon)	H. Pla y Deniel	2337	16	–	
GC 7	10/26/1962	Roman	W. Kempf (Germany)	D. Yougbare (Upper Volta)	J. Frings	2325	22	–	
GC 8	10/27/1962	Roman	P. Felici (Italy)	M. Miranda y Gomez (Mexico)	E. Ruffini	2303	24	–	
GC 9	10/29/1962	Roman	P. Nabaa (Lebanon)	P. Yamaguchi (Japan)	A. Caggiano	2279	19	–	
GC 10	10/30/1962	Roman	C. Morcillo Gonzales (Spain)	J. Mangers (Norway)	B. Alfrink	2257	23	–	
GC 11	10/31/1962	Dominican	J. Villot (France)	J. Lemieux (Canada)	E. Tisserant	2230	25	–	
GC 12	11/5/1962	Maronite (concelebrated)	J. Krol (USA)	J. Khoury (Lebanon), M. L. Bostani (Sup. Gen. Aleppians), and M. Harika (Sup. Gen. Antonin Maronite Order)	A. Liénart	2129	24	–	
GC 13	11/6/1962	Roman	W. Kempf (Germany)	A. Hamvas (Hungary)	I. Tappouni	2211	24	–	
GC 14	11/7/1962	Roman	R. Dosseh (Togo)	P. Nguyen van-Binh (Vietnam)	N. Gilroy	2214	26	–	
GC 15	11/9/1962	Roman	M. Perrin (Tunisia)	E. Cunial (Italy)	J. Frings	2216	20	–	
GC 16	11/10/1962	Bracarense	C. A. Minali (Brazil)	F. Da Silva (Portugal)	E. Ruffini	2172	24	–	
GC 17	11/12/1962	Roman, in Paleo-Slavic	A. Beras (Santo Domingo)	J. Arneric (Yugoslavia)	A. Caggiano	2186	21	–	
GC 18	11/13/1962	Roman	A. Corso (Uruguay)	M. Serrano Abad (Ecuador)	B. Alfrink	2209	23	–	

Sources: The table is modeled after the one published in the special 1965 issue of *L'Osservatore della domenica* on the council, 52–53. The only data taken from this source is the time of the congregations, which is more exact than can be found elsewhere, while the remaining data is from *Concilio Vaticano II. Cronache del Concilio Vaticano II* by *La Civiltà Cattolica*, edited by G. Caprile and by *Acta synodalia*. In particular, Caprile, from the second session onwards, counted the number of fathers based on attendance records—a count which would have excluded latecomers—but revised based on the maximum number of votes at a congregation.

Duration	Theme	Topic Discussed	Subject of Vote
8:30/13:30	Solemn opening liturgy—John XXIII's speech, *Gaudet mater ecclesia*		
9:00/9:50	Election of conciliar commissions—vote postponed to give episcopal commissions time to prepare lists of candidates	Conciliar Commissions	
9:00/10:25	Election of conciliar commissions	Conciliar Commissions	Conciliar Commissions
9:05/12:45	Discussion and vote on the message of the council fathers to the world	Message of the council fathers to the world	Message of the council fathers to the world
9:05/12:10	Discussion of draft *De sacra liturgia* [On the sacred liturgy]	*De sacra liturgia*	
9:00/12:10	Discussion of draft *De sacra liturgia*—introduction and ch. I		
9:00/12:15	Discussion of draft *De sacra liturgia*—introduction and ch. I		
9:00/12:20	Discussion of draft *De sacra liturgia*—introduction and ch. I		
9:00/12:20	Discussion of draft *De sacra liturgia*—introduction and ch. I		
9:00/12:10	Discussion of draft *De sacra liturgia*—ch. I and II		
9:00/12:15	Discussion of draft *De sacra liturgia*—ch. II		
9:00/12:20	Discussion of draft *De sacra liturgia*—ch. II		
9:03/12:15	Discussion of draft *De sacra liturgia*—ch. II		
9:00/12:10	Discussion of draft *De sacra liturgia*—ch. II and III		
9:00/12.15	Discussion of draft *De sacra liturgia*—ch. III and IV		
9:02/12:20	Discussion of draft *De sacra liturgia*—ch. IV		
9:00/12:30	Discussion of draft *De sacra liturgia*—ch. IV and following		
9:00/12:22	Discussion of draft *De sacra liturgia*—final chapter		
9:00/12:15	Discussion of draft *De sacra liturgia*—final chapter. Vote on the conclusion of the debate on the *De sacra liturgia*.		

GC 19	11/14/1962	Roman	P. Leclerc (Mali)	P. Cheng (Formosa)	E. Tisserant	2215	15	1
GC 20	11/16/1962	Armenian	P. Kiredjian (Turkey)	G. Layek (Syria)	A. Liénart	2213	21	
GC 21	11/17/1962	Roman	L. Bianchi (China)	A. Baraniak (Poland)	N. Gilroy	2207	18	4
GC 22	11/19/1962	Roman	C. Quintero Arce (Mexico)	M. Beovich (Australia)	F. Spellman	2197	18	–
GC 23	11/20/1962	Roman	J.-B. Gahamanyi (Rwanda)	C. Rodriguez-Quiros (Costa Rica)	J. Frings	2211	13	1
GC 24	11/21/1962	Ukrainian Byzantine (concelebrated)	G. Bukatio (Yugoslavia)	G. Bukatio (Yugoslavia)	E. Ruffini	2186	16	–
GC 25	11/23/1962	Roman	A. Scola (Italy)	G. Tredici (Italy)	A. Caggiano	2157	17	–
GC 26	11/24/1962	Roman	M. McGrath (Panama)	F. Charriere (Switzerland)	B. Alfrink	2136	24	–
GC 27	11/26/1962	Roman	A. Cazzaniga (Italy)	J. Rosales (Philippines)	E. Tisserant	2133	17	–
GC 28	11/27/1962	Roman	L. Chavez y Gonzalez (El Salvador)	L. Rodriguez Ballon (Peru)	A. Liénart	2156	15	1
GC 29	11/28/1962	Ethiopian	A. M. Yemmeru (Ethiopia)	A. M. Yemmeru (Ethiopia)	I. Tappouni	2144	17	–
GC 30	11/30/1962	Roman	J. Domingues de Oliveira (Brazil)	A. Charue (Belgium)	F. Spellman	2145	15	9
GC 31	12/1/1962	Roman	A. Plaza (Argentina)	F. Grimshaw (Great Britain)	J. Frings	2115	14	1
GC 32	12/3/1962	Syro-Malabar	G. Alapatt (India)	G. J. Parecattil (India)	E. Ruffini	2116	16	2
GC 33	12/4/1962	Roman	A. Santin (Italy)	H. Rakotomalala (Madagascar)	A. Caggiano	2104	17	–
GC 34	12/5/1962	Roman	S. Splett (Poland)	E. Da Silveira d'Elboux (Brazil)	B. Alfrink	2113	8	8
GC 35	12/6/1962	Roman	A. Lazik (Czechoslovakia)	B. Gantin (Dahomey)	E. Tisserant	2085	12	5
GC 36	12/7/1962	Chaldean	J. Cheikho (Iran)	G. Ganni (Lebanon)	A. Liénart	2118	10	1
PS	12/8/1962	Roman		P. Marella (Italy)	John XXIII			

1. Journalists and the faithful watch the procession of council fathers in St. Peter's Square (Archivio Fscire).

2. Opening ceremony of the second session (photo Pais/Archivio 1 Rodrigo Pais–Ceub Università di Bologna).

9:00/12:25	Vote on *De sacra liturgia*; discussion of draft *De fontibus revelationis* [On the Sources of Revelation]		*De sacra liturgia*
9:00/12:25	Discussion of draft *De fontibus revelationis*	*De fontibus revelationis*	
9:00/12:15	Discussion of draft *De fontibus revelationis*—four votes on amendments to *De sacra liturgia*		*De sacra liturgia*
9:00/12:20	Discussion of draft *De fontibus revelationis*		
9:00/12:25	Discussion of draft *De fontibus revelationis*—ch. I—debate interrupted by inconclusive vote (no quorum)		*De fontibus revelationis*
9:00/12:15	Discussion of draft *De fontibus revelationis*—ch. I—communication of John XXIII's decision to suspend discussion, per previous day's vote, on *De fontibus revelationis*		
9:00/12:15	Discussion of draft *De instrumentis communicationis socialis* [On the Instruments of Social Communication]	*De instrumentis communicationis socialis*	
9:00/12:20	Discussion of draft *De instrumentis communicationis socialis*		
9:00/12:15	Discussion of draft *De instrumentis communicationis socialis*— start of debate on draft *De ecclesiae unitate* [On the Unity of the Church]		
9:00/12:10	Discussion of draft *De ecclesiae unitate*—vote on *De instrumentis communicationis socialis*	Discussion of draft *De ecclesiae unitate*— preliminary vote on De instrumentis communicationis socialis	*De instrumentis communicationis socialis*
9:00/12:15	Discussion of draft *De ecclesiae unitate*		
9:00/12:15	Discussion of draft *De ecclesiae unitate*—vote on nine amendments to *De sacra liturgia*		
9:00/12:10	Discussion of draft *De ecclesia*		*De sacra liturgia*
9:00/12:30	Discussion of draft *De ecclesia*—vote on *De sacra liturgia*		
9:00/12:26	Discussion of draft *De ecclesia*	*De ecclesia*	
9:00/12:20	Discussion of draft *De ecclesia*—eight votes on *De sacra liturgia*		
9:00/12:10	Discussion of draft *De ecclesia*—five votes on *De sacra liturgia*		*De sacra liturgia*
9:00/12:15	Discussion of draft *De ecclesia*—general vote on preface and ch. I of *De sacra liturgia*—visit and speech of John XXIII		
	Solemn celebration of the eucharist for the closing of session one of the council—visit and speech of John XXIII		

SECOND SESSION (September 29-December 4, 1963)

PS	9/29/1963	Roman	P. Felici (Italy)	E. Tisserant (Italy)	Paul VI			
GC 37	9/30/1963	Ambrosian	P. Felici (Italy)	G. Colombo (Italy)	G. P. Agagianian	2258	8	–
GC 38	10/1/1963	Roman	P. Nabaa (Lebanon)	J. C. Mcquaid (Ireland)	G. Lercaro	2229	12	1
GC 39	10/2/1963	Roman	C. Morcillo Gonzales (Spain)	T. Cooray (Ceylon)	J. Döpfner	2288	17	–
GC 40	10/3/1963	Roman	J. Villot (France)	G. B. Zoa (Cameroon)	L.-J. Suenens	2262	19	–
GC 41	10/4/1963	Roman	J. Kroll (USA)	F. Filippini (Somalia)	G. P. Agagianian	2256	18	–
GC 42	10/7/1963	Roman	W. Kempf (Germany)	P. M. Théas (France)	G. Lercaro	2275	16	–
GC GC	10/8/1963	Syro-Antiochene	A. J. D. Bakose (Iraq)	I. Tappouni (Cardinal Patriarch of Antioch (Syrian)	J. Döpfner	2298	9	5
GC 44	10/9/1963	Roman	J. C. Garner (South Africa)	A. Rohracher (Austria)	L.-J. Suenens	2278	14	7
GC 45	10/10/1963	Roman	P. Kimbondo (Congo)	P. Kinam Ro (Korea)	G. P. Agagianian	2265	17	7
GC 46	10/11/1963	Roman	V. Kennally (Caroline and Marshall Is.)	A. Fernandez Feo-Tinoco (Venezuela)	G. Lercaro	2249	16	–
GC 47	10/14/1963	Roman	C. Sipovic (Poland)	M. Mihayo (Tanzania)	J. Döpfner	2242	19	1
GC 48	10/15/1963	Mozarabic	E. Martinez Gonzales (Spain)	A. Granados Garcia (Spain)	L.-J. Suenens	2239	9	4
GC 49	10/16/1963	Alexandrian-Coptic	Y. Kabes (Egypt)	A. Scandar (Egypt)	G. P. Agagianian	2259	13	4
GC 50	10/17/1963	Roman	J. Scanlan (Scotland)	G. Aramburu (Argentina)	G. Lercaro	2259	17	2
GC 51	10/18/1963	Roman	A. Abed (Lebanon)	A. Djajasepoetra (Indonesia)	J. Döpfner	2217	16	1
GC 52	10/21/1963	Romanian Byzantine	B. Cristea (Romania)	B. Cristea (Romania)	L.-J. Suenens	2204	8	3
GC 53	10/22/1963	Roman	G. Pearce (Polynesia)	Manuel Sanchez Beguiristain (Chile)	G. P. Agagianian	2238	15	5
GC 54	10/23/1963	Roman	J. Wolff (Madagascar)	J. Shehan (USA)	G. Lercaro	2234	15	5
GC 55	10/24/1963	Roman	A. Lopez Aviña (Mexico)	P. Bertoli (France)	J. Döpfner	2236	7	6
GC 56	10/25/1963	Roman	A. Kozlowiecki (Northern Rhodesia)	D. Gomez Junqueira (Angola)	L.-J. Suenens	2192	16	5
CG 57	10/29/1963	Ukrainian Byzantine	G. Bukatko (Yugoslavia)	G. Slipyi (Ukraine)	G. P. Agagianian	2204	7	5
GC 58	10/30/1963	Roman	F. Gomez Leon (Mexico)	M. de Miranda Vilas-Bôas (Brazil)	G. Lercaro	2157	13	3
CG 59	10/31/1963	Roman	W. O'Connor (USA)	P. C. Van Lierde (Belgium)	J. Döpfner	1941	20	1

	Solemn celebration of the opening of the second session of the council—speech by Paul VI		
9:23/12:30	Discussion of draft *De ecclesia*		
9:05/12:10	Discussion of draft *De ecclesia*—vote on draft prior to review of individual chapters		
9:05/12:06	Discussion of draft *De ecclesia*—introduction and ch. I		
9:05/12:05	Discussion of draft *De ecclesia*—introduction and ch. I		
9:00/12:05	Discussion of draft *De ecclesia*—introduction and ch. I–II		
9:10/12:12	Discussion of draft *De ecclesia*—ch. II		
9:03/12:18	Discussion of draft *De ecclesia*—ch. II—votes on amendments to draft *De sacra liturgia* [On the Sacred Liturgy]		*De sacra liturgia*
9:02/12:15	Discussion of draft *De ecclesia*—ch. II—votes on amendments to draft *De sacra liturgia*		
9:00/12:13	Discussion of draft *De ecclesia*—ch. II—votes on amendments to draft *De sacra liturgia*		
9:00/12:13	Discussion of draft *De ecclesia*—ch. II		
9:00/12:20	Discussion of draft *De ecclesia*—ch. II—vote on ch. II of draft *De sacra liturgia*	*De ecclesia*	*De sacra liturgia*
9:00/12:08	Discussion of draft *De ecclesia*—ch. II—vote in favor of ending debate on ch. II of draft *De ecclesia*—votes on amendments to ch. III of draft *De sacra liturgia*		
9:05/12:07	Discussion of draft *De ecclesia*, ch. II—votes on amendments to ch. III of draft *De sacra liturgia*		
9:03/12:07	Discussion of draft *De ecclesia*, ch. III—votes on amendments to ch. III of draft *De sacra liturgia*		
9:00/12:15	Discussion of draft *De ecclesia*, ch. III—general vote on ch. III of draft *De sacra liturgia*		
9:02/12:10	Discussion of draft *De ecclesia*, ch. III—votes on amendments to ch. IV of draft *De sacra liturgia*		
9:02/12:10	Discussion of draft *De ecclesia*, ch.III—votes on amendments to ch. IV of draft *De sacra liturgia*		
9:04/12:07	Discussion of draft *De ecclesia*, ch. III—votes on amendments to ch. IV of draft *De sacra liturgia*		
9:02/12:06	Discussion of draft *De ecclesia*, ch. III—vote, by remaining seated or standing, for concluding discussion on ch. III—general vote on ch. IV of draft *De sacra liturgia* and on amendments to ch. V		
9:00/12:13	Discussion of draft *De ecclesia*, ch. III (supplementary interventions) and IV—votes on amendments to ch. V of draft *De sacra liturgia*		
9:03/12:12	Discussion of draft *De ecclesia*, ch. IV—vote on whether to insert ch. VI on Bl. Virgin Mary in draft *De ecclesia*—General vote on ch. V of draft *De sacra liturgia*, amendments to ch. VI		
9:05/12:14	Discussion of draft *De ecclesia*, ch. IV—vote on five questions regarding approach to *De ecclesia*—Vote on amendments to ch. VI of draft *De sacra liturgia*		*De ecclesia*
9:02/12:07	Discussion of draft *De ecclesia*, ch. IV—Single vote on amendments to ch. VII of draft *De sacra liturgia*		*De sacra liturgia*

	11/4/1963							
GC 60	11/5/1963	Chaldean	R. Rabban (Iraq)	Paul II Cheikho (Iraq)	L.-J. Suenens	2107	12	–
GC 61	11/6/1963	Roman	A. Brandao Vilela (Brazil)	N. Mosconi (Italy)	L.-J. Suenens	2136	19	1
GC 62	11/7/1963	Roman	H. Berlier (Niger)	S. Nierman (Holland)	G. P. Agagianian	2155	18	–
GC 63	11/8/1963	Roman	J. B. Llosa (France)	A. Ddungu (Uganda)	G. P. Agagianian / G. Lercaro	2148	17	–
GC 64	11/11/1963	Roman	L. Hoch (USA)	J. Khiamsum Nittayo (Thailand)	G. Lercaro	2141	18	
GC 65	11/12/1963	Roman	M. Serrano Abad (Ecuador)	B. Gut (Abbot Primate OSB)	G. Lercaro / J. Döpfner	2166	16	1
GC 66	11/13/1963	Byzantine Russian	A. Katkoff (Russia)	A. Katkoff (Russia)	J. Döpfner	2164	16	–
GC 67	11/14/1962	Roman	P. Kalwa (Poland)	R. Tchidimbo (Guinea)	J. Döpfner / L.-J. Suenens	2168	16	2
GC 68	11/15/1963	Roman	P. Dalmais (Chad)	T. Botero Salazar (Colombia)	J. Döpfner / L.-J. Suenens	2123	16	–
GC 69	11/18/1963	Roman	E. Mabathoana (Basutoland)	P. Felici (Italy)	G. P. Agagianian	2090	10	1
GC 70	11/19/1963	Syro-Malankar	A. Polachirakal (India)	G. Thangalathil (India)	G. P. Agagianian	2182	9	–
GC 71	11/20/1963	Roman	M. Maradan (Seychelles)	D. Vendargon (Malaysia)	G. P. Agagianian	2182	13	5
GC 72	11/21/1963	Roman in Paleo-Slavic	M. Bernard (Congo)	A. G. Grutka (USA)	G. Lercaro	2186	12	6
GC 73	11/22/1963	Roman	V. Gonzales y Robleto (Nicaragua)	E. Duval (Algeria)	G. Lercaro	2178	9	3
GC 74	11/25/1963	Roman	P. Martin (New Caledonia)	A. Antezanas y Rojas (Bolivia)	G. Lercaro / J. Döpfner	2168	15	2
GC 75	11/26/1963	Maronite	F. Ayoub (Syria)	J. Khoury (Lebanon)	J. Döpfner	2131	17	–
GC 76	11/27/1963	Roman	F. Minerva (Italy)	G. Gray (Scotland)	J. Döpfner / L.-J. Suenens	2122	17	–
GC 77	11/28/1963	Roman	B. Yago (Ivory Coast)	A. Sépinski (Minister Gen. OFM)	L.-J. Suenens	2192	19	–
GC 78	11/29/1963	Greek Byzantine	G. Perniciaro (Italy)	H. Gad (Greece)	L.-J. Suenens	2094	11	–
GC 79	12/2/1963	Roman	A. Lefevre (Morocco)	P. Ngo Dinh Thuc (Vietnam)	G. P. Agagianian	2110	12	–
	12/3/1963	Roman	A. G. Cicognani (Italy)	Paul VI		–		-
PS III	12/4/1962	Roman	Paul VI	E. Tisserant	P. Felici (Italy)	2152	1	2

Time			
	Commemoration of the fourth centenary of the decree of Trent on the establishment of seminaries. Keynote by Cardinal S. Wyszyński		
9:00/12:07	Discussion of draft *De episcoporum ac de dioecesium regimine* [On the Bishops and Governance of Dioceses], introduction and overall content	*De episcoporum ac de dioecesium regimine*	
9:03/12:18	Discussion of draft *De episcoporum ac de dioecesium regimine*, preface and ch. I—vote in favor of suspending general debate to examine the chapter		
9.02/12:10	Discussion of draft *De episcoporum ac de dioecesium regimine*, ch. I—summary report on last intervention on ch. IV of draft *De ecclesia*		
9:00/12:20	Discussion of draft *De episcoporum ac de dioecesium regimine*, ch. I and II		
9:00/12:12	Discussion of draft *De episcoporum ac de dioecesium regimine*, ch. II		
9:00/12:10	Discussion of draft *De episcoporum ac de dioecesium regimine*, ch. II and III—simple vote to suspend debate on ch. II—vote to defer ch. V to the Commission for the Revision of the Code of Canon Law, avoiding discussion at meeting		
9:00/12:13	Discussion of draft *De episcoporum ac de dioecesium regimine*, ch. III, last three interventions on ch. II		
9:02/12:20	Discussion of draft *De episcoporum ac de dioecesium regimine*, ch. III—simple vote to suspend debate on ch. III—Discussion of ch. IV—voting on texts of amendments to draft *De instrumentis communicationis socialis*		*De instrumentis communicationis socialis*
9:00/11:46	Discussion of draft *De episcoporum ac de dioecesium regimine*, ch. IV, last three interventions on ch. III		
9:02/12:22	Start of discussion of draft *De oecumenismo* [On ecumenism]—vote on preface and ch. I of De sacra liturgia—Final intervention on ch. IV of draft De episcoporum ac de dioecesium regimine	*De oecumenismo*	
9:02/12:14	Discussion of draft *De oecumenismo* in general		
9:03/12:18	Discussion of draft *De oecumenismo* in general—vote on ch. II of *De sacra liturgia*		*De sacra liturgia*
9:02/12:23	Discussion of draft *De oecumenismo* in general and on ch. I—simple vote on suspending the general discussion–vote on ch. III of De sacra liturgia		
9:00/12:07	Final intervention on draft *De oecumenismo* in general, discussion of ch. I—vote on last four chapters of *De sacra liturgia* and vote on draft in general		
9:03/12:22	Discussion on draft *De oecumenismo*, ch. I and II—simple vote to suspend discussion of ch. I—General vote on draft of De instrumentis communicationis socialis		
9:08/12:20	Discussion on draft *De oecumenismo*, ch. II—final interventions on ch. I		
9:03/12:13	Discussion on draft *De oecumenismo*, ch. II and III—simple vote on suspending discussion of ch. II		
9:02/12:17	Last fifteen interventions on ch. II of draft *De oecumenismo*—Discussion of ch. III (4 interventions)		
9:00/12:10	Discussion of draft *De oecumenismo*, ch. III		
9:03/11:56	Discussion of draft *De oecumenismo*, ch. III		
9:00/...	Solemn commemoration of the Council of Trent—opening address by Cardinal Urbani—intervention by lay auditors J. Guitton and V. Veronese		
	Final vote and promulgation of the constitution on the liturgy, *Sacrosanctum Concilium* and the decree on social communication, *Inter Mirifica*—second session closes with speech by Paul VI		

THIRD SESSION (September 14–November 21, 1964)

PS IV	9/14/1964	Roman (concelebrated)		Paul VI, with 24 others	Paolo VI				
GC 80	9/15/1964	Roman	P. Felici (Italy)	C. Vanuytven (Belgium)	G. P. Agagianian	2170	14	–	
GC 81	9/16/1964	Roman C. Morcillo Gonzales (Spain)	J. Thiandoum (Senegal)	G. Lercaro	2204	17	2	2	
GC 82	9/17/1964	Roman	J. Krol (USA)	G. Angrisani (Italy)	G. Lercaro	2210	16	4	
GC 83	9/18/1964	Roman	W. Kempf (Germany)	M. Larrain (Chile)	J. Döpfner	2190	16	1	
GC 84	9/21/1964	Roman	A. Noser (New Guinea)	F. Donaghy (China)	J. Döpfner	2220	6	4	
GC 85	9/22/1964	Roman	G. Michelotto Pellanda (Brazil)	M. Roy (Canada)	J. Döpfner	2248	19	8	
GC 86	9/23/1964	Roman	(Relic of St. Andrew enthroned instead of Gospel)	P. Marella (Italy)	L.-J. Suenens	2254	12	6	
GC 87	9/24/1964	Roman	J. Holterman (Curaçao)	J. Cordeiro (Pakistan)	L.-J. Suenens	2228	18	6	
GC 88	9/25/1964	Syro-Antiochian	J. Karroum (Syria)	C. E. Benni (Iraq)	L.-J. Suenens	2198	11	6	
GC 89	9/28/1964	Roman	E. Sosa Gaona (Paraguay)	F. Tomasek (Czechoslovakia)	G. P. Agagianian	2176	18	6	
GC 90	9/29/1964	Roman	L. Lommel (Luxembourg)	J. Amissah (Ghana)	G. P. Agagianian	2229	21	3	
GC 91	9/30/1964	Roman	F. Marty (France)	M. Rodriguez Rozas (Cuba)	G. Lercaro	2242	4	6	
GC 92	10/1/1964	Roman	A. Ramos (Brazil)	R. Campelli (Italy)	G. Lercaro	2169	20	–	
GC 93	10/2/1964	Roman	P. Hagarty (Bahamas)	N. Farren (Ireland)	G. Lercaro / J. Döpfner	2119	18	–	
GC 94	10/5/1964	Roman	J. E. Malenfant (India)	P. McKeefry (New Zealand)	J. Döpfner	2112	15	4	
GC 95	10/6/1964	Roman	E. Nowicki (Gdansk)	H. Santos (Mexico)	J. Döpfner	2168	13	5	
GC 96	10/7/1964	Roman	A. Fernandez (Master Gen. Dominicans)	A. Signora (Pompei)	L.-J. Suenens	2177	9	4	
GC 97	8.10.1964	Roman	C. Chitsulo (Malawi)	G. Pedicini (Italy)	L.-J. Suenens	2169	18	1	
GC 98	10/9/1964	Chaldean (Syria)	Z. Dachtou (Iran)	L.-J. Suenens	2070	19	–	-	
GC 99	10/12/1964	Roman	L. Bentivoglio (Italy)	A. Ferreira de Macedo (Brazil)	G. P. Agagianian	2065	17	–	
GC 100	10/13/1964	Roman	J. Gunnarsoh (Iceland)	E. Mason (Sudan)	G. P. Agagianian	2152	17	–	
GC 101	10/14/1964	Roman	M. Gonzi (Malta)	V. Brizgys (Lithuania)	G. P. Agagianian	2119	19	–	
GC 102	10/15/1964	Roman	G. Garrone (France)	S. Moro Briz (Spain)	G. P. Agagianian/ G. Lercaro	2130	11	–	

Time	Description	Category	
	Solemn celebration of the opening of the third session of the council—speech by Paul VI		
9:20/12:38	Discussion of draft *De ecclesia*, ch. VII	*De ecclesia*	*De ecclesia*
9:03/12:29	Discussion of draft *De ecclesia*, ch. VII and VIII—preliminary vote on voting procedure for *De ecclesia* and first vote on ch. I		
9:04/12:31	Discussion of draft *De ecclesia*, ch. VIII—vote on amendments to ch. II		
9:03/12:30	Final three interventions on ch. VIII of *De ecclesia*—final vote on ch. II of same– start discussion of draft *De pastorali episcoporum munere in Ecclesia*	*De pastorali episcoporum munere in Ecclesia*	
9:12/12:32	Discussion of draft *De pastorali episcoporum munere in Ecclesia*—vote on ch. III of De ecclesia		
9:00/12:40	Discussion of draft *De pastorali episcoporum munere in Ecclesia*— eight votes on ch. III of *De ecclesia*		
9:09/12:34	Ceremony in honor of St. Andrew the apostle, as the relic is returned to Patras—Final two interventions on the draft *De pastorali episcoporum munere in Ecclesia*—discussion of declaration on religious freedom—voting on ch. III of draft *De ecclesia*	*De libertate religiosa*	
9:03/12:32	Discussion of declaration on religious liberty—voting on ch. III of draft *De ecclesia*		
9:08/12:30	Discussion of declaration on religious liberty—simple vote on closing the debate— vote on ch. ch. III of draft *De ecclesia*—report on Cardinal Bea's statement regarding *De iudaeis et de non christianis*		
9:05/12:33	Final intervention on religious liberty—voting on ch. III of *De ecclesia*— first fourteen interventions on *De iudaeis*	*De iudaeis*	
9:03/12:35	Discussion of declaration *De iudaeis et de non christianis*—final vote on ch. III of *De ecclesia*		
9:03/12:28	Final intervention on *De iudaeis*—voting on draft *De ecclesia*—first intervention on the draft *De divina revelation* [On divine revelation]	*De divina revelatione*	*De oecumenismo*
9:03/12:27	Discussion of draft *De divina revelatione*: preface, ch. I and II		
9:03/12:30	Discussion of draft *De divina revelatione*: ch. I, II, III, IV, V, VI		
9:03/12:26	Discussion of draft *De divina revelatione*: ch. III, IV, V, VI—vote on ch. I on *De oecumenismo*		
9:03/12:28	End of discussion on *De divina revelatione*—voting on draft *De oecumenismo*— report on draft on the lay apostolate		
9:03/12:28	Discussion of draft on the lay apostolate—vote on draft of *De oecumenismo*, ch. II and III	*De apostolatu laicorum*	
9:00/12:21	Discussion of draft on the lay apostolate—general vote on ch. III of draft *De oecumenismo*		
9:00/12:30	Discussion of draft on the lay apostolate		
9:02/12:13	Discussion of draft on the lay apostolate—simple vote to suspend the discussion		
9:00/12:33	Three interventions on the draft *De apostolatu laicorum*—intervention in English by the auditor Patrick Keegan—discussion of proposals for *De vita et ministerio sacerdotali* [On the life and ministry of priests]	*De vita et ministerio sacerdotali*	
9:00/12:28	Discussion of proposals for *De vita et ministerio sacerdotali*		
9:00/12:26	Discussion of proposals for *De vita et ministerio sacerdotali*—beginning of discussion of proposals for *De ecclesiis orientalibus* [On eastern churches]	*De ecclesiis orientalibus*	

GC 103	10/16/1964	Byzantine	P. Achkar (Siria)	G. Hakim (Israel), Patriarch Maximos IV Saigh presiding	G. Lercaro	2092	10	-	
GC 104	10/19/1964	Roman	P. Saburo Hirata (Japan)	J. Descuffi (Turkey)	G. Lercaro	2135	14	5	
GC 105	10/20/1964	Roman	M. Arattukulam (India)	K. Wojtyła (Poland)	J. Döpfner	2191	11	2	
GC 106	10/21/1964	Romanian Byzantine (concelebrated)	S. Kocisco (USA)	B. Cristea (Romania)	J. Döpfner	2176	12	5	
GC 107	10/22/1964	Roman	J. Taylor (Sweden)	B. Printesis (Greece)	J. Döpfner	2157	15	2	
GC 108	10/23/1964	Roman	N. Elko (USA)	L. Sangaré (Mali)	J. Döpfner / L.-J. Suenens	2076	14	1	
GC 109	10/26/1964	Roman	B. Alvarez Restrepo (Colombia)	C. Alvim Pereira (Mozambique)	L.-J. Suenens	2007	18	-	
GC 110	10/27/1964	Maronite (concelebrated)	I. Ziadé (Lebanon)	A. Abed (Lebanon)	L.-J. Suenens	2042	17	-	
GC 111	10/28/1964	Roman (concelebrated)	L. Rosa (Italy)	P. Felici (Italy)	G.P. Agagianian	2077	15	-	
GC 112	10/29/1964	Roman (concelebrated)	A. Corso (Uruguay)	J. Döpfner (Germany)	G.P. Agagianian	2092	13	1	
GC 113	10/30/1964	Roman	N. Calmels (Sup. Gen. Premonstratensians)	J. Gay (Antilles)	G.P. Agagianian G. Lercaro	1929	17	2	
GC 114	11/41964	Ambrosian	C. Himmer (Belgium)	E. Forni (Italy)	G. Lercaro	2011	11	6	
GC 115	11/51964	Roman	M. Rossell y Arellano (Guatemala)	C. Kabukasanska (Zambia)	G. Lercaro	2063	9	8	
GC 116	11/61964	Ethiopian Coptic	G. J. Jacob (Ethiopia)	H. Cahsay (Ethiopia)	J. Döpfner (in presence of Paul VI)	2129	5	7	
GC 117	11/71964	Roman	J. McCarthy (Nigeria)	C. Jurgens Byrne (Peru)	J. Döpfner	1911	17	-	
GC 118	11/91964	Roman	T. Parker (Great Britain)	B. Aloisi Masella (Italy)	J. Döpfner / L.-J. Suenens	1964	15	-	
GC 119	11/101964	Roman	S. Ferrando (India)	L. Mathias (India)	L.-J. Suenens	2119	11	1	
GC 120	11/111964	Roman	S. Kovacs (Hungary)	L. Ferrand (France)	L.-J. Suenens	2109	17	1	
GC 121	11/121964	Roman	A. Bagnoli (Italy)	J. Rancans (Latvia)	L.-J. Suenens	2042	12	1	
Cap. papale	11/131964	Byzantine (concelebrated)	Maximos IV Saigh with 14 others	Paolo VI					
GC 122	11/141964	Roman	F. Seper (Yugoslavia)	G. Bukatko (Yugoslavia)	G.P. Agagianian	1963	13	7	
GC 123	11/161964	Malabar	M. Potanamuzhi (India)	S. Valloppilly (India)	G.P. Agagianian	2122	12	3	
GC 124	11/171964	Roman	A. Tranfaglia (Italy)	A. Gori (Latin Patriarch of Jerusalem)	G. Lercaro	2146	8	8	

Time	Description		
9:00/12:12	Discussion of proposals for *De ecclesiis orientalibus*	*De ecclesiis orientalibus*	*De vita et ministerio sacerdotali*
9:01/12:29	Discussion of proposals for *De ecclesiis orientalibus* and simple vote on interrupting the discussion on the draft on eastern churches—preliminary vote on draft *De vita et ministerio sacerdotali*—report and vote on ch. VII of *De ecclesia*		*De ecclesia*
9:01/12:26	Last three interventions and preliminary vote on draft *De ecclesiis orientalibus*—vote on ch. VII of *De ecclesia*—report and first intervention on draft *De ecclesia in mundo huius temporis*	*De ecclesia in mundo huius temporis*	*De ecclesiis orientalibus*
9:02/12:27	General discussion on draft *De ecclesia in mundo huius temporis*— five votes on draft *De ecclesiis orientalibus*		
9:00/12:31	General discussion on draft *De ecclesia in mundo huius temporis*— Final two votes on draft *De ecclesiis orientalibus*		*De ecclesia in mundo huius temporis*
9:00/12:30	General discussion of draft *De ecclesia in mundo huius temporis*— simple vote to interrupt the general debate—preliminary vote on draft– beginning of discussion of preface and ch. I		
9:03/12:13	Discussion of draft *De ecclesia in mundo huius temporis*: ch. I, II, and III		
9:03/12:27	Discussion of draft *De ecclesia in mundo huius temporis*: ch. II–III		
8:58/12:27	Discussion of draft *De ecclesia in mundo huius temporis*: ch. IV		
9:01/12:29	Discussion of draft *De ecclesia in mundo huius temporis*: the dignity of the human person, peace, problems concerning marriage and the family— report and vote on ch. VIII of *De ecclesia*		*De ecclesia*
9:01/12:13	Dicussion of n. 21 in draft *De ecclesia in mundo huius temporis*— simple vote to interrupt debate on n. 21 and to start discussion of n. 22—voting on *De ecclesia*		
8:58/12:25	Discussion of n. 22 and 23 of draft *De ecclesia in mundo huius temporis*— vote on *De pastorali episcoporum munere in Ecclesia*		
9:01/12:24	Simple vote to interrupt debate on n. 23 of draft *De ecclesia in mundo huius temporis*: last supplementary three interventions on the paragraph; discussion of n. 24—eight votes on ch. II of *De pastorali episcoporum munere in ecclesia*		*De pastorali episcoporum munere in ecclesia*
8:47/12:29	Speech of Paul VI on the draft on the missions— Report and discussion on the draft on the missions— voting on ch. II and III of *De pastorali episcoporum munere in Ecclesia*	*De activitate missionali ecclesiae*	
9:00/12:21	Discussion of draft *De activitate missionali ecclesiae* [On the church's missionary activity]		
9:05/12:25	Last six interventions and the end (approved by simple vote) of debate on draft on the missions—Resumption of debate on n. 24–25 of draft *De ecclesia in mundo huius temporis* (nine interventions)		
9:02/12:27	Conclusion of debate on draft *De ecclesia in mundo huius temporis*— intervention by the audit or J. Vasquez—voting on ch. I of *De oecumenismo*— report and initial discussion on the draft on religious life (1 intervention)	*De ecclesia in mundo huius temporis*	*De oecumenismo*
8:59/12:26	Discussion of draft on religious life—vote on ch. II on *De oecumenismo*	*De accomodata renovatione vitae religiosae*	
9:00/12:31	End of discussion on religious life and preliminary vote (eight interventions before the simple vote in favor of suspending debate)—report and initial debate on *De institutione sacerdotali* [On the institution of the priesthood] (four interventions)	*De institutione sacerdotali*	*De accomodata renovatione vitae religiosae*
	Feast of St. John Chrysostom—The papal tiara is given to the poor.		
8:56/12:22	Debate on the draft on priestly formation—Voting on *De oecumenismo* (ch. III) and on first fourteen propositions regarding religious life (six votes)—distribution of "Nota explicativa praevia" on ch. III of *De ecclesia*	*De institutione sacerdotali*	*De oecumenismo*
9:00/12:18	Simple vote on concluding the debate on the draft on priestly formation and the final intervention—Felici's communication of the "Nota explicativa praevia"— last three votes on the draft on religious life		*De accomodata renovatione vitae religiosae*
8:59/12:33	Last three interventions on the draft *De institutione sacerdotali*—beginning of discussion of draft on Christian education– voting on *De ecclesia*, including the "Nota explicativa praevia"—first votes on *De institutione sacerdotal*	*De educatione christiana*	*De ecclesia*

GC 125	11/18/1964	Armenian	N. Tayroyan (Iraq)	Ignace Pierre XVI Batanian (Armenian Patriarch), in presence of Paul VI	G. Lercaro	2131	9	6
GC 126	11/19/1964	Roman	C. J. Lemaire (France)	J. Ijjas (Hungary)	J. Döpfner	2145	8	6
GC 127	11/20/1964	Roman	L. Rodriguez Pardo (Bolivia)	J. Heenan (Great Britain)	J. Döpfner	2129	13	8
PS V	11/21/1964	Roman (concelebrated)	P. Felici (Italy)	Paul VI with 24 others	P. Felici (Italy)	2156	–	3

3

3. St. Peter's Basilica, September 14, 1964. The third session of the council opens, bringing in one of the approved liturgical reforms: concelebration. In fact, the opening liturgy will be the first celebrated by Paul VI along with twenty-four concelebrants from nineteen different countries symbolizing, as the pope wrote "the council as representative of the universal Church gathered in unity of mind and

Time	Description		
8:55/12:35	Mass commemorating the fiftieth anniversary of the Armenian genocide—interventions on the draft *De educatione christiana*—voting on *De ecclesia* (ch. VI, VII, VIII) and on *De institutione sacerdotali*	*De educatione christiana*	*De institutione sacerdotali*
			De ecclesia
8:59/12:44	Simple vote to conclude the discussion of *De educatione christiana* and final interventions—beginning of discussion of the draft on marriage (one intervention)—vote on entire *De ecclesia* and on *De educatione christiana*—vote on *De libertate religiosa* [On religious liberty] postponed to the fourth session		*De educatione christianachristiana*
9:00/12:51	Discussion of *De matrimonio* [On marriage], simple vote on interrupting the discussion and voting, deferring to the pope—vote on *De ecclesiis orientalibus catholicis* [On eastern Catholic chuches], *De oecumenismo* and *De ecclesiae habitudine ad religiones non christianas* [Declaration on the relation of the church with non-Christian religions]	*De matrimonio*	*De ecclesiis orientalibus*
			De oecumenismo
			De ecclesiae habitudine ad religiones non christianas
	Voting and promulgation of three documents: the dogmatic constitution *Lumen gentium*, the decree *Orientalium ecclesiarum* and the decree *Unitatis redintegratio*—Paul VI's speech to close the session		

4

will." In the photo, concelebrants around the altar. The area was expanded especially for this occasion (Archivio Fscire).

4. Paul VI, at the presidents' table, reads the account of his trip to the United Nations on October 5, 1965 (photo O. Semmelroth from *Erneuerung in Christus*).

FOURTH SESSION (September 14–December 8, 1965)

PS VI	09/14/1965	Roman (concelebrated)	Paul VI	Paul VI	P. Felici (Italy)	2245			
GC 128	09/15/1965	Roman	P. Felici (Italy)	B. Cazzaro (Chile) G. P. Agagianian		2265	8	–	-
GC 129	09/16/1965	Roman	F. Nabaa (Lebanon)	M. Callens (Tunisia)	G. P. Agagianian	2252	17	–	
GC 130	09/17/1965	Roman	C. Morcillo (Spain)	J. K. Aggey (Nigeria)	G. P. Agagianian	2114	18	–	
GC 131	09/20/1965	Roman	J. Krol (USA)	F. Torres Oliver (Puerto Rico)	G. P. Agagianian	2204	13	6	
GC 132	09/21/1965	Roman	W. Kempft (Germany)	B. Heiser (Minister Gen. OFMConv)	G. P. Agagianian / G. Lercaro	2257	9	6	
GC 133	09/22/1965	Roman	J. Le Cordier (France)	F. Ndong (Gabon)	G. Lercaro	2260	16	9	
GC 134	09/23/1965	Roman	J. Krol (USA)	A. G. Cicognani (Italy)	G. Lercaro / J. Döpfner	2229	11	7	
GC 135	09/24/1965	Roman	M. A. Yemmeru (Ethiopia)	F. Janssen (Ethiopia)	J. Döpfner	2182	12	8	
GC 136	09/27/1965	Roman	J. Attipetty (India)	S. Loosdregt (Laos)	J. Döpfner	2147	13	8	
GC 137	09/28/1965	Roman	M. Moloney (Gambia)	J. Beran (Czechoslovakia)	J. Döpfner	2161	15	–	
GC 138	09/29/1965	Roman	A. Cesarano (Italy)	L. Haller (Switzerland)	L.-J. Suenens	2190	10	7	
GC 139	09/30/1965	Roman	L. Magliacani (Arabia)	J. Martin (Burundi)	L.-J. Suenens	2177	14	5	
GC 140	10/1/1965	Syro-Antiochene	B. P. Habra (Egypt and Sudan)	A. Bakose (Iraq)	L.-J. Suenens	2128	12	4	
GC 141	10/4/1965	Roman	P. Clementino da Vlissingen (Minister Gen. OFMCap)	S. Silvestri (Italy)	L.-J. Suenens	1944	17	–	
GC 142	10/5/1965	Roman	G. A. Raballand (France)	A. Bengsch (Germany)	L.-J. Suenens	2174	16	–	
GC 143	10/6/1965	Roman	J. J. McEleney (Jamaica)	J. Chucherousset (Central African Rep.)	L.-J. Suenens	2180	12	7	
GC 144	10/7/1965	Roman	W. Cobben (Finland)	G. Bolatti (Argentina)	L.-J. Suenens / G.P. Agagianian	2147	12	7	
GC 145	10/8/1965	Alexandrian-Coptic	P. Nousseir (Egypt)	I. Ghattas (Egypt)	G. P. Agagianian	2143	12	6	
GC 146	10/11/1965	Roman	S. St. Kuijpers (Dutch Guyana)	I. Gillet (Abbot Gen., Trappists)	G. P. Agagianian	2128	11	10	
GC 147	10/12/1965	Roman	D. Liston (Mauritius)	A. Cousineau (Haiti)	G. P. Agagianian	2126	17	7	
GC 148	10/13/1965	Roman	J. Rupp (Monaco)	A. Schmitt (Southern Rhodesia)	G. Lercaro	2210	10	10	

Time	Description		
9:10....	Solemn opening of the fourth session—Speech by Paul VI. In the afternoon, a penitential procession from St. Peter's Basilica to the Lateran with a relic of the True Cross.		
9:04/12:31	Presentation and promulgation of the motu proprio *Apostolica sollicitudo*—first intervention on *De libertate religiosa*	*De libertate religiosa*	
9:02/12:29	Interventions on *De libertate religiosa*		
9:01/12:20	Interventions on *De libertate religiosa*		
9:01/12:23	Interventions on *De libertate religiosa*—six votes on *De divina revelatione*		
9:00/12:27	Four interventions on *De libertate religiosa*, simple vote to conclude the debate and voting on the draft—report and discussion of the draft *De ecclesia in mundo huius temporis* (five interventions)—five votes on *De divina rivelatione*		*De divina revelatione*
			De libertate religiosa
9:00/12:29	Four supplementary interventions on *De libertate religiosa*—general discussion of draft *De ecclesia in mundo huius temporis*—voting on *De divina rivelatione*		*De divina revelatione*
9:00/12:36	Final intervention on the draft *De ecclesia in mundo huius temporis*; voting and approval of preface—report and first six votes on the draft *De apostolatu laicorum* [On the apostolate of the laity]		*De apostolatu laicorum*
9:01/12:24	*De ecclesia in mundo huius temporis*: discussion of introduction and ch. I—voting on draft *De apostolatu laicorum*		
9:00/12:29	*De ecclesia in mundo huius temporis*: discussion of part one—final vote on draft *De apostolatu laicorum*	*De ecclesia in mundo huius temporis*	
9:00/12:20	*De ecclesia in mundo huius temporis*: discussion part one		
9:00/12:23	*De ecclesia in mundo huius temporis*: discussion of part two on marriage and family—voting on *De pastorali episcoporum munere in ecclesia*		*De pastorali episcoporum munere in ecclesia*
9:01/12:17	*De ecclesia in mundo huius temporis*: discussion of part two on marriage and family–voting on *De pastorali episcoporum munere in ecclesia*		
9:01/12:28	*De ecclesia in mundo huius temporis*: discussion of part two on marriage and culture—votes on *De pastorali episcoporum munere in ecclesia*		
9:00/12:25	*De ecclesia in mundo huius temporis*: discussion of part two on culture and socio-economic context		
9:00/13:07	*De ecclesia in mundo huius temporis*: discussion of part two on socio-economic and political context and peace. Paul VI's speech on his return from his visit to the UN		
9:02/12:28	*De ecclesia in mundo huius temporis*: discussion of part two on peace– voting on entire draft of *De pastorali episcoporum munere in ecclesia*—voting on *De accomodata renovatione vitae religiosae* [On the renewal of religious life]		*De pastorali episcoporum munere in ecclesia*
			De accomodata renovatione vitae religiosae
9:01/12:26	Final eight interventions on draft XIII—report and interventions on *De activitate missionali ecclesiae*—voting on *De accomodata renovatione vitae religiosae*	*De ecclesia in mundo huius temporis*	*De accomodata renovatione vitae religiosae*
9:02/12:28	Supplementary interventions on draft XIII—interventions on *De activitate missionali ecclesiae*—voting on *De accomodata renovatione vitae religiosae*		
9:00/12:30	Interventions on De activitate missionali ecclesiae—concluding votes on *De accomodata renovation vitae religiosae*—voting on *De institutione sacerdotali*	*De activitate missionali ecclesiae*	
9:01/12:34	Interventions on *De activitate missionali ecclesiae* and concluding debate—six votes on *De institutione sacerdotali*		*De institutione sacerdotali*
9:00/12:39	Supplemental interventions on *De activitate missionali ecclesiae*—voting on entire draft of *De institutione sacerdotali* and on *De educatione christiana*—intervention by auditor Asjakpley		*De educatione christiana*

GC 149	10/14/1965	Roman	M. Bergonzini (Italy)	P. Mazé (Polynesia)	G. Lercaro	2189	12	11
GC 150	10/15/1965	Maronite	A. Khoreiche (Lebanon)	F. Ayoub (Syria)	G. Lercaro	2122	16	4
GC 151	10/16/1965	Roman	V. Bertoli (Libya)	P. Arrupe (Sup. Gen. Jesuits)	G. Lercaro	1696	16	1
GC 152	10/25/1965	Roman	J. Colaço (P)	J. T. Suhr (Denmark)	J. Döpfner	2028	7	–
GC 153	10/26/1965	Roman (concelebrated)	J. M. Mueller (USA)	V. De Zanche (Italy), N. C. Gavilanes Chamorro (Ecuador), N. Grimley (Liberia), G. Gassongo (Congo), S. Kleiner (Abbot Gen. Cistercians)	L.-J. Suenens	2220	5	6
GC 154	10/27/1965	Roman	M. Olçomendy (Singapore)	J. Ireland (Falkland Is.)	G. P. Agagianian	2240	1	5
PS VII	10/28/1965	Roman (concelebrated)	P. Felici (Italy)	Paul VI	P. Felici (Italy)	2325	–	5
GC 155	10/29/1965	Armenian	J. Gennangi (Syria)	N. Tayroyan (Iraq)	G. Lercaro	2240	–	7
GC 156	11/9/1965	Melkite Byzantine	G. Perniciaro (Italy)	E. Youakim, Maximos IV Saigh presiding	J. Döpfner	2159	–	6
GC 157	11/10/1965	Roman	U. Murphy (South African Rep.)	A. Cicognani (Italy)	L.-J. Suenens	2228	6	11
GC 158	11/11/1965	Roman	P. Tavares (Macao)	E. Blanchet (France)	G. P. Agagianian	2204	6	10
GC 159	11/12/1965	Ukrainian Byzantine (concelebrated)	C. Sipovic (Russia)	J. Slipyj (Ukraine), N. Savaryn (Canada)	G. Lercaro	2182	–	9
GC 160	11/13/1965	Roman	C. Stella (Italy)	I. Phakoe (Basutoland)	J. Döpfner	2090	–	6
GC 161	11/15/1965	Roman	F. Cleret de Langavant (Reunion Is.)	J. Schröffer (Germany)	L.-J. Suenens	2201	–	7
GC 162	11/16/1965	Roman	E. Schlotterback (Southwest Africa)	N. Jubany Arnau (Spain)	G. P. Agagianian	2211	–	15
GC 163	11/17/1965	Roman	W. Fitzgerald(Trinidad and Tobago)	G. Tomzinski (Poland)	G. Lercaro	2262	–	11
PS VIII	11/18/1965	Roman (concelebrated)	P. Felici (Italy)	Paul VI	P. Felici (Italy)	2347	–	2
GC 164	11/19/1965	Hungarian Byzantine	P. Brezanoczy (Hungary)	N. Dudas (Hungary)	J. Döpfner	2268	–	5
GC 165	11/30/1965	Maronite (concelebrated)	J. Khoury (Lebanon)	P. Meouchi (Maronite Patriarch)	G. P. Agagianian	2241	–	10
GC 166	12/2/1965	Roman (concelebrated)	A. Creemers (Congo)	J. A. Neto (Brazil), G. Pronti (Italy), A. Fletcher (USA), T. Moreno Quintana (Peru), M. Rigaud (France), G. Garavito Jimenez (Colombia), R. Caceres (Uruguay)	G. Lercaro	2296	–	6
GC 167	12/4/1965	Roman	L. Dagaglio (Venezuela)	I. Dud (Sudan)	J. Döpfner	2246	–	12
GC 168	12/6/1965	Ruthenian Byzantine in English	M. Johnson (Canada)	N. Elko (USA)	L.-J. Suenens	2387	–	1
PS IX	12/7/1965	Roman (concelebrated)	Paul VI	Paul VI	P. Felici (Italy)	2394		
PS X	12/8/1965	Roman		Paul VI				

Time	Description		
			De educatione christiana
9:00/12:23	Start of discussion on the draft *De ministerio et vita presbyterorum* [On priestly life and ministry]—final vote on the draft *De educatione christiana*—report of Bea and initial vote on draft *De ecclesiae habitudine ad religiones non christianas*		*De ecclesiae habitudine ad religiones non christianas*
9:03/12:32	Discussion of draft *De ministerio et vita presbyterorum*—voting on draft *De ecclesiae habitudine ad religiones non christianas*		
9:00/12:26	Discussion on draft *De ministerio et vita presbyterorum*—vote on conclusion of debate and acceptance of text as basis for future work	*De ministerio et vita presbyterorum*	*De ministerio et vita presbyterorum*
9:00/11:47	Supplemental interventons on the draft *De ministerio et vita presbyterorum*—report on amendments to *De libertate religiosa*		
9:00/11:31	Supplemental interventions on the draft *De ministerio et vita presbyterorum*—six votes on *De libertate religiosa*		*De libertate religiosa*
9:01/11:17	Voting on *De libertate religiosa*—intervention by pastor T. Falls (USA) on *De ministerio et vita presbyterorum*		
	Voting and promulgation of five documents: *Christus Dominus*, *Perfectae Caritatis*, *Optatam Totius*, *Gravissimum educationis*, and *Nostra aetate*		
9:02/11:47	Reports and voting on the draft *De divina revelatione*		*De divina revelatione*
9:32/12:32	Reports and voting on *De apostolatu laicorum*—presentation and report on *De sacrarum indulgentiarum recognitione*		*De apostolatu laicorum*
9:10/12:31	Interventions on *De sacrarum indulgentiarum recognitione*—voting on entire draft *De apostolatu laicorum*—report and vote on *De activitate missionali ecclesiae*	*De sacrarum indulgentiarum recognitione*	*De activitate missionali ecclesiae*
9:30/12:25	Interventions on *De sacrarum indulgentiarum recognitione*—voting on *De activitate missionali ecclesiae*		
9:29/12:33	Reports and nine votes on *De ministerio et vita presbyterorum*		*De ministerio et vita presbyterorum*
9:30/11:20	Six votes on *De ministerio et vita presbyterorum*		
9:30/12:33	Report and seven votes on *De ecclesia in mundo huius temporis*		*De ecclesia in mundo huius temporis*
9:01/12:21	Fifteen votes on *De ecclesia in mundo huius temporis*		
9:01/11:49	Eleven votes on *De ecclesia in mundo huius temporis*		
	Voting and promulgation of two documents: *De divina revelatione* and *De apostolatu laicorum*		
9:05/11:12	Report and voting on *De libertate religiosa*		*De libertate religiosa*
9:01/12:07	Report and voting on *De activitate missionali ecclesiae*		*De activitate missionali ecclesiae*
9:00/11:36	Report and six votes on *De ministerio et vita presbyterorum*; general report on draft XIII		*De ministerio et vita presbyterorum*
9:02/11:56	Twelve votes on draft XIII		*De ecclesia in mundo huius temporis*
9:02/12:17	Final general vote on *De ecclesia in mundo huius temporis*—farewell greetings—gift of commemorative rings to council fathers		
9:00/...	Revocation of reciprocal excommunications between the Roman Catholic Church and the Orthodox Church of Constantinople—Final vote and promulgations of four documents: the declaration *Dignitatis humanae*, the decree *Ad gentes*, the decree *Presbyterorum ordinis* and the pastoral constitution *Gaudium et spes*		
10:00/...	Concluding speech by Paul VI—reading of messages from the council fathers: to rulers, to men of thought and science, to artists, to women, to the poor, sick and suffering, to workers, and to youth		

52. DESTINIES

In this section are excerpts on Vatican II by council fathers and theologians, as well as by one individual Christian, all of whom later became popes.

Albino Luciani—John Paul I (August 26–September 28, 1978)

A Day in the Life of a Council Father

During the council, Albino Luciani, later elected pope under the name John Paul I on August 26, 1978, was bishop of Vittorio Veneto, a position he had assumed in December 1958. He participated in all four sessions of the council, but never intervened in a discussion. However, he contributed a written intervention on episcopal collegiality during the 42nd General Congregation of October 7, 1963, during the debate on *De ecclesia.*

Shortly after the Mass, I take the car provided. As usual, the archbishop of Gorizia and the bishop of Padua have already been picked up, and by 8:30 we are on the steps of St. Peter's. By this time dozens of busses from all over Rome have arrived; the bishops disembark and start conversing, greeting people at the entrance—and I with them. Once inside, I stop to say a prayer at the altar of Saint Pius X; many others do the same. Down the aisle, I stop for a prayer in the transept, where the altar of Saint Joseph is located. For convenience, the Blessed Sacrament is preserved there during the days of the General Congregation, and there are already about three hundred council fathers kneeling in prayer. The confessionals are located in this part of the basilica, and by this time are busy with the council fathers. It does something to one to see a cardinal, clad in mantelletta and mozetta [garments worn by high-ranking clerics], kneeling where we usually just see the good laywomen [...].
I continue along the transept with hundreds other fathers, who, until the clock strikes nine, stop to chat in various groups as they go to their seats. The tables of the cardinals "presidents" and that of the "moderators" are still empty. However there is a small crowd before the table of the five secretaries: bishops delivering their written interventions, signing up to speak, seeking written permission to bring in guests from outside of the body of the council. It is understood that these guests will leave when the robust voice of Monsignor Felici, Secretary General, announces "Extra omnes." Then out go the guests; the Swiss Guards and the police scour the basilica to flush out any of the curious hiding there to listen in [...].
I go through the transept and another aisle until I reach the stairs that enter the back of the seats, and I arrive at my place, n. 834, the top of the fifth level, left. Some greetings and compliments to bishops and neighbors, and in a few more minutes, I sit and I enjoy the show. On my left are the doors: the bishops arrive there in waves. The central corridor between the two tiers is a swarm of red, lively and noisy, because bishops chat as they go up the aisles to their seats. On the right, I see the altar and the cardinals' places almost completely filled. And now the learned and venerable Cardinal Bea enters, stooped, with his leather bag in hand as if he were a mere schoolboy.
The organ resounds: it is a sign that we are about to begin and, in fact, while the fathers rush to their places, the bell rings and the secretary announces, "Incipit missa celebrata ab eximo domino...." A great silence falls. The celebrant begins, "In nomine Patris," and the Mass proceeds as usual; only the congregation is unusual. After Mass, following the enthronement of the Gospel, there's debate, solemn and compelling. However, this does not offset the impression that we're sitting at school desks: I have a notebook for notes, I have a printed syllabus; the small desktop can be

1. On December 27, 1958, Albino Luciani was consecrated bishop by Pope John XXIII. He was created cardinal by Paul VI in 1973 and elected pope on August 26, 1978, taking the name John Paul I.

2. On November 25, 1962, Pope John XXIII received in audience the Polish bishops who had arrived in Rome for the council. Among them was Karol Wojtyla, auxiliary bishop of Krakow. On October 16, 1978, he would be elected pope and take the name John Paul II.

raised as in school. Sometimes it happens that some passages are not easily understood, some interventions seem boring and then my pen stops, discouraged. On the other hand, sometimes I'm very interested and my pen rushes to jot the best thoughts down on paper.

Then we want to hear our neighbors' opinions. "Quid tibi videtur—What do you think?" I ask my neighbor on the left, Monsignor Quezada, the bishop of Acapulco (Mexico). And he, not without a little fear of offending charity, responds, "Mihi videtur quod iste Canat extra chorum—I think this intervention is a bit off." Later, I turn to the right: "Placet— Please?" "Ja, das ist fein—Yes, that's fine," replies Monsignor Fürstenberger. ...I put down my pen and look at the assembly. At first, they all sit motionless, but towards eleven o'clock, while continuing to follow the debate (the PA system can be heard throughout the basilica) several fathers get up and stroll the aisles..... However, I never saw Archbishop Fulton Sheen, the famous American writer and speaker, move from his place. He sits in front of me, carefully taking notes, but does not comment. Monsignor Rupp is attentive but more lively, frequently gesturing and commenting. He asked to take the floor, and we certainly were happy because he was exciting, announcing that he spoke on behalf of the whole episcopate of his nation. "We are absolutely united," he said, but it turned out that he was the bishop of Monaco and the entire national episcopate...was him!

At ten after twelve, the cardinal moderator says, "Loquatur excimus Tal dei Tali—So-and-so speaks well," and adds, "Qui erit ultimus—and will be the last." Can you believe it? One of my neighbors heaves a sigh of relief. After three hours, the council fathers also tire of speeches, however beautiful, and are happy to pick up their agendas, notebooks, and pens and get ready to go [...]. All in the assembly appreciate the speaking style of those who are not tiresome and say what they have to say clearly and briefly; few appreciate a speaker who first announces what he will say, then decides what to say, and finally comes back to repeat what he just said!

["Lettere dal Concilio: ai seminaristi di Oderzo," November 25, 1963, in *Bollettino della diocesi di Vittorio Veneto*, LI (1963), 395–398]

2

Karol Wojtyla—John Paul II (October 16, 1978–April 2, 2005)

We Must Be Called by Name

Bishop Karol Wojtyla participated in the first session at the Vatican Council, initially as an auxiliary bishop and later, from January 1964, as archbishop of Krakow, Poland.

▶ **INTERVENTIONS BY KAROL WOJTYLA DURING THE COUNCIL**

1. 14th General Assembly (November 7, 1962): intervention, chapters III and IV of schema on the liturgy
2. 24th General Assembly (November 21, 1962): intervention, schema on the sources of revelation
3. 27th General Assembly (November 26, 1962): intervention in writing, unity of the church
4. 52nd General Assembly (October 21, 1963): intervention, liturgical schema
5. 88th General Assembly (September 25, 1964): intervention, freedom of religion
6. 97th General Assembly (October 8, 1964): intervention, lay apostolate
7. 106th General Assembly (October 21, 1964): intervention, Schema XIII
8. 133rd General Assembly (September 22, 1965): intervention, declaration on religious liberty
9. 137th General Assembly (September 28, 1965): intervention, Schema XIII

When I went to the first session of the council two years ago, we all still had a very general idea of it. But even then, it appeared to be an extraordinary initiative of the unforgettable Pope John XXIII, an initiative inspired by God. We have heard this inspiration!

The first session of the council in which I participated was like a collective mapping out of the road toward the real goal. In general, we knew the expectations of the Church and of humanity, but we were trying to define more precisely and to determine concretely the central theme of the council and its proper objectives.

Last year, in the second session of the council, in which I had the grace to participate, this central theme, the critical task of the council, was unearthed. Pope John XXIII wanted a pastoral council, one to serve the salvation of souls. The Holy Father wished the council to be ecumenical, to serve the unity of Christians. Finally, he wanted a council that was universal, that would serve contemporary humanity.

In the second session of the council, we realized that in order to accomplish all these tasks, the council first had to define and formulate what is the reality of the Church. What is the Church? We answered this especially during the second session.

Today's world is so rich, so diversified, and at the same time so troubled and divided, that the Church, which is in this world, must know its essence, must discover in depth, and should know what it is and what it should serve. For this reason, the main work of the council fathers focused on the schema *De Ecclesia*.

In order to save souls, to achieve the unity of Christians, and finally, so that we who are the Church can take care of contemporary questions, we must know who we are and what we represent. We must reveal the great divine energies that dwell in us. We need to call them by name. The council does all this with the schema—and will in the future with the constitution—on the Church's teaching on the Mystical Body of Christ, the people of God, the vocation of the bishops, priests, and laity, the vocation of consecrated persons, the holiness toward which we must strive [...].

Among the work planned during the third session of the council, the schema, that is, the draft of the council declaration on the presence of the Church in the modern world, *De Ecclesia in Mundo Huius Temporis*, deserves particular attention. The title alone—"The Church in the modern world"—piques our curiosity. It seems that discussion of this issue is unprecedented in the history of the Church, especially in the history of the councils. Indeed, if the Church feels the need to define its essence, to become aware of all its energies and forces, of what it is, all this is so that it will be equal to its tasks in today's world.

My dear brothers and sisters, perhaps it is already evident, perhaps you can feel that the Church in the modern world is not marginal, does not just look outside from within at what happens in this world, at what humanity endures today. After all, the Church wants to elevate contemporary humanity out from the problems, the difficulties, and the sufferings that beset it. In fact, this is the Church's redemptive mission for every man individually and for all humanity. If the Church is Christ, the Mystical Body of Christ, and Christ is our Savior, the Redeemer of all, then based on this truth, it must discover its redemptive mission toward humanity today. We must be convinced of this mission and then—as far as possible—convince others. The Church cannot remain on the sidelines of contemporary human life. It must find its place at the heart of the problems that afflict humanity today! We must want to find this place! I confess that going into this session, I anticipate with particular trepidation the discussion of the schema *De Ecclesia in Mundo Huius Temporis* [...].

["Dalla verità sulla Chiesa deriva la sua missione redentrice. Discorso nella cattedrale del Wawel," September 10, 1964, in *Notificationes e Curia Metropolitana Cracoviensi*, (1964), 10–11, 247–251]

3. Joseph Ratzinger participated in the work of the commissions as a *peritus*. He was elected pope on April 19, 2005, and took the name Benedict XVI (Photo archive of *L'Osservatore Romano*).

3

Joseph Ratzinger—Benedict XVI (April 19, 2005–February 28, 2013)

My Council

Joseph Ratzinger participated in the Second Vatican Council as a *peritus* of Cardinal Josef Frings, archbishop of Cologne. Professor of fundamental theology at age thirty-one, he taught on the ordinary Catholic faculty at the University of Bonn from 1959 to 1963 and from 1963 to 1966 at Münster, where he taught dogmatic theology and history of dogma.

At the time of the council, I was a young professor at the University of Bonn, near Cologne. The archbishop responsible for this university was Cardinal Frings. I gave a lecture on the theology of the council before the cardinal, who very much appreciated it, and he invited me to accompany him. Previously, Frings had given a speech in Genoa, at the invitation of Cardinal Siri, about the issues to be discussed in the council. This conference, which perhaps could appear to be both a little unrevolutionary but certainly a little bold, was very much liked by Pope John, who, embracing Frings, said, "These were my very intentions when I called for the council."
Seeing the living Church, with three thousand bishops pres-

ent, is an exceptional experience: rarely in history can you see it, touch it in its universality, and share in a moment of great accomplishment.
I lived with the cardinal in the Collegio dell'Anima in the via della Pace: the Austrian atmosphere was nice. The cardinal met all the German-speaking bishops in the hall of the college, and I was instructed to organize their conference and introduce the whole German-speaking episcopate to the work of the council. For a young professor—I was only thirty-two and had just started teaching at the university—it was really impressive, but in a sense it weighed heavily on me: the burden of mapping the road that the German bishops would take was largely on my shoulders. On one hand, I was filled with great joy to actually participate in the work of the council, but on the other, I felt a great responsibility before God and before history. The council was for me, personally, a historical event: I was with so many people I had previously known only through books.
For a young professor who had lived until then in academia, Roman life was a whole new reality. In the Collegio dell'Anima I could see the world, hear the sounds of old Rome, go to coffee with others and learn about Roman life. It was so different from the university, and it made a great impression that marked my life […].
I was in the grandstand where the *periti* sat so I could follow the work of the council. However, for the first two months I was not an official *peritus*, just a private *peritus* for the cardinal. The pope appointed me only in November, and then I attended all the meetings in an official capacity. At first, I could participate in the work, but not regularly in all meetings. These meetings were great events, with all the *periti,* great personalities whom I previously only knew through study: Henri de Lubac, Jean Daniélou (1905–1974), Yves Congar (1904–1995), Marie-Dominique Chenu (1895–1990) and other big names. It was amazing to meet these revered men; they were people I had admired. It was also great to see representatives of other churches and Christian denominations; and then, of course, the pope himself […].
In my official position, I witnessed many historic moments, but I will never forget that famous evening, lit by torchlight and the moon, when the Holy Father said to the mothers present "Kiss your children, and tell them it's from the pope."

[J. Ratzinger, "Vi racconto il mio Concilio," in *Reset*, (2005), 89, 18–20]

J. Ratzinger, The Issue of So-called "Nota praevia"

I believe this expression is further strengthened if you take the so-called *Nota praevia Explicativa*, which, as is well known, gave a bitter taste to the final days of the third session of the council that had been filled previously with daring hopes. We would digress too far if we were to do an exact analysis here, as this text is very complicated. The result—to which we have to limit ourselves—does not create a substantially new situation, but in principle, the dialectic remains the same, resulting in ambiguity regarding the actual competence of the college of bishops, which is already inherent in the same conciliar text. Undoubtedly, this dialectic is further aggravated in favor of primacy. But for every statement that pushes this trend, the text makes another statement alongside and restores balance, which makes it possible to interpret it either more in a "primatial" sense or more toward the principle of collegiality. Therefore, you may very well speak of a certain disharmony intrinsic to the text of the *Nota*, reflecting the lack of agreement among those who have worked and attempted to reconcile the contradictory trends. If the text gives the impression of disharmony, this is a sign that full harmonization was not successful and not even possible.

The task that the council bequeaths looks surprisingly light in the gloom of the *Nota praevia Explicativa*. On the one hand, we face an idea that starts with all of Christian tradition, and according to it tries to describe the breadth of ecclesial possibilities; on the other, we have purely systematic thought that admits only the present legal status of the Church as the norm of its reflections and therefore must fear every move beyond it. This conservatism is based on its strangeness to history and, at its base, a lack of tradition that is opening up for the whole of Christian history. It is important to realize this, because it allows a view of the intrinsic form of contrasting trends present in the council, falsely described as opposition of liberals and conservatives. More rightly, one could speak of opposition between historical thought and systematic thought. For "progressives" (at least for the bulk of them) it was just the "tradition," the return to the breadth and richness of the Christian tradition, where at the same time they were the rules of renewal that enabled them to be bold and wide, according to its intrinsic width of the Church.

Returning to the *Nota praevia*. We have said that these statements have not created a new situation substantially against the conciliar text. The same result appears, even considering only the legal value. On the one hand, it is placed as the normative, valid interpretation, but the other was not accepted in the same conciliar text, so it was not even duly signed by the pope and the council fathers, but only by General Secretary Felici. We then need to say that attributing to this *Nota* the taste of bitterness, is not due to its content, but rather the circumstances surrounding its appearance.

[J. Ratzinger, *Problemi e risultati del concilio Vaticano II*, Queriniana, Brescia 1967, 64–67]

4. Jorge Mario Bergoglio, elected pope with the name Francis on March 13, 2013, after the resignation of Pope Benedict XVI (Archival photograph from *L'Osservatore Romano*).

4

us.…Today we all seem to be glad for the presence of the Holy Spirit, but it is not true. This temptation is still with us today. For just one example, think of the council. The council is a beautiful work of the Holy Spirit. Think of Pope John, such a good pastor and so obedient to the Holy Spirit. But after fifty years, have we done everything the Holy Spirit inspired in the council? Have we continued the growth of the Church since the council? No. We celebrate this anniversary, we erect a monument, but we do not want to change. What's more, there are rumors that some want to go back. This is called stubbornness, this is called wanting to tame the Holy Spirit, this is being fools and slow of heart.

[Pope Francis, "Concilio, opera dello Spirito Santo, ma c'è chi vuole andare indietro. Messa dedicata a Benedetto XVI," Vatican Radio, April 16, 2013]

Jorge Mario Bergoglio—Francis (March 13, 2013–)

The Council, a Work of the Holy Spirit

During the years of the council, Bergoglio was a novice of the Society of Jesus (he was ordained a priest on December 13, 1969). He had entered the archdiocesan seminary in Villa Devoto in Buenos Aires in 1957 but left to enter the Jesuits and started his novitiate on March 11, 1958. From 1964–1965, he taught literature and psychology in the Colegio de la Inmaculada Concepción in Santa Fe and in 1965–1966 in the Colegio del Salvador in Buenos Aires.

Even Jesus rebukes the disciples of Emmaus: "Oh, how foolish you are, and how slow of heart to believe all that the prophets have declared!" Still, even among us, there is that resistance to the Holy Spirit. To say it clearly: the Holy Spirit makes us uncomfortable because it moves us, makes us walk, impels the Church to move forward. And we are like Peter at the Transfiguration: "Lord, it is good for us to be here" …but that does not bother us. We want to tame the Holy Spirit. And that's wrong because he is God; he is the wind that comes and goes and you do not know where. It is the power of God that gives us the consolation and strength to go on. This bothers

LIST OF VATICAN II DOCUMENTS

Conciliorum oecumenicorum generaliumque decreta, ed. G. Alberigo-A. Melloni, 3, Turnhout, 2010

MESSAGE TO THE WORLD FROM THE COUNCIL FATHERS	October 20, 1962
CONSTITUTION ON THE SACRED LITURGY, *SACROSANCTUM CONCILIUM*	December 4, 1963
DECREE ON MEANS OF SOCIAL COMMUNICATION, *INTER MIRIFICA*	December 4, 1963
DOGMATIC CONSTITUTION ON THE CHURCH, *LUMEN GENTIUM*	November 21, 1964
DECREE ON ECUMENISM, *UNITATIS REDINTEGRATIO*	November 21, 1964
DECREE ON EASTERN CATHOLIC CHURCHES, *ORIENTALIUM ECCLESIARUM*	November 21, 1964
DECLARATION ON CHRISTIAN EDUCATION, *GRAVISSIMUM EDUCATIONIS*	October 28, 1965
DECLARATION ON THE RELATIONSHIP OF THE CHURCH TO NON-CHRISTIAN RELIGIONS, *NOSTRA AETATE*	October 28, 1965
DECREE ON PRIESTLY FORMATION, *OPTATAM TOTIUS*	October 28, 1965
DECREE ON THE RENEWAL OF RELIGIOUS LIFE, *PERFECTAE CARITATIS*	October 28, 1965
DECREE ON THE PASTORAL OFFICE OF BISHOPS, *CHRISTUS DOMINUS*	October 28, 1965
DOGMATIC CONSTITUTION ON DIVINE REVELATION, *DEI VERBUM*	November 18, 1965
DECREE ON THE APOSTOLATE OF THE LAITY, *APOSTOLICAM ACTUOSITATEM*	November 18, 1965
DECLARATION ON RELIGIOUS LIBERTY, *DIGNITATIS HUMANAE*	December 7, 1965
DECREE ON THE MISSIONARY ACTIVITY OF THE CHURCH, *AD GENTES*	December 7, 1965
DECREE ON THE LIFE AND MINISTRY OF PRIESTS, *PRESBYTERORUM ORDINIS*	December 7, 1965
PASTORAL CONSTITUTION ON THE CHURCH IN THE MODERN WORLD, *GAUDIUM ET SPES*	December 7, 1965
APPROVAL OF THE LIFTING OF THE MUTUAL EXCOMMUNICATIONS BETWEEN ROME AND CONSTANTINOPLE	December 7, 1965
MESSAGES ON BEHALF OF THE COUNCIL TO RULERS, TO INTELLECTUALS AND SCIENTISTS, TO ARTISTS, TO WOMEN, TO THE POOR, SICK AND SUFFERING, TO WORKERS, AND TO YOUTH	December 8, 1965

LIST OF COUNCIL FATHERS

Each council father's name is followed by indication of his ecclesiastical rank, nationality, and the periods of the council in which he participated. RA: Resident Archbishop; TA: Titular Archbishop; TB: Titular Bishop; RB: Resident Bishop; PN: Prelate Nullius; AP: Apostolic Prefect; AA: Apostolic Administrator; SG: Superior General

A

Abascal y Salmerón Emilio, TB Abziri and Aux. Puebla de los Ángeles Puebla (Mexico)—II, IV

Abasolo y Lecue John Ambrose OCD, RB Vijayapuram (India)—I, II, III, IV

Abed Antoine, RA Tripoli of Maronites (Lebanon)—I, II, III, IV

Ablewicz Jerzy Karol, RB Tarnów (Poland)—I, IV

Abou-Saada Gabriel, TA Cesarea in Palestine (Jordan)—I, II

Abraha François, RB Asmara (Ethiopia)—I, II, III, IV

Absolem McCabe Thomas, RB Wollongong (Australia)—I, II, III, IV

Acciari Florido, RA Rodi (Greece)—I, II, III, IV

Ach-Chaer Athanase, RB Bāniyās (Lebanon)—I, II, III, IV

Achkar Paul, RA Lattaquié (Syria)—I, II, III, IV

Ackerman Richard, RB Covington (USA)—I, II, III, IV

Adam François-Nestor, RB Sion (Switzerland)—I, II, III, IV

Adam Jean, RA Libreville (Gabon)—I, II, III, IV

Addazi Reginaldo, RA Trani e Barletta (Italy)—I, II, III, IV

Adem Gennadios, SG Order of dell'Ordine Antoniano Aleppino dei Maroniti—II, III, IV

Adrover Julià, SG Theatines—I, II, III

Agagianian Grégoire-Pierre XV [Krikor Bedros XV] card., pref. Congr. Propaganda of the Faith—I, II, III, IV

Agboka Lucien, RA Abomey (Benin)—I, II, III, IV

Aggey John, RA Lagos (Nigeria)—I, II, III, IV

Aglialoro Filippo, TB Germa di Galazia (Italy)—I, II, III, IV

Agniswami Thomas Roch, RB Kottar (India)—I, II, III, IV

Agnozzi Nicola, TB Adramitto (Zambia)—I, III, IV

Aguilera Narbona Pedro, RB Iquique (Chile)—I, II, III, IV

Aguirre Antonio, RB San Isidro (Argentina)—I, II, III, IV

Aguirre Garcia Lino, RB Culiacán (Mexico)—I

Agustin Rémy, TB Turuzi (Haiti)—I, II, III, IV

Ahern John, RB Cloyne (Ireland)—I, II, III, IV

Ahr George, RB Trenton (USA)—I, II, III, IV

Alapatt George, RB Trichur (India)—I, II, III, IV

Alaupovič Marko, RA Vrhbosna (Yugoslavia)—I, II, III, IV

Alba Palacios José, RB Tehuantepec (Mexico)—I, II, III, IV

Albanese Adelchi, RA Viterbo (Italy)—I

Albareda y Ramoneda Joaquín Anselmo María OSB, card. prefect, Vatican Library—I, II, III, IV

Alberione Giacomo, SG Society of St. Paul—I, II, III, IV

Albers Antoine, RB Malang (Indonesia)—I, II, III, IV

Albers Joseph, RB Lansing (USA)—I

Alberti Romeu, RB Apucarana (Brazil)—III, IV

Alberto y Valderrama Teopisto, RA Caceres (Philippines)—III, IV

Alcaraz y Figueroa Estanislao, RB Matamoros (Mexico)—I, II, IV

Alcedo Otoniel, RB Ayacucho (Peru)—I, II, IV

Alcini Ilario, TA Nicea (Italy)—I, II, III, IV

Aldegunde Dorrego Francisco, RA Tanger (Morocco)—I, II, III, IV

Alfrink Bernard Jan card., RA Utrecht (The Netherlands)—I, II, III, IV

Alibrandi Gaetano, TA Binda (Lebanon)—II, III, IV

Alix Bernard, TB Mediana (France)—IV

Allen Francis, TB Avensa (Canada)—I, II, III, IV

Allorio Carlo, RB Pavia (Italy)—I, II, III, IV

Almarcegui Angelus de la Virgen de Valentuñana, SG Augustinian Recollects—I, II, III, IV

Almarcha Hernández Luis, RB León (Spain)—I, II, III, IV

Almeida de Andrade Climerio, RB Vitória da Conquista (Brazil)—II, III, IV

Almeida y Merino Adalberto, RB Zacatecas (Mexico)—I, II, III, IV

Almeida Trindade Manuel, RB Aveiro (Portugal)—I, II, III, IV

Almici Giuseppe, RB Alessandria (Italy)—I, II, III, IV

Aloisi Masella Benedetto card., RB Palestrina (Italy), pref. Congr. for the Discipline of the Sacraments—I, II, III, IV

Alonso Aparicio Gregório, TB Pogla (Brazil)—I, II, IV

Altamirano y Bulnes Luis María, RA Morelia (Mexico)—IV

Alter Karl, RA Cincinnati (USA)—I, II, III

Altomare Umberto, RB Muro Lucano (Italy)—I, II, III, IV

Alvarez Diaz Alquilio, PN Marajó (Brazil)—IV

Alvarez Eduardo, TB Tabunia (El Salvador)—IV

Alvarez Lara Rafael, RB Mallorca (Spain)—I, II, III, IV

Alvarez Macua José, TB Colibrasso (Brazil)—I, II, III, IV

Alvarez Restrepo Baltasar, RB Pereira (Colombia)—I, II, III, IV

Alvarez Tena Vittorino, RB Apatzingan (Mexico)—I, II, III, IV

Alves Acácio Rodrigues, RB Palmares (Brazil)—I, II, III, IV

Alves De Pinho Moisés, RA Luanda São Tomé (Angola)—I, II, III, IV

Alves de Siqueira Antônio, TA Calcide di Syria (Brazil)—I, II, III, IV

Alves Trindade José, RB Montes Claros (Brazil)—I, II, III, IV

Alvim Pereira Custódio, RA Lourenço Marques (Mozambique)—I, II, III, IV

Amadouni Garabed, TB Amathus in Cypro (France)—I, II, III, IV

Ambrosi Giacinto, TA Anchialo (Italy)—I, II

Amici Giuseppe, RA Modena (Italy)—I, II, III, IV

Amissah John Kodwo, RA Cape Coast (Ghana)—I, II, III, IV

Ammann Joachim, TB Petnelisso (Germany)—I, II, III, IV

Anasagasti Zulueta Carlos, TB Caltadria (Bolivia)—I, II, III, IV

Anastasio del SS. Rosario, SG Carmelitani Scalzi—I, II, III, IV

Anaya y Diez de Bonilla José, RB Zamora (Mexico)—I, II, III, IV

Ancel Alfred-Jean-Félix, TB Myrina (France)—I, II, III, IV

Angelelli Carletti Enrique, TB Lystra (Argentina)—I, III, IV

Angeleri Carlo, TB Ptolemais in Libya (Italy)—I, II, III, IV

Angelini Fiorenzo, TB Messene (Italy)—I, II, III, IV

Angerhausen Julius, TB Eminentiana (Germany)—I, II, III, IV

Angioni Antonio, TB Hippo Diarrhytus (Italy)—I, II, III, IV

Anglim Mário Roberto Emmett, PN Coari (Brazil)—I, II, III, IV

Angrisani Giuseppe, RB Casale Monferrato (Italy)—I, II, III, IV

Angulo del Valle y Navarro José, RB Tabasco (Mexico)—I, II

Añoveros Ataún Antonio, RB Cadiz y Ceuta (Spain)—I, II, III, IV

Antezana y Rojas Abel, RA La Paz (Bolivia)—I, II, III, IV

Antiporda Hernando, TB Edessa in Macedonia (Philippines)—I

Antoniutti Ildebrando card. prefect Congregation for Religious—I, II, III, IV

Anyogu John, RB Enugu (Nigeria)—I, II, III

Aparicio y Quintanilla Pedro, RB San Vicente (El Salvador)—I, II, III, IV

Apcar John, RB Ispahan (Iran)—I, II

Aponte Martínez Luis, RA S. Juan de Puerto Rico (Puerto Rico)—I, III, IV

Arai Lucas Katsusaburo, RB Yokohama (Japan)—I, II, III, IV

Aramburu Juan Carlos, RA Tucumán (Argentina)—I, II, III, IV

Arámburu Urquiola Zenón SJ, RB Wuhu (China)—I

Arango Henao Bernardo, RB Barranca Bermeja (Colombia)—I, II, III, IV

Arango Velasquez José, AP Guapí (Colombia)—II, III, IV

Arattukulam Michael, RB Aleppey (India)—I, II, III, IV

Arbulú Pineda Ignacio, RB Huánuco (Peru)—I, II

Arcaira Leopoldo, TB Acrassus (Philippines)—I

Arce Mostajo Augustin, TB Philadelphia in Lydia (Bolivia)—I

Arcilla Arnulfo, RB Sorsogón (Philippines)—I, II, III, IV

Arduino Michele, RB Gerace-Locri (Italy)—I, II, III, IV

Argaya Goicoechea Jacinto, RB Mondoñedo-Ferrol (Spain)—I, II, III, IV

Arinze Francis, TB Fissiana (Nigeria)—IV

Ariola Flaviano, RB Legazpi (Philippines)—I, II, III, IV

Ariz Huarte Javier, TB Bapara (Peru)—I, II, III, IV

Arkfeld Leo, TB Bucellus (New Guinea)—I, II, III, IV

Armas Lerana Florentius, PN Chota (Peru)—II, III, IV

Arnaud Jean, TB Tentyris (Laos)—I, II, IV

Arnerič Josip, RB Šibenik (Yugoslavia)—I, II, III, IV

Arntz Pierre, RB Bandung (Indonesia)—I, II, III

Arrieta Villalobos Roman, RB Tilaran (Costa Rica)—I, II, III, IV

Arroyo Ignacio Lehonor, RB Tuxpan (Mexico)—II, III, IV

Arroyo Valeriano, TB Gomphi (Peru)—I, II, III, IV

Arrupe Pedro, SG Society of Jesus—IV

Artazcor Lizarrage Gennaro, AA El Petén (Guatemala)

Arteaga Yepes Alonso, RB Ipiales (Colombia)—II, III, IV

Arthurs Eugen, RB Tanga (Tanzania)—I, II, III, IV

Arulswami Daniel, RB Kumbakonam (India)—I, II, III, IV

Ashby Brian Patrick, RB Christchurch (New Zealand)—III, IV

Assaf Michel, RA Petra e Filadelfia (Jordan)—I, II

Asta Salvatore, TA Aureliopolis in Lydia (Iran)—III, IV

Athaide Dominic, RA Agra (India)—I, II, III, IV

Atkielski Roman, TB Stobi (USA)—I

Attipetty Joseph, RA Verapoly (India)—I, II, III, IV

Atton Alfred, RB Langres (France)—I, II, III, IV

Audet Lionel, TB Thibaris (Canada)—I, IV

Audet René, TB Chonochora (Canada)—III, IV

Audrain Henri, RA Auch (France)—I, II, III, IV

Aufderbeck Hugo, TB Arca in Phoenicia (Germany)—II, III, IV

Aurrecoechea Palacios Miguel, TB Doliche (Venezuela)—I, II, III, IV

Austregésilo de Mesquita Francisco, RB Afogados da Ingàzeira (Brazil)—I, II, III, IV

Ayala y Ayala Rafael, RB Tehuacán (Mexico)—II, III, IV

Ayoub François, RA Alep of Maronites (Syria)—I, II, III, IV

Azcárate de Andrade Fernando, TB Cefala (Cuba)—III, IV

Azzolini Augusto, RB Makeni (Sierra Leone)—I, II, III, IV

B

Baaken Heinrich, TB Gordo (Germany)—I, II, III, IV

Babcock Allen, RB Grand Rapids (USA)—I, II, III, IV

Babini Paolo, RB Forlì (Italy)—I, II, III, IV

Bacci Antonio, TA Colonia in Cappadocia; cardinal-deacon Saint'Eugenio (Italy)—I, II, III, IV

Baccino Luis, RB San José de Mayo (Uruguay)—I, II, III, IV

Bacile Pasquale, RB Acireale (Italy)—I, II, III, IV

Badré Jean, TB Aquae Novae in Proconsulari (France)—III, IV

Baeten Jozef, TA Stauropolis (Netherlands)—I

Bafile Corrado, TA Antiochia in Pisidia (Germany)—I, II, III, IV

Baggio Sebastiano, TA Ephesus (Brazil)—I, II, III, IV

Bagnoli Antonio, RB Fiesole (Italy)—I, II, III, IV

Bakache Joseph, TA Edessa in Osrhoëne dei Siri (UAR-Egypt)—I

Bakose Athanase, RA Baghdad (Syrian) (Iraq)—I, II, III, IV

Balaguer Miguel, TB Castellum Minus (Uruguay)—II, III, IV

Balconi Lorenzo, TA Hierapolis in Phrygia (Italy)—I, II

Baldassarri Salvatore, RA Ravenna (Italy)—I, II, III, IV

Baldelli Ferdinando, TB Aperlae (Italy)—I

Baldini Carlo, RB Chiusi e Pienza (Italy)—I, II, III, IV

Baldini Faustino, RB Massa Marittima (Italy)—I, II, III, IV

Baldwin Vincent, TB Bencenna (USA)—I, II, III, IV

Bampi Candido, TB Tlos (Brazil)—I, II, III, IV

Bandini Carlo, RB Sarsina (Italy)—I, II, III, IV

Bánk Jozsef, TB Materiana (Hungary)—IV

Bannwarth Gérard, RB Soissons (France)—II, III, IV

Bantigue y Natividad Pedro, TB Catula (Philippines)—III

Baraniak Antoni, RA Pozna (Poland)—I, II, III, IV

Baranzini Ettore, RA Siracusa (Italy)—I, II

Baratta Raffaele, RA Perugia (Italy)—I, II, III, IV

Barbado y Viejo Francisco, RB Salamanca (Spain)—I, II

Barbero Luigi, RB Vigevano (Italy)—I, II, III, IV

Barbetta Giulio, TB Pharan (Italy)—I, II, III, IV

Barbieri Antonio card., RA Montevideo (Uruguay)—I, IV

Barbieri Ezio, RB Città della Pieve (Italy)—I, II, III, IV

Barbieri Raffaele, RB Cassano all'Ionio (Italy)—I, II, III, IV

Barbisotti Angelo, TB Caunus (Ecuador)—I, II, III, IV

Barbosa Aguiar Otávio, RB Palmeira dos Indios (Brazil)—I, II, III, IV

Barbosa Antonio, RB Campo Grande (Brazil)—I, II, III, IV

Barda Franciszek, RB Przemyśl (Poland)—I

Barela Stefan, RB Czestochowa (Poland)—II, III, IV

Barneschi Attilio, RB Manzini (Swaziland)—I, II, III

Barni Julián, TB Coracesium (Nicaragua)—II, III, IV

Baroncelli Emilio, RB Recanati (Italy)—I, II, III, IV

Baroni Agostino, TB Balecium (Sudan)—I, II

Baroni Gilberto, RB Reggio Emilia (Italy)—I, II, III, IV

Barrachina Estevan Pablo, RB Orihuela-Alicante (Spain)—I, II, III, IV

Barrera y Reyes Benjamin, RB Santa Ana (El Salvador)—I

Barthe Gilles, RB Fréjus-Toulon (France)—I, II, III, IV

Bartholome Peter, RB Saint Cloude (USA)—I, III, IV

Bartoletti Enrico, TB Mindo (Italy) –I, II, III, IV

Bascuñana Llópez José, RB Solsona (Spain)—I, II, III, IV

Basoli Lorenzo, RB Ogliastra (Italy)—I, II, III, IV

Bassi Assuero Teofano SX, RB Loyang (China)—I, II, III, IV

Bassoul Jean, RA Homs of Melkites (Syria)—I, II, III, IV

Batanian Ignace Pierre XVI, P Cilicia of the Armenians (Lebanon)—I, II, III, IV

Battaglia Giuseppe, RB Faenza (Italy)—I, II, III, IV

Battaglierin Dante, RB Khulna (Pakistan)—I, II, III, IV

Battistelli Stanislao, RB Teramo-Atri (Italy)—I, II, III, IV

Baud Alphonse, RB Berbérati (Central African Republic)—I, II, III, IV

Baud Joseph, RB Visakhapatnam (India)—I, II, IV

Baudoux Maurice, RA Saint Boniface (Canada)—I, II, III, IV

Bäuerlein Stjepan, RB Bosna (Djakovo)-Srijem (Yugoslavia)—I, II, III, IV
Baumgartner William, RB Agaña (Micronesia)—I, II, III, IV
Bayan Raphael, RB Iskanderiya (URA-Egypt)—I, II, III, IV
Bayet Claudius, TB Cidyessus (Thailand)—I, II, III, IV
Bazin Victor MEP, RA Rangoon (Burma)—I, II, III
Bea Augustin SJ, card. president of the Secretariat for Christian Unity—I, II, III, IV
Beccaro Felice, RB San Miniato (Italy)—I, II, III, IV
Beck George, RA Liverpool (Great Britain)—I, II, III, IV
Beckmann Francisco, RA Panamà (Panama)—I, II
Bednorz Herbert, TB Bulla Regia (Poland)—I, II, III, IV
Beel Hendrik, TB Sucarda (Netherlands)—IV
Begin Floyd, RB Oakland (USA)—I, II, III, IV
Beitia Aldazabal Eugenio, TB Verrona (Spain)—I, II, III, IV
Béjot Georges, TB Cassandria (France)—I, II, III, IV
Beize Bogdan, TB Idassa (Poland)—III, IV
Bekkers Willem, RB s'Hertogenbosch (The Netherlands)—I, II, III, IV
Bélanger Valérien, TB Cyrene (Canada)—I, II, III, IV
Bell Alden John, RB Sacramento (USA)—I, II, III, IV
Belleau Henri, TB Perrhe (Canada)—I, II
Bellec Joël, RB Perpignan (France)—I, II, III, IV
Bello Stéphane, RB Alep dei Caldei (Syria)—I, II, III, IV
Bellotti Luigi, TA Voncariana (Nigeria)—III, IV
Beltrami Giuseppe, TA Damascus (Netherlands)—II, III, IV
Beltramino Attilio, RB Iringa (Tanzania)—I, II
Beltritti Giacomo, TB Cana (Palestine)—IV
Benavent Escuín Emilio, TB Cercina (Spain)—I, III
Benavides Morriberón José, RB Chachapoyas (Peru)—II, III, IV
Benedetti Cesar, TB Tiddi (Bolivia)—I, III, IV
Benedetti Tarcisio, RB Lodi (Italy)—I, II, III, IV
Bengsch Alfred, RA Berlino (Germany)—I, II, III, IV
Benincasa Pius, TB Buruni (USA)—III, IV
Benitez Avalos Felipe, RB Villarica (Paraguay)—I, II, III, IV
Benítez Fontúrvel Crispulo, RB Barquisimeto (Venezuela)—I, II, IV
Benjamin Eric, RB Darieeling (India)—I, II, III, IV
Benni Cyrille, RA Mossul (Syrian) (Iraq)—I, II, III, IV
Bentivoglio Guido, RA Catania (Italy)—I, II, III, IV
Beovich Matthew, RA Adelaide (Australia)—I, II, III, IV
Beran Josef, RA Praga (Czechoslovakia)—IV
Beras Rojas Octavio, RA Santo Domingo (Dominican Republic)—I, II, III
Bereciartúa y Balerdi Lorenzo, RB San Sebastián (Spain)—I, III, IV
Berenguer Prado Jackson, RB Feira de Santana (Brazil)—I, III, IV
Beretta Alfoso, RB Warangal (India)—I, II, III, IV
Bergamaschi Antonio, RB Montefeltro (Italy)—I, II, III, IV
Bergamin Raimondo, RB Padang (Indonesia)—I, II, III, IV
Bergan Gerald, RA Omaha (USA)—I, II, IV
Bergonzini Marino, RB Volterra (Italy)—I, II, III, IV
Berlier Hippolyte, RB Niamey (Niger)—I, II, III, IV
Bernacki Lucjan, TB Mela (Poland)—I
Bernal Ortiz Juan, RA Los Toques (Venezuela)—I, II, III, IV
Bernard Michel, TA Arae in Mauretania (France)—I, II, III, IV
Bernarding George Elmer, TB Belabitene (New Guinea)—I, II, III, IV
Bernasconi Giovanni, SG Barnabites—III, IV
Bernier Paul, RA Gaspé (Canada)—I, II, III
Berry Joseph, RA Halifax (Canada)—I, II, III
Bertazzoni Augusto, RA Potenza e Marsico Nuovo (Italy)—I, II, III, IV
Berti Leonello, TB Germanicopolis (Laos)—I, II, III, IV
Bertoglio Francesco, TB Paros (Italy)—I, II, III, IV
Bertoli Paolo, TA Nicomedia (France)—I, II, III, IV
Bertoli Vitale Bonifacio, TB Attaea (Libya)—I, II, III, IV
Bertrand Gerard, RB Navrongo (Ghana)—I, II, III, IV
Bessone Lawrence, RB Meru (Kenya)—I, II, III, IV
Bettazzi Luigi, TB Tagaste (Italy)—II, III, IV
Bézac Robert, RB Aire (France)—I, II, III, IV
Bezerra Coutinho José, RB Estância (Brazil)—I, II, III, IV
Bezmalinovič Celestin, TB Hadrumetum (Yugoslavia)—I, II, III, IV
Biancheri Emilio, RB Rimini (Italy)—I, II, III, IV
Bianchi Giovanni, TB Seleuciana (Italy)—III, IV
Bianchi Lorenzo PIME, RB Hong Kong (China)—I, II, III, IV
Bianconi Giulio, RB Tarquinia-Civitavecchia (Italy)—I, II, III, IV
Biard George, RB Mopti (Mali)—IV
Bidawid Raphaël, RB Amadiyah (Iraq)—I, II, III, IV
Bieniek Juliusz, TB Dascylium (Poland)—III
Bigirumwani Louis, RB Nyundo (Rwanda)—I, III, IV
Bignamini Egidio, RA Ancona (Italy)—I, II, III, IV
Bihonda Nestor, TB Siminina (Burundi)—IV
Bilgeri Joseph, RB Eshowe (South Africa)—I, II, III, IV
Billington Vincent, TB Fallaba (Great Britain)—I, II, III, IV
Binaschi Gaudenzio, RB Pinerolo (Italy)—I, II, III
Binni Adolfo, RB Nola (Italy)—I, II, III, IV
Binz Leo, RA Saint Paul (USA)—I, II, III, IV
Birch Peter, RB Ossory (Ireland)—II, III, IV
Biskup George, RB Des Moines (USA)—I, II, III, IV
Black James, RB Paisley (Great Britain)—I, II, III, IV
Blais Léo, TB Hieron (Canada)—III, IV
Blanchet Conrad, SG Missionaries of Our Lady of La Sallette—III, IV
Blanchet Emile-Arsène, TA Philippopolis in Thracia (France)—I, II, III, IV
Blanchet Maturino, RB Aosta (Italy)—I, II, III, IV
Blanchette Romeo Roy, TB Maxita (USA)—IV
Blanchoud Moises, RB Rio Quarto (Argentina)—I, II, III, IV
Blanquet du Chayla Armand, RA Bagdad (Iraq)—I
Bliestle Heinrich, SG Missionaries of the Holy Family—I, II, III, IV
Blomjous Joseph, RB Mwanza (Tanzania)—I, II, III, IV
Bluyssen Johannes Willem, TB Aëtus (The Netherlands)—I, II, III, IV
Boardman John, TB Gunela (USA)—I, II, III, IV
Boccadoro Luigi, RB Montefiascone e Acquapendente (Italy)—I, II, III, IV
Boccella Giovanni, SG Third Order of St. Francis—I, II, III
Boeris Giuseppe, SG Somaschans—II, III, IV
Bodewes Martin, PA Bangassou (Central African Republic)—II
Boerkamp John, PA Kashmir-Jammu (India)—II, III, IV
Bogarín Argaña Ramón, RB S. Juan B. de las Misiones (Paraguay)—I, II, III, IV
Boghaert Arnold, RB Roseau (Trinidad and Tobago)—I, II, III, IV
Boiardi Carlo, RB Apuania (Italy)—I, II, III, IV
Boilleau George, TB Ausuccura (USA)—III
Boillon Pierre, RB Verdun (France)—I, II, III, IV
Boisguérin René-Desiré-Romain MEP, RB Suifu (China)—I, II, III, IV
Bokenfohr John, RB Kimberley (South Africa)—I, II, III, IV
Boland Thomas, RA Newark (USA)—I, II, III, IV
Bolaños Quesada Enrique, TB Andropolis (Costa Rica)—II, IV
Bolatti Guillermo, RA Rosario (Argentina)—I, II, III, IV
Bolognini Danio, RB Cremona (Italy)—I, II, III, IV
Bolte Adolf, RB Fulda (Germany)—I, II, III, IV
Bona Stanislaus Vincent, RB Green Bay (USA)—II
Bonacini Giuseppe, RB Bertinoro (Italy)—I, II, III, IV
Bonamin Victorio, TB Bita (Argentina)—II, IV
Bonfiglioli Giuseppe, TA Darnis (Italy)—I, II, III, IV
Bong-kil Sye John, RA Tae Gu (Korea)—I, II, III, IV
Bonhomme Joseph, TB Tulana (Canada)—I, II, III, IV
Bonomini Felice, RB Como (Italy)—I, II, III, IV
Bontempi Alfredo, TB Palmyra (Italy)—I
Bontems André-Georges, RB S. Jean-de-Maurienne (France)—I, II, III, IV
Borecky Isidore, RB Toronto degli Ucraini (Canada)—I, II, III, IV
Borgatti José, RB Viedma (Argentina)—I, II, III, IV
Borge y Castrillo Carlos, TB Lappa (Nicaragua)—I, II, III, IV
Borić Crnosija Vladimir, RB Punta, Arenas (Chile)—I, II, III, IV
Borne Pietro, SG Benedictine Congregation of Beuron—IV
Bornigia Domenico, RB S. Sepolcro (Italy)—I
Borra Dionisio, RB Fossano (Italy)—I
Borromeo Luigi, RB Pesaro (Italy)—I, II, III, IV
Bortignon Girolamo, RB Padua (Italy)—I, II, III, IV
Bosio Giovanni Battista, RA Chieti (Italy)—I, II, III, IV
Bossi Adolfo, TB Parnassus (Brazil)—II, III, IV
Bostani Luigi, SG Aleppians (Maronite) (Lebanon)—I
Botero Salazar Tulio, RA Medellín (Colombia)—I, II, III, IV
Bottino Francesco, TB Sebaste in Palaestina (Italy)—I, II, III, IV
Botto Paolo, RA Cagliari (Italy)—I, II, III, IV
Boucheix Noël, RB Porto Novo (Benin)—I, II, III, IV
Bouckaert Pierre SJ, RB Popokabaka (Congo-Leopoldville)—I, II, III, IV
Boudon René, RB Mende (France)—I, II, III, IV
Boudreaux Warren, TB Calynda (USA)—I, II, III, IV
Bougon François, RB Moulins (France)—I, II, III, IV
Bouque Paul, TB Abbir Germaniciana (France)—I, II, III, IV
Boussard Auguste, RB Vannes (France)—III, IV
Bouter William, RB Nellore (India)—I, II, IV
Bouve Gustave, RB Kongolo (Congo-Leopoldville)—I, II, III, IV
Bowers Joseph, RB Accra (Ghana)—I, II, III
Boyle Hugh, RB Johannesburg (South Africa)—I, II, III, IV
Boza Masvidal Eduardo, TB Vinda (Cuba)—I, II, III, IV
Bracci Francesco card., TA Idassa (Italy)—I, II, IV
Brandão de Castro José, RB Propriá (Brazil)—I, II, III, IV
Brandão Vilela Avelar, RA Teresina (Brazil)—I, II, III, IV
Brasseur William, TB Agathonice (Philippines)—I, II, III, IV
Brault Henri, RB Saint Dié (France)—I, II
Braunstorfer Karl, SG Cistercian Congregation of the Sacred Heart of Jesus—I, II, III, IV
Brazys Franz, TB Zella (Italy)—IV
Brechter Heinrich, SG Congregation of St. Ottilien (Benedictine)—I, II, III, IV
Breen George, PA Haflong (India)—II, III, IV
Bréheret André, RB Cahors (France)—I, II, III, IV
Breitenbeck Joseph, TB Tepelta (USA)—IV
Brellinger Leopold SJ, RB Kinghsien (China)—II, III, IV
Brennan William, RB Toowoomba (Australia)—I, II, III, IV
Bressane de Araújo Hugo, RA Mārilia (Brazil)—I, II, III, IV
Bresson Edoardo, TB Cetrus (Melanesia)—I
Bretault Joseph, RB Koudougou (Upper Volta)—I, II, III, IV
Brezanóczy Pavol, TB Rotaria (Hungary)—III, IV
Briacca Sebastiano, RB Mondoví (Italy)—I
Briani Gaetano, SG Sons of the Sacred Heart of Jesus—I, II, III, IV
Bright Humphrey, TB Soli (Great Britain)—I, II
Brini Mario, TA Algiza (URA-Egypt)—II, III, IV
Brizgys Vincentas, TB Bosana (Lithuania)—I, II, III, IV
Brizi Domenico, RB Osimo e Cingoli (Italy)—I, II
Brodeur Rosario, RB Alexandria (Canada)—I, III, IV
Broers Filippo Tiago, RB Caravelas (Brazil)—II, III, IV
Bronsveld Cornelius, TA Leontopolis in Augustamnica (Tanzania)—I, II
Brosnahan Thomas, RB Freetown and Bo (Sierra Leone)—I, II, III, IV
Brot Pierre, TB Marciana (France)—I, III
Brown Carlos, TB Vallis (Bolivia)—I, II, III, IV
Browne Michael, RB Galway and Kilmacduagh (Ireland)—I, II, III, IV
Browne Michael OP, TA Idebessus (Ireland)—I, II, III, IV
Bruls Francisco, RB Villavicencio (Colombia)—I, III, IV
Bruniera Alfredo, TA Claudiopolis in Honoriade (Ecuador)—I, III, IV
Brunini Joseph, TB Axomis (USA)—I, II, III, IV
Brunner George, RB Middlesbrough (Great Britain)—I, II
Brunon Jean, TB Vagal (France)—IV
Brustia Francesco, RB Andria (Italy)—I, II, III, IV
Brzana Stanislaus Joseph, TB Cufruta (USA)—III, IV
Buchkremer Joseph, TB Aggar (Germany)—I, II, III, IV
Buchholz Matthias MSC, PA Shihtsien (China)—II, III, IV
Buckley Jospeh, SG Marists—I, II, III, IV
Buckley William, SG Oblates of St. Francis de Sales—I, II, III, IV
Bučko Ivan, TA Leucas (Italy)—I, II, III, IV
Buddy Charles, RB San Diego (USA)—I
Budelacci Biagio, TB Nyssa (Italy)—I, II, III, IV
Bueno Couto Gabriel, TB Leuce (Brazil)—I, II, III, IV
Bueno Miele Bernardo, TB Bararus (Brazil)—II, III, IV
Bueno y Monreal José card., RA Siviglia (Spain)—I, II, III, IV
Bühl Berthold, TB Methone (Germany)—I, II, III
Builes Miguel, RB Santa Rosa de Osos (Colombia)—I, II, IV
Buis James, TB Astypalaea (Malaysia)—I, II, III, IV
Bukatko Gabriel, RA Belgrado (Yugoslavia)—I, II, III, IV
Burić Viktor, RB Senj (Yugoslavia)—I, II, III, IV
Burke James, PN Chimbote (Peru)—IV
Burke John, RB Simla (India)—I, II, III
Burzio Giuseppe, TA Gortyna (Italy)—I, II, III, IV
Busimba Joseph, RB Goma (Congo-Leopoldville)—I, II, III, IV
Buswell Charles, RB Pueblo (USA)—I, II, III, IV
Buteler Alfonso Maria, RA Mendoza (Argentina)—I, I, IV
Butibubage Lwamosa Renatus, TB Casius (Tanzania)—I, IV
Butler Christopher, SG English Benedictine Congregation—I, II, III, IV
Butler Eugene Joseph, RB Mombasa (Kenya)—I, II, III, IV
Butorac Pavao, RB Dubrovnik (Yugoslavia)—I
Buttarazzi Nivardo, SG Congregation of Casamari-Cistercians (Italy)—I, II, III, IV
Buyse Marcel, RB Lahore (Pakistan)—I, II, IV
Byrne Edwin, RA Santa Fe (USA)—I
Byrne Henry, TB Lamia (Philippines)—I, II, III, IV
Byrne James, RA Dubuque (USA)—I, II, III, IV
Byrne Leo, TB Sabadia (USA)—I, II, III, IV

C

Cabana Georges, RA Sherbrooke (Canada)—I, II, III, IV
Cabana Louis, TA Carallia (Canada)—I, II, III, IV
Cabrera Cruz Luis, RB S. Luis Potosi (Mexico)—I, II, III, IV
Cabrera Urdangarin Enrico, RB Mercedes (Uruguay)—I, II, III, IV
Cáceres González Roberto Reinaldo, RB Melo (Uruguay)—I, II, III, IV
Cadoux Theophile, RB Kaolack (Senegal)—II, III, IV
Cafferata Carlos, RB San Luis (Argentina)—I, II, III, IV
Caggiano Antonio card., RA Buenos Aires (Argentina)—I, II, III, IV
Cagna Mario, TA Heraclea in Europa (Japan)—II, III, IV
Cagnoni Emiliano, RB Cefalú (Italy)—I, II, III
Cahill Thomas, RB Cairns (Australia)—I, II, III, IV
Cahsay Hailé, RB Adigrat (Ethiopia)—II, III, IV
Caillot Antoine, RB Evreux (France)—I, II, III, IV
Caillouet Louis, TB Setea (USA)—I, II, III, IV
Calabretta Angelo, RB Noto (Italy)—I, II, III, IV
Calabria Raffaele, RA Benevento (Italy)—I, II, III, IV
Calderón José, RB Cartago of Colombia (Colombia)—I, II, III, IV
Calderón y Padilla Octavio, RB Matagalpa (Nicaragua)—I
Calewaert Karel, RB Ghent (Belgium)—I, II
Calheiros de Novaes Waldyr, TB Mulia (Brazil)—III, IV
Caliaro Marco, RB Sabina e Poggio Mirteto (Italy)—I, II, III, IV
Callens Michel, TA Moxori (Tunisia)—IV
Callori di Vignale Federico card., TA Maiuca (Italy)—IV
Calmels Norbert, SG Premonstratensians —I, II, III, IV
Calzolari Pacifico OFM, PA Xiangtan (China)—II, III
Camagni Ernesto, TB Suava (Italy)—III, IV
Cambiaghi Placido, RB Novara (Italy)—I, II, III, IV

Caminada Costantino, RB Ferentino (Italy)—I, II, III, IV
Camomot Bastida Teofilo, TA Marcianopolis (Philippines)—I, III, IV
Camozzo Ugo, RA Pisa (Italy)—I, II, III, IV
Campbell Donald, RA Glasgow (Great Britain)—I
Campelli Raffaele, RB Cagli e Pergola (Italy)—I, II, III, IV
Campos Paulo, RA Campinas (Brazil)—I, II
Campuzano Juan de Dios, PA Galapagos (Ecuador)—II, III, IV
Canestri Giovanni, TB Tenedus (Italy)—I, II, III, IV
Cannonero Giacomo, RB Asti (Italy)—I, II, III, IV
Canonne Michel, RB Tulear (Madagascar)—I, II, III, IV
Cantero Cuadrado Pedro, RA Saragozza (Spain)—I, II, III, IV
Canyes Santacana Eduardo, PA Leticia (Colombia)—II
Canzonieri Carmelo, RB Caltagirone (Italy)—I, II, III, IV
Capasso Nicola, RB Acerra (Italy)—I, II, III, IV
Capobianco Giovanni, RB Urbania (Italy)—I, II, III
Capozi Domenico Luca OFM, RA Taiyüan (China)—I, II, III, IV
Caprio Giuseppe, TA Apollonia (China)—II, III, IV
Capucci Hilarion, TA Cesarea in Palestina (Melkite-Greek) (Jordan)—II, III, IV
Carata Giuseppe, TB Praesidium (Italy)—IV
Carberry John, RB Columbus (USA)—I, II, III, IV
Carboni Romolo, TA Sidon (Peru)—I, II, III, IV
Cardenas Manuel, TB Aulon (Argentina)—II, III, IV
Cardijn Joseph-Léon card., TA Tusuros (Belgium)—IV
Cardinale Igino, TA Nepte, Apostolic Delegate to Great Britain (Belgium)—II, IV
Cardoso Cunha Antonio, TB Baris in Pisidia (Portugal)—I, II, III, IV
Carinci Alberto, RB Campobasso (Italy)—I, II, III, IV
Carinci Alfonso, TA Seleucia in Isauria (Italy)—I, II
Carli Luigi, RB Segni (Italy)—I, II, III, IV
Carpino Francesco, TA Serdica (Italy)—I, II, III, IV
Carranza Chévez José, RB S. Rosa de Copán (Honduras)—I, II, III, IV
Carranza Lopez Clemente, RB Estele (Nicaragua)—IV
Carrara Benigno, RB Imola (Italy)—I, II, III, IV
Carraro Giuseppe, RB Verona (Italy)—I, II, III, IV
Carrasco Bartolomeo, RB Huejutla (Mexico)—IV
Carreras Jorge, RB San Rafael (Argentina)—I, IV
Carretto Pietro, TB Zenobia (Thailand)—I, II, III, IV
Carrizzo Villareal José, RB Chitre (Panama)—II, III, IV
Carrieri Leonardo, SG Congregation of the Sacred Hearts of Jesus and Mary (Italy)—II, III, IV
Carroll Coleman, RB Miami (USA)—I, II, III, IV
Carroll Francis, TA Gabula (Liberia)—I, II, III, IV
Carroll Francis Patrick, RB Calgary (Canada)—I
Carroll James, TA Amasea (Australia)—II, III, IV
Carta Paolo, RA Sassari (Italy)—I, II, III, IV
Carter Alexander, RB Sault Saint Marie (Canada)—I, II, III, IV
Carter Gerald, RB London (Canada)—I, II, III, IV
Carvajal Rosales Luis Alfredo, TB Coptus (Ecuador)—I, IV
Carvalho Augusto, RB Caruarú (Brazil)—I, II, III, IV
Casariego Mario, RA Guatemala (Guatemala)—I, II, III, IV
Casas Artemio, RB Imus (Philippines)—I, II, III, IV
Cascón Luis, RB S. Cristobal de la Laguna (Spain)—I, II, IV
Caselle Alfredo, TB Lugura (Italy)—IV
Casey James, RB Lincoln (USA)—I, II, III, IV
Casey Lawrence, TB Cea (USA)—I, II, III, IV
Cashman David, RB, Arundel Brighton (Great Britain)—I, II, III, IV
Cassulo Silvio, RB Macerata e Tolentino (Italy)—I, II, III, IV
Castaldo Alfonso card., RA Napoli (Italy)—I, II, III, IV
Castán Lacoma Laureano, RB Sigüenza e Guadalajara (Spain)—I, III, IV
Castellano Ismaele Mario, RA Siena (Italy)—I, II, III, IV
Castellano Ramón, RA Cordoba (Argentina)—I, II
Castelli Alberto, TA Rhusium (Italy)—I, II, III, IV
Castro Becerra Jesús, RB Palmira (Colombia)—I, II, IV
Castro Cabrera José, RB San Felipe (Chile)—II, III
Castro Ramirez Francisco Santiago de Maria (El Salvador)—I, III
Castro Ruiz Manuel, TB Cincari (Mexico)—IV
Casullo Guido Maria, TB Utica (Brazil)—I, II, III, IV
Catani Aliprando, SG Camaldolese Benedictines– II, III, IV
Catarella Antonino, RB Piazza Armerina (Italy)—I, II, III, IV
Catarzi Danilo, RB Uvira (Congo-Leopoldville)—I, II, III, IV
Catry Hector, TB Semta (Belgium)—III, IV
Cavagna Alfredo, TB Tium (Italy)—I, II, III, IV
Cavallera Charles, RB Marsabit (Kenya)—I, II, III, IV
Cavallero José Maria, RB Minas (Uruguay)—I
Cavanna Nicola, RB Rieti (Italy)—I, II, III, IV
Cayer Jean de Capistran Aimé, TB Cissi (URA-Egypt)—I, II, III, IV
Caza Percival, TB Albulae (Canada)—I, II, III, IV
Cazaux Antoine-Marie, RB Luçon (France)—I, II, III, IV
Cazzaniga Anacleto, RA Urbino (Italy)—I, II, III, IV
Cazzaro Bernardo, TB Pyrgos (Chile)—III, IV
Cecchi Vittorio, RB Fossombrone (Italy)—I, II, III, IV
Cece Antonio, TB Damiata (Italy)—I, II, III, IV
Čekada Smiljan, RB Skoplje (Yugoslavia)—I, II, III, IV
Cento Fernando card. penitenziere maggiore—I, II, III, IV
Centoz Luigi, TA Edessa di Osroene (Italy)—I, II, III, IV
Ceól Orazio Ferruccio OFM, RB Kichow (China)—I, II, III, IV
Cerqua Arcangelo, TB Olbia (Brazil)—I, II, III, IV
Cesana John, RB Gulu (Uganda)—I, II, III, IV
Cesarano Andrea, RA Manfredonia (Italy)—I, II, III, IV
Chabukasanska Clemente, RB Kasama (Zambia)—II, III, IV
Chacón Acacio, RA Mérida (Venezuela)—I
Chalup Jorge, RB Gualeguaychù (Argentina)—I, II, III, IV
Chambon Léon, RB Bossangoa (Central African Republic)—II, III, IV
Chami Pierre, RA Bosra (Syria)—I, IV
Champagne Gabriel, RB Tamale (Ghana)—I, II, III, IV
Chan Francis, RB Penang (Malaysia)—I, II, III
Chang Tso-huan Vito SVD, TB Cyanae (China)—I, II, III, IV
Chantoux Alphonse, PA Fada N'Gourma (Upper Volta)—II
Charbonneau Paul, RB Hull (Canada)—I, II, III, IV
Charles de la Brousse André, RB Dijon (France)—I, II, III, IV
Charrière François, RB Lausanne, Genève e Fribourg (Switzerland)—I, II, III, IV
Charue André, RB Namur (Belgium)—I, II, III, IV
Chauvin Marcel, RB Fada N'Gourma (Upper Volta)—III, IV
Chaves Orlando, RA Cuiabá (Brazil)—I, II, III, IV
Chávez y González Luis, RA San Salvador (El Salvador)—I, II, III, IV
Chedid Jean, TB, Arca di Fenicia (Lebanon)—II
Cheikho Joseph, RA Sehna (Iran)—I, II, III, IV
Cheikho Paul II P Babilonia dei Caldei (Iraq)—I, II, III, IV
Chelucci Ireneo, RB Montalcino (Italy)—I, II, III, IV
Ch'eng Shih-kuang Paul, TB Uccula e Tainan, Taiwan—I, II, III, IV
Cheng Tien-Siang Joseph OP, RB Kaohsiung (China)—I, II, III, IV
Chevalier Paul, RB Le Mans (France)—I, II, III, IV
Chiappero Pier Giorgio, TB Cibira (Palestine)—I
Chiarlo Carlo card.—I, II
Chichester Aston, TA Velebusdo (Rhodesia)—I
Chilouet Camille, RB Farafangana (Madagascar)—I, II, III, IV
Chiocca Secondo, TB Cesarea di Bitinia (Italy)—I, II, III, IV
Chiriboga Benigno, RB Latacunga (Ecuador)—II, III, IV
Chitsulo Cornelius, RB Dedza (Malawi)—I, II, III
Chizzini Cornelio, TB Ege (Brazil)—I, II, III, IV
Choi Jae-seon John, RB Pusan (South Korea)—I, II, III, IV
Chopard Lallier Robert, PA Parakou (Benin)—II
Choquet Maurice, TB Diospoli Inferiore (Haiti)—I, III, IV
Choromański Zygmunt, TB Panopoli (Poland)—I, III
Chu-Kim-Tuyen Emanuel, SG Congregazione Cistercense della Sacra Famiglia– III, IV
Cialeo Francis, RB Lyallpur (Pakistan)—I, II, III, IV
Cibrian Fernandez Ubaldo, TB Bida (Bolivia)—I, II, III
Cicognani Amleto Giovanni, card. segretario di Stato—I, II, III, IV
Cicuttini Luigi, RB Città di Castello (Italy)—I, II, III, IV
Ciesielski Augustyn, SG Congregazione Cistercense di Maria Regina– I, III
Cifuentes Gómez Alfredo, RA La Serena (Chile)—I, III
Cimichella Adrien, TB Quiza (Canada)—IV
Cinense y Abera Emilio, RB S. Fernando (Philippines)—I, II, III, IV
Cioli Telesforo, RB, Arezzo (Italy)—I, II, III, IV
Ciona Giacomo, TB Bacanaria (Malawi)—IV
Cirarda Lachiondo José, TB Drusiliana (Spain)—I, II, III, IV
Ciriaci Pietro card. prefetto della congregazione del Concilio—I, II, III, IV
Cirio Armando, RB Toledo (Brazil)—I, III
Ciuchini Adolfo, RB Alghero (Italy)—I, II, III, IV
Civardi Luigi, TB Tespia (Italy)—I, II, III, IV
Civelli Mario PIME, RB Jixian (China)—I, II, III, IV
Clabaut Armand, TB Troade (France)—I, II, III, IV
Clarizio Emanuele, TA Claudiopoli di Isauria (Dominican Republic)—II, III, IV
Clavel Méndez Tomás, RA Panama (Panama)—I, II, III, IV
Cleary Joseph, TB Cresima (Great Britain)—IV
Cleary Patrick SSCME, RB Nancheng (China)—I, II, III, IV
Cleire Richard, TB Tadamata (Italy)—I, II, III, IV
Clemente da Milwaukee, SG Frati Minori Cappuccini—I, II
Clementino da Vlissingen, SG Frati Minori Cappuccini—III, IV
Cléret de Langavant François, TB Mactaris (Reunion Island)—I, II, III, IV
Clerici Alberto, SG Congregazione Benedettina Cassinese—IV
Cleven Wilhelm, TB Sasima (Germany)—I, II, III, IV
Clinch Henry, TB Badie (USA)—III, IV
Cobben William, RB Helsinki (Finland)—I, II, III, IV
Coderre Gérard, RB S. Jean de Québec (Canada)—I, II, III, IV
Cody John C., RB London (Canada)—I, II
Cody John P., RA Chicago (USA)—I, II, III, IV
Coelho Jaime Luiz, RB Maringá (Brazil)—I, II, III, IV
Coggin Walter AN Mary Help of Christians (USA)—I, II, III, IV
Cognata Giuseppe, TB Farsalo (Italy)—II, III, IV
Cogoni Francesco, RB Ozieri (Italy)—I, II, III, IV
Coimbra José, RB Patos de Minas (Brazil)—I, II, IV
Colaço José, RB Santiago de Cabo Verde (Cape Verde)—I, II, III, IV
Colli Evasio, RA Parma (Italy)—I, II, III, IV
Collignon Jean, RB Les Cayes (Haiti)—IV
Collin Bernardin, RB Digne (France)—I, II, III, IV
Colling João Cláudio, RB Passo Fundo (Brazil)—I, II, III, IV
Collini André, TB Zefirio (France)—I, II, III, IV
Collins Thomas, TB Sufetula (Bolivia)—I, II, III, IV
Colombo Carlo, TB Vittoriana (Italy)—III, IV
Colombo Giovanni card., RA Milano (Italy)—I, II, III, IV
Comber John, TB Foraziana (USA)—I, II, III, IV
Compagnone Enrico, RB Anagni (Italy)—I, II, III, IV
Concha Luis card., RA Bogotá (Colombia)—I, II, III, IV
Condon William, RB Great Falls (USA)—I, II, III, IV
Confalonieri Carlo card. arciprete della Basilica di S. Maria Maggiore e segretario della congregazione Concistoriale—I, II, III, IV
Conigli Abele, RB Sansepolcro (Italy)—II, III, IV
Connare William, RB Greensburg (USA)—I, II, III, IV
Connolly James, RB Fall River (USA)—I, II, III, IV
Connolly Thomas, RA Seattle (USA)—I, II, IV
Conti Servilio, PN Roráima (Brazil)—IV
Conway William card., RA, Armagh (Ireland)—I, II, III, IV
Coque Terence, TB Summa (USA)—IV
Cooray Thomas card., RA Colombo (Ceylon)—I, II, III, IV
Copas Virgil, TB Bennefa (New Guinea)—I, II, III, IV
Copello Santiago card.—I, II, III, IV
Corboy James, RB Monze (Zambia)—I, II, III, IV
Cordeiro Joseph, RA Karachi (Pakistan)—I, II, III, IV
Cornejo Ravadero Mario, TB Sanavo (Peru)—II, III, IV
Cornelis Joseph, RA Elizabethville (Congo-Leopoldville)—I, II, III, IV
Cornelli Leone, SG Benedettini Silvestrini– I, II, III, IV
Coroli Eliseu, TB Zama Maggiore (Brazil)—I, II, III, IV
Coronado Caro Jesús PA, Ariari (Colombia)—III, IV
Coronado Romani Florencio, RB Huancavelica (Peru)—I, II, III, IV
Correa José, RB Caratinga (Brazil)—I, II, III, IV
Correa León Pablo, RB Cúcuta (Colombia)—I, II, III, IV
Correa Yepes Heriberto, PA Mitú (Colombia)—II, III, IV
Corripio y Ahumada Ernesto, RB Tampico (Mexico)—I, II, III, IV
Corso Antonio, TB Moglena (Uruguay)—I, II, III, IV
Cortés Peréz Fidel, RB Chilapa (Mexico)—I, II, III, IV
Coscia Benedetto, RB Jataí (Brazil)—I, II, III, IV
Cosme do Amaral Alberto, TB Tagaria (Portugal)—III, IV
Costa Campos José, RB Valença (Brazil)—I, II, III, IV
Costa Franco, TB Emmaus (Italy)—II, III, IV
Costa João, TB Scilio (Brazil)—I, IV
Costa José, RB Caetité (Brazil)—I, II, III, IV
Costantini Vittorio, RB Sessa Aurunca (Italy)—I, II, III, IV
Costello Joseph, TB Coma (USA)—II, III, IV
Côté Philip SJ, RB Xuzhou (China)—I, II, III, IV
Cotter Kiernan, PA Máiduguri (Nigeria)—II, III, IV
Coty, Arnold, RB Nachingwea (Tanzania)—II, III, IV
Coucherousset Joseph, RA Bangui (Central African Republic)—I, II, III, IV
Couderc Alfred, RB Viviers (France)—I, II, III, IV
Coudert John, TB Rodiapoli (Canada)—I, II, III, IV
Coudray Jean, PA Kankan (Guinea)—II, III, IV
Courbe Stanislas, TB Castoria (France)—I, II, III, IV
Courtemanche Firmin, RB Fort Jameson (Zambia)—I, II, IV
Courtois Etienne, RB Kayes (Mali)—II, III, IV
Cousineau Albert, RB Cap Haïtien (Haiti)—I, II, III, IV
Cousins William, RA Milwaukee (USA)—I, II, III, IV
Couturier Gérard, RB Hauterive (Canada)—I, II, III, IV
Cowderoy Cyril, RA Southwork (Great Britain)—I, II, III, IV
Cowley Leonard, TB Pertusa (USA)—I, II, III, IV
Craven George Laurence, TB Sebastopolis in Armenia (Great Britain)—I
Crawford John, TB Caffa—I, II, III, IV
Creemers André, RB Bondo (Congo-Leopoldville)—I, II, III, IV
Crespo Chiriboga Luis Alfonso, RB Loja (Ecuador)—III
Cristea Vasile, TB Lebedo (Italy)—I, II, III, IV
Crivellari Pio, RB Trivento (Italy)—I, II, IV
Cronin Patrick, TB Ubaza (Philippines)—I, II, III, IV
Crous y Salichs Camilo, TB Crazia (Colombia)—I, II, III, IV
Cserháti József, TB Melzi (Hungary)—III, IV
Cuenco José, RA Jaro (Philippines)—I, III, IV
Cueter Elias, TB Taua (Brazil)—III, IV
Cueto Gonzalez Felipe, RB Tlalnepantla (Mexico)—III, IV
Čule Petar, RB Monstar (Yugoslavia)—I, II, III, IV
Cullinane John, TB Flumenzer (Australia)—I, II, IV
Cunial Antonio, RB Lucera (Italy)—II, III, IV
Cunial Ettore, TA Soteropoli (Italy)—I, II, III, IV
Cuniberti Angelo, TB Arsinoe di Cipro (Colombia)—I, II, III, IV
Cunningham David, TB Lampsaco (USA)—I, II, III, IV
Cunningham James, RB Hexham e Newcastle (Great Britain)—I, II, III, IV
Curtis Walter, RB Bridgeport (USA)—I, II, III, IV
Cushing Richard card., RA Boston (USA)—I, II, III, IV
Cuyper Alfonso, PA Vichada (Colombia)—III
Czapliński Bernard, TB Faustinopolis (Poland)—II, IV
Czerniak Jan, TB Eudocia (Poland)—II, IV

Durán Moreira Alejandro, RB S. Carlos de Ancud (Chile)—I, II, III, IV
Durick Joseph, TB Cerbali (USA)—I, III, IV
Durkin John Thomas, PA Louis Trichardt (South Africa)—II, III, IV
Durning Dennis, RB, RAusha (Tanzania)—II, III, IV
Durrheimer Emile, RB Katiola (Ivory Coast)—I, II, III, IV
Durrieu Louis, RB Ouahigouya (Upper Volta)—I, II, III
Duschak Wilhelm Josef, TB Abidda (Philippines)—I, II, III, IV
Dutil Joseph Alphonse, SG Missionari di N. S. de la Salette—I, II
Duval Léon card., RA Algeri (Algeria)—I, II, III, IV
Dworschak Baldwin Wilfred, SG Congregazione Benedettina Americana Cassinese—IV
Dworschak Leo Ferdinand, RB Fargo (USA)—I, II, III, IV
Dwyer George, RA Birmingham (Great Britain)—I, II, III, IV
Dwyer Robert, RB Reno (USA)—I, II, III, IV

E

Eccher Jacinto, TB Garriana (Bolivia)—I, II, III, IV
Echeverría Ruiz Bernardino, RB Ambato (Ecuador)—I, II, III, IV
Edelby Néophytos, TA Edessa in Osrhoëne dei Greco-Melkiti (Syria)—I, II, III, IV
Edezath Alexander, RB Cochin (India)—I, II, IV
Eijo y Garay Leopoldo, P Indie Orientali (Spain)—I
Ekandem Dominic, RB Ikot Ekpene (Nigeria)—I, II, III, IV
Elchinger Léon-Arthur, TB Antandro (France)—I, II, III, IV
Elko Niklos, RB Pittsburgh (USA)—I, II, III, IV
Ellis Edward, RB Nottingham (Great Britain)—I, II, III, IV
Elorza Legaristi Martin Fulgencio, TB Baliana (Peru)—I, II, IV
Elwell Clarence, TB Cone (USA)—II, III, IV
Emanuel Isidor Markus, RB Speyer (Germany)—I, II, III, IV
Enciso Viana Jesus, RB Mallorca (Spain)—I, II
Enrici Domenico, TA Ancusa (Australia)—I, III
Enrique y Tarancón Vicente, RA Oviedo (Spain)—I, II, III, IV
Erviti Félix, PA Sahara Spagnolo e Ifni (Western Sahara)—II, III, IV
Escalante y Escalante Alfonso Manuel, TB Sora (Mexico)—I, II, III, IV
Escobar Vélez Guillermo, RB Antioquia (Colombia)—I, II, III, IV
Esorto Germiniano, RA Bahía Blanca (Argentina)
Espelage Bernard, RB Gallup (USA)—I
Espiga y Infante Gregorio, TB Afneo (Philippines)—I, II, III
Espino y Silva Alfonso, RA Monterrey (Mexico)—I, II, III, IV
Esser Francis, RB Keimoes (South Africa)—I, II, III, IV
Essuah Joseph, RB Kumasi (Ghana)—I, II, III, IV
Esteves Dias Francisco, RB Luso (Angola)—II, III, IV
Etges Alberto Frederico, RB S. Cruz do Sul (Brazil)—I, II, III, IV
Etoga Paul, RB Mbalmayo (Cameroon)—I, II, III, IV
Etrillard Jean, RB Gagnoa (Ivory Coast)—I, II, III, IV
Etspueler Odilo, TB Fata (Philippines)—I, II, III, IV
Etter Tadeusz, TB Bonizza (Poland)—II
Eugenín Teodoro Bernardo Eugenín, TB Hierissus (Chile)—I, II, III, IV
Evangelisti Giuseppe, RA Meerut (India)—I, II, III, IV
Evrard Joseph, TB Dionisiopoli (France)—I, II, III, IV

F

Facchini Edoardo, RB Alatri (Italy)—I
Fady Joseph, RB Lilongwe (Malawi)—I, II, III, IV
Fahy Eugene SJ, PA Yangzhou (China)—II, III
Falconieri Gregorio, RB Conversano (Italy)—I, II
Falcucci Benedetto, TA Preslavo (Italy)—I, II, III, IV
Falkowski Czeslaw, RB Łomża (Poland)—III, IV
Fallani Giovanni, TB Partenia (Italy)—III, IV
Farah Augustin, RB Tripoli del Lebanon, Greco Melchita (Lebanon)—I, II, III, IV
Farah Elie, RA Cipro, Maronita (Cyprus)—I, III, IV
Fares Armando, RA Catanzaro (Italy)—I, II, III, IV
Faresin Camillo, TB Bubastis (Brazil)—I, II, III, IV
Farrelly Patrick, RB Lismore (Australia)—I, II, III, IV
Farren Neil, RB Derry (Ireland)—I, II, III, IV
Fasola Francesco, RA Messina (Italy)—I, II, III, IV
Fasolino Nicolas, RA Santa Fe (Argentina)—I, II, III, IV
Fauret Jean Baptiste, RB Pointe Noire (Congo-Brazzaville)—I, II, III, IV
Fauvel André, RB Quimper (France)—I, II, III, IV
Favé Vincent, TB Andeda (France)—I, II, III, IV
Faveri Luigi, RB Tivoli (Italy)—I, II, III, IV
Fearns John Michael, TB Geras (USA)—I, II, III, IV
Fedders Edward Luis, TB Antiochia ad Maeandrum (Peru)—I, II, III, IV
Federal Joseph, RB Salt Lake City (USA)—I, II, III, IV
Federici Michele, RA Santa Severina (Italy)—I, II, III, IV
Feeney Daniel, RB Portland (USA)—I, II, III, IV
Felici Pericle, TA Samosata, Council secretary (Italy)—I, II, III, IV
Feltin Maurice card. Paris (France)—I, II, III, IV
Fenech Francis, RB Jhansi (India)—I, II, III, IV
Fenocchio Giuseppe, RB Pontremoli (Italy)—I, II, III, IV
Ferche Joseph, TB Vina (Germany)—I, II, III
Fergus James, RB Achonry (Ireland)—I, II, III, IV
Fernandes Angelo Innocent, TA Novae Patrae (India)—I, II, III, IV
Fernandes de Araújo Serafim, TB Verinopolis (Brazil)—I, II, IV
Fernandes Geraldo Bijos, RB Londrina (Brazil)—I, II, III, IV
Fernandes Joseph, RA Delhi (India)—I, II, III, IV
Fernandes Luis, TB Mididi (Brazil)—I
Fernandes Mathias Sebastião Francisco, RB Mysore (India)—III, IV
Fernández Alonso Aniceto, SG Domenicani—I, II, III, IV
Fernández-Conde Manuel, RB Córdoba (Spain)—I, II, III, IV
Fernández Feo-Tinoco Alejandro, RB San Cristobal (Venezuela—I, II, III, IV)
Fernández Jerome, RB Quilon (India)—I, II, III, IV
Fernández Pérez Celestino, RB San Marcos (Guatemala)—I, II, III, IV
Fernández y Fernández Celestino, RB Huajuapan de León (Mexico)—IV
Fernández y Fernández Doroteo, TB Castabal (Spain)—I, II, III, IV
Fernando Frank Marcus, TB Oliva (Ceylon)—IV
Fernando Thomas, RB Tuticorin (India)—I, II, III, IV
Ferrand Louis, RA Tours (France)—I, II, III, IV
Ferrando Stephen, RB Shillong (India)—I, II, III, IV
Ferrara Dominico, PA Mupoi (Sudan)—II, III, IV
Ferrari Carlo, RB Monopoli (Italy)—I, II, III, IV
Ferraz Salomão Barbosa, TB Eleutherna (Brazil)—I, II, III, IV
Ferreira Arreola Francisco, RB Texcoco (Mexico)—II, III, IV
Ferreira Cabral Manuel, TB Obbi (Portugal)—IV
Ferreira da Silva Manuel, TA Cizico (Portugal)—I, II, III, IV
Ferreira de Macedo Antônio, TA Gangra (Brazil)—II, III, IV
Ferreira Gomes António, RB Porto (Portugal)—I, II, III, IV
Ferreira João, PA Guinea Portoghese (Portuguese Guinea)—II, III, IV
Ferreira Reis Gerardo, RB Leopoldina (Brazil)—I, II, III, IV
Ferrero di Cavallerleone Carlo, TA Trebisonda (Italy)—I, II, III, IV
Ferretto Giuseppe card., RA Sabina e Poggio Mirteto (Italy)—I, II, III, IV
Ferro Giovanni, RA Reggio Calabria (Italy)—I, II, III, IV
Ferro Juan, RB Concepción (Argentina)—III, IV
Ferrofino Giovanni, TA Zenopoli Isauria (Italy)—IV
Ferroni Alfonso Maria Corrado OFM, RB Laohekou (China)—I, II, III
Feuga René, TB Fornos Maggiore (France)—I, II
Fey Schneider Bernardo, TB Filadelfia Minore (Bolivia)—I, II, III, IV
Field Justin, RB S. George's e Grenada (Trinidad and Tobago)—I, II, III, IV
Field William, RB Ondo (Nigeria)—I, II, III, IV
Filipak Pedro, RB Jacarézinho (Brazil)—I, II, III, IV
Filippini Francesco, TB Tinisia di Numidia (Somalia)—I, II, III, IV
Finn Richard, RB Ibadan (Nigeria)—I, II, III, IV
Fiordelli Pietro, RB Prato (Italy)—I, II, III, IV
Fiorina Domenico, SG Istituto Missioni Consolata—I, II, III, IV
Fitzgerald Edward, RB Winona (USA)—I, II, III, IV
Fitzgerald William, TB Zarna (Trinidad and Tobago)—I, II, III, IV
Fitzgibbon Edmond, PA Minna (Nigeria)—IV
Flahiff George, RA Winnipeg dei Latini (Canada)—I, II, III, IV
Flanagan Bernard, RB Worcester (USA)—I, II, III, IV
Flannelly Joseph, TB Metelis (USA)—I
Flavin Glennon, TB Janina (USA)—I, II, III, IV
Fletcher Albert, RB Little Rock (USA)—I, II, III, IV
Floersh John, RA Louisville (USA)—I
Flores Martin Jaime, RB Barbastro (Spain)—I, II, III, IV
Flórez Hernández José, RB Ibagué (Colombia)—I, II, III, IV
Florit Ermenegildo card., RA Firenze (Italy)—I, II, III, IV
Flusin Claude, RB Saint Claude (France)—I, II, III, IV
Foery Walter, RB Syracuse (USA)—I
Fogar Luigi, TA Patrasso (Italy)—I
Foley Brian, RB Lancaster (Great Britain)—I, II, III, IV
Foley Theodore, SG Passionisti—III, IV
Foley Victor, TB Petinesso (Polynesia)—I, II, IV
Fondalinski Jan, TB Dobero (Polynesia)—I, IV
Font y Andreu Jaime, RB San Sebastián (Spain)—I
Forer Enrico, TB Menfi (Italy)—I, II, III, IV
Forero y García Norberto, RB Santa Marta (Colombia)—I, II
Forni Efrem card.—I, II, III, IV
Forni Raffaele, TA Egina (Uruguay)—II, III, IV
Forst Francis, RB Dodge City (USA)—I, II, III, IV
Fortier Joseph, RB Gaspé (Canada)—II, IV
Forzoni Aldo, RB Diano Teggiano (Italy)—I, II, III, IV
Fossati Maurilio, RA Torino (Italy)—I, II
Fougerat André, RB Grenoble (France)—I, II, III, IV
Fourrey René, RB Belley (France)—I, II, III, IV
Fox Arthur, TB Rinocorura (Australia)—I, III
Fox Thomas, RB Wilcannia Forbes (Australia)—II
Foylan Michael, RB Aberdeen (Great Britain)—IV
Fraghí Sebastiano, RA Oristano (Italy)—I, II, III, IV
Fragoso Antônio Batista, RB Crateus (Brazil)—I, II, III, IV
Franciolini Giuseppe, RB Cortona (Italy)—I, II, III, IV
Franco Arango Julio, RB Duitama (Colombia)—III, IV
Franco Francesco, TB Ilio (Italy)—I, II, III, IV
Franić Franjo, RB Split-Makarska (Yugoslavia)—I, II, III, IV
Franz John, RB Peoria (USA)—I, II, III, IV
Franzoni Giovanni Battista, AN S. Paolo fuori le Mura (Italy)—III, IV
Fratteggiani Bruno, RA Camerino (Italy)—III, IV
Freeman James, TB Ermopoli Minore (Australia)—I, IV
Freking Frederik, RB La Crosse (USA)—I, II, III, IV
Frenette Emilien, RB di Saint-Jérôme (Canada)—I, II, III, IV
Fresnel Alphonse, RB Fort Dauphin (Madagascar)—I, II, III, IV
Fresno Larraín Juan, RB Copiapó (Chile)—I, II, III, IV
Freundorfer Joseph, RB Augsburg (Germany)—I
Frias Hurtado Hernán, TB Bareta (Chile)—I
Frings Josef card., RA Köln (Germany)—I, II, III, IV
Frondosa Antonio José, RB Capiz (Philippines)—I, II, III, IV
Frotz Agostino, TB Corada (Germany)—I, II, III, IV
Fryns Jean, RB Kindu (Congo-Leopoldville)—I, II, III
Fukahori Senyemon Dominic, RB Fukuoka (Japan)—I, II, III, IV
Furey Francis, TB Temno (USA)—I, II, III, IV
Furlong Philip, TB, Arassa (USA)—I, II, III, IV
Fürstenberg Adolf, RB Abercorn (Zambia)—I, II, III, IV
Furura Yoshiyuki Paul, RB Kyōto (Japan)—I, II, III, IV
Fustella Antonio, RB Todi (Italy)—I, II, III, IV

G

Gabro Jaroslaw, RB Saint Nicholas (USA)—I, II, III, IV
Gachet Charles, RB Castries (Trinidad and Tobago)—I, II, III, IV
Gad Hyakinthos, TB Gratianopolis (Greece)—I, II, III, IV
Gaddi Clemente, RA Bergamo (Italy)—I, II, III, IV
Gaddo Giovanni, SG Rosminiani– I, II, III, IV
Gagnon Joseph, RB Edmundston (Canada)—I, II, III, IV
Gagnor Giuseppe, RB Alessandria (Italy)—I, II, III
Gahamanyi Jean-Baptiste, RB Astrida (Rwanda)—I, II, III, IV
Galbiati Amerigo (Ambrogio), RB Jalpaiguri (India)—I, II, III, IV
Galea Emanuele, TB Tralle di Asia (Malta)—I, II, III, IV
Galeazzi Paolo, RB Grosseto (Italy)—I
Galindo Mendoza Alfredo, RB Tijuana (Mexico)—II, IV
Gallagher Bryan, RB Port Pirie (Australia)—I, II, III, IV
Gallagher Normam, TB Adraso (Australia)—III, IV
Gallagher Raymond, RB Lafayette in Idiana (USA)—IV
Galvin Anthony, TB Lete (Malaysia)—I, II, IV
Gamboa Igino, PA Aguarico (Ecuador)—II
Gand Adrien, TB Macriana Minore (France)—III, IV
Ganguly Theotonius Amal, TA Drizipara (Pakistan)—I, II, III, IV
Ganni Gabriel, RB Beirut dei Caldei (Lebanon)—I, II, III, IV
Gantin Bernardin, RA Cotonou (Benin)—I, II, III, IV
Garavito Gregorio Jiménez, TB Ciparissia (Colombia)—I, II, III, IV
Garaygordóbil Berrizbeitia Victor, TB Pudenziana (Ecuador)—III, IV
Garcia Ayala José, TB Lacedemonia (Mexico)—III
Garcia De Sierra y Méndez Segundo, RA Burgos (Spain)—I, II, III, IV
García Franco Miguel, RB Mazatlán (Mexico)—I, II, III, IV
García Goulart Jaime, RB Dili (India)—I, II, III
García Lahiguera José, RB Huelva (Spain)—I, II, III, IV
García Martinez Fidel, TB Sululi (Spain)—I, II, III, IV
García Rodríguez Argimiro, TB Coropissus (Venezuela)—I, II, III, IV
García Segundo, TB Olimpo (Venezuela)—I, II, III, IV
García Villa José, RB San Pedro Sula (Honduras)—II, III
García y Aráuz Miguel, RB Jalapa (Guatemala)—I, II, III, IV
García y García de Castro Rafael, RA Granada (Spain)—I, II, III, IV
García y Goldaraz José, RA Valladolid (Spain)—I, II, III, IV
García y Suárez Marco Antonio, RB Granada (Nicaragua)—I, II
Gargitter Joseph, RB Bolzano (Italy)—I, II, III, IV
Gargiulo Lorenzo, TA Germa di Ellesponto (Italy)—I, II, III, IV
Garibi y Rivera José card., RA Guadalajara (Mexico)—I, II, III, IV
Garković Mate, RA Zadar (Yugoslavia)—I, II, III, IV
Garner John, RA Pretoria (South Africa)—I, II, III, IV
Garneri Giuseppe, RB Susa (Italy)—I, II, III, IV
Garriga Mariano Simon, RB Corpus Christi (USA)—I
Garrone Gabriel-Marie, RA Toulouse (France)—I, II, III, IV
Gasbarri Primo, TB Tenneso (Italy)—I, II, III, IV
Gassongo Georges Benoit, TB Cubda (Congo-Brazzaville)—IV
Gatimu Caesar, RB Nyeri (Kenya)—I, IV
Gauci Redento Maria, PN Chuquibamba (Peru)—I, II, III, IV
Gaudreau William, SG Redentoristi—I, II, III, IV
Gaudron Alphonse-Paul-Désiré, RB Evreux (France)—I
Gaumain Samuel, RB Moundou (Chad)—I, II, III, IV
Gavazzi Egidio, AN Subiaco (Italy)—II, III, IV
Gavilanes Chamorro Nicanor, RB Portoviejo (Ecuador)—I, II, III, IV
Gaviola y Garcés Mariano, RB Cabanatuan (Philippines)—II, III, IV
Gawlina Józef, TA Madytus (Poland)—I, II, III
Gay Jean, RB Basse Terre (Guadeloupe)—I, II, III, IV

Gazza João, TB Circesio (Brazil)—II, III, IV
Gerbermann Hugo Mark, TB Amatunte di Palestina (Guatemala)—I, III, IV
Geeraerts Xavier, TB Lagania (Belgium)—I, II, III, IV
Geiger Clemente, TB Olena (Brazil)—I, II, IV
Geise Paternus, RB Bogor (Indonesia)—I, II, III, IV
Gelain Henrique, RB Vacaria (Brazil)—I, II, III, IV
Gennangi Joseph, RB Kamichlíe (Syria)—I, III, IV
Gerin y Boulay Marcel, PN Choluteca (Honduras)—III, IV
Gerlier Pierre card., RA Lyon (France)—II, III
Geromini Carlos Luis, TB Zabi (El Salvador)—III, IV
Gerow Richard, RB Natchez-Jackson (USA)—I
Gerrard James, TB Forma (USA)—IV
Ghattas Isaac, RA Tebe (URA-Egypt)—I, II, III, IV
Ghiga Mario, RB Ampurias e Tempio (Italy)—I
Ghedighian Hemaiagh, SG Ordine Mechitarista di Venezia– III, IV
Ghiglione Ernesto, TB Gauriana (Libya)—I, II
Ghizzoni Paolo, TB Tene (Italy)—I, II, III, IV
Giabbani Anselmo, SG Congregazione dei Monaci Eremiti Camaldolesi– I
Gianfranceschi Augusto, RB Cesena (Italy)—I, II, III, IV
Gill Thomas, TB Lambesi (USA)—I, III
Gillet Jacques, SG Trappisti– III, IV
Gillmore Stock Francisco, TB Auzia (Chile)—II, III, IV
Gilroy Norman card., RA Sydney (Australia)—I, II, III, IV
Giobbe Paolo card. emerito della Dataria Apostolica—I, II, III, IV
Giordani Juán, PA La Paz California (Mexico)—II, III, IV
Giorgi Emilio, RB Montepulciano (Italy)—I, II
Giraldo Restrepo Jorge, RB Pasto (Colombia)—I, II, III, IV
Gleen Lawrence, RB Crookston (USA)—I, II, III, IV
Gleeson Francis, RB Fairbanks (USA)—I, II, III, IV
Gleeson James, TA Aurusuliana (Australia)—I, III, IV
Glennie Ignatius Philip Trigueros, RB Trincomalee (Ceylon)— I, II, III, IV
Gnädinger Karl, TB Celerina (Germany)—I, II, III, IV
Gobbato Giovanni Battista PIME, RB Taunggyi (Burma)—I, II, III
Godfrey William card., RA Westminster (Great Britain)—I
Gogué Joseph, RA Bassorah (Iraq)—I
Gólinski Zdzislaw, RB Czestochowa (Poland)—I
Golland Trindade Henrique, RA Botucatú (Brazil)—I, II, III, IV
Gomes de Almeida João, TB Gerafi (Portugal)—I, II, III, IV
Gomes dos Santos Fernando, RA Goiânia (Brazil)—I, II, III, IV
Gomes José, RB Bagé (Brazil)—I, II, IV
Gomes Junqueira Daniel, RB Nova Lisboa (Angola)—I, II, III, IV
Gomes William Zephryne, TB Parlais (India)—II, III, IV
Gómez Serrano Ciro, RB Girardot (Colombia)—I
Gomez Davila Horacio, RB La Rioja (Argentina)—I, IV
Gómez Frande Manuel, PA S. Miguel de Sucumbios (Ecuador)— II, III, IV
Gomez Gregory, AN New Norcia (Australia)—I, II, III, IV
Gómez León, RA Antequera (Mexico)—I, II, III, IV
Gomez Marijuan Francisco, TB Sinna (Equatorial Guinea)— I, II, III, IV
Gómez Tamayo Diego, RA Popayan (Colombia)—I, II
Gómez Villa Constantino, TB Cucuso (Venezuela)—I, II, III, IV
Gonçalves Cerejeira Manuel card., RA Lisbona (Portugal)—I, II, III, IV
Gonçalves da Costa Ernesto, RB Inhambane (Mozambique)— II, III, IV
Gonçalves da Costa José, TB Rodopoli (Brazil)—II, III, IV
Gonçalves do Amaral Alexandre, RA Uberaba (Brazil)— I, II, III, IV
Gonzaga y Rasdesales Lino, RB Palo (Philippines)—I, II, III, IV
Gonzales Ruiz Julio, RB Puno (Peru)—I, II, III, IV
González Arbeláez Juan, TA Ossirinco (Colombia)—I, II, III, IV
González Ascanio Feliciano, RB Maracay (Venezuela)— I, II, III, IV
González Estrada Rafael, TB Matrega (Guatemala)—III, IV
González Ferreiro Amedeo, TB Metre (Brazil)—I, II, III, IV
Gonzalez Ibarra Miguel, RB Autlan (Mexico)—I, II, III, IV
González Martín Marcelo, RB Astorga (Spain)—I, II, III, IV
González Moralejo Rafael, TB Dardano (Spain)—I, II, III, IV
González Ramirez Rafael Angel, RB Barinas (Spain)—IV
Gonzaléz y Robleto Vicente, RA Managua (Nicaragua)— I, II, III, IV
Gonzi Michele, RA Malta (Malta)—I, II, III, IV
Goody Launcelot John, RB Bumbury (Australia)—I, II, III, IV
Gopu Ignatius, TB Feradi Maggiore (India)—III, IV
Gopu Joseph, RA Hyderabad (India)—I, II, III, IV
Gordon John, TA Nicopoli al Nesto (Algeria)—II, IV
Gori Alberto, P Gerusalemme (Palestine)—I, II, III, IV
Gori Giuseppe, RB Nepi e Sutri (Italy)—I, II, III, IV
Gorman Thomas, RB Dallas e Fort Worth (USA)—I, II, III, IV
Gottardi Alessandro, RA Trento (Italy)—II, III, IV
Gottau Jorge, RB Añatuya (Argentina)—I, II, III, IV
Gottwald George, TB Cedamusa (USA)—I, II, III
Goupy Joseph, RB Blois (France)—I, II, III, IV
Gouvêa Coelho Carlos, RA Olinda e Recife (Brazil)—I, II
Gouyon Paul, RA Rennes (France)—I, II, III, IV
Graber Rudolf, RB Regensburg (Germany)—I, II, III, IV
Gracias Valerian card., RA Bombay (India)—I, II, III, IV
Graffin René, TA Mistia (France)—I, II, III, IV
Graham John, TB Sabrata (USA)—III, IV
Gran John Willem, RB Oslo (Norvegia)—II, III, IV
Granados García Anastasio, TB Cidramo (Spain)—I, II, III, IV
Graner Lawrence, RA Dacca (Pakistan)—I, IV
Grano Carlo, TA Tessalonica (Italy)—I, II, III, IV
Grant Charles, TB Alinda (Great Britain)—I, II, III, IV
Grasar William, RB Shrewsbury (Great Britain)—I, II, III, IV
Grau y Arola Pedro, TB Pella (Colombia)—I, II, III, IV
Grauls Antoine, RA Gitega (Burundi)—II
Gray Gordon, RA S. Andrews e Edinburgo (Great Britain)— I, II, III, IV
Graziano Lorenzo Michele Joseph, TB Limata (El Salvador)— II, III, IV
Greco Charles, RB Alexandria (USA)—I, II, III, IV
Green Ernest, RB Port Elizabeth (South Africa)—I, II, III, IV
Green Francis, RB Tucson (USA)—I, II, III, IV
Green Michael, TB Trisipa (USA)—I, II, III, IV
Grégoire Paul, TB Curubi (Canada)—I, II, III, IV
Greif John, RB Tororo (Uganda)—I, II, IV
Grellinger John, TB Siene (USA)—I, II, III, IV
Gremigni Gilla, RA Novara (Italy)—I
Grent Jacques, TB Betagbarara (Indonesia)—I, II, IV
Greteman Frank, TB Vissalsa (USA)—IV
Griffiths James, TB Gaza (USA)—I, II
Grimley Nicholas, TB Tuburbo Minore (Liberia)—I, II, III, IV
Grimm Peter Gratian OFM Cap, RB Tsínchow (China)— I, II, III, IV
Grimmelsman Henry, TB Tabla (USA)—I, II, III, IV
Grimshaw Francis, RA Birmingham (Great Britain)—I, II, III
Groblicki Julian, TB Filadelfia di Arabia (Poland)—III, IV
Groner Heinrich, AN Wettingen (Austria)—I, II, III, IV
Grossi José, RB Bom Jesu de Lapa (Brazil)—I, II, III, IV
Grotti Giocondo Maria, TB Tunigaba (Brazil)—II, III, IV
Grovas Rafael, RB Caguas (Puerto Rico)—IV
Grueter Joseph, RB Umtata (South Africa)—I, II, IV
Grutka Andrew, RB Gary (USA)—I, II, III, IV
Grzondziel Henryk, TB, TAribi (Poland)—II, IV
Guano Emilio, RB Livorno (Italy)—I, II, III
Guercilena Fernando PIME, RB Kengtung (Burma)—I, II, III
Guerra Campos José, TB Muzia (Spain)—III, IV
Guerry Emile Maurice, RA Cambrai (France)—I, II, III, IV
Guffens Joseph, TB Germaniciana (Belgium)—I, II, III, IV
Gufflet Henri, TB Calama (France)—I, II, III, IV
Gugić Giovanni, TB Bonusta (Yugoslavia)—I, II, III, IV
Guibert Georges, RB Réunion (Reunion Island)—I, II, III, IV
Guichet Pierre, TB Strettorio (Micronesia)—I, II, III, IV
Guilford Clyde, RA Hobart (Australia)—IV
Guilfoyle George, TB Marazane (USA)—I, II, III, IV
Guilfoyle Merlin, TB Bulla (USA)—I, II, III, IV
Guilhem Jacques, RB Laval (France)—I, II, III, IV
Guilly Richard, RB Georgetown (Guyana)—I, II, III, IV
Guiot Albert, RB Port-de-Paix (Haiti)—I, II, III, IV
Guízar Barragán Luis, RB Saltillo (Mexico)—I, II, III, IV
Guízar Valencia Antonio, RA Chihuahua (Mexico)—I
Gunnarson Johann, TB Holar (Iceland)—I, II, III, IV
Gúrpide Beope Pablo, RB Bilbao (Spain)—I, II, III, IV
Gusi Pietro, SG Congregazione Sublacense—I, II, III, IV
Gut Benno, SG Benedettini Confederati—I, II, III, IV
Gutiérrez Diéz Thomas, RB Cadice (Spain)—I
Gutierrez Granier José, RB Cochabamba (Bolivia)—I, II, III, IV
Guyot Louis, RB Coutances (France)—I, II, III, IV

H

Habozian Mesrop, TA Camaco (France)—II, III, IV
Habra Basile Pierre Charles, TB Batne per i Siri (URA-Egypt)—II, III, IV
Hacault Antonio, TB Media (Canada)—III, IV
Hacker Hilary, RB Bismarck (USA)—I, II, III, IV
Hackett John, TB Elenopoli di Palestina (USA)—I, II, III, IV
Haddad Georges, RA Tiro dei Melchiti (Lebanon)—IV
Haddad Emmanuel, SG Ordine antoniano di S. Ormisda—I
Hadda Grégoire, TB Palmira per i Melchiti (Lebanon)—IV
Haelg Anthony, TB Baia (Tanzania)—I, II, III, IV
Haene Aloysius, RB Gwelo (Rhodesia)—I, II, III, IV
Häring Edgar Anton OFM, RB Shohchow (China)—I, II, III, IV
Hagan James, RB Makurdi (Nigeria)—I, II, III, IV
Hagarty Paul, RB Nassau (Bahamas)—I, II, III, IV
Hage Atanasio, SG Ordine Basiliano S. Giovanni Battista– I, II, III, IV
Hage Nicola, TA Damiata dei Melchiti (Syria)—IV
Hagendorens Joseph, RB Tshumbé (Congo-Leopoldville)— I, II, IV
Hains Gaston, TB Belesasa (Canada)—III, IV
Hakim George, RA Akka (Israel)—I, II, III, IV
Hall Federick, TB Castra Nova (Great Britain)—I, II, III, IV
Haller Louis, TB Betlemme (Switzerland)—I, II, III, IV
Hallinan Paul, RA, Atlanta (USA)—I, II, IV
Hammes George, RB Superior (USA)—I, II, III, IV
Hamvas Endre, RA Kalocsa (Hungary)—I, II, III, IV
Han Kong-ryel Peter, RB Jeon Ju (South Korea)—I, II, III, IV
Hanly Vincent, RB Elphin (Ireland)—I, II, III, IV
Hannan Jerome, RB Scranton (USA)—I, II, III, IV
Hannan Philip, RA New Orleans (USA)—I, II, III, IV
Hanrion Barthélemy, RB Dapango (Togo)—II, III, IV
Hardman Lawrence, RB Zomba (Malawi)—I, II
Harika Maroun, SG Ordine Antoniano S. Isaia dei Maroniti— I, II, III, IV
Haro Alvear Silvio, RB Ibarra (Ecuador)—I, II, III, IV
Harper Edward, TB Eraclea Pontica (Puerto Rico)—I, II, III, IV
Harrington Michael, RB Kamloops (Canada)—I, II, III, IV
Hart William, RB Dunkeld (Great Britain)—I, II, III, IV
Hartl Carlos, TB Stratonicea di Caria (Chile)—I, II, III, IV
Hascher José, TB Elie (Brazil)—I, II, IV
Hasler Joseph, RB San Gallo (Switzerland)—I, II, III, IV
Hastrich Jerome, TB Gurza (USA)—II, III, IV
Hász Istvan, TB Sura (Switzerland)—I, II, III, IV
Hayek Ignace Antoine II, RA Aleppo dei Siri (Syria)—I, II, III, IV
Hayes James, TB Reperi (Canada)—IV
Hayes Nevin, TB Novasinna (Peru)—I, II, III, IV
Hayes Ralph, RB Davenport (USA)—I, II, III, IV
Healy John, RB Gibilterra (Gibilterra)—I, II, III, IV
Healy Kilian, SG Carmelitani Antica Osservanza—I, II, III, IV
Heard William Theodore card. emerito della Rota romana— I, II, III, IV
Heenan John card., RA Westminster (Great Britain)—I, II, III, IV
Heerey Charles, RA Onitsha (Nigeria)—I, II, IV
Heiligers Cornelius, SG Monfortani—I, II, III, IV
Heim Bruno Bernard, TA Xanto (Denmark)—I, II, III, IV
Heiser Herman, SG Frati Minori Conventuali—I, II, III, IV
Helmsing Charles, RB Kansas City (USA)—I, II, III, IV
Hendriksen Theodoor, TB Eumenia (The Netherlands)— I, II, III, IV
Hengsbach Franz, RB Essen (Germany)—I, II, III, IV
Henriquez Jiménez Luis, TB Lamdia (Venezuela)—I, II, III, IV
Henry Harold William, RA Kwang Ju (South Korea)—I, II, IV
Henschke Francis, RB Wagga Wagga (Australia)—I, II, III, IV
Herlihy Donald, RB Ferns (Ireland)—III, IV
Hermaniuk Maxim, RA Winnipeg degli Ucraini (Canada)— I, II, III, IV
Hermelink Albert, RB Tandjung e Karang (Indonesia)— I, II, III, IV
Hintringer da Losenstein Isidor Hermenegild OFM Cap, PA Kiamusze (China)—II, III, IV
Hermil Jean, TB Marida (France)—II, III, IV
Hernández Hurtado Adolfo, RB Tapachula (Mexico)—I, II, IV
Herrera Augustin, RB San Francisco (Argentina)—I, IV
Herrera Riera Eduardo, TB Sesta (Venezuela)—IV
Herrera y Oria Angel card., RA Malaga (Spain)—II, III, IV
Hervás y Benet Juan, TB Dora (Spain)—I, II, III, IV
Hess Gilbert, SG Congregazione Benedettina Elveto-Americana—I, II, III
Hettinga Nicholas, RB Rawalpindi (Pakistan)—I, II, III, IV
Heuschen Jozef-Maria, TB Drua (Belgium)—I, II, III, IV
Hidalgo Ibáñez Angel, RB Jaca (Spain)—I, II, III, IV
Hillerich Rupert, PA Solwezi (Zambia)—II, III, IV
Hillinger Raymond, TB Derbe (USA)—I, II, III, IV
Hiltl Josef, TB Costantina (Germany)—I, II, III, IV
Himmer Charles, RB Topurnai (Belgium)—I, II, III, IV
Hines Vincent, RB Norwich (USA)—I, II, III, IV
Hinojosa Hurtado Erasmo, RB Piura (Peru)—I, II, IV
Hippel Bruno, RB Oudtshoorn (South Africa)—I, II, III, IV
Hirata Saburo Peter, RB Oita (Japan)—I, II, III, IV
Hnilica Paolo, TB Rusado (Italy)—I, II, III, IV
Hoang-van-Doan Dominique, RB Quinhon (Vietnam)—I, II, IV
Hoa Nguyen-van-Hien Simon, RB Dalat (Vietnam)—I, II, III, IV
Hoang Min Syeng Peter, RB Tae Jeon (South Korea)—IV
Hoch Lambert, RB Sioux Falls (USA)—I, II, III, IV
Hodapp Robert, RB Belize (British Honduras)—I, II, III, IV
Hodges Joseph, RB Wheeling (USA)—I, II, III, IV
Höck Johannes, SG Congregazione Benedettina di Baviera— I, II, III, IV
Höffner Josef, RB Münster (Germany)—I, II, III, IV
Hoenen François, RB Kenge (Congo-Leopoldville)—II, IV
Höfer Alfonso, TB Tebe di Ftiotide (Costa Rica)—II, IV
Hoffer Paul-Joseph, SG Marianisti—I, II, III, IV
Hoffmann Henri, RB Djibouti (Somalia)—I, II, III, IV
Hoffmann João, RB Frederico Westphalen (Brazil)—I, II, III, IV
Hoffmann Anton, TB Berenice (Germany)—I, II, III, IV
Hogan James, RB Filomelio (USA)—I, II, III, IV
Höhne Johannes, TB Urima (New Guinea)—II, III, IV
Holland Joseph, TB Cinopoli di Egitto (Great Britain)—I
Holland Thomas, RB Salford (Great Britain)—I, II, III, IV
Holmes-Siedle James, RB Kigoma (Tanzania)—I, II, III, IV
Holterman Joannes Maria Michael, RB Willemstad (Curaçao)— I, II, III, IV
Hornyak Augustine, TB Ermontis (Great Britain)—I, II, III, IV
Horsthuis Artur, RB Jales (Brazil)—I, II
Houlihan Joseph, RB Eldoret (Kenya)—I, II, III, IV
Howard Edward, RA Portland in Oregon (USA)—I
Howe John James SSCME, RB Myitkyina (Burma)—I, II, III
Hubert Amand, TB Sais (URA-Egypt)—I, II, III, IV

Liverzani Luigi, RB Frascati (Italy)—I, II, III, IV
Livraghi Carlo, TB Tagora (Italy)—I, II, III
Lizardi Ramón, TB Assava (Venezuela)—I, II
Llopis Ivorra Manuel, RB Coira e Cáceres (Spain)—I, II, III, IV
Llorente y Federico Daniel, RB Segovia (Spain)—I, II, III, IV
Llosa Jean-Baptiste, RB Ajaccio (France)—I, II, III
Loayza Gumiel Cleto, RB Potosì (Bolivia)—I
Loewenau João Floriano, TB Drivasto (Brazil)—I, II, III, IV
Loftus Giuseppe, SG Servi di Maria—IV
Lojali Vincenzo, RB Amelia (Italy)—I, II, III, IV
Lokuang Stanislaus, RB Tainan (China)—I, II, III, IV
Lombardi Armando, TA Cesarea di Filippo (Brazil)—I, II
Lommel Léon, RB Luxembourg (Luxembourg)—I, II, III, IV
Lonati Emiliano, TB Epifania di Cilicia (Brazil)—I
Longinotti Ferdinando, RB San Severino (Italy)—I, II, III, IV
Longo Dorni Mario, RB Pistoia (Italy)—I, II, III, IV
Longo Vittorio, TB Lorima (Italy)—I, II, III, IV
Loosdregt Etienne, TB Amaura (Laos)—I, II, III, IV
Lopes De Moura Agostinho, RB Portalegre-Castelo B. (Portugal)—I, II, III, IV
López Aviña Antonio, RA Durango (Mexico)—I, II, III, IV
Lopes de Castro Pinto José, TB Gerapoli di Isauria (Brazil)—III, IV
López Estrada Manuel, RA Jalapa (Mexico)—I, II, III, IV
López Ortiz José, RB Tuy Vigo (Spain)—I, II, III, IV
López Umaña José, RA Cartagena (Colombia)—I, II, IV
López Vitoria Juan, TB Metropoli di Asia (Puerto Rico)—III, IV
Lorscheider Aloísio Leo Arlindo, RB Santo Angelo (Brazil)—I, II, III, IV
Lorscheiter Ivo, TB Tamada (Brazil)—IV
Loucheur André, PA Bafia (Cameroon)—IV
Louis Georges, RB Périgueux (France)—I, II, III
Lourdusamy Duraisamy Simon, TA Filippi (India)—II, III, IV
Lovey Angelin Maurice, SG Congregazione Ospedaliera di San Bernardo—I, II, III, IV
Lucas Martin, TA Aduli (The Netherlands)—II, III, IV
Lucas Rojo Sinforiano, TB Boreo (Paraguay)—I, II, III, IV
Lucey Cornelius, RB Cork e Ross (Ireland)—I, II, III, IV
Lucey Robert, RA San Antonio (USA)—I, II, III, IV
Luciani Albino (Pope John Paul I), RB Vittorio Veneto (Italy)—I, II, III, IV
Lueck John, RB Aliwal (South Africa)—I, II, III, IV
Luí Raimundo, RB Paracatù (Brazil)—I, II, III, IV
Luisi Renato, RB Nicastro (Italy)—I, II, III, IV
Luna Pianegonda Costantino, RB Zacapa (Guatemala)—I, II, III, IV
Lussier Philippe, RB Saint Paul in Alberta (Canada)—I, II, III, IV
Lyons Patrick, RB Sale (Australia)—I, II, III, IV

M

Maanicus Antoine Marie, RB Bangassou (Central African Republic)—III, IV
Mabathoama Emanuel, RA Maseru (Basutoland)—I, II, III, IV
Mabutas y Lloren Antonio, RB Laoag (Philippines)—I, II, III, IV
Macario Raffaele, TB Tiberiade (Italy)—I, II, III, IV
Maccari Carlo, RA Mondovì (Italy)—I, II, III, IV
MacEachern Malcolm, RB Charlottetown (Canada)—I, II, III, IV
Machado Cavalcanti Adelmo, RA Maceió (Brazil)—I, II, III, IV
Machado y Escobar Miguel, RB San Miguel (El Salvador)—I
Macheiner Eduard, TB Selja (Austria)—II, III, IV
MacNamee James, RB, RAdagh (Ireland)—I, II, III
MacNeely Anthony, RB Raphoe (Ireland)—I, II
Madriaga Mariano, RA Lingayen Dagupan (Philippines)—I, II
Maggi Giuseppe PIME, RB Hanchung (China)—I
Maginn Edward, TB Curio (USA)—I, II, III, IV
Magliacani Irzio Luigi OFMCap, TB Diu e VA di Arabia (Arabia)—I, II, III, IV
Magliano Mauricio Eugenio, RB Rio Gallegos (Argentina)—I, II, III, IV
Maguire John, TA Tabalta (USA)—III, IV
Maher Leo, RB Santa Rosa (USA)—I, II, III, IV
Mahon Gerald, SG S. Giuseppe Mill Hill—II, III, IV
Mahony William, PA Ilorin (Nigeria)—I, II, III, IV
Maillat Eugene, RB N'Zérékoré (Nigeria)—I, II, III, IV
Majdanski Casimiro, TB Zorolo (Poland)—II, IV
Majewski Waclaw, TB Docimio (Poland)—II, IV
Makarakiza Andreas, RB Ngozi (Burundi)—I, II, III, IV
Malanchuk Vladimiro, TB Epifania di Syria (France)—I, II, III, IV
Malbois Albert, TB Altava (France)—I, II, III, IV
Malchiodi Umberto, RA Piacenza (Italy)—I, II, III, IV
Maleddu Pietro OFMConv, PA Hinganfu (China)—II, III, IV
Malefant Joseph, PA Benares Gorakhpur (India)—II, III
Malké Flavien Zacharie, TA Amida per i Siri (Lebanon)—II, IV
Malone James, TB Alabanda (USA)—I, II, III, IV
Maloney Charles, TB Capsa (USA)—I, II, III, IV
Maloney David, TB Ruspe (USA)—I, II, III, IV
Malouf Joseph, RB Baalbeck dei Melchiti (Lebanon)—I, II, III, IV
Malula Joseph, RA Léopoldville (Congo-Leopoldville)—I, II, III, IV
Malzone Hugo, RB Governador Valadares (Brazil)—I, II, IV
Mancini Tito, TB Vartana (Italy)—I, II, III, IV
Mancuso Giuseppe, RB Mazara del Vallo (Italy)—I, II, III, IV
Manek Gabriel, RA Endeh (Indonesia)—I, II, III
Mangers Jacques, TB Afufenia (Luxembourg)—I, II, III, IV
Mangino Bartolomeo, RB Caserta (Italy)—I, II
Manning Timothy, TB Lesvi (USA)—I, II, III, IV
Manning Tomás Roberto Patricio, TB Arsamosata (Bolivia)—I, II, III, IV
Manresa Formosa Luis, RB Quezaltenango (Guatemala)—I, II, III, IV
Manrique Hurtado Jorge, RB Oruro (Bolivia)—I, II, III, IV
Mansfeld Carlo, SG Ministri degli Infermi—I, II, III
Mansilla Reoyo Demetrio, RB Ciudad Rodrigo (Spain)—I, II, III, IV
Mansourati Ignace, TA Apamea di Syria (Italy)—II, III, IV
Manziana Carlo, RB Crema (Italy)—III, IV
Maradan Marcel, RB Port Victoria (Seychelles)—I, II, III, IV
Maradei Costantino, RB Cabimas (Venezuela)—IV
Marafini Giuseppe, RB Veroli e Frosinone (Italy)—IV
Maranta Edgard, RA Dar-es-Salaam (Tanzania)—I, II, III, IV
Marcante Luciano, RB Valva e Sulmona (Italy)—I, II, III, IV
Marchesani Francesco, RB Chiavari (Italy)—I, II, III, IV
Marchesi Giovanni, TB Cela (Brazil)—I, II, III, IV
Marchetti-Zioni Vicente, RB Bauru (Brazil)—II, III, IV
Marchioni Ambrogio, TA Severiana (Italy)—I, III, IV
Marella Paolo card. arciprete della Basilica Vaticana e prefetto della congregazione della Fabbrica di San Pietro; presidente del segretariato per i Non cristiani—I, II, III, IV
Marena Aurelio, RB Ruvo e Bitonto (Italy)—I, II, III, IV
Marengo Manuel, RB Azul (Argentina)—I, II, III, IV
Marengo Orestes, RB Tezpur (India)—I, III, IV
Maresma Olimpo, TB Gegi (Argentina)—IV
Margiotta Nicola, RA Brindisi (Italy)—II, III, IV
Mari Septimio, TB Pacnemunis (Colombia)—I, II, III, IV
Maricevich Fleitas Anibal, RB Concepción (Paraguay)—I, II, III, IV
Marie Alfred, RB Cayenne (Guyane)—III, IV
Marinoni Giovanni, TA Amorio (Italy)—I, II, III, IV
Marinucci Gabriele, SG Romitani Scalzi di S. Agostino– III, IV
Markall Francis, RA Salisbury (Rhodesia)—I, II, III, IV
Marling Joseph, RB Jefferson City (USA)—I, II, III, IV
Marozzi José, RB Resistencia (Argentina)—I, II, IV
Marques Ferreira Almir, RB Uberlandia (Brazil)—I
Márques y Toríz Octaviano, RA Puebla de los Angeles (Mexico)—I, II, III, IV
Marquez Gomez Tomás, TB Tapso (Venezuela)—IV
Marrocco Francis, TB Limne (Canada)—II, III, IV
Martenetz José, TB Soldaia (Brazil)—I, II, III, IV
Martensen Joannes, RB Copenaghen (Denmark)—IV
Martin Del Campo Padilla Manuel, TA Vadesi (Mexico)—I, II, III, IV
Martin Giacomo, TB Neapoli di Palestina (Italy)—III, IV
Martin Joseph, RB Bururi (Burundi)—I, II, IV
Martin Joseph A., RB Nicolet (Canada)—I, II, III, IV
Martin Joseph card., RA Rouen (France)—I, II, III, IV
Martin Pierre, TB Selinonte (Melanesia)—I, II, III, IV
Martin Raimundo, RB Vera Paz (Guatemala)—I, IV
Martín Raimondo Enrico, Iles de Saint-Pierre (Canada)—IV
Martinez Aguirre Salvador, TB, Arca di Armenia (Mexico)—I, II, III, IV
Martínez Vivas Angel, RB Tsiroanomandidy (Madagascar)—I, II, III, IV
Martínez Betancourt José, RB Tacámbaro (Mexico)—I, II, IV
Martínez Gonzáles Eduardo, RB Zamora (Spain)—I, II, III, IV
Martinez Silva Salvador, TB Jaso (Mexico)—I, II, III
Martínez Vargas José, RB Armenia (Colombia)—I, II, III
Martinez y Dalmau Eduado, TB Teuzi (USA)—II, III
Martini Carlo, TA Abari (Philippines)—II
Marty François, RA Reims (France)—I, II, III, IV
Marx Adolph, RB Brownsville (USA)—I, II, III, IV
Marzi Adalberto, TB Sesina (Brazil)—I, II, IV
Mascariñas y Morgia Manuel, RB Tagbilaran (Philippines)—I
Masnou Boixeda Ramón, RB Vich (Spain)—I, II, III, IV
Mason Edoardo, TB Rusicade (Sudan)—II, III, IV
Massa Pedro, TB Ebron (Brazil)—I
Massa Pietro PIME, RB Nanyang (China)—I, II, III, IV
Massimiliani Roberto, RB Civita Castellana, Orte, Gallese (Italy)—I, II, III, IV
Mata Cova Crisanto, RB Cumaná (Venezuela)—I, II, IV
Matagrin Gabriel, TB Floriana (France)—IV
Mathew David, TA Apamea di Bitinia (Great Britain)—I
Mathias Alfonso, RB Chikmagalur (India)—III, IV
Mathias Louis, RA Madras (India)—I, II, III
Matsuoka Magoshiro Peter, RB Nagoya (Japan)—I, II, III, IV
Matthysen Alphonse, RB Bunia (Congo-Leopoldville)—I
Maung Kyaw George, RB Bassein (Burma)—I, II
Maurer José, RA Sucre (Bolivia)—I, II, III, IV
Mauro dell'Addolorata, SG Carm. B.V.M. Immacolata—IV
Maury Jean, TA Laodicea di Frigia (Congo-Leopoldville)—I, II, III, IV
Maverna Luigi, TB Vannida (Italy)—IV
Maya Guzman Vincenzo, TB Comana Pontica (Ecuador)—III, IV
Mayer Jorge, RB Santa Rosa (Argentina)—I, II, III, IV
Mazé Jean, TB Sauatra (France)—I, II
Mazé Paul, TB Ascalone (Polynesia)—I, II, III, IV
Mazerat Henri, RB Angers (France)—I, II, III, IV
Maziers Félix-Antoine Marius, TB Augustopoli di Frigia (France)—I, II, III, IV
Mazur Jan, TB Bladia (Poland)—II
Mazzarella Bernardino, RB Comayagua (Honduras)—I, II, III, IV
Mazzarotto Antonio, RB Ponta Grossa (Brazil)—I
Mazzarotto Jerônimo, TB, Arsinoe di Arcadia (Brazil)—IV
Mazzieri Francis, RB Ndola (Zambia)—I, II, III, IV
Mazzocco Guido, RB Adria (Italy)—I, II, III
Mazzoldi Sisto, TB Lamo (Uganda)—I, IV
Mbali Jacques, RB Buta (Congo-Leopoldville)—I, II, IV
Mbemba Théophile, RA Brazzaville (Congo-Brazzaville)—I, III, IV
Mbuka-Nzundu Alexander, TB Cataquas (Congo-Leopoldville)—I, II, III, IV
McBride John, RB Kokstad (South Africa)—I, II, III, IV
McCann Owen card., RA Cape Town (South Africa)—I, II, III, IV
McCarthy Edward, TB Tamascani (USA)—IV
McCarthy John, RA Kaduna (Nigeria)—I, II, III, IV
McCarthy John Joseph, RA Nairobi (Kenya)—I, II, IV
McCarthy Thomas, RB Saint Catharines (Canada)—I, II, III, IV
McCarthy William, RB Rapid City (USA)—I, II, III, IV
McCauley Vincent, RB Fort Portal (Uganda)—I, II, III, IV
McCormick Joseph, RB Altoona Johnstown (USA)—I, II, III, IV
McCoy Owen, RB Oyo (Nigeria)—II, III, IV
McDevitt Gerald, TB Tigia (USA)—I, II, III, IV
McDonald William, TB Acque Regie (USA)—III, IV
McDonough Thomas, RB Savannah (USA)—I, II, III, IV
McEleney John, RB Kingston (Jamaica)—I, II, III, IV
McEntegart Bryan, RB Brooklyn (USA)—I, II, III, IV
McFeely Anthony, RB Raphoe (Ireland)—IV
McGarry Urban, RB Bhagalpur (India)—II, III, IV
McGee Joseph, RB Galloway (Great Britain)—I, II, III, IV
McGeough Joseph Francis, TA Hemesa (South Africa)—I, II, III, IV
McGettrick Thomas, RB Ogoja (Nigeria)—I, II, III, IV
McGill Stephen, RB, Argyll (Great Britain)—I, II, III, IV
McGrath Marcos Gregorio, RB Santiago di Veraguas (Panama)—I, II, III, IV
McGucken Joseph, RA San Francisco (USA)—I, II, III, IV
McGuigan James card., RA Toronto (Canada)—I, II, III
McGurkin Edward, RB Shinyanga (Tanzania)—I, II, III, IV
McHonde Elias, RB Mahenge (Tanzania)—I, II, III, IV
McHugh Francis, PN Itacoatiara (Brazil)—IV
McIntyre James card., RA Los Angeles (USA)—I, II, III, IV
McKeefry Peter, RA Wellington (New Zealand)—I, III, IV
McKeon Myles, TB Antipirgo (Australia)—I, III, IV
McLaughlin Charles, TB Risinio (USA)—III, IV
McManaman Edward, TB Floriana (USA)—I, II
McManus James, TB Benda (USA)—I, II, IV
McNabb Juan Conway, PN Chulucanas (Peru)—III, IV
McNamara Martin, RB Joliet (USA)—I
McNaughton William, RB Inchon (South Korea)—I, II, III, IV
McNulty James, RB Buffalo (USA)—I, II, III, IV
McQuaid John, RA Dublino (Ireland)—I, II, III, IV
McShea Joseph, RB Allentown (USA)—I, II, III
McSorley Francis, TB Sozusa di Palestina (Philippines)—I, II, III, IV
McVinney Russell, RB Providence (USA)—I, II, III, IV
Medawar Pierre, TA Pelusio (Syria)—III
Medina José, TB Termesso (Argentina)—II, III
Medina y Medina Miguel Antonio, RB Montería (Colombia)—I, II, III, IV
Mekkelholt Henri, TB Dausara (The Netherlands)—II, III, IV
Melancon Davide, SG Congregazione Benedettina Elveto-Americana– IV
Melas Giuseppe, RB Nuoro (Italy)—I, II, III, IV
Mele Giovanni, RB Lungro (Italy)—I, II, III, IV
Melendro y Gutiérrez Federico SJ, RA Anking (China)—I, II, III, IV
Melhado Campos José, TB Ospita (Brazil)—I, II, III, IV
Melillo Aniger, RB Piracicaba (Brazil)—I, II, III, IV
Melis Fois Giovanni, RB Ampurias e Tempio (Italy)—II, III, IV
Melotto Mazzardo Angelico, RB Solola (Guatemala)—I, II, IV
Mels Bernard, RA Luluabourg (Congo-Leopoldville)—I, II, III, IV
Mena Arroyo Luis, TA Siniti (Mexico)—III, IV
Mena Porta Juan, RA Asunción (Paraguay)—I, III
Ménager Jacques, RB Meaux (France)—I, II, III, IV
Ménard Jean-Ernest, RB Rodez (France)—II, III, IV
Menchaca Lira Alejandro, TB Pinara (Chile)—I, II, III, IV
Méndez Alfredo, RB, Arecibo (Puerto Rico)—I, IV
Méndez Arceo Sergio, RB Cuernavaca (Mexico)—I, II, III, IV
Mendiharat Marcelo, TB Zerta (Uruguay)—I, II, III, IV
Mendonça James, RB Tiruchirapalli (India)—I, II, III, IV
Mendonça Monteiro António, RB Bonfim (Brazil)—I, II
Mendoza Castro Alcides, RB Abancay (Peru)—I, II, III, IV
Menéndez Manuel, RB San Martin (Argentina)—I, II, III, IV
Mennonna Antonio, RB Nardó (Italy)—I, II, III, IV

Mensa Albino, RB Ivrea (Italy)—I, II, III, IV
Meouchi Paul Pierre card. P Antiochia (Lebanon)—I, II, III, IV
Mercier Georges, RB Laghouat (Algeria)—I, II, III, IV
Merkle Atanasio, SG Ordine Cistercense di Santa Croce—II
Mery Beckdorf, RAturo, TA Fasi (Chile)—I, II, IV
Messmer León, RB Ambanja (Madagascar)—I, II, III, IV
Metzger Sidney, RB El Paso (USA)—I, III, IV
Metzinger Lucien, TB Autenti (Peru)—I, II, III, IV
Meyer Albert Gregory card., RA Chicago (USA)—I, II, III
Mezza Fausto, AN SS. Trinità di Cava dei Tirreni (Italy)—I, II, III, IV
Micci Costanzo, RB Larino (Italy)—I, II, III, IV
Michelato Antonio, TB, Archelaide (Italy)—I, II, III, IV
Michele di Gesù, SG Ordine SS.ma Trinità—I, II, III, IV
Micheletto Pellanda Geraldo, RB Ponta Grossa (Brazil)—I, II, III, IV
Michetti Gaetano, TB Irenopoli di Cilicia (Italy)—I, II, III, IV
Michler Martino, AN Nostra Signora di Monserrate (Brazil)—I, II, III, IV
Michon Roger, RB Chartres (France)—I, II, III, IV
Mignani Gaetano CM, RB Kian (China)—I, II, III, IV
Mihayo Marc, RA Tabora (Tanzania)—I, II, III, IV
Minali Cesário, TB Achirao (Brazil)—I, II, III, IV
Minerva Francesco, RB Lecce (Italy)—I, II, III, IV
Mingo Corrado, RA Monreale (Italy)—I, II, III, IV
Minihan Jeremiah, TB Pafo (USA)—I, II, III, IV
Minisci Teodoro, AN S. Maria di Grottaferrata (Italy)—I, II, III, IV
Miranda y Gómez Miguel, RA Mexico (Mexico)—I, II, III, IV
Mistrorigo Antonio, RB Treviso (Italy)—I, II, III, IV
Mocellini Giovanni, RB Comacchio (Italy)—I, II, III, IV
Modrego y Casáus Gregorio, RA Barcellona (Spain)—I, II, III, IV
Modzelewski Jerzy, TB Daonio (Poland)—IV
Möhler Wilhelm, SG Pallottini—I, II, III, IV
Moietta Vittorio, RB Nicastro (Italy)—I
Mojaisky Perrelli Gastone, RA Nusco (Italy)—I, II, III, IV
Mojoli Giuseppe, TA Larissa di Tessalia (Ethiopia)—II, III, IV
Molin Paul, TB Garba (Mali)—I, II, III, IV
Moll y Salord Manuel, RB Tortosa (Spain)—I, II, III, IV
Moloney Michael, RB Bathurst (Gambia)—I, II, III, IV
Monaco Francesco, RB Caltanisetta (Italy)—I, II, III, IV
Mondè Enrico, SG Società Missioni Africane—II, III, IV
Mongeau Gerard, TB Diana (Philippines)—I, II, III, IV
Mongo Thomas, RB Douala (Cameroon)—I, II, III, IV
Montà Alfonso Maria, SG Servi di Maria—I, II, III
Monte Nivaldo, TB Eluza (Brazil)—II, III, IV
Montini Giovanni Battista card. (Pope Paul VI), RA Milano (Italy)—I
Moors Pieter Jan Antoon, RB Roermond (The Netherlands)—I, II, III, IV
Moran Lawrence, TB Cesarea di Filippo (Australia)—IV
Morano Francesco card.—I, II, III, IV
Morcillo González Casimiro, RA Madrid (Spain)—I, II, III, IV
Morel Louis, TA Eno (Belgium)—I, II, III, IV
Moreno Quintana Teodosio, RB Huaraz (Peru)—I, II, III, IV
Moretti Pietro OFM, PA Tungchow (China)—II, III, IV
Morgante Marcello, RB Ascoli Piceno (Italy)—I, II, III, IV
Morilleau Xavier, TB Cappadocia (France)—III, IV
Morin Laurent, RB Prince Albert (Canada)—I, II, III, IV
Morkovsky John, TB Tigava (USA)—I, II, III, IV
Morlion Urbain, RB Baudouinville (Congo-Leopoldville)—I, II, III, IV
Moro Briz Santos, RB Avila (Spain)—I, II, III, IV
Morris Thomas, RA Cashel (Ireland)—I, II, III, IV
Morstabilini Luigi, RB Brescia (Italy)—I, II, III, IV
Morta Figuls Angel, TB Gubaliana (Spain)—IV
Moscatelli Teobaldo, SG Congregazione Cistercense di S. Bernardo d'Italia—I, II, III, IV
Moscato Demetrio, RA Salerno (Italy)—I, II, III, IV
Mościcki Aleksander, TB Doara (Poland)—II
Mosconi Natale, RA Ferrara (Italy)—I, II, III, IV
Mosquera Corral Cesar, RA Guayaquil (Ecuador)—I, II, III, IV
Motolese Guglielmo, RA Taranto (Italy)—I, II, III, IV
Motta Othon, RB Campanha (Brazil)—I, II, III, IV
Mouisset Jean, RB Nice (France)—I, II, III, IV
Moynagh James, RB Calabar (Nigeria)—I, II, III, IV
Moynihan Denis, RB Kerry (Ireland)—I, II, III, IV
Mozzoni Umberto, TA Side (Argentina)—I, II, III, IV
Msakila Charles, RB Karema (Tanzania)—I, II, III, IV
Muccin Gioacchino, RB Feltre e Belluno (Italy)—I, II, III, IV
Mudartha Giovanni, TB Idebesso (India)—II, III, IV
Mueller Joseph, RB Sioux City (USA)—I, II, III, IV
Muguerza Francisco, RB Oran (Argentina)—I, III, IV
Muhn Enrique, RB Jujuy (Argentina)—I
Muldoon Thomas, TB Fessei (Australia)—I, II, III, IV
Mulrooney Charles, TB Valentiniana (USA)—I, II, III, IV
Mummadi Ignacius, RB Guntur (India)—I, III, IV
Munita Eyzaguirre Ramón, RB San Felipe (Chile)—I
Munive Escobar Luis, RB Tlaxcala (Mexico)—I, II, III
Muniz João Batista, RB Barra do Rio Grande (Brazil)—I, II
Muñoyerro Alonso Luis, TA Sion (Spain)
Muñoz Duque Anibal, RA Nueva Pamplona (Colombia)—I, II, III, IV
Muñoz Vega Paolo, TB Ceramo (Ecuador)—III, IV
Murphy Henry, RB Limerick (Ireland)—I, II, III, IV
Murphy John, RA Cardiff (Great Britain)—I, II, III, IV
Murphy Thomas, RB Juázeiro (Brazil)—II, IV
Murphy Thomas A., TB Appiaria (USA)—I
Murphy Urban, PA Bechuanaland (Bechuanaland)—II, III, IV
Mussio Anthony, RB Steubenville (USA)—I, II, III, IV
Musto Biagio, RB Aquino (Italy)—I, II, III, IV
Musty Jean, TB Botriana (Belgium)—I, II, III, IV
Muszyński Edward, TB Mastaura di Asia (Poland)—II
Muthappa Francis, RB Coimbatore (India)—I, II, III, IV
Muzzolón Angel, TB Tirieo (Paraguay)—I, II, III, IV
Myskiw Paolo, SG Ordine Basiliano di s. Giosafat—I

N

Nabaa Philippe, RA Beirut (Lebanon)—I, II, III, IV
Nanayakkara Leo, RB Kandy (Ceylon)—I, II, III, IV
Nardone Beniamino, TA Aureopoli di Asia (Italy)—I
Navagh James, RB Paterson (USA)—I, II, III, IV
Navarrete y Guerrero Juan, RA Hermosillo (Mexico)—I, II, III, IV
Navarro Allende Bernardo, SG Mercedari– I, II, III, IV
Navarro Ramirez Juan, RB Ciudad Altamirano (Mexico)—IV
Ndong François, TB Rafanea (Gabon)—I, II, III, IV
Ndongmo Albert, RB Nkongsamba (Cameroon)—III, IV
Ndudi Raymond, TB Matara di Procosolare (Congo-Leopoldville)—I, II, III, IV
Nécsey Eduard, TB Velicia (Czechoslovakia)—I, II, III, IV
Nelligan Charles Leo, TB Fenice (Canada)—I, II, III, IV
Nepote-Fus José, TB Elo (Italy)—I, II, III, IV
Neuhäusler Johannes, TB Calidone (Germany)—II, III, IV
Neves José, RB Assis (Brazil)—I, II, III, IV
Newell Hubert, RB Cheyenne (USA)—I, II, III, IV
Newman Thomas Albert MS, RB Prome (Burma)—I, II, III
Nežić Dragutin, RB Parenzo e Pola (Yugoslavia)—I, II, III, IV
Nganga Louis, RB Lisala (Congo-Leopoldville)—I, II, IV
Ngô-dinh-Thuc Pierre, RA Hué (Vietnam)—I, II, III, IV
Nguyên-Khác-Ngu Michel, RB Long-Xuyen (Vietnam)—I, II, III, IV
Nguyên-Kim-Diên Philippe, TA Pario (Vietnam)—I, II, III, IV
Nguyên-Ngoc-Quang Jacobus, RB Cantho (Vietnam)—IV
Nguyên-van-Binh Paul, RA Saigon (Vietnam)—I, II, IV
Nguyên-van-Thien Antoine, RB Vinh-Long (Vietnam)—I, II, III, IV
Niccolai Juan, RB Tarija (Bolivia)—I, II, III, IV
Niccoli Francesco, RB Colle di Val d'Elsa (Italy)—I, II, III, IV
Nicodemo Enrico, RA Bari (Italy)—I, II, III, IV
Nicolini Giuseppe, RB Assisi (Italy)—I, II, III, IV
Nicolosi Salvatore, RB Lipari (Italy)—II, III, IV
Niederberger Basil, SG Congregazione Benedettina Switzerland—I, II, III, IV
Niedhammer Matthew, TB Caloe (Nicaragua)—I, II, III, IV
Niehues Alfonso, TA Aptuca (Brazil)—I, II, III, IV
Nierhoff Francisco, RB Floresta (Brazil)—III, IV
Nierman Pieter, RB Groningen (The Netherlands)—I, II, III, IV
Nigris Leone, TA Filippi (Italy)—I, II
Nilmar Juan, TB Zapara (Philippines)—II
Niu Hui-ching Thomas, RB Yangku (China)—I, III, IV
Niza Ribeiro Felix, RB Tete (Mozambique)—II, III, IV
Nkalanga Placidus Gervasius, TB Balbura (Tanzania)—I, III, IV
Nkongolo Joseph, RB Luebo (Congo-Leopoldville)—I, II, III, IV
Nkou Pierre-Célestin, RB Sangmélina (Cameroon)—II, III, IV
Noa Thomas, RB Marquette (USA)—I, II, III, IV
Noël Laurent, TB Agatopoli (Canada)—II, III, IV
Noguchi Dominicus, RB Hiroshima (Japan)—I, II, III, IV
Nold Wendelin, RB Galveston e Houston (USA)—I, II, III, IV
Nolker Bernardo José, RB Paranaguà (Brazil)—II, III, IV
Nordhues Paul, TB Cos (Germany)—I, II, IV
Noronha Marcos Antonio, RB Itabira (Brazil)—IV
Norton John Francis, RB Bathurst (Australia)—I
Noser Adolph, TB Gerpiniana (New Guinea)—I, II, III, IV
Nousseir Paul, RA Minya (URA-Egypt)—I, II, III, IV
Nóvoa Fuente Miguel, TB Chitri (Spain)—I, II, III, IV
Nowak Lodovico, SG Monaci S. Paolo Primo Eremita—I
Nowicki Edmund, RB Gda sk (Poland)—I, II, III, IV
Ntuyahaga Michel, RB Bujumbura (Burundi)—I, II, III, IV
Nuer Jean, RB Assiut dei Copti (URA-Egypt)—I, II, III, IV
Nujaim Abdallah, RB Baalbeck dei Maroniti (Lebanon)—II, III, IV
Nunes Gabriel, TA Metimna (Angola)—I, IV
Nunes Teixeira Francisco, RB Quelimane (Mozambique)—I, II, III, IV
Nuñez Núñez Daniel Enrique, RB David (Panama)—III, IV
Nuño Francisco, TA Garella (Mexico)—I
Nuti Oreste, RB Canelones (Uruguay)—I, II, III, IV
Nuzzi Jolando, RB Campagna (Italy)—I, II, III, IV
Nwedo Anthony, RB Umuahia (Nigeria)—I, II, III, IV
Nze Abui Raffaele, TB Sutunurca (Equatorial Guinea)—IV
Nzita Simon, TB Gindaro (Congo-Leopoldville)—I, II, IV

O

Obert Joseph, RB Dinajpur (Pakistan)—I, II, III, IV
Oblak Jan, TB Abbir Maggiore (Poland)—II, IV
Oblak Marijan, TB Flaviade (Yugoslavia)—I, II, III, IV
O'Boyle Patrick, RB Killala (Ireland)—I, II, III, IV
O'Boyle Patrick L., RA Washington (USA)—I, II, III, IV
O'Brien Eris, RA Canberra e Goulburn (Australia)—I, II, III, IV
O'Brien Henry, RA Hartford (USA)—I
Obviar y Aranda Alfredo, TB Linoe (Philippines)—I
O'Callaghan Eugene, RB Clogher (Ireland)—I
Ocampo Berrío Angel, RA Tunja (Colombia)—I, II, III, IV
Ochoa Francisco, TB Remesiana (Spain)—I, II, III, IV
O'Collins James, RB Ballarat (Australia)—I, II, III, IV
O'Connor Martin, TA Laodicea di Syria (Italy)—I, II, III, IV
O'Connor William, RB Springfield in Illinois (USA)—I, II, III, IV
O'Connor William P., RB Madison (USA)—I, II
Oddi Silvio, TA Mesembria (Belgium)—I, II, III, IV
O'Doherty Eugene, RB Dromore (Ireland)—I, II, III, IV
Odongo James, TB Baanna (Uganda)—IV
O'Donnell Cletus, TB Abritto (USA)—I, III, IV
O'Donnell Patrick, RA Brisbane (Australia)—I, II, III, IV
O'Flanagan Dermot, RB Juneau (USA)—I, II, III, IV
O'Gara Cutbert Martin CP, RB Yüanling (China)—I, II, III, IV
Ogez John, RB Mbarara (Uganda)—I, II, III, IV
O'Grady John, TB Aspendo (Canada)—I, II, III, IV
Oguki Atakpah Bernard, RB Atakpame (Togo)—III, IV
O'Hara Gerald, TA Pessinonte (Great Britain)—I
O'Keefe Gerald, TB Candiba (USA)—I, II, III, IV
Okoye Godfrey, RB Port Harcourt (Nigeria)—I, II, III, IV
Olaechea Loizaga Marcelino, RA Valencia (Spain)—I, II, III, IV
Olalia Alejandro, RB Lipa (Philippines)—I, II
Olano y Urteaga León, TB Lagina (Spain)—I, II, III, IV
Olazar Muruaga Gregorio, TB Prusa (Peru)—I, II, III, IV
Olbert Augustin SVD, RB Tsíngtao (China)—I, II
Olçomendy Michael, RA Malacca (Singapore)—I, II, III, IV
Oldani Luigi, TB Gergi (Italy)—I, II, III, IV
Olivotti Giuseppe, TB Samo (Italy)—I, II, III, IV
O'Loughlin John, RB Darwin (Australia)—I, II, III, IV
Olu Chukwuka Nwaezeapu Lucas, RB Warri (Nigeria)—III, IV
Olwell Charles Quentin Bertram, TB Tabraca (Philippines)—I, III, IV
Oña de Echave Antonio, RB Lugo (Spain)—I, II, III, IV
O'Neill John, RB Grand Falls (Canada)—I, II, III, IV
O'Neill Michael, RA Regina (Canada)—I, II, III, IV
O'Reilly Michael, RB Saint George's (Canada)—I, II, III, IV
Oscoz Mariano, SG Congregazione Eremitani Camaldolesi di Monte Corona—I, II, III
O'Shea Thimothy, RB Livingstone (Zambia)—I, II, III, IV
Oste Joseph Julian CICM, RB Jehol (China)—I, II, III, IV
O'Sullivan Joseph, RA Kingston (Canada)—I, II, III, IV
Ottaviani Alfredo card., segretario del s. Uffizio—I, II, III, IV
Ottaviani Vittorio, RB Alatri (Italy)—II, III, IV
Otunga Maurice, RB Kisii (Kenya)—I, II
Ouellette Joseph, RB Mont Laurier (Canada)—I, II, III, IV
Oviedo Cavada Carlos, TB Benevento (Chile)—III, IV
Oviedo y Reyes Isidro, RB León (Nicaragua)—I

P

Pace Joseph, RB Gozo (Malta)—I, II, IV
Pacheco Ribeiro Altivo, RB Barra do Piraí (Brazil)—II, III, IV
Pachowiak Heinrich, TB Fitea (Germany)—I, II, III, IV
Pacini Alfredo, TA Germia (Switzerland)—I, IV
Padilla Lozano José, RB Veracruz (Mexico)—II, III, IV
Padin Candido, TB Tremitonte (Brazil)—II, III, IV
Padiyara Anthony, RB Ootacamund (India)—I, II, III, IV
Pailler André, TA Marcelliana (France)—I, II, III, IV
Pailloux René, RB Fort Rosebery (Zambia)—I, II, IV
Palathuruthy Januarius Paul, Ordinario Chanda (India)—III, IV
Palazzini Pietro, TA Cesarea di Cappadocia (Italy)—I, II, III, IV
Palha Luis, TB Lunda (Brazil)—I
Palmas Angelo, TA Vibiana (Vietnam)—IV
Palmerini Achille, RB Isernia e Venafro (Italy)—I, II, III, IV
Palombella Giacomo, RA Matera (Italy)—I, II, III, IV
Pangrazio Andrea, RA Gorizia (Italy)—I, II, III, IV
Papp Kalmán, RB Györ (Hungary)—II
Pappalardo Paolo, TA Apamea di Syria (Italy)—III
Pardini Giovanni, RB Iesi (Italy)—I, II, III, IV
Pardy James Vincent, RB Cheong-Ju (South Korea)—I, II, III, IV
Paré Marius, RB Chicoutimi (Canada)—I, II, III, IV
Parecattil Joseph, RA Ernakulam (India)—I, II, III, IV
Parent Charles, RA Rimouski (Canada)—I, II
Parente Pietro, TA Tolemaide di Tebaide (Italy)—I, II, III, IV
Parenty André, TB Sitifi (France)—I, II, III, IV
Parker Thomas, RB Northampton (Great Britain)—I, II, III, IV
Paro Gino, TB Diocesarea di Isauria (Italy)—I, II, III, IV
Parodi Diego, TB Centenaria (Brazil)—I, II, III, IV

Parodi Giovanni B., RB Savona e Noli (Italy)—I, II, III, IV
Parteli Keller Carlos, RB Tacuarembo (Uruguay)—I, II, III, IV
Paschang John, RB Grand Island (USA)—I, II, III, IV
Pasini Ferdinando Fulgencio OFM, RB San-yüan (China)—I, II, III, IV
Pastorino Giustino, TB Babra (Libya)—IV
Paternain Miguel, TA Acrida (Uruguay)—I, II, III, IV
Patria Jacques, RB Périgueux (France)—I, II, III, IV
Patroni Aldo Maria, RB Calicut (India)—I, II, III, IV
Paupini Giuseppe, TA Sebastopoli di Abasgia (Colombia)—II
Pavlišić Iosip, TB Bruzo (Yugoslavia)—I, II, III, IV
Pawłowski Antoni, RB Włocławek (Poland)—I, II, III, IV
Paz Ladislau, RB Corumbá (Brazil)—I, II, III, IV
Pearce George, TB, Attalea di Pamfilia (Polynesia)—I, II, III, IV
Pearson Thomas, TB Sinda (Great Britain)—I, II, III, IV
Pechillo Arthur Gerolamo, TB Nuova Spagna (Paraguay)—I, II, IV
Pechuán Marin Enrique, RB Cruz del Eje (Argentina)—II, III, IV
Pedicini Gioacchino, RB Avellino (Italy)—I, II, III, IV
Pedroni Angelo, TA Novica (Thailand)—IV
Peeters Julius Joseph Willem, RB Buea (Cameroon)—I, II, III, IV
Peiris Edmund, RB Chilaw (Ceylon)—I, II, III, IV
Pękala Karol, TB Trocmade (Poland)—I, IV
Pelaia Bruno, RB Tricarico (Italy)—I, II, III, IV
Pellecchia Raffaele, RB Alife (Italy)—I, II, III, IV
Pellegrino Michele, RA Torino (Italy)—IV
Pelletier Georges, RB Trois Rivières (Canada)—I, II, III, IV
Pellin Jesús Maria, TB Acque Tibilitane (Venezuela)—IV
Peluso Luis Gonzaga, RB Cachoeiro de Itapemirin (Brazil)—I, III, IV
Pennisi Francesco, RB Ragusa (Italy)—I, II, III, IV
Pepén y Soliman Juan, RB N.S. de la Altagracia (Dominican Republic)—I, II
Peralta y Ballabriga Francisco, RB Vitoria (Spain)—I, II, III, IV
Perantoni Pacifico, RA Lanciano ed Ortona (Italy)—I, II, III, IV
Pereira da Costa Manuel, RB Campina Grande (Brazil)—I, II, III, IV
Pereira Longinus Gabriel, TB Vada (India)—II, IV
Pereira Manuel, RB Bragança e Miranda (Portugal)—I, II, III, IV
Pereira Corrêa Milton, TB Coronea (Brazil)—II, III, IV
Pereira Peter, TB Urusi (India)—I, IV
Pereira Venâncio João, RB Leiria (Portugal)—I, II, III, IV
Pérez Cisneros Angel, RB Barcelona (Venezuela)—I, II, III, IV
Pérez Eslava Carlos, RA Salta (Argentina)—I, II, III, IV
Pérez Pérez José, PA San Andrés y Providencia (Colombia)—II
Pérez Platero Luciano, RA Burgos (Spain)—I
Pérez Silva Federico, RA Trujillo (Peru)—I, II
Périer Ferdinand, TA Roina (India)—I, II
Perini Norberto, RA Fermo (Italy)—I, II, III, IV
Perniciaro Giuseppe, TB Arbano (Italy)—I, II, III, IV
Pernicone Joseph, TB Adrianopoli (USA)—I, II, III, IV
Perraudin André, RA Kabgayi (Rwanda)—I, II, III, IV
Perrin Maurice, RA Bagdad dei Latini (Iraq)—I, II, III, IV
Perris Ioannis, RA Naxos (Greece)—I, II, III, IV
Perrot Joseph, RB San (Mali)—III, IV
Perry Harold, TB Monte di Mauritania (USA)—IV
Person Urbain, TB Cime (Ethiopia)—I, II, III, IV
Peruzzo Giovanni Battista, RA Agrigento (Italy)—I
Pesce Anthony, RB Dodoma (Tanzania)—I, II, III
Pessers Quintinus OFM, PA Kiangchow (China)—II, III, IV
Pessôa Câmara Hélder, RA Olinda e Recife (Brazil)—I, II, III, IV
Petit John, RB Menevia (Great Britain)—I, II, III, IV
Petralia Giuseppe, RB Agrigento (Italy)—II, III, IV
Petrilli Enrico, TB Apolloniade (Italy)—II, III, IV
Petro Augusto, RB Uruguaiana (Brazil)—I, II, III, IV
Petroni Domenico, RB Melfi (Italy)—I, II, III, IV
Peyrou Eugenio Santiago, RB Comodoro Rivadavia (Argentina)—III, IV
Pezzullo Federico, RB Policastro (Italy)—I, II, III, IV
Pflaum Jorge, TB Iziriana (Bolivia)—I, II, IV
Phakoe Ignatius, RB Leribe (Basutoland)—I, II, III, IV
Pham-ngoc-Chi Pierre, RB Danang (Vietnam)—I, II, IV
Philbin William, RB Down e Connor (Ireland)—I, II, III, IV
Philippe Paul-Pierre OP, TA Eracleopoli Maggiore (Italy)—I, II, III, IV
Piana Agostinetti Edoardo, TB Eurea di Fenicia (Italy)—I, II, III, IV
Piasentini Giovanni, RB Chioggia (Italy)—I, II, III, IV
Piazera Honorato, RB Nova Iguaçú (Brazil)—I, II, III, IV
Piazza Alessandro, RB Albenga (Italy)—IV
Piazzi Giuseppe, RB Bergamo (Italy)—I
Picachy Trevor Lawrence, RB Jamshedpur (India)—I, II, III, IV
Picão David, TB Tois (Brazil)—I, II, III, IV
Picard de la Vacquerie Robert, RB Orléans (France)—I
Picchinenna Domenico, RA Cosenza (Italy)—I, II, III, IV
Picco Giovanni, TB Anea (Italy)—II, III, IV
Piché Paul, TB Orcisto (Canada)—I, II, III, IV
Pichler Alfred, RB Banjaluka (Yugoslavia)—I, II, III, IV
Piérard Henri, RB Beni (Congo-Leopoldville)—I, II, III, IV
Piérard René, RB Chalons (France)—I, II, III, IV
Piersanti Fiorello, SG Caracciolini– I, II, III, IV

Pietraszko Jan, TB Torreblanda (Poland)—III, IV
Pietrulla Anselmo, RB Tubarão (Brazil)—I, II, III, IV
Pietsch Leo, TB Narona (Austria)—I, II, III, IV
Pignedoli Sergio, TA Iconio (Canada)—I, II, III, IV
Pildáin y Zapiáin Antonio, RB Islas Canarias (Spain)—I, II, III, IV
Pillai Jerome Emiliano, RB Jaffna (Ceylon)—I, II, III, IV
Pimiento Rodriguez José, RB Garzon Neiva (Colombia)—I, II, III, IV
Piña Torres José, TB Milevi (Mexico)—I, II, III, IV
Pinault Henri-Marie-Ernest-Désiré MEP, RB Chengtu (China)—I, II, III, IV
Pinci Antonino, TA Tarasa di Numidia (Panama)—II, III, IV
Piñera Carvallo Bernardino, RB Temuco (Chile)—I, II, III, IV
Pinger Henry Ambrose OFM, RB Chowtsun (China)—I, II, III, IV
Pinier Paul, RB Constantine (Algeria)—I, II, III, IV
Pintado José, TB Foba (Ecuador)—I, II, III, IV
Pinto Edwin, RB Ahmedabad (India)—I, II, III, IV
Pintonello Arrigo, TA Teodosiopoli di Arcadia (Italy)—I, II, III, IV
Pioger André, RB Sées (France)—I, II, III, IV
Piquet Marcel, RB Nhatrang (Vietnam)—I, II
Pirastru Giovanni, RB Iglesias (Italy)—I, II, III, IV
Pirelli Luigi, RB Sovana e Pitigliano (Italy)—I, II
Pires José, RB Arassuaí (Brazil)—I, II, III, IV
Pires Manuel, RB Silva Porto (Angola)—I, II, III, IV
Pirolley Emile, RB Nancy (France)—I, II, III, IV
Pironio Edoardo, TB Ceciri (Argentina)—III, IV
Pirotto Antonio, RB Troia (Italy)—I, II, III, IV
Pirovano Aristide, TB Adriani (Italy)—I, II, III, IV
Pirozzi Felice, TA Graziana (Madagascar)—I, II, IV
Pizzardo Giuseppe card. prefect, Congregation for Seminaries and Studies—I, II, III, IV
Pizzoni Emilio, RB Terracina (Italy)—I, II, III, IV
Planas Muntaner Francisco, RB Ibiza (Spain)—I, II, III, IV
Pla y Deniel Enrique card., RA Toledo (Spain)—I
Plaza Antonio, RA La Plata (Argentina)—I, II, III, IV
Plourde Joseph, TB Lapda (Canada)—IV
Plumey Yves, RB Garoua (Cameroon)—I, II, III, IV
Pluta Wilhelm, TB Leptis Magna (Poland)—I, III
Pobožný Robert, TB Neila (Czechoslovakia)—II, III, IV
Pocci Filippo, TB Gerico (Italy)—I, II, III, IV
Pocock Philip, TA Isauropoli (Canada)—I, II, III, IV
Podestá Jerónimo José, RB Avellaneda (Argentina)—II, III, IV
Pogacnik Jože, RA Ljubljana (Yugoslavia)—II, III, IV
Poggi Luigi, TA Forontoniana (Cameroon)—IV
Pohlschneider Johannes, RB Aachen (Germany)—I, II, III, IV
Poirier François, RA Port-au-Prince (Haiti)—I, II, III, IV
Polachirakal Athanasios Cheriyan, RB Tiruvalla (India)—I, II, III, IV
Polanco Brito Hugo, RB Santiago de los Caballeros Rep. Dominicana)—II, III, IV
Poledrini Alfredo, TA Vazari (Italy)—IV
Poletti Ugo, TB Medeli (Italy)—I, II, III, IV
Polge Eugène, TB Tiava (France)—IV
Polidori Amedeo, TB Metellopoli (Italy)—I
Pollio Gaetano, RA Otranto (Italy)—I, II, III, IV
Poma Antonio, RB Mantova (Italy)—I, II, III, IV
Ponce de Léon Carlo, TB Rodosto (Argentina)—I, II, IV
Poncet Alexandre, TB Basilinopoli (Polynesia)—I
Pont y Gol José, RB Segorbe e Castellón (Spain)—I, II, III, IV
Portalupi Sante, TA Cristopoli (Honduras)—I, II, III, IV
Portela de Araujo Pena Cristiano, RB Divinópolis (Brazil)—I, II, IV
Porter William, TA Lemno (Great Britain)—I, II, IV
Posada Peláez Gustavo, TB Zaliche (Colombia)—I, II, IV
Potanamuzhi Matthew, RB Kothamangalam (India)—I, II, III, IV
Pourchet Maurice, RB Saint Flour (France)—I, II, III, IV
Power William, RB Antigonish (Canada)—I, II, III, IV
Prada Carrera Francisco, RB Uruaçu (Brazil)—I
Prado Tello Elias, TB Teveste (Peru)—IV
Prasko Ivan, TB Zigri (Australia)—I, II, IV
Prata Gennaro, TB Adriania (Bolivia)—I, II, III, IV
Prati Artemio, RB Carpi (Italy)—I, II, III, IV
Prendiville Redmond, RA Perth (Australia)—I, II
Previtali Guido, PA Misurata (Libya)—II, III, IV
Prévost Joseph, TB Ammaedara (Peru)—I, II, III, IV
Primatesta Raúl Francisco, RA Cordoba (Argentina)—I, II, III, IV
Principe Enrique, TB Abila di Lisania (Argentina)—II, III, IV
Principi Primo, TA Tiana (Italy)—I, II, III, IV
Primeau Ernest John, RB Manchester (USA)—I, II, III, IV
Prinetto Angelo, TB Adriane (Italy)—I, II, III, IV
Printesis Venedictos, RA Atene (Greece)—I, II, III, IV
Proaño Villalba Leonidas, RB Riobamba (Ecuador)—I, II, III, IV
Proni Giovanni, RB Termoli (Italy)—I, II, III, IV
Pronti Giuseppe, RB Nocera Umbra (Italy)—I, II, III, IV
Prost Tadeu, TB Fronta (Brazil)—II, IV
Prou Jean, SG Congregazione Benedettina di Francia—I, II, III, IV
Proulx Adolphe, TB Missua (Canada)—IV
Przyklenk João Batista, RB Januária (Brazil)—I, II, III, IV

Puchol Montiz Vicente, RB Santander (Spain)—IV
Puech Pierre, RB Carcassonne (France)—I, II, III, IV
Pulido Mendez José, TA Cirro (Venezuela)—II, III, IV
Pullano Giuseppe, RB Patti (Italy)—I, II, III, IV
Punzolo Luigi, TA Sebastea (Syria)—I, II, III, IV
Pursley Leo Aloysius, RB Fort Wayne (USA)—I, II, III, IV
Puset Jules, RB Tamatave (Madagascar)—I, II, III, IV

Q

Quadri Santo, TB Villanova (Italy)—III, IV
Quaglia Martinez Edmondo, RB Minas (Uruguay)—III, IV
Quaremba Pasquale, RB Gallipoli (Italy)—I, II, III, IV
Quarracino Antonio, RB Nueve de Julio (Argentina)—I, II, III, IV
Quéguiner Maurice, SG Società per le Missioni Estere di Parigi—III, IV
Quereketa Joseph, TB Eresso (Philippines)—III
Quesada Castro Delfin, RB San Isidro (Costa Rica)—II
Quezada Limón Salvador, RB Aguascalientes (Mexico)—I, II, III, IV
Quezada Valdés José, RB Acapulco (Mexico)—I, II, IV
Quinlan Thomas, RB Chunchon (Korea)—I, III, IV
Quinn Augustine, RB Kilmore (Ireland)—I, II, III, IV
Quint Edward Gabriel OFM, PA Weihaiwei (China)—II, III, IV
Quintanilla Manzanares del Rosario Arturo ORA, RB Kweiteh (China)—I, II, III, IV
Quintero Arce Carlos, RB Ciudad Valles (Mexico)—I, II, III, IV
Quintero José card., RA Caracas (Venezuela)—I, II, III, IV
Quiroga y Palacios Fernando card., RA Santiago de Compostela (Spain)—I, II, III, IV

R

Raballand Gustave-André-Ferdinand MEP, TB Eguga e VA Em Phnom-Penh (Cambodia)—I, II, IV
Rabban Ablahad, SG Ordine Antoniano di S. Ormisda dei Caldei—III, IV
Rabban Raphael, RA Kerkūk (Iraq)—I, II, III, IV
Rabbani Joseph, TA Nacolia (Syria)—I, II, III
Rada Senosiain Candido, RB Guaranda (Ecuador)—I, II, III, IV
Radicioni Vincenzo, RB Montalto e Ripatransone (Italy)—I, II, III, IV
Radossi Raffaele, RA Spoleto (Italy)—I, II, III, IV
Raeymaeckers Felicissimo Alphonse, TB Aperle (Pakistan)—III, IV
Raible Otto, TB Anemurio (Germany)—I, II
Raimondi Luigi, TA Tarso (Mexico)—I, II, III, IV
Raimondi Pietro, RB Crotone (Italy)—I, II, III, IV
Raimondo G. M. del SS. Sacramento, SG Romitani Scalzi—I, II
Rajaonarivo François Xavier, RB Miarinarivo (Madagascar)—I, II, III, IV
Rakotomalala Jérôme, RA Tananarive (Madagascar)—I, II, III, IV
Ramalho de Alarcón Santiago Giuseppe Mauro, RB Iguatú (Brazil)—I, II, III, IV
Ramanantoanina Gilbert, RA Fianarantsoa (Madagascar)—I, II, III, IV
Ramirez Salaverría Antonio, RB Maturín (Venezuela)—I, II
Ramirez Taboada Pablo, RB Huacho (Peru)—I, III
Ramos Alberto Gaudêncio, RA Belém do Parà (Brazil)—I, II, III, IV
Ramousse Ives-Georges-René MEP, TB Pisita e VA Phnom-Penh (Cambodia)—II, III, IV
Rancans Jazeps, TB Marcopoli (Latvia)—I, II, III, IV
Raspanti Miguel, RB Morón (Argentina)—I, II, III, IV
Raspini Maurizio, TB Sebarga (Italy)—I, II, III, IV
Rast Maurinus, SG Salvatoriani—IV
Rastouil Louis, RB Limoges (France)—I, II, III, IV
Ratsimamotoana Bernard Charles, RB Morodan (Madagascar)—IV
Rau Enrique, RB Mar del Plata (Argentina)—I, II, III, IV
Ravagli Antonio, RB Modigliana (Italy)—I, II, III, IV
Ravetta Umberto, RB Senigallia (Italy)—I, II
Rayappan Ambrose, RA Pondicherry e Cuddalore (India)—I, II, III, IV
Raymond Leonard, RA Nagpur (India)—I, II, III, IV
Raymundos Timoteo, TB Cariopoli (France)—I, II, III, IV
Re Carlo, TB Aspona (Italy)—I, II, III
Rea Ildefonso, TB Corone (Italy)—I, II, III, IV
Reddington John, RB Jos (Nigeria)—I, II, III, IV
Redois Patient, RB Natitingou (Benin)—III, IV
Reed Victor, RB Oklahoma City (USA)—I, II, III, IV
Reetz Benedikt, SG Congregazione Benedettina di Beuron—I, II, III
Regan Joseph, TB Isinda (Philippines)—I, II, III, IV
Regno Bernardo, TB Bagai (Ceylon)—I
Reh Francis, TB Macriana di Mauritania (Italy)—I, II, III, IV
Rehring George, RB Toledo (USA)—I, II, III, IV
Reicher Louis, RB Austin (USA)—I, II, III, IV
Reilly Tomás, TB Temisonio (Dominican Republic)—II, III, IV
Reis Thomas, RB Zaku Zākhō (Iraq)—I, III

Reiterer Anthony, RB Lydenburg-Witbank (South Africa)—I, II, III, IV
Renard Alexandre, RB Versailles (France)—I, II, III, IV
Rencoret Donoso Alberto, RA Puerto Montt (Chile)—I, II, III, IV
Rendeiro Francisco, TB Benepota (Portugal)—I, II, III, IV
Restieaux Cyril, RB Plymouth (Great Britain)—I, II, III, IV
Reuss Joseph, TB Sinope (Germany)—I, II, III, IV
Reyes Vicente, RB Borongan (Philippines)—I, II, III, IV
Rezende Costa João, TA Martiropoli (Brazil)—I, II, III, IV
Ribeiro Camelo Abel, RB Goiás (Brazil)—I, II, III, IV
Ribeiro de Oliveira Antonio, TB Arindela (Brazil)—IV
Ribeiro De Santana Altino, RB Sá da Bandeira (Angola)—I, II, III, IV
Ribeiro Guedes Delfim, RB São João del Rei (Brazil)—I, III, IV
Ribeiro José, TB Egee (India)—I, II, III, IV
Riberi Antonio, TA Dara (Spain)—II, III, IV
Ricceri Francesco, RB Trapani (Italy)—I, II, III, IV
Ricceri Luigi, SG Salesiani—IV
Richaud Paul card., RA Bordeaux (France)—II, III, IV
Ricote Alonso, TB Miletopoli (Spain)—I, II, IV
Riesco Carbajo Angel, TB Limisa (Spain)—I, III, IV
Riezzo Nicola, RB Castellaneta (Italy)—I, II, III, IV
Rigaud Maurice, RB Pamiers (France)—I, II, III, IV
Righi-Lambertini Egano, TA Doclea (Chile)—I, II, III, IV
Righi Vittore Ugo, TA Bilta (Paraguay)—I, II, IV
Riha Mauro, SG Congregazione Benedettina d'Austria—I, II, III, IV
Riley Thomas, TB Regie (USA)—I, II, III, IV
Rinaldi Luigi, RB S. Marco e Bisignano (Italy)—I, II, III, IV
Rincón Bonilla José, TB Tamaso (Venezuela)—I
Rintelen Friedrich, TB Cusira (Germany)—I, II, III, IV
Riobé Guy, RB Orléans (France)—I, II, III, IV
Riopel Marcel, TB Neocesarea di Syria (France)—I, II, III, IV
Ritter Joseph card., RA Saint Louis (USA)—I, II, III, IV
Riu Anglés Carlos, TB Lari Castello (Cuba)—I, II, III
Rivato Angelo Maria, PN Ponta de Pedras (Brazil)—IV
Rivera Damas Arturo, TB Legia (El Salvador)—I, II, III, IV
Rivera Mejía Pedro, RB Socorro y San Gil (Colombia)—I, II, III, IV
Rivera Meza Nemesio, TB Diospoli Superiore (Peru)—III, IV
Rizzo Giovanni, RA Rossano (Italy)—I, II, III, IV
Roa Perez Domingo, RB Maracaibo (Venezuela)—I, III, IV
Roatta Ilario, RB S. Agata dei Goti (Italy)—I, II, III, IV
Robert Paul, RB Les Gonaïves (Haiti)—I, II, III, IV
Roberti Francesco card. prefetto della Segnatura Apostolica—I, II, III, IV
Roberti Vito, RA Caserta (Italy)—I, II, III, IV
Roberts Thomas, TA Sugdaea (Great Britain)—I, II, III, IV
Robichaud Norbert, RA Moncton (Canada)—I, II, III, IV
Róbles Jimenez José, RB Tulancingo (Mexico)—I, II, III, IV
Roborecki Andrew, RB Saskatoon degli Ucraini (Canada)—I, II, III, IV
Rocco Carmine, TA Giustinianopoli di Galizia (Bolivia)—I, II, III, IV
Ródenas Garcia Alfonso, RB Almería (Spain)—I, II, III, IV
Rodgers John, TB Sbida (Polynesia)—I, III, IV
Rodgers Joseph, RB Killaloe (Ireland)—I, II, III, IV
Rodríguez Augustin, TB Castello di Tingizio (Paraguay)—I, IV
Rodriguez Ballón José, RA Arequipa (Peru)—I, II, III, IV
Rodríguez Benito, TB Aricanda (Argentina)—II, III, IV
Rodríguez Diez Inocencio, RB Cuenca (Spain)—I, II, III, IV
Rodríguez Herrera Adolfo, RB Camaguey (Cuba)—III, IV
Rodriguez Gamoneda Angel, TB Gazera (Peru)—I, II, III, IV
Rodríguez Pardo Luis, RB S. Cruz de la Sierra (Bolivia)—I, II, III, IV
Rodriguez-Quírós Carlos, RA S. José de Costa Rica (Costa Rica)—I, II, III, IV
Rodríguez Rozas Manuel Pedro, RB Pinar del Rio (Cuba)—I, III, IV
Rodríguez y Olmos Audino, RA San Juan de Cuyo (Argentina)—II
Rohracher Andreas, RA Salzburg (Austria)—I, II, III, IV
Roig Damián Nicolau, PN Huamachuco (Peru)—II, III, IV
Roig y Villalba Vicente, TB Arad (Colombia)—I, II, III, IV
Rojas Chaparro José, RB Trujillo (Venezuela)—I, II, III, IV
Rolando Ottorino, SG Dottrinari—III, IV
Rolim De Moura Zacarias, RB Cajazeiras (Brazil)—I, II, III, IV
Rolim-Loureiro Paulo, RB Mogi das Cruzes (Brazil)—I, II, III, IV
Rolland Claude, RB Antsirabe (Madagascar)—I, II, III, IV
Rolón Silvero Ismael Blas, TB Fornos Maggiore (Paraguay)—I, II, III, IV
Romaniello John Angel MM, PA di Kweilin (China)—II, III, IV
Romeijn Jacques, RB Samarinda (Indonesia)—I, II, III, IV
Romero Arvizu Manuel, TB Dusa (Mexico)—I, II, III, IV
Romero de Lema Maximino, TB Orta (Spain)—III, IV
Romero Menjibar Felix, RB Jaén (Spain)—I, II, III, IV
Romo Gutierrez Fernando, RB Torreón (Mexico)—I, II, III, IV
Romoli Dino, RB Pescia (Italy)—I, II, III, IV
Ronca Roberto, TA Lepanto (Italy)—I, II, III, IV
Roques Clément-Emile card., CP Rennes (France)—I
Rosa Luigi, RB Bagnoregio (Italy)—I, II, III, IV
Rosales Julio, RA Cebù (Philippines)—I, II, III, IV
Rosario Joseph, RB Amravati (India)—I, II, III, IV
Rosch Ricardo, RB Concordia (Argentina)—I, II, IV
Rosenhammer José, TB Ampora (Bolivia)—I, II, III, IV
Rosenthal John, RB Queenstown (South Africa)—I, II, III, IV
Rosina Marcello, TB Ezani (Italy)—II, III, IV
Rossel y Arellano Mariano, RA Guatemala (Guatemala)—I, II, III
Rossi Agnelo card., RA São Paulo (Brazil)—I, II, III, IV
Rossi Carlo, RB Biella (Italy)—I, II, III, IV
Rossi Fortunato, RB Venado Tuerto (Argentina)—I, II, III, IV
Rossi Francesco, RB Tortona (Italy)—II, III, IV
Rossi Giuseppe, TB Palmira (Italy)—II, III, IV
Rossi Opilio, TA Ancira (Austria)—I, II, III, IV
Rossini Angelo, RA Amalfi (Italy)—I, II, III
Rotolo Salvatore, TB Nazianzo (Italy)—I
Rotta Angelo, TA Tebe di Greece (Italy)—I, II
Rouanet Pierre, RB Daloa (Ivory Coast)—I, II, III, IV
Rougé Pierre, RB Nîmes (France)—I, II, III, IV
Rousseau Maurice, TB Ausafa (France)—I, II, III, IV
Rousset Agostino, RB Ventimiglia (Italy)—I, II
Rousset André, TB Vaga (France)—II, III, IV
Routhier Henri, TB Naisso (Canada)—I, II, III, IV
Roy Alexandre, TB Ambia (France)—I, II, III, IV
Roy Maurice card., RA Québec (Canada)—I, II, III, IV
Rubin Wladyslaw, TB Serta (Poland)—III, IV
Rubio Diaz Alfredo, RB Sonsón (Colombia)—I, II, III, IV
Rubio Luciano, SG Eremitani S. Agostino—I, II, III
Rubio Repulles Mauro, RB Salamanca (Spain)—III, IV
Rubio y Montiél Saturnino, RB Osma e Soria (Spain)—I, II, III, IV
Rudderham Joseph, RB Clifton (Great Britain)—I, II, III, IV
Rudin John James, RB Musoma (Tanzania)—I, II, III, IV
Rueda Hernández Héctor, RB Bucaramanga (Colombia)—I, II, III, IV
Ruffini Ernesto card., RA Palermo (Italy)—I, II, III, IV
Rugambwa Laurean card., RB Bukoba (Tanzania)—I, II, III, IV
Ruiz Garcia Samuele, RB Chiapas (Mexico)—I, II, III, IV
Ruiz y Solórzano Ferdinando, RA Yucatán (Mexico)—I, II
Rummel J. Francis, RA New Orleans (USA)—I
Ruotolo Giuseppe, RB Ugento (Italy)—I, II, III, IV
Rupp Jean, RB Monaco (Monaco)—I, II, III, IV
Rusch Paul, RB Innsbruck (Austria)—I, II, III, IV
Rush Francis, RB Rockhampton (Australia)—I, II, III, IV
Rusnack Michele, TB Zernico (Canada)—III, IV
Russell John, RB Richmond (USA)—I, II, III, IV
Russell Michele, RB Waterford (Ireland)—IV
Russo Innocenzo, TB Pege (Italy)—I, II, III, IV
Russo Salvatore, RB Acireale (Italy)—I
Rüth Johann, TB Amudarsa (Norvegia)—I, II, III, IV
Ryan Hugh, RB Townsville (Australia)—I, II, III, IV
Ryan James, TB Margo (Brazil)—I, II, III, IV
Ryan Joseph, RB Hamilton (Canada)—I, II, III, IV
Ryan Patrick, RA Port of Spain (Trinidad and Tobago)—I, II, III, IV
Ryan Thomas, RB Clonfert (Ireland)—II, III, IV

S

Sabbattani Aurelio, TA Giustiniana Prima (Italy)—IV
Sabóia Bandeira De Mello Carlos, RB Palmas (Brazil)—I, II, III, IV
Sagrera Antonio, SG Teatini—IV
Sahagun de la Parra José de Jésus, RB Tula (Mexico)—I, II, IV
Saigh Maximos IV card., P Antiochia dei Melchiti (Syria)—I, II, III, IV
Salas Miguel, RB Calabozo (Venezuela)—I, II, IV
Salas Valdés Ramòn, PN, RAica (Chile)—III, IV
Salatka Charles, TB Cariana (USA)—I, II, III, IV
Salazar Mejia, RAturo, TB Avitta Bibba (Colombia)—IV
Salinas Fuenzalida Augusto, RB Linares (Chile)—I, II, III, IV
Salmon Pietro, TB Giocondiana (Italy)—III, IV
Salvini Alfonso, SG Benedettini Vallombrosani—I, II, III, IV
Salvucci Achille, RB Molfetta (Italy)—I, II, III, IV
Samorè Antonio, TA Tirnovo (Italy)—I, II, III, IV
Sana Abdul-Ahad, RB Alquoch (Iraq)—I, III, IV
Sana André, RB Akkra dei Caldei (Iraq)—I, II, III, IV
Sanahuja y Marcé Raimundo, RB Cartagena (Spain)—I, II
Sanchez Beguiristain Manuel, RA Concepción (Chile)—I, II, III, IV
Sánchez-Moreno Lira Luis, TB Nilopoli (Peru)—I, II, III, IV
Sánchez Tinoco Alfonso, RB Papantla (Mexico)—I, II, III, IV
Sangaré Luc Auguste, RA Bamako (Mali)—I, II, III, IV
Sanguon Souvannasri Francis Xavier, TB Enoanda (Thailand)—I, III, IV
Sani Paul Kleden, RB Den Pasar (Indonesia)—I, II, III, IV
Sanschagrin Albert, TB Bagi (Canada)—I, II, III, IV
Sansierra Robla Ildefonso Maria, TB Oreo (Argentina)—I, II, III, IV
Santin Antonio, RA Trieste e Capodistria (Italy)—I, II, III, IV
Santos Ascarza José, RB Valdivia (Chile)—I, II, III, IV
Santos Hernández Héctor, RA Tegucigalpa (Honduras)—I, II, III, IV
Santos Rufino Jiao card., RA Manila (Philippines)—I, II, III, IV
Santos Songco Pedro, RA Cáceres (Philippines)—I, III
Sapelak Andrés, TB Sebastopoli di Tracia (Argentina)—I, II, III, IV
Sargolini Federico, TB Lisiade (Italy)—II, III, IV
Sarmiento Peralta Rafael, RB Ocaña (Colombia)—II, III, IV
Sartori Luís, RB Santa Maria (Brazil)—II, III, IV
Sartre Victor, TA Beroe (Cameroon)—I, II, III, IV
Satoshi Nagae Laurentius, RB Urawa (Japan)—I, II, III, IV
Satowaki Joseph, RB Kagoshima (Japan)—I, II, III, IV
Sauvage Jean, RB Annecy (France)—I, II, III, IV
Savarese Francesco, SG Minimi—I, II, III, IV
Savaryn Niel, RB Edmonton degli Ucraini (Canada)—I, II, III, IV
Savino Paolo, TB Cesarea di Tessalia (Italy)—I, II, III, IV
Scalais Félix, TB Acque di Numidia (Italy)—I, II, III, IV
Scandar Alexandros, RB Assiut (URA-Egypt)—I, II, III
Scanlan James, RA Glasgow (Great Britain)—I, II, III, IV
Scanlan John, TB Cene (USA)—I, II, III, IV
Scapinelli di Léguigno Giovanni Battista, TA Laodicea al Lebanon (Italy)—I, II, III
Schaffran Gerhard, TB Semnea (Germany)—II, III, IV
Schäufele Hermann Josef, RA Freiburg im Breisgau (Germany)—I, II, III, IV
Scheerer Aloysius Louis, RB Multan (Pakistan)—I
Scheffer Lionel, TB Isba (Canada)—I, II, III, IV
Schell Alejandro, RB Lomas de Zamora (Argentina)—I, II, III, IV
Schenk Francis, RB Duluth (USA)—I, II, III, IV
Scherer Alfredo Vicente, RA Pôrto Alegre (Brazil)—I, II, III, IV
Schexnayder Maurice, RB Lafayette (USA)—I, III, IV
Schiavini Giuseppe, TA Famagosta (Italy)—I, II, III, IV
Schick Eduard, TB, Aradi (Germany)—I, II, III, IV
Schilling Bernhard, TB Callipoli (New Guinea)—I, II, III, IV
Schladweiler Alphonse, RB New Ulm (USA)—I, II, III, IV
Schlotterback Edward, TB Balanea (South West Africa)—I, II, III, IV
Schmidt Carl, TB Taso (Germany)—I, II, III, IV
Schmidt Firmin Martin, TB Conana (New Guinea)—II, III, IV
Schmitt Adolph, RB Bulawayo (Rhodesia)—I, II, III, IV
Schmitt Carlos, RB Dourados (Brazil)—I, II, IV
Schmitt Paul, RB Metz (France)—I, II, III, IV
Schmitz Quirino, RB Teófilo Otoni (Brazil)—I, II, III, IV
Schmondiuk Joseph, RB Stamford degli Ucraini (USA)—I, II, III, IV
Schneider Josef, RA Bamberg (Germany)—I, II, III, IV
Schneiders Nicolas, RA Makassar (Indonesia)—I, II, III, IV
Schoemaker Guillaume, RB Purwokerto (Indonesia)—I, II, III, IV
Schoenmaeckers Paul Constant, TB Acarasso (Belgium)—I, II, III, IV
Schoiswohl Joseph, RB Graz (Austria)—I, II, III, IV
Scho Emilio, SG Barnabiti—I, II
Schott Lawrence Frederik, TB Eluza (USA)—I
Schräder Bernhard, TB Sciro (Germany)—I, II, III, IV
Schröffer Joseph, RB Eichstätt (Germany)—I, II, III, IV
Schu Theodore SVD, RB Yenchow (China)—I, II, III
Schuck Jaime, TB Avissa (Brazil)—I, II, III, IV
Schulte Paul, RA Indianapolis (USA)—I, II, III, IV
Schuster Eldon, TB Amblada (USA)—I
Schütte Johannes, SG Verbiti—I, II, III, IV
Schweiger Peter, SG Claretiani—I, II, III, IV
Schweizer Bonaventura Josef, SG Salvatoriani—I, II, III, IV
Scola Alberto, RB Norcia (Italy)—I, II, III, IV
Scozzina Pacifico, RB Formosa (Argentina)—I, II, III, IV
Scrivano Francesco, SG Dottrinari– I, II
Scully William, RB Albany (USA)—I, II
Secondo Ludovico, SG Terz'Ordine S. Francesco—IV
Sedlmeier Wilhelm, TB Aulona (Germany)—I, II, III, IV
Segedi Gioacchino, TB Gissaria (Yugoslavia)—II, III, IV
Segura Ernesto, TB Carpi (Argentina)—I, II, III, IV
Seitz Paul, RB Kontum (Vietnam)—I, II, IV
Selis Enea, TB Cesarea di Mauritania (Italy)—III, IV
Selvanaden Lurdu, RB Salem (India)—I, II, III, IV
Semeraro Alberico, RB Oria (Italy)—I, II, III, IV
Semeraro Orazio, RB Cariati (Italy)—I, II, III, IV
Sena De Oliveira Ernesto, RA Coimbra (Portugal)—I, II, III, IV
Senner Juan, TB Equizeto (Bolivia)—I, II, III, IV
Sensi Giuseppe Maria, TA Sardi (Ireland)—I, II, III, IV
Senyshyn Ambrozij, RA Filadelfia degli Ucraini (USA)—I, II, III, IV
Šeper Franjo card. RA Zagabria (Yugoslavia)—I, II, III, IV
Sépinski Augustin-Joseph Antoine, TA Assura (Jordan)—I, II, III, IV
Serafini Anunciado, RB Mercedes (Argentina)—I
Serena Carlo, RA Sorrento (Italy)—I, II, III, IV
Serra Ruy, RB São Carlos (Brazil)—I, II, III, IV
Serrano Abad Manuel, RA Cuenca (Ecuador)—I, II, III, IV
Serrano Pastor Jesús, TB Ipseli (Panama)—I, II, III, IV
Severi Pietro, TB Pergamo (Italy)—I, II, III, IV
Sevrin Oscar, TB Mossina (India)—I, II, III, IV
Sfair Pietro, TA Nisibi (Italy)—I, II, III, IV
Shanley Patrick, TB Sofene (USA)—I, II, IV
Shannon James, TB Lacubaza (USA)—IV
Sheen Fulton, TB Cesariana (USA)—I, II, III, IV
Sheenhan Daniel, TB Capso (USA)—III, IV
Shehan Lawrence card., RA Baltimora (USA)—I, II, III, IV

Sheil Bernard, TA Selge (USA)—II
Shwe Yauk Sebastian U, RB Toungoo (Burma)—I
Sibomana Joseph, RB Ruhengeri (Rwanda)—I, II, III, IV
Sidarouss Stephanos I card., P Alessandria dei Copti (URA-Egypt)—I, II, III, IV
Sigismondi Pietro, TA Neapoli di Pisidia (Italy)—I, II, III, IV
Signora Aurelio, TA Nicosia (Italy)—I, II, III, IV
Siino Salvatore, TA Perge (Philippines)—II
Sikorski Bogdan, RB Płock (Poland)—III, IV
Sillekens Guillaume, RB Ketapang (Indonesia)—I, II, III, IV
Silva Henriquez Raul card., RA Santiago del Cile (Chile)—I, II, III, IV
Silva Santiago Alfredo, TA Petra di Palestina (Chile)—I, II, III, IV
Silva Silva Raul, TB Eudossiade (Chile)—III, IV
Silveira De Mello Alonso, TB Nasai (Brazil)—I, II, III, IV
Silvestri Siro, RB Foligno (Italy)—I, II, III, IV
Simaan Neemeh, TB Termesso (Jordan)—IV
Simões Mendes Elizeu, RB Campo Mourão (Brazil)—I, II
Simonds Justin, RA Melbourne (Australia)—I, II, III, IV
Simons Francis, RB Indore (India)—I, II, III, IV
Sipović Ceslao, TB Mariamme (Italy)—I, II, III, IV
Siri Giuseppe card., RA Genova (Italy)—I, II, III, IV
Sison Jesus, RB Tarlac (Philippines)—II, III, IV
Sison Juan, TA Nicopsi (Philippines)—I, II, III, IV
Skinner Patrick, RA Saint John's (Canada)—I, II, III, IV
Skomorucha Waclaw, TB Zoara (Poland)—II, IV
Skutans Stanslaus, SG Mariani—I
Slattery Guglielmo, SG Lazzaristi—I, II, III, IV
Slipyj Josyf card., RA Lviv (USSR/Ukraine)—II, III, IV
Sloskāns Boleslavs, TB Cillio (Belgium)—I, II, III, IV
Smit Giovanni, TB Paralo (Italy)—I, II, III, IV
Smith Eustache, TB Apamea Ciboto (Lebanon)—I, II, III, IV
Smith Leo, RB Ogdensburg (USA)—I, II
Smith William, RB Pembroke (Canada)—I, II, III, IV
Snedden Owen, TB Acheloo (New Zealand)—II, III, IV
Soares de Resende Sebastião, RB Beira (Mozambique)—I, II, III, IV
Soares Idilio José, RB Santos (Brazil)—I, II
Socche Beniamino, RB Reggio Emilia (Italy)—I, II, III
Socquet Emile, TA Selimbria (Italy)—I, II, III, IV
Soegijapranata Albert, RA Semarang (Indonesia)—I
Soenneker Henry, RB Owensboro (USA)—I, II, III, IV
Soetemans Giuseppe, SG Congregazione del SS. Salvatore Lateranense—I, II, III, IV
Sol Andreas, RB Amboina (Indonesia)—III, IV
Solá y Farrell Matias, TB Colofone (Spain)—I, II, III, IV
Solis Fernández Juan, RB Alajuela (Costa Rica)—I
Sorrentino Aurelio, RB Bova (Italy)—I, II, III, IV
Sorrentino Salvatore, TB Gerasa (Italy)—I, II, III, IV
Sortais Gabriele, SG Trappisti—I, II
Sosa Gaona Emilio, TB Sergenza (Paraguay)—I, II, III, IV
Soudant Joseph, RB Palembang (Indonesia)—I, II, III, IV
Souto Vizoso José, RB Palencia (Spain)—I, II, III, IV
Spallanzani Renato, TB Mazaca (Italy)—III, IV
Spanedda Francesco, RB Bosa (Italy)—I, II, III, IV
Spellman Francis card., RA New York (USA)—I, II, III, IV
Speltz George Henry, TB Claneo (USA)—II, III, IV
Spence John, TB Aggersel (USA)—III, IV
Sperandeo Matteo, RB Calvi e Teano (Italy)—I, II, III, IV
Spiess Hermann, TB Cemeriniano (Tanzania)—I, II, III, IV
Spiller Maximiliano, TB Mirica (Ecuador)—I, II, III, IV
Splett Carl, RB Gda sk (Poland)—I, II
Spülbeck Otto, RB Meissen (Germany)—I, II, III, IV
Staeb Placido, SG Congregazione Benedettina del Brasile– I, III
Staffa Dino, TA Cesarea di Palestina (Italy)—I, II, III, IV
Stangl Josef, RB Würzburg (Germany)—I, II, III, IV
Stanton Martin, TB Cizio (USA)—I, II, III, IV
Stappers Camille, TB Cerano (Belgium)—I
Staunton James, RB Ferns (Ireland)—I
Staverman Rudolf, TB Mosinopoli (Indonesia)—I, II, III, IV
Stein Bernhard, TB Dagno (Germany)—I, II, III, IV
Stella Costantino, RA L'Aquila (Italy)—I, II, III, IV
Stella Giuseppe, RB La Spezia (Italy)—I, II, III, IV
Stella Ubaldo Teofano OCD, TB Anteopoli e VA Kuwait (Arabia)—I, II, III, IV
Stemper Alfred, TB Eleuteropoli di Palestina (New Guinea)—I, II, III, IV
Stété Iwannis Georges, RA Damas (Syria)—I, II, III, IV
Stewart Bernard, RB Sandhurst (Australia)—I, II, III, IV
Stimpfle Joseph, RB Augsbourg (Germany)—II, III, IV
Stoppa Carlo, RB Alba (Italy)—I, II, III
Stourm René, RA Sens (France)—I, II, III, IV
Strakowski Henryk, TB Girba (Poland)—I
Strebler Joseph, TA Nicopoli di Epiro (France)—I, II, III, IV
Strecker Ignacio, RB Springfield-Cape Girardeau (USA)—I, II, III, IV
Streit Alphonse, RB Mariannhill (South Africa)—I, II
Strittmatter Denis, SG Congregazione Benedettina Americana Cassinese—I, II, III
Stroba Jerzy, TB Arado (Poland)—IV
Stuyvenberg Daniel, TB Dionisiade (Melanesia)—I, II, III, IV
Sudres Michele, SG Chierici di S. Viatore)—I, II, III, IV
Suenens Léon-Joseph card., RA Mechelen-Brussel (Belgium)—I, II, III, IV
Suhr Johannes Theodor, TB Apisa Maggiore (Denmark)—I, II, III, IV
Sundaram Rajarethinam, RB Tanjore (India)—I, II, III, IV
Surban Belmonte Epifanio, RB Dumaguete (Philippines)—I, II, III, IV
Swain John, VG Gesuiti—III
Swamidoss Pillai David, RB Vellore (India)—I, II, IV
Swanstrom Edward, TB Arba (USA)—I, II, III, IV
Sweeney James, RB Honolulu (USA)—I, II
Sweeney Paschal, PA Vanino (New Guinea)—III, IV
Swrarbrick Alban, PA Jullundur (India)—II, III, IV
Systermans Henry, SG Congregazione dei Sacri Cuori—I, II, III, IV
Szabó Imre, TB Tiatira (Hungary)—II, III
Szwagrzyk Tadeusz Stanislaw, TB Ita (Poland)—IV
Szymanski Ramírez Arturo, RB S. Andrés Tuxtla (Mexico)—I, II, III, IV

T

Tabera Araoz Arturo, RB Albacete (Spain)—I, II, III, IV
Taborski Boleslaw Lukasz, TB Dices (Poland)—III, IV
Taffi Antonio, TA Sergiopoli (Italy)—I, II, III, IV
Tagle Covarrubias Emilio, RA Valparaiso (Chile)—I, II, III, IV
Tagliabue Secondo, RB Anglona (Italy)—I, II, III, IV
Taguchi Yoshigoro Paul, RB Osaka (Japan)—I, II, III, IV
Talamás Camandari Manuel, RB Ciudad Juárez (Mexico)—I, II, III, IV
Talleur Vunibaldo, TB Magido (Brazil)—I, II, III, IV
Tanaka Eikichi Franciscus Xaverius, RB Takamatsu (Japan)—II, III, IV
Tani Antonio, TA Scitopoli (Italy)—I, II, III, IV
Tanner Paul, TB Lamasba (USA)—IV
Tappouni Ignace Gabriel I (Théophile) card., P Antiochia dei Siri (Lebanon)—I, II, III, IV
Tarantino Angelo, RB Arua (Uganda)—I
Tato Losada Eloy, TB Cardicio (Colombia)—I, II, III, IV
Tato Manuel, RB Santiago del Estero (Argentina)—I, II, III, IV
Tavares Baêta Neves Daniel, RB Sete Lagôas (Brazil)—I, II, III, IV
Tavares de Araújo Manuel, RB Caicó (Brazil)—I, II, III
Tavares Paulo, RB Macau (India)—I, II, III, IV
Tavares Rebimbas Júlio, RB Faro (Portugal)—IV
Tavella Roberto José, RA Salta (Argentina)—I
Távora José, RA Aracajú (Brazil)—I, II, III, IV
Tawil Joseph, TA Mira (Syria)—I, II, III, IV
Taylor John, RB Stockholm (Sweden)—I, II, III, IV
Taylor Leo, RA Lagos (Nigeria)—I
Tayroyan Nersès, RA Baghdad degli Armeni (Iraq)—I, II, III, IV
Tchidimbo Raymond-Maria, RA Conakry (Guinea)—I, II, III, IV
Tedde Antonio, RB Ales e Terralba (Italy)—I, II, III, IV
Teixeira Vieira Walfrido, TB Laranda (Brazil)—I, II, III, IV
Temiño Saiz Angel, RB Orense (Spain)—I, II, III, IV
Tenhumberg Heinrich, TB Tuburnica (Germany)—I, II, III, IV
Tenreiro Francia Pedro, RB Auzegera (Venezuela)—I, II, III, IV
Terceiro de Souza José, RB Penedo (Sudan)—I, II, III, IV
Te Riele Gerard, PA Malakal (Sudan)—II, III, IV
Terrienne Octave-Marie, TB Menelaites (France)—I, II, III, IV
Terzi Cristoforo, TB Diocleziana (Italy)—I, II, III, IV
Terzian Mesrob, TB Comana di Armenia (Lebanon)—II, III, IV
Tessier Maxime, RB Timmins (Canada)—I, II, III, IV
Testa Gustavo card. segretario della congregazione per le Chiese orientali—I, II, III, IV
Testa Zenone Albino, TB Tinista (Canada)—I, II, III, IV
Teutonico Antonio, RB Aversa (Italy)—III, IV
Thangalathil Benedict Varghese Gregorios, RA Trivandrum (India)—I, II, III, IV
Tharayil Thomas, RB Kottayam (India)—I, II
Théas Pierre, RB Tarbes e Lourdes (France)—I, II, III, IV
Theissing Heinrich, TB Mina (Germany)—II, III, IV
Theunissen John, RA Blantyre (Malawi)—I, II, III, IV
Thiandoum Hyacinthe, RA Dakar (Senegal)—I, II, III, IV
Thibault Joseph, TB Canata (Philippines)—I, II, III, IV
Thijssen Antoine, RB Larantuka (Indonesia)—I, II, III, IV
Thomas Albert, RB Bathurst (Australia)—II, III, IV
Thomas Francis, RB Geraldton (Australia)—I, II, III, IV
Thoyer François, TA Odesso (Madagascar)—I, II, III, IV
Thomson Francis, RB Motherwell (Great Britain)—IV
Thurler José, TB Capitoliade (Brazil)—I, II, III, IV
Tickle Gerard William, TB Bela (Great Britain)—III, IV
Tielbeek Joannes, TB Tipasa di Numidia (Brazil)—I, II, III, IV
Tien Kenh-hsin Thomas SVD card., RA Beijiing (China)—I
Tigga Leo, RB Dumka (India)—I, II, III, IV
Tigga Stanislaus, RB Raigarh e Ambikapur (India)—I, II, III, IV
Tillemans Herman, TB Berissa (Indonesia)—I, II, III, IV
Tinivella Felicissimo, TA Utina (Italy)—I, II, III, IV
Tinti Macario, RB Fabriano e Matelica (Italy)—I, II, III, IV
Tirado Pedraza José, RB Ciudad Victoria (Mexico)—II, III, IV
Tirilly Louis, TB Butrinto (Polynesia)—I, II
Tisserant Eugène-Gabriel-Gervais-Laurent card. decano del Sacro Collegio; archivista e bibliotecario di S.R. Chiesa—I, II, III, IV
Tissot Faustino M. SX, RB Zhengzhou (China)—I, II, III, IV
Tji Hak Soun Daniel, RB Won Ju (South Korea)—IV
Tobar Gonzáles Paul, RB Cuttak (India)—I, II, III, IV
Tokič Aleksandar, RA Bar (Yugoslavia)—I, II, III, IV
Tomášek František, TB Buto (Czechoslovakia)—I, II, III, IV
Tomassini Dino, RB Ischia (Italy)—I, II, III, IV
Tomé Luis, RB Mercedes (Argentina)—II, III, IV
Tomek Vincent, SG Scolopi—I, II, III, IV
Tomizawa Benedict Takahiko, RB Sapporo (Japan)—I, II, III, IV
Tomzičski Jerzy, SG Monaci di S. Paolo Primo Eremita—IV
Tonetti Guido, RA Cuneo (Italy)—I, II, III, IV
Tonna Eduardo, TA Mileto (Italy)—I
Tonna Umberto, RB Florida (Uruguay)—I, II, III, IV
Toohey John, RB Maitland (Australia)—I, II, III, IV
Toolen Thomas, RA Mobile-Birmingham (USA)—I
Topel Bernard, RB Spokane (USA)—I, II, III, IV
Torbay Giuseppe, SG Ordine Antoniano Libanese dei Maroniti—I, II, IV
Toriz Cobián Alonso, RB Querétaro (Mexico)—I, II
Torpigliani Bruno, TA Malliana (El Salvador)—III, IV
Torres Alfonso Pedro, RB Catamarca (Argentina)—II, III
Torres Oliver Juan Fremiot, RB Ponce (Puerto Rico)—IV
Torres y Castañeda José, RB Ciudad Obregón (Mexico)—I, II, III, IV
Torrini Antonio, RA Lucca (Italy)—I, II
Tortolo Adolfo, RA Paraná (Argentina)—I, II, III, IV
Tortora Francesco, TB Liviade (Italy)—I, II, III, IV
Tou Pao-Zin Petrus, RB Hsínchu (China)—I, II, III, IV
Tourel Cyprien-Luis-Pierre, RB Montpellier (France)—I, II, III, IV
Touissant René, RB Idiofa (Congo-Leopoldville)—I, II, IV
Toutoungy Athanasios, RA Alep dei Melchiti (Syria)—I, II, III, IV
Tracy Robert, RB Baton Rouge (USA)—I, II, III, IV
Traglia Luigi card. pro-vicario generale di Roma—I, II, III, IV
Tranfaglia Anselmo, AN Monte Vergine (Italy)—I, II, III, IV
Trān-Vān-Thiên Joseph, RB My-Tho (Vietnam)—I, II, III, IV
Trapani Costantino, RB Nicosia (Italy)—I, II, III, IV
Trapè Agostino, SG Ordine Eremitano di S. Agostino—IV
Treacy John Patrick, RB La Crosse (USA)—I, II
Tredici Giacinto, RB Brescia (Italy)—I, II
Treinen Sylvester, RB Boise (USA)—I, II, III
Trindade Salgueiro Manuel, RA Évora (Portugal)—I, III
Trinidad Sepulveda José, RB Tuxtla Gutierrez (Mexico)—IV
Trudel Joseph, TB Noba (Canada)—II, III, IV
Trujillo Arango Augusto, RB Jericó (Colombia)—I, II, III
Truong-cao-Dai Joseph, TB Sila (Vietnam)—I, II, III, IV
Tscherrig José Alfonso, TB Nefeli (Bolivia)—I, II, III, IV
Tschudy Raymund, AN Maria Einsiedeln (Switzerland)—I, II, III, IV
Tsiahoana Albert Joseph, TB Abtugni (Madagascar)—III, IV
Tubino Mongilardi Fidel, TB Cernizza (Peru)—II, IV
Tumler Marian, SG Ordine Teutonico—I, II, III, IV
Turner Kenneth Roderick SFM, RB Lishui (China)—I, II, III, IV

U

Ubaldi Beniamino, RB Gubbio (Italy)—I, II, III ć
Ujčić Josip Antun, RA Beograd (Yugoslavia)—I
Uluhogian Seraphin, TA Chersoneso di Zechia (Italy)—I, II, III
Ukec Gabriel, RB Bunia (Congo-Leopoldville)—IV
Ulyatt Christopher, PA Volksurst (South Africa)—II, III
Ungarelli Alfonso, TB Azura (Brazil)—I, II, III, IV
Unterkoefler Ernest, RB Charleston (USA)—I, II, III, IV
Urban Wincenty, TB Abitine (Poland)—IV
Urbani Giovanni card., RA Venezia (Italy)—I, II, III, IV
Urbss Antonijis, RB Liepaja (Latvia)—I, II
Urgel y Villahermosa Cipriano, RB Calbayog (Philippines)—I, IV
Uribe Jaramillo Alfonso, TB Aureliopoli di Asia (Colombia)—II, III
Uribe Urdaneta Alberto, RA Cali (Colombia)—I, II
Urrutia Enrique Alvear, RB San Felipe (Chile)—II, III, IV
Urrutia Jean-Baptiste, TA Carpato (Vietnam)—I, II, III, IV
Ursi Corrado, RA Acerenza (Italy)—I, II, III, IV
Urtasun Joseph, RA Avignone (France)—I, II, III, IV
U Win John Joseph, RA Mandalay (Burma)—I, II

V

Vagnozzi Egidio, TA Mira (USA)—I, II, III, IV
Vailati Valentino, RB San Severo (Italy)—I, II, III, IV
Vairo Giuseppe, RB Gravina (Italy)—I, II, III, IV
Vaivods Julijans, TB Macriana Maggiore (Latvia)—IV
Valdés Subercaseaux Maximiano, RB Osorno (Chile)—I, II, III, IV
Valdivia y Ortiz Mariano Jacinto, RB Huancayo (Peru)—I, II, III, IV
Valencia Cano Gerardo, TB Resaina (Colombia)—I, II, III, IV
Valente da Fonseca António, RB Vila Real (Portugal)—I, II, III
Valenzuela Rios Francisco, RB Antofagasta (Chile)—I, II, III, IV
Valeri Valerio card. prefetto della congregazione dei Religiosi—I
Valerii Domenico, RB Marsi (Italy)—I, II, III, IV

Valle Gallardo José, TB Germania di Numidia (Chile)—III, IV
Vallejo Bernal Enrique, PA Tierradentro (Colombia)—II, III, IV
Valloppilly Sebastian, RB Tellicherry (India)—I, II, III, IV
Van Bekkum Wilhelm, RB Ruteng (Indonesia)—I, II, III, IV
van Beurden Victor, PA Kole (Congo-Leopoldville)—II, III
van Cauwelaert Jean, RB Inongo (Congo-Leopoldville)—
    I, II, III, IV
Van de Bergh François, RB Budjala (Congo-Leopoldville)—
    I, II, III, IV
Van den Bosch Alphonse, RB Matadi (Congo-Leopoldville)—
    I, II, III, IV
van den Bronk Andrew, RB Parakou (Benin)—I, II, III, IV
van den Elzen Guillaume, PA Doruma (Congo-Leopoldville)—
    II, III, IV
van den Hurk Antoine, RA Medan (Indonesia)—I, II, III, IV
van den Ouwelant Charles, RB Surigao (Philippines)—I, II, III, IV
Van den Tillaart Theodor, RB, Atambua (Indonesia)—I, II, III, IV
Van der Burgt Herculanus Joannes, RA Pontianak (Indonesia)—
    I, II, III, IV
Vanderkerckhove Camille Jean-Baptiste, RB Bikoro (Congo-
    Leopoldville)—I, II, III, IV
van der Westen Nicolas Pierre, RB Pangkal-Pinang (Indonesia)—
    I, II, III, IV
van Diepen Petrus Malachias, PA Manokwari (Indonesia)—II,
    III, IV
van Dodewaard Jan, RB Haarlem (The Netherlands)—I, II, III, IV
van Elswijk Herman Jan, RB Morogoro (Tanzania)—I, II, III, IV
van Engelen Johannes, SG Congregazione Cistercense di Maria
    Mediatrice—I, II, III, IV
van Gaver Alain, TB Capra (Thailand)—IV
van Hees Wilhelmus Joannes Leo, SG Crocigeri—I, II, III, IV
van Heygen Lambert, RB Doumé (Cameroon)—I, II, III, IV
van Hoeck Francis, TB Cissita (South Africa)—I, II, III, IV
Van Kerckhoven Jozef, SG Missionari del S. Cuore—I, II, III, IV
van Kessel Lambert, RB Sintang (Indonesia)—I, II, III, IV
van Kester Guillaume, RB Basankusu (Congo-Leopoldville)—
    I, II, IV
van Lierde Petrus Canisius, TB Porfireone (Italy)—I, II, III, IV
Van Melckebeke Charles Joseph CICM, RB Ningsia (China)—
    I, II, III, IV
Van Melis Estanislau Arnoldo, TB Polemonio (Brazil)—II, III, IV
van Miltenburg James, RA Hyderabad (Pakistan)—I, II, III, IV
Vanni Pacifico, TA Proconneso (Italy)—I, II, III, IV
van Oorschot Antoon, RB Mbeya (Tanzania)—I, II, III
van Peteghem Léonce Albert, RB Gent (Belgium)—III, IV
van Rengen Marcel, PA Mweka (Congo-Leopoldville)—II, III, IV
van Sambeek John, TB Tracula (Tanzania)—II
van Steene Louis, RA Bukavu (Congo-Leopoldville)—I, II, III
Vanuytven Charles, TB Megara (Belgium)—I, II, III, IV
van Valenberg Tarcisio, TB Comba (Italy)—I, II, III, IV
van Velsen Gerard, RB Kroonstad (South Africa)—I, II, III, IV
van Waeyenbergh Honoraat, TB Gilba (Belgium)—I, II, III, IV
van Zuylen Guillaume, RB Liège (Belgium)—I, II, III, IV
Vaquero Tomàs, RB São João do Bôa Vista (Brazil)—II, III, IV
Varani José, RB Jaboticabal (Brazil)—I, II, III, IV
Varin de la Brunelière Henri, RB Fort-de-France et S. P.
    (Martinique)—I, III, IV
Varthalitis Antónios, RA Corfú (Greece)—I, II, III, IV
Vásquez Díaz José, TB Usula (Brazil)—I, II, III, IV
Vásquez Ochoa Jacinto, RB Espinal (Colombia)—I
Vayalil Sebastian, RB Palai (India)—I, II, III, IV
Vaz das Neves Abilio, RB Bragança e Miranda (Portugal)—I
Veerman Cornelio, TB Numida (Brazil)—II
Vega Ignacio Prieto, RB Wankie (Rhodesia)—II, III, IV
Veigle Adrian, PN Borba (Brazil)—III, IV
Velasco Díaz Juan Bautista OP, RB Hsíamen (China)—I, II, III, IV
Vélez Martínez, RAturo, RB Toluca (Mexico)—I, II
Vendargon Dominic, RB Kuala Lumpur (Malaysia)—I, II, III, IV
Vendola Domenico, RB Lucera (Italy)—I
Venezia Pasquale, RB Ariano (Italy)—I, II, III, IV
Véniat Henri, RB Fort Archambault (Chad)—I, II, III, IV
Venini Diego, TA Adana (Italy)—I, II, III, IV
Vennera Francisco, RB S. Nicolás del los, RAroyos (Argentina)—
    I, II, III, IV
Verdet Félix, RB La Rochelle (France)—I, II, III, IV
Verfaillie Camille, TB Oea (Belgium)—I, II, III, IV
Verhille Emile, RB Fort Rousset (Congo-Brazzaville)—I, II, III, IV
Verhoeven Nicolas, RB Manado (Indonesia)—I, II, III, IV
Vérineux André-Jean MEP, RB Yingkou (China)—I, II, III, IV
Vermeiren Hilaire, TA Pedactoe (Belgium)—I, II, III, IV
Verolino Gennaro, TA Corinto (Italy)—I, II, III, IV
Verschuren Paul, TB Acque Sirensi (Finland)—III, IV
Verstraete Daniel, PA Western Transvaal (South Africa)—IV
Verwimp Alphonse, TB Gibba (Italy)—I, II
Verwoort Karl, TB Barica (Germany)—I, II, III, IV

Verzich Maura, SG Congregazione Benedettina Slava—
    I, II, III, IV
Veuillot Pierre Marie Joseph, TA Costanza di Tracia (France)—
    I, II, III, IV
Vezzani Forsennio, SG Ministri degli Infermi—IV
Vial Michel, RB Nevers (France)—I, II, III, IV
Vicentín Francisco, RA Corrientes (Argentina)—I, II, III, IV
Vicuña Aránguiz Eladio, RB Chillán (Chile)—I, II, III, IV
Vieira Alvernaz José, RA Goa e Damao (India)—I, II, III, IV
Vieira Florencio, RB Amargosa (Brazil)—I, II
Vielmo Cesare, TB Ariasso (Chile)—I
Vignancour Paul, RB Valence (France)—I, II, III, IV
Villa Gaviria German, RB Barranquilla (Colombia)—I, II, III, IV
Villena Oscar, TB Musti (Argentina)—III
Villepelet Jean, RB Nantes (France)—I, II, III, IV
Villot Jean-Marie card., RA Lyon (France)—I, II, III, IV
Villuendas Polo León, RB Teruel (Spain)—I
Vincent Jean, RB Bayonne (France)—III, IV
Viola Alfredo, RB Salto (Uruguay)—I, II, III, IV
Vion Henri, RB Poitiers (France)—I, II, III, IV
Vogel Cyril John, RB Salina (USA)—III, IV
Volk Hermann, RB Magonza (Germany)—I, II, III, IV
Völker Leo, SG Padri Bianchi—II, III, IV
Vòllaro François, RB Ambatondrazaka (Madagascar)—
    I, II, III, IV
Vonderach Johannes, RB Chur (Switzerland)—I, II, III, IV
von Rudloff Johannes, TB Busiri (Germany)—I, II, IV
von Streng Franz, RB Basel and Lugano (Switzerland)—
    I, II, III, IV
Vos Jan, TB Cnido (Malaysia)—I, III, IV
Vovk Anton, RA Ljubljana (Yugoslavia)—I
Vozzi Alfredo, RB Cava e Sarno (Italy)—I, II, III, IV
Vroemen Eugen Joseph Frans, RB Chikwawa (Malawi)—IV
Vuccino Antonio, TA Apro (France)—I, II, III, IV

W

Wade Thomas James, TB Barbalissus (USA)—I, II, III, IV
Wall Bernard Patrick, RB Brentwood (Great Britain)—
    I, II, III, IV
Walsh Emmet Michael, RB Youngstown (USA)—I, II
Walsh Francis Raymond, RB Aberdeen (Great Britain)—I
Walsh Joseph, RA Tuam (Ireland)—I, II, III, IV
Ward James, TB Sita (Great Britain)—I, II, III, IV
Ward John James, TB Bria (USA)—III, IV
Warmeling Gregório, RB Joinville (Brazil)—I, II, III, IV
Waters Vincent Stanislaus, RB Raleigh (USA)—I, II, III, IV
Waterschoot Ignace Joseph, RB Lolo (Congo-Leopoldville)—I, II
Watson Alfred Michael, TB Naziona (USA)—IV
Watters Loras Joseph, TB Fidoloma (USA)—IV
Weber Charles SVD, RB Ichow (China)—I, II
Weber Jean-Julien, RA Strasbourg (France)—I, II, III, IV
Weber Jerome, AN S. Peter-Muenster (Canada)—I, II, III, IV
Webster Benjamin Ibberson, RB Peterborough (Canada)—
    I, II, III, IV
Wechner Bruno, TB Cartenne (Austria)—I, II, III, IV
Wehr Matthias, RB Trier (Germany)—I, II, III, IV
Weidner John, PA Raipur (India)—III
Weigl Joseph, RB Ikela (Congo-Leopoldville)—I, II, III, IV
Weinbacher Jakob, TB Thala (Austria)—I, II, III, IV
Weldon Christopher Joseph, RB Springfield (USA)—I, II, III, IV
Welykyj Atanasij Hryhor, SG Ordine Basiliano S. Giosafat—
    II, III, IV
Wember Johann, TB Vasada (Norway)—I, II, III, IV
Westermann Hermann, RB Sambalpur (India)—I, II, III, IV
Whealon John Francis, TB Andrapa (USA)—I, II, III, IV
Wheeler William Gordon, TB Theudalis (Great Britain)—III, IV
Whelan Joseph Brendan, RB Owerri (Nigeria)—I, II, III, IV
Whelan William Patrick, RA Bloemfontein (South Africa)—
    I, II, III, IV
Wichrowski Walmor Battú, TB Phelbes (Brazil)—I, II, III, IV
Wien Dud Ireneus, TB Barcuso (Sudan)—I, II, IV
Wiesen Johannes, TB Telmisso (Paraguay)—I, II, III, IV
Wijnants Pierre, RA Coquilhatville (Congo-Leopoldville)—IV
Wilczyński Tomasz, TB Poliboto (Poland)—I, III
Wildermuth Augustine Francis, RB Patna (India)—I, II, III, IV
Wilhelm Joseph Lawrence, TB Saccea (Canada)—II, III, IV
Willebrands Johannes, TB Mauriana (Italy), segretario del
    segretariato per l'Unità dei cristiani—III, IV
Willinger Aloysius Joseph, RB Monterey-Fresno (USA)—I
Windle Joseph Raymond, TB Uzita (Canada)—II, III, IV
Winkelmolen Henry, PA Same (Tanzania)—III, IV
Winkler József, TB Dadima (Hungary)—III, IV
Winters Patrick, RB Mbulu (Tanzania)—I, II, III, IV

Wittebols Joseph-Pierre-Albert, RB Wamba (Congo-
    Leopoldville)—I, II
Wittler Helmut Hermann, RB Osnabrück (Germany)—
    I, II, III, IV
Wójcik Walenty, TB Baris di Ellesponto (Poland)—I, II
Wojtyła Karol Józef, RA Cracovia (Poland)—I, II, III, IV
Wolff Edmond-Marie-Jean, RA Diego Suarez (Madagascar)—I,
    II, III, IV
Worlock Derek John, RB Portsmouth (Great Britain)—IV
Wosinski Jan, TB Abaradira (Poland)—III, IV
Woznicki Stephen Stanislaus, RB Saginaw (USA)—I, IV
Wright John Joseph, RB Pittsburgh (USA)—I, II, III, IV
Wronka Andrzej, TB Vatarba (Poland)—I, IV
Wycisk Waclaw, TB Cesarea di Numidia (Poland)—II, III, IV
Wycislo Aloysius John, TB Stadia (USA)—I, II, III, IV
Wyszyński Stefan card., RA Gniézno-Warszawa (Poland)—I, II,
    III, IV

X

Xenopulos Georges, RB Syra e Milo (Greece)—I, II, III, IV

Y

Yago Bernard, RA Abidjan (Ivory Coast)—I, II, III, IV
Yamaguchi Paul Aijirô, RA Nagasaki (Japan)—I, II, III
Yáñez Ruiz Tagle Luis, RB Los Angeles (Chile)—III, IV
Yednapally Ambrose Papaiah, RB Bellary (India)—III, IV
Yemmeru Asrate Mariam, RA Addis Abeba (Ethiopia)—I, II, III,
    IV
Yerena y Camarena Manuel, RB Huejutla (Mexico)—I
Youakim Eftimios, RB Zahleh e Furzol (Lebanon)—I, II, III, IV
Youakim Saba, SG Ordine Basiliano SS. Salvatore dei Melchiti—
    I, II, III, IV
Yougbare Dieudonné, RB Koupéla (Upper Volta)—I, II, III, IV
Youn Kong-hi Victorinus, RB Su Won (Korea)—II, III, IV
Yüen K'ai-chih (Ching-Ping) Joseph Marie, RB Chumatien
    (China)—I
Yü-Pin Paul, RA Nanking (China)—I, II, III, IV

Z

Zaffonato Giuseppe, RA Udine (Italy)—I, II, III, IV
Žak Franz, RB Sankt Pölten (Austria)—I, II, III, IV
Zaleski Alexander, RB Lansing (USA)—I, II, III, IV
Zambarbieri Angelo, RB Guastalla (Italy)—I, II, III, IV
Zambarbieri Giuseppe, SG Piccola Opera della Divina
    Provvidenza—II, III, IV
Zambrano Camader Raúl, RB Facatativa (Colombia)—III, IV
Zambrano Palacios Alberto, TB Case di Numidia (Ecuador)—
    I, II, III, IV
Zanchin Mario, RB Fidenza (Italy)—I, II, III, IV
Zanini Lino, TA Adrianopoli di Emimonto (Palestine)—
    I, II, III, IV
Zaplana Bellizza Alfonso, RB Tacna (Peru)—I, II, III
Zareba Jan, TB Bitilio (Poland)—IV
Zarranz y Pueyo Juan, RB Plasencia (Spain)—I, II, III, IV
Zarza Bernal Anselmo, RB Linares (Mexico)—I, II, III, IV
Zattera Antônio, RB Pelotas (Brazil)—I, II, III, IV
Zauner Franz, RB Linz (Austria)—I, II, III, IV
Zayek Francesco Mansour, TB Callínico (Brazil)—I, II, III, IV
Zazinović Karmelo, TB Lebesso (Yugoslavia)—I, II, III, IV
Zazpe Vicente Faustino, RB Rafaela (Argentina)—I, II, III, IV
Zerba Cesare card. segretario della congregazione per il Culto
    divino e la disciplina dei sacramenti—I, II, III, IV
Ziadé Ignace, RA Beirut dei Maroniti (Lebanon)—I, II, III, IV
Ziggiotti Renato, SG Salesiani—II, III
Zilianti Pietro Romualdo, AN Monte Oliveto Maggiore (Italy)—
    I, II, III, IV
Zimmermann Joseph, RB Morombe (Madagascar)—I, II, III, IV
Zimmermann Joseph, TB Cerinia (Germany)—I, II, III, IV
Zinato Carlo, RB Vicenza (Italy)—I, II, III, IV
Zoa Jean, RA Yaoundé (Cameroon)—I, II, III, IV
Zoghbi Elias, TA Nubia (URA-Egypt)—I, II, III, IV
Zohrabian Cyrille Jean, TB Acilisene (Italy)—I, II, III, IV
Zoppas Fortunato, RB Nocera de' Pagani (Italy)—I
Zorzi Benedito, RB Caxias (Brazil)—I, II, III, IV
Zoungrana Paul card., RA Ouagadougou (Upper Volta)—
    I, II, III, IV
Zuccarino Pietro, RB Bobbio (Italy)—I, II, III, IV
Zupi Saverio, TA Serra (Pakistan)—II, III, IV
Zuroweste Albert Rudolph, RB Belleville (USA)—I, II, III, IV
Zvekanović Matija, TB Burca (Yugoslavia)—I, II, III, IV

LIST OF OBSERVERS, DELEGATES, AND GUESTS OF THE SECRETARIAT

Abraham T. S. – III
Abrecht Paul A. – IV (s)
Abdel-Messih Marcos Elias – III
Adams James Luther – I (s)
Afanassieff Nicolas, guest of the secretariat – IV
Afinogenov Nikolaj – I (s), II (s), IV
Aghiorgoussis Maximos – III, IV
Aldenhoven Herwig – III (s)
Amvrosij (Pogodin, Amvrosij) – III, IV
Antonij (Bartoševič) – I, II
Antonios – IV
Ariga Tetsutaro – IV
Arndt Elmer J. F. – II (s)
Arseniev Nicholas, guest of the secretariat – IV
Athanasius (Thomas) – IV
Bader Jesse Moren – I
Baker William George – II, III
Bekmezyan Grigor – II, III, IV
Berkouwer Gerrit Cornelis, guest of the secretariat – I, II, III, IV
Blakemore William Barnett – III, IV
Boegner Marc, guest of the secretariat – III, IV
Borovoij Vitalij – I, II, III, IV
Brauer Jerald C. – III, IV
Burns Chalmers A. – III
Caird George B. – I, II, III, IV
Canavatis Vasso – IV
Cannon William R. – III (s), IV (s)
Cassien (Bezobrazov, Sergej Sergeevič) guest of the secretariat – I, II, III
Chandler Edgar H. S. – IV (s)
Chrysostom (Oommen, Philipose) – III
Corson Fred Pierce – I, II, III (s), IV
Cramer Albert W. – IV
Cuba'In Najib Atallah – IV
Cullmann Oscar, guest of the secretariat – I, II, III, IV
Cushman Robert E. – I (s), II (s), III (s), IV (s)
Cuttriss Frank Leslie – IV
Dagne Haile Gabriel – II
Davidson Richard H. N. – IV
Day Peter – IV (s)
Der Hagopian Zgon V. – IV
De Soysa Harold – I, II
Dietzfelbinger Wolfgang – III (s), IV (s)
Dimetros (Gebremariam, Melake Selam Dimetros) – II
Dodds Robert C., guest of the secretariat – IV
Doi Masatoshi, guest of the secretariat – II, III
Du Plessis David, guest of the secretariat – III
Eapen C. T. – IV
Eley Stanley – II (s)
El-Pharaony Farid – II, IV
El-Moharaky Pakhoum A. – II
Emilianos (Timiadis) – IV
Evdokimov Pavel, guest of the secretariat – IV
Faber Heije – IV (s)
Fairweather Eugène R. – III, IV
Findlow John – III, IV

Galiatsatos Nicodimos – IV
Grant Frederick C. – I
Grotoff Sergej – I (s), II (s), III (s), IV (s)
Guirguis Youhanna – I, IV
Hayward Victor E. W. – IV (s)
Hildebrandt Franz – I (s)
Hoffmann Oswald C. J., guest of the secretariat – III, IV
Holt Basil – IV
Horton Douglas – I, II, III, IV
Hubben William – I (s)
Huenermann Ruben H. – IV (s)
Hyslop Ralph D. – IV (s)
Ilič Jakov – II
Iwas Ramban Zakka B. – I, II
Jackson Joseph M. – I
Joan (Nikolov, Petrov) – IV
John Ernst – III
Juvenalij (Poiarkov, Vladimir) – IV
Kantzenbach Friedrich W. – IV (s)
Kasič Dušan – IV
Keighley David Alan – II (s), III (s), IV (s)
Kevorkian Parkev – II, III, IV
Kissack Reginald – I (s)
Kniazeff Alexis, guest of the secretariat – IV
Koukoulatis Cyrillos – III
Küppers Werner – II (s), IV (s)
Lamsa George W. – I
Lawrence John W. – IV (s)
Legg Arnold Henry – II, III
Leibrecht Walter – I (s)
Le Roy Anderson Stuart – IV (s)
Lindbeck George A. – I, II, III (s)
Littel Franklin H. – III (s)
Maan Peter J. – I, II, III, IV
Mathew C. P. – II
Matthews Zachariah Keodirelang – III
McAfee Brown Robert – II
McArthur Allan – III
McLean Greeley Dana – I, II
Meyer Carl S., guest of the secretariat – IV
Miguez-Bonino José – I (s), II (s), IV (s)
Milin Lazar – IV
Moorman John R. H. – I, II, III, IV
Morrison Angus W. – II
Mosconas Theodoros, guest of the secretariat – II, III, IV
Moss Robert V. – I (s)
Muelder Walter G. – III
Nacpil Emer P. – IV (s)
Nelubin Boris – III, IV (s)
Nichols James – I
Nissiotis Nikos A. – II, III, IV
Norgren William A., guest of the secretariat – II, III, IV
Oberman Heiko A. – I (s), II (s), III (s), IV (s)
Outler Albert Cook – I, II, III, IV
Pawley Bernard – I, II, III, IV (s)
Philipos Korah – II
Potter Philip – III (s)

Quanbeck Warren A., – II (s), III, IV
Rehana Quashisha Isaac – III
Reid John K. S. – IV
Roberts Harold – I, II, III, IV
Rodger Patrick – IV (s)
Rodopoulos Panteleimon – III
Romanides John – III
Root Howard E. – II (s), III (s), IV (s)
Roux Hébert – I, II, III, IV
Rupp Ernest Gordon – IV (s)
Sadiq John – II
Samuil – III
Sarkissian Vardapet Karekin – I, III, IV
Satterthwaite John R. – IV
Schlink Edmund – I, II, III, IV
Schmemann Alexander, guest of the secretariat – I, II, III, IV
Schmidt Wilhelm, guest of the secretariat – III, IV
Schomer Howard – II (s)
Schutz Roger, guest of the secretariat – I, II, III, IV
Scrima André – III, IV
Selassie Petros Gabre – I, IV
Selassie Sergew Hable – IV
Shamoon Saliba – III, IV
Shaw Douglas W. D. – I
Shepherd Massey Hamilton – III (s)
Short Howard E. – III (s)
Silén Sven – II (s), III, IV
Skydsgaard Kristen Ejner – I, II, III, IV
Solomon Pereji – IV
Staack Hagen A. K. – IV (s)
Steere Douglas Van – II, III, IV
Stuber Stanley I., guest of the secretariat* – I, II
Subilia Vittorio – I (s), II (s), III, IV
Tadros Mikhail – I
Teinonen Seppo Antero – IV (s)
Terterian Ardavazt – II, III, IV
Teshome Haile Mariam – I
Thomas John Newton – III
Thompson Bard – III (s)
Thurian Max, guest of the secretariat – I, II, III, IV
Troyanoff Igor – I, II, III, IV
Tuttle Lee F. – II (s)
Ullmann Richard Karl – I
Vajta Vilmos – I (s), II, III (s), IV
Van Holk L. J. – I, II, III, IV
Verghese Paul – IV (s)
Vischer Lukas – I, II, III, IV
Vladimir (Kotliarov, Vladimir) – I
Von Rohr John R. – III (s)
Voronov Liverij – III, IV
Welsh Clement W. – IV
Williams George Huntston – I (s), II (s), III (s), IV (s)
Wolbrecht Walter F., guest of the secretariat – IV
Wolf William J. – I (s), II
Woodward Max W. – II (s), III (s), IV (s)
Zulu Alphaeus – II (s)

Legend
(s) = substitute
* = Executive director, Missouri Council of Churches, not of the Missouri Synod as indicated on p. 195.

NOTES

NOTES TO INTRODUCTION

1. G. Alberigo, *L'annuncio del concilio, in Storia del concilio Vaticano II diretta da G. Alberigo*, Italian edited by A. Melloni, 2012–2015 (new edition), vol. 1, 31 (for the English version, see *History of Vatican II*, edited by G. Alberigo and J. Komonchak, Maryknoll-Leuven 1995–2006); the thesis on the pointlessness comes from *Conciles* of J. Forget in *Dictionnaire de Théologie Catholique*, by A. Vacant- E. Mangeot, Paris 1906, column 636–676, especially column 669 and here ch. 4.

2. Y. Congar, *Journal d'un théologien: 1946–1956*, edited by É. Fouilloux, Paris 2001, and my introduction to *Vera e falsa riforma nella chiesa*, edited by A. Melloni, Milan 2015.

3. Riccardi. *Il potere del papa da Pio XII a Giovanni Paolo II*, Rome-Bari 1993, 319; regarding Montini cf. F. De Giorgi, *Paolo VI, il papa del moderno*, Brescia 2015; his recent beatification should have opened the reasons of secrecy which for decades kept Montini's motives secret outside the Vatican and even those within the Vatican which, based on the same standards Paul VI applied to the prefect of the archives secret to the cardinals, should have been available for study for a long time; cf. Pagano, S., "Riflessioni sulle fonti archivistiche del concilio Vaticano II. In margine ad una recente pubblicazione," in *Cristianesimo nella storia*, 23 (2002), 775–812 and Doria, P, "L'Archivio del Concilio Vaticano II: storia e sviluppo," in *Anuario de Historia de la Iglesia*, 21 (2012), 135–155.

4. Melloni, A. "La semplicità del bene. Indagine sui primi lettori del Giornale dell'Anima di A.G. Roncalli-Giovanni XXIII," in *Un cristiano sul trono di Pietro. Studi storici su Giovanni XXIII*, works by E. Bianchi et al., Gorle 2003, 326–349.

5. Cf. Melloni, A. *L'altra Roma. Politica e S. Sede durante il concilio Vaticano II (1959–1965)*, Bologna 2000, with the edition of the diary of Bartolomeo Migone, ch. 9

6. Cf. *Chiesa e progetto educativo nell'Italia del secondo dopoguerra (1945–1958)*, Brescia 1988.

7. Cf. Melloni. *L'altra Roma* cit., and ch. 21

8. The critical edition in A. Melloni, *Papa Giovanni. Un cristiano e il suo concilio*, Turin 2009, 299–335.

9. Regarding the speech, edited in a version taken from speeches in *Discorsi Messaggi Colloquio del S. Padre Giovanni XXIII*, IV, Vatican City 1964, 593, cf. F. Ruozzi, *Il concilio in diretta. Il Vaticano II e la televisione tra informazione e partecipazione*, Bologna 2012.

10. Grootaers, J. *Actes et acteurs à Vatican II*, Leuven 2000, 44, ch 18, 22.

11. Cf. Theobald, Ch. *"Dans les traces . . ." de la constitution "Dei Verbum" du concile Vatican II. Bible, théologie et pratiques de lecture*, Paris 2009, ch. 23.

12. Cf. *Chiesa ed ebraismo oggi. Percorsi fatti, questioni aperte*, edited by N. Hofmann, J. Sievers, M. Mottolese, Rome 2005, 153–179 [English. "*Nostra ætate* and the discovery of the sacrament of otherness," in The *Catholic Church and the Jewish People: Recent Reflections from Rome*, Philip A. Cunningham, Norbert J. Hofmann, Joseph Sievers editors., Fordham 2007; *Nostra Aetate -Origins, Promulgation, Impact on Jewish-Catholic Relations*, edited by Neville Lamdan and Alberto Melloni, Münster 2007, ch. 10 and 47

13. M. Velati created a veritable library of research: *Una difficile transizione. Il cattolicesimo tra unionismo ed ecumenismo (1952–1964)*, Bologna 1996; *Dialogo e rinnovamento. Verbali e testi del segretariato per l'unità dei cristiani nella preparazione del concilio Vaticano II (1960–1962)*, Bologna 2011; *Separati ma fratelli. Gli osservatori non cattolici al Vaticano II (1962–1965)*, Bologna 2014; though in an anthology of declarations it is interesting that Th. Stransky, *Doing the Truth in Charity. Statements of Paul VI Popes John Paul I, John Paul II and the Secretariat for Promoting Christian Unity, 1964–1980*, New York 1982 excludes the podromes and the beginning of the council.

14. Cf. De Giorgi. *Paolo VI* cit., ch 28.

15. For the procedure cf. studies by G. Alberigo, *Transizione epocale. Studi sul Concilio Vaticano II*, Bologna 2009, 152–220.

16. An initial reconstruction in V. Martano, *L'abbraccio di Gerusalemme. Cinquant'anni fa lo storico incontro tra Paolo VI e Athenagoras*, Cinisello B. 2014.

17. Cf. Miccoli, G. *La chiesa dell'anticoncilio. I tradizionalisti alla riconquista di Roma*, Rome-Bari 2011.

18. Cf. Grootaers, J. *Primauté et Collégialité. Le dossier de Gerard Philips sur la Nota Explicativa Praevia*, Leuven 1986; on the modest scope, the following had already intervened: E. Olivares, "Anàlisis e interpretaciones de la 'Nota praevia explicative'," in *Estudios Eclesiasticos* 42 (1967), 183–205; on the subversive value cf. G. Alberigo, "L'episcopato al Vaticano II," in *Cristianesimo nella storia* 8(1987), 156–162, while for a fair explanation on the Grootaers critique of U. Betti, in *Antonianum*, 62 (1987)/2–3 357–360, ch. 44.

19. Cf. Alberigo. *Transizione epocale* cit.

20. Cf. Vilanova, E. "L'intersessione," in *Storia del concilio Vaticano II* cit., IV, 367–478, and ch. 33.

21. Komonchak, J.A. "Le valutazioni sulla Gaudium et spes: Chenu, Dossetti, Ratzinger," in *Volti di fine concilio: studi di storia e teologia sulla conclusione del Vaticano II*, edited by Joseph Doré and A. Melloni, Bologna 2000, 115–153.

22. Ch. Theobald. *La réception del concile Vatican II, I. Accéder à la source*, Paris 2009.

23. Cf. the Congar-Chenu dialogue in the end of Y. Congar, *Mon Journal du Concile*.

24. Cf. Menozzi, D. *I papi del '900*, Florence 2000.

25. The issue is still being developed as posed by *Storia vissuta del Popolo Cristiano*, directed by Jean Delumeau (Italian edition edited by F. Bolgiani), Turin 1979.

26. The category of anti-council coined by G. Alberigo was based on this misunderstanding at once historical and theological, which was studied first by D. Menozzi, *L'anticoncilio, in Il VaticanoII e la Chiesa*, edited by G. Alberigo and J.P. Jossua, Brescia 1985, 433–464.

27. Cf. Von Balthasar, H.U. *Der anti-romische Affekt. Wie lasst sieh das Papsttum in der Gesamtkirche integrieren?*, Freiburg 1974; cf. K. Lehmann and W. Kasper (editors), *Hans Urs von Balthasar. Gestalt and Werk*, Cologne 1989.

28. Cf. *Araldo del Vangelo. Studi sull'episcopato e sull'archivio di Giacomo Lercaro, 1952–1968*, edited by N. Buonasorte, Bologna 2004.

29. Scatena, S. *In populo pauperum. La Chiesa latino-americana dal Concilio a Medellín (1962–1968)*, Bologna 2008.

30. Barba, M. "La riforma conciliare" from *Ordo Missae*, Padua 2008.

31. Cf. Galavotti, E. *Processo a Papa Giovanni. La causa di canonizzazione di A. G. Roncalli (1965–2000)*, Bologna 2005 and the paper "Francesco e san Giovanni XXIII. La canonizzazione del Concilio," in *Ioannes XXIII*, 2(2014), 55–67. The very good *positio* put down for the canonization is substantial in S. Falasca, *Giovanni XXIII, in una carezza la rivoluzione*, Milan 2014.

32. Melloni, A. *Le cinque perle di Giovanni Paolo II*, Milan 2011, 113

33. Cf. Melloni, A. *Inizio di Papa Ratzinger. Lezioni sul conclave del 2005 e sull'incipit del pontificato di Benedetto XVI*, Turin 2006.

34. McDonnell, K. "The Ratzinger/Kasper Debate: The Universal and the Local Churches," in *Theological Studies* 63(2002) 1–24.

35. As is shown by J. Komonchak, "Benedict XVI and the Interpretation of Vatican II," in "*Cristianesimo nella storia*" 28(2007), 323–337, the speech of Ratzinger as used by anticonciliar groups also points to positions of the lefebrian schismatics.

36. For a framework "Il Vaticano II e la sua storia. Introduzione alla nuova edizione," in *Storia del Vaticano II* cit., 1, Bologna 2012, IX–LVI, taken up again in "Vatican II and the history of Vatican II," in *Pacifica* 26(2013)/2, 134–154 and "Fare storia del concilio. Criteri ermeneutici, problemi storiografici e processi di ricezione del Vaticano II," in *Schweizerische Zeitschrift für Religions- und Kulturgeschichte / Revue suisse d'histoire religieuse et culturelle* 107(2013), 63–95; for its development and discussion cf. M. Lamberigts, "Alberigo and/on the History of Vatican II," in *Cristianesimo nella storia* 29(2008), 875–902 and along the lines of future works again G. Alberigo, "Le concile Vatican II. Perspectives de recherche," in *Revue d'Histoire Ecclésiastique* 97(2002), 562–573.

37. On these authors cf. G. Alberigo, "Concili (storia dei)," in *Dizionario del sapere storico religioso del 900*, edited by A. Melloni, 2 vols., Bologna 2009, 540–566.

38. On its production cf. Th. Hainthaler, "Grillmeier," in *Biographisch-Bibliographisches Kirchenlexikon* 17(2000), 493–505.

39. Cf. Valliere, P. *Conciliarism. A History of Decision-Making in the Church*, Cambridge 2014.

40. Cf. *Christian Unity: The Council of Ferrara-Florence: 1438/39–1989*.

41. Ganzer, K. "Hubert Jedin e il concilio di Trento," in *Cristianesimo nella storia* 22(2001), 339–354.

42. O'Malley, J. *What Happened at Vatican II*, Cambridge Mass.-London 2008.

43. Cf. Sale, G. *Giovanni XXIII e la preparazione del Concilio Vaticano II nei diari inediti del direttore della Civiltà Cattolica padre Roberto Tucci*, Milan 2012.

44. Cf. the edition of Vatican II in *Conciliorum oecumenicorum genraliumque decreta*, edited by G. Alberigo–A. Melloni, 3, Turnhout 2010, edited by me where I reestablished the text voted on and its extrinsic characteristics, restoring those documents approved in council by acclamation either by rising or by remaining seated, even if not passed by the commissions or by a debate, as messages to the world at the beginning and end of the council and the lifting of the excommunications.

45. Exemplary regarding this, Theobald, Ch, *La réception* cit.

46. Cf. on this the position of G. Galasso, *Nient' altro che storia*, Bologna 2000, who makes the position of Hannah Arendt his own in which the event is that which illuminates the past, but which can never be deducted.

47. So said, at the end of the pontificate of Montini, the thesis based on the De Lubac cards on which the author was silent and the placement of Ph. Levillain, *La mécanique politique de Vatican II. La majorité et l'unanimité dans un concile*, Paris 1975.

48. Jedin, H. *Storia del concilio di Trento*, 3, Brescia 1982 (ed. or. 1970), 12.

49. Cf. Vatican II, "1962–2012: The History after the History? Contributions and Perspectives of the Studies on the Council, Ten Years after *The History of Vatican II*," edited by S. Scatena, in *Cristianesimo nella storia* 34(2013).

50. So states G. Battelli, "La recente storiografia sulla Chiesa in Italia nell'età contemporanea," in *Rivista di storia della chiesa in Italia* 2(2007), 463–500; some examples in R. Burigana, *Storia del concilio Vaticano II*, Torino 2012; or R. De Mattei, *Il Concilio Vaticano II. Una storia mai scritta*, Turin 2010 from the decisively traditionalist point of view.

51. It's a very nice formula of Delio Cantimori as a part of the Italian historiography, regarding which cf. G. Miccoli, "Cantimori Delio," in *Il Contributo italiano alla storia del pensiero - Storia e Politica*, directed by G. Galasso, Rome 2013, in treccani.it *ad vocem*.

52. Cf. Zamagni, G. M. *Chenu e il Vaticano II come "fine dell'era costantiniana". Categoria della storia e imperativo pastorale*, in *Constantino I. Una enciclopedia internazionale sulla figura, il mito, la critica e la funzione dell'imperatore dell'editto di Milano*, directed by A. Melloni, P. Brown, E. Prinzivalli, S. Ronchey, 3, Rome 2013, 433–443 and M. Pesce, Introduzione to the re-edition of M.D. Chenu, *La fine dell'era costantiniana*, Brescia 2013.

53. Faggioli, M. "Concilio Vaticano II: bollettino bibliografico," in various sections: for 2000–2002, in *Cristianesimo nella Storia* 24 (2003), 335–360; for 2002–2005, therein 26 (2005), 743–767; for 2005–2007, therein 29 (2008), 567–610; for 2007–2010, in 31 (2010), 755–791 and with the title *Vatican II. Bibliographical Survey, 2010–2013*, therein 34 (2013), 927–995 an overview to the debate is now in M. Faggioli, *Vatican II. The Battle for Meaning*, New York-Mahwah, NJ, 2012.

54. Cf. *Le devenir de la théologie catholique mondiale depuis Vatican II: 1965–1999*, directed by J. Doré, Paris 2000 and P. Pietrusiak, "La catholicité de l'église dans la pensée d'Yves Congar," in *Roczniki Teologiczne* 53–54(2006–2007) 39–59.

55. A critical reflection on the naivety of this matter was assembled by S. Scatena in *Vatican II, 1962–2012: The history after the History?* cit.

56. Valliere. *Conciliarism* cit.

57. Cf. Pié-Ninot, S. "*Ecclesia in et ex Ecclesis* (LG 23): la Catolicidad de la *communio ecclesiarum*," in *Revista Catalana de Teologia* (1997) 75–89. The best developed position is that of J.M.R. Tillard, *L'Église locale. Ecclésiologie de communion et catholicité*, Paris 1995; on the opposite position in De Lubac cf. G. Chantraine, *La "corrélation radicale" des églises particulières et de l'église universelle chez Henri de Lubac*, in F. Chica, S. Panizzolo, H. Wagner H. (ed.), Casale Monferrato 1997, 68–85.

58. Cf. the papers of *La théologie catholique entre intransigeance et renouveau : la réception des mouvements préconciliaires à Vatican II*, G. Routhier, Ph.J. Roy, K. Schelkens (directed), Louvain-la-Neuve 2011.

59. Cf. Del Re, N. *La curia romana. Lineamenti storico-giuridici*, Rome 1970.

60. "André Scrima (1925–2000). Un Moine hésychaste de notre temps," in *Contacts. Revue française de l'Orthodoxie*, 55(2003) and 56(2004).

61. Duval, A. *Le message au monde*, 105–118; cf. also M.-D. Chenu, *Notes quotidiennes au Concile*, Paris 1995, [tr. it. Bologna 1996]; on the message H. Küng, *My Struggle for Freedom: An Autobiography*, 1, London 2003 (ed. now Munich 2002), 279; on the contemporary position of the Dutch Dominican theologian, E. Schillebeeckx, *The council notes of Edward Schillebeeckx 1962–1963*, ed. K. Schelkens, Leuven 2011.

62. Cf. Schelkens, K. *Catholic Theology of Revelation on the Eve of Vatican II: A Redaction History of the schema De fontibus revelationis (1960–1962)*, Leiden 2010.

63. Cf. Marangoni, R. *La Chiesa mistero di comunione. Il contributo di Paolo VI nell'elaborazione dell'ecclesiologia di comunione (1963–1978)*, Rome, 2001.

64. Cf. the recovery of a well-known thesis of G. Dossetti in M. Faggioli, *True Reform: Liturgy and Ecclesiology in Sacrosanctum Concilium*, Collegeville 2012.

65. Melloni. *L'altra Roma* cit.

66. *Christian Unity 550 Years after the Council of Ferrara-Florence* cit.; for this as for the other councils a recent bibliography cited in COGD.

67. García y García, A. "Les constituciones del concilio IV Lateranense de 1215," *in Innocenzo III. Urbs et orbis*, I, Rome 2003, 200–224.

68. The literature in K. Schatz. *Storia dei Concili. La Chiesa nei suoi punti focali*, Bologna 2006, 245–247 beginning with its history in three volumes *Vaticanum I: 1869–1870*, Paderborn 1992–1994 (*Vor der Eröffnung*, 1992; *Von der Eröffnung bis zur Konstitution "Dei Filius,"* 1993; *Unfehlbarkeitsdiskussion und Rezeption*, 1994).

69. Beginning with the classic A. Grillmeier-H. Bacht. *Das Konzil von Chalkedon. Geschichte und Gegenwart*, 2 vols., Würzburg 1953.

70. O'Malley, J. *What Happened at Vatican II*, Harvard 2008.

71. *Herders Theologischer Kommentar zum Zweiten Vatikanischen Konzil*, 5 vols., directed by P. Hünermann and B.J. Hilberath, Frankfurt a.M. 2004–2006.

72. Melloni. *Papa Giovanni. Un cristiano e il suo concilio* cit.

73. Ruggieri. *Ritrovare il concilio* cited for references to a long reflection on this point.

74. Cf. *L'evento e le decisioni. Studi sulle dinamiche del concilio Vaticano II*, edited by A. Melloni and M.T. Fattori, Bologna 1997.

75. Cf. Ch. Théobald. "L'herméneutique de réforme implique-t-elle une réforme de l'herméneutique?" in "*Recherches de science religieuse*" 100(2012)/1, 65–84.

76. Faggioli, M. *Il vescovo e il concilio. Modello episcopale e aggiornamento al Vaticano II*, Bologna 2005.

77. *The Catholic Church and the Jewish People* cit.

78. On this theme, the following work was begun but not finished, G. Thils, "Hierarchia Veritatum (Décret sur l'oecumenisme n. 11)," in *Revue Théologique de Louvain* 2 (1979): 208–215.

79. Dossetti, G. *Per una "chiesa eucaristica". Rilettura della portata dottrinale della Costituzione liturgica del Vaticano II. Lezioni del 1965*, edited by G. Alberigo and G. Ruggieri, Bologna 2002.

80. Corecco, E. "Considerazioni sul problema dei diritti fondamentali del cristiano nella chiesa e nella società," in *Les droits fondamentaux du chrétien dans l'Église et dans la société: Actes du IVe Congrès International de Droit Canonique* [6–11.X.1980., E. Corecco, N. Herzog, A. Scola (ed.), Freiburg i.B.-Milan 1981.

81. O'Collins, G. *Living Vatican II: The 21st Council for the 21st Century*, Maryknoll 2006.

82. The documentary comparison lies in the fact that there are dozens and dozens of passages, phrases, titles, and elements of the council of which dozens and dozens of fathers and theologians were sincerely convinced of being the sole and primary author.

83. Curnow, R.M. "John O'Malley on Vatican II and Bernard Lonergan's Realms of Meaning," in *Irish Theological Quarterly* 75(2010), 188–203.

84. Melloni, A. "Concili, ecumenicità e storia. Note di discussione," in *Cristianesimo nella storia* 28 (2007), 509–542.

85. Sieben, H.J. *Die katholische Konzilsidee von der Reformation bis zur Aufklärung*, Paderborn 1988.

86. Alberigo, G. "Ekklesiologie im Werden. Bemerkungen zum Pastoralkonzil und zu den Beobachtern des II. Vatikanums," in *ÖkRun* 40 (1991): 109–128.

87. E.g. Cassidy, E. *Ecumenism and Interreligious Dialogue: Unitatis Redintegratio, Nostra Aetate*, New York-Mahwah 2005; the following contributions are awaited: A. Birmelé and C. Hovorun in the acts of seminary *Historicizing Ecumenism*, Bose 2015.

88. Legrand, H. "Primato e collegialità al Vaticano II. Valutazione ecumenica di una formulazione dottrinale incompiuta," in *Il ministero del Papa in prospettiva ecumenica*, edited by A. Acerbi, Milan 1999, 211–231.

89. Routhier, G. *Vatican II. Herméneutique et réception*, Montréal 2006.

90. Mennini, M. "Paul Gauthier e la povertà della chiesa durante il Vaticano II," in *Cristianesimo nella storia* 34(2013), 391–422.

91. *Herders Theologischer Kommentar* cit.

92. On a possible payback of *Lex ecclesiæ fundamantalis* one study is missing; on the effects of a lexical detail cf. A. Melloni, "Definitivus, definitive," in *Cristianesimo nella storia* 21(2000), 171–205.

93. Cf. Melloni. *Il Vaticano II e la sua storia* cit.

94. The booklet "Sinodo 1985—una valutazione di *Concilium*" 22(1986)/6, edited by G. Alberigo and J. Provost contains writings of great importance by editors among whom A. Dulles, J.A. Komonchak, J.M. Tillard, A. Lorscheider, A.Melloni, E. Zoghby, H.J. Pottmeyer, H. Teissier, G. Ruggieri.

95. Orsy, L. *Receiving the Council. Theological and Canonical Insights and Debates*, Collegeville 2010.

96. Quinn, J. R. *The Reform of the Papacy: The Costly Call to Christian Unity*, New York 1999.

97. Ruggieri, G. "Ricezioni e interpretazioni del Vaticano II. Le ragioni di un dibattito," in *Chi ha paura del Vaticano II?*, edited by A. Melloni and G. Ruggieri, Rome 2009, 17–44

98. Melloni, A. "Francesco," in *Il conclave di papa Francesco*, directed by A. Melloni, Rome 2013, 63–95.

99. Lindbeck, J.A. *The Nature of Doctrine: Religion and Theology in a Postliberal Age*, Louisville 1984.

100. Nickel, J.W. "Rethinking Indivisibility: Towards A Theory of Supporting Relations between Human Rights," in *Human Rights Quarterly* 30(2008)/4, 984–1001.

101. Théobald. *La réception du concile* cit. e *"Dans les traces…" de la constitution Dei Verbum* cit.

FOREWORD

Massimo Faggioli

If we have historically reliable accounts of what happened at Vatican II and trustworthy commentaries of the final documents approved by the council, it is because of the work of people such as the bishops, *periti*, ecumenical observers, journalists, diplomats, and other participants who made Vatican II and kept their journals, diaries, and letters, and used them to write the first commentaries of the final documents of the council; John XXIII and Paul VI, who decided to create and make available the archives of the council immediately after Vatican II, in a sharp departure from the policy regarding the archives of the council of Trent; historians and theologians who wrote on Vatican II after its conclusion on December 8, 1965; Catholics, non-Catholic Christians and other observers worldwide, who in these last fifty years never lost interest in Vatican II. In this sense, the memory of Vatican II is a collective enterprise on which nobody has total control, not the magisterium, not the mass media, even less academia.

But there are some who, in the last few years, have been particularly committed to the continuation of the historical and theological inquiry on Vatican II. It is no accident that the Bologna-based scholars who took on that gigantic mass of documents, archives, and testimonies about Vatican II are at the basis of what this book accomplishes. The group of scholars mentored by Alberigo and his team, who worked on this book, walked in the footsteps of those who, after the 1985 Extraordinary Synod on the reception of Vatican II, decided to work on the history of the council and published the multilingual, multi-author, five-volume *History of Vatican II* starting in 1995, and innumerable more analytical studies in books and articles published starting in the late 1980s.

This book will not be used only by the insiders of the debate on the council's interpretation. Vatican II is crucial to the understanding of contemporary Catholicism as such. Its role is sometimes evident, sometimes active in more subtle ways, as we can see from the complex reception of the pontificate of Francis—a pope who takes Vatican II as the basis of the Church of today, and not something that needs to be discussed once again. But for a long time Vatican II has been identified as merely a set of texts whose theological meaning was to be understood separately from the awareness of the process through which those texts came to be—something that not even the most literalist interpreter of a text would do.

The *final documents* approved by Vatican II—constitutions, decrees, declarations—are part of a richer corpus of conciliar *texts* (including John XXIII's opening speech *Gaudet Mater Ecclesia* of October 11, 1962, the "Message to the World" of October 20, 1962, and the messages of the final day on December 8, 1965) and all of them live in a plurality of texts that make Vatican II intelligible.

Though the authors do not use these categories themselves, I see the final documents of Vatican II as *contextual*: the social and political context of a newly globalized Catholicism after World War II is a necessary element for the comprehension of the conciliar debates and acquisitions. The documents of Vatican II are *intertextual*, with the effective presence of other texts in the final text (sometimes explicitly referenced, sometimes not) approved by the council fathers and promulgated by the pope. The final documents of Vatican II are *hypertextual*, with references to other texts that had a given role and position in the Catholic tradition during Vatican II but now, fifty years later, may have a different role and position. The final documents of Vatican II live also in a world of *para-textuality*, where the authors' invisible notes on the margins, the story of their distribution and dissemination, the early reception and comments, surround every text. The final documents of Vatican II need to be considered in an environment of *meta-textuality*, of comments to the final text and the previous drafts that are part of the formation of the Catholic theological tradition at Vatican II. The final documents of Vatican II are part of an *archi-textual* dimension, with the literary genre of the constitutions, decrees, and declarations finding their place in the history of the conciliar tradition.[1]

But Vatican II requires especially to be inserted in the history of the Church of these last few decades, where no Catholic can avoid calling himself or herself a "Vatican II Catholic." This book helps the reader to see the "lived history of Vatican II" not as something that belongs to post-Vatican II Catholics only, but also to those who were there. The iconographic and photographic sections of this book give us back Vatican II and its actors in their everyday life at the council, their diverse geographic and cultural backgrounds, and the composition of the commissions and of the other formal and informal groups that built the mechanics of the council. In this sense, this is a necessary companion to every book on the history of Vatican II and to every edition of its final documents because, in order to understand Vatican II and its texts, we need to be aware of all the other elements that build the architecture of meaning of the conciliar event.

---

1. See Markus Pohlmeyer, "Er war nicht das Gute, sondern das Ganze. Transtextuelle Lektüre von Thomas Manns Joseph-Roman," *Literatur in Wissenschaft und Unterricht*, 46 (2013): 23–30.

2015. 11. 18

in dedicatione basilicarum
Petri et Pauli, apostolorum

79.95 (57.50)